ENCYCLOPEDIA OF TERRORISM

REVISED EDITION

ENCYCLOPEDIA OF TERRORISM

REVISED EDITION

CINDY C. COMBS AND MARTIN SLANN

Facts On File
An imprint of Infobase Publishing

Encyclopedia of Terrorism, Revised Edition

Facts On File, Inc.
An imprint of Infobase Publishing
132 West 31st Street
New York NY 10001

ISBN-10: 0-8160-6277-3
ISBN-13: 978-0-8160-6277-5

Library of Congress Cataloging-in-Publication Data

Combs, Cindy C.
Encyclopedia of terrorism / Cindy C. Combs and Martin Slann.—Rev. ed.
p. cm.
Includes bibliographical references and index.
ISBN 0-8160-6277-3 (hc : alk. paper)
1. Terrorism—Encyclopedias. I. Slann, Martin W. II. Title.
HV6431.C65 2007
363.32503—dc22 2006015853

Facts On File books are available at special discounts when purchased in bulk quantities for businesses, associations, institutions, or sales promotions. Please call our Special Sales Department in New York at (212) 967-8800 or (800) 322-8755.

You can find Facts On File on the World Wide Web at http://www.factsonfile.com

Text design by Cathy Rincon
Cover design by Cathy Rincon/Salvatore Luongo
Ilustrations by Jeremy Eagle and Melissa Ericksen

Printed in the United States of America

VB CGI 10 9 8 7 6 5 4 3 2 1

This book is printed on acid-free paper.

CONTENTS

LIST OF ENTRIES

INTRODUCTION TO THE REVISED EDITION

This edition of *Encyclopedia of Terrorism* derives from a world that, while coping with the events of September 11, 2001, finds itself now engaged in a "war on terrorism." Not only have the vulnerabilities of modern societies to terrorism become vivid, but we have also become more aware of the global nature of the threat of terror and the diversity of the individuals, groups, and causes that generate terror today. The events of 9/11 have been described as a "wake-up call" to Americans, most of whom had not been personally touched by the violence of terrorism, and who consequently had believed themselves to be somehow secure from terrorism in its most lethal forms.

September 11 dramatically demonstrated the power of terrorism to touch the life of America and many of its allies. It also evoked from the community of nations meeting in New York at the United Nations a joint declaration of "war" on terrorism worldwide. For many nations that had experienced terrorism in many forms for far too many years, this united resolution against terrorism was a turning point in history. For the first time, nations agreed that terrorism is a global problem, one which cannot be solved by one nation alone, but which must be resolved by united effort. It is a scourge that will not be quickly or easily reduced, and it will probably never be eliminated completely; however, collective global determination to deal with the problem may seriously impact the ability of terrorists to act with impunity.

Terrorism is not, certainly, a phenomenon of modern times; it has occurred throughout the ages in a wide range of forms. Many nations have had to deal with terrorism by individuals, groups, cults, militias, and corrupt state officials for centuries. Modern terrorism, however, has set new patterns of lethality and endurance, with unique patterns of networks forming across national borders, linking peoples by ethnic identity, religion, and hatred of a common enemy. While leaders in the United Nations have stressed that the "war on terrorism" is not a war between cultures, the clash of cultures has been highlighted by the religious zealotry of many who carry out terrorist acts today. For many current terrorist organizations, the West, particularly the United States, is viewed as a threat to fundamentalist religious values and traditional ways of life. Globalization is blamed in many societies as bringing destructive elements of permissiveness and materialism, placing the family unit at risk by pressure for a two-worker income, and jeopardizing religiously mandated moral codes. The increasing industrialization and networking of modern societies is perceived by those resorting to terrorism as a threat to morality, destructive of values and beliefs, and thus justifying the commission of horrendous acts of violence by those whose values are "threatened" by our modern world.

Terrorism has become, during the past few years, a topic of intense interest to scholars and government agencies. Academic interest in terrorism was moderate during the last few decades, with journals, books, monographs, and national reports reasonably accessible and courses taught in most colleges on terrorism and political violence, but interest in this issue has exploded since the events of 9/11. Although many democracies have, in recent years, developed departments or agencies to deal with terrorism, in the wake of 9/11 and the subsequent declaration of "war on terrorism" by the global community, nations throughout the world are now publishing annual reports on terrorism, creating joint task forces to gather information, and creating multinational centers to deal with this problem.

Even so, there is still a lack of consensus for what precisely terrorism is, although there is general agreement on certain primary features, such as the targeting of civilian noncombatants, the intent to create a mood of fear and intimidation in a population, the use of violence, and the advocacy of a political or social cause. But these characteristics are very broad and may not encompass all acts of terrorism today. The attacks on America in 2001, Indonesia in 2002, Spain in 2004, and Britain in 2005 highlighted, for example, the growing strength of religious fundamentalism as a cause for terrorism. Suicides in the name of religion are not new, but the rapidly growing number of willing suicide bombers committing terrorism for their faith is unique to this century.

Modern terrorism, too, now encompasses tools not associated with terrorism of previous centuries and, in some cases, previous decades. The threat of cyberterror, for instance, was not a concern for governments only 20 years ago, but today it is considered a serious threat to many systems, and much effort is now expended on protecting systems from cyber attacks. "Weapons of mass destruction" were only a few years ago regarded as very unlikely terrorist tools; today governments expend considerable effort to determine who has such weapons and whether they might be used effectively.

The impact of so-called failed states on the world at large was made clear by the role that Afghanistan played in the attacks of 9/11. The ability of a terrorist group to use such a state as a "breeding ground" for terrorism was dramatically demonstrated, leading to concern for such states that has led, productively, to more collective efforts by states to monitor and support the formation of stable governments and economies in such states. Fear that terrorist groups might gain access to weapons of mass destruction prompted, in part, the U.S.-led war in Iraq in 2003, and awareness of the dangers of a "failed state" in that country has led to concern about the impact of this war on the growth of terrorism.

The U.S. State Department, which until 2004 had produced an annual "Global Report on Terrorism," decided that its report should be altered to reflect some of these new concerns and uncertainties. Its definition of terrorism was broadened, and thus the statistics generated were not immediately released and could not be used for annual comparative graphs to track the increases and decreases of terrorist acts. At the same time, the shift in emphasis from a focus on terrorist groups to a report on global cooperative efforts on combating terrorism led to a dramatically different annual report.

This edition of the *Encyclopedia of Terrorism* reflects, in some part, many of these changes. Global awareness of terrorism has led to a dramatically increased knowledge base about the incredible number of terrorist groups active today. Thus this edition seeks to reflect the updated information about groups that have splintered, reformed, and networked across national borders. It also includes information about new agencies and policies generated by the events of 9/11 in the United States, its allies, and in international organizations.

As in the first edition, the focus in on modern terrorism, with descriptions and analyses of what its contributors consider to be among the most serious and influential terrorist personalities and organizations, motivations and targets of terrorism today. Since terrorism is not a modern phenomenon, there are occasional historical examples or references, offered to provide context and content for more recent events. Since any analysis of terrorism can be distorted, to some extent, by the source of the information, some groups have been excluded in spite of being listed by one government source as "terrorists," if their activities are primarily revolutionary or insurgent rather than terrorist in nature. It is impossible to rule out all bias, of course, but serious effort has been made to be fair and consistent, applying the term *terrorist* to acts that fit the definition and without bias for or against the motive for the acts.

As noted in the first edition, too, we have had to be selective. Encyclopedic does not mean all-inclusive. The amount of material generated since 9/11 about terrorists and terrorism has been staggering, too often unedited and biased, with conflicting sources and conclusions. Our conclusions will continue to change as we explore this challenging field, but we have sought to provide in this work a large number of entries, some updated and expanded from the first edition and others included for the first time generated by that expanding base of information. As such, we have again no doubt failed to include topics important to some of our readers and missed some topics that are even now growing in significance. We therefore welcome your suggestions for future inclusions. This is not a subject that will cease to be important or cease to change as the world seeks to understand, and cope, with all of its many forms.

The horrific attacks of September 11, 2001, on the World Trade Center in New York City and the Pentagon in Washington, D.C., have left no doubt as to how vulnerable a modern society is to the menace of terrorism. Many if not most Americans had come to view the United States as somehow secure from terrorism or at least secure from its more lethal forms. However, September 11 also conclusively demonstrated that terrorism is a global scourge that will not be ended quickly or, in all likelihood, completely. Terrorism's durability and its increasing lethality are explained at least in part by the rapid evolution over the last few decades of technology and the spread of religious zealotry.

For many current terrorist organizations, the United States and, to a somewhat lesser extent, the European industrial democracies are viewed as threats to absolute religious values and traditional ways of life. Democracy and the global economy are feared as harbingers of permissiveness and materialism that place at risk the family unit and divinely inspired moral codes. Thus, those whom we generally acknowledge to be terrorists perceive reality as destructive of all that they believe and hold dear. What most modern societies consider progress, terrorists consider blasphemy or the spoliation of the environment or, in some cases, both.

Terrorism is a phenomenon of international politics that has a long history and appears in a variety of forms. Terrorism's causes and manifestations are varied and complicated. While terrorism is far from a recent phenomenon—its roots can be traced back at least two millennia—its modern incarnation is unprecedented in frequency, scope of activities, and overall ferocity. The dissolution of the Soviet Union, the termination of the cold war, and the intensification of ethnic conflict and religious radicalism have all contributed to the proliferation of terrorism. Ironically, democratization and globalization have also produced or enforced the menace of terrorism. Open borders and the increase in commercial exchange have made it easier for terrorists to move about and to acquire new and more lethal weapons. Finally, the acceleration of computer and other forms of electronic technology have contributed to the impact of terrorism and can be expected to continue to do so into the future.

Over the last few decades, terrorism, has become a topic of increasing academic interest. Scholarly publications, including journals, books, and monographs, have proliferated; this literature has been authored by scholars, by police officials, and in a few cases by terrorists themselves. Undergraduate and graduate courses in political terrorism and violence have appeared on numerous campuses and attract substantial enrollments. Institutes and centers have been established to study the many aspects of terrorist phenomena. Countless movies and novels have used terrorism as a plot line. The activity and study of political terrorism have become permanent features in the lives of large numbers of people. Some governments have asked every citizen to be on the alert for terrorist threats to public safety and to immediately report them. In several countries, entire government departments have been created to blunt or stop the scourge of terrorism, and their budgets have steadily increased; in others, governments allocate significant resources to support and perpetuate terrorism.

Terrorism is not a subject that is easily defined or fully understood. There is general agreement on its main features, which may include purposeful attacks on random selected targets, a desire to intimidate governments and entire populations, and the goal of gaining publicity for a particular cause. There is also general agreement that terrorism is a lot more than those characteristics. Some forms of terrorism may not even be politically motivated. Part of the difficulty in either defining or understanding terrorism is that the activity of terrorism is itself dynamic. Terrorism not only takes on different forms, but the forms themselves are constantly changing, sometimes in unanticipated ways. A generation ago, for example, neither the term nor the activity of cyberterrorism was a consideration. Finally, we can also be confident that there is general agreement that terrorism is a permanent feature of our times and for the foreseeable future.

This volume is an attempt to offer brief descriptions and analyses of what its contributors have found to be among the most serious and influential terrorist personalities and organizations and the most significant motivations and victims of terrorism. The emphasis is on the features of modern terrorism, although there are occasional references to historical examples, in great part because of the models they provide for more current activities. Opposing governments frequently accuse one another of condoning or supporting terrorism, while terrorists usually see themselves as victims of regimes bereft of any sense of morality, so for some it is difficult to be sure where terrorism ends and counterterrorism begins.

September 11 changed, among other things, the ways we perceive terrorism, and we will be reassessing our understanding of terrorism well into the future. The usual limitations of time and space have enabled the contributors to this work to provide a selection of entries in the knowledge that other topics, important to individual readers, have not been included. Any work such as the current one will inevitably omit topics that have a significant or growing importance. We have genuinely tried to be comprehensive but recognize the likelihood that we have been incompletely successful.

CONTRIBUTING AUTHORS

Salmane Belayachi, University of North Carolina, Charlotte

Ivan Blackwell, U.S. Air Force

Robert Broughton, University of North Carolina, Charlotte

Loryn Buckner, University of North Carolina, Charlotte

Elizabeth A. Combs, Chatham Emergency Management Agency, Savannah, GA

Evan Cooney, University of North Carolina, Charlotte

Michael Dasher, U.S. Department of Defense

Erin Graves, Catholic University

Steve Harris, University of Georgia Emergency Management

Burl E. Holland, University of North Carolina, Charlotte

Brock Long, Federal Emergency Management Agency

Melissa Gayan, Emory University

Lydia Marsh, University of North Carolina, Charlotte

Timothy Linker, North Carolina State University

Caleb McIntosh, University of North Carolina, Charlotte

Gary Mitchell, Congressional Liaison

Earl Sheridan, Univeristy of North Carolina,Wilmington

Anthony Spotti, U.S. Department of State Security

ENTRIES A–Z

A

Abu Abbas *See ACHILLE LAURO,* HIJACKING OF.

Abu Nidal *See* AL-BANNA, SABRI.

Abu Nidal Organization (ANO; Fatah Revolutionary Council, Arab Revolutionary Brigades, Black September, and Revolutionary Organization of Socialist Muslims)

International organization carrying out terrorist acts, led by SABRI AL-BANNA, the ANO split from the PALESTINE LIBERATION ORGANIZATION (PLO) in 1974. It is comprised of various functional committees, including political, military, and financial. It has a membership of a few hundred, as well as a limited overseas support structure, including safe haven, training, logistic assistance, and financial aid from IRAN, LIBYA, and Syria (until 1987), including close support for selected operations.

ANO has carried out terrorist attacks in 20 countries, killing or injuring nearly 900 persons. Targets have included the United States, the United Kingdom, France, Israel, moderate Palestinians, the PLO, and various Arab countries. Major attacks include the MUNICH MASSACRE OF ISRAELI ATHLETES at the Olympic Games in 1972, the Rome and Vienna airport attacks in December 1985, the Neve Shalom synagogue in Istanbul and the Pan Am flight 73 hijacking in Karachi in September 1986, and the City of Poros day-excursion ship attack in Greece in July 1988. It was suspected of assassinating PLO deputy chief Abu Iyad and PLO security chief Abu Hul in Tunis in January 1991. The ANO assassinated a Jordanian diplomat in Lebanon in January 1994 and has been linked to the killing of the PLO representative there. It has not attacked Western targets since the late 1990s.

Al-Banna relocated to IRAQ in December 1998, where the group maintains a presence. It has an operational presence in LEBANON in the Bekaa Valley and several Palestinian refugee camps in coastal areas of Lebanon. The ANO also has a limited presence in Sudan, although financial problems and internal disorganization have reduced the group's activities and capabilities. Government authorities shut down the ANO's operations in Libya and Egypt in 1999.

On Friday, January 14, 2000, the Austrian police announced the arrest of a female activist of the Abu Nidal group, Fatah-Revolutionary Council (FRC). The activist, Halima Nimer, was arrested while attempting to withdraw the sum of about $7.5 million from a bank in downtown Vienna. Several newspapers claimed that Nimer was responsible for the finances of the group, but no further details were revealed. The Abu Nidal group was not active in the latter part of the 1990s. This was due in part to the loss of support of Iraq and later Libya, as well as the death of its leader, SABRI AL-BANNA, a.k.a. "Abu Nidal." One of the last known operations was the murder of a Jordanian diplomat in Beirut in January 1994. In October of the previous year, the Lebanese authorities arrested Mahmud Khalid 'Aynatur, a.k.a. Abu 'Ali Majid, who was head of special operations for the group. He was accused of orchestrating the kidnapping of the Belgian passengers on a yacht near Lebanon in 1987 and sentenced to imprisonment.

Reference: Naval Postgraduate School. Terrorist Group Profiles, "Abu Nidal Organization (ANO)." Available online: URL: http://library.nps.navy.mil/home/tgp/abu.htm. Accessed February 15, 2006.

Abu Sayyaf Group (ASG)

The ASG is the smallest and perhaps the most radical of the Islamic separatist groups operating in the southern Philippines. Some ASG members have studied or worked in the Middle East and have thus developed ties to mujahideen while fighting and training in AFGHANISTAN. Under the leadership of Abdurajik Abubakar Janjalani, the group split from the Moro National Liberation Front in 1991. Janjalani was killed in a clash with the Philippine police on December 18, 1998, and the ASG is still trying to fill the leadership void left by his death. Press reports indicate that his younger brother, Khadafi Janjalani, is the head of the ASG's operations in the Basilan Province.

Bombs, assassinations, kidnappings, and extortion payments to promote an independent Islamic state in western Mindanao and the Sulu Archipelago (areas in the southern Philippines heavily populated by Muslims) are among the acts carried out by this group in the 1990s. The ASG's first large-scale action occurred when it raided the town of Ipil in Mindanao in April 1995. In May 2001, Abu Sayyaf forces attacked a tourist resort in Malaysia and kidnapped 21 foreigners, and in May of that year, they kidnapped 20 people from a resort in Palawan. The latter group included three American citizens, one of which, Guillermo Sobero, was beheaded by the terrorists. In June 2002, the Philippine military staged a rescue operation, during which American missionary Gracia Burnham was rescued, but her husband Martin Burnham was killed in the firefight that ensued in the encounter. In July 2002, the U.S. attorney general handed down indictments against five leaders of the Abu Sayyaf Group for their participation in these crimes and offered a reward for their capture. In 2004, a faction of the ASG bombed a ferry in Manila Bay, killing 132 passengers. All of its activities have been carried out by a membership of about 200 to 500 active fighters.

References: Naval Postgraduate School. Terrorist Group Profiles, "Abu Sayyaf Group (ASG)." Available online. URL: http://library.nps.navy.mil/home/tgp/asc.htm. Accessed February 15, 2006; U.S. Department of Justice. "Five Leaders of Abu Sayyaf Group Indicted for Hostage-taking of Americans and Others in the Philippines." Available online. URL: http://www.usdoj.gov/opa/pr/2002/July/02_crm_419.htm. Accessed February 15, 2006.

Aceh Merdeka *See* FREE ACEH MOVEMENT.

Achille Lauro, hijacking of

In October 1985, a group of American and European tourists were taken hostage aboard a pleasure ship, the *Achille Lauro,* by a small group of Palestinians. The ship, with 80 passengers and 320 crew aboard, wandered north along the coast of LEBANON as the hijackers sought a safe haven. During this time, 60-year-old Leon Klinghoffer of New York City was murdered in his wheelchair.

The Egyptian government called in a negotiator, Abu Abbas, leader of the PALESTINE LIBERATION FRONT, the splinter group to which the hijackers claimed to belong. He ordered them to release the ship and come into port, where they were promised safe passage out of Egypt.

At the same time, U.S. intelligence sources, who were monitoring the exchanges between Egyptian president Hosni Mubarak and YASIR ARAFAT, leader of the PALESTINE LIBERATION ORGANIZATION (PLO) gained enough information to enable the United States to spring a trap. The Egypt Air plane, aboard which the hijackers were being smuggled out of Egypt, was ambushed by U.S. warplanes and forced to land in Italy, where the hijackers were taken into custody by the Italian government.

The United States and Italy fought over jurisdiction in the case, but the Italians refused to extradite. The

Italian authorities then released Abbas and the Palestinians, indicating that there was insufficient evidence to hold them. Subsequently, an Italian court convicted Abbas and sentenced him in absentia to life in prison. Abbas moved to Gaza, where in 2003 he expressed regret over Klinghoffer's death, but Klinghoffer's family insisted that he serve his sentence. Abbas eventually made his way to Iraq, where he was captured by U.S. forces on April 15, 2003. He died in U.S. custody on March 10, 2004.

References: Bohn, Michael K. *The* Achille Lauro *Hijacking: Lessons in the Politics and Prejudice of Terrorism* (Washington, D.C.: Brassey's, 2004); Johnston, David. "Ship Highjack Plotter Abu Abbas Dead." *San Diego Union Tribune* (March 10, 2004). Available online. URL: http://www.signonsandiego.com/uniontrib/20040310/news_1n10abbas.html. Accessed February 15, 2006.

Action Direct (AD)

Based in France, this group was active during the 1980s, networking with other groups in anti-NATO attacks in Europe. A communiqué on January 15, 1986, declared that the RED ARMY FACTION (RAF) of West Germany and Action Direct would together attack the multinational structures of NATO. Shortly after this, assassins killed the general in charge of French arms sales and a West German defense industrialist. On August 8, 1985, two Americans were killed in a bomb blast at a U.S. air base in Frankfurt, West Germany. The RAF and AD claimed joint responsibility for this attack. This attack was followed by the bombing of a U.S. antiaircraft missile site. Authorities believed that these attacks also involved Belgium's Fighting Communist Cells (FCC) since the explosives used were stolen from a Belgian quarry. The FCC bombed NATO pipelines and defense-related companies.

The organization ceased to claim operations in the 1990s, and it is believed to be defunct.

Adams, Gerry *See* SINN FÉIN.

aerial hijacking

Beginning around 1968 and continuing through most of the 1980s, airplane hijacking was a preferred operation of political terrorists. Typically, a commercial flight, usually crowded with unsuspecting passengers and crew members, would become the hostages of a few terrorists who boarded the aircraft posing as tourists or students (most hijackers were in their late teens or early twenties). The odds of surviving a hijacking were generally good. The hijackers themselves only infrequently were intent on hurting people. The discomfiture of the airplane's passengers and crew members usually lasted only several hours. Typically, a hijacked plane was allowed to land by very few countries. The passengers and crew were then returned to their point of origin. Often the hijackers themselves were arrested by the government allowing landing rights. On other occasions they were considered heroes.

One of the more notorious exceptions to this rule occurred in June 1985 when a TWA flight from Athens to Rome was diverted to Beirut. One American passenger who was in the military was murdered. Thirty-nine other Americans were held hostage in Beirut. They were freed at the end of the month after Israel agreed to release 700 Shiite Muslim prisoners. While Palestinian extremists in the public eye became increasingly associated with these activities, it is important to point out that numerous hijackings occurred that were unrelated to developments in the Middle East. Flights departing Miami, for example, were for a time, mostly during the 1960s and 1970s, regularly diverted to Cuba, usually by lone activists. Airplane hijackings began to occur less and less as airports developed better security systems, making it more difficult to smuggle weapons on board. However, many terrorists then resorted to more lethal methods by bombing planes rather than merely hijacking them.

Airplane hijacking developed a new and even more frightening dimension on September 11, 2001. The hijackers who directed commercial aircraft into the World Trade Center in New York City and the Pentagon in Washington, D.C., had carefully prepared for their enterprise. For several of them, this included enrolling in flight schools and successfully completing courses that enabled them to fly the airborne craft. In this case, no one survived the hijacking because the plane itself was the weapon of attack.

Reference: B. Taillon, J. Paul de. *Hijacking and Hostages: Government Responses to Terrorism* (Westport, Conn.: Praeger Publishers, 2002).

Afghanistan, U.S. bombing in *See* OPERATION INFINITE REACH.

Ahl-e Hadees *See* JAMIAT-E-AHL-E-HOLEES.

airport security

Many nations have managed to institute some security measures at one of terrorism's favorite targets: airports. Travelers on commercial airlines are routinely subjected to electronic or manual luggage inspection and to electronic or physical body searches, a relatively recent phenomenon. In most European airports, and in some of the larger airports in the United States, individuals without purchased airline tickets can no longer meet arriving passengers at the arrival gates, nor can they take their friends or relatives to the departure gates.

Such PHYSICAL SECURITY measures, of course, offer only a measure of protection, in some countries, against only one type of terrorism. Since such measures are not universally applied, the potential for SKYJACKING or bombing remains substantial, even for citizens of countries having such security systems. Moreover, physical security dependent on this technology is unable to completely screen against terrorist weapons. X-ray procedures for carry-on luggage have been proven to miss about 20% of the time on average for such weapons. With the advent of plastic weapons, and plastique, these security devices are even less effective. The plastique in the device used to cause the crash of the Pan Am 103 flight over LOCKERBIE, Scotland, in 1989 was of such small quantity that the extremely expensive sensing devices being installed at major airports would probably not have detected it.

OPERATIONAL SECURITY and personnel security are also critically important aspects of airport security. Procedures that match luggage with on-board passengers are not universally applied, particularly on domestic flights. This allows the possibility of an individual or group placing an explosive device aboard a flight, via luggage, while boarding another flight to safety. While many airports use employee identification badges to restrict access to sensitive areas of airport security systems, thousands of these badges are reported "missing" each year. A few examples illustrate airport security problems not yet resolved universally:

1. A reporter with a suitcase, at a large national airport, walked past a security checkpoint on the side where arriving passengers walk out of the arrival gate. The reporter pretended to make a call at a row of pay phones near the checkpoint, then slipped by when the guards' backs were turned.
2. At another international airport, a visitor found a baggage-room security door open. He walked through with his briefcase into the baggage truck passageway, onto the tarmac where planes fuel and load, and up a jetway staircase. He then entered the terminal as if deplaning and caught another flight—without ever going through security. He could have sabotaged either the luggage or the plane, without any contact with security.
3. A reporter watched, at yet another international airport, as janitors pushed large trash cans up to the passenger checkpoints. The janitors went through the metal detectors, but they pulled the cans through on the unscreened side. Guards neither inspected the trash cans—a serious security breach—nor did they check parcels brought into the same area by food vendors.

Such lapses in operational and personnel security worry those responsible for such security and the passengers and crew whom such security is designed to protect. Balancing a need to make air travel as pleasant as possible—since this is a service industry dependent upon happy customers—and a need to maintain an increasingly intense level of security against terrorism, airlines are faced with an almost impossible task. Airports throughout the world are increasingly challenged to "harden" themselves as targets for possible terrorist attacks, facing terrorists who are continuously working to discover more effective ways to breach that security.

Following the hijacking of four planes in the ATTACK ON AMERICA in September 2001, the U.S. government initially responded by tightening security at airports nationwide. This included requiring that only passengers with plane tickets be allowed into the arrival and departure areas at airports, that curbside check-in be suspended at airport terminals, and that security at the passenger-screening areas be substantially improved. The airlines initiated internal security improvements, such as equipping the cockpit with doors that can be sealed by the cockpit crew to prevent a hijacking initiated by passengers, as apparently occurred on September 11.

Although curbside check-in and the use of e-tickets was resumed in many airports in the months following the incident, efforts to improve airport security continued. Congressional decisions resulted in laws making passenger and luggage security personnel federal employees, although the implementation of these rules remained problematic. Screeners were at least temporarily more likely to seize potential weapons that might be smuggled aboard aircraft, including knives and other cutting instruments since this was the type of weapon used in the September 11 attack.

Increased security efforts extended in other directions as well. Food services, both at the airports and abroad the planes, could not supply cutting utensils to the customers/passengers, which forced a change in menu at many restaurants and in the first-class menus of most airlines. Most passengers were advised to assume that there would be longer lines at check-in points and therefore to plan to be at the airports well in advance of their flight times. Security was further increased on August 11, 2006, when British authorities uncovered a terror plot that involved the detonation of explosive liquids (disguised as ordinary items such as baby formula or shampoo) on flights originating from the United Kingdom and the United States. It was also the first time the U.S. Terror Alert ever reached the red level. As a result, airports have placed tighter restrictions on the amount of liquid material that passengers can bring on a plane.

The intensity of the security at most U.S. airports remained inconsistent, in spite of efforts by the government. Airports, facing heavy financial losses as a result of the extensive shut-down of flights in the days following the incident, found the loss of clients at food courts and passenger lounge areas difficult to bear. Passengers, confronted with long lines caused by the increased security screening efforts and fearing to travel by air until reassured that such travel was "safe," complained of both too many problems caused by security (lack of curbside check-in, limitations on family and friends in terms of access to arrival and departure areas, etc.) and a lack of confidence in the security of the planes. Responding in part to this ambivalence, the U.S. government found it difficult to decide who should be responsible for the training and maintenance of airport personnel, first placing portions of the U.S. military, including the National Guard, at airports to improve passenger safety, but only as a temporary measure. The decision to make airport security personnel federal employees was not immediately implemented, as the transition would be difficult and costly.

In the September 11 attack, the hijackers did not try to smuggle bombs aboard the four planes they hijacked from three different airports nor did they try to hijack the planes for ransom; instead, they used them as explosives. Thus, it is not clear that airport security, in the United States or in any other country, could be improved to the point where terrorism could not take place in this venue. The impact of spiraling costs, customer dissatisfaction, passenger perceptions of personal safety, and the ingenuity of those committing terrorist acts make each step toward improvement uncertain.

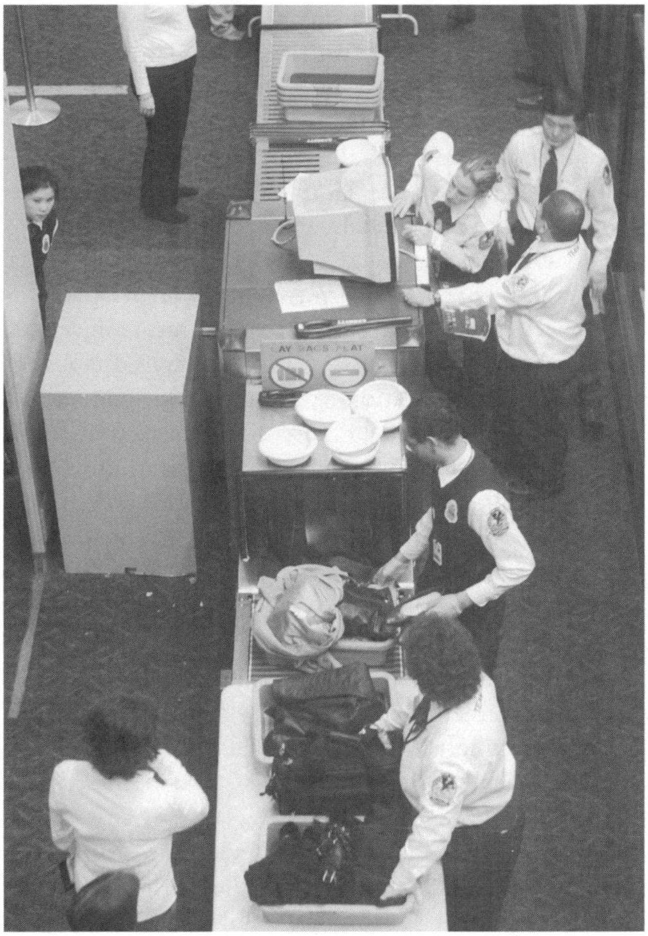

People pass through airport security, 2002. (CORBIS)

In the wake of the events of 9/11, the former Sky Marshal Program, initiated in 1968 and continued through the 1970s as a program designed to stop aerial hijackings to and from Cuba, was renewed. The Federal Aviation Administration (later replaced by the Transportation Security Administration [TSA]) greatly expanded this program in late 2001, augmenting the Federal Air Marshal Program (FAMS) with law-enforcement officers from other federal agencies within the Department of Justice and the Department of Treasury and actively recruited new trainees. All Federal Air Marshals were required to meet stringent physical fitness expectations and the highest firearm proficiency standards.

Regarded by the TSA as a fundamental tool in the security-challenged airline industry, only limited information about the Federal Air Marshal Program is normally made public. The TSA will not reveal the number or identity of the marshals, the details of their training, their budget, or the routes they fly. There is not necessarily an air marshal on every flight, but the potential for their presence is presumed to deter future hijackers.

The Federal Air Marshal Program was established in the Federal Aviation Administration one month after the events of 9/11, and FAMS was transferred to the Transportation Security Administration when it was established. With the creation of the Department of Homeland Security in 2003, the TSA was transferred into the Directorate for Border and Transportation Security in November 2001. On November 25, 2003, DHS secretary Tom Ridge announced that FAMS would be transferred to U.S. Immigration and Customs Enforcement, thus bringing the air marshals back "home" to where the sky marshals had been so successful 30 years ago.

See also ATTACK ON AMERICA.

References: Combs, Cindy C. *Terrorism in the Twenty-First Century.* 4th ed. (Upper Saddle River, N.J.: Prentice-Hall, 2006; Thomas, Andrew R. *Aviation Insecurity: The New Challenge of Air Travel* (Amherst, N.Y.: Prometheus Books, 2003).

Alex Boncayao Brigade (ABB)

The ABB was formed in the mid-1980s in the Philippines, emerging as a breakaway urban "hit squad" of the Communist Party of the Philippines New People's Army. It was responsible for more than 100 murders, and it is believed to have been involved in the murder in 1989 of U.S. Army colonel James Rowe.

In March 1997, the ABB announced that it had formed an alliance with another armed group, the Revolutionary Proletarian Army.

Although it did not carry out many attacks during the next few years, in March 2000 the group claimed credit for a rifle grenade attack against the Department of Energy building in Manila and for strafing the Shell Oil offices in the Central Philippines, allegedly to protest rising oil prices.

Although the exact size of this group remains unclear, the best approximation of its size is about 500 members. The largest ABB groups are on the Philippine islands of Luzon, Negros, and the Visayas. It is unclear how much external aid the group receives. Most of its activities continue to focus in Manila. The group was added to the U.S. Terrorist Exclusion list in December 2001, apparently due to its purported links to al-Qaeda cells.

Reference: U.S. Department of State, *Patterns of Global Terrorism: 2003* (Washington, D.C.: Department of State, 2004).

Allied Democratic Forces (a.k.a. National Army for the Liberation of Uganda [NALU])

Comprised of a diverse coalition of former members of the National Army for the Liberation of Uganda, as well as Islamists from the Salaf Tabliq group, this conglomeration of fighters formed in 1995 to oppose the government of Ugandan president Yoweri Museveni. It has carried out kidnappings and murders of civilians to create a mood of fear in the local population and to undermine citizen confidence in the government. It is suspected of being responsible for dozens of bombings in public areas as well.

Although the group has perhaps a few hundred members, the efforts of the Ugandan military in 2000 to destroy several ADF camps has diminished its strength. In the past, the ADF received funding, supplies, and training from the government of Sudan, as well as from sympathetic Hutu groups. It is unclear at present whether it continues to enjoy this support.

American Front

The American Front (AF) is a skinhead group founded around 1990, in either Portland, Oregon, or San Francisco, California, by Bob Heick that within a few years had spread from California to Florida. Its members have been arrested in Napa, San Francisco, and Sacramento, California; Pennsylvania; Florida; Maryland; and Washington, indicating the breadth of its spread.

Heick, an American high school dropout, first encountered the racist skinhead culture in Britain in 1984. During that time, the racist organization National Front was engaged in a "war" with antiracist skinheads for control of the British skinhead movement. Since the National Front won, when Heick returned to the United States, he launched his own skinhead organization, the American Front, with membership by application only. The application is intended to be intimidating, implying that if a member betrays the organization, the punishment is "death by crucifixion." Clearly, the "war" between skinheads in Britain impacted Heick's new organization.

AF members have committed terrorist crimes. In California and Washington in July 1993, AF members were arrested for the bombing of the Elite Tavern (a gay club) and an NAACP meeting hall. According to the U.S. attorney involved in the cases, the individuals involved in these bombings—Wayne Paul Wooten, Jeremiah Gordon Knesal, and Mark Kowaalski—were part of an effort to incite a race war. The bombings were timed, apparently, to coincide with the sentencing of police officers convicted in the Rodney King case, presumably to heighten racial tension connected with the case.

James Porazzo, American Front's new leader, moved AF headquarters to Harrison, Arkansas, and embarked on an effort to unify the extreme right and the extreme left to fight against the "global capitalist system," which he regards as "the REAL ENEMY." According to his propaganda, "The forces of capitalism are controlled by the Zionists and the Race that spawned them . . . a filthy, evil people the world would be better without."

Reference: Ridgeway, James. *Blood in the Face: The Ku Klux Klan, Aryan Nations, Nazi Skinheads and the Rise of a New White Culture* (New York: Thunder's Mouth Press, 1995).

Amin, Idi (in full, Idi Amin Dada Oumee) (1924/25–2003)

Born in 1924 or 1925 in Koboko, Uganda, Amin was president of Uganda from 1971–1979. A member of the small Kakwa tribe of northwestern Uganda, he had little formal education. Joining the King's African Rifles of the British colonial army in 1943, he served in World War II and in the British action against the Mau Mau revolt in Kenya in the mid-1950s. Following Uganda's independence in 1962, he became closely associated with the new nation's prime minister and president, Milton Obote who made him chief of the army and air force in 1966. On January 25, 1971, he staged a successful military coup against Obote and became president and chief of the armed forces in 1971, field marshal in 1975, and president-for-life in 1976.

Amin was often extreme in his nationalism, expelling all Asians from Uganda in 1972, an action that led to the breakdown of the Ugandan economy. A Muslim, he broke the pattern of Uganda's peaceful relationship with Israel and became friends with LIBYA and the Palestinians. In 1976, he was personally involved in the Palestinian hijacking of the French airliner to ENTEBBE.

Taking tribalism to an extreme as well, Amin ordered the persecution of Acholi, Lango, and other tribes. Under his rule, reports emerged of the torture and murder of between 100,000 and 300,000 Ugandans, a level of state terrorism that provoked an attack by his own people and Tanzanian forces in late 1978. Amin fled the capital, Kampala, in April 1979 when the invading troops reached the city's outskirts, going first to Libya and finally settling in Saudi Arabia, where he later died on August 16, 2003.

References: "Former Ugandan dictator Idi Amin dies," CNN.com (August 16, 2003). Available online. URL: http://www.cnn.com/2003/WORLD/africa/08/16/saudi.amin. Accessed February 15, 2006; Omara-Otunnu, Amii. *Politics and the Military in Uganda, 1890–1985* (New York: St. Martin's Press, 1985).

Amir, Yigal (1972–)

One of the best and brightest students at Bar-Illan University at Ramat Gan, just outside Tel Aviv in Israel, a computer science and a law major, Amir in the fall of 1995 assassinated Prime Minister Yitzak Rabin. Frequently involved in treks beyond the campus for fist-shaking, epithet-slinging demonstrations against Israel's withdrawal from the West Bank and Gaza Strip, he carried a licensed Beretta 9-mm pistol with him, even on campus. Amir was part of a radical group known as Eyal, a Hebrew acronym for "Jewish Fighting Organization." This organization was similar to KACH but had no more than 10 to 20 members.

Amir started elementary school and junior high at state-run religious schools in Herzliyya, then went to a more religious, privately run high school in Tel Aviv. Later he went to Karem D'Yavneh, a yeshiva that the Israeli army allowed religious youths to attend as part of their three-year mandatory military service. A professor at Bar-Ilan noted that most religious public schools and yeshivas espouse a brand of religious nationalism, placing the holiness of "Eretz Yisrael" (Land of Israel) above every other value.

Amir, according to his friends, saw his world of unshakable precepts and unalterable truths coming apart, a feeling shared by many ardently religious Jews who believed that the peace process through which

Rabin was leading the nation was nothing less than a democratic challenge to divine plan. Like many religiously Orthodox Jews, he believed that the West Bank and Gaza belong to the Jews as a biblical commandment and as a precursor to the coming of the Messiah. For Amir, as for many right-wing hardliners, Rabin was a traitor to Israel, an anathema to Jewish destiny. From their perspective, he deserved to be killed.

For Amir, this was not just an idea; it was a duty. Few shared his ruthless interpretation of those beliefs. Indeed, though there was a strong conservative tendency at Bar-Ilan, only about 20 students identified with the extreme right. While authorities determined that he had not, as he claimed initially, worked completely alone on the assassination, police arrested less than 10 others, including his older brother Hagai, for assisting him in the plot to kill Rabin. His "sacred mission," as Amir described it, was not shared by most of his closest friends. Amir was sentenced to a mandatory term of life in prison and continues to be unrepentant about his crime to this day.

See also IMAGES, HELD BY TERRORISTS; PALESTINE.

Amn Araissi *See* HAWARI GROUP.

amplification effect, of the media

Terrorism often benefits from what has been called an amplification effect when the actions are broadcast through the media to a much larger audience than would be available on the spot where the action is occurring. For instance, insurgents carried out rural guerrilla warfare in several countries, including Angola and Mozambique, for more than a decade without receiving much attention from the rest of the world. But when a similar number of Palestinians carried their warfare into the urban centers of Europe and the Middle East, their actions and their causes became dinner table conversation for television audiences around the world, because in the urban centers of Europe and the Middle East, the terrorists were within reach of TV news reporters and their cameras.

This confluence of interest between the media—who thrive on sensational news—and terrorists—who are only too happy to provide the sensational events—has raised questions about the possible complicity of the media in modern terrorism. The amplification, to a worldwide audience, of the news events created by terrorists certainly fulfills one of the GOALS OF TERRORISTS, publicity, and perhaps lends more significance to the acts than would ordinarily accrue. The endless guerrilla struggles that remain largely unnoticed in more remote settings for decades cause at least as many casualties and destruction but seldom attract an international audience or provoke international reaction. This amplification effect, then, dramatizes the theatrical crime of terrorism in ways that can enhance the message sent by the terrorists to their audience.

References: Alali, A. Odasno, and Kenoye K. Eke. "Terrorism, the News Media, and Democratic Political Order," *Current World Leaders* 39, no. 4 (August 1996): 64–72; Perl, Ralph F. *Terrorism, the Media, and the 21st Century* (Washington, D.C.: Congressional Research Service, 1998); Kidder, Rushworth M. "Manipulation of the Media," in *Violence and Terrorism 98/99* (New York: McGraw-Hill/Dushkin, 1998).

anarchists

These are adherents of a social philosophy whose central tenet is that human beings can live justly and harmoniously without government and that the imposition of government upon human beings is in fact harmful and evil. Anarchists are distinguished from Marxists and other socialists in that the latter believe that the state must first be taken over before it can "wither away." Anarchists are generally too suspicious of the corruption of power to believe that this is desirable or even possible.

MIKHAIL BAKUNIN was the architect of a brand of anarchism that became known as collectivism. He and his followers agreed with Karl Marx in stressing the role of the workers' associations and the need for violent revolutionary action but protested what Bakunin called Marx's German authoritarianism in favor of a looser confederation of associations. When the First International disbanded in 1872, Bakunin and his followers retained control of the workers' organizations in countries such as Spain and Italy, the countries in which the anarchist movements attained their greatest strength.

Bakunin's emphasis on violence and revolutionary action as a means of revealing the vulnerability of the state inspired many assassinations, including President Sadi Carnot of France (1894), Empress Elizabeth of Austria (1898), King Umberto of Italy (1900), and President William McKinley of the United States (1901).

Not all anarchist movements were associated with violence. Many forms, such as that developed by

Pierre-Joseph Proudhon, the French writer, and known as mutualism, rejected revolutionary activity.

See also CYCLICAL NATURE OF TERRORISM.

Reference: Nozick, Robert. *Anarchy, State and Utopia* (New York: Basic Books, 1974).

ancient terrorism

Terrorism has a long history. As an activity, it has a lineage of at least two millennia and has been traced back to Roman times. Most of the terrorism identified during this period was religiously inspired. Extremists associated with Christianity, Hinduism, Judaism, and Islam have instigated terrorism. This characteristic is particularly noticeable during times of great religious change and unrest. This was certainly the case in the examples indicated below.

During the Roman occupation of Palestine in the early centuries of the Christian era, groups existed known as Zealots and Sicarii, who in the first case assassinated Romans and Greeks and in the second their Jewish collaborators. The preferred weapon was the knife (Sicarii means "daggermen"). The terrorist would stab the victim in busy and public places and attempt, usually with success, to melt back into the crowd. Interestingly, ancient terrorists were no more successful in provoking large-scale uprisings than their modern counterparts. There were several failed uprisings of Jews against Roman authority, but these occurred separately from terrorist activities.

Even during Muhammad's lifetime, assassins were dispatched to murder especially annoying critics of his teachings. Many of the victims were local Jewish or Christian leaders whose followers often converted to Islam after community leaders were eliminated. Terrorism in this instance was motivated by both political and religious considerations since political and religious authority tended to be combined into one. Similar practices were found in much of the history of Christianity, especially in the early centuries when it was attempting to eliminate heresies and paganism. In this case, though, terrorist episodes were promulgated by members of the clergy against those perceived to behave in contradiction to scripture.

See also BROTHERHOOD OF ASSASSINS.

Reference: Sinclair, Andrew. *An Anatomy of Terror: A History of Terrorism* (London: Macmillan, 2003).

Andrés Castro United Front (Frente Unido Andrés Castro or FUAC)

The FUAC formed from the ashes of the Sandinista-Contra civil war, which tore Nicaragua apart during the 1980s. When the conflict ended in 1990, as the Sandinistas lost the Nicaraguan presidency in a free election, former soldiers were left with no job prospects and little training. These soldiers formed armed rebel groups in the early 1990s to pressure the new Nicaraguan government for aid, led by a group of former Nicaraguan military officers who named this movement the Andrés Castro United Front in 1995. FUAC leaders pledged to keep fighting until the government provided its members with aid, in the form of land, food, and job training.

The Nicaraguan government negotiated with FUAC and other armed rebel groups with similar demands, reaching an agreement with FUAC leaders in 1997. FUAC agreed to demobilize their approximately 400 members in exchange for economic aid. Not surprisingly, a rebel group emerged two years later, calling itself FUAC, embarking again on a terrorist campaign, claiming that the Nicaraguan government had not fulfilled its promise to provide economic assistance.

Reference: National Memorial Institute for the Prevention of Terrorism (MIPT). "Group Profile: Andrés Castro United Front (FUAC)." Available online. URL: http://www.tkb.org/Group.jsp?groupID=3086. Accessed February 15, 2006.

Animal Liberation Front (ALF)

This group began in the United Kingdom with a group calling itself Band of Mercy. Initially, Band of Mercy, led by activists Ronnie Lee and Cliff Goodman, focused its efforts on preventing fox hunting in the countryside of England from occurring, by disabling the hunt vehicles, usually leaving a message explaining why the action had occurred. The band then turned to attempts to stop the vivisection of animals in labs, targeting first the research laboratory being built near Milton Keynes for a company called Hoechat Pharmaceutical. On November 10, 1973, Band of Mercy set fire to the half-completed building, with another fire set six days later in the same building, leaving a note that the fire was set "in an effort to prevent the torture and murder of our animal brothers and sisters by evil experiments."

Band of Mercy then turned its efforts to stopping the annual seal cull of the Wash along the Norfolk coast in 1974, trying to destroy the two boats licensed by the Home Office to hunt the seals. Although only one boat was totally destroyed, there was no seal hunt that year or in that location in any following year. But the escalating level of violence by this group began to fracture the animal protection movement. While the group launched eight raids against vivisection labs between June and August of 1974, culminating in an attack on the Oxford Laboratory Animal Colonies in Bicester, the two leaders were spotted, arrested, and sentenced to three years in prison.

Although Lee and Goodman only served a third of their sentence, paroled after only 12 months in the spring of 1976, this marked a radical change in the movement. Goodman made the decision to stick to legal campaigning for animal rights in the future, even offering information to the police about Band of Mercy. Lee, in contrast, gathered new recruits to the remains of Band of Mercy and decided to become more revolutionary, renaming the movement the Animal Liberation Front (ALF).

During the succeeding years, the violence and destructive activities of this animal rights group has extended to the United States, as well as to parts of Europe, increasing in frequency and intensity. In the United States, ALF has used arson, harassment, death threats, animal releases, and razor blade threat letters to intimidate individuals and businesses. The victims include fur farmers and retailers, research laboratories and personnel, circuses, zoos, fast-food restaurants, forestry services, and large corporations.

ALF's ideology is one of unwavering support for the liberation of captive animals by any means, including criminal activity. Activists in this group engage in very few "symbolic" acts of terrorism, choosing instead to launch attacks specifically designed to cause a sufficient level of economic hardship to drive individual enterprises out of operation. ALF activities in the United States during the last quarter of the 20th century included significant criminal activity, ranging from graffiti, broken windows, and other petty acts of vandalism to pipe-bombings, large-scale mink releases, destruction of research documentation, and arson. In January 2005, ALF was designated a "terrorist threat" by the U.S. Department of Homeland Security. On January 20, 2006, the U.S. Department of Justice filed charges against nine American and two Canadian activists who are alleged to have engaged in acts of arson between 1996 and 2001 in the name of ALF and the Earth Liberation Front. These arrests were part of Operation Backfire, an ongoing investigation led by the FEDERAL BUREAU OF INVESTIGATION (FBI) into the violent acts of animal rights and evironmental groups.

ALF maintains a website through its Information Service that provides information about how and when to strike a fur farm, encouraging activists to "scout out" the targeted farm to determine the types of security measures in place, the best time to hit the facility, and the impact on "pelting season" on security measures. While ALF continues to target fur farms in its campaign for animal liberation, its activists also continue to carry out numerous multimillion-dollar arson attacks on corporations engaged in animal testing or related industries.

References: BBC News. "Animal Rights, Terror Tactics." Available online. URL: http://news.bbc.co.uk/1/hi/uk/902751.stm. Accessed February 24, 2006; Smith, Brent L. *Terrorism in America: Pipe Bombs and Pipe Dreams* (Albany: State University of New York Press, 1994).

E.C.G.

Ansar al-Islam (a.k.a. Partisans of Islam, Helpers of Islam, Supporters of Islam)

Ansar al-Islam is a radical Islamist group of Arabs and Kurds who seek to establish an independent Islamic state in Iraq. Formed in December 2001 and closely allied with AL-QAEDA, some of its members trained in al-Qaeda camps in Afghanistan. The group provided, according to American reports, safe haven for al-Qaeda fighters before the U.S.-led OPERATION IRAQI FREEDOM (OIF). Since OIF, this has been one of the leading groups engaged in anti-Coalition attacks.

Most of the attacks of this group have focused on one of the two main Kurdish political factions—the Patriotic Union of Kurdistan (PUK). Ansar-al-Islam has mounted ambushes and attacks in PUK areas, including assassination attempts (some of which were successful) against PUK officials. It has worked closely with al-Qaeda operatives and associates in Abu Mus'ab AL-ZARQAWI's network.

With between 700 and 1,000 members, primarily in central and northern Iraq, Ansar al-Islam receives funding, training, equipment, and combat support from al-Qaeda as well as other individuals and groups supporting an international JIHAD. Some of its members claim to have produced cyanide-based toxins, RICIN, and alfatoxin, though none have been used in recent attacks.

Reference: Naval Postgraduate School. Terrorist Group Profiles, "Ansar Al-Islam (AI)." Available online. URL: http://library.nps.navy.mil/home/tgp/al.htm. Accessed February 15, 2006.

A.B.

anthrax, as a biological weapon

Anthrax is an acute infectious disease caused by the spore-forming bacterium *Bacillus anthracis*. It occurs most commonly in mammals, including sheep, goats, camels, and antelope, but can also occur in humans. Humans infected with anthrax normally have been exposed to infected animals, tissue from infected animals, or infected animals' products through their occupations (in agriculture or animal husbandry). Anthrax, however, has been used throughout history as a biological weapon.

Anthrax is linked to several devastating plagues that killed both humans and livestock. In 1500 B.C., the fifth Egyptian plague, which affected livestock, and the sixth, known as the plague of boils, were linked to anthrax; the Black Bane of the 1600s is also thought to have been anthrax and killed 60,000 cattle in Europe.

Robert Koch confirmed the bacterial origin of anthrax in 1876. Not long after this discovery, anthrax began to emerge as a biological weapon. German agents in the United States are believed to have injected horses, mules, and cattle with anthrax on their way to Europe during World War I. In 1937, Japan began a biological warfare program in Manchuria that included tests of anthrax. The United Kingdom experimented with anthrax at Guinard Island off the east coast of Scotland in 1942, an area that was only decontaminated more than 50 years later. During the years of World War II, several other countries, including the United States, began to develop anthrax as a weapon.

The biological weapons programs involving anthrax continued after World War II through the 1950s and '60s at various military bases. In the United States, Fort Detrick in Maryland became the focal point for this program until 1969, when President Richard Nixon formally ended the U.S. biological weapons program, signing in 1972 an international convention outlawing the development or stockpiling of biological weapons.

The ratification of this convention did not end the production, testing, and use of biological agents, including anthrax. In 1978–80, Zimbabwe experienced an outbreak of human anthrax that infected more than 6,000 people and killed as many as 100. Evidence of continued development of anthrax as a biological weapon emerged in 1979 when aerosolized (weaponized) anthrax spores were accidentally released at Compound 19, a military part of the city of Sverdlovsk (now called Yekaterinburg) in the Soviet Union. An explosion at this secret military base near an industrial complex in the Ural Mountains sent a cloud of deadly microbes over a nearby village. Death tolls from this accident vary, with as few as 68 deaths attributed and as many as 1,000 eventually dying from this contact with a weaponized form of anthrax.

The group AUM SHINRIKYO released anthrax in Tokyo several times between 1990 and 1993 but without causing any reported deaths or infections. Anthrax, even in weaponized form, is difficult to disseminate over a city since warm air generated by the traffic and compression of population generally forces the air up, not down, making it difficult to spray above the city with any success. In theory, a cloud of anthrax spores inhaled by a city's population would create widespread, severe flulike symptoms, killing 80% of those infected within one or two days after their symptoms appeared. As yet, no successful dissemination of this sort has been recorded. Nevertheless, states continue to seek to produce anthrax as a weapon. In 1995, Iraq admitted to United Nations inspectors that it produced 8,500 liters of concentrated anthrax as part of its biological weapons program.

In 2001, a letter containing anthrax spores was mailed to the NBC television offices in New York City, one week after the ATTACK ON AMERICA of September 11. This was the first of a number of incidents at locations in the eastern part of the country, including letters in Florida and Washington, D.C. Five deaths to date have been credited to anthrax attacks.

Anthrax infection can occur in three forms: cutaneous (skin), inhalation, and gastrointestinal. About 95% of cutaneous anthrax infections occur via a cut or abrasion on the skin, such as when someone is handling wool, hides, or hair products of infected animals. It begins as a raised, itchy bump that resembles an insect bite but soon turns into a painless ulcer, about one to three centimeters in diameter, with a black center in the middle. About 20% of untreated cases of cutaneous anthrax result in death. One person who contracted anthrax in the U.S. incident had the cutaneous form of anthrax.

In the case of inhalation anthrax, once spores enter the lungs, the bacteria require from two to 43 days to incubate. Initial symptoms for this form of anthrax may resemble a common cold but will lead to severe breathing problems and to shock after several days. Inhalation anthrax is fatal in about 90% of cases because its symptoms initially appear in a form that does not require a visit to a doctor. An employee of a Florida tabloid and four mail handlers in a New Jersey postal service died of inhalation anthrax in the 2001 attack.

The intestinal form of anthrax generally follows consumption of contaminated meat. It is characterized by an acute inflammation of the intestinal tract and includes symptoms of nausea, loss of appetite, vomiting, and fever, followed by abdominal pain, vomiting blood, and severe diarrhea. Usually between 25% and 60% of cases of intestinal anthrax are fatal. This is the type of anthrax that the Soviet Union initially blamed for the deaths in Sverdlovsk.

Anthrax is not contagious and can be treated with antibiotics. To be effective, the treatments must be initiated early; if untreated in a timely fashion, the disease can be fatal. A cell-free filtrate vaccine, which contains no dead or live bacteria in the preparation, exists for anthrax.

Anthrax is a particularly attractive candidate for a successful bioweapon because its spores are hardy, resisting sunlight, heat, and disinfectant, and can remain active in soil and water for years. However, manufacturing sufficient quantities of any bacteria in stable form is a technical and scientific challenge, and dissemination of anthrax remains a challenge. The use of crop duster planes, for instance, as a tool for dissemination is difficult, since the planes are designed to spray pesticides in a heavy, concentrated stream; anthrax as a bioweapon, in contrast, would preferably be scattered in a fine mist over as large an area as possible. The nozzles of crop dusters are best suited to discharge relatively large particles—100 microns in diameter—not tiny one-micron specks of bacteria.

In its natural state, anthrax has a low rate of infection among humans. Experts state that it takes a sophisticated lab and advanced skills to turn the natural anthrax spore into an aerosol that can cause death from lung infection. The organism, *Bacillus anthracis,* can be grown in a lab to produce a weapons-grade form of the bacteria. Removed from a nutrient-rich environment, the bacteria turn into spores, which naturally clump together. These spores are then purified, separated, and concentrated, then combined with fine dust particles to maintain separation and increase the time that the spores can be suspended in the air.

Used as a weapon in the 2001 attacks, the powdery mixture was apparently put into an envelope. When released into the air, often during the processing of mail at mail centers, a high concentration of spores could be drawn deep into the lungs, where the spores returned to their bacterial state and a rapidly developing anthrax infection released deadly toxins into the person's system.

In addition to the apparent use of anthrax as a weapon through the mail system in the United States after the September 11 attack, several other countries reported mail that tested initially positive to anthrax contamination. In Pakistan, at least one of four suspected letters received at three locations in Islamabad contained anthrax, while in Lithuania, one mailbag at the U.S. embassy at the capital tested positive, revealing trace elements of anthrax. Although similarly suspicious letters received in Kenya, Brazil, Argentina, and Germany tested initially positive to anthrax, none resulted in confirmed contamination of workers, and most tested negative in subsequent tests for exposure. As a result of the heightened threat from anthrax attack, the United States Army instituted the Anthrax Vaccine Immunization Program (AVIP) for its service members, and between 1998 and 2005, more than 1.3 million people have been vaccinated against anthrax.

See also BIOLOGICAL AND CHEMICAL ATTACKS.

References: Centers for Disease Control and Prevention. "Anthrax." Available online. URL: http://www.bt.cdc.gov/agent/anthrax. Accessed February 16, 2006; Miller, Judith, Stephen Engelberg, and William Broad, *Germs: Biological Weapons and America's Secret War* (New York: Simon & Schuster, 2001).

anthrax, attack in the United States

In the fall of 2001, the United States was the victim of a serious bioterror attack, with a total of four anthrax-tainted parcels recovered. This included letters to NBC news anchor Tom Brokaw and the editor of the *New York Post.* The first victim of the anthrax attack, Robert Stevens, was an employee of American Media Incorporated (AMI), the nation's largest publisher of tabloid newspapers. Mr. Stevens sought medical attention on September 30 when he began experiencing flu-like symptoms. Laboratory results indicated pulmonary anthrax on October 4, and Stevens died the following day.

Several days later, a second victim, also an employee of AMI, fell ill of pulmonary anthrax, but this individual was treated promptly with antibiotics and subsequently recovered fully. Swabbings indicated the presence of *Bacillus anthracis* at several locations in the AMI building, which was then closed while further testing and cleaning took place.

Letters were also mailed to the *New York Post* and to NBC news anchor Tom Brokaw, postmarked in Trenton, New Jersey, on September 18, just one week after the September 11 ATTACK ON AMERICA. A CBS employee and a seven-month-old baby of an ABC producer also tested positive for cutaneous anthrax, making it clear that additional letters were sent to the New York offices of CBS and ABC, although no letters were recovered from those locations.

In October of that year, letters addressed to U.S. senators Tom Daschle and Patrick Leahy containing anthrax powder and references to "September 11, 2001," "anthrax," and "Allah" were received. When a staff member of Senator Daschle opened his letter, a small cloud of anthrax spilled out of the envelope, resulting in the notification of the U.S. Capitol Police and the FBI and the subsequent vacating and securing of the area. The letter to Senator Leahy, who was chairman of the Senate Judiciary Committee, was discovered from a quarantined postal facility on November 16. The envelope included the same fictitious return address that was printed on the Daschle letter. All four anthrax-infected letters were mailed in envelopes that were prestamped and embossed with a blue "Federal Eagle" design on the front, processed at the Hamilton Distribution Center in Hamilton Township, New Jersey, and postmarked in Trenton, New Jersey.

While the four letters that were recovered were similar in many ways, there were also several differences. The two letters mailed to the senators had a more refined form of anthrax powder, and some differences in the texts from those sent to the media. All four included the statements "DEATH TO AMERICA. DEATH TO ISRAEL. ALLAH IS GREAT." However, the punctuation was different, and several differing phrases were included in the two sets.

By the end of December, 2001, 11 cases of pulmonary anthrax were confirmed, seven cases of cutaneous anthrax were also confirmed, and four additional cases were still under investigation. The five deaths resulting from these attacks were from the pulmonary anthrax infections, the first-known deaths in the United States from criminal use of a biological agent. The FBI investigation of these attacks remains ongoing.

Reference: Thompson, Marilyn W. *The Killer Strain: Anthrax and a Government Exposed* (New York: HarperCollins, 2003).

antiabortion clinic attacks

While nonviolent forms of protest are the preferred methods for most who oppose abortion, violence and threats of violence have been an increasing part of the antiabortion movement since the Supreme Court's *Roe v. Wade* decision legalized abortion. During the last two decades of the 20th century, antiabortion terrorists have been responsible for six murders and 15 attempted murders. They have also carried out around 200 bombings and arsons, 72 attempted arsons, 750 death and bomb threats, and hundreds of acts of vandalism, intimidation, stalking, and burglary.

The first arson attack against an clinic where abortions took place occurred in 1977, four years after the U.S. Supreme Court decision on the landmark case of *Roe v. Wade*. The attack was aimed at a Long Island, New York, clinic owned by abortion rights advocate Bill Baird. During the next six years, the pace of attacks picked up, with a total of 29 bombings and arsons by 1983. In fact, the attacks were increasingly made against individuals, not just buildings. In 1982, a man claiming to represent the ARMY OF GOD (AOG) kidnapped, and eventually released, an abortion doctor and his wife. Don Benny Anderson was convicted of the kidnapping and of three clinic bombings in Florida and Virginia.

The year 1984, dubbed the "Year of Fear and Pain" by militant activists of Joseph Scheidler's Pro-Life Action Network (PLAN), was marred with 25 clinic arsons and bombings, resulting in millions of dollars in damage. At least seven of these attacks were planned and carried out by a group headed by Rev. Michael Bray, of Bowie, Maryland, an activist who engaged in nonviolent protests by day but waged covert terrorism by night against abortion.

Although most of the people involved in clinic protests were not involved in and did not support violence, these protests remained the common ground of expression for antiabortion sentiment. Those willing to use violence to stop abortions, such as Michael Bray or Paul Hill in Florida and John Salvi in Boston, used the occasion of peaceful protest to blend in and to gather intelligence and recruits for violent attacks on clinics. In fact, in this "Year of Fear and Pain," Bray indicated on a note left at the site of a Norfolk, Virginia, bombing that a group of violent antiabortionists was forming, calling itself, the "Army of God" (AOG). U.S. Supreme Court justice Harry Blackmun, who wrote the *Roe v. Wade* decision, received a threatening letter from a group using that name, and that same year, a caller claiming responsibility for several bombings said he was from the Army of God. Letters signed by Army of God took credit for the bombing of an abortion clinic in Birmingham, Alabama; the 1997 bombings of a clinic and a lesbian bar in the Atlanta area; and the attempted assassinations of abortion physicians in Canada.

The primary document reaching the public from the Army of God, other than the occasional letter claiming responsibility for a bombing, has been its training manual, an underground handbook on how to commit clinic violence. This manual describes itself as "a manual for those who have come to understand that the battle against abortion is a battle not against flesh and blood, but against the devil and all of the evil he can muster among flesh and blood to fight at his side." It calls the United States "a nation ruled by a godless civil authority that is dominated by humanism, moral nihilism and new age perversion of the high standards upon which a Godly society must be founded, if it is to endure."

This manual not only offers detailed instructions on how to build ammonium nitrate bombs and "homemade C-4 plastic explosive," but it also advocates maiming abortion doctors by cutting off their hands. While it could be argued that the Army of God of the 1980s was reasonably careful not to harm people, attacking clinics only when empty or leaving messages with threats, the AOG's widely circulated manual suggests that those who now claim to be part of the Army of God, whoever they may be, are willing to kill and maim.

High-profile murder in the early 1990s marked a turning point in the antiabortion violence, transforming the movement and catching the attention of the nation as never before. In fact, Michael Bray, one of the earlier leaders of the less violent 1980s AOG, was by the early 1990s advocating the murder of abortion doctors and calling for a theocratic revolution with the aim of instituting biblical law. During this time, Rachelle "Shelley" Shannon, who had already launched butyric acid and arson attacks on clinics in the western United States, attempted to murder Dr. George Tiller, in Wichita, Kansas, wounding him badly.

A new faction, Rescue America, emerged during this time, highlighted by the murder of Dr. David Gunn by activist Michael Griffin in 1993. Paul Hill, an early leader with Bray from Florida, came to the nation's attention through his efforts to promote the notion that the murder of Dr. Gunn, as well as that of other abortion providers, should be considered "justifiable homicide" under U.S. law. Joseph Scheidler presided over a summit meeting of militant pro-life (antiabortion) leaders in Chicago after Dr. Gunn's murder, from which emerged the hard-line American Coalition of Life Activists (ACLA), most of whose leaders signed the "justifiable homicide" statement generated by Hill.

In 1994, Hill murdered a doctor and his escort outside a Pensacola, Florida, clinic. He drew moral support of ACLA leaders like Andrew Burnett, who appeared in a photograph holding a sign saying "Free Paul Hill! JAIL Abortionists." By that year, the number of arsons and bombings grew to 180, a trend partly attributable to the evolution of the revolutionary theology of those originally associated with Operation Rescue and its links to CHRISTIAN IDENTITY activists.

During this period, the line between antiabortion activists and Patriot and militia groups was beginning to blur. The 1996 bombing of Planned Parenthood offices in Spokane, Washington, for instance, was carried out by Identity-motivated white supremacists—so-called Phineas Priests—from Idaho. Moreover, the nature of those willing to kill changed. The first wave of those who attacked doctors and others saw themselves as public martyrs; the second, informed by a revolutionary hatred of the government that is shared by many Patriot groups, is composed of assassins with no desire to go public or be sentenced to prison.

Around the same time as the attack in Spokane, a novel, *Rescue Platoon,* that would have the same impact on the antiabortion movement that *The Turner Diaries* had on the militia movement, appeared on a website sponsored by David Leach. *Rescue Platoon* is set in the "near future," focusing on the execution of Paul Hill (who at the time was awaiting execution in Florida). Hill's "martyrdom" in the novel ignites a war against abortion, from "deep, deep down in the soul of America." In the book, "(t)hese were the conditions when the 'Rescue Platoon' came out of training and entered into active service in the Army of God." The novel is built around the Army of God's campaign to blow up clinics and murder doctors, culminating in the former Confederate states and Utah outlawing abortion, Texas seceding from the Union, joined by the Rescue Platoon and other "patriots."

Antiabortion activism remains a source of violence against clinics and doctors in the United States, although the number of attacks diminished in the late

1990s, as the federal hunt for ERIC RUDOLPH riveted the nation's attention after the 1996 Olympics bombing.

References: Clarkson, Frederick. "Anti-Abortion Violence." *Intelligence Report.* Southern Poverty Law Center. Available online. URL: http://www.splcenter.org/intel/intelreport/article.jsp?pid=701. Accessed February 16, 2006; Mason, Carol. *Killing for Life: The Apocalyptic Narrative of Pro-Life Politics* (Ithaca, N.Y.: Cornell University Press, 2002).

Anti-Imperialist International Brigade *See* JAPANESE RED ARMY.

Anti-Imperialist Territorial Nuclei (NTA)

This group first appeared in the Fruili region of Italy in 1995, adopting the class-struggle ideology of the RED BRIGADES and a similar logo (an encircled five-point star). The NTA has sought to form an "anti-imperialist fighting front" with other Italian leftist groups, including the Revolutionary Proletarian Initiative Nuclei and the New Red Brigades. Drawing on its opposition to what it calls "US and NATO imperialism" and Italy's foreign and labor policies, the NTA in January 2002 issued a leaflet listing experts in four Italian government sectors—federalism, privatizations, justice reform, and jobs and pensions—as potential targets for attack.

However, the NTA has, during its first decade of existence, primarily conducted its attacks against property rather than individuals. Responsibility for arson attacks against three vehicles belonging to U.S. troops serving at the Ederle and Aviano bases in Italy in 2003 was claimed by the NTA, as was the bomb attack in September 2000 against the Central European Initiative Office in Trieste and the bomb attack on the Venice Tribunal building in August 2001. In response to the NATO intervention in Kosovo, NTA activists threw gasoline bombs at the Rome and Venice headquarters of the then-ruling party.

There is no evidence of external support, and the membership of this organization continues to be fairly small, perhaps 20 members. While it presumably still exists in northeastern Italy, none of its members were arrested or prosecuted in 2003.

Reference: Overseas Security Advisory Council. Profiled Groups, "Anti-Imperialist Territorial Nuclei (NTA) a.k.a. Anti-Imperialist Territorial Units" Available online. URL: http://www.ds-osac.org/Groups/group.cfm?contentID=1306. Accessed February 15, 2006.

April 19 Movement (M-19)

The April 19 Movement was precipitated by the outcome of the Colombian presidential election in 1970. Former Colombian dictator Rojas Pinilla ran as a populist candidate in this election as a member of the National Popular Alliance Party (ANAPO). This party, and Pinilla, enjoyed wide support among the urban poor in the election, but lost, coming in a close second. Although ANAPO publicly rejected violence as an answer to the electoral defeat, some members of the party broke ranks and formed M-19, embarking on a violent spree of terrorist attacks for two decades.

Drawing its name from the date of Pinilla's presidential loss, M-19 claimed to support the poor of Colombia. It differs from other groups in Colombia engaged in terror, such as the FARC and ELN, in that it followed, not marxism, but a generally left-wing ideology, supporting the poor and calling for reform within the Colombian government rather than a socialist revolution. In November 1985, members of M-19 attacked the Supreme Court of Colombia in the Palace of Justice in Bogotá, with the intention of holding the court hostage. After several hours, the military raided the building, and many hostages were caught in the crossfire. More than 100 people died, including 11 of the 25 Supreme Court justices and all of the rebels. Some claim that Pablo Escobar and the Medellin drug cartel of Colombia were behind the attack because of their fear of the Extradition Treaty between the U.S. and Colombia. The Supreme Court judges were in favor of the treaty, which would allow Colombia to extradite any drug trafficker to stand trial in the United States.

The group ceased to exist, essentially, in 1990, when, under intense pressure from the Colombian government's security forces and right-wing paramilitary groups, M-19 agreed to a cease-fire. Shortly after this, the group laid down its arms permanently to become the Colombian political party Democratic Alliance M-19. A few members, however, rejected this cease-fire and formed new groups to continue the violent struggle for populist reform.

Reference: National Memorial Institute for the Prevention of Terrorism (MIPT). "April 19 Movement." Available online. URL: http://www.tkb.org/Group.jsp?groupID=26. Accessed February 15, 2006.

al-Aqsa Martyrs' Brigade

The al-Aqsa Martyrs' Brigade is comprised of an unknown number of small cells of FATAH-affiliated activists emerging at the beginning of the current intifada targeting Israeli presence in the West Bank and Gaza Strip. Its political aim is to establish a Palestinian state. Members of al-Aqsa have carried out bombings, shootings, and suicide operations against Israelis, both military personnel and civilians. This group has also killed Palestinians who it believed were collaborating with Israel.

In January 2002, al-Aqsa claimed responsibility for the first suicide bombing carried out by a female. In March 2002, the U.S. State Department added the group to the list of foreign terrorist organizations. The brigade also uses children in its attacks. In March 2004, a Palestinian teenager was caught at an Israeli checkpoint wearing an explosive belt, and in September 2004, a 15-year-old suicide bomber was arrested by Israeli security forces. The group has also carried out joint attacks with other militant groups, such as HAMAS and PALESTINIAN ISLAMIC JIHAD.

A leader of the Fatah movement, Marwan Barghouti, was arrested by Israel on charges of being involved as a leader in al-Aqsa. In May 2004, he was convicted of murder and sentenced to life imprisonment. The brigade continues to operate primarily in the West Bank, although it claims attacks inside Israel and the Gaza Strip as well.

Reference: National Memorial Institute for the Prevention of Terrorism (MIPT). "Al-Aqsa Martyrs Brigade." Available online. URL: http://www.tkb.org/Group.jsp?groupID=3855. Accessed February 15, 2006.

Arab Revolutionary Brigades

See ABU NIDAL ORGANIZATION.

Arafat, Yasir (Yasser Arafat) (1929–2004)

The longtime leader of the Palestine Liberation Organization (PLO) and, since 1996, president of the Palestinian Authority, was born in Jerusalem on August 24, 1929, and spent most of the first three decades of his life there. He was the fourth of seven children. Arafat's full name is Abd al-Rahman Abd al-Rauf Arafat al-Qudwa al-Husseini. Yasir is a family nickname that means "no problems." Like his nemesis, Israeli prime minister Ariel Sharon, Arafat's political outlook was formed in great part during the first Arab-Israeli war in 1948–49, though, of course, the two came to different and opposing conclusions. Arafat's career can easily be called remarkable, including damages not many of which, according to biographers, were self-inflicted. He has often been referred to as the "Teflon terrorist" for good reason.

Arafat co-founded the FATAH organization in 1957 and guided it to dominance as the primary faction of what became the Palestinian Authority. He assumed the leadership of the PLO in 1969. He had already taken on a military role in planning and launching attacks against Israel from a base in Jordan. Arafat became known to his followers and admirers as ra'is, or boss. By 1970, the Jordanians had had enough of Arafat's attempts to undermine the Hashemite monarchy. Arafat's forces were driven out of the kingdom and went to Lebanon. However, the Black September terrorist organization was created and operated loosely under PLO auspices as it attacked not only Israeli targets but also Jordanian ones considered to be less than supportive of, or perceived as opposed to, the PLO's agenda. Lebanon by 1975 was being destroyed in a civil war, was partly occupied by Syrian military units, and was the target of retaliatory strikes by Israelis because of attacks by the PLO's military arm's (Fatah's) attacks on northern Israeli towns. In 1982, Israel invaded Lebanon and forced Arafat to again flee, this time to Tunis, where he remained for the next decade.

While Arafat and his PLO leadership suffered military defeat, they were still able to achieve diplomatic successes. On November 13, 1974, for example, Arafat addressed the United Nations and was cordially received. The Palestinian cause clearly had a great deal of global sympathy as the underdog in the struggle with Israel. And because of his relentless identification with the Palestinian effort, Arafat now personified both the nation and its struggles. Throughout the 1980s, Arafat continued to solicit and in many instances receive diplomatic, military, and financial support from several Arab governments and Eastern European communist regimes. In the mind of most Israelis and Americans, however, Arafat remained a terrorist and not a statesman.

By 1987, however, the world was beginning to change in drastic fashion. The First Intifada began in Gaza. The phenomenon caught both the PLO and the Israelis by surprise. The appearance of young Islamic extremists whose entire lives had been spent under the Israeli occupation and who operated independently from the PLO produced nervousness in the veteran leadership. By 1988, Arafat publicly announced that he recognized the existence of Israel, and by 1993, secret meetings were going on between Israelis and Palestinians that resulted in the Oslo Agreement. In the early summer of 1993, Arafat shook hands with Israeli prime minister Yitzhak Rabin at the White House. The peace process seemed finally underway. The expectation was widespread that the peace process would eventually lead to an independent Palestinian state.

The optimism that Oslo inspired did not last. Both Israelis and Palestinians had significant numbers of rejectionists in their ranks who condemned any negotiation with the other side. Rabin was assassinated in 1995 by a Jewish religious fanatic. Rabin's immediate successor was his foreign minister, Shimon Peres, one of the primary architects of Oslo. Peres, however, was defeated in the 1996 elections by Benjamin Netanyahu, a hard-liner who did not trust Arafat and was suspicious of the benefits of any Israeli withdrawals from the territories.

The peace process stalled and eventually broke down completely. Arafat had another opportunity with Ehud Barak, a Rabin protégé, who defeated Netanyahu in the 1999 elections. With the encouragement and support of the Clinton administration, Barak offered between 95 and 97% of the West Bank and most of East Jerusalem to Arafat and all of the Gaza Strip. Arafat refused the offer and did not provide a counteroffer. The outgoing American president, Bill Clinton, publicly blamed Arafat for the failure of the negotiations. In the 2001 elections, Barak lost in a landslide, unusual for Israeli elections, to ARIEL SHARON, the former Israeli general who had led the 1982 invasion of Lebanon to destroy the PLO and who expressed regret that he had not killed Arafat in Beirut when he had the opportunity.

The Sharon government gradually reduced Arafat's position to one of powerlessness. The Israeli Defense Forces almost completely destroyed the PA compound in Ramallah where Arafat lived and worked. Arafat was understandably afraid to leave the compound for fear the Israelis would not allow him to return. During the Sharon regime, Arafat was basically reduced to house arrest, though he still met with his cabinet and gave interviews to the media. He remained a popular figure with rank-and-file Palestinians because of the defiance shown to Israel's policies and despite the fact that meaningful accomplishments were rare. The economy and standard of living steadily deteriorated because of the Israeli reluctance to allow Palestinian workers

Yasir Arafat (CORBIS)

into Israel, the corruption of PA officials, and Arafat's refusal or inability to blunt or stop terrorist attacks on Israeli targets that invited retaliatory strikes.

By the summer of 2004, different Palestinian factions began to attack one another in great part because of the rampant corruption, nepotism, and cronyism that seemed to characterize Arafat's political style. The appointment of a cousin as chief of security in the Gaza Strip was, for many, the last straw. After Palestinians, apparently members of the AL-AQSA MARTYRS' BRIGADE, attacked and burned down a security installation in Gaza, Arafat withdrew the appointment. Arafat's second prime minister in only two years, Ahmed Queria, threatened to resign because of an inability to exert control over Palestinian security forces. Arafat refused to accept the resignation, and Queria was persuaded to stay on at least as the prime minister of a caretaker government. The episode was symptomatic of the increasingly restive members of the Palestinian Authority who were growing weary of the institutionalized corruption that had become pervasive. By this point in time, Arafat was having more difficulty within his own Palestinian Authority than he was with the Israelis.

With Israeli withdrawal imminent, the strong possibility of a civil war between Islamists in Gaza, such as Hamas, versus secular nationalists began to evolve. Arafat's health problems by 2004, when he turned 75, worsened. By October, he was in a serious quandary as well as seriously ill. He needed to go where he could secure necessary medical treatment. Arafat had not left his Ramallah compound since 2002 and was afraid to do so because of his conviction that the Israelis would not allow him to return. By November 2004, his health had deteriorated, and he was evacuated to Paris for treatment at a military hospital. The Israeli government guaranteed that he would be allowed to return following recovery.

Reports began to go out in early November that Arafat's condition was critical, and on November 4, a report circulated that he had died, but this report was denied by the hospital where he was receiving his medical treatment. Yasir Arafat was declared dead on November 11, 2004, after he went into a coma and while he was on life support. Mahmoud Abbas, having been elected chairman of the PLA on November 11, was in January of 2005 elected president of Palestine, replacing Arafat as leader of the Palestinians.

References: Aburish, Said K. *Arafat from Defender to Dictator* (New York: Bloomsbury, 1998); Rubin, Barry, and Judith Colp Rubin. *Yasir Arafat: A Political Biography* (Oxford University Press, 2003). Shikaki, Khalil. "Let Us Vote." *Wall Street Journal,* July 30, 2004, A10; Stephens, Bret. "A Gangster with Politics." *Wall Street Journal,* November 5, 2004, A12.

Argentina, state terrorism in

In spite of the fact that Argentina's 1853 constitution places strong emphasis on protecting individuals from abuse by authority, repressive military rule has made this a difficult tradition to maintain. In 1930, the military deposed President Hipólito Yrigoyen, beginning a trend of regimes. After five military coups and 30 out of 46 years spent under military rule, the 1976 military coup that overthrew President Isabel Perón was hardly remarkable in itself, but the "dirty war" carried out during the next seven years remains a dark period of state terrorism tarnishing Argentina's history.

General Juan Domingo Perón was president of Argentina twice, from 1946 to 1955 and again briefly from 1973 to 1974. Perón's advocacy of social justice and a "third way" between capitalism and socialism generated animosity from both the military and the Catholic bishops, leading to his ouster and flight into exile in 1955. In exile, he remained a powerful political figure, and Peronism continued to make the country difficult to govern for a succession of anti-Peronist military regimes. The Peronist movement splintered into various factions, several of which were violent and carried out terrorist activities.

To combat the activities of opposition groups, the Argentine government resorted to the use of death squads as a form of counterterrorism. The Argentine Anti-Communist Alliance (AAA, or Triple A)—established under the government of Isabel Perón, who became president upon the death of her husband, Juan, in 1975—was the most notorious of the death squads during this time. Isabel Perón's Social Security minister, Jose López Rega, created the Triple A, and his close relationship with her gave him the freedom to carry out operations under the Social Welfare Ministry. About 200 of the security forces were recruited to carry out "special tasks," including terrorism against political opposition groups and any individuals thought to have "leftist" ideas or contacts. Among these suspect individuals were journalists, actors, singers, socialists, academicians, and many university professors. During what came to be called Black September in 1975, these individuals were given 72 hours to leave the country, following a warning by Triple A.

In 1976, a new military junta, comprised of three commanders of the military (representing army, navy, and air force), took control of the government. General Jorge Rafael Videla was leader of the coup and became president of Argentina from 1976 to 1981. Under his direction, the government issued a Process of National Reorganization (PRN), which sought to eliminate all opposition. Together with General Robert Viola, who succeeded him as president in 1981, Videla developed a myth of necessary counterterrorism and security activities, which later became known throughout the world as the dirty war. Exaggerating the violence of the Peronist left, Videla called for increases in counterterrorism measures in the form of secret police, death squads, and censorship of the media and the universities. Although the Montoneros, a group whose members were drawn from the Peronist left, had engaged in acts of violence and terrorism, they were all but extinct by the time Videla came to office. Yet this group became the focus of the Videla government's counterterrorism movement and the basis for his claim that a "civil war" was occurring that required strong government action in the subsequent dirty war.

While it is impossible to be certain of the exact number of deaths generated in this state terrorism, which included extrajudicial killings, abductions, and torture executed by the military regime from 1976 to 1983, at least 30,000 people were killed and another 9,000 "disappeared" during that time. The *desaparecidos,* or "disappeared ones," count among them those who, after being kidnapped by secret police or military units, were never found. Secret police and military units maintained secret lists of names of those targeted for abduction, torture, and murder. Clandestine places of detention were known as holes, and many of those taken to these secret camps were tortured for information. Most were eventually killed and their bodies disposed of secretly.

Victims of this period of state terrorism included trade unionists, artists, teachers, human rights activists, politicians, Jews, and all of their respective relatives. Virtually no one was safe, and the intense mood of fear generated by this state terrorism lingered long after the "war" ended. One well-documented example of this state terrorism was known as the Night of the Pencils. High school students decided to protest for lower bus fares, specifically a half-rate fare, already in existence for younger children. The government labeled these protests "subversion in the schools" and ordered the death of those who participated. More than 20 students were kidnapped from two schools. One-third of the 15 children seized in La Plata survived. One of them was 16-year-old Pablo Días, who described how his captives blindfolded him, put him in front of a mock firing squad, asked questions, stripped him, tied him down, and began to burn his lips. His captors subjected him to electric torture in his mouth and on his genitals. They pulled out one of his toenails with tweezers, an action that became almost signature of army torture. He was also beaten with clubs and fists and kicked repeatedly. He related that his friend Claudia, who was also kidnapped, had been raped at the detention camp. The ordeal lasted from September to December of 1976.

Scholar Martin Andersen in his book *Dossier Secreto: Argentina's Desaparecidos and the Myth of the "Dirty Wars"* notes that the Argentine military practiced a forged disappearance of people that was modeled on the tactics of Adolf Hitler's might-and-fog decrees—a systematic, massive, and clandestine operation. The government built 340 secret camps in which victims were housed and prepared mass graves for their burial. Prisoners in these camps were, like those in Nazi concentration camps, lined up or made to kneel in front of large, previously dug graves, then blindfolded and gagged. Some were put in the grave alive. Victims were doused with oil and burned with tires to cover the smell. Indeed, disposal of bodies became an exercise in creativity, and many were dumped in rivers or even in the South Atlantic from airplanes or ships. According to Andersen, detainees were usually tortured to the maximum extent before being killed. Torture methods used by the military were intended to produce pain, a breakdown of resistance, fear and humiliation, a strong sense of imminent death, and weakness. Anyone who escaped or survived these camps was changed forever by the terrorism endured.

Nine of the top officials responsible for these acts of violence and mass terror were brought eventually to trial under the rule of President Razúl Alfonsín. Two of them, Videla and Viola, were sentenced to life imprisonment, with the others also receiving substantial prison terms. In 1990, however, President Carlos Menem issued pardons to every official involved in the dirty war, intending to help Argentina "move forward." In August 2003, under a new government, the amnesty given by Menem was annulled, providing a major victory to human-rights advocates and families of the victims.

See also OVERVIEW OF LATIN AMERICA, BY REGION; STATE TERRORISM.

References: Andersen, Martin Edwin. *Dossier Secreto: Argentina's Desaparecidos and the Myth of the "Dirty Wars"* (Boulder, Colo.: Westview Press, 1993); Arditti, Rita. *Searching for Life: The Grandmothers of the Plaza de Mayo and the Disappeared Children of Argentina* (Berkeley: University of California Press, 1999); Guest, Ian. *Behind the Disappearances: Argentina's Dirty War against Human Rights and the United Nations* (Philadelphia: University of Pennsylvania Press, 1990).

Arizona Patriots

This loosely organized group subscribed to the Posse Comitatus and the CHRISTIAN IDENTITY ideology, portraying themselves as white supremacists and anti-Semites who sought to overturn the American government. While initially involved in primarily "paper" threats, including a document in 1984 threatening to indict all Arizona public officials before a "Patriot" grand jury, their plots became more violent. The FBI in 1986 arrested 10 members of the group, charging them with plotting to bomb the Simon Wiesenthal Center, the LA office of the FBI, two offices of the Jewish Defense League, a Utah IRS office, and an armored car in Nevada. The plans were extraordinarily complex, including the planned use of arrows with exploding tips, homemade mortars, and sleeping gas. The crimes were allegedly inspired by *The Turner Diaries,* the same novel that inspired both Timothy McVeigh and The Order to commit heinous crimes. The arrest of the members in 1986 signaled the end of the Patriots as an organized group.

Armed Islamic Group (GIA)

An Islamic extremist group with a membership of at least several hundred (and perhaps as many as several thousand), the GIA has as its goal the overthrow of the secular Algerian regime, replacing it with an Islamic state. In the first round of the Algerian legislative elections in December 1991, Algiers voided the victory of the Islamic Salvation Front (FIS)—the largest Islamic party. The GIA began its violent activities in early 1992 in response to this action.

Its activities have included attacks against civilians, journalists, and foreign residents. During the latter part of the 1990s, the GIA conducted a campaign of civilian massacres, sometimes wiping out entire villages in its areas of operation and frequently killing hundreds of civilians. Since announcing its campaign against foreigners living in Algeria in September 1993, this group has killed more than 100 expatriate men and women (predominately European) living in the country. While the early 1990s activities of this group comprised primarily bombings (including car bombings), assassinations, and kidnappings (usually involving slitting the throat of the kidnap victims) in Algeria, the GIA in December 1994 carried out an aircraft hijacking of an Air France flight to Algiers. In late 1999, several GIA members were convicted by a French court for conducting a series of bombings in France in 1995.

References: Council on Foreign Relations. Terrorism: Questions and Answers, "Armed Islamic Group." Available online. URL: http://cfrterrorism.org/groups/gia.html. Accessed February 16, 2006; Naval Postgraduate School. Terrorist Group Profiles, "Armed Islamic Group (GIA)." Available online. URL: http://library.nps.navy.mil/home/tgp/gia.htm. Accessed February 16, 2006.

armed militias in the United States

Numerous local or state militias are in the forefront of the antigovernment movement in the United States. Several armed militias are very well armed and have assumed that they need to be for the ultimate conflict with federal authority they believe will inevitably occur. They have adopted as their national day April 19, the anniversary date of the Battle of Lexington in 1775 that launched the American Revolution. Militia personnel consider themselves to be instrumental in restoring the pristine values that the revolution fought to protect. The bombing of the Alfred P. Murrah Federal Building in Oklahoma City on April 19, 1995, is the most violent expression of antigovernment sentiment. This was the most lethal terrorist attack ever perpetrated on American soil: 168 people were killed and 850 others were injured. By coincidence, April 19 was also the date of a 1992 shoot-out between federal authorities and Randall Weaver on Ruby Ridge. A year later on April 19, after a 51-day siege by the FBI and the ATF, a fire broke out at Mount Carmel where David Koresh and his followers had stockpiled a large supply of illegal weapons. All of these events have provided the militia movement with inspiration and martyrs.

The militias firmly believe that the federal government is an aggressive force intent on undermining liberty in the United States and that they are only preparing to defend themselves against unconstitutional authority. However, not all militia members are advocates of violence or desirous of committing violent acts. The U.S. Constitution protects free speech even if it is offensive or extremist. Only those militia members accumulating arsenals composed of illegal weapons have been targeted by government agencies. However, most militia members possess a conspirational view of the government and are convinced that its officials are determined to confiscate handguns and deliver their owners to isolated reeducation camps in the western desert.

References: Levitas, Daniel. *The Terrorist Next Door: The Militia Movement and the Radical Right* (New York: St. Martin's, 2002); Mulloy, D. J. *American Extremism: History, Politics and the Militia Movement* (Philadelphia: Taylor & Francis, 2004).

Armed Revolutionary Nuclei (ARN; a.k.a. Ordine Nuovo [New Order])

Founded by Pino Rauti, this outlawed fascist Italian group is an offshoot of the Ordine Nuovo. The Ordine Nuovo bombed the Piazza Fontana in Milan in December 1969, killing 16 and wounding 90. The following year, this same group bombed the Rome-Messina train, killing six and wounding 100. An antifascist march was attacked with hand grenades by the Ordine Nuovo in May 1974, killing eight.

The Armed Revolutionary Nuclei (ARN), as it emerged in early 1980, was responsible for the bombing of the Bologna train station, which killed 85 people. This massacre was put together by Stafano Delle Chiaie, a member of the ARN. Much of the ARN's activity appears to have been generated by a desire to force the Italian government to take a stronger stand against terrorism, by carrying out terrorist attacks. The subsequent government crackdown on terrorism diminished significantly the strength of this group.

armed right-wing groups in the United States

Armed right-wing groups have given evidence of several disturbing differences between the left-wing "college radicals" of the 1960s and 1970s. Unlike the isolated, crudely unsophisticated pipe-bomb manufacturers who dominated most of the U.S.-based terrorist groups of the past, these groups are often militias, well trained in the use of arms and explosives. They often have skilled armorers and bomb makers and many who are adept in guerrilla-warfare techniques and outdoor survival skills. Usually coupled with racial and religious intolerance, and even an apocalyptic vision of imminent war, these groups bring more potential to engage in lethal and increasingly sophisticated terrorist operations, as the OKLAHOMA CITY BOMBING demonstrated.

This form of right-wing activity has wide-ranging geographical dimensions, a diversity of causes its adherents espouse, and overlapping agendas among its member groups. There are militia groups from Idaho to California, Arizona to North Carolina, Georgia to Michigan, Texas to Canada. Almost every state has at least one such group, and most have several. These groups share motivations that span a broad spectrum, including antifederalism, sedition, racial hatred, and religious hatred. Most have masked these unpleasant-sounding motives under a rather transparent veneer of religious precepts.

Literature from these groups indicate that they are bound together by a number of factors. These include a shared hostility to any form of government above the county level and even an advocacy of the overthrow of the U.S. government (or the Zionist Occupation government, as some of them call it). Vilification of Jews and nonwhites as children of Satan is coupled with an obsession with achieving the religious and racial purification of the United States and a belief in a conspiracy theory of powerful Jewish interests controlling the government, banks, and the media.

These facets of right-wing ideology give interesting insights in light of the images that terrorists have of their world, their victims, and themselves. To view the "enemy" as "children of Satan" is to dehumanize them, as terrorists must in order to kill. To view the struggle of the group as an effort to "purify" the nation is to view it as a battle between good and evil, as terrorists must. The view of a coming racial war fits the "millenial" view that many terrorists maintain. A "warrior" fighting in a cause to "purify" a state from the "children of Satan" will have little problem in justifying the use of lethal force.

Right-wing groups capable of terrorism in the United States are widespread, intricately linked by many overlapping memberships, and bound together in a political and religious doctrine that defines the world in terms that make the use of violence not just acceptable but necessary. Since many of the members of these groups are skilled in the use of weapons and utilize survival training in camps throughout the country in planning for an "inevitable" racial war, the impact of these groups may well be formidable in the 21st century.

See also AMERICAN FRONT; ARIZONA PATRIOTS; ARYAN NATIONS; ARYAN REPUBLICAN ARMY; COVENANT, SWORD, AND ARM OF THE LORD.

References: Dyer, Joel. *Harvest of Rage: Why Oklahoma City Is Only the Beginning* (Boulder, Colo.: Westview Press, 1998); Michael, George. *Confronting Right Wing Extremism and Terrorism in the USA* (New York: Routledge, 2003).

Armenian Secret Army for the Liberation of Armenia (ASALA; Orly Group, 3rd October Organization)

ASALA was formed in 1975 with the stated purpose of pressuring the Turkish government to acknowledge and apologize publicly for its alleged responsibility for the deaths of 1.5 million Armenians in 1915, an event that may have inspired the Jewish Holocaust in Europe a quarter of a century later. The group demands that Turkey also pay reparations and cede territory for an Armenian homeland. By the 1990s, however, the former Soviet republic of Armenia became a sovereign state and became occupied with territorial disputes with neighboring Azerbaijan. Possibly for this reason and also because of internal dissension, ASALA was relatively inactive throughout the closing years of the 20th century.

ASALA strategy has been to target Turkish installations and personnel mostly in Europe and the Middle East. The Syrian government, probably because of its own differences with Turkey (and the Turkish military alliance with ISRAEL), has provided assistance to ASALA. ASALA also has ties to some of the more radical Palestinian organizations such as the POPULAR FRONT FOR THE LIBERATION OF PALESTINE and POPULAR FRONT FOR THE LIBERATION OF PALESTINE-GENERAL COMMAND. ASALA's strength is estimated at around a few hundred members and sympathizers.

Reference: United States Department of State Publication, *Patterns of Global Terrorism, 1997* (Washington, D.C.: Department of State, 2000).

Army for the Liberation of Rwanda (ALIR; a.k.a. Interahamwe, Former Armed Forces [ex-FAR])

The FAR was the army of the Rwandan Hutu regime that carried out the genocide of at least 500,000 Tutsi and regime opponents in 1994. The Interahamwe was the civilian militia force that carried out much of the killing. These groups merged after they were forced from Rwanda into the Democratic Republic of the Congo (DRC; then Zaire) in 1994. The ALIR now operates as the armed branch of the PALIR, or Party for the Liberation of Rwanda.

The ALIR seeks to topple Rwanda's Tutsi-dominated government, desiring to restore Hutu control. It may also be seeking to complete the genocide begun in 1994. In 1996, a message alleged to have been from the ALIR threatened to kill the U.S. ambassador to Rwanda and other U.S. citizens. In 1999, ALIR guerrillas kidnapped and killed eight foreign tourists in a game park on the Congo-Ugandan border, apparently in protest of alleged U.S.-U.K. support for Rwanda's government.

Several thousand ALIR regular forces worked with the Congolese Army in the Congo civil war. At the same time, an indeterminate number of ALIR guerrillas operate behind Rwanda lines in eastern Congo close to the Rwandan border, and sometimes even within Rwanda.

In 2001, the ALIR, while not formally disbanded, was supplanted by the Democratic Front for the Liberation of Rwanda (FLDR). The exact strength of the FLDR is not known today, but several thousand FLDR members operate in the eastern part of the Democratic Republic of the Congo, near the Rwandan border. In 2003, the United Nations, with the assistance of Rwanda, repatriated about 1,500 of the FLDR combatants from the DRC. The government of the Democratic Republic of the Congo provided training, arms, and supplies to the ALIR forces but halted that support in 2002. In 2006, one of the ALIR rebels involved in the 1999 killing in the game park along the Congo-Ugandan border was convicted of murder in an Ugandan court. Despite FDLR's claim that they have given up their armed struggle, some groups descended from ALIR continue to operate in eastern Congo.

Reference: Federation of American Scientists (FAS). "Army for the Liberation of Rwanda." Available online. URL: http://www.fas.org/irp/world/para/interahamwe.htm. Accessed February 15, 2006.

Army of God

The Army of God is an underground movement whose members believe that the use of violence is an appropriate tool for fighting abortion. Michael Bray, the chaplain of the Army of God, hosts an annual "White Rose Banquet" honoring those imprisoned for antiabortion violence. Bray has written a book, *A Time to Kill,* offering theological justification for violence against abortion providers and has served time in jail for bombing abortion clinics.

According to the manual of this organization, the Army of God "is a real Army, and God is the General and the Commander-in-Chief." This manual provides instruction for abortion clinic violence, detailing methods for blockading entrances, attacking with butyric acid, arson, bomb making, and a variety of other equally illegal activities. In fact, the manual begins with a "declaration of war" on the abortion industry, stating that "We are forced to take up arms against you. Our life for yours—a simple equation . . . You shall not be tortured at our hands. Vengeance belongs to God only. However, execution is rarely gentle."

Several members of the Army of God have been involved in highly publicized incidents of terrorism, including ERIC ROBERT RUDOLPH, convicted of an abortion clinic bombing as well as the Atlanta Olympic bombing, and James Kopp, convicted in the fatal shooting of clinic doctor Barrett Slepian in 1998. Clayton Waagner, the individual who claimed responsibility for sending anthrax letters to abortion clinics in 2001, signed many of his threat letters with the name Army of God and posted (on the Army of God website) threats to kill several dozen people working at abortion clinics.

Antiabortion extremist Clayton Lee Waagner escaped from a county jail in Clinton, Illinois, on February 22, 2001, where he was being held after his conviction on federal charges for possession of a firearm by a felon and interstate transportation of a stolen vehicle. On September 7, he was involved in a hit-and-run accident in Memphis, Tennessee, abandoning his vehicle at the scene. Police discovered a pipe bomb and bomb-making components in the car and more such materials in a hotel room that Waagner also abandoned in Tunica, Mississippi.

During a three-day period, from the 15th to the 17th of October 2001, Waagner allegedly mailed more than 300 ANTHRAX threat letters to reproductive health clinics on the east coast of the United States. The envelopes, marked "Urgent Security Notice Enclosed" and "Time Sensitive," had the return address of the U.S. Marshall's Service or the U.S. Secret Service. The letters, which contained a white powdery substance (which was not, however, anthrax), were signed "Army of God—Virginia Dare Cell." A similar batch of letters, also signed in this fashion that tested negative for anthrax in spite of the white powdery substance, was sent to reproductive health clinics. Bomb threats were also telephoned during this time to businesses located in the building that housed the national headquarters of Planned Parenthood and the National Abortion Federation.

Following his arrest in December of 2001, Waagner suggested to investigators that he was preparing a third wave of fake anthrax letters to abortion providers and that he had intended to place the pipe bomb recovered from the vehicle in Memphis at a local Planned Parenthood office. Waagner was also charged with two bank robberies—one in Harrisburg, Pennsylvania, in May and the other in Morgantown, West Virginia, in November—allegedly to finance his antiabortion activities while he was a fugitive. In December 2003, Waagner was convicted on 51 counts out of a 53-count indictment.

In recent months, the Army of God website has contained a growing rhetoric against gays and lesbians, but violence in this direction has not yet been documented by members of this group.

See also ANTIABORTION CLINIC ATTACKS.

Reference: National Memorial Institute for the Prevention of Terrorism (MIPT). "Army of God" Available online. URL: http://www.tkb.org/Group.jsp?groupID=28. Accessed February 15, 2006.

Aryan Nations

This group traces its origins back to the 1950s and early 1960s. Its current structure was organized in the early 1970s under the leadership of Richard Butler, with headquarters in Hayden Lake, Idaho. Butler, who created the group in 1973, also established a religious arm of the organization a few years later known as the Church of Jesus Christ Christian. Its ideology is a mixture of theology and racism, being anti-Semitic and antiblack. The literature of this group indicates that its beliefs are couched under a religious doctrine of "identity," which holds that Jesus Christ was not a Jew but an Aryan, that the lost tribes of Israel were in fact Anglo-Saxon and not Semitic, and that Jews are the children of Satan.

The operational profile for this group derives from a book written by an American NEO-NAZI, William Pierce. This book, *The TURNER DIARIES*, offers a blueprint for revolution in the United States based on a race war. It is a disturbing book, freely available on the market, and used by many groups that have splintered from the Aryan Nations for tactical reasons, focusing on certain elements of the doctrine. These groups include, but are not limited to, the Order, the Silent Brotherhood, the White American Bastion, Bruder Schweigen Strike Force II, POSSE COMITATUS, the Arizona Patriots, and the White Patriot Party.

These groups have been linked to armored-car and bank robberies, counterfeiting, assassinations, and assaults on federal, state, and local law enforcement personnel and facilities. One leader in the Aryan Nations, who was also the head of the KU KLUX KLAN in Texas, proposed a point system to achieve "Aryan Warrior" status. One could achieve this status (which required achieving a whole point) by killing:

Members of Congress = 1/5 point
Judges and FBI Director = 1/6 point

FBI agents and U.S. Marshalls = 1/10 point
Journalists and local politicians = 1/12 point
President of the U.S. = 1 point (Warrior status)

This form of right-wing terrorism has wide-ranging geographical dimensions, a diversity of causes its adherents espouse, and overlapping agendas among its member groups. The Aryan Nations is regarded as an umbrella group for many factions involved in violent, often terrorist, activity.

In 2001, as a result of a case filed by a family injured by security guards at the Idaho compound of this group, the court found the group criminally negligent and the resulting fine cost the Aryan Nations the loss of this property, which included the home of its founder. A new headquarters was not immediately established.

The planned celebration, to be held in front of the county courthouse in York, Pennsylvania, on April 21, 2002, by the Aryan Nations of the 113th anniversary of Adolf Hitler's birth, gave a dramatic sense of the diminishing power of this group. Only 14 white supremacists, including 84-year-old Richard Butler, showed up for the celebration. They shuffled along the police barricades and orange mesh fencing, unfurled their Nazi flags, and stood for only about 20 minutes of the hour their permit allowed. While Butler spoke, his remarks were completely drowned out by the shouts of a local street preacher and the drone of a police helicopter hovering overhead. The police actually outnumbered the white supremacists, who had begun targeting York in 2001 after nine white men, including then-mayor Charlie Robertson, were arrested and charged with the murder of a black minister's daughter, Lillie Belle Allen, killed in a torrent of gunfire in 1969 as she and her family unknowingly drove into a hostile white neighborhood at the height of 10 days of racial violence.

By June 2003, the annual "world congress" held by the Aryan Nations had diminished considerably. Since the group had lost its north Idaho headquarters in the civil rights lawsuit, it met with other white supremacist groups at the Farragut State Park on Lake Pend Oreille in Idaho. Although the event featured several speakers and neo-Nazi SKINHEAD rock bands, drawing between 100 and 200 people, the planned marches through downtown Coeur d'Alene were not possible, since other groups had already bought the permits for parades on the same dates.

At this rally, however, Aryan Nations founder Richard Butler's successor, Ray Redfeairn, was formally named the next leader of the racist organization. Indeed, this year's congress, which pulled together a full menu of racist leaders from around the country, suggested the Aryan Nations had crept back from the brink. In the lineup were

- Redfeairn, the newly anointed successor to lead Butler's Aryan Nations. In ascending to the leadership of the white supremacist organization, Redfeairn stated that his greatest enemies were Jews, and he proclaimed that the Bible demanded their genocide. He also preached hatred of all nonwhites and called the federal government a betrayer of the "white race," which in his view is endangered with extinction as a consequence.
- Bradley Jenkins, the Imperial Wizard of the Aryan Nations Knights of the Ku Klux Klan, an Alabama-based group that focuses most of its wrath against blacks and all non-Western immigrants. Jenkins's presence was a result of an alliance of these groups by Redfeairn earlier in the year, which pulled dozens of southern KKK clans into alliance with the Aryan Nations.
- Billy Roper, leader of a new group called White Revolution, which splintered from the neo-Nazi National Alliance the previous year. This group is an unusual mixture of genetics and white supremacist interpretations of Christianity and appears to have more of an appeal for young people, as Roper was, at the time of this rally, in his 30s and a former high school history teacher.
- Hal Turner, a New Jersey talk-show host whose daily broadcast of fiercely anti-immigrant, anti-Jewish and anti-federal commentary on shortwave radio and the Internet appears to draw easily on the current politics of the day to support his case.
- Jeff Schoep and Tim Bishop, leaders of the Minneapolis-based National Socialist Movement, a neo-Nazi organization appealing to young SKINHEAD racists.

The death of William Pierce, the neo-Nazi author of *The Turner Diaries,* in July 2002, and the arrest of Matthew Hale, the so-called Pontifex Maximus of the anti-Semitic and racist group calling itself the World Church of the Creator, may have weakened the strength of the Aryan Nations groups. Hale was charged with soliciting the murder of a federal judge who presided over an Oregon church's trademark infringement suit against Hale and who had ordered him to stop using the name of the World Church of the Creator.

The Aryan Nations, under Butler's leadership, became increasingly interested in using local elections as a platform for vocalizing racist ideology. On November 5, 2003, Butler lost the Hayden, Idaho, mayoral election. With 100% of votes counted, Butler had only 50 votes (2%). Incumbent mayor Ronald B. McIntire had 1,924 votes (92%), far outpacing the other candidate in the race, Gordie Andrea, who had 148 votes (7%). During the race, Butler's followers passed out racist literature in city neighborhoods. The fliers urged white people to wake up or face extinction.

Since only about 10,000 residents live in Hayden, a municipal election in the resort town would ordinarily get little notice outside of the county. However, Butler's candidacy drew national attention because the vote would show exactly how many Hayden residents support his racist views. Two of Butlers supporters also ran for city council seats. City Councilwoman Nancy Taylor, a one-term incumbent who was being challenged by one of Butler's followers, won with 1,236 votes (60%). Aryan Nations member Karl Gharst had 42 votes (2%). The remainder went to Roger Saterfiel. City Councilman Chris Beck won his race with 1,986 votes (97%) against Aryan member Zachary L. Beck, who had posted 69 votes (2%). The two are not related.

Following the September 8, 2004, death of Richard Girnt Butler, the Church of Jesus Christ Christian/Aryan Nations, moved the mailing address of the organization from Hayden, Idaho, to Lincoln, Alabama. In the post–September 11 security environment, both the white supremacists and their detractors say they have been tracked more closely by federal agents who are better funded and more vigilant about potential domestic terrorists.

Reference: National Memorial Institute for the Prevention of Terrorism (MIPT). "Aryan Nations (AN)." Available online. URL: http://www.tkb.org/Group.jsp?groupID=29. Accessed February 15, 2006.

Aryan Republican Army

The Aryan Republican Army (ARA) was a militant group consisting of members of the Aryan Nations and of the CHRISTIAN IDENTITY MOVEMENT. This organization committed bank robberies in the midwest during 1994 and 1995. Adopting the "leaderless resistance" structure advocated by KU KLUX KLAN leader Louis Beam, members of the ARA were staunchly paramilitary and radically neo-Nazi, with stated goals of the overthrow of the U.S. government, the extermination of Jews, and the establishment of an Aryan state in North America.

Members of this group were "required" to read *THE TURNER DIARIES*, the white supremacist novel that served as an inspiration for The Order and for Timothy McVeigh, the Oklahoma City bomber. The primary base of operations for the ARA was Elohim City, Oklahoma, a haven for militant racists and a place that McVeigh called two weeks before the bombing.

Bank robbery and the stockpiling of weapons were the primary activities during the brief history of this group. They reportedly carried out 22 robberies in the two-year period and gave part of the proceeds for these robberies to fund "White Terror Productions," a racist record label that recorded a CD dedicated to Sam and Vicki Weaver (who were killed at Ruby Ridge) and Richard Wayne Snell (a white supremacist militant who was executed on the day of the OKLAHOMA CITY BOMBING for his role in an earlier plot to bomb the Alfred P. Murrah Federal Building in Oklahoma City).

When one of the members arrested in a January 1996 robbery told police about the ARA and identified four of his accomplices (who were subsequently arrested), the ARA apparently carried out no further crimes.

Reference: National Memorial Institute for the Prevention of Terrorism (MIPT). "Aryan Republican Army (ARA)." Available online. URL: http://www.tkb.org/Group.jsp?groupID=3412. Accessed February 15, 2006.

al-Asad, Hafiz (1930–2000)

Asad's date of birth is in some dispute, and he may have been born a few years before 1930. The name means "lion" in Arabic but was changed from *Wahsh*, which means "wild beast." Asad was president of the Syrian Arab Republic during 1971–2000 after taking power in a bloodless coup. Asad had served as defense minister during 1965–1970. During his ministership, Syria lost the Golan Heights to ISRAEL during the Six-Day War in 1967. He won national elections in 1991 and 1999 for a fourth and fifth term with 99.98% of the popular vote. Because Asad was a member of the Alawite minority (about an eighth of the Syrian population), he broadened his base by appointing a Sunni prime minister, since Sunnis represent nearly three-quarters of the Syrian population. His efforts did not prevent numerous Sunni demonstrations against the regime. Though Asad also pursued some economic liberalization policies, Syria still suffers from an economy unable to keep pace with a rapidly growing population, which during the 1990s reached a rate of 3.4% annually.

During the 1970s and 1980s, Asad accepted military assistance from the Soviet Union. After that time, he attempted to pursue negotiations with Israel for peace and the return of the Golan Heights. The negotiations have not produced any lasting results as yet. Moreover, Asad was more consumed with preparing for his succession, hoping that his son would be the next Syrian leader. This was no guarantee, but at the time of his death, his son did indeed succeed to power. However, at the time of his succession, the economy was weak, and the country had strained relations with its eastern neighbor, IRAQ. It was still in a state of belligerency with Israel and remained nervous about the close military contacts between Israel and Turkey, the country on Syria's western borders.

Under Asad, Syria became more identified with the sponsorship of terrorism against American and Israeli targets. Syria was listed by the U.S. Department of State as a state that directed or encouraged terrorist acts against American citizens and installations. In addition, Asad had in effect "Syrianized" Lebanon by maintaining approximately 20,000 soldiers there and encouraging a million Syrians, who now may form a fourth of Lebanon's population, to move there to live and work.

Syria, under his leadership, also supported numerous training camps for terrorist organizations in some of the areas of Lebanon that its military controls. Asad supported Palestinian organizations in their attacks on Israel in concert with his own war against the Jewish state. However, Asad supported the allied side during the 1990–91 Persian Gulf War. He later cultivated closer and more cordial relations with the West, especially the United States, in an effort to gain concessions from Israel over the Golan Heights.

Reference: Maoz, Moshe. *Syria and Israel: From War to Peace Making* (New York: Oxford University Press, 1995); Pipes, Daniel. "Syria's 'Lion' Was Really a 'Monster,'" *Wall Street Journal* (June 12, 2000); Van Dam, Nikolaos. *The Struggle for Power in Syria: Politics and Society under Asad and the Ba'ath Party* (London: I. B. Taurus, 1996).

Asbat al-Ansar

Asbat al-Ansar (The League of the Followers or Partisans' League) is a Sunni-based extremist group operating in Lebanon that is composed primarily of Palestinians and allied with BIN LADEN's AL-QAEDA organization. The group adheres to an extreme version of Islam, justifying violence against civilian targets to accomplish "holy" goals. These goals include the overthrow of the Lebanese government, thwarting perceived anti-Islamic and pro-Western influences in the region.

This group has carried out multiple terrorist attacks in Lebanon since the early 1990s. It was responsible for the assassination of Lebanese religious leaders and the bombing of nightclubs, theaters, and liquor stores during the last decade of the 20th century. Asbat al-Ansar's profile changed somewhat in 2000 with attacks against international targets and Lebanese political leaders, carrying out a rocket-propelled grenade attack on the Russian embassy. In 2003, suspected members of this group were responsible for the attempt in April to use a car bomb against a McDonald's in a Beirut suburb. They were also involved with a member of ARAFAT's FATAH movement in a rocket attack on the Future TV building in Beirut.

Asbat al-Ansar's leader, Abu Juhjin, remains at large, although he has been sentenced to death in absentia for the murder in 1994 of a Muslim cleric. The group has about 300 fighters in Lebanon, with a primary base of operations in the Ayn al-Hilwah Palestinian camp near Sidon in southern Lebanon. It is believed to receive monetary support from Bin Laden's al-Qaeda network and from extremist Sunnis in the region.

Reference: National Memorial Institute for the Prevention of Terrorism (MIPT). "Asbat al-Ansar." Available online. URL: http://www.tkb.org/Group.jsp?groupID=4639. Accessed February 15, 2006.

attack on America: September 11, 2001

During the bloodiest day on American soil since the Civil War, the United States experienced a well-coordinated terrorist attack on two of its major cities, New York and Washington, D.C. A country of nearly 300 million people nearly came to a standstill, while 3,000 died and billions of dollars were lost to the national economy. For a time, the United States went into a recession, and many people were afraid to fly. Subsequent investigations, most notably the 9/11 Commission, concluded that the nation was unprepared for and shocked by violence that was designed to cause as many casualties as possible and to destroy symbols of American financial, military, and political supremacy.

The World Trade Center had been attacked previously in 1993 when terrorists had packed explosives in a parked van in the underground parking lot. The destruction killed six people and injured dozens of others. On September 11, 2001, the approach was different; the terrorists had learned from the previous attack that destroying the World Trade Center would require a greater and better-planned effort. Commercial planes full of jet fuel could be made into missiles; seizing control of them and flying them to their targets would require meticulous planning and training. Al-Qaeda operatives took flying lessons (though flight instructors reported that they were uninterested in taking off and landing aircraft) while living seemingly normal lives.

Sequence of Events

The tragic string of events on September 11 began with the departure of two planes from Boston's Logan airport. One was a Boeing 767, American Airlines flight 11, bound for Los Angeles with 81 passengers, which departed at 7:59 A.M. and headed west, over the Adirondacks, before taking a sudden turn south and diving toward the heart of New York City and lower Manhattan. The second flight, United Airlines 175, also a Boeing 767, left at 7:58 with 63 passengers. Another two Boeing 757s took off that were also part of the attack plan: American flight 77 departed from Dulles airport in Washington, D.C., at 8:10 A.M., bound for Los Angeles; and United flight 93 left Newark, New Jersey, at 8:01 A.M., bound for San Francisco. All of these flights were transcontinental and therefore loaded with jet fuel.

At 8:45 A.M., American flight 11 hit the World Trade Center's 110-floor north tower, ripping through the building and setting the upper floors on fire. Plane parts, office furniture, glass, and body parts began falling all around, stunning people in the street below. Inside the building, workers desperately began running down the stairways. The lower stairs, however, began filling with water from broken pipes and sprinklers. The smell of jet fuel permeated the building. Still others leaped to their deaths since they were trapped in the upper floors and preferred a relatively quick death to being burned alive. Some crawled outside the building in an attempt to escape the fire, only to fall to their deaths. Many of those able to escape suffered from burns and smoke inhalation. At this point in time, few believed that what was going on was a terrorist attack. Most understandably believed that a tragic accident had occurred. America's age of innocence would last for a few more minutes.

United flight 175 departed from the airport 20 minutes late. After passing the Massachusetts-Connecticut state line, the plane made a 30-degree turn, one more sharp turn, and then descended rapidly to Manhattan, flying between buildings until slamming into the south tower of the World Trade Center at 9:06 A.M. The departure delay probably saved thousands of other lives since the 20-minute interval provided precious time to escape from the north tower.

The north tower was at this point a scene of human misery. The dead and dying were seemingly everywhere. According to one survivor, the emergency phone on the 20th floor was dead, and an emergency alarm switch failed when pulled. Each of the towers contained a central steel core surrounded by open office space. Eighteen-inch tubes ran vertically along the outside and provided support for the buildings. American flight 11 damaged the building's central core, and the weight was distributed to the outer steel tubes. These were slowly deformed by the additional weight and the intense heat of the fires. The floors above where the second plane hit 1 Trade Center were resting on steel that was gradually softening from the heat of the burning jet fuel, until the girders could no longer carry the load. As one retired investigator explained, "All that steel turns to spaghetti, and then all of a sudden that structure is untenable, and the weight starts bearing down on the floors that were not designed to hold that weight, and you start having collapse." Because each floor dropped down to the one below, neither building toppled. Instead, each one came straight down, each floor collapsing on the one below it.

The south tower collapsed first, followed by the north tower less than a half-hour later, trapping hundreds of

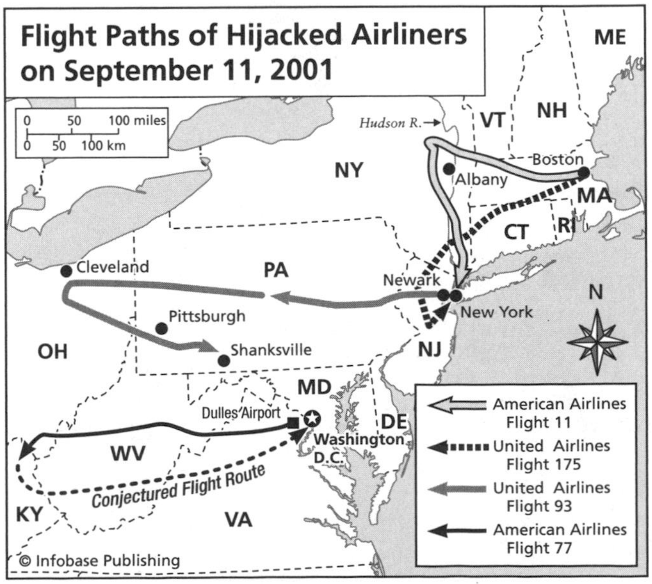

rescue workers below, in addition to the thousands of workers still in the building. The debris from this collapse gutted the 4 World Trade Center building below it. A third building, 7 World Trade Center, collapsed several hours later at 5:25 in the afternoon.

The second crash made everyone realize that this event was not a horrible accident. New York City basically shut down at 9:35 as tunnels and bridges were sealed. There were also evacuations from landmarks such as the Empire State Building, the Metropolitan Museum of Art, and the United Nations buildings. Airports were shut down across the country for the first time in history, and they would not reopen for several days.

World Trade Center: Damage Assessment, Done Soon after September 11, 2001

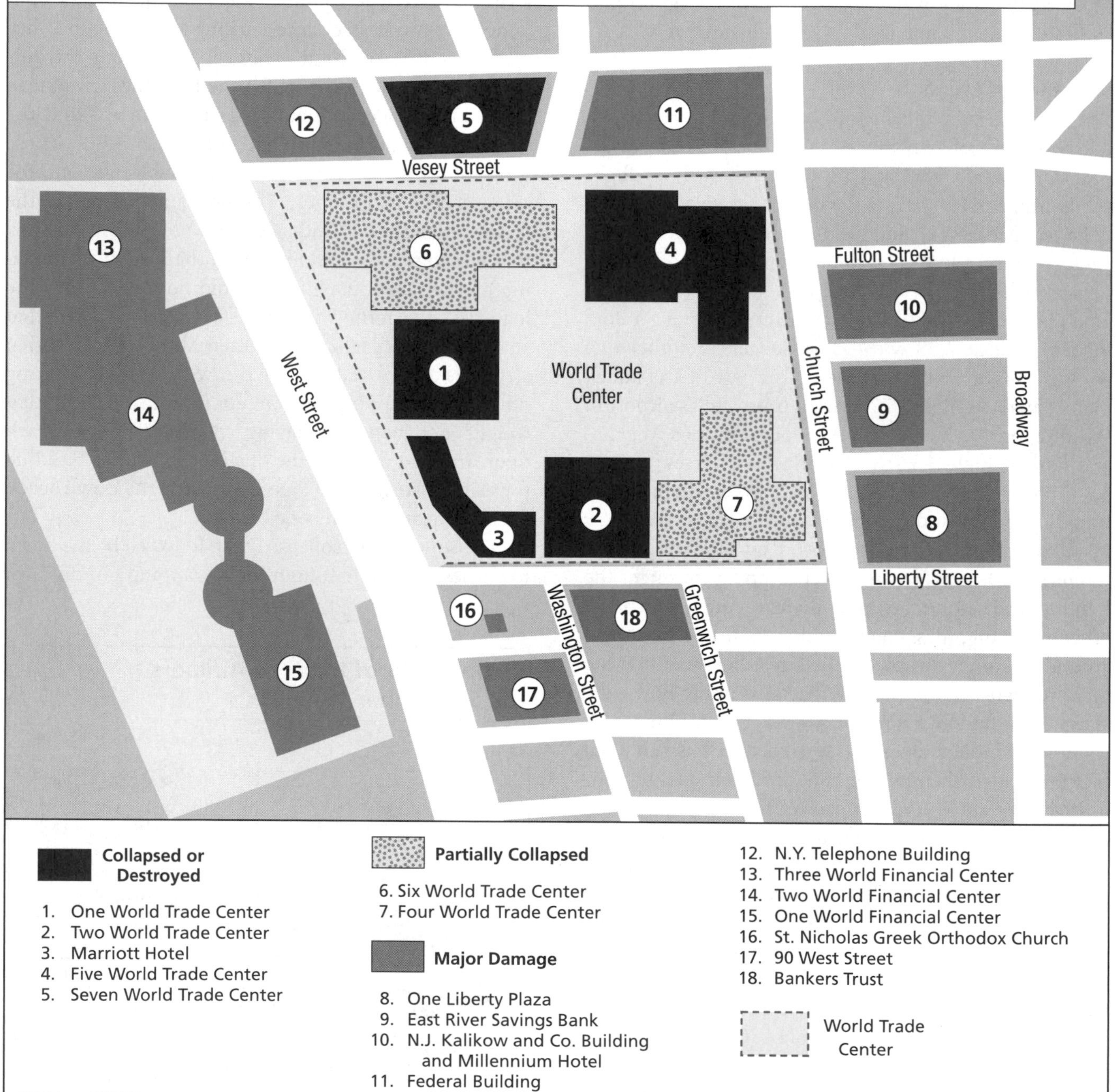

Two days after the 9/11 terrorist attacks, fires still burn amidst the rubble and debris of the World Trade Center in New York City in the area known as Ground Zero. (DEPARTMENT OF DEFENSE)

In fact, there were additional attacks already underway. In Washington, D.C., American Airlines flight 77 hit the Pentagon at 9:40. Within minutes, the White House was evacuated, as were federal office buildings. A little more than an hour later, Washington itself was gridlocked, as thousands attempted to drive away from the city. Top government officials, including the vice president, the Senate's president pro tempore, and some cabinet officials (all of whom were in the line of presidential succession) were evacuated. The president himself was sent from a Florida school he had been visiting to a military base. *Air Force One* was escorted by several military jets.

A fourth attack was by this time underway. United Airlines flight 93 had departed from Newark and was heading west when it suddenly turned back toward Washington. Several of the passengers on this flight had some sense of what was happening. One called from his cell phone to announce that the plane was being hijacked. Others called later to tell their families they planned to regain control of the plane. Their efforts were partially successful. The plane did not reach Washington; instead, it crashed into a reclaimed section of an old coal strip mine in Pennsylvania at 10:06 A.M. All on board were killed.

Insights into Those Responsible

The 19 hijackers, led by Mohamad Atta (a possible 20th hijacker, Moussawi, was found guilty in early 2006 at the end of a trial that took several months), all died in the attacks they perpetuated. The ease in which they were allowed to board their flights, take control of the aircrafts, and transform commercial planes into lethal missiles combined to provide a shock to the nation and a large part of the world. Moreover, the hijackers had developed the appearance of normalcy. They looked and behaved as though they were merely average passengers. Previously, they had led comfortable and seemingly quiet lives that were essentially similar to those of their neighbors: They did not stand out; they wore

Aerial view of the Pentagon Building located in Washington, District of Columbia (DC), showing emergency crews responding to the destruction caused when a high-jacked commercial jetliner crashed into the southwest corner of the building, during the 9/11 terrorists attacks. (DEPARTMENT OF DEFENSE)

khakis and polos, ate at pizzerias, and lived in nondescript apartments. A few occasionally even visited strip clubs. The detailed investigations that followed 9/11 revealed, however, that Atta and his collaborators were part of large network that received financing and help with planning the attacks. Some of the hijackers, such as Atta and Hani Hanjour, had lived quietly in the United States for years, scattered in locations from Florida to Arizona. Several took flying lessons, hardly an abnormal activity and certainly not one that caused attention.

The Moussaoui trial also gave some insight into the sort of phenomenon that threatened American lives and economic well-being. During the penalty phase of the trial when the jury was charged to decide whether to recommend the death penalty or life imprisonment, Moussaoui behaved in ways that caused his own defense lawyers to express concern. He was the last witness in his own trial, an appearance his lawyers advised against. Moussaoui maintained that he and Richard Reid, a would-be terrorist arrested in a shoe-bombing attempt while aboard a transatlantic flight, were to collaborate in the hijacking of a fifth plane on 9/11 and fly it into the White House. But, according to the 9/11 mastermind, Khalid Sheikh Mohammed, Moussaoui was regarded as too "problematic" to be trusted to carry through an assignment. Rather, it was hoped he would be available for a second wave of attacks on the United States's west coast. Moussaoui also regularly cursed the United States during his trial and stated that he considered "every American to be my enemy." He seemed undecided himself about whether it would be best to die as a martyr or spend the rest of his life in prison.

While Moussaoui's behavior was mercurial, it was also instructive. Observers and terrorism experts received confirmation that, while the 9/11 attacks were a success for al-Qaeda, they were only a first step in a process to destroy the United States or at least bring it to its knees. Moreover, the fact that he was not allowed to participate in 9/11 suggests that AL-QAEDA carefully selects personnel who are devoted to their task, unafraid to die, and determined to cause as much devastation as possible.

America's Initial Response

Following the attacks hundreds of people were taken into custody. Within a short time the links of at least some of the hijackers to OSAMA BIN LADEN were established. Atta had apparently met bin Laden years earlier. President Bush also received intelligence that linked the al-Qaeda network to its headquarters in Afghanistan where it was protected by the Taliban government. In a speech to a joint session of Congress, Bush demanded that the Taliban turn bin Laden and his principal associates over to the United States. They refused and the United States immediately prepared to launch a military campaign in Afghanistan to locate the al-Qaeda leadership and bring it to justice or, in the president's words, "bring justice to them." The American initiative in Afghanistan received support from several allies, including some NATO countries and even acquiescence from several Islamic states. Pakistan's government cooperated with the United States to overthrow the Taliban regime. However, while the Taliban government was removed, its top leadership as well as the top leadership of al-Qaeda remained at large. A government, obligated to democratize Afghanistan and protected by the United States, has been in control since 2002.

Aftermath of 9/11

During the months and years that followed 9/11, American officials as well as the American public mostly refrained from engaging in the "blame game." In fact, in the immediate post-9/11 era, Americans at least appeared to be more united than they had been in some time. The spilling of American blood on American soil was understood as the beginning of new chapter in the country's national history. For reasons that seemed incompletely understood, the United States was at war with an enemy that was both elusive and determined.

The 9/11 COMMISSION'S REPORT, however, revealed a good many problems with the American ability to cope with this threat to national security, especially the inability or unwillingness of government bodies and their personnel to share information and collaborate on behalf of the common interest. Air force fighter pilots who were ordered into the air after the World Trade Tower attacks at first assumed they were responsible for repelling a "Russian" attack. Simple communication systems on the ground were inadequate, and there was at least a partial communication breakdown between different public safety units attempting to rescue survivors of the attacks.

Americans experienced a near-universal shock that they could be attacked in their own country by an organization, al-Qaeda, that most of them had never heard of, that civilians would be the primary target, and that the objective of the attackers was simply to kill as many people as possible. Comparisons were quickly made to December 7, 1941, the date of the Japanese attack on Pearl Harbor, in which nearly 2,000 Americans had perished. The comparisons quickly faded as soon as the realization sank in that this war would have no obvious frontlines, that no countries had declared war on the United States, and that there was no foreseeable estimate as to how long the conflict would endure.

The situation was further complicated because of what the 9/11 Commission referred to as "failure of imagination." Americans were suddenly made to realize that terrorism was not simply an annoyance that would not go away, but that did not have global reach. Terrorism had become a sophisticated enemy with substantial financial support, a global agenda, an organization in dozens of different countries, fanatical operatives willing and even looking forward to dying for their cause, and had designated the United States as the target of choice.

Most experts also assumed that 9/11 was not simply a single event but was the culmination of planning and earlier attacks that had been going on against Americans for several years and that could easily be traced to the first attack on the World Trade Center in 1993. At the same time, there was every reason to take Islamic terror organizations and spokespersons at their word: They would attack again, and they would not hesitate to use weapons of mass destruction if they could acquire any. By 2007, the United States's annual defense budget was nearing the half-trillion-dollar level. There was no longer any hesitation or doubt that Americans were engaged in a global conflict that would endure for an indefinite time. Even optimists remained convinced that the war on terror would take decades and that the outcome was not at all certain. Part of the challenge for the U.S. government has been to prevent terrorist strikes before they happen, and so far there have been no major terrorist incidents since 9/11 on U.S. soil. This is partly accomplished by the justice system using any and all legal tools in the U.S. code, such as the USA PATRIOT ACT, in order to make a case and detain suspects. However, a recent study has found that only of fraction of the cases brought forward receive a conviction. By the end of 2006, the U.S. Department of Justice had had 510 cases since September 11, 2001, that the government said were terrorism-related, but only 30% of the defendants were prosecuted on a terrorism charge. Most of the others faced charges such as fraud, racketeering, or conspiracy. While 169 cases are still pending, only four people charged since the 2001 attacks were convicted of trying to commit an act of terrorism. Three of the four are Richard Reid; Shahawar Matin Siraj, who plotted to to blow up Herald Square in New York City; and Zacarias Moussaoui.

See also 9/11 COMMISSION REPORT; USA PATRIOT ACT.

References: Dyer, Jim, and Kevin Flynn. *102 Minutes: The Untold Story of the Fight to Survive Inside the Twin Towers* (New York: Henry Holt & Company, 2005); National Commission on Terrorist Attacks. *The 9/11 Commission Report: The Final Report of the National Commission on Terrorist Attacks upon the United States* (New York: W. W. Norton & Company, 2004).

Aum Shinrikyo (Supreme Truth)

The religious cult Aum Shinrikyo, or the Supreme Truth, was established in 1987 and headquartered in Japan. The cult's blind leader, Shoko Asahara (whose real name is Chizuo Matsumoto) allegedly masterminded most, if not all, of its activities until his arrest in May 1995. Asahara prophesied that 30,000 souls had to be saved so that their awakening spiritual energy would prevent a nuclear war in 1999. Aum's plan to save the world was its top priority, and believers were willing to commit heinous acts in order to inform the public of Aum's agenda.

Aum effectively spread its message via the Internet. During the early 1990s the cult's membership in Japan numbered in the thousands. But they also operated internationally. Moscow and its surrounding areas contained dozens of Aum facilities and thousands of disciples. At one time Aum's membership numbered well over 10,000, and Asahara may have actually achieved his goal of saving 30,000.

Aum Shinrikyo was a pioneer in modern terrorism. The sect effectively used communication and information in carrying out the March 20, 1995, sarin gas attack in the Tokyo subway system. The Japanese police had actually been planning to raid Asahara's Tokyo compound on March 22; Aum, however, understood the importance of information and had infiltrated two disciples into the police department. These two moles were able to warn Asahara of the upcoming raid, which would be prepared to find and face chemical agents. Aum leaders, realizing they had little time to act, organized a plan to attack the subway during the police shift change on March 20. These effective communication lines and information sources enabled Aum to carry out one of the most terrifying crimes in the 1990s with little planning and preparation.

The 1995 Tokyo attack was not the cult's first successful foray into chemical terror. Aum had spent more than $30 million on developing poisonous gases and even built a special $10-million facility called Satyan 7 to produce sarin gas. Seven people died in the city of Matsumoto in 1994 when Aum disciples sprayed sarin from a van. Also in 1994, Asahara allegedly ordered a chemical attack on the leader of a rival cult in order to test Aum's sarin and to incite an internal religious war in Japan, but the attack failed due to a faulty sprayer. Less than two months after the successful sarin attack in Tokyo, Aum followers left bags of cyanide in a men's bathroom at Tokyo's Shinjuku train station to distract the authorities from their search for Asahara.

The cult owned and operated a billion-dollar computer empire in Japan, running legitimate stores across the country, as well as selling software and hardware over the Internet. One of Aum's companies was suspected of developing software for government agencies, including the Japan Defense Agency, and major corporations. Legitimate revenues taken in by this business front were supplemented by the personal contributions of all believers (Asahara preached that followers would attain salvation by denying the world and giving their money and belongings to the organization).

Although Aum did not finance its activities with drug and arms sales like many other terrorist organizations have done, the sect certainly did not shrink from dealing with them. The cult manufactured drugs and even its own assault rifles. It produced amphetamines, mescaline, thiopental, and LSD but did not attempt to sell them. Drug manufacturing charges against Asahara were dropped in 2000 because the crimes had no victims. The weapons manufacturing charges still stand even though the weapons produced were proved to be useless. Aum did not intend to sell the weapons for profit, but the Japanese authorities believe Aum wanted to use them to overthrow the government.

The cult used its money to build facilities for the disciples to live, work, and train. It also built and fully equipped laboratories in order to create or modify deadly chemical and biological toxins. The sect was even able to purchase electron microscopes. Aum's biological research team traveled all over the world to find deadly bacteria and viruses. Asahara himself went to Zaire during the Ebola outbreak on the pretense of spreading his gospel. However, authorities believe that his real motive was to obtain a culture of the virus to take back to Japan for genetic manipulation into a biological warfare agent. The scientists at Aum attempted to develop virulent strains of *Clostridium botulinum* and anthrax, as well. While Aum's forays into biological warfare research and production are frightening, its willingness to use biological weapons is scarier still. In a five-year period, Aum disciples were involved in nine attacks using biological agents.

The attacks were usually indiscriminate acts of random terror. Twice in 1993, disciples sprayed what they believed to be anthrax as an aerosol from the roof of their eight-story compound in Tokyo. Followers also confessed to spraying a botulinum toxin on the walls outside the American embassy in Tokyo. Fortunately, Aum's willingness to use lethal biological agents was coupled with its inability to produce effective strains, and no casualties were reported from any of its biological attacks.

Although the sarin attacks produced a relatively low number of casualties given its capabilities, Aum's merciless tactics attracted international public attention that established the group as a legitimate terrorist organization. But their time in the international spotlight would end soon after it began. The Japanese government systematically hunted down and captured the key leaders in the subway attack. Most important, it captured the elusive Asahara less than 60 days after the incident. Already the five cultists directly involved

Doomsday cult Aum Shinrikyo followers work in front of a computer screen showing a picture of guru Sahoko Asahara, 1999. (REUTERS/ERIKO SUGITA/ARCHIVE PHOTOS)

in the attack have been sentenced. Four of the culprits have been condemned to die, and one other has been sentenced to life in prison. Japanese police arrested Asahara in May 1995, charging him with 17 counts of murder. In 2004, a Tokyo court sentenced Asahara to death, but that sentence is under appeal.

From 1997 to 1999, the cult recruited new members, built up a profitable commercial business, and bought several properties. In September 1999, Aum declared that it would cease most of its activities, and in December of that year, it apologized for the sarin attack. Aum maintains an Internet home page but shut down almost all its links after these announcements. Under the leadership of Fumihiro Joyu, the Aum changed its name to Aleph in January 2000, claiming to have rejected the violent and apocalyptic teachings of Asahara. Joyu took formal control of the entire organization in early 2002. Although the cult continued to recruit new members, engage in commercial espionage, and acquire property, it scaled back these activities in 2001, in response to public outcry, and in 2002, with the change in leadership.

However, in July 2001, Russian authorities arrested a group of Russian Aum activists who were planning to set off bombs near the Imperial Palace in Tokyo as part of an effort to free Asahara from jail. The group planned to smuggle Asahara to Russia.

While the Aum's membership at the time of the Tokyo subway attack was claimed (by the group) to be about 9,000 in Japan and nearly 40,000 worldwide, its current membership is estimated to be less than 1,000 persons. While its primary base of operation and principal membership is in Japan, it clearly has at least one brand of followers in Russia, but it receives no known external aid.

References: Brackett, D. W. *Holy Terror: Armageddon in Tokyo* (New York: Weatherhill, 1996); Lifton, Robert Jay. *Destroying the World to Save It: Aum Shinrikyo, Apocalyptic Violence, and the New Global Terrorism* (New York: Henry Holt, 2000); National Memorial Institute for the Prevention of Terrorism (MIPT). "Aum Shinrikyo." Available online. URL: http://www.tkb.org/Group.jsp?groupID=3956. Accessed February 15, 2006.

M.D.

Autodefensas Unidas de Colombia (AUC)

See UNITED SELF-DEFENSE FORCES OF COLOMBIA.

auto-genocide

Auto-genocide differs from the usual interpretation of genocide in which a government follows a murderous policy against an entire community of people based on race, religion, ethnicity, social class, or even gender. In contrast, auto-genocide is characterized by a regime that pursues an interest in murdering a large proportion of its own citizenry. The concept is an ancient one: the Roman emperor Tiberius, a political recluse who despised and was contemptuous of the people under his authority, once remarked how he wished the Roman people had only one neck so that he could cut off its head with one blow of the sword.

More modern interpretations have resulted in unprecedented lethality. The Nazi regime in Germany (1933–45), when it was clear that World War II was lost, initiated policies of great destruction during the war's final weeks against the Germans themselves. The Nazis felt that if they did not survive, there was no point in the German nation enduring. In this case, a partially successful effort was made to destroy the country's industrial and communication infrastructure and reduce life to a primitive level or even wreck any hope of continuing life altogether.

The KHMER ROUGE regime in Cambodia (1975–1979) wiped out between 1 and 2 million Cambodians out of a total population of 7 million in a similar fashion by expelling urban dwellers from the capital city and forcing them to grow their own food. Cambodia was to become a purified country without the contaminants provided by the sophistication of the city. Hundreds of thousands starved before a crop came in. Journalists, teachers, and engineers were simply shot. The Khmer Rouge was considering the murder of all Cambodians over the age of 18 in order to prepare a new generation for a perfect society unscarred by any memories of a past that they considered to be corrupt and decadent.

Auto-genocide is more deadly than any other kind since the victims are readily available. Some form of it is readily and unhesitatingly practiced by numerous current authoritarian regimes, including Sudan and Uganda.

References: Kressel, Neil Jeffrey. *Mass Hate: The Global Rise of Genocide and Terror* (Boulder, Colo.: Westview Press, 2002). Robertson, Geoffrey. *Crimes against Humanity: The Struggle for Global Justice* (New York: New Press, 2003).

B

Baader-Meinhof gang *See* RED ARMY FACTION.

Babbar Khalsa International (a.k.a., International Sikh Youth Federation, Dal Khalsa, Bhinderanwala Tiger Force, Saheed Khalsa Force, Khalistan Liberation Tiger Force, Khalistan Commando Force, Khalistan Liberation Front, Khalistan National Army) Khalistan, the Sikh homeland in India's Punjab Province, declared its independence on October 7, 1987, and a bitter struggle ensued, since more than 60% of India's grain comes from Punjab, and there are about a half-million Indian soldiers occupying this province. Sikh violence has been sponsored by expatriate and Indian Sikh groups seeking the liberation of an independent Sikh state—Khalistan, Land of the Pure—from Indian territory. In recent years, groups active in this violence have included Babbar Khalsa, the International Sikh Youth Federation, Dal Khalsa, and the Bhindeeranwala Tiger Force. A previously unknown group, the Saheed Khalsa Force, claimed credit for the marketplace bombings that occurred in New Dehli in 1997. Many of the groups operate under umbrella organizations, the most significant of which appears to be the Second Panthic Committee.

Sikh attacks in India have included assassinations, bombings, and kidnappings of Indian officials and facilities, other Sikhs, and Hindus. Actions by Indian security forces aimed at killing or capturing senior Sikh militant leaders since 1992 have resulted in a marked drop in Sikh attacks. The Indian government was responsible for taking the lives of 250,000 Sikhs in Punjab between 1984 and 1992. Total civilian deaths in Punjab have declined more than 95% since more than 3,300 civilians died in 1991. The drop is attributed, according to reports, to Indian army, paramilitary, and police successes against the extremist groups. There have also been internicine feuds, further weakening the group in the 1990s, though they are still active. In 1995, a man claiming to be part of BKI assasinated the Punjab chief minister, while four other members also claimed responsibility. In 2005, two alleged BKI members were arrested and charged with bombing a cinema in New Delhi. The Babbar Khalsa is listed as a terrorist organization by the United Kingdon, the European Union, and Canada.

Reference: National Memorial Institute for the Prevention of Terrorism (MIPT). "Babbar Khalsa International (BKI)." Available online. URL: http://www.tkb.org/Group.jsp?groupID=4568. Accessed February 15, 2006.

al-Badr Mujahideen

The al-Badr Mujahideen was formed in June 1998 with the professed aim of supporting the "Kashmiri freedom struggle" and liberating the Indian state of Jammu and Kashmir and integrating it into Pakistan. The group advocates that Kashmiris are entitled to the right of self-determination in agreement with the United Nations resolutions.

Al-Badr reportedly traces its birth to 1971, when a similarly labeled group was accused of participating in the massacre of 10,000 Bengali intellectuals throughout the Pakistani civil war. Al-Badr then disappeared for nearly two decades. The group also operated as part of the Hizb-e-Islami, the most radical among the seven parties that made up the anti-Soviet Afghan mujahideen as well as a key ally of Pakistan's Inter-Services Intelligence.

The group has opposed the cease-fire on the Line of Control declared by India and Pakistan in November 2003. Al-Badr has constantly been opposed to any route of talks between India and Pakistan. The al-Badr leader Bakht Zameen declared in an interview on September 5, 2001, that India was not genuine about holding a dialogue for the agreeable resolution of the Kashmir issue. While urging Pakistan to focus on intensification of jihad instead of "wasting time seeking a negotiated settlement," he also asked the military regime to abstain from initiating any steps that would destabilize the "freedom movement" in Jammu and Kashmir. Following the September 11th attacks on the United States, al-Badr denied any affiliation with al-Qaeda, even though the group remained critical of President Musharraf's restrictions on jihadi groups and his support for the U.S. War on Terrorism.

Al-Badr was responsible for several major attacks, including one involving an improvised explosive device blast targeted at an Indian security forces convoy that killed 11 policemen on February 18, 2000. Spokesman Salim Hashmi claimed on April 26, 2001, that its mujahideen had killed 51 Indian soldiers, injured 137, and destroyed 34 barracks during a two-day operation after the group had given an ultimatum to the Indian army that it would carry out at least 35 attacks between the nights of April 23 and 24, 2001.

Reference: GlobalSecurity.org. Military. "Al-Badr/Al-Badr Mujahideen." Available online. URL: http://www.globalsecurity.org/military/para/Al-Badr.htm. Accessed February 27, 2006.

S.B.

Bakunin, Mikhail Aleksandrovich (1814–1876)

Born on May 30, 1814, in Premukhine, Russia, Mikhail Bakunin was the chief propagator of 19th-century anarchism. He was both a prominent Russian revolutionary agitator and a prolific political writer.

The eldest son of a small landowner, he began what became a lifetime of revolt when he was sent to the Artillery School in St. Petersburg and later posted to a military unit on the Polish frontier. Absenting himself without permission and resigning his commission, he spent the next five years in study of various philosophers, particularly Hegel. Studying in Berlin, Bakunin fell under the influence of the Young Hegelians, the radical followers of Georg W. H. Hegel, and in 1842 published his first revolutionary credo, ending with the now-famous aphorism: "The passion for destruction is also a creative passion."

With this publication, Russia ordered him to return home, and, on his refusal, he lost his passport. He then settled, after brief stays in other cities, in Paris and got his first taste of street fighting in the February Revolution of 1848. After participating enthusiastically for a few days, he went on to try to spread the revolutionary fervor to Germany and Poland. Indeed, he was at the Slav congress in Prague in June, which ended when Austrian troops bombarded the city.

From these experiences, Bakunin wrote his first major manifesto, *An Appeal to the Slavs,* in which he called for the overthrow of the Hapsburg Empire and the creation in central Europe of a free federation of Slav peoples. This was not quite anarchistic but began to build in that direction. He had begun to be dissatisfied with all forms of government and sought instead a "free federation."

His involvement in the Dresden insurrection of May 1849 resulted in his arrest and his return, under arrest, to Russia. After spending more than six years in prison, the last part of which was in Siberia, he married and, with help from his mother's cousin, escaped the country for good. Landing in London, he embarked only two years later on an effort to take volunteers to aid in the Polish insurrection in 1863. He only made it as far as Sweden, and in 1854, he moved to Italy, where he remained for four years, where his writings became the principal outline for the anarchist creed that he preached with unsystematic but undaunted vigor for the rest of his life.

In 1866, his *National Catechism* advocated the use of "selective, discriminate terror" in the pursuit of anarchism. From this articulation of creed, both terrorists and anarchists would draw philosophical support for the next century of activities. From Bakunin's linkage, too, of anarchism and terror would come the confusing blend of anarchism, revolution, and terror-violence that has confronted states from Europe and Asia to North and South America, as many groups claimed his philosophy as their own.

Bakunin died on July 1, 1876, but anarchist movements owing allegiance to him continued to flourish in Italy and Spain, with small groups existing in Great Britain, Switzerland, and Germany.

See also ANARCHISTS.

References: Maximoff, G. P., ed. *Political Philosophies of Bakunin* (New York: 1953); "Bakunin, Mikhail Alexandrovich," *Encyclopaedia Britannica* (Chicago: Encyclopaedia Britannica, 1992) 817–818.

al-Banna, Sabri (Abu Nidal) (1937–2002)

Sabri al-Banna was one of the most notorious individuals engaged in terrorist acts during the 1970s through the early 1990s. The architect of the Rome and Vienna airport massacres of 1985, he was a mastermind of countless other atrocities as well as the leader of the ABU NIDAL organization, whose original group, BLACK SEPTEMBER, was responsible for the MUNICH MASSACRE OF ISRAELI ATHLETES in 1972.

Sabri al-Banna was born in May 1937 in Jaffa. His father, Khalil, was one of the wealthiest men in Palestine, with homes in Marseilles, France; Iskenderun; Turkey; and Syria. Khalil also owned several houses in Palestine itself. All of the al-Banna land in Palestine was confiscated by the newly formed Israeli government in 1948. Sabri's father was dead by this time, and he and his family were forced to flee, first to their house near Majdal, then to the al-Birj refugee camp in the Gaza Strip. In early 1949, they moved again to Nablus, on the West Bank of the Jordan River, under the sovereignty at the time of the state of Jordan.

From a position of incredible wealth, Sabri saw, at age 12, his family reduced to life in the teeming refugee camps. Formerly taught at private schools and by tutors in his early years, he now entered school provided by the government of Jordan, graduating from the city high school in 1955. Although he entered Cairo University in Egypt, he returned to Nablus two years later without having completed his degree.

Through his brother, Zakzriya, he obtained a job as an electrician's assistant with a construction company in Saudi Arabia. While there, he became involved in the illegal Ba'ath Party (which later stood him in good stead with the Iraqi regime). His involvement was noted by his employers and the Saudi regime. He was fired, and later imprisoned, tortured, and expelled from the country.

Sabri returned to Nablus a few months before the Israeli tanks rolled in during the 1967 Six-Day War. Although he had been a passive member of Fatah for years, he became an active member after this traumatic experience. Again a refugee, he moved to Amman, where he chose the nom de guerre Abu Nidal (which can be translated to mean "father of the struggle").

Of his career since that time, no single account exists, although many stories of his exploits abound. He certainly broke with the PALESTINE LIBERATION ORGANIZATION leadership of YASIR ARAFAT after the end of the intifadah, contending that its policy of accommodation and moderation was "selling out the Palestinians." He established ties with several former communist nations as well as with some Arab states, between which he traveled with impunity.

In addition to the Rome and Vienna airport attacks, he directed assaults on a group of British invalids in an Athens hotel, on the Israeli ambassador to London, and on his own nephew's family. In August 1998, there were reports that Abu Nidal was seriously ill with leukemia and undergoing clandestine treatment in an Egyptian hospital, after he was expelled from Libya. The Egyptian authorities denied this, and there was no official confirmation of his whereabouts at that time. Among those who actively sought his arrest were the PLO and the Palestine Authority since Nidal was responsible for the murder of several prominent Palestinian figures, such as 'Issam Sirtawi, Salah Khalaf "Abu 'Iyad," and Hail 'Abd al-Hamid, between 1983 and 1991. His connection with the serious injury of the Israeli ambassador in the United Kingdom, Shlomo Afgov, in June 1980, led Israel to invade southern Lebanon in order to oust his and other Palestinian organizations from their bases there.

On January 19, 1999, the London-based Arab daily *Al-Sharq al-Awsat* reported some conflicting rumors about Abu Nidal, his location, his illness, and his relations with several Arab states. About a month later, in Damascus, a member of the FRC read a message from Abu Nidal at the convention of the Palestinian groups opposed to Arafat. In March, the same newspaper noted above quoted the eminent British Middle East expert Patrick Seale, stating that Nidal was well and living in Cairo. Again, this report was denied by the Egyptian authorities. Sabri al-Banna died on August 6, 2002. On August 19, 2002, the Palestinian newspaper *Al Ayyam* reported that Abu Nidal was suffering from a serious illness and apparently committed suicide in his Baghdad apartment. Nidal was 65 at the time of his death, about which some dispute still remains.

References: BBC News. "Abu Nidal Found Dead." World–Middle East. Available online. URL: http://news.bbc.co.uk/1/hi/world/middle_east/2203004.stm. Accessed February 22, 2006; Seale, Patrick. *Abu Nidal: A Gun for Hire* (New York: Random House, 1992).

Basque Fatherland and Liberty (Euzkadi ta Askatasuma [ETA], Basque Homeland and Freedom)

Concentrated in the northwest corner of Spain, in the provinces of Vizcaya, Guipuzcoa, Alava, and Navarra, the Basque people have lived for centuries under semi-autonomous rule. During Franco's reign, however, this autonomy was dramatically reduced. As a result, Basque nationalists, in conjunction with the newly formed (1959) Euskadi ta Askatasuna (ETA), began to carry out acts of violence against a variety of targets. As the Basque movement grew, so did ETA, with the result that ETA decided to "divide" into two entities: a political-military branch and a strictly military branch.

The political branch, Herri Batsuna, essentially became dormant after a limited home rule was granted in 1982 but resurfaced in 1994. During this period, little was heard from ETA, but it was later revealed that Herri Batsuna sent a three-man delegation to Northern Ireland, where they met the IRISH REPUBLICAN ARMY (IRA) leaders. This may have resulted in the networking that clearly occurred through the next decade between these two groups and may also explain, in part, why ETA was willing to institute a unilateral cease-fire in 1998 as the IRA began similar cease-fire efforts with the British authorities.

The military wing, led by José Ternera, remained strong. In January 1995, Gregorio Ordonea, spokesman for the conservative Popular Party (PP) and a leading mayoral candidate for the town of San Sebastian, was assassinated. A car bomb detonated in April 1995 injured eight, including the head of the PP, Josi Maria Asnar. A smaller bomb exploded just an hour later near a Madrid railway depot, causing no injuries, believed to be the result of the car bombers' blowing up their escape vehicle.

ETA has been primarily involved in bombing and assassinations of Spanish government officials, especially security and military forces, politicians, and judicial figures. In response to French operations against the group, ETA has also targeted French interests. Kidnapping for ransom is an important fund-raising tactic employed by this group, which also employs robbery and extortion to generate funds. With a support network comparable to that enjoyed by the IRA, throughout not only the Basque regions but also the rest of the country, ETA has established cells in most of the major cities.

Notable here is the existence of native "Y" Groups, who appear to operate independently but in support of ETA and its goals. Two teenage members of a "Y" Group were arrested in 1995 after being observed guarding a substantial arms cache for several days. A police crackdown on these elements was intense and resulted in 33 arrests in February 1995. This crackdown, however, appears to have generated the creation of a previously unknown group known as the Anti-Terrorist Liberation Group (GAL), which was discovered to have carried out an illegal "dirty war" against Basque separatists, in particular ETA. Rafael Vera, former secretary of state for security, was arrested in February on suspicion that he was involved with this group, which an investigation revealed had secured moneys for its operations from the manipulation of existing government accounts.

In November 1994, an autonomous Basque police force known as the Ertzaintza successfully attacked the Vascaya Command, almost wiping the cell out. Spanish authorities have been aided in their fight against the ETA by the French government in recent years, as the French have regularly raided suspected hideouts and weapons caches. The French also arrested Maria Idoia Lopez Raino, "The Tigress," in Aix-en-Provence on August 25, 1994. Raino, a member of the ETA cell "Madrid Command," was responsible for the deaths of 17 Civil Guards and a number of soldiers and civilians between 1980 and 1986.

ETA power has diminished considerably in recent years. Though more than 800 have been killed in ETA attacks since the 1960s, in 2003, for example, only three people were killed in ETA violence. The turning point in public opinion towards the group is seen by many to be the 1997 kidnapping of 29-year-old politician Miguel Angel Blanco in the Basque region. ETA demanded the release of 460 prisoners as the ransom for his release, but Spanish officials refused to comply. Soon afterward, Blanco's body was found with two bullet wounds to the head. As a result of this brutal murder, more than 6 million people across Spain took to the streets over four days to protest ETA's bloody violence. This in turn moved some of ETA's own members to publicly condemn the killing. Another factor was the March 11, 2004, MADRID TRAIN BOMBINGS that were originally blamed on ETA by some officials, though ETA has denied involvement in the attacks. It is now thought by some commentators that ETA no longer believes it can achieve its goals through violent means, though others believe it is due more to better law-enforcement methods than to any kind of shift in ETA tactics. In March 2006, ETA leadership announced a "permanent cease-fire" but the cease-fire was disrupted by the December 2006 bombing at Madrid Barajas Airport, for which the ETA was blamed.

See also TRAINING CAMPS FOR TERRORISTS.

Reference: National Memorial Institute for the Prevention of Terrorism (MIPT). "Basque Fatherland and Freedom (ETA)." Available online. URL: http://www.tkb.org/Group.jsp?groupID=31. Accessed February 15, 2006.

Begin, Menachem (1913–1992)

Begin became Israeli prime minister in 1977, after nearly three decades as leader of the conservative parliamentary opposition to a succession of left-of-center governments, and served until 1983. During the immediate years before Israeli statehood (1943–48) Begin led an underground organization, the IRGUN ZVAI LEUMI, that attacked both Arab and British authorities and favored a heavy-handed approach to establishing an independent Jewish state. The Irgun was a much more hard-line organization than the mainstream Zionist structure led by David Ben-Gurion. Begin was branded as a terrorist by the British after an Irgun attack on their headquarters in Jerusalem at the KING DAVID HOTEL.

Yet, as prime minister, Begin welcomed Egyptian President Anwar Sadat to Israel in November 1977 and concluded a peace treaty with him in 1979. The peace arrangements included mutual recognition, a peace treaty, and the return of the Sinai, which Israel had occupied since 1967, to Egypt. The United States had critical involvement during the Carter Administration (1977–81) and hosted many of the deliberations at Camp David. The peace accords were in fact signed in Washington. Begin and Sadat shared the 1978 Nobel Peace Prize.

In 1982 Begin authorized the Israeli attack on Lebanon that succeeded in driving the PALESTINE LIBERATION ORGANIZATION (PLO) from its guerilla bases in the southern part of the country. During the Israeli attack some Christian militia units, allied with Israel's army, massacred thousands of Palestinians in refugee camps. The Israeli military was accused and the Begin government condemned by much of the world community for not preventing the deaths of many Palestinian civilians.

Begin left public life in 1983 depressed and saddened by the deaths of his wife and several close friends from prestate days.

References: Begin, Menachem. *White Nights: The Story of a Prisoner in Russia* (New York: Harper and Row, 1977); Safer, Sasson. *Begin: An Anatomy of Leadership* (Oxford: Oxford University Press, 1988).

Beria, Lavrenti Pavlovich (1899–1953)

Lavrenti Pavlovich Beria was born on March 29, 1899, in Merkheuli, Russia, and died December 23, 1953, in Moscow. He was the director of the Soviet secret police who played a major role in the purge of JOSEPH STALIN's opponents.

Joining the Communist Party in 1917, Beria participated in revolutionary activity in Azerbaijan and Georgia. He was drawn into intelligence and counterintelligence work and appointed head of the Cheka (secret police) in Georgia. As party boss of the Transcaucasian republics, he personally oversaw the political purges in those republics during Stalin's Great Purge (1936–38). Brought to Moscow in 1938 as the deputy to Nikolai Yezhov, head of the People's Commissariat for Internal Affairs (NKVD), the Soviet secret police, Beria became head of the secret police that same year, after Yezhov was apparently arrested and shot on Stalin's orders.

As head of the NKVD, Beria supervised a purge of the police bureaucracy itself and administered the huge network of labor camps set up throughout the country. The millions who died in these camps offer grim evidence of the state terrorism carried out under his rule.

Beria was arrested, deprived of his government and party posts, and publicly accused of being an "imperialist agent" and of conducting "criminal antiparty and antistate activities." He was convicted of these charges in December 1953 and immediately executed.

Beslan school hostage crisis

Many Russians consider the terrorism at Beslan to be their own 9/11. In fact, Russia had suffered previous attacks by terrorists, most of whom were from CHECHNYA, a predominantly Islamic republic of about 1 million in the southern part of the Russian Federation. Throughout the Russian Federation, "First September" is considered a national "Day of Knowledge." September 1 is the traditional beginning of the fall semester. In 2004, however, the date took on a more ominous meaning. Students, parents, and teachers usually begin the new school year together in an atmosphere of celebration. Older students normally mentor younger ones through the day. Beslan, a Russian town in North Ossetia, a member of the federation, was targeted by terrorists for an attack. The building of School Number One was seized by approximately 30 male and female terrorists who took approximately 1,300 students, parents, and teachers hostage. The terrorists installed wired explosive devices throughout and around the school building. They herded the hostages into the school gym where, because of the hot weather, all became uncomfortable.

Russian security forces quickly surrounded the building, and a siege was begun that was to last for several days. The security police at first were determined to work toward a peaceful outcome that would be achieved through negotiation. The terrorists were quickly identified as mostly Chechen separatists, although there is some dispute over the national and ethnic origins of the terrorists. For nearly two days, negotiations ensued but were unsuccessful. The terrorists refused food and water for their hostages or themselves despite the intense heat. On the afternoon of September 2, the terrorists did allow 26 nursing women to leave the building with their infants after negotiations with Ruslan Aushev, the former Inguish president. The terrorists demanded the withdrawal of Russian troops from Chechnya and also that certain Russian officials be present at the scene. By the next day, the terrorists agreed to permit medical workers to remove the five bodies, four police officers, and one terrorist who had been killed in a gun battle at the beginning of the siege outside of the school building and to remove another 20 adult male bodies. These had been murdered by the terrorists after they had occupied the building. However, as the medical workers approached the building, the terrorists opened fire and killed two of them. About 30 of the hostages tried to escape during this violent interlude, and many of them were shot to death by the terrorists.

By this point, the Russian authorities had had enough. Accounts of what occurred next are conflicting and contradictory. What is undisputed is that a great deal of carnage and bloodshed were the result of shooting. Civilians, whose children were inside the school, joined police and security forces in the shooting. The most accepted version of what started the shooting is that a special forces sniper shot a terrorist who had propped his leg on a detonator. The terrorists were especially vicious and even shot fleeing children in the back. They seemed determined to kill as many as possible before being killed themselves. In the end, 31 terrorists were counted among the dead, with only one terrorist taken alive. Two weeks after the attack, the Chechen terrorist Shamil Basayev—who also claimed responsibility for the Moscow theater siege in 2002—issued a statement that he was responsible for organizing the Beslan attack.

According to official data, 344 civilians were killed (186 of them children) and hundreds more wounded. While this number is hardly more than a 10th of the total who died during 9/11, the target on schoolchildren and the overall brutality associated with the attack outraged all areas of Russian society. It also intensified the already well-established distrust and antipathy Russians felt toward Chechens and reminded them of previous terrorist attacks on Russian soil. The fact that a relatively small Russian town could experience a terrorist attack at all, let alone one on such a lethal scale, suggested that Russians could be attacked anywhere in their own country and that terrorists were not restricting their targets to large urban areas such as Moscow.

Beslan was also a reminder that the reach of terrorists was global. Radical Islam apparently considered its conflict to be universal and against those considered enemies who were as disparate as the United States and the Russian Federation. The Russians were confused as well: They did not have soldiers in Iraq and had indeed opposed the American attack on Saddam Hussein's regime. They and others were reminded that terrorists inspired by radical Islam consider all non-Muslims to be the enemy.

References: BBC News. Europe. "School Seige: Eyewitness Accounts." Available online. URL: http://news.bbc.

co.uk/2/hi/europe/3627406.stm. Accessed February 22, 2006; National Memorial Institute for the Prevention of Terrorism (MIPT). "Riyad Us-Saliheyn Martyrs' Brigade Attacked Educational Institutions Target (Sept. 1, 2004, Russia)." *Incident Reports*. Available online.URL:http://www.tkb.org/Incident.jsp?incID=19321. Accessed February 15, 2006.

bin Laden, Osama bin Mohammad (1957–)
Millionaire, Islamic fundamentalist, and financier of international terrorism, Osama bin Laden was born in the city of Riyadh, Saudi Arabia, in 1957. He was raised in Al-madina Alunawwara and Hijaz, and received his education in the schools of Jedda, completing a study of management and economics at King Abdul Aziz University in Jedda.

Bin Laden began his interaction with Islamic groups in 1973, working during the early 1980s with the mujahideen against the Communist Party in South Yemen, and remained involved until the beginning of the struggle to overthrow the communist government in Afghanistan. Coming to see this conflict in terms of "Muslim believers versus heretics," he established, with Sheikh Dr. Abdullah Azzam, the office for mujahideen services in Peshawar and the Sidda camp for the training of Arab mujahideen who came for jihad ("holy war") in Afghanistan. After the Russians entered the war, bin Laden established "Ma'sadat Al-Ansar," a base for Arab mujahideen in Afghanistan. Although in 1986 he participated in the battles of Jalalabad, bin Laden became more concerned with the growing American influence in the region since the United States was the nation supplying much of the arms and training to many of the mujahideen. As a strongly committed Muslim, he opposed the incursion of non-Islamic influences into the heart of the Islamic holy places.

The Saudi government asked bin Laden to return home in the early 1990s, presumably to discuss his activities. He refused, and then his citizenship was canceled, his passport revoked, his assets frozen, and he became, in effect, a stateless person. In the course of an ABC interview, he described his view of "heretics" to include "pragmatic" Arab regimes (including his homeland, Saudi Arabia) and the United States, which he viewed as "taking over the Muslim holy sites of Mecca and Medina, and assisting the Jews in their conquest of Palestine." This point of view led him to encourage perpetration of acts of terrorism, sanctifying these acts by religious edict. Based on these perceptions, he founded the "International Islamic Front for Jihad against the Jews and the Crusaders" in 1998.

Poster depicting Osama bin Laden (GETTY)

Long before September 11, 2001, the U.S. government had already concluded that bin Laden was an important and resourceful terrorist leader. He had been connected to the August 7, 1998, bombings of the American embassies in Nairobi, Kenya, and Dar es Salaam, Tanzania, causing the deaths of hundreds of people. Two years later bin Laden's organization was viewed as responsible for the bombing of the USS Cole in the port of Aden, Yemen. As elsewhere, suicide bombers were used to commit the crime.

Bin Laden's name has also been connected with the attacks in Riyadh (November 1995) and Dhahran (June 1996), in which 30 people were killed; attacks on a Yemenite hotel (December 1992) resulting in several casualties; the assassination attempt on Egyptian president Mubarak in Ethiopia (June 1995); and the WORLD TRADE CENTER BOMBINGS (February 1993), which killed six and injured hundreds. While his specific connections to each of these acts is somewhat tenuous, he has openly praised those responsible for many of them, calling them "shahids," or martyrs, whose deeds paved the way for other true believers.

Bin Laden played an important role in supporting and enlarging the pool of Islamic fighters know as the "Afghan Veterans," a large number of whom owe allegiance to him. He maintains extensive ties with a number of international organizations and individuals engaged in terrorism, in EGYPT, India, the Philippines, Tajikistan, Bosnia, CHECHNYA, Somalia, Sudan, Yemen, and Eritrea. These contacts enjoy the use of his funding and training camps. Those who see themselves as Islamic "crusaders" enjoy the logistical, financial, and communications support network of bin Laden's economic empire. A hero of the Afghan war and a loyal supporter of The Islamic Movement, bin Laden remained at the beginning of the 21st century intensely involved in contemporary international terrorism, funding and equipping groups of trained and experienced fighters, steeped in Islamic indoctrination, prepared to be "crusaders" in battlefields that cover the entire world.

Stating in several interviews that he regarded it as a "sin" for Muslims not to try to possess the weapons that would prevent the "infidels" from inflicting harm on Muslims, he made serious efforts to obtain nonconventional weapons, in particular, biological and chemical weapons. In combination with his worldview of an ongoing "holy war," his view of the conflict as a zero-sum game, supported by scriptural decree and supplied with proven conventional capabilities, this potential for nonconventional capabilities by bin Laden and his organizations increased the level of the threat of terrorism substantially.

Already sought by legal authorities in several countries, bin Laden became the world's most wanted criminal on September 11, 2001, when the ATTACK ON AMERICA was immediately blamed by the U.S. and British governments on bin Laden and his AL-QAEDA network. Bin Laden did not accept responsibility for the atrocities but approved of them. The Taliban regime of Afghanistan was accused of harboring bin Laden, and the American government demanded that the Taliban surrender bin Laden and his lieutenants to U.S. jurisdiction. To no one's surprise, the Taliban refused, and on October 7, 2001, American air strikes were launched against Taliban military installations and al-Qaeda bases in Afghanistan. These operations led to the fall of the Taliban and ushered in the American occupation, but all attempts to locate bin Laden had proved futile. Since then, there have been numerous rumors reporting bin Laden's failing health or death, but as recently as January 2006, there has been audiotape with what is claimed to be a recent authentic recording of bin Laden's voice. Many officials believe that bin Laden is hiding somewhere along the vast borderland region between Afghanistan and Pakistan.

In a number of video and audio tapes released to the media, bin Laden has demonstrated his hatred of Americans and Jews. He has reiterated his call to Muslims to kill both military personnel and civilians who are American and/or Jewish. The consensus about bin Laden is that his hatred is genuine and that he is prepared to die for his beliefs, preferably in battle against his enemies. Whether or not he is apprehended, it seems clear that bin Laden's operations have both inspired and supported numerous terrorist acts and may continue to do so whether he is alive or dead. The U.S. government seems to agree with this assessment. Several officials, including high-ranking cabinet secretaries, have publicly stated their expectation that the conflict with terrorism will be a long and arduous one and will require a global strategy.

References: Bergen, Peter. *The Osama Bin Laden That I Know: An Oral History of Al-Qaeda's Leader* (New York: Free Press, 2006); Randal, John. *Osama: The Making of a Terrorist* (New York: I. B. Tauris, 2005).

biological agents

There are four categories of living microorganisms: bacteria, viruses, rickettsiae, and fungi. Bacteria are small, free-living organisms; they can be grown on solid or liquid media and produce diseases that often respond to specific treatment with antibiotics. A familiar example of a bacteria used recently in a terrorist attack is ANTHRAX, an acute infectious disease caused by the spore-forming bacterium *Bacillus anthracis*. Although anthrax most often occurs in hoofed mammals, it can also infect humans, as the anthrax attack in the mail system of the United States in the fall of 2001 clearly proved.

Viruses are organisms that require living cells in which to replicate. This type of organism does not respond to antibiotics but is sometimes responsive to viral compounds, few of which are available. Again, the most familiar example of viruses as a weapon of terror is smallpox, an infection caused by the *Variola* virus, whose use was mentioned in the chapter on domestic terrorism.

The latter two groups are less familiar to the general public. Rickettsiae are microorganisms that have characteristics of both bacteria and viruses. Like bacteria, rickettsiae have metabolic enzymes and a cell membrane, utilize oxygen, and are susceptible to a broad spectrum of antibiotics. Like viruses, they grow only within living cells. Q fever is a zoonotic disease caused by rickettsiae *Coxiella burnettii*. Fungi, primitive plants which do not utilize photosynthesis, are capable of anaerobic growth and draw nutrition from decaying vegetable matter. They are a little more familiar, but not in terms of a biological weapon. A diverse group of more than 40 compounds produced by fungi, *Trichothecene Mycotoxins*, have been generated in recent years since they can inhibit protein synthesis, impair DNA synthesis, alter cell and membrane structure and function, and inhibit mitochondrial respiration. T-2, as this is called, used as a biological warfare agent aimed at causing acute exposure via inhalation could result in the onset of illness within hours of exposure and death within 12 hours.

Biotoxins, poisonous substances produced naturally by microorganisms, plants, or animals that may be produced or altered by chemical means, will be discussed later, in the context of chemical weapons. This category would include agents such as ricin, abrin, and strychnine.

A quick look at five biological agents currently available today illustrates the breadth of the threat of attack from such weapons. A more in-depth case study of one of these—ANTHRAX—will offer further clues as to the danger which such agents pose.

Botulinum toxin (*Clostridium botulinum*) is the single most poisonous substance known. While it is usually food-borne, it could be developed as an aerosol weapon. After infection with this biological agent, symptoms

Covered in Chemical Protective Overgarments, members of a Chemical, Biological, Radiation investigative team search compartments for possible contamination. (DEPARTMENT OF DEFENSE)

generally include blurred vision as well as difficulty swallowing and speaking within 24 to 36 hours. This agent, a nerve toxin, paralyzes muscles, leading to respiratory failure and death. The Aum Shinrikyo cult in Japan was accused of trying to use botulinum toxin sprayed from airplanes over Tokyo, fortunately without success, at least three times in the 1990s.

Plague (*Yersinia pestis*) is an incredibly virulent, but not always lethal, biological agent. If 110 pounds of this agent were released over a city of 5 million people, about 150,000 would contract the disease, but most would survive if treated early in the infection period. Within one to six days after exposure to the plague bacteria, victims would begin to show symptoms of severe respiratory and gastrointestinal distress. Treatment with antibiotics, however, would be effective as long as it was administered within the early stages of infection.

Tularemia is a potentially lethal infectious organism developed by the United States as a possible weapon in the 1950s and 1960s. As a weapon, it could be sprayed in an aerosol cloud. Within three to five days of infection, the victims would suffer fever, chills, headaches, and weakness. Subsequent inflammation and hemorrhaging of the airways can be fatal, and no vaccine is currently available.

Smallpox is an infectious agent that several nations have tried for decades to effectively weaponize, but which was eradicated in 1980. Some strains of this disease are maintained, however, in only two nations, officially: the United States and Russia. The former Soviet Union reportedly stockpiled large amounts of this virus for use as weapons, and several other nations, such as Iraq and North Korea, may have covert stashes of smallpox today. The smallpox virus is highly contagious, and would quickly spread, because even in the United States, vaccinations for this disease stopped more than 25 years ago. An aerosol release of smallpox, infecting only 50 people, could easily unleash an epidemic, killing about 30% of those infected with the painful, disfiguring disease.

Anthrax is an acute infectious disease caused by the spore-forming bacterium *Bacillus anthracis*. It most commonly occurs in mammals such as cattle, sheep, goats, camels, and antelopes, but it can also occur in humans exposed to infected animals or tissue from infected animals. Anthrax is unusual in that its spores are hardy: They are resistant to sunlight, heat, and disinfectant and can remain active in soil and water for years. Anthrax spores tend to clump together in humid conditions, making it somewhat difficult to spray as an aerosol. Anthrax, unlike smallpox, is not contagious—that is, it is highly unlikely that it could be transmitted from direct person-to-person contact.

Since this particular bacterium was used in 2001 as a biological agent, a closer look at anthrax as a biological weapon would be useful at this point. This case study of anthrax is not an account of the attack, but an evaluation of anthrax as a biological weapon.

References: Mangold, Tom, and Jeff Goldberg. *Plague War: The Terrifying Reality of Biological Warfare* (New York: St. Martin's Press, 2001); Preston, Richard. *The Demon in the Freezer* (New York: Random House, 2003); Tucker, Jonathan B. *Scourge: The Once and Future Threat of Smallpox* (New York: Grove/Atlantic, 2002).

Black Hand

The Black Hand was a secret Serbian society of the early 20th century that used terrorist methods to promote the liberation of Serbs outside Serbia from either Hapsburg or Ottoman rule. This organization was instrumental in planning the assassination of Archduke Franz Ferdinand in 1914, an act that precipitated the outbreak of World War I.

Formed in 1911 and led by Colonel Dragutin Dimitrijević, most of the members of this organization were army officers, along with a few government officials. Operating from Bulgaria, the Black Hand carried out propaganda campaigns and organized armed bands in Macedonia. It effectively established a network of revolutionary cells throughout Bosnia. The Black Hand dominated the army and held enormous influence over the government in Serbia, terrorizing government officials.

Responding to this internal threat, Prince Alexander, who was commander in chief of the expatriate Serbian Army, brought Dimitrijević to trial in 1917. Dimitrijević and two other officers were executed, and more than 200 members were imprisoned, effectively ending this group's role in the cycle of violence.

Reference: Hoffman, Bruce. *Inside Terrorism* (New York: Columbia University Press, 1998).

Black September

This group derived its name from events following the 1967 war involving Israel and its Arab neighbors. Palestinians living in the West Bank, many in refugee camps from the earlier conflicts, fled into Jordan after the 1967 war. With Syria's backing, Palestinian guerrillas took over many parts of Jordan, much to King Hussein of Jordan's dismay.

The crisis came at the height of an international hijacking and hostage incident in September 1970 that began when guerrillas of the POPULAR FRONT FOR THE LIBERATION OF PALESTINE hijacked four aircraft (one of the four attempts failed). Two of the three planes were taken to a remote desert airstrip, Dawson's Field, in Jordan. One of their commanders, LEILA KHALED, was being held in London after the failed attempt to take an El Al flight. Demanding her release, the Palestinians blew up the three airliners, after releasing most of the hostages through behind-the-scenes negotiations with the United Kingdom and others.

King Hussein feared that because the United Kingdom released Khaled and appeared to be "siding" with the Palestinians, the entire country could fall into Palestine hands. Syrian forces were already entering Jordan "in support" of the Palestinians. Hussein ordered the Jordanian army to destroy the Palestinian bases in what came to be known by Palestinians as Black September. A faction of the Palestinians, regarding this as a betrayal and, radicalized to seek vengeance, formed a group using this name and carried out the MUNICH MASSACRE OF ISRAELI ATHLETES in 1972. In 1974, Black September split from the PALESTINE LIBERATION ORGANIZATION to become the ABU NIDAL ORGANIZATION.

Reference: BBC News. In Depth. UK Confidential. "Black September: Tough negotiations." Available online. URL: http://news.bbc.co.uk/1/hi/in_depth/uk/2000/uk_confidential/1089694.stm. Accessed December 4, 2006.

Bombay, India, train bombings

On the evening of July 11, 2006, at least eight powerful bombs detonated in the first-class compartments of commuter trains and stations during the rush hour in Bombay (Mumbai), India's commercial capital, killing at least 190 people and wounding more than 660. Indian authorities called the explosions a coordinated terrorist attack on the city that in many respects embodies India's global ambitions. Train doors were blown off, and luggage and other debris littered the platforms, as rescue workers helped injured and bewildered survivors from the mangled train cars. The blasts occurred between 6 and 6:30 P.M., as the local trains were running in the hectic rush hour.

Bombay, also called Mumbai, is the capital of Maharashtra state. The city's commuter rail system is one of the most heavily used in the world, carrying an average of 6 million of the Arabian seaport's 16 million people daily. All of the explosions occurred along a single rail corridor in a western portion of the port city, catching passengers in very congested cars.

Suspicion quickly fell on Kashmiri militants, who have carried out similar though smaller nearly simultaneous blasts in other Indian cities, including bombings last year at three markets in New Delhi. Pakistan, India's rival over the disputed territory of Kashmir, quickly condemned the bombings, aware that a Kashmiri link to the blasts could slow or derail a peace process that has gained momentum in recent years.

Indian prime minister Manmohan Singh blamed terrorists and called the attacks "shocking and cowardly attempts to spread a feeling of fear and terror among our citizens." Security was tightened in cities worldwide from New Delhi to New York after the eight blasts, which hit seven trains within minutes of each other during the early evening rush hour.

Emergency crews struggled to treat survivors and recover the dead during monsoon downpours. Survivors clutched bandages to their faces, and many frantically tried to use their cell phones, but the mobile phone network collapsed, adding to the sense of panic. With train services down until midnight, thousands were stranded and had no way of reaching their families.

The attacks were similar to the terrorist attacks on the London public transportation system last July and the MADRID TRAIN BOMBINGS in March 2004. Initially, there was no concrete evidence linking the blasts to a particular group, nor any claim of responsibility. It was not clear how the bombs had been planted, what materials had been used, or whether suicide bombers were involved. Police inspector Ramesh Sawant said most of the victims suffered head and chest injuries, leading authorities to believe the bombs were placed in overhead luggage racks. Officials in Washington suggested that the attack was the work of LASHKAR-E-TAYYIBA or JAISH-E-MOHAMMED, another Islamic extremist group. Washington considers them AL-QAEDA affiliates.

The Press Trust of India, citing railway officials, said all the blasts hit first-class cars, a sign the assailants were targeting the professional class. Bombay is the center of India's financial industry, a city of striking contrasts between its bustling cosmopolitan metropolis and its streets crowded with the desperately poor. In the wake of the blasts, the prosperous and poor worked together to help survivors.

bonuses, for terrorist success/injury

Assistance to terrorist groups by Libya's QADHAFI was not confined to the financing of a terrorist operation itself. Israeli intelligence suggested that Qadhafi paid a $5 billion bonus to the BLACK SEPTEMBER terrorists who were responsible for the MUNICH MASSACRE OF ISRAELI ATHLETES in 1972. Western intelligence also believed that Qadhafi paid CARLOS "THE JACKAL" a large bonus, around $2 billion, for his role in the seizure of the OPEC oil ministers in Vienna in December 1975.

Bonuses were given for success, such as that paid to Carlos, and for "injury or death on the job." By the 1990s, these significantly decreased in amount. Qadhafi reportedly paid only between $10,000 and $30,000 to the families of terrorists killed in action in the late 1980s, down considerably from the $100,000 reportedly paid to a terrorist injured in the OPEC incident in 1975.

Qadhafi has taken his support of terrorists to great lengths with the offer of bonus payments for terrorist acts. When the United States carried out air raids on Libya on April 15, 1986, Qadhafi was, of course, furious. He offered to buy an American hostage in Lebanon so that he could have him killed. On April 17, Peter Kilburn, a 62-year-old librarian at American University who had been kidnapped on December 3, 1984, was "executed" after Qadhafi paid a $1 million to the group holding him. He paid a $1-million bonus to the group able to kill an elderly librarian in order to inflict harm on the United States.

Declining oil revenues, particularly due to UN sanctions, diminished Libya's role in financing terrorism, and since 2003 Libya appears to have renounced terror altogether by normalizing relations with Western nations. There is little evidence to support the premise that he is still involved in offering "bonuses" for terrorist acts.

SADDAM HUSSEIN's offer of thousands of dollars to the "martyrs" killed in the Palestinian attacks in the West Bank against Israeli settlers and soldiers has been described in the press as a new offer of "bonuses" for violent, possibly terrorist acts occurring in the early 21st century.

Bosnia, genocide in

For centuries, the Balkans have endured savage conflicts that usually included massacres of one ethnic group by another. The unraveling of Yugoslavia in the early 1990s initiated the latest episode of ethnic and religious violence. Bosnia, a former member of the Yugoslav federation, contains 4 million people divided into Croatian, Islamic, and Serbian communities. There has been traditional rivalry and distrust among all three for several centuries. The Balkans is as much an extension of the Near East as it is a part of southeastern Europe. The region is a meeting ground not only between competing ethnic and national groups but also a place where three major religions—Roman Catholicism, Islam, and Orthodox Christianity—impact on one another.

In Bosnia, Catholic Croatians, Muslims, and Orthodox Serbs in effect fought a three-way civil war. At different times, two of the three would ally against the other. Perhaps the most horrific genocidal activities were committed by Bosnian Serbs (with the probable assistance of regular military personnel from Serbia proper) against Muslims. Several mass graves were found during and after the conflict of Muslims who had been executed. In addition, a systematic rape of Muslim women by Serbs also occurred.

In 1993, the United Nations formed the International Criminal Tribunal for the former Yugoslavia (ICTY) to prosecute war crimes in the former Yugoslavia. Many of these atrocities are being blamed on several paramilitary groups run by local warlords that would operate outside the normal chain of military command. One of the more notorious examples was Željko Ražnatović, or Arkan as he was commonly known. Arkan was a criminal and psychopath who formed the Serb Volunteer Guard in 1990, also known as "Arkan's Tigers," which boasted up to 10,000 members at its peak and is suspected of being involved in several atrocities, including the Srebrenica massacre. So far only the Srebrenica massacre—the 1995 killing of an estimated 8,000 Bosniak males by Serbian forces—has been officially recognized as genocide by the United Nations tribunal. The prosecution of Serbian war criminals has been difficult, as several of them have been murdered, such as Arkan in 2000.

Serbian president Slobodan Milošević was found dead early on the morning of Saturday, March 11, 2006, in the cell where he was being detained while on trial at a United Nations war crimes tribunal in The Hague. Defending himself before the UN's International Criminal Tribunal for the Former Yugoslavia on 66 charges, including genocide, Milošević's trial was nearing its end, after more than four years. Milošević

A Muslim family in Bosnia stands in front of their destroyed home. (UNITED NATIONS)

suffered from a heart condition and high blood pressure, which repeatedly interrupted his trial. Although it was announced that Milošević died of natural causes, reports following an autopsy indicated that nonprescription drugs were found in his system. This was the first time that a sitting head of state had been tried for war crimes.

Each side claims to have been wronged by the others. Each has also chosen different sides during major conflicts. Croatia, for example, supported Germany in World War II and was instrumental in the elimination of large numbers of Serbs, Jews, and Muslims. Genocide is the ultimate form of "ETHNIC CLEANSING." In the Balkans, genocide has become the weapon of choice. It should also be pointed out that in Bosnia and elsewhere, Croatians, Muslims, and Serbs have demonstrated the capacity to live and work together in the same society in relative harmony. However, there is evidence that a great deal of bloodletting seems to occur either as the result of unscrupulous political leadership or because some event triggers a renewed and lethal hostility.

References: Burg, Steven L., and Paul S. Shoup. *War in Bosnia-Herzegovina: Ethnic Conflict and International Intervention* (Armonk, N.Y.: M.E. Sharpe, 1999). Federation of American Scientists (FAS). "Serb Volunteer Guard [SDG/SSJ] 'Arkan's Tigers'" Available online. URL: http://www.fas.org/irp/world/para/sdg.htm. Accessed February 22, 2006.

Brotherhood of Assassins

Based on stories told by Marco Polo and other travelers to this region about "gardens of paradise" where drugged devotees were introduced to receive a foretaste of eternal bliss, and not confirmed by any known Isma'ili source, the Brotherhood of Assassins comprised a sect with both religious and political elements whose members believed that murdering enemies was a religious duty. The Arabic name *hashashin* means "hashish smoker," a reference to the alleged practice of the Assassins of taking hashish to induce visions of paradise before setting out to kill and perhaps die in the attempt. Historical evidence of this practice is marginal, but the use of this name resulted in the eventual derivation of the term "assassin."

This group came into existence under the rule of IBN SABBAH AL-HASAN, caliph of a network of strongholds all over Persia and Iraq near the end of the 11th century. He created among his followers in the Nizari Isma'ili political-religious sect of Islam a corps of devoted men who carried out acts of terror-violence against his political and religious enemies in the cities and villages under his control. They were reportedly sent out to kill statesmen and generals, women and children, even other caliphs, if these people posed any threat to Hasan's rule. They were believed to have been motivated not only by religious promises of eternal reward for service to Islam but also by promises of unlimited access to hashish upon their return. Even the Crusaders made mention of this group and the terror it inspired.

This Brotherhood of Assassins offers one of the earliest links between terrorism, drugs, and religious zealotry. The potent combination of religious and political fanaticism with intoxicating drugs made the legacy of this brotherhood formidable. This lethal combination is still evident to some extent in several regions of the world today.

References: "Assassin," *New Encyclopaedia Britannica,* vol. 1 (Chicago: Encyclopaedia Britannica, Inc., 1992), 640; "Religious Fanaticism as a Factor in Political Violence." *International Freedom Foundation* (publication data December 1986); Combs, Cindy. *Terrorism in the Twenty-First Century* (Upper Saddle River, N.J.: Prentice Hall, 2000).

C

Cambodia, state terrorism in *See* KHMER ROUGE (PARTY OF DEMOCRATIC KAMPUCHEA).

Canada and the FLQ

Canada offers an instructive example of emergency legislation, enacted and applied on a limited scale, in terms of both scope and time, to combat terrorism. As the first North American nation to face a vigorous and violent native terrorist campaign, Canada from the late 1960s through the early 1970s was forced to create its own answer to terrorism. Faced with a series of violent attacks by the FRONT DU LIBÉRATION DU QUÉBEC (FLQ), in early 1970, culminating in the kidnapping of James Cross (British trade commissioner for Quebec) and Pierre Laporte (Minister of labor in the Quebec provincial government), Prime Minister Pierre Elliott Trudeau decided to take firm, and extraordinary, measures.

In 1970, Trudeau invoked the War Measures Act, which empowered him to call in the army to enforce his refusal to be coerced by kidnappers. Although Trudeau agreed to deal with the kidnappers of Mr. Cross, allowing them to be flown to Cuba in return for Cross's release, he was determined to rid Canada of the terrorists in the FLQ.

Trudeau was willing to use any means at his disposal to accomplish this aim. He was willing to subordinate civil rights to the preservation of public order. As he noted:

> When terrorists and urban guerrillas were trying to provoke the secession of Quebec, I made it clear that I wouldn't hesitate to send in the army and I did, despite the anguished cries of civil libertarians.

To a large extent, Trudeau succeeded in ridding Canada of its indigenous terrorist organization. In order to do so, he saturated the Montreal area with troops, which acted to pin down terrorist cells, and used the Royal Canadian Mounted Police to concentrate on locating the cells that had organized the terrorist attacks. Using broad local powers of search and arrest, more than 300 suspects were apprehended.

Excesses were no doubt committed during the course of this crisis. Nevertheless, the crisis had an end point, when civil liberties were restored, the army withdrawn, and local police once again constrained by strict laws on search-and-seizure operations. It may be true, as David Barrett, head of the opposition New Democratic Party once stated, that

> . . . the scar on Canada's record of civil liberties which occurred (at that time) is a classic illustration of how

the state, in an attempt to combat terrorism, overstepped its boundaries and actually threatened its own citizens.

It is also true that after Trudeau's crackdown Canada enjoyed a decade relatively free of terrorism, with civil rights and liberties fully restored. It is also worth noting that Trudeau was astute enough to accompany the repression of this period with political measures designed to end some of the grievances that may have contributed to the terrorism. These political initiatives included creating compulsory French courses for English-speaking persons in Quebec and heavy government investment in the French-speaking minority areas. Such measures helped to deprive those advocating terrorist actions of the support of the moderates among the French community.

The problems, ironically, that Canada faced in the 1990s over the efforts of Quebec to secede stem at least in part from the success of the government in "co-opting" segments of the frustrated French-speaking population that had offered some support to the FLQ. By making the option of "working with the system" to achieve their objectives more attractive, Canada diminished its terrorism problems but may well have enhanced the attraction of secession.

See also ITALY, LEGAL INITIATIVES AGAINST TERRORISM IN; NORTHERN IRELAND ACT; PREVENTION OF TERRORISM ACT (TEMPORARY PROVISIONS).

References: Bothwell, Robert. *Canada and Quebec: One Country, Two Histories* (Seattle: University of Washington Press, 1999); Moore, Brian. *The Revolution Script* (New York: Holt, Rinehart, and Winston, 1971).

Carlos "the Jackal"

The nom de guerre of Ilyich Ramírez Sánchez, born in Caracas, Venezuela, on October 12, 1949. His father, José, was a wealthy lawyer and dedicated communist, while his mother, Elba, was a devout Catholic who desired her three sons to know and accept her faith. During his early childhood, his parents struggled over their marriage and the proper course of life for their children. Elba left José, who was a womanizer, for a time when Ilyich was a young boy, taking the children to Jamaica, then to Mexico, back to Jamaica, and finally back to Colombia, where José had taken the family years before after being expelled from Venezuela. The traveling, while disruptive, showed Ilyich that he had a flair for learning new languages.

Ilyich Ramírez Sánchez, otherwise known as Carlos the Jackal (CORBIS)

Back in Bogotá, José sent Ilyich to a radical left-wing high school. From this school, Ilyich became interested in violent protests and revolutions. He was sent to a Cuban indoctrination camp to study sabotage, the use of explosives, automatic weapons, mines, encryption, and false documents, skills he would later put to use.

In 1966, Elba took the boys to London, where Ilyich, remembered by his teachers as a somewhat lazy student, passed his exams and continued his education. José planned in 1968 to take them to Paris and enroll Ilyich in the Sorbonne but found the protests and upheaval in the city at that time unappealing and instead sent the two older boys, Ilyich and Lenin (all three sons were named after José's hero, Vladimir Ilyich Lenin), to Patrice Lumumba University in Moscow. Continuing his lifestyle of heavy drinking, womanizing, and eventually supporting a rebel faction of the Venezuelan Communist Party, which had supported him at the university, Ilyich was expelled from the university in 1970.

At the university, however, he formed ties with Palestinian students that would lead him to work with

Wadi Haddad and George Habash in the POPULAR FRONT FOR THE LIBERATION OF PALESTINE (PFLP). He left Moscow in July 1970 and traveled first to Beirut, Lebanon, where he met with Habash and went to a training camp in the Bekaa Valley. His first real action with the Palestinians occurred in that year, when King Hussein of Jordan, responding to clashes in the street with Palestinians who had been allowed to have as many as 50 terrorist groups in the country, became concerned that the attacks on Israel might make Jordan vulnerable to reprisals. When a royal decree to surrender their arms and explosives instead triggered three days of street clashes, Hussein declared martial law and had his army drive the Palestinians out of Jordan. Ilyich, or "Carlos" as he called himself after his meeting with Habash, fought with the Palestinians in this conflict in which more than 3,000 were killed.

Carlos was sent by Habash to London to infiltrate the "cocktail party set" to which his mother still belonged and to make a list of high-profile targets for assassination or kidnapping. With this list completed, he was sent to Paris and told to work with the PFLP agent in charge there. This arrangement lasted until his partner was detained in LEBANON, gave information that was passed on to Paris, and finally led police to Carlos, who escaped by shooting his way out of the apartment and fleeing back to Lebanon.

He was then told to put a team together to hit the coming OPEC ministers meeting in Vienna in December of 1975. His instructions were to hold the ministers for ransom and to execute two of them: Saudi Arabia's Sheik Yamani and Iran's Jamshid Amonzegar. He recruited three Germans, Wilfred Bose, Joachim Klein, and Gabrielle Krocher-Tiedeman, two Palestinians, and one Lebanese to carry out this plan. The assault was carried out with success, preceded by careful surveillance, planning, information from an informant, a large supply of weapons, and Carlos's flair for the dramatic. He in fact changed his appearance for this attack, growing his hair longer with sideburns, and wearing a goatee beard and a black beret, looking somewhat like his hero, Che Guevara. After taking the ministers hostage, he negotiated successfully with Austrian authorities for a bus to the airport, a plane, and safe passage out.

After a circuitous route, including stops in Algeria, Libya, and a return to Algiers, he completed a release of the passengers, but he did not execute the two ministers as instructed. It remained unclear what, if any, ransom was paid and by whom. Some evidence suggested that QADHAFI of Libya had commissioned/paid for the raid and paid Carlos $1 million a year as a reward. His failure to follow orders concerning the executions angered Habash, and he evicted Carlos from the PFLP.

In March 1978, Carlos offered his services to Arab states as a "terrorist for hire." He began recruiting people to work for him as mercenaries, using contacts in the RED ARMY FACTION (RAF) and several other European groups. While he carried out a number of bombing attacks in subsequent years, he began to alienate most of the countries for whom he had depended for support and safe haven. At the age of 39, he had in fact been forced into "early retirement," since in order to secure sanctuary, he had to agree to be inactive in order not to draw international attention to the state sheltering him.

With the end of the cold war and the announcement after the Gulf War by SADDAM HUSSEIN that he would use Carlos to strike back at the West, Carlos became intensely hunted once more. Living in "retirement" in relative luxury with his wife and daughter in Syria had already become impossible. Syria had asked that he leave, and his wife left him (he was again womanizing). After the Gulf War, he tried to go to LIBYA, Lebanon, Cyprus, and Iran and was rejected or allowed to stay only a few days by each state. He finally secured sanctuary in the Sudan, but this came to an end as French authorities, who had been actively seeking him, found his location and put pressure onto Sudan to allow them to pick him up and bring him to France for trial. The Sudanese government finally agreed, and he was apprehended, sedated, and smuggled out of the country and back to France.

Carlos stood trial in 1997 and was convicted of all charges. He was sentenced to life in prison and is currently a guest of the French prison authorities.

Reference: Yallop, David. *Tracking the Jackal: The Search for Carlos, the World's Most Wanted Man* (New York: Random House, 1993).

censorship, of media concerning terrorist incidents

The term censorship, in this context, refers to efforts by a government to limit and edit what is said by the press about an incident in its coverage of terrorist events. Many democratic states are hard-pressed not to desire to filter what reporters say to a general (and possibly credulous) public about the motives, lives, intentions, actions, and individuals involved in perpetrating terrorist events. The power of the press to create heroes is sometimes frightening, and democratic governments are not blind to this danger. But few are willing to sacrifice cherished liberal values in order to keep the press from depicting a person who bombs a supermarket as a heroic "freedom fighter."

To impose censorship on the press in a democratic society would be to give to the perpetrators of the terrorist events a significant and unearned victory. When a democratic society, in panic and anger, abandons one of the cherished principles of law that make it democratic, the society has inflicted on itself a greater wound than the terrorists could achieve were they to bomb a hundred buildings.

Yet anger, frustration, and unrelenting problems have led some democratic systems into just that situation. The problems in NORTHERN IRELAND, for example, taxed the patience and the ingenuity of the British security forces to the breaking point. The fabric of democracy has sometimes worn thin in this troubled area, as restrictions have been placed on the press as a kind of "damage control." The damage done by censorship in such situations is difficult to calculate.

This issue has been of serious interest to many Western democracies since most have been challenged to resolve the tension between a need to guarantee as unfettered a media as possible while maintaining control over terrorist events. While most of the studies conducted have focused on the ability of the British government to cope with the continuous flow of terrorist events that, until recently, emanated from Northern Ireland, several studies of other Western democracies have also yielded significant insights into this problem.

Abraham Miller, a Bradley Resident Scholar at The Heritage Foundation who conducted the study of the U.S. Supreme Court case law on this issue, expanded his study of this topic in 1990 with research into the struggles of the British government to balance the media's desire to be unfettered against special security needs generated by the struggle in Northern Ireland. As in the study of the U.S. Supreme Court decisions, Miller concluded that media access to information was not guaranteed by British law. Miller found no evidence, however, to support claims by the government of a need for censorship that extended beyond the limiting of access.

One of the most comprehensive research studies on terrorism and the media was conducted during the 1980s, examining the relationship between terrorist violence, the Western news media, and the political actors. This study was empirical, and it included careful scrutiny of terrorist violence, beginning with 19th-century anarchists. The study evaluated interaction between terrorists, the media, and political actors in many regions of the world. It concluded that much of the blame for the increase in terrorism could be attributed to the media.

Schmid and de Graff, the authors of this study, summarize the arguments for and against censorship of terrorist news reporting. At the bottom of their list of 11 arguments against censorship is the only argument even marginally relevant to the legality of such censorship. This argument was simply that the assertion of insurgent terrorists that democratic states are not really "free" would gain credibility if the freedom of the press were suspended. In this sense, censorship in such events would not necessarily be unconstitutional, but it might be counterproductive in constitutional democracies.

Government-directed censorship has been most often studied in the context of the United Kingdom's efforts to restrain the media on the subject of the conflict in Northern Ireland. Of particular interest in this situation is the legislation banning television and radio broadcasts of interviews or direct statements by members of the outlawed IRISH REPUBLICAN ARMY (IRA) along with nine other organizations. Two of the organizations are legitimate (or at least not proscribed) groups: SINN FÉIN and the Protestant ULSTER DEFENSE ASSOCIATION (UDA).

This broadcasting ban was intended, in the words of the prime minister at that time, Margaret Thatcher, to deprive terrorists of "the oxygen of publicity" on which they thrive. Ian Stewart, minister of state for Northern Ireland when the ban was enacted, stated that it was designed to put an end to the practice of providing an easy platform for people who represented groups such as Sinn Féin and the UDA in Northern Ireland, who at that time supported political action by means of violence.

While the British system of government does not have a formal written constitution, it does possess a strong legal tradition of protection of civil liberties. There is considerable difference of opinion as to whether such measures are attacks on that legal tradition or simply reasonable precautions taken by a government faced with an extraordinarily difficult situation. As Henrik Bering-Jensen noted in his article "The Silent Treatment for Terrorists," "Nobody calls it censorship when Mafia spokesmen are not allowed to explain, over the airwaves, why it is advisable to pay protection money."

British governmental restraint of media reporting on terrorism was not limited to the 1988 ban. Occasionally pressure rather than legislation enabled the government to limit media coverage of terrorism. In his analysis, *Terrorism and the Liberal State,* Paul Wilkinson noted that the home secretary was able to pressure the British Broadcasting Company into banning the documentary *Real Lives: At the Edge of the Union,* which was a portrayal of Northern Ireland extremism.

The controversy in Northern Ireland highlights one dilemma faced by law enforcement officials assigned the task of coping with terrorism. Terrorism is, by definition, a political crime in that it involves political motives. Yet most of the laws created by democracies to deal with it have been crafted with a desire to prevent its classification as a political crime in order to prevent the use of the "political crime exception" included in most extradition agreements. Democracies, in general, allow a wide range of political dissent, with political parties and interest groups representing extremes on both the right and the left of the ideological spectrum operating legally within the system. Thus, it is generally not the political motive that is "illegal" but the action taken by the individual or group.

Most formal agreements and legislation concerning terrorism today focus on the illegality of the action taken, not on the group or its motive. Prevention of terrorist acts, not designation of terrorist groups, is the stated focus of law enforcement today. The motives of the group may be legal, even laudable; its actions may properly be subject to censure.

It is easier to censure such actions than to censor them. If the motive is not illegal, few democratic systems can realistically expect the press not to investigate, evaluate, and report on the motive as it relates to a specific act of terrorist violence. In a system in which the press is allowed to interview perpetrators of violent crime (such as murder, rape, torture, etc.), and to interview their family, friends, coworkers, and any other "relevant" individuals, it seems unlikely that a clear standard could be established for the need to censor stories about individuals and groups involved in terrorist acts.

If terrorist acts are not legally designated as "political crimes," then the press cannot reasonably be censored from reporting information on the individuals and their motivations in such cases, as long as they are permitted to publish similar insights relating to other violent crimes. Such reporting may be in poor taste or reflect bad judgment, but it is viewed by most democratic governments as unworthy of the serious punishment of censorship.

Broadcasters in the United Kingdom, confronted with the censorship system created by the government to control media coverage of the situation in Northern Ireland, were quick to note the ambiguity of this policy. Certainly it was inconsistent to prohibit Sinn Féin from having access to the broadcast media, and to censor news stories about this political group, when it was by law allowed to function openly as a political party. Since it was legal to report on the activities and the causes espoused by other legal political parties, it was not rational for it to be illegal to report on those same items with regard to Sinn Féin.

Neither the United States nor the United Kingdom has been willing to recognize violent acts carried out by radical political groups as acts of war. Had they done so, it would have been a fairly simple matter to justify censoring media reporting that might give "aid or comfort to the enemy during time of war." But if the governments declare that a state of war exists, then they would also be bound by international law to treat the individuals captured during the commission of those violent acts of terrorism as prisoners of war, combatants actively involved in a war who have been captured by the opposing side. This would make such prisoners subject to the appropriate Geneva Convention provisions and eligible for exchange. Governments are aware that such a step would encourage the endless taking of hostages by groups committing acts of terror in order to "exchange" them for the "prisoners of war" held by the government. This could create an intolerable situation, one not worth the comparatively small advantage that the legitimization of censorship would give.

Other Western democracies also offer interesting viewpoints on the utility and effect of governmental restriction on the media's dissemination of information regarding terrorism. A study by Christopher Kehler, Greg Harvey, and Richard Hall offers interesting perspectives on the delicate balance that democracies are expected to maintain between the need for some form of media regulation and the need for a free press.

Kehler and his associates argue that some form of media regulation is essential simply because media coverage of terrorist events can endanger lives. They cite cases in which the press negotiated with terrorists; cases where press corps members entered lines of fire and secured zones; and cases in which hostage rescue efforts were endangered by live broadcasts of the rescue forces moving in for assault. While such cases led these researchers to agree that it would be legally permissible for governments to regulate the media in its access to the scenes of these violent acts, it is interesting to note that these authors concluded that responsible standards created and enforced by the broadcast industry itself would be a preferable solution.

The conclusions of Kehler and his associates are consistent with those of most other researchers on this subject. While most deplore the reckless endangering of lives that sometimes takes place when an unrestricted media abuses its privileges of access, few scholars advocate government censorship as a solution. Most appear to agree with Paul Wilkinson's assessment, published in *Terrorism and the Liberal State,* that:

> [A]ny suggestion that any external body is bringing pressure to bear and altering editorial judgement as a result of political considerations undermines not only the credibility of the media, but the credibility of democratic government.

This is, in effect, the dilemma faced by the media and the Bush administration's "War on Terror." There have been several incidents where a member of the media has leaked classified intelligence that the Bush adminstration considers to be of a "sensitive and secretive" nature. Two examples are when the *New York Times* ran a story in December 2005 about a National Security Agency program that monitored international phone calls and e-mails to and from people in America suspected of being linked to terrorism, and again when the *Times* revealed in June 2006 a U.S. Treasury Department program to monitor an international database of financial wire transfers. The Bush adminstration maintains that these disclosures of classified intelligence do "great harm" to U.S. security, while other experts point out that organized terror groups are already aware of these efforts, so nothing has been lost. The media is caught between the desire to reveal new information that is important for the public to know (such as the NSA wiretapping and privacy issues) and the risk that such revelations may aid the terrorists.

See also RIGHT OF ACCESS, GOALS OF MEDIA TO TERRORIST EVENTS IN THE UNITED STATES; GOALS OF MEDIA, IN TERRORIST EVENT; GOALS OF GOVERNMENT, CONCERNING MEDIA IN TERRORIST EVENT; GOALS OF TERRORIST, CONCERNING MEDIA; NORTHERN IRELAND.

References: Alexander, Yonah P., and Robert Latter, eds. *Terrorism and the Media: Dilemma for Government, Journalism, and the Public* (Washington, D.C.: Brassey's, 1990); Norris, Pippa. *Framing Terrorism: The News Media, the Government and the Public* (Philadelphia: Taylor & Francis, 2003); Schmid, Alex P., and Janny F. A. de Graff. *Violence as Communication* (Newbury Park, Calif.: Sage Publications, 1982); Wilkinson, Paul. *Terrorism and the Liberal State* (New York: New York University Press, 1986).

Central Intelligence Agency (CIA)

The Central Intelligence Agency (CIA) is the principal intelligence and counterintelligence agency of the U.S. government. It was formally created in 1947, evolving from the Office of Strategic Services, which carried out these functions during World War II. In 1947, Congress created the National Security Council (NSC) and, under its direction, the CIA. Prior to its creation, U.S. intelligence and counterintelligence efforts had been carried out by the army and navy and by the Federal Bureau of Investigation (FBI), and frequently suffered from duplication, competition for resources, and a lack of coordination. The CIA was created to help correct these problems.

Under the legislation creating it, the CIA was tasked with advising the NSC on intelligence matters bearing on national security, making recommendations on coordinating intelligence activities of government agencies generally, correlating and evaluating intelligence and ensuring its proper communication within government, and carrying out such other national security intelligence functions as the NSC might direct.

The CIA is limited by the same legislation to carrying out its activities on foreign soil, although it has been permitted occasionally to move beyond its legal mandate. The FBI is charged instead with domestic intelligence and counterintelligence operations. This has created a system that, depending on the leadership of the two agencies, has generated the earlier problems of competition, duplication, and lack of coordination of information. On the issue of terrorism, however, there was a serious effort in the 1990s to create a renewed coordination of information and activities.

In the wake of the attacks of September 11, 2001, the CIA has been increasingly criticized for its role in counterterrorism. The 9/11 COMMISSION REPORT cited the lack of accurate intelligence about the reality of the threat posed by AL-QAEDA, suggesting the need to create a new leader in intelligence gathering—a National Intelligence Director—who would presumably assume the role of the director of the CIA in briefing the president about threats. This suggestion, which has been implemented, diminishes the role of the CIA as the primary intelligence-gathering and analysis agency. The subsequent faulty intelligence concerning the presence of weapons of mass destruction in Iraq, which was used to justify the U.S.-led war in Iraq, was also attributed to the CIA, further damaging its credibility in intelligence analysis.

Recent charges that the CIA had picked up individuals believed to be connected to terrorism and placed them in secret prisons in other countries (called "extraordinary rendition"), where they were allegedly tortured for information, have caused international concern. The CIA's role under President Clinton had been focused on creating a global partnership in the gathering of information. The recent errors and abuses of which the agency has presumably been guilty have seriously impaired the willingness of other nations to cooperate with intelligence operations in the war on terror.

See also USA PATRIOT ACT.

References: Baer, Robert. *See No Evil: The True Story of a Ground Soldier in the CIA's War on Terrorism* (New York: Crown Publishing Group, 2003); Schroen, Gary C. *First In: An Insider's Account of How the CIA Spearheaded the War on Terror in Afghanistan* (New York: Random House, 2005).

Chechnya

This is a small region of approximately 1 million people located in the Russian Federated Republic. It is a very oil-rich and very Islamic area. The Russian Empire forcibly annexed Chechnya during the 19th century. Many Chechens have since attempted to secede from Russia. During 1994–95, the Chechens fought a brutal war with the Russians that left the country destroyed. Fighting flared up again by 1999 and is continuing.

The fighting between Chechens and Russians is extremely brutal with neither side granting or expecting mercy from the other. Some Chechens fight alongside Russians as allies. Chechnya is a country that is basically divided into tribal associations and loyalties. Russian government statements have frequently referred to Chechens as terrorists and have officially linked them to bomb explosions in Moscow. Chechens consider Russians as terrorists who bomb their cities and villages and murder innocent civilians. Moreover, Russian brutality in Chechnya has a long history. The Soviet Union deported as much as a third of the population after the Germans were driven out of the region during 1943–44. At least a fourth of those who were deported died in Siberia.

Chechen rebels carried out terrorist attacks during the early part of the new millennium, two of which received substantial worldwide attention. The first occurred on October 23, 2002, when armed Chechen men and women seized a crowded theater in Moscow, demanding that the Russian government withdraw its forces from Chechnya. After a two-and-one-half-day siege, Russian "special forces" raided the theater in which more than 900 were being held hostage and pumped an aerosol anesthetic into the theater. Waiting 30 minutes for the anesthetic to take effect, the Russian force entered the building from the roof and other entrances.

In spite of the ensuing gun battle between the Chechens and the Russian security forces, the senior doctor from the Moscow public health department announced that all but one of the hostages that were killed in the raid had died from the effects of the anesthetic gas, rather than from the gunfire. The 42 terrorists and at least 120 hostages were killed in the Russian forces assault on the theater. While this qualifies as terrorism on the part of the Chechens who took the theater hostage, it is also arguably a counterterror action by a state that meets the criteria of terrorism as well, since many innocent victims died as a result of the gas attack, although their deaths were not perhaps intended by the state.

A similar Chechen attack, and Russian forces response, resulted in multiple deaths of innocent civilians. On September 1, 2004, an attack on a school in BESLAN, a Russian town in North Ossetia, was carried out by Chechens demanding, as had the group attacking the theater in Moscow, a complete and unconditional Russian troop withdrawal from Chechnya. The building of School Number One was seized by about 30 terrorists, taking approximately 1,300 students, parents, and teachers hostage and wiring explosive devices throughout the school building.

Public news reports as well as official government accounts of what occurred in the ensuing government attempt to end this hostage situation are conflicting and contradictory, but certainly many were killed in the resulting gun battle. Civilians, whose children were inside the school, joined police and security forces in the shooting. As many as 300 people or more perished during the siege, some killed by the hostage-takers, some by Russian forces, and some by civilian family members of trapped victims. Again, the response to the terrorist attack arguably exceeded the trauma of the attack itself.

The Chechen resistance to Russian occupation received a serious setback with the death of Shamil Salmanovich Basayev (also know as Abdullah Shamil Abu-Idris) on July 10, 2006. Basayev's family had a tradition of fighting Russia and, later, the Soviet Union that could be traced as far back as the late 19th century. Basayev never really held a steady job until he became a leader of the more extreme elements fighting for Chechen independence. He spent a lot of his youth sleeping during the day, playing video games at night, and considered Che Guevara his hero and inspiration.

Basayev fought in the first Chechen war that began at the end of 1994, the second Chechen war that began in 1999, and sporadically continued, associating himself with some of the more outrageous acts of terrorism against Russia. These included the 2002 Moscow theater siege, the 2004 assassination of the pro-Russian Chechen president Akhmad Kadyrov, and the Beslan school murders in which more than 350 people lost their lives—most of them schoolchildren.

In 2006, Basayev was killed in an explosion that occurred while he was in a car that was part of a convoy. The Russians claimed credit, though there is speculation that Basayev was killed by a rival Islamic extremist group. His Chechen supporters, though, argued that the episode was simply an accident. All agreed, however, that Basayev was dead, at the age of 41.

Reference: Meier, Andrew. *Chechnya: To the Heart of the Conflict* (New York: W. W. Norton & Company, 2004).

chemical weapons

The attack by the AUM SHINRIKYO on the Tokyo subway system in Japan illustrates both the strength, in terms of the psychological disruptive effects, and the weaknesses, in light of the relative non-lethality of the attack and the problems in dissemination, inherent in the use of chemical weapons by terrorists today.

Chemical weapons are a much more recent addition to the arsenals of nations and terrorists than are biological agents. For the most part, this type of weapon was not used in conflict until the 20th century, existing only in the form of "plans" never carried out in the decades at the end of the 19th century. The idea of using poison gas against an enemy has been reported in connection with several groups, including the Finians in the 1870s, who allegedly planned to spray it in the House of Commons in London. Similar plans were apparently made, but not carried out, during the Boer War and even the Japanese War with the Russians in 1905.

It was not until World War I that a chemical weapon—chlorine gas—was used on a large scale, with shocking success, by the Germans in 1915 at the Battle of Ypres. The gas killed 5,000 Allied troops and injured many more. Five months later, in Loos, Belgium, the Allies used poison gas against German troops, again with dreadful success. Military on both sides continued to use gases as weapons, with varying levels of success. While chlorine gas continued to be used in gas artillery shelling in a number of battles, including but not limited to the battles of Fey-en-Haye, Verdun, and the Somme, an equally effective mixture of chlorine and phosgene (mustard gas) was also used.

About 25 poison gases were used ultimately in the First World War. The exact casualty count from the use of this type of weapon is unclear; estimates vary between 500,000 and 1.2 million of both troops and civilians from both sides. History indicates that the Russians may have suffered the worst losses from this weapon when it was used against them in conflict east of Warsaw in 1915. They reportedly lost about 25,000 soldiers in the first such attack, with countless casualties among civilians in towns near the front line.

Gas attacks, though clearly technologically possible, do not appear to have occurred in the Second World War. Even the Germans, who had clear technical superiority in the range of chemical weaponry developed, decided for a variety of reasons not to use these weapons. Believing, apparently, that Allied forces had also developed tabun and sarin, toxic gases produced in Germany by 1944, Hitler decided not to use these newest lethal weapons (although it turned out that the Allies had *not* developed these toxins during the war).

The next reported use of chemical weapons occurred when Iraq used them during its war with Iran, against both Iranians and later against members of Iraq's own citizenry. A few accounts of the use of these agents in this eight-year conflict follow:

1983—Mustard gas was used at Haj Umran.
1984—Nerve gases were again used, at Al Basra, when Iraqi troops were on the defensive, in retreat.

Inspectors measure the volume of nerve gas in a container. (UNITED NATIONS)

1985 and 1986—Thousands of Iranian soldiers were reportedly killed by gas attacks at Um Rashrash, Hawiza marsh, and other locations.

1986 and 1987—Poison gases were used against the Kurds at Panjwin and Halabah.

Reports indicate that Saddam Hussein used tabun in these attacks. News reports depicted men, women, and children lying in agonized death-sprawls on the streets, after planes passed over the villages spraying the toxins.

- In 1991, sheriff's deputies in Alexandria, Minnesota, learned of a shadowy group of tax protestors called the Patriots Council. One informant reported discussions of blowing up a federal building. Another turned over a baby food jar containing ricin, one of the most deadly poisons known. In 1995, three of the plotters, whose plans included the assassination of IRS agents, were convicted under the Biological Weapons Antiterrorism Act.
- In December 1995, an Arkansas man, Thomas Levy, who had survivalist connections, was arrested by the FBI for having possession of a biological agent for unlawful purposes. He had 130 grams of ricin, enough to kill thousands of people when used with skill.

If terrorists want such weapons, they can make potent agents from such substances as isopropyl alcohol (easily available at drug stores and supermarkets), from pesticides and herbicides (available at most home and farm supply stores), and from a host of other equally accessible products. Most experts agree that it does not take great skills in chemistry to manufacture many different chemical agents. Some are, of course, more difficult than others; but a wide range is possible for someone with perhaps a few graduate courses in chemistry.

Chemical weapons are less attractive to terrorists primarily because of the difficulty in their delivery. As evidenced in the sarin gas attack in Tokyo, if the agent is not administered properly, it may afflict many but kill few. If the desire is for dramatic effect, this may not be a critical factor. But if the desire is to disable as well as frighten an enemy, to punish severely rather than merely inconvenience a target, then this problem in dissemination can be a major stumbling block. Factors such as wind direction, temperature, enclosure of space, and moisture can affect the dissemination process. Nerve gas, for example, rapidly hydrolyzes in water and therefore cannot be put, as many biological agents can, into the water system of a city.

As weapons of terrorists, then, chemical agents are relatively easy to obtain, potentially very lethal, but are limited in usefulness to date by the difficulty in dissemination, unless the desired effect is primarily psychological rather than physical in nature.

References: Center for Nonproliferation Studies (CNS). Chemical & Biological Weapons Resource Page. Available online. URL: http://cns.miis.edu/research/cbw. Accessed February 22, 2006; Harris, Robert. *A Higher Form of Killing: The Secret History of Chemical and Biological Warfare* (New York: Random House, 2002); Laqueur, Walter. *The New Terrorism: Fanaticism and the Arms of Mass Destruction* (Oxford: Oxford University Press, 1999); Mayor, Adrienne. *Greek Fire, Poison Arrows & Scorpion Bombs: Biological and Chemical Warfare in the Ancient World* (New York: Overlook Press, 2003); Tucker, Jonathan B. *War of Nerves: Chemical Warfare from World War I to Al-Qaeda* (New York: Pantheon Books, 2006).

Chile, state terrorism in

On September 11, 1973, the Chilean Armed Forces, led by its commander-in-chief General Augusto Pinochet, staged a military coup to overthrow the constitutionally elected president Salvador Allende and his Popular Unity government. President Allende was killed in La Moneda presidential palace, and his ministers and collaborators were arrested and sent to concentration camps. Many of them were later killed or "disappeared." The armed forces, through Decree Law No. 5, declared the existence of an "internal war" in the country and continued to wage this war until March 11, 1990.

In addition to the "war," a state of siege was declared throughout Chile and continued, with only brief interruptions, until 1987. This meant that all legal cases involving infractions of state of siege regulations were transferred from civilian courts to military tribunals, and it was used to justify the repression and killing of Chile's civilian population, with thousands of people detained for "political" reasons. According to Amnesty International and the United Nations Human Rights Committee, 250,000 Chileans had been detained under these rules by the end of 1973. Summary executions, disappearances, and killings in fake armed confrontations became the norm, with neighbors and colleagues denouncing one another to the dictatorship.

In June 1975, the regime officially created the DINA secret police agency, but this unit was dissolved two years later and replaced with the CNI secret policy. The National Congress and the Constitutional Tribunal were closed down by the junta at the beginning of its rule. All left-wing political parties were officially dissolved and made illegal associations. Other political parties were declared to be in recess, voter registration rolls were incinerated, and the functions of mayors and city councilors were annulled.

During the period from 1973 to 1990, particularly in the earliest years of the Pinochet regime, human rights violations were widespread and systematic. These included arbitrary arrests, raids on private households, imprisonment, extrajudicial executions, torture, and exile. Records of the abuses of civilians by the state only began to be revealed after 1990. While the Chilean delegate to the UN General Assembly emphatically denied allegations of state terrorism, claiming that "many of the supposedly disappeared do not legally exist," evidence of mass murder under Pinochet's regime continued to grow.

One painful incident in the history of Chile's disappeared came to light on November 30, 1978, when the human remains of 15 men arrested on October 7, 1973, were discovered in limestone ovens in Lonquen, a town just outside Santiago. The 15 men, between ages 17 and 51, had last been seen alive in the Isla de Maipo police headquarters. Sergio Maureira Lillo and his four sons, Rodolfo Antonio, Sergio Miguel, Segundo Armando, and José Manuel; the brothers Oscar, Carlos, and Nelson Hernández Flores; Enrique Astudillo Alvarez and his two sons, Omar and Ramón; Miguel Brant; Iván Ordoñez; José Herrera; and Manuel Navarro had disappeared after being arrested by police under orders of the police chief Lautaro Castro Mendoza.

The remains of many of the disappeared, however, will never be recovered. The National Truth and Reconciliation Commission, formed in April 1990, evoked confessions from officers who recounted loading civilians into airplanes and taking them many miles out to sea, where their bodies were dropped from the planes. Such tactics leave little evidence, except in the memories of those who participated. Pinochet was indicted for his role in a number of the deaths that occurred under his regime. Pinochet remained under house arrest until his death on December 10, 2006. One month before his death Pinochet released a statement that he accepted "political responsibility" for acts committed during his rule.

References: Constable, Pamela. *A Nation of Enemies: Chile under Pinochet* (New York: W. W. Norton & Company, 1993); Dinges, John. *The Condor Years: How Pinochet and His Allies Brought Terrorism to Three Continents* (New York: New Press, 2004).

Christian Identity Movement

The Christian Identity Movement (CIM) in the United States involves individuals linked by opposition to gun control, federal regulations, environmental regulation, and, to a lesser degree, abortion. Christian Identity teaches that Aryans are God's chosen people, that Jews are the offspring of Satan, and that minorities are not human. Many Identity adherents are driving forces in the militia movement and believe that the "system" no longer works because it has been taken over by the "New World Order," a secret group that actually runs the world. The membership of this secret group is less clearly defined; for some, it is "the Jews," for others, the United Nations.

Many Identity members, particularly those in militias, define the enemy as the U.S. government, which is recast into the role of King George III, with members of the movement defining themselves as true "patriots." They reject the normal democratic processes of change, including election, petition, assembly, and constitutional amendment, believing instead that they alone are the defenders of freedom in their country.

Norman Olson, a militia movement leader in Michigan, suggested that:

> The militia is the militant or the right wing, if you will, the front line, of the patriot community. The patriot community is a broad spectrum . . . involving the militia all the way down to the Religious Right and the political action groups and jury reform legislative action groups.

It is important to distinguish between the Christian Identity Movement and the Christian Patriotism Movement, even though there is considerable overlap in membership and philosophy. Christian Identity came from a 19th-century belief called "British Israelism." A person can be an Identity member in Australia, Canada, and other former British colonial territories. Christian Patriots, in contrast, are found only in the United States. One could be a Christian Patriot without subscribing to Identity religious ideology.

It would constitute a large step for those who would go from the Christian Coalition, which as a part of the Religious Right wants to impose its ways on American society within the rules, not by breaking them, to a militia movement, which rejects the rules and flouts them with enthusiasm to "save" America. It is a much smaller step to go to the militias from the Christian Identity Movement since CIM also despises much of what comprises the system today and can rationalize, by religious doctrine, the death/destruction of "children of Satan" and other non-Aryan types. It is as unlikely that a militia leader will be elected to the U.S. Congress as it is that a Christian Coalition leader will consider poisoning a town's water supply. The Christian Identity Movement members could do either.

The Religious Right and the Christian Identity were, for a long time, separated by many theological gaps. The cross-fertilization of these movements began occurring in the 1990s, sparked in part by the collapse of the Soviet Union. While the Christian Identity religion, with its focus on hatred of certain peoples and its distortion of biblical texts, has been anathema to legitimate Christian groups, this began to change as the uncertainty of the 1990s engendered a fear that American society was "under attack," not from without but from within. Instead of an "evil empire" upon which both the Religious Right and the Christian Identity could project its worst fears and personify as "Satan," the enemy became internal: the U.S. government. It became easier to bridge the theological gaps when a common enemy was perceived at home.

The Christian Identity Movement has links in many directions, including groups that focus on issues like gun control and abortion. Larry Pratt, an activist in the antiabortion movement and head of the 100,000-member Gun Owners of America, attended a meeting in 1992 convened by Christian Identity leader Peter Peters in Estes Park, Colorado. Held shortly after the surrender of Randy Weaver at Ruby Ridge, the meeting attracted a vast array of leaders from the white supremacist world.

Researchers believe that this 1992 meeting was the "birthplace" of the militia movement.

See also ARMED MILITIAS IN THE UNITED STATES; ARYAN NATIONS.

References: Barkun, Michael. *Religion and the Racist Right: The Origins of the Christian Identity Movement* (Chapel Hill: University of North Carolina Press, 1994); Kaplan, Jeffrey. *Radical Religion in America* (Syracuse, N.Y.: SUNY Press, 1995).

Christian militia movements in the United States

The Christian militia offers a significantly different challenge to government efforts to provide security than did the left-wing "college radicals" of the 1960s and 1970s. Unlike the isolated, crudely unsophisticated pipe-bomb manufacturers who dominated most of the U.S.-based terrorist groups for at least two decades, members of Christian militia groups are often well trained in the use of arms and explosives. Some of these groups even have skilled armorers and bomb-makers and members with outdoor survival skills who are adept at guerrilla-warfare techniques. They are also strongly motivated by fundamental religious beliefs that advocate the use of violence for "holy" causes, making them susceptible to "crusader" impulses.

Christian militia groups in the United States are widespread, intricately linked by overlapping memberships, and bound together by a religious and political doctrine that defines the world in terms that make the use of violence, not just acceptable, but necessary, and offers an apocalyptic vision of imminent war. Since many of the members of these groups are skilled in the use of weapons and utilize survival training in camps throughout the country, planning for an "inevitable" racial war, the impact of these groups may well be formidable in the 21st century.

Although the United States has produced many different types of right-wing extremist groups, particularly during last two decades of the 20th century, Christian militia group cells share striking similarities in ideology and overlapping membership that help to explain several important factors: the broad popular base enjoyed by militia groups; the assumption on the part of the general public—and much of the law-enforcement community, until the Oklahoma City bombing—that such groups are nonthreatening as a whole; and the festering of support for hatred that such groups provide to individuals seeking someone or something to blame for the loss of jobs, income, family farms, etc.

As Abraham Foxman, national director of the Anti-Defamation League (ADL), noted in 2004, such religiously motivated militias are able to quietly reorganize and retool without attracting public notice. Foxman, in his ADL report, highlighted several significant trends in the modern militia movement. These trends have their roots in the *Free Militia Training Manual,* which is heavily couched in Christian doctrine, and they include, but are not limited to:

Efforts to maintain a low profile: While Christian militias have begun to increasingly connect with each other and to seek recruits, this has been done in low-profile arenas, such as online discussion forums and mailing lists from websites. This fits the *Training Manual's* precepts precisely.

Fear of the government: Christian militias have been reenergized by post–September 11 fears of conspiracies and government power, viewing the "war on terrorism" and the USA PATRIOT Act as being directed at them. This also fits the "paranoia" pattern suggested in the manual.

The perception that time is running out: Christian militia members are unifying around the idea that the country is headed toward a violent end-time confrontation between its citizens and the government. This anticipation of a millennial conflict between good and evil has also been noted as fundamental to the worldview of someone willing to carry out a terrorist act and is strongly portrayed in the *Training Manual.*

Christian militia groups in the United States today fit easily into the all-channel network pattern of groups, with no specific "group leader" or hub; each cell is capable of acting independently, with varying degrees of skill and success, against a common target—frequently a government individual or facility. When an individual such as Timothy McVeigh has membership in both the Religious Right (in the form of the CHRISTIAN IDENTITY MOVEMENT) and a local militia group, his or her ability to act independently is enhanced, but it is also more likely that the individual would see himself or herself as a "holy warrior" in a good cause supported by his or her religious beliefs. This combination of independence, military expertise, and religious zeal can clearly be lethal.

Christian militias and non-faith-based militias are very similar, often sharing memberships. McVeigh was a member of the Christian Identity Movement (which was a precursor to the ARYAN NATIONS and THE ORDER) as well as a member of a local militia organization; this overlap can create difficulty in determining the "support network" sustaining and perhaps invoking such terrorist events as the Oklahoma City bombing. While groups like the ARIZONA PATRIOTS and the Aryan Nations tend to coalesce around a white-supremacist doctrine, they also usually perceive themselves as political "patriots" rather than religious "crusaders," making them less likely to be suicide bombers and more likely to be vigilante warriors.

Since many militias in the United States today draw from the theology of the Christian Identity Movement, there are traces of "Christian militia" elements in many militia groups today. But these are "traces," not compelling motivating factors. Most militia members have been in military service, like working with weapons, and will never, in all likelihood, break the law by carrying out vigilante actions, since their motivation is less intense. Christian militia members, however, are potentially crusaders and, like McVeigh, willing to die for doing what they believe is "right," according to their faith.

One last conclusion is relevant here. The actions of McVeigh proved that Christian militia groups, while not directly responsible for the actions of their members, may offer social and psychological support that will enable individuals to carry out lethal acts on their own. However, since the training manuals of such militia groups today stress paranoia and a lack of overt leadership structure, it is unlikely that the militia movement will be responsible for an event on the scale of the September 11 tragedy. This is not particularly encouraging, since the Oklahoma City bombing was incredibly destructive. But compared to that of 9/11, it was a modest effort. The danger may lie in the ability of individuals, motivated by militia propaganda, to launch unilateral attacks on disparate targets, coordinated only by timing—and that danger remains clear and not yet preventable.

See also CHRISTIAN PATRIOTISM; THE COVENANT, THE SWORD, AND THE ARM OF THE LORD.

References: Abanes, Richard. *American Militias: Rebellion, Racism and Religion.* (Downers Grove, Ill.: InterVarsity Press, 1996); Foxman, Abraham H. "The Quiet Retooling of the Militia Movement." New York: Anti-Defamation League (September 7, 2004). Available online. URL: http://www.adl.org. Accessed March 6, 2006.

E.A.C.

Christian Patriotism

Christian Patriotism (CP), a key ideological and theological tenet of many in the militia movement in the United States, teaches that the United States is the biblical promised land, promised to white/Aryan/Nordic types. Members of this movement hold that the U.S. Constitution and the Bill of Rights are divinely inspired and should be treated like scripture, while the amendments to the Constitution that follow the first 10 (like those guaranteeing equality under the law, votes for women and those of nonwhite races, and freeing the slaves) are regarded as "man-made" and hence flawed "derogations" of the "original" Constitution.

Christian Patriots frequently file documents announcing that they are "sovereign citizens" with no link to the "corporate entity" known as the United States of America, which they regard as an "evil" government that pays attention to those "derogating" post-Bill of Rights amendments. Terry Nichols, involved in the OKLAHOMA CITY BOMBING and Militia of Montana leader John Trochmann have made such pronouncements.

The MONTANA FREEMEN group, involved in the Ruby Ridge standoff, were advocates of Christian Patriotism as well. Their refusal to pay their taxes was defended in terms of CP belief that America is promised to the white race, and by opposing and even severing ties to an evil government that tolerates and even advocates equal rights for minorities, white Americans can "reclaim their birthright." Rodney Skurdal, a Freeman, stated that he based his belief that he owed no taxes on the theological premise that "We the white race are God's chosen people . . . and our Lord God stated that 'the earth is Mine,' so there is no reason for us to be paying taxes on His land."

Christian Patriots have links with militia groups, the CHRISTIAN IDENTITY MOVEMENT, and the Christian Coalition, but there are significant differences between each. Transition from a member of the nonviolent Christian Coalition to the militia groups, Christian Patriots, or the Christian Identity Movement is often a large step. James Nichols, brother of Terry Nichols (mentioned earlier as being involved in the Oklahoma City bombing), was a Christian Patriot who considered, but was convinced not to accept, Identity theology by a Christian friend. For him, as for many others, the theology rather than the willingness to commit violence was a critical factor for such a transition.

NETWORKING of such groups does occur in the United States. Christian Patriots exist only in the

United States since their ideology focuses only on the U.S. government, its history, and related documents. Christian Identity Movement adherents and militia groups, however, have appeared in other countries, and members elsewhere network with members of CP in the United States. Networking also occurs inside the country based on common positions on issues such as gun control and abortion.

coerced conversion

See STATE TERRORISM.

Colombia, narco-terrorism and

In order to understand the link between narcotics and terrorism as it emerged in Colombia, it is essential to understand three critical elements: insurgent groups such as the REVOLUTIONARY ARMED FORCES OF COLOMBIA (FARC) and the NATIONAL LIBERATION ARMY (ELN); the drug cartels, with their "drug lords" who often used drug money; and the victims of the cartel violence, who often became guilty of terrorism as well, such as "Los Pepes." All had enormous impact on the conflict and narco-terrorism that characterized Colombia until the beginning of the 21st century.

FARC and ELN

The FARC, the ELN, and other leftist paramilitary groups generated much of their funding and support by protecting narcotics trafficking. Estimates of the profits to groups from their involvement in narcotics ranged into the hundreds of millions of dollars. The United States includes both groups on its list of foreign terrorist organizations. Plan Colombia started in 2000 by the United States is a multibillion-dollar aid package designed to help Colombia's weak government deal with narcotrafficking. With the assistance of the United States, the Colombian army trained, equipped, and fielded its first counternarcotics battalion, designed to support national police efforts to break terrorist links to narcotics production. A third group, the right-wing UNITED SELF-DEFENSE FORCES OF COLOMBIA (AUC), is also on the U.S. foreign terrorist list, and is comprised of several paramilitary squads supported by wealthy landowners, drug cartels, and certain parts of the Colombian military itself. In an example of the nexus between the war on terror and the war on drugs, in August 2002 the United States authorized Colombia to use U.S. aid previously allocated for drug interdiction to directly combat FARC, ELN, and the AUC.

Pablo Escobar and the Medellín cartel

Pablo Escobar, born in 1949 to a peasant farmer and a schoolteacher, was perhaps the most successful criminal in history, and his life seriously impacted the population and government of Colombia, in the context of narco-terrorism. Before his death, at the age of 44, Escobar amassed a personal fortune of approximately $3 billion, and he remains a folk hero in his home town of Envigado, a suburb of the city of Medellín. He grew up during a violent time in Colombia's history, often called "La Violencia," a period of about 40 years during which two factions waged war. Marxist insurgents, controlling large parts of the country, waged a long guerrilla war, with daily clashes with security forces.

As a teenager, Escobar was expelled from school, drifted into petty crime, and got his start in the drug business driving coca paste from the Andean Mountains to the laboratories in Medellín. He was caught once, but the charges were dropped on a technicality, and by the time he was 26, Escobar had made the transition from courier to smuggler, carrying cocaine that was worth $35,000 a kilo.

A small plane could make big money, and Escobar soon was making millions. Within a few flights, he was a multimillionaire; he invested his money and purchased land, buying Haciendo Napoles for a reported $63 million before he was 30 years old. Escobar owned his own helicopter at this point, a private zoo, thousands of acres of land in Colombia, and a car once owned by U.S. gangster Al Capone, with whom Escobar felt a kinship.

The drug planes had to run the gauntlet of U.S. Customs, who had planes of their own, but few of the drug planes were detected, and Escobar ran a very tight organization. His planes were smuggling about 400 kilos of cocaine a trip, where one flight could net $10 million. The bales of cocaine were off-loaded at remote airstrips or dropped into the water. High-speed motor boats made the final run.

Cocaine was perceived by the American public at that time very much like alcohol had been during the days of Prohibition: not addictive and "fashionable," a "harmless" vice whose demand in the United States was growing almost too quickly to be met by the suppliers, like Escobar. As a result, at 32, Escobar was earning about $500,000 per day, but his competition with other drug dealers in Medellín was becoming intense. Cooperation and risk-sharing, by diversifying and creating a transshipment network, strengthened the hands of all of the dealers, creating what became known as the Medellín cartel.

Violence became a trademark of this cartel, which shared the U.S. market with its competitors from Cali. With five or more planes taking cocaine into the United States each week from this cartel, and Escobar making a million dollars each day, his "enforcers"—known for their hits with snub-nosed machine guns fired from motorbikes—were valued employees in his multimillion-dollar business.

Escobar was a study in contrasts, strategically ruthless in eliminating "problems" by murdering whole families, but a devoted family man. His title of "El Patrón" derived not only from his role as head of a business but also for his role in taking several trucks to poor neighborhoods to distribute food to people who were hungry. Escobar built a soccer field and sponsored a soccer team. He hired local people to do construction, to run businesses for him, and to teach in the local schools, which he built. He was much more involved in the local community life than the local government or the Colombian government in many ways, and he clearly created for himself a power base in Medellín; not surprisingly, he was elected as a member of Congress from this area in 1982.

In the United States, a change in policy emerged in 1982, with President Reagan announcing a "war on drugs," a crusade to rid the country of drug abuse. When the Drug Enforcement Administration (DEA) made cocaine a higher priority, it ran a sophisticated sting operation that enabled the agency to track the cocaine all the way back to one of Escobar's processing laboratories, deep in the Colombian jungle. Using information supplied by the DEA, the anti-narcotics unit of the Colombian national police raided the location in March 1984.

Colombian narcotics officials found a complex of airstrips and laboratories capable of refining and shipping cocaine on an industrial scale, which the drug lords had named "Tranquilandia," with almost 14 metric tons of cocaine, worth more than a billion dollars. The weighbills, receipts, and accounts offered even more important information: the existence of the Medellín cartel, which until that time, the DEA had not even known existed.

Airstrips and laboratories continued to be found over the next few days, drawing the attention of the head of the anti-narcotics division in Colombia, Colonel Jaime Ramirez. It was the greatest drug bust globally, at this point.

Escobar and the cartel personally offered Ramirez's brother a multimillion-dollar payment, if the colonel would cease all operations in this sting, and withdraw his forces. Instead, Ramirez's forces poured gallons of ether into the laboratories and lit fires, explosively demolishing the facilities. The response of the cartel was to write a death list, which included Ramirez's name and that of his boss, the minister of justice.

Escobar and many of the other cartel leaders left the country as the government raided their haciendas. Escobar found sanctuary in revolutionary Nicaragua, where the cartel had been doing business with both the Sandinistas and with Castro's Cuban regime. His money was used to pay government officials there, ensuring his welcome.

With help from a pilot turned informant, the DEA was able to get photos of Nicaraguan soldiers loading cocaine into an airplane to be delivered to the United States. At the urging of White House adviser Oliver North, the photo was shared with the nation, generating outrage and support for the war on drugs—and a call to bring Escobar to the United States for trial.

Those who knew him said that there was nothing Escobar feared more than the American justice system, where prison guards cannot be routinely bribed or judges easily intimidated. He was known to have said, "Better a grave in Colombia than a cell in the USA," and he clearly feared extradition.

The cartel brought Colombia to a state of virtual civil war. When terrorists in the APRIL 19TH MOVEMENT group in 1985 kidnapped the justices of the Supreme Court, government troops had to lay siege to the Palace of Justice. While a direct connection between M-19 and the drug cartels has never been proved, Escobar and the other cartel leaders believed that the destruction or intimidation of the judiciary system in Colombia was essential, since the Court was to have ruled on that day on the law of extradition. In the fighting that followed, nearly 100 people were killed—including half of the members of the Court—and all the files on extradition cases were destroyed.

The cartel's relentless campaign of murder and intimidation took on new strength as Escobar and several other Medellín leaders became known as the EXTRADITABLES. The money from drugs financed the car-bomb attacks that ripped through the cities. A new word was added to the vocabulary: *narco-terrorism*. A bomb exploded outside the police headquarters in Bogotá, killing 63 and wounding 600. On November 27, 1989, an Avianca jet blew up in mid-air, killing 107 passengers and crew. Faced with this growing violence, the newly elected president of Colombia changed the

Pablo Escobar (ARCHIVOS PRIVADOS)

Constitution in 1990 to appease the drug traffickers, eliminating the provision for extradition to the United States.

Escobar, having seen one cartel leader deported earlier to America and another killed, with his son, in a hail of police bullets, decided to surrender to the police, go to jail, and let the government protect him and his family, which had been threatened by his rivals in the drug business. But he went to jail on special terms: The jail was built on his land, to his designs, jokingly called "Club Medellín," with maximum comfort. He had a suite, with a Jacuzzi, an office, and parties, often in the discotheque and bar that the prison also possessed.

After Escobar had four of his own lieutenants brought to the prison and tortured, then murdered in a dispute over money, the authorities—who had not stopped his continued narcotics trafficking—decided to move Escobar to a "regular" prison. Escobar, fearing this move, walked away from his "club" and spent the next months on the run.

With help from other governments, who provided tracking equipment, Escobar was finally located. On December 2, 1993, Escobar died during a rooftop gun battle. His death did not end the cartel or its business; it did not change the pace of drug trafficking or impact the price of cocaine. But through this, Colombia, the United States, and much of the world became aware of the violence and danger in narco-terrorism.

Los Pepes

People Persecuted by Pablo Escobar, or Los Pepes, also generated a form of violence in Colombia. This short-lived vigilante group comprised, as the name suggests, of those who had been victims of Escobar's violence, is alleged to have committed acts of torture, murder of civilians, and rape in Colombia. For example, this group was responsible for the murder of the 18-year-old son of one of Escobar's lawyers and of the man who was Escobar's horse trainer (neither individuals were involved in committing any of Escobar's violence).

Although the name this group assumed suggests that its members were persecuted by Escobar, many were simply rival drug traffickers. One of Escobar's rivals in the drug business, the Cali cartel, was one of those providing funds for this group. Several of the leaders of Los Pepes eventually became leaders instead in the national paramilitary alliance, the AUC, which is considered responsible for massive human rights violations in Colombia. Some of these leaders, such as Diego Murillo-Bejarano, became drug lords as well as leading members in the AUC. The cycle of violence initiated by drug dealers like Escobar continues, as Colombia seeks to cope with the AUC today.

Reference: Bowden, Mark. *Killing Pablo: The Hunt for the World's Greatest Outlaw* (New York: Penguin Group, 2002).

Comitatus *See* GUERRILLA WARFARE.

complicity, between media and terrorists

The relationship between terrorism and the media does not flow in a single direction; rather, terrorism reacts to and utilizes the media in a fashion similar to that in which the media reacts to and uses (to sell papers) the terrorist events. This interactive relationship has allowed serious charges of complicity, a legal charge indicating active participation of a primary or secondary nature, in terrorist events to be leveled at the media by law enforcement and government counterterrorism officials.

Terrorism is a crime of theater. In order for terrorism to be effective, the terrorists need to be able to communicate their actions and threats to their audience as quickly and dramatically as possible. Statistically, terrorist incidents worldwide are significant, both in terms of the number of dead and injured and in terms of the number of incidents reported annually. But massive media coverage of individual terrorist attacks reach a vast audience, creating an impact far beyond that which the incident, in the absence of this media, could be expected to effect. Without intensive media coverage, it could be argued that few would know of terrorist actions, motivations, and actors. As Brian Jenkins noted:

> Terrorism is violence for effect—not primarily, and sometimes not at all for the physical effect on the actual target, but rather for its dramatic impact on an audience. Developments in world communications, particularly the news media, have expanded the potential audience to national and, more recently, to international proportions.

The interaction of the media with terrorists in the Hanafi Muslim siege in Washington, D.C., in March 1977, is an interesting example of interference by the media in law enforcement efforts, and of the proactive role of some media in terrorist events. Live broadcasts from the scene continued throughout the siege, and overzealous journalists interviewing the terrorists tied up the telephone lines. This constitutes nuisance, perhaps, but not necessarily interference.

However, at least two incidents during the siege occurred that highlight the interactive nature of the media and the terrorists in this event. One of the reporters, observing law enforcement officers bringing something (food) to the terrorists, broadcast that the police were preparing for an assault. Eventually, the police were able to convince the Hanafi that the reporter was incorrect, but valuable negotiating time and trust-building efforts were lost. Another reporter called the leaders of the hostage-takers, Hamas Abdul Khaalis, and suggested that the police were trying to trick him. Khaalis selected 10 of the older hostages for execution, and police again had to try to defuse the situation by removing some of their sharpshooters from the area.

This certainly constituted interference in the hostage negotiation process, and it generated much legitimate criticism of the press. A reporter who was one of the hostages in this siege observed:

> As hostages, many of us felt that the Hanafi takeover was a happening, a guerrilla theater, a high impact propaganda exercise programmed for the TV screen, and . . . for the front pages of newspapers around the world. . . . Beneath the resentment and the anger of my fellow hostages toward the press is a conviction gained . . . that the news media and terrorism feed on each other, that the news media and particularly TV, create a thirst for fame and recognition. Reporters do not simply report the news. They help create it. They are not objective observers, but subjective participants.

This charge suggests that the media play an active role in terrorist events, sometimes even impacting the course of the event. Such a claim goes well beyond that commonly made by many who research this issue, namely, that terrorists use the media for their own purposes. Few would argue that terrorists do indeed use the media to reach a large audience and to carry a specific message to that audience as quickly as possible. The hijacking of TWA FLIGHT 847 in 1985 was, as Grant Wardlaw noted, cleverly structured to ensure maximum media coverage and maximum exposure of their propaganda. It remains a disturbing example of the manipulation of the free world's news media by groups involved in terrorist acts.

An interactive relationship suggests that it is possible that the media's impact on terrorism goes beyond that of a reluctant tool, tending instead toward that of a generator of action. This does not mean that the media plan, or deliberately suggest, terrorist attacks to groups or individuals. But the actions of the media have been scrutinized intensely in recent years to determine whether media coverage of terrorist events caused, for instance, terrorists to choose one particular course of action over another (for example, bombings over hijackings).

Alex Schmid offered three hypotheses that explain the media's effect on terrorism. The first, called the arousal hypothesis, suggests that unusual or unique media content can increase a person's desire to act aggressively; that, in fact, any news story detailing some form of aggressive behavior can increase the potential for more aggressive behavior from members of the media's audience. A second hypothesis concerns what is termed disinhibition. This hypothesis suggests that violence portrayed in the media weakens the inhibition of the viewer to engage in similar behavior, which in turn increases the person's readiness to engage in aggressive behavior.

A great deal of time and attention have been devoted to determining whether the media encourages violent behavior in viewers, particularly young people. Results of research into these hypotheses have been mixed, but findings have generated sufficient concern for the attorney general of the United States to issue a not-too-veiled warning to the television networks, strongly suggesting that they initiate self-regulation systems for limiting TV violence before the government decides that it must regulate the industry on this issue.

The third hypothesis suggested by Schmid involves the social learning theory. This is premised on the belief that all behavior is learned by observation. Thus, if television depicts successful terrorist acts, then viewers will learn all about them; this will in turn increase the likelihood of terrorism. The media would thus be engaged in training individuals in terrorist behavior each time it reported such acts.

This is an extreme assessment of the relationship between media and terrorism. While live media coverage has, perhaps, given greater importance to events in remote parts of the world, it is unlikely that an individual would decide, on the basis of a news report of a terrorist incident, to begin engaging in terrorist activities. Although TV newscasts are more visually exciting than printed news articles, efforts have been made to test this hypothesis by tracking the articles generated by terrorist events over a decade to determine whether or not increased coverage of terrorist events actually resulted in an increase in the number of such events.

All that was determined by such an analysis was that an interactive relationship appears to exist; that is, that one of the variables acts upon or influences the other. It was not possible, with the type of data available, to determine much more than a rough estimate of the strength of the relationship and its apparent direction. Since other variables could also be acting upon the ones being studied, without controlling for all other potential influences on terrorist behavior, it would be difficult to generalize about the results of this research. It did, however, become possible to comment more on the utility of the third hypothesis posited by Schmid, using this limited study.

According to the list generated by the U.S. Department of State of terrorist incidents that took place during the years 1981–89 (this was a time of fairly intense terrorist activity), a total of 119 incidents were recorded involving an American citizen in some respect. Since all of these incidents involved at least one U.S. citizen, it was assumed that they would be reported in national newspapers, such as the *Washington Post* and the *New York Times*. By using these two papers, most of whose stories on these incidents were supplied by the Associated Press (thus eliminating most of the anomalies in the reporting of the data), and categorizing the incidents by type (to discover whether any type of event served better as a "learning tool"), it was possible to note several interesting phenomena:

1. Cumulative regression analysis of the data resulted in a multiple r of .843 and a square multiple of r of .710. This generally indicates a strong relationship, in this case between the type of event and the amount of coverage.
2. During the period 1981–89, inclusive, the number of terrorist incidents increased overall, whereas the number of articles generated in response to these incidents actually decreased.
   a. There were exceptions to these trends. The number of bombings resulting in deaths remained relatively constant, actually decreasing toward the end of the period. This occurred in spite of the enormous increase in the number of articles generated by these attacks.
   b. The incidence of assassination (defined, in Department of State terms as "any time an American is shot and killed) peaked in 1984, with four incidents that generated a record 14 articles. In spite of the spate of press coverage, however, the number of incidents fell the following year to the 1981 level (one incident), producing only four articles. The following year there were three incidents, clearly not impacted by the previous year's limited press coverage of these types of events. In other words, many articles in one year did not generate many attacks in the following year; nor, in a year when the number articles dropped to only four, was there a decrease in the subsequent number of incidents.
   c. Hijackings (involving the willful seizure of a means of transportation for a political purpose) occurred only in three years during the decade

studied. After three incidents generated a phenomenal 16 articles, there was only one further incident for the remainder of the decade.

d. Kidnappings of American actually generated fewer articles than incidents, meaning that some incidents were not even reported in the national news. Nor was there a directional relationship between the number of articles and the number of incidents. Four incidents in 1985 generated only one article, while fewer incidents (three) in 1986 provoked seven articles. The same number of incidents (three) in 1987 produced only one article.

This data suggests that, while a relationship appears to exist between the number of terrorist incidents in a given year and the number of articles that they generate, this relationship varies with the type of incident. Moreover, even in the same category of incident, there is considerable variation in the number of articles provoked by the same number of incidents. This suggests that there are, as suggested earlier, other factors at work in this process not accounted for by so simplistic an assumption as the "learned behavior" hypothesis. If all that was necessary for a terrorist to repeat the action or to attempt a similar action were news coverage of the event, then all of the types of events should have produced parallel growth lines between incident and article numbers. This was clearly not the case.

Instead, it was obvious that other factors influence the decision of an individual or group to engage in terrorist activities. While the media may have some impact, it would be erroneous to assume that the action of the media causes terrorist events to happen by the coverage of previous events. Hijacking incidents did not become less frequent because of limited press coverage; instead, press coverage was extensive. However, the enactment of several aerial hijacking conventions and the subsequent closing of most safe havens for hijackers by the "extradite or prosecute" provisions in international agreements may as easily be given credit for reducing the number of hijacking incidents.

This limited study of news media in a role of "motivation" for terrorism suggests that, while terrorism and the media show a strong relationship, this does not mean that media coverage results in terrorist acts. The mass media does serve to extend experience, present models, stimulate aspirations, and indicate goals for terrorists. But media is clearly not "responsible" for terrorist acts occurring.

It is possible to infer from a variety of studies on this issue that the media can impact terrorists by what Schmid terms a "built-in escalation imperative" that requires that terrorists must commit more and more bizarre and cruel acts to gain media attention. Since kidnapping failed to generate continued media attention, even though most articles suggested that many times the ransom demands were met, terrorists turned increasingly to the use of assassination. When the shooting of a single American stopped generating many articles (as it did between 1985 and 1989), then bombings, which resulted in multiple deaths, became the weapon of choice.

A relationship certainly exists between terrorists and the media. The strength and direction of that relationship is dependent upon many variables, of which there are insufficient data to reach firm conclusions to date.

See also CENSORSHIP, OF MEDIA CONCERNING TERRORIST INCIDENTS; CONVENTIONS ON AERIAL HIJACKING; GOALS OF GOVERNMENT, CONCERNING MEDIA IN TERRORIST EVENT; GOALS OF MEDIA, IN TERRORIST EVENT; GOALS OF TERRORIST, CONCERNING MEDIA; MEDIA AS A "SHOWCASE" FOR TERRORISM; RIGHT OF ACCESS, OF MEDIA TO TERRORIST EVENTS IN THE UNITED STATES.

References: Nacos, Brigitte L. *Terrorism and the Media: From the Iran Hostage Crisis to the Oklahoma City Bombing* (New York: Columbia University Press, 1994); Schmid, Alex P., and Janny F. A. de Graff, *Violence as Communication* (Newbury Park, Calif.: Sage, 1982).

computers *See* CYBERTERRORISM.

Continuity Irish Republican Army *See* IRISH REPUBLICAN ARMY.

conventions on aerial hijacking

Convention on Offenses and Certain Other Acts Committed on Board Aircraft

This convention, signed in Tokyo on September 14, 1963, provided a general basis for the establishment of jurisdiction—that is, legal authority to exercise control—in cases of SKYJACKING. The hijacking of the aircraft is an act that often takes place in flight en route between countries. Such planes are often registered to yet another country and carry citizens of many countries. So a decision as to which country has the right to bring the hijacker to justice is often a difficult one.

Article 3 of the Tokyo Convention provides that the state of registration is the one that has first and primary right to exercise jurisdiction. But this convention does not place on any signatory nation the responsibility to ensure that all alleged offenders will be prosecuted. Thus, a nation may accept jurisdiction and then refuse or neglect to bring the offenders to justice before a court of law.

Convention for the Suppression of Unlawful Seizure of Aircraft

This convention, signed in The Hague on December 16, 1970, deals more specifically with the issues of extradition and prosecution of individuals involved in aerial hijacking. The Hague Convention obliges contracting states (those who sign and ratify the treaty) to make the offense of unlawful seizure of aircraft a crime under their own law, punishable by severe penalties.

In this convention can be found a definition of the actions that may constitute, by law, the offense of skyjacking. Article 1 states that any person commits an offense on board an aircraft in flight who

1. Unlawfully, by force or threat thereof, or by any other means of intimidation, seizes, or exercises control of, that aircraft, or attempts to perform any such act; or,
2. Is an accomplice of a person who performs or attempts to perform any such act.

Although not as explicit as the later convention drawn up in Montreal, this convention provides an important legal framework for prosecution of an offense, reasonably and clearly defined in legal terms that are directly applicable in the legal systems of many states. Thus, the states are not given the sticky, politically difficult task of creating laws to make such acts a legal offense.

Under this convention, too, provisions for jurisdiction are extended. The states party to this document were legally given the responsibility for jurisdiction, in the following order of precedence: (1) the state of registration; (2) the state of first landing; and (3) the state in which the lessee has its principal place of business or permanent residence. Moreover, this convention requires each contracting state to take measures to establish jurisdiction if the offender is within its territory and is not to be extradited.

The Hague Convention also addresses the issue of prosecution, obligating each contracting state either to extradite an alleged offender (i.e., to send the person to another state seeking to prosecute) or to submit the case "without exception whatsoever to its competent authorities for the purpose of prosecution." While this does not create an absolute obligation to extradite, the convention states that the offense referred to is deemed to be included as an extraditable offense in any existing treaties between contracting states and in every future extradition treaty concluded between such states.

Convention for the Suppression of Unlawful Acts Against the Safety of Civil Aviation

Signed in Montreal on September 23, 1971, this convention adds more detail to the description of the offenses affecting aircraft and air navigation. The offenses include:

1. Acts of violence against a person on board an aircraft in flight if that act is likely to endanger the safety of that aircraft; or
2. Destruction of an aircraft in service or damage to such an aircraft which renders it incapable of flight or which is likely to endanger its safety in flight; or
3. Placing or causing to be placed on an aircraft in service, by any means whatsoever, a device or substance which is likely to destroy that aircraft, or to cause damage to it which is likely to endanger its safety in flight; or
4. Destruction or damage of air navigation facilities or interference with their operations, if such an act is likely to endanger the safety of the aircraft in flight; or
5. Communication of information which is known to be false, thereby endangering the safety of the aircraft in flight.

This convention also made aerial hijacking an international crime, for which every state has jurisdiction. Thus, the ability of individuals engaged in skyjacking to escape to a country not given jurisdiction by earlier conventions (Tokyo and The Hague, noted earlier) is legally denied. Every contracting state to this convention has legal jurisdiction to prosecute the crime.

Covenant, Sword, and Arm of the Lord (CSA)

The Covenant, Sword, and Arm of the Lord (CSA) was a CHRISTIAN IDENTITY MOVEMENT survivalist group founded by James Ellison, a former minister. Ellison ran a Christian retreat on his property, which was near the Missouri-Arkansas border. In 1978, Ellison had a "vision" of a race war that would soon engulf America, and as a result, he transformed his property into a white-supremacist paramilitary training camp, dedicated to the principles of Christian Identity. Ellison envisioned the CSA as being an "Ark for God's people" during the coming race war. Since Ellison accepted Christian Identity theology, by referencing "God's people" he meant white Christians, since Jews were, by this theology, not really God's chosen people, but rather a demonic and inferior race.

CSA recruited at gun shows, inviting people to sign up for CSA's "Endtime Overcomer Survival Training School." Students who attended CSA training received training in weapons usage, urban warfare, wilderness survival, and "Christian martial arts." At the gun shows, CSA also made money from the sales of homemade machine guns, silencers, and explosives. Ellison also encouraged his "disciples" to steal, citing the Israelites' plundering of the Philistines' tents after David killed Goliath, as biblical justification.

The CSA embarked on a crime spree in 1983, including the firebombing of an Indiana synagogue, an arson attack on a Missouri church, and the attempted bombing of a Chicago gas pipeline. On April 19, 1985, 300 federal officers surrounded the CSA compound and demanded that the 100 or more heavily armed residents surrender, which they did, after a tense four days of negotiations. The compound was found to contain homemade landmines, U.S. Army antitank rockets, and a large supply of cyanide that the CSA was apparently planning to use to poison the water supply of an unspecified city. The capture and imprisonment of the leaders of this group effectively destroyed the CSA.

See also MILITIAS IN THE UNITED STATES; WHITE SUPREMACIST GROUPS.

Reference: Tucker, Jonathan. *Toxic Terror: Assessing Terrorist Use of Chemical and Biological Weapons* (Boston: MIT Press, 2000).

criminals, crusaders, and crazies, as terrorist types

Understanding the individual who commits terrorism is vital, not only for humanitarian reasons but also for making decisions about how best to deal with these individuals while they are engaged in terrorist activities. From a law enforcement perspective, it is important to appreciate the difference between a criminal and a crusading terrorist involved in a hostage-taking situation. Successful resolution of such a situation often hinges on an understanding of the mind of the individuals who are driven to commit terrorism.

Frederick Hacker has suggested three categories of persons who commit terrorism: criminals, crusaders, and crazies. While it is true that one is seldom "purely" one type or another, each type offers some insights into why an individual will resort to terrorism. Analysis of the characteristics of each of these types, and comparison of the similarities and differences that exist, offers tools to better understand, and respond to, individuals committing terrorist acts.

One point of distinction made, by Hacker and others, among these types focuses on the motive or goal sought by the terrorist. Crazies are emotionally disturbed individuals who are driven to commit terrorist acts for reasons of their own that often do not make sense to anybody else. They frequently state that their actions were directed by a command of a dog, or billboard sign, or toaster, or song on the radio. Criminals perform terrorist acts for reasons understood by most—that is, some form of personal gain. Such individuals transgress the rules of society knowingly and, usually, in full possession of their faculties. Both the motives and the goals of criminal terrorists are usually clear, if still deplorable, to most people.

Crusaders, however, commit terrorism for reasons that are often unclear both to themselves and to those witnessing the acts. Frequently their goals are not understandable. Although such individuals are usually idealistically inspired, their idealism tends to be a rough blend of several philosophical and/or ideological concepts. Crusaders rarely seek personal gain, desiring instead prestige and power for a collective "higher" cause.

This can be a significant difference for law enforcement called upon to resolve hostage situations. Criminals can presumably be offered some form of personal gain (i.e., money) to induce them to release the hostages. Crusaders are far less likely to be talked by law enforcement out of carrying out their threats to the hostages by inducements of personal gain since to accept such an offer would be to betray, in an ideological sense, the higher cause for which the crusader is committing the act.

In a similar context, it would be useful for security agents to know what type of individual is likely to commit a terrorist act within their province. A criminal, for example, would be more likely to try to smuggle a gun aboard an aircraft than a bomb since the criminal type usually anticipates living to enjoy the reward of his/her illegal activities. Crusaders, however, are more willing to blow themselves up with their victims, because their service to the "higher cause" often carries with it a promise of a reward in the life to come.

The distinction between criminals and crusaders with respect to terrorism needs some clarification. Clearly, when an individual breaks the law, as in the commission of a terrorist act, he/she becomes a criminal, regardless of the reason for the transgression. The distinction between criminals, crazies, and crusaders, in this typology, focuses on the differences in the motives/goals, willingness to negotiate, and expectation of survival of the perpetrators.

The willingness of the individual carrying out the terrorist act to negotitate is also a useful variable in distinguishing between criminals, crusaders, and crazies. Criminals are usually willing to negotiate in return for profit and/or safe passage from the scene. Crusaders, in contrast, are usually far less willing to negotiate for at least two reasons. One is that to negotiate might be viewed as a betrayal of a sublime cause; the other is that there is little that the negotiator for the law enforcement authorities can offer that would be meaningful since neither personal gain nor safe passage out of the situation are particularly desired by the true crusaders.

Similar problems exist with crazies, depending on how much in touch with reality such an individual is at the time of the incident. Negotiation is difficult, but not impossible, if the negotiator can ascertain the goal/motive of the perpetrator and offer some hope (even if it is not real) of success in the achieving of that goal by other, less destructive, means.

The expectation of survival is also a critical differentiating element. For a crusader, belief in the cause makes death not a penalty but a path to reward and glory; therefore, the threat of death and destruction can have little punitive value. According to Hacker's evaluation, crazies have a limited grip on the reality that they themselves might die in the course of their action. Thus, the threat of death by a superior force carries diminished weight if the perpetrator cannot grasp the fact that he/she may die in the encounter. Just as very young children find the reality of death a difficult concept to grasp, crazies also offer serious difficulties for negotiators because they do not grasp this reality.

Criminals, then, are the preferred perpetrators of terrorist acts, because they will negotiate; their demands are quite logical (although often outrageous) and are based on terms that can be met or satisfied with rational alternatives. Criminals know that they can be killed, and they have a strong belief/desire to live to enjoy the tangible rewards of the actions they are taking. Thus, negotiators have specific demands to be bartered, and their "opponents" can be expected to recognize superior force and to respond accordingly in altering demands and resolving the incident.

These differences can be critically important to those agencies tasked with resolving situations in which hostages are held by terrorists as well as those involved in providing security against terrorist attack. Insights into the type of person/persons likely to commit acts of terrorism enhance an ability to predict behavior patterns with some accuracy and to respond in forms most suited to the type of individual involved.

It is interesting to note that there is an increase in the number of terrorists who are defined as crusaders by this analysis. This is the most difficult type of terrorist for law enforcement to deter or confound successfully since the goals for such an individual are idealistic rather than rooted in tangible terms, there is little to negotiate, and death is a reward instead of a punishment.

See also BROTHERHOOD OF ASSASSINS; TERRORISM.

Reference: Hacker, Frederick J. *Criminals, Crusaders, Crazies: Terror and Terrorism in Our Time* (New York: W. W. Norton, 1976).

Cuba

During the 1970s and 1980s, Cuba actively supported armed struggle in Latin America and other regions of the world, providing a safe haven for many individuals involved in terrorist incidents in other countries as well as providing arms and training for carrying out a wide variety of violent acts to members of an array of groups engaged in terrorism. This ability to support and/or sponsor terrorism was seriously curtailed by the demise of the Soviet Union in the early 1990s since much of the arms and the support came from this source. Cuba's economic problems following the collapse of the U.S.S.R. limited but did not end Cuba's involvement with many of the groups.

In the earlier years of Fidel Castro's regime in Cuba, significant levels of military training, weapons, funding, and guidance were provided to many revolutionary organizations. Even with the economic problems that it faced at the end of the 20th century, Cuba remained a safe haven for several individuals involved in international terrorism, maintained close relations with other states engaged as sponsors of terrorism, and continued to network with many groups in Latin America. Several members of BASQUE FATHERLAND AND LIBERTY (ETA) sought and were granted sanctuary in Cuba. Some of members of the MANUEL RODRIGUEZ PATRIOTIC FRONT (FPMR), having escaped from a Chilean prison in 1990, were also given refuge in Cuba.

Colombia's two main guerrilla groups, the REVOLUTIONARY ARMED FORCES OF COLOMBIA (FARC) and the NATIONAL LIBERATION ARMY (ELN), maintained representatives in Havana. This enabled Cuba, near the end of 1999, to host a series of meetings between Colombian government officials and ELN leaders, who until that time had not been included, as had FARC leaders, in the ongoing peace process. Since Cuba does seem to lend support to these guerrilla groups (though not direct military aid), the United States continues to list Cuba as a state sponsor of terrorism, although some contend that Cuba has helped further the peace process. Another reason for being on the list is Cuba's ties to states that support terrorism, such as Iran and North Korea. In 2002, the United States accused Cuba of having a limited biological weapons program and selling dual-use biotechnology to rogue states.

Reference: Council on Foreign Relations. "Cuba, Terrorism: Questions and Answers." Available online. URL: http://cfrterrorism.org/sponsors/cuba.html. Accessed February 16, 2006.

cultural terrorism

Throughout history, governments or religious movements have targeted institutions or elements within a population for destruction. In the fourth century, Christianity was adopted by the Roman government as the state religion. The Catholic Church proceeded to encourage the overthrow of remaining pagan installations. Not only were pagan idols destroyed, however; anything else that was a product of pagan civilization was similarly eliminated. For example, although historical sources differ, the destruction of the great library of Alexandria may have occurred because of the Church's hostility toward much of the pagan learning that was housed in the institution.

Other examples include book burnings of works authored by individuals that the Nazis in Germany (1933–45) disapproved of, such as Jews and "degenerates," and the banning of works of literature that were not consistent with the Communist Party line in the Soviet Union. In a similar vein, in some Islamic countries, governments have been hostile to pre-Islamic cultures. A recent and notorious example occurred in Afghanistan in early 2001, when the radical Taliban regime ordered the leveling of statues of Buddha that had been built centuries before Islam arrived. Many cultural antecedents that include works of art and accumulated wisdom have often been tragically eradicated to satisfy the ideological or theological motivations of extremist groups or governments.

Reference: Romey, Kristin M. "Cultural Terrorism." *Archaeology* (May/June 2001). Available online. URL: http://www.archaeology.org/0105/newsbriefs/afghan.html. Accessed February 28, 2006.

cyberterrorism

Perhaps the most recent and most threatening dimension of political terror, cyberterrorism is defined as the use of computing resources to intimidate and/or coerce others or an entire society. Cyberterrorists represent a new generation of terrorists who have the potential to cause considerably more harm than any previous generation. There are several variants of cyberterror.

1. Many organizations as disparate as HIZBALLAH in Lebanon and racist groups in the United States possess their own websites with chat rooms. These websites offer propaganda, weapons systems for sale, and literature. A 2004 report on terrorism and the Internet by the United States Institute of Peace found that in 2003–04 there were hundreds of websites serving terrorist organizations. Ease of access and little or no censorship makes the the Internet the ideal arena for these groups to keep in touch with supporters, raise funds, plan attacks, and recruit new members.
2. Cyberterror can be activated by anyone with the skill to use a computer. Viruses that erase computer programs, worms that damage computers by behaving as independent programs, and Trojan horses that appear as free gifts to an unsuspecting computer user and then destroy

the computer's programming after being downloaded are but some of its forms.

3. Cyberterrorists have the capability of disrupting services or endangering the welfare of literally millions of people. Emergency services, electric power, financial systems, and airports can be shut down. Hospital records and even national-security computer programs can be interfered with or even permanently destroyed. However, some experts contend that terrorist groups will more likely make use of the vast amounts of easily available information found on the Internet. For example, a computer captured from al-Qaeda in Afghanistan was found to contain engineering and structural features of a dam—information that could then be used to plan a terrorist strike.

Efforts are being made by both governments and the private sector to block cyberterrorist activities; however, given the rapid changes that are accompanying computer technology, no system is likely to become foolproof. According to the CENTRAL INTELLIGENCE AGENCY, "Terrorist groups, including Hizballah, Hamas, and bin Laden's al-Qaeda group, are using computerized files, e-mail and encrypton to support their operations."

Presently, there is no completely foolproof system that offers protection against cyberterrorism. Most of us who use computers have learned to be wary of suspicious e-mail messages from an unknown (or unknowable) origin. Perhaps the most serious and threatening form of cyberterrorism for the individual is the possibility of bank and hospital records being altered. Substantial funds can be deleted or added to savings accounts, and medical files can be changed in such a fashion that harm is done to patients.

A disconcerting example of cyberterrorism is the Chaos Computer Club, a group that during the late 1990s had the capability of stealing money from those using Quicken software installed on their computers. Cyberterror can also be surprisingly lethal. It is possible for a hacker to change the ingredients of a medication to the point that it kills a particular patient, then change the medication back to the original helpful dosage.

Cyberterrorists can also spread rumors that alarm or panic large numbers of people. They can simply post messages that an entire city's water supply is contaminated and cause a disruption of order. A lone individual never even has to leave home to cause injury, emotional distress, or even death to large numbers of people. Some hackers have the ability to enter corporate computer files and render them useless, causing companies to spend a great deal of time and money repairing the damage. Interestingly, most cyberterrorists are amateurs, sometimes refereed to as "cyberjoyriders," who may not even be aware of the damage they are causing. A smaller group is composed of professional hackers who are mostly corporate spies. Some experts contend that it is unlikely that a cyberattack will harm critical systems—such as the power grid—since these systems are usually inaccessible through the Internet. There is even doubt about a serious threat to the infrastructure of the Internet itself. This skepticism would seem to be supported by various drills and mock "cyber attacks" conducted by law enforcement over the past decade. In 2002, the U.S. Naval War College contracted a group of security analysts and government hackers for a war game dubbed "Digital Pearl Harbor." The Internet withstood the attack from the hackers, albeit with minor disruptions, which led the researchers to conclude that it would take a group with "significant resources" to be able to stage a similar attack. In February 2006, the U.S. Department of Homeland Security staged a massive electronic war game called Cyber Storm to see how the Internet would hold up to mock attack from antiglobalization activists, underground hackers, and bloggers. While the full report is not yet complete, the Internet did survive this particular scenario.

It is more likely, experts contend, that terrorists will continue to use the Internet as a tool for information, recruitment, fund-raising, propaganda, and psychological warfare. A recent example of this was seen in 2002 when a videotape of a Pakistani militant group beheading journalist Daniel Pearl made its way onto several terrorist websites. In December 2001, the U.S. government seized the the assets of the Holy Land Foundation of Relief and Development (HDF), a Texas-based charity that was collecting funds for Hamas via its website. The U.S. government has been using its own computer resources to combat terrorists, including a practice called data mining. Data mining uses supercomputers to sift through all electronic communications in order to detect possible patterns of criminal activity, like monitoring Internet chatrooms used by al-Qaeda. This practice, however, raises its own questions concerning privacy issues, such as was shown in the recent furor involving the National Security Agency and domestic wiretapping.

References: Council on Foreign Relations. Terrorism: Questions and Answers, "Cyberterrorism." Available online. URL: http://cfrterrorism.org/terrorism/cyberterrorism.html. Accessed February 16, 2006; Gerstein, Daniel M. *Securing America's Future: National Strategy in the Information Age* (Westport, Conn.: Greenwood Press, 2005); Verton, Dan. *Black Ice: The Invisible Threat of Cyberterrorism* (New York: McGraw-Hill, 2003); Weimann, Gabriel. *Terror on the Internet: The New Arena, the New Challenges* (Washington, D.C.: Potomac Books, 2006). Weimann, Gabriel. "www.terror.net: How Modern Terrorism Uses the Internet." Special Report. United States Institute of Peace. Available online. URL: http://www.usip.org/pubs/specialreports/sr116.html. Accessed February 28, 2006.

cyclical nature of terrorism

Violence, particularly terrorist violence, has too often created a cycle of violence, with those against whom the terror-violence is first carried out becoming so angered that they resort to terrorism in response, directed against the people or institutions regarded as being responsible for the initial terrorist acts. Each violent act frequently causes equally violent reactions. When the violence is unselective, when innocent people are victimized, the reactive violence is also likely to "break all the rules" in the selection of targets and thus to be defined as "terrorist."

Most revolutionary groups assert that it is terrorism by the state that provokes, and by its presence justifies, acts of terror-violence by nonstate groups seeking to change the government or its policies. The relationship between terror-violence by the state and that of nonstate groups and individuals is evident in the history of many modern nation-states. But the nature of that relationship is still the subject of much debate.

EXAMPLES OF CYCLES

Russian Anarchists under the Late Czarist Regime

From the time of the French Revolution, terrorism and guerrilla movements have become inextricably intertwined. Perhaps the most prominent proponents of individual and collective violence as a means of destroying governments and social institutions were the Russian ANARCHISTS, revolutionaries within Russia who sought an end to the Czarist state of the latter 19th century. Force only yields to force, and terror would provide the mechanism of change, according to Russian radical theorist Alexander Serno-Solovevich. In the writings of two of the most prominent spokesmen for revolutionary anarchism, MIKHAIL ALEKSANDROVICH BAKUNIN and Sergei Nechaev, one finds their philosophies often echoed by modern terrorists. Bakunin, for example, advocated in his *National Catechism* (1866) the use of "selective, discriminate terror." Nechaev, in his work, *Revolutionary Catechism,* went further in advocating both the theory and practice of pervasive terror-violence. He asserted of the revolutionary:

> (D)ay and night he must have one single thought, one single purpose: merciless destruction. With this aim in view, tirelessly and in cold blood, he must always be prepared to kill with his own hands anyone who stands in the way of achieving his goals.

This is surely a very large step in the evolution of a terrorist from the lone political assassin of earlier centuries. Even the religious fanatics of the Assassins genre and the privateers of Elizabethan times were arguably less willing to kill "anyone" to achieve a political objective. But this difference may well have existed more on paper than in practice. In spite of this written willingness to kill "anyone" who stood in the way, even the Socialist Revolutionary Party in Russia resorted primarily to selective terror-violence and took special pains to avoid endangering the "innocent" bystanders. For instance, the poet Ivan Kalialev, who assassinated the Grand Duke Sergius on the night of February 2, 1905, passed up an opportunity earlier that evening to throw the bomb because the Grand Duchess and some of her nieces and nephews were also in the Grand Duke's carriage. Although an attempt was made to kill Czar Alexander II as early as 1866, the first generation of Russian "terrorists" generally resorted to violence only to punish traitors and police spies or to retaliate against brutal treatment of political prisoners.

With the creation of the Zemiya I Volva (The Will of the People) in 1879, political assassination of a wide range of targets began to become a normal form of political protest, becoming part of an intense cycle of terror and counterterror. This revolutionary group believed that terrorism should be used to compromise the best of governmental power, to give constant proof that it is possible to fight the government, and to strengthen thereby the revolutionary spirit of the people and its faith in the success of the cause.

It is quite easy to note the blending of revolutionary and state terror-violence during this time. The assassinations of Czar Alexander II in 1881 and of First

Minister Peter Stolypin in 1911 were incidents that produced periods of counterterrorism (in the form of state repression). This repression probably accelerated the revolutionary movement responsible for those assassinations. Thus, the terrorist acts of assassination, inspired by brutal repression in the czarist state, provoked further state terrorism, which in turn inspired the revolutionary movement to further acts of violence.

The formation of the Union of Russian Men to combat the growing revolutionary movement "by all means" was not only sanctioned by the czar but granted special protection by him. This reactionary group engaged in a variety of "terrorist" activities, including but not limited to political murders, torture, and bombing. The Okrana (the czarist secret police) also wreaked fierce "counterterror" against the militant revolutionaries in an unabated attack until World War I.

George Kennan, commenting on the rising tide of "terrorism" in Russia during the last half of the 19th century, explained the relationship of state and revolutionary terrorism in this way:

> Wrong a man . . . deny him all redress, exile him if he complains, gag him if he cries out, strike him in the face if he struggles, and at the last he will stab and throw bombs.

Still, while some of the seeds of a more widespread and random terror-violence were sown in the revolutionary and anarchistic movements of the late 19th century, by the beginning of the 20th century, terror-violence was still principally directed toward political assassination. Between 1881 and 1912, at least 10 national leaders had lost their lives to assassins.

Northern Ireland

Perhaps nowhere else in this century has the role of liberationist combined more thoroughly, until recently, with that of "terrorist" than in the actions of the militant group usually known as the IRISH REPUBLICAN ARMY (IRA). This group's guerrilla campaign of murder and terror, growing out of the SINN FÉIN movement in 1916, provoked the British to respond in kind with a counterterror campaign. While this revolutionary terrorism may be said to have stimulated the creation of an independent Irish Republic, the violence did not end with this "success." In the mid-1950s, the provisional IRA began a second wave of anti-British terror, which continued until 1994.

This struggle offers insights in several historical respects. In addition to being, in part, a blend of nationalism and terrorism, it is also a contemporary example of the potent mixture of religion and politics. Catholic Ireland had long resented Protestant Britain's domination of its politics. Northern Ireland, which remains under British rule, is predominantly Protestant, with a Catholic minority.

Thus, the lines of battle were drawn along both nationalistic and religious lines. Catholics in Northern Ireland tended to support a unification of those northern provinces with the Irish Republic, while Protestants in Northern Ireland demanded continued British rule. The legacy of hatred and mistrust bred by generations of violence is still so bitter than an end to the violence seemed, until the end of the 20th century, unlikely. The cyclical nature of violence can indeed create a deadly spiral.

The Holocaust and the State of Israel

The cyclical nature of terror is also evident in the events surrounding the creation of the State of Israel. The terrorism spawned in Nazi Germany helped to create a cycle of violence that still grips the Middle East today. After the military collapse of the Central Powers and the Armistice Agreement of November 1918, within Germany a large number of largely right-wing paramilitary organizations grew. In ideology, terrorist method, and political role, these groups were in many respects the historical heirs of the Brotherhood of Assassins. They were also the nucleus for the German Reichswehr.

Under the leadership of such men, Germany perpetrated upon innocent persons the greatest atrocities the world has ever recorded. Organized state terrorism reached its zenith in Nazi Germany, and its victims numbered in the millions. Of those victims, the majority were Jewish. Many who sought to flee the terror tried to emigrate to Palestine, which at that time was under British mandate. But the British mandate government, by 1940, was engaged in closing the gates to Jewish immigration into this land, which was, in fact, already occupied by Arabs. As the population balance began to swing away from the indigenous Arab population toward the immigrant Jews, the British government sought to stem the tide of refugees.

The HAGANAH, a Zionist underground army, and the IRGUN ZVAI LEUMI, a Zionist militant force willing to use terrorist tactics, waged terrorist warfare on the British forces in Palestine. Bombing, murder, and assassination became the order of the day as British counterviolence met with escalating Irgun and Haganah intransigence. With the Irgun bombing of the KING DAVID HOTEL, in which many innocent persons died or were seriously injured, British determination to quell the rebellion diminished.

However, during the struggle to gain a homeland free of Nazi terror, the Irgun had practiced terror against the indigenous population. When Israel declared itself to be an independent state in 1948, some of the dispossessed people within its borders and those who fled to surrounding states began a war of revolution and of terror against Israel.

Israel's revolutionary counter-terror-violence against the Palestinian radicals has spurred a conflict that continues to rend the fragile fabric of peace in the Middle East. Born in bloodshed, violence, and desperation, Israel continues to struggle against the terrorist violence that its very creation evoked.

References: Laqueur, Walter. "Post-modern Terrorism," *Foreign Affairs* (September/October 1996); Schultz, George. "Low-Intensity Warfare: The Challenge of Ambiguity," Address to Low-Intensity Warfare Conference, Washington, D.C. (January 15, 1986); Slann, Martin. "The State as Terrorist," *Multidimensional Terrorism,* edited by Martin Slann and Bernard Schechterman (New York: Reinner, 1987).

D

Darfur

Darfur is a term that is translated as "home of the Fur," a non-Arab people inhabiting the expansive westernmost region of Sudan, a huge area about the size of Texas. The area includes only 6 million inhabitants, though, because of the violence that has been almost continuous since the early months of 2003; hundreds of thousands of people have fled to neighboring countries. Moreover, a British Parliamentary Report in 2004 estimated the loss of over 300,000 lives, or 5% of the total population. The inhabitants of entire villages have been completely wiped out. Many of these were murdered outright, though an uncertain number have perished from hunger and exposure. Around 2 million people, a third of the total population, have been driven from their homes. Most of the killing has been orchestrated by the *Janjaweed* (in Fur, the term means "evil horsemen"). However, refugees from the fighting include Arabs and non-Arabs. The Janjaweed have both Arab and non-Arab victims to their credit.

The violence has a strong ethnic/religious dimension that was apparent long before the conflict began. The Sudanese government is predominantly Arab and Sunni Muslim. However, the Arab population is less than two-fifths of the whole, while the black African population is more than 50%. A significant proportion of blacks are Muslims, but most are either animist or Christian. The government has worked for decades to Arabize the country, at least in terms of advocating Arabic as Sudan's overall language. In addition to ethnic and religious differences, there is also an economic aspect to the conflict. Most non-Arabs are farmers, and most Arabs are pastoralists, a difference that immediately invites economic competition over land rights.

In the Darfur region, the Fur and Arab communities have historically refrained from intermingling with one another even though Fur and Arab villages are usually within easy walking distance from one another. Outrages against human rights have been committed by both sides, including wholesale murder, mass rape, and ethnic cleansing. However, the Arab side usually has the support of the Sudanese military that, like the government, is overwhelmingly Arab and Muslim. Elements of the Janjaweed have been indiscriminate in their destructive activities and have burned dozens of mosques in the region to the ground.

The Sudanese government maintains that it opposes all outside interference, whether from the United Nations or any individual government. There is little doubt that acts of genocide are occurring in Darfur

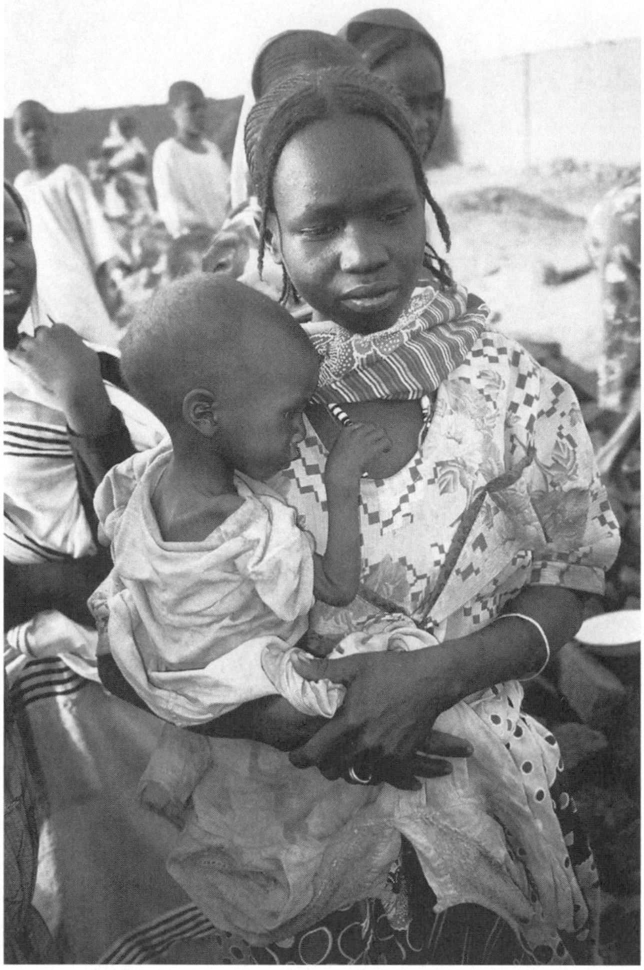

A displaced mother holds her malnourished child in North Darfur, Sudan. (USAID)

even though Sudan rejects that assumption. The reality remains, though, that the Sudanese government has done little to nothing to protect the non-Arab residents of Darfur. Neither the United Nations nor the African Union has officially determined that genocide is happening. If the United Nations did decide that genocide was in fact occurring, intervention from other countries would become an option. Several member states of the African Union are engaged in their own genocidal activities and most likely do not desire to establish what for them would be an unpleasant precedent.

Reference: Africa Crisis Foundation. "Crisis in Western Sudan (Darfur)." Available online. URL: http://www.africacrisis.org/sudancrisis.html. Accessed February 28, 2006.

Dayak

In West Kalimantan, violence between Dayak and Madurese was recurrent during the last two decades of the 20th century. Bloody clashes between the Dayak people, who are indigenous, and migrants from Madura between December 1996 and January 1997 resulted in a death toll of over 600 according to the humanitarian organization Human Rights Watch. Violent conflict between the Dayak and the Madurese began in 1983. Clashes in Pontianak caused many landless peasants from Java and the island of Madura (which is southeast of Java) to move to West Kalimantan, where the Dayak live, as part of a government resettlement program offering free land, housing, and food aid.

Relations between the Dayak, who make up 40% of West Kalimantan's population and who have converted to Christianity, and the Muslim Madurans have been tense, and the Dayak fear that the immigrants will take away land and jobs from their indigenous population. Dayak communities have been dispossessed, as their traditional forest lands are appropriated in the building of government-supported settlements.

The Indonesian army sent 3,000 troops to fight the Dayaks, including six battalions of troops and the Army Strategic Reserve, eventually forcing a fragile truce in the area by late 1999. An eruption of violence in Central Kalimantan in February 2001 around the logging port of Sampit, Kotawaringin Timur district, led to indigenous Dayaks killing some 500 immigrants from the island of Madura, off the coast of East Java, and displacing more than 150,000. Many of the killings involved decapitation, and little distinction was made between men, women, and children. The outbreak had complex roots but appeared to be linked to long-standing economic and social grievances of the Dayaks, competition over local resources, and new opportunities for political mobilization along ethnic lines. Muhamad Usop, a Dayak leader who sought the Central Kalimantan governorship, was arrested on May 4, 2001, and held briefly on incitement charges.

Reference: Human Rights Watch. "Indonesia: The Violence in Central Kalimantan (Borneo)." Available online. URL: http://www.hrw.org/backgrounder/asia/borneo0228.htm. Accessed March 3, 2006.

Dayr Yassin massacre (April 9, 1948)

The British Mandate in Palestine expired on May 15, 1948. During the preceding several weeks, however, the British military and police presence in Palestine was gradually withdrawn from most areas outside of the major urban areas. The absence of authority enabled Arab and Jewish paramilitary forces to move freely and to occasionally commit outrages on one another's populations. One of the worst atrocities occurred on April 9 in the Arab village of Dayr Yassin, a Palestinian community outside of Jerusalem. Elements of the Irgun and LEHI (a Hebrew acronym for "Fighters for the Freedom of Israel," formerly the STERN GANG), groups operating outside of and often in opposition to the mainstream HAGANAH units, apparently believed they had located Palestinian militants hiding from them in villagers' homes. Village leaders and the Haganah had previously established what basically amounted to a nonaggression pact, but this agreement was not respected by either the Irgun or LEHI.

Most historians concur that Irgun and LEHI encountered armed Palestinian militants in Dayr Yassin and overcame them. That should have been the end of the matter. Irgun and LEHI, though, went on a rampage that only ended when between 245 and 250 of the village residents were murdered. Neither age nor gender provided immunity against the massacre. For all practical purposes, the village was wiped out.

The massacre's consequences were immediate and far-reaching. On April 13, an Arab retaliation resulted in another slaughter, this time of 70 Jewish physicians and nurses who were caught in a medical convoy near Jerusalem. By this time, the events of Dayr Yassin had become well known throughout both the Jewish and Arab communities. The mass murder at the village was strongly condemned by the Jewish leadership. Several Jewish local leaders also individually expressed their disgust and shame at the episode. It was pointed out that the mainstream Jewish military forces, the Haganah (or self-defense) was not involved and had no knowledge beforehand of the event. Many Arabs, however, panicked and feared for their lives. Many Jews who condemned the outrage were at the same time not upset to see streams of Arabs leaving their homes. Some, though, correctly viewed the exodus as the beginning of a humanitarian disaster and strove to discourage the flight. Haifa, the third-largest city in Palestine, contained a significant Arab community. Its Jewish mayor, Abba Houshi, personally pleaded with the city's Arabs to remain. He was only partially successful. As many as 300,000 Arabs throughout Palestine, a fourth of the Arab population, were already leaving their homes, many of them in despair, because they genuinely believed that the Israelis would do to them what had been in done in Dayr Yassin. This number would double over the next several months. A permanent refugee problem was created in a matter of weeks that would endure for generations afterward. Moreover, Dayr Yassin became a reminder to later Palestinian terrorist organizations that, in their belief, only violence would dislodge the Jewish state.

After a cease-fire was established between Israel and the invading Arab armies during the early spring in 1949, large numbers of the Arabs who had fled applied to Israel to be allowed to return to their homes. With rare exceptions, these requests were denied by the Israeli government. In general, Christian Arabs and Druses received better responses than the Muslims. The government was already encouraging Israeli Jews to move into and occupy homes and farms vacated by the departure of hundreds of thousands of Arabs. Palestinian refugees were now to become and indefinitely remain a serious international problem and perennial obstacle to future efforts to establish and sustain a peace process. They would also eventually contribute to periods of political instability in Jordan and Lebanon, where the greatest numbers settled. It seems reasonable to conclude that Dayr Yassin produced both intended and unintended consequences that continue to apply to the Israeli-Palestinian conflict.

References: Morris, Benny. *The Birth of the Palestinian Refugee Problem, 1947–1949* (Cambridge: Cambridge University Press, 1987); Nazzal, Nafez. *The Palestinian Exodus from Galilee, 1948* (Beirut: Institute for Palestine Studies, 1978).

Democratic Front for the Liberation of Palestine (DFLP)

This organization splintered from the POPULAR FRONT FOR THE LIBERATION OF PALESTINE (PFLP) in 1969, espousing a belief that Palestinian national goals can only be achieved through revolution of the masses. In the early 1980s, it established a political stance somewhere between YASIR ARAFAT and the so-called rejectionists. The PFLP itself split into two factions: a majority, hard-line faction led by Nayif Hawatmah, and a smaller, more moderate faction.

Led by Hawatmah's faction, the DFLP joined other rejectionist groups to form the Alliance of Palestinian Forces (APF), opposing the Declaration of Principles signed in 1993 by Arafat in the initiation of the Oslo

Accords. The DFLP then broke, along with the PFLP, from the APF over ideological differences and has been making limited movements toward merger with the PFLP since that time.

The DFLP has, since the 1970s, carried out numerous small bombings and minor assaults, along with a few more spectacular operations in Israel and the occupied territories. But since 1988, it has only been involved in border raids, and it continues to oppose the Israel-PLO peace agreement. It has received limited financial and military aid from Syria and conducts occasional guerrilla operations in southern Lebanon. Including both of its factions, its strength is estimated at about 500.

References: Council on Foreign Relations. "PFLP, DFLP, PFLP-GC: Palestinian Leftists," Terrorism: Questions and Answers. Available online. URL: http://cfr-terrorism.org/groups/pflp.html. Accessed February 16, 2006; National Memorial Institute for the Prevention of Terrorism (MIPT). "Democratic Front for the Liberation of Palestine (DFLP)" Available online. URL: http://www.tkb.org/Group.jsp?groupID=39. Accessed February 15, 2006.

Democratic Front for the Liberation of Rwanda (FLDR)

See ARMY FOR THE LIBERATION OF RWANDA.

demography

In indirect but real ways, changing or shifting population trends can help provoke original or renewed terrorist activities. Relevant examples include Catholics and Protestants in Northern Ireland, Arabs and Jews in Palestine and Israel, and Christians and Muslims in Lebanon. Communities and political leaderships were aware of demographic shifts even in biblical times. One theory about the Hebrew exodus from Egypt more than 3,000 years ago focuses on the indigenous Egyptians' fear that the Jewish slaves were multiplying too quickly and might eventually overwhelm the native population. Ethnic cleansing and its accompanying violence is associated with fear of the "other," especially if the other's population is growing quickly.

Lebanon has not conducted a national census since 1932, when a Christian majority was in place. The outcome of a new census can be easily guessed: Christians would be in a decided minority, and political power might have to be redistributed among an Islamic majority, itself divided into Sunni and Shiite Muslims. The Alawite sect in Syria, only an eighth of the total population, has controlled that country's government and the military for the last two generations, a monopoly of power resented by the rest of the population. A similar if slightly less extreme situation prevailed in Iraq from at least the late 1950s until 2003, when the Ba'ath (renaissance) party, which controlled the country in a totalitarian fashion, was itself dominated by the Arab Sunni fifth of the population. Treatment of ethnic or religious communities distrusted by the regime can be exceptionally brutal. The regime of Saddam Hussein in Iraq was so distrusting of its Kurdish and Shiite populations that the regime did not shrink from the mass murder of hundreds of thousands of its own citizens.

State terrorism in the form of GENOCIDE of demographic groups has occurred elsewhere and in recent times. During the Khymer Rouge domination of Cambodia during 1975–79, as much as 20% of the total population of 7 million was executed, starved, or worked to death. A large proportion of the victims belonged to the upper middle class—academicians, physicians, engineers, teachers—who were singled out for their professions and expertise. Most of these were driven out of cities and forced into an agricultural society, though they had little understanding of the requirements to survive in a subsistence economy. The regime even considered eliminating anyone over the age of 18 in order to build a new and (in the minds of the Khymer Rouge leadership) perfect society by wiping out those whose cultural norms were already set.

Demographic pressures have been instrumental in Israeli policies in the West Bank and Gaza Strip. The fear that Arabs will outnumber Jews in the near future has encouraged the government's decision to withdraw from heavily Arab areas such as the Gaza Strip. With no available Jews to attack, Palestinians will have to curtail their acts of terrorism, according to this theory.

Ethnic and/or religious communities that are dispersed from their homeland may encounter acts of terrorism or perpetrate them. Islamic communities in Europe, for example, have frequently been the object of attacks by the indigenous populations. At the same time, elements within these communities have planned and, in some instances, executed terrorist acts against their hosts. Jews are the best known and one of the most dispersed groups in the world and in history. For most of this history of perhaps 2,500 years, they have also been the victims of terrorist acts that culminated in the Holocaust during World War II (1939–45).

Demographic changes can make people fearful of the "other." The growth of Islamic communities in Europe has produced a backlash among elements of the more indigenous population that occasionally produces violence. Attacks by extremist right-wing groups in Germany on citizens of Turkish descent, by French extremists on Islamic arrivals from North Africa, and by Russians on Chechens living in Moscow are examples.

Reference: Brown, Michael E. E. *Grave New World: Security Challenges in the Twenty-First Century* (Washington, D.C.: Georgetown University Press, 2003).

De Regis Institutions *See* ANARCHISTS.

Devrimci Sol (Revolutionary Left; Dev Sol, Revolutionary People's Liberation Party/Front [DHKP/C])

Originally formed in 1978 as Devrimci Sol, the DHKP/C is a splinter faction of the Turkish People's Liberation Front. It was renamed in 1994 after factional infighting, and it currently endorses a Marxist ideology. It is violently anti-United States and anti-NATO in its orientation, and its actions have focused primarily on robbery and extortion.

Most of the attacks by this group until the late 1980s occurred against current and retired Turkish security and military officials. In 1990, however, a new campaign was initiated against foreign interests, resulting in the assassination of two U.S. military contractors and the wounding of a U.S. Air Force officer in an effort to protest the Gulf War against IRAQ. The launching of rockets at the U.S. consulate in Istanbul in 1992 was similarly described as a protest against the Gulf War.

Dev Sol was responsible for the assassination of prominent businessmen in early 1996, in what has been described as the group's first significant terrorist act (since the previous acts had military, not civilian, targets). Turkish authorities thwarted Dev Sol's attempt in June 1999 to fire an antitank rocket at the U.S. consulate in Istanbul.

DHKP/C added suicide bombings to its repertoire in 2001, with successful attacks against Turkish police in January and September. However, security operations in Turkey weakened the group, and it did not conduct any major terrorist attacks for the next two years, although an operative prematurely detonated her explosive belt in May 2003.

The DHKP/C has typically used improvised explosive devices against official Turkish targets and soft U.S. targets of opportunity. Attacks against U.S. targets beginning in 2003 probably came in response to the U.S.-led war in Iraq. This group did not carry out any major attacks in 2003, but on June 24, 2004, an explosive device detonated, apparently prematurely, aboard a passenger bus in Istanbul while a DHKP/C operative was transporting it to another location. The explosion killed the operative and three passengers.

The strength of this group has not been accurately determined, although it continues to have perhaps several dozen operatives. It has confined its area of operation to Turkey, primarily focusing attacks in Istanbul, Ankara, Izmir, and Adana, although it has a large support network throughout Europe. Indeed, most of its funds appear to come from supporters in western Europe, which appears to be its only source of external aid.

Reference: National Memorial Institute for the Prevention of Terrorism (MIPT). "DHKP-C." Available online. URL: http://www.tkb.org/Group.jsp?groupID=38. Accessed February 15, 2006.

diplomatic personnel and heads of state, as targets of terrorism

In 1833, Belgium enacted a law providing for nonextradition of political offenders, a principle incorporated into a Franco-Belgian treaty in 1834. Following attempts, both successful and unsuccessful, on the lives of heads of state in subsequent years, however, an attendant clause began to be incorporated into treaties. This clause made the murder or attempted murder of any head of state or his/her immediate family a common (not a political) crime. These clauses stated that such attempts should not be considered a political offense or an act connected with such an offense.

In 1957, the European Convention on Extradition invoked the principle of the attendant clause by making assaults on heads of state and their immediate families legally nonpolitical offenses. The Vienna Convention on Diplomatic Relations gave evidence of a broadening concern for diplomats as well as heads of state. Under this convention, the contracting states assume the responsibility of preventing attacks on a diplomatic agent's person, freedom, or dignity.

This broadly stated concern and general delegation of authority has not been translated into significant enforceable protections for diplomats. There still remains a need, as one expert noted, for a constant vigilance on the part of states, acting both individually and collectively in an organized way, to prevent the occurrence of incidents.

Although subsequent treaties on this subject have attempted to make clear the specific acts that are prohibited, and the states that have a right to claim jurisdiction over the crime, there remain serious flaws in the protection afforded to diplomatic agents today. No "collective, organized" approach to the problem has evolved.

Moreover, the delegation of responsibility for protecting and punishing in the event of attacks on diplomats can generate serious legal problems when the government of a state is itself a party, or a tacit accessory, to the taking of diplomatic hostages. It is unreasonable to expect a government that actively or tacitly approves of such a crime to prosecute the perpetrators of the crime. Such a requirement would mean that the government must at some point prosecute itself for committing what it clearly did not regard as an illegal act (the attack on the diplomats), a most unlikely scenario.

There has been one further development in the law regarding the protection of diplomatic personnel. The Venice Statement on Taking of Diplomatic Hostages, issued by the heads of state and government of the seven summit countries during their meeting in Venice in 1980, not only expressed grave concern about the Iranian hostage situation but also called on nations to ratify the completed Convention Against the Taking of Hostages, adopted by the UN General Assembly on December 17, 1979.

Completed shortly after the seizure of the U.S. embassy in Teheran, this convention made it a crime to take any person as a hostage. Through this convention, the protection of international law is extended to every individual, regardless of his or her position (or lack of one), with the exception of those in armed forces engaged in armed conflict.

This broadening of the law in this respect indicated that the community of nations consider the action of hostage taking to be completely unacceptable. Just as in laws of war, certain actions were prohibited at all times, whether at war or at peace, so it is that, by law, there are some actions that the international community has come to regard as unacceptable, regardless of the cause.

The bombing attacks on U.S. Embassies in Kenya and Tanzania in the late 1990s brought this convention under public scrutiny again. It has been used, but only tangentially, in the prosecution of the individuals indicted for planning and/or perpetrating these attacks. As a result of these and other more recent attacks on diplomatic personnel, particularly in Iraq, more nations have become signatories to the convention, and regional centers for counterterrorism initiated by the United States since 2003 have used this law to fashion regional legislative measures that are plausibly applicable as domestic law for participating nations seeking to enhance legal counterterrorism measures.

See also OPERATION INFINITE REACH.

disinhibition hypothesis

See COMPLICITY, BETWEEN MEDIA AND TERRORISTS.

drugs and terrorism

See NARCO-TERRORISM.

dynastic assassination

This is an attack upon a head of state or a ruling elite, precisely the kind of terrorism that the international community tried to criminalize in the mid-19th century. Dynastic assassination generally involves individuals or groups, is targeted against the head of state or the ruling elite in a system, and utilizes very selective forms of violence. Russian anarchists during the end of the 19th and beginning of the 20th centuries utilized this form of terrorism.

E

Earth Liberation Front (ELF)

The Earth Liberation Front is thought to have splintered off from the Earth First movement and is associated with ecoterrorism. This split is thought to have taken place in Brighton, England, during an Earth First meeting in 1994. The notable difference between the Earth First movement and the Earth Liberation Front is that the ELF advocates the destruction of property belonging to corporations that they believe are hurting the environment.

The Federal Bureau of Investigation upgraded the Earth Liberation Front to a terrorist organization in January 2001. This upgraded status was due to an incendiary attack on a ski resort together with other destructive tactics. During the attack on the Vail Mountain ski resort in Colorado, the ELF burned three buildings and caused a partial destruction of four ski lifts. The estimated cost of this damage exceeded $12 million. The ELF immediately claimed responsibility for the attack via an e-mail sent out of Denver, Colorado. The reason for the attack, according to the e-mail, was that the Vail resort was planning an expansion of the ski resort that would encroach on the best lynx habitat in the state.

At the time of this publication, the FBI has failed to make arrests and uncover the identity of the group's members. One of the main reasons contributing to this is the lack of a central hierarchy to the organization. The FBI believes that members of the Earth Liberation Front work in small groups composed of members who are well known to each other and do not keep membership lists or release their identities outside of the organization. Because the Earth Liberation Front was formed from a grassroots movement, the members are likely to remain in small groups and continue to lack a central governing apparatus or leader.

In March 2001, the Federal Bureau of Investigation classified ELF as the top domestic terror threat in the United States. While the events of 9/11 drove ELF from headlines, it clearly did not stop the actions of ELF activists.

In 2002, three students at Douglas S. Freeman High School in Henrico County, Virginia, engaged in a spree of destruction in the name of the Earth Liberation Front, using kerosene-soaked wicks to set fire to the fuel tanks of vehicles being used to construct a mall in Henrico. The three young men also vandalized 25 sports utility vehicles (SUVs) at an auto dealership, as well as several other SUVs parked at private homes. The three students, Adam Blackwell, Aaron Linas, and John Wade, pled guilty in January 2004 and agreed

Emergency personnel walk past an automobile destroyed at a car dealership, with one bearing the scrawl "ELF" for the Earth Liberation Front. (CORBIS)

to provide in excess of $200,000 in restitution for the damage; they were also sentenced to short terms in jail.

Extremists from ELF caused about $30,000 in damage to a Charlottesville, Virginia, building site in February 2004, setting fire to a bulldozer and damaging other construction equipment at the site. The site was being developed into a mix of retail, commercial, and residential units, to which ELF obviously had objections. The ELF members responsible for this attack left behind a banner reading "YOUR CONSTRUCTION = LONG-TERM DESTRUCTION—ELF."

Activities by ELF were not limited, in the early years of the 21st century, to the east coast of the United States. Fires set by Earth Liberation Front extremists early on the morning of April 20, 2004, in Snohomish County, Washington, caused an estimated $1 million in damages. The arsonists destroyed two new houses. According to a local newspaper, at a separate home-construction site near the firebombing the next morning, workers arrived to find soft drink and Gatorade bottles filled with flammable liquid and a threatening note written on a piece of cardboard.

In February 2006, a self-proclaimed member of ELF was charged in California with demonstrating the use of a destructive device. Rodney Adam Coronado was arrested in Tucson, Arizona, by agents of the FBI and the Bureau of Alcohol, Tobacco, Firearms and Explosives. According to the indictment, on August 1, 2003, at a gathering in San Diego, Coronado taught and demonstrated the construction and use of a destructive device, with the intent that the device be used to commit arson. The FBI has identified Coronado as a "national leader" of ELF, although Coronado describes himself as an "unofficial spokesman."

According to FBI reports, ELF has committed more than 1,200 acts of vandalism and arson in the United States, causing more than $200 million in damage, but without causing loss of life.

Reference: National Memorial Institute for the Prevention of Terrorism (MIPT). "Earth Liberation Front (ELF)." Available online. URL: http://www.tkb.org/Group.jsp?groupID=41. Accessed February 15, 2006.

I.B.

Eastern Shan State Army (ESSA)

The ESSA, also known as the Mong Tai Army (MTA), is the drug trafficking group that today produces the bulk of the world's supply of opium. Myanmar, formerly known as Burma, is the source for about 84% of the world's opium, much of it produced in the ethnic minority areas of Myanmar's Shan State, including Kokang and Wa territories. In spite of a cease-fire, negotiated more than a decade before the turn of the century, and the "arrest" of leaders of this army, there has been little disruption of the drug trade, although the terms for the "arrest" stipulated an end to the insurgency by this organization. The group leaders and their armies accepted temporary disruption of the trafficking routes and the destruction of several heroin refineries in the area, but they did not disband or disarm.

Focus by the State Law and Order Restoration Council (SLORC), created in 1989, has been on disrupting the insurgency led by Khun Sa and his MTA, rather than on disrupting the flow of opium. Indeed, the cease-fire agreements negotiated by the SLORC with several of the Khun Sa have left other leaders, including U Sai Lin of the ESSA and U Mahtu Naw of the Kachin Defense Army, also drug-trafficking leaders, in control of much of this part of Mynamar. The MTA was offered in the late 1990s, in return for its cooperation, limited autonomy and development assistance in return for an end to its insurgency. The ESSA is able under these agreements, in 2006, to remain armed, to continue to be heavily involved in the drug trade, and to continue to exercise substantial control over the Shan States.

Egypt, extremist attacks

In 1997, the number of fatalities from terrorist incidents in Egypt rose, reversing a trend since 1995 of decreasing death tolls. In the latter half of 1997, AL-GAMA'AT AL-ISLAMIYYA carried out a series of violent attacks. The group claimed responsibility for an attack at a pharaonic temple site in Luxor on November 17, in which 62 people were killed. This was the group's most lethal attack, and six members of the group were killed in a shoot-out with Egyptian police during their escape. According to al-Gama'at, the group's goal was to take the tourists hostage and use them to effect an exchange for the release of Shaykh Umar al-Rahman, who was serving a life prison term in the United States after being convicted of several conspiracies, including the WORLD TRADE CENTER BOMBING in New York City. Several people were arrested for the attack but none stood trial.

Foreign tourists were also attacked in September by two Egyptian gunmen who claimed support for the Egyptian al-Jihad but who were not found to be linked to an established group. Nine Germans and their Egyptian bus driver were killed in the attack outside the National Museum in Cairo. One of the gunmen was an escaped mental hospital patient who had previously killed four foreign nationals in an attack at a restaurant in the Semiramis Intercontinental Hotel in Cairo in October 1993.

In response to these attacks, Egyptian authorities intensified security at tourist sites in Cairo, Luxor, and other parts of southern Egypt. However, the loss of tourism trade by these attacks seriously harmed Egypt's economy for a time.

Egyptian Islamic Jihad (EIJ; a.k.a. al-Jihad, Islamic Jihad, Jihad Group, Vanguards of Conquest, Talaa' al-Fateh)

This Egyptian Islamic extremist group has been active since the late 1970s. Islamic Jihad appears to be divided into two factions: one based in Afghanistan that is a key player in OSAMA BIN LADEN'S AL-QAEDA; the other faction, the Vanguards of Conquest (Talaa' al-Fateh), initially Dr. Ayman al-Zawahir, operates mainly in the Cairo area, although it has members outside Egypt, in Afghanistan, Pakistan, and Sudan. The initial goal of Islamic Jihad was apparently the overthrow of the Egyptian government and the replacement of that government with an Islamic state. This group, in both of its factions, specialized in armed attacks against high-level Egyptian government personnel, although it demonstrated an increasing willingness to target interests of the United States in Egypt.

Islamic Jihad threatened to strike against the United States in retaliation for its incarceration of Shaykh Umar Abed al-Rahman (in connection with the bombing of the WORLD TRADE CENTER in New York City). It also threatened retaliation against the United States for the arrests of its members in Albania, Azerbaijan, and the United Kingdom, on warrants based on information supplied by the United States.

An Islamic fundamentalist, Ayman al-Zawahiri joined the outlawed Egyptian Islamic Jihad group as a teenager. As a 16-year-old medical student in the 1960s, he became involved in the Islamic fundamentalist movement sweeping Egypt, and was arrested and charged with being a part of a Muslim Brotherhood plot to overthrow President Gamal Abdel Nasser.

Islamic Jihad was responsible for the assassination in 1981 of Egyptian president Anwar Sadat, shortly after the conclusion of the Camp David Peace Accords, stabilizing relations between Egypt and Israel. This attack was crucial in that it was intended to derail the peace process, and it did indeed alter the momentum of this process. The next significant steps toward peace within this turbulent community would not take place for another decade. In a 1981 trial, as defendant number 113, al-Zawahiri was convicted on weapons charges, but not for being part of the assassination plot, and sentenced to three years in prison, where he was (by his own and other accounts) tortured severely.

By the time al-Zawahiri got out of prison, he had moved into the top ranks of the militants, a leader in Islamic Jihad. Zawahiri left Egypt in 1985, making his way to Peshawar, Pakistan, where he worked as a surgeon treating fighters injured in the "holy war" against the Soviet troops in Afghanistan. Here he met Bin Laden, already a prominent Mujahedeen leader who, like Zawahiri, had left a privileged upbringing to join the war in Afghanistan.

After the Soviets pulled out of Afghanistan, Zawahiri was unable to return to Egypt, choosing instead to join bin Laden in Sudan, where he helped to plan an attack on the Egyptian embassy in Islamabad, Pakistan, and assassination attempts on several Egyptian politicians, linking his Islamic Jihad organization to these attacks and to the attack on the U.S. embassy in Albania in 1998. Islamic Jihad continued to concentrate its efforts on attacks of high-level, high-profile Egyptian government officials, including cabinet ministers. It claimed responsibility for the attempted assassination of Interior Minister Hassan al-Alfi in August 1993 and of Prime Minister Atef Sedky in November of that year.

Upon their return to Afghanistan, bin Laden and al-Zawahiri appeared together in early 1998 to announce the formation of the World Islamic Front for the Jihad Against the Jews and the Crusaders, an organization that completed the formal merger of Islamic Jihad and al-Qaeda, bin Laden's group. Zawahiri and bin Laden issued a fatwa, declaring that "(T)he judgment to kill and fight Americans and their allies, whether civilians or military, is an obligation for every Muslim." Al-Zawahiri and Osama bin Laden were indicted in U.S. courts for allegedly masterminding the twin bombings of the U.S. embassies in Kenya and Tanzania on August 7, 1998.

With the merger of their organizations, Zawahiri became Osama bin Laden's personal physician and closest confidant. His influence on bin Laden was profound, according to many people who knew both men. Zawahiri, according to these associates, encouraged bin Laden to become more anti-American, more radical, and more violent. From this merger of groups and powerful individual forces would come the impetus and the planning for the events of 9/11.

Reference: National Memorial Institute for the Prevention of Terrorism (MIPT). "Egyptian Islamic Jihad (EIJ)." Available online. URL: http://www.tkb.org/Group.jsp?groupID=3611. Accessed February 15, 2006.

Elizabethan Sea Dogs, as terrorists

From the 16th century forward, pirates and piracy have been considered by lawmakers to be the "common enemies of humanity." Blackstone's *Commentaries* referred to piracy as "an offense against the universal law of society." Yet both England (for whom Blackstone wrote) and America (whose law frequently cites his precepts) licensed privateers, private ships that were outfitted as war ships and given letters of marque and reprisal, allowing them to make war on vessels flying foreign flags.

Under the reign of Queen Elizabeth I of England, the Elizabethan Sea Dogs, privateer ships sailing under the protection of the English flag, carried out violent acts of piracy against the Spanish fleet and against Spanish ports. British and American privateers, too, played a relatively significant role in both the American Revolution and the War of 1812. Both nations commissioned pirates to carry out acts of terror-violence for them on the high seas, acts that both nations publicly deplore as "offenses against humanity" in their courts today. Modern terrorism continues to take the form of piracy occasionally, although today's piracy is usually that of aircraft rather than sea vessels.

See also PIRACY, AS A FORM OF TERRORISM; STATE TERRORISM.

References: Hurstfield, Joel. *Queen Elizabeth and the Making of Policy, 1572–1588.* (Boston: Little, Brown, 1981); MacCaffrey, Wallace. *The Shaping of the Elizabethan Regime* (New York: Putnam, 1968); Slann, Martin. "The State as Terrorist," *Multidimensional Terrorism* (New York: Reinner, 1987).

Entebbe, rescue operation

When an Air France Airbus, flight 139 en route from Tel Aviv to Paris, was hijacked after a stop at Athens airport, Israel responded by organizing a brilliant and successful military rescue operation. The plane, which landed at Entebbe airport in Uganda, carried 248 passengers and crew members. All but 106 of these hostages were released by the terrorists before the Israeli raid. Only the Israeli citizens and Jews of other nationalities were kept hostage, to increase pressure on Israel to agree to the release of 53 "freedom fighters" imprisoned in Israeli prisons.

The military incursion mounted by Israel succeeded in freeing all of the hostages held at the airport, with the exception of three who either misunderstood or did not hear orders by the commandos to lie down as they opened fire on the terrorists. All seven of the terrorists (two of whom were German and five of whom were Palestinian members of the POPULAR FRONT FOR THE LIBERATION OF PALESTINE [PFLP]) were killed, along with a number of Ugandan soldiers, who tried to prevent the Israeli commandos from escaping with the hostages.

International opinion, for the most part, supported Israel in spite of the fact that Israel militarily invaded Uganda. Part of this approbation derives, no doubt, from a common love for a "winner." But part is due to the perceived legal right of a nation to intervene for "humanitarian" purposes in another country. While this right of "humanitarian intervention" is limited, it seemed to most of the community of nations to be acceptable in this case.

Thus, Israel had the first, and arguably the most highly trained, of the strike forces. Their greatest liability may lie in the fervor with which they pursue their enemies. This zeal has caused them to cross not only national boundaries in their quest for vengeance but also to transgress international law.

Reference: Schiff, Ze'ev, Ethan Haber, and Yeshayahu Ben-Porat. *Entebbe Rescue* (New York: Dell, 1977).

environmental groups, terrorism and

Most environmental groups do not engage in actions that could be classified as "terrorist." Instead, most are merely politically oriented or semi–politically oriented political action groups. Only a few are genuinely civilly disobedient organizations, engaging in actions that meet the criteria for terrorism.

Groups such as the Rainforest Action Network, the Sierra Club, the World Wildlife Foundation, and the Earth Island Institute operate legally within existing political systems, creating support networks at the grass-roots level to stimulate public concern about environmental issues. Most groups focus their efforts on educating the general public about environmental issues, lobbying with state and national legislatures for or against legislation impacting the environment, and raising money through donations to finance these efforts. Groups such as these, whose goals are accomplished using nonviolent weapons (e.g., letter writing, consumer education, nonviolent protests, boycotts of products), are not, by definition, terrorists groups.

The semi–politically oriented groups also use a variety of nonviolent methods, including boycotts, letters, nonviolent protest, and civil disobedience. Organizations such as Greenpeace, which rely primarily on nonlethal weapons such as Internet websites to share information, will use this last optional "weapon" from time to time, making these groups easier to distinguish from the primarily politically "correct" groups described in the first category.

There are environmental groups that are willing to commit violence for their cause. Such groups do not rely on efforts to convince a public "apathetic" or even "hostile" to their efforts to prevent environmental harm. Rather, they make use of explosives and arson to make dramatic statements about their concern for protecting "Mother Earth." They have been willing to harm people in their efforts to save trees, habitats, and other things environmentally threatened by mankind. Use of spikes in bike and hiking trails to theoretically protect such trails from the encroachment and abuse of people's usage have resulted in injuries to joggers who reside in the area. Similar use of spikes to deter logging in areas in which timber companies are engaged in legally approved foresting have injured several, including an older man reaching retirement, whose face was devastated by the impact of his chain saw hitting such a spike.

In the United States, the most lethal of these environmental groups is the EARTH LIBERATION FRONT

(ELF), which has been responsible for serious arson attacks. Such extremist approaches among committed environmentalists are rare since most are able to translate serious concern for the environment and its destruction into more peaceful efforts, which the Rainforest Action Network and Greenpeace have demonstrated.

References: Anti-Defamation League. Law Enforcement Agency Resource Network. "Ecoterrorism: Extremism in the Animal Rights and Environmentalists Movements" Available online. URL: http://www.adl.org/Learn/Ext_US/Ecoterrorism.asp. Accessed March 6, 2006; Manes, Christopher. *Green Rage: Radical Environmentalism and the Unmaking of Civilization* (Boston: Back Bay Books, 1991).

Eritrean Islamic Jihad Movement (a.k.a. Islamic Salvation Movement, Harakat al-Jihad al-Islami)

The Eritrean Islamic Jihad Movement engaged in armed opposition to the Eritrean government, from its base in Sudan. In 1998, at a congress held in Khartoum in September, the group changed its name to Harakat al Khalas al Islami (Islamic Salvation Movement) and declared its support for the forceful overthrow of Eritrea's government and its replacement by an Islamic government. Its violent opposition continues to claim civilian lives.

Reference: Federation of American Scientists (FAS). "Eritrean Islamic Jihad Movement" Available online. URL: http://www.fas.org/irp/world/para/ism.htm. Accessed August 24, 2006.

ethnic cleansing

The term refers to a form of terrorism that is comprehensive and usually very lethal. Ethnic cleansing is simply the removal of all or most members of an ethnic community from a particular territory. The territory may include an entire country. Several states throughout the world have engaged in ethnic cleansing as a government policy. In other situations, the government may simply condone or ignore ethnic cleansing efforts. Several notorious examples of state-sponsored ethnic cleansing occurred in the 20th century. These include the German state machinery applied to rid Europe of its Jewish inhabitants during the Holocaust (1939–45) as well as the Roma (Gypsies) and other ethnic communities by mass murder. The Soviet Union during the Stalinist era (1924–53) was nearly as inhumane. The regime moved millions of people off their ancestral lands only to perish or be worked to death in Siberia. In effect, the Soviet Union and Nazi Germany pursued genocidal agendas against targeted ethnic communities. After it annexed Tibet in 1950, the People's Republic of China attempted a form of GENOCIDE by moving large numbers of Han Chinese into Tibet to the extent that native Tibetans began to feel submerged under a Chinese demographic and cultural imperialism.

Ethnic cleansing has probably been practiced throughout human history. The Bible provides examples. The practice usually assumes a posture of self-righteousness, racial superiority, or historical justice on the part of those doing the ethnic cleansing.

During the early 1990s, ethnic cleansing appeared in regions of the former Yugoslavia when Croatians removed Serbs from the eastern part of the country or when both Croatians and Serbs attempted to rid Bosnia of Muslims. In Rwanda and Burundi, at least a half million Tutsi were murdered by Hutus. Even democracies may experience a nascent form of ethnic cleansing when there are calls for the removal of "foreigners" who are viewed as becoming too numerous or too competitive in the job market.

See also BOSNIA, GENOCIDE IN; DARFUR; KHMER ROUGE (THE PARTY OF DEMOCRATIC KAMPUCHEA); OVERVIEW OF TERRORISM, BY REGION; STALIN, JOSEPH.

References: Gow, James. *Triumph of the Lack of Will: International Diplomacy and the Yugoslav War* (New York: Columbia University Press, 1997); Naimark, Norman M. *Fires of Hatred: Ethnic Cleansing in Twentieth-Century Europe* (Cambridge, Mass.: Harvard University Press, 2002); Shaw, Paul, and Yuwa Wong. *Genetic Seeds of Warfare: Evolution, Nationalism, and Patriotism* (Boston: Unwin Hyman, 1989).

Euzkadi ta Askatasuma (ETA)

See BASQUE FATHERLAND AND LIBERTY.

Exercise ELIGIBLE RECEIVER

With the increasing dependence on computer networks to run all aspects of military, government, and civilian organizations, it has become apparent that one of the world's growing threats is cyber-terrorism. In the summer of 1997, the chairman of the Joint Chiefs of Staff authorized Exercise ELIGIBLE RECEIVER, the first-ever no-warning attack of government computer and networking systems. This exercise was conducted by less than 30 individuals from several agencies such as the National Security Agency to test the Department of Defense's ability to combat network intrusions while working with other government agencies to stop the intrusions and fix those problems that were caused.

It is reported that the group of "hackers" was able to gain control of the Pacific Military Command Center, U.S. power grids, as well as disable nine major U.S. cities' 911 emergency response centers. What shocked the U.S. military the most was that the "hacking" was accomplished using commercially bought (as well as free) hardware and software that is available to anyone.

In response to Exercise ELIGIBLE RECEIVER, the U.S. military took steps to prevent and curb damage that could be caused by unauthorized intrusions. Some of the steps included opening networking watch centers that are manned 24 hours a day, installing more and better intrusion detection systems, and establishing the Joint Task Force-Computer Network Defense (JTF-CND).

References: Magnan, Stephen W. "Are We Our Own Worst Enemy? Safeguarding Information Operations," Central Intelligence Agency. Available online. URL: http://www.cia.gov/csi/studies/summer00/art08.html. Accessed January 29, 2006; Robinson, Colin. "Military and Cyber-Defense: Reactions to the Threat." Center for Defense Information. November 8, 2002 Available online. URL: http://www.cdi.org/terrorism/cyberdefense-pr.com. Accessed January 29, 2006.

B. H.

explosives, taggants for

Taggants are chemically identifiable agents used to track many types of explosives today. This assumes that the explosive can be traced only after it has been used and thus is not a preventive measure. It is possible, although not simple, to use trace detectors for chemical agents, which would enable security agents to detect the presence of dangerous or hazardous chemicals in innocuous-looking containers.

The use of tagging devices and trace elements for human-portable rocket security, in addition to more complete inventory control measures, is being considered by many nations. The advantage in the use of taggants, in addition to an ability to detect certain substances, is an ability to determine the country, and sometimes even the company, of origin for the explosive device used in a terrorist incident. Although this would not necessarily be of immediate use in preventing terrorist attacks, it would be of considerable use in determining responsibility, perhaps thereby making future such attacks less likely.

However, companies and countries manufacturing such materials, from explosives to handguns, from nuclear to chemical and biological weapons, have resisted many attempts to institute a comprehensive tagging effort. Most have argued that laws requiring such security measures violate the rights of businesses engaged in lawful enterprises.

Following the OKLAHOMA CITY bombing on April 19, 1995, an Antiterrorism and Effective Death Penalty Act was passed by both houses of the United States Congress and signed by the president on April 24, 1996. Section 603 of this act proscribes the manufacture, import/export, or possession of plastic explosives that do not contain a detection agent with (1) a 15-year exception for preexisting explosives manufactured or imported for federal military or law-enforcement agencies or a state national guard, (2) a 3-year exception for preexisting explosives made or imported for anyone else, and (3) a 120-day exception for civilian reporting of preexisting explosives. Section 732 instructs the secretary of the Treasury to study the following important aspects relating to taggants:

- The feasibility of tagging explosives and precursor chemicals to permit post-explosion tracing;
- The feasibility of regulating the sale and distribution of precursor chemicals other than black or smokeless powder; and
- State regulation of high explosives for commercial use.

Having completed this study, the Treasury Secretary is authorized to promulgate regulations requiring the addition of tracer taggants to all manufactured and imported explosives to the extent he or she finds that the additions can be made without posing a risk to human life, will aid law enforcement, will not impair the effectiveness of the explosives, will not adversely affect the environment, and will not cost more than they are worth.

The Antiterrorism and Effective Death Penalty Act of 1996 was subsequently amended with respect to the secretary of the Treasury's mandated study of taggants involved in the marking, rendering inert, and licensing of explosive materials. The amendment repealed (1) the exclusion of black or smokeless powder from such study and (2) the requirement for congressional review of such study and congressional hearings on the secretary's recommendations. It also shortened, from 270 to 90 days, the period before proposed regulations for the addition of tracer elements to explosive materials become effective (unless modified or disapproved by an Act of Congress).

Extraditables, The

This group was formed by drug traffickers in the Medellín cartel in order to prevent their extradition to the United States. Colombia's administration at that time had made an agreement with the U.S. government to extradite certain cartel leaders for trials in the U.S. legal system, since members of both governments preferred that leaders of cocaine cartels be sent to the United States for trial, rather than being held for trial in Colombia's judicial system. Even after the Colombian Supreme Court annulled the Colombia–United States extradition treaty in 1987, cartel leaders feared the possibility of such extradition, since Colombian policy was somewhat murky and allegedly corrupt.

The Extraditables was formed in response to the threat of extradition, and its attacks were focused on politicians and journalists suspected of supporting extradition. This group was thought to be responsible for the murders of government officials as well as for high-profile kidnappings.

In 1991, the Colombian government adopted a new constitution, with specific prohibition on the extradition of Colombian citizens. The most well-known figure involved in this group, Medellín cartel leader Pablo Escobar, surrendered to authorities shortly after this constitution was ratified. He escaped from jail about a year later and was shot by Colombian police in 1993. By the mid-1990s, the Medellín cartel had been effectively disbanded, and The Extraditables ceased to exist as an organization.

See also APRIL 19TH MOVEMENT; COLOMBIA AND NARCO-TERRORISM.

Reference: National Memorial Institute for the Prevention of Terrorism (MIPT). "The Extraditables." Available online. URL: http://www.tkb.org/Group.jsp?groupID=4284. Accessed February 15, 2006.

Extradition, European Convention on

Legally, to extradite means to send the person to another state seeking to prosecute a person accused of committing a crime within or against that other state. In 1957, the European Convention on Extradition invoked the principle of the attendant clause by making assaults on heads of state and their immediate families nonpolitical offenses. The CONVENTION FOR THE SUPPRESSION OF UNLAWFUL SEIZURE OF AIRCRAFT, signed at the Hague on December 16, 1970, also deals specifically with the issue of extradition in application of law against terrorists, but only in SKYJACKING incidents.

The process of extradition depends upon the relations between the states involved and the political ramifications of such a cooperative move. In the LOCKERBIE case, Libya and the United States did not enjoy good relations, and the compromise of the use of the Hague as the site for extradition and a Scottish court for prosecution was agreed to by both parties, after years of negotiation. The efforts of Spain to have the United Kingdom extradite Augusto Pinochet to Spain for crimes allegedly committed by him against Spanish citizens living in Chile while he was president were complicated by the legal issue of his immunity from prosecution granted to him by his government in return for his relinquishing power. The relations between the United Kingdom and Spain were not the problem, but the United Kingdom was reluctant to set aside the legal protection offered to Pinochet by Chile, with whom the United Kingdom also had favorable relations.

See also CONVENTIONS ON AERIAL HIJACKING.

F

Farabundo Martí National Liberation Front (a.k.a Frente Farabundo Martí para la Liberación Nacional [FMLN])

Farabundo Martí, in 1932, led an uprising of workers and peasants in El Salvador in the wake of the devastating volcanic eruption of Izalco in an attempt to use this upheaval to spur a transformation of Salvadoran society. The attempted uprising failed and caused more than 30,000 workers and peasants to be massacred.

In the late 1970s and early 1980s, U.S. presidents approved large military aid packages, along with a small number of military advisers, to help the Salvadoran government "fortify" against "subversives." With this assistance, the Salvadoran Armed Forces began using counterinsurgency tactics learned, with U.S. assistance, from the Vietnam War. The ensuing bloody armed conflict, from 1979 until the cease-fire, cost more than 80,000 lives.

In the 1970s, violence by both left- and right-wing groups increased substantially, culminating in the ouster of the government in a coup in 1979. The junta that seized control promised reform, order, and free elections, which were held in 1982. The conservative government that emerged did not satisfy the demands of groups within the FMLN for greater redistribution of wealth and better access to health and education for those living in rural areas.

The FMLN formed in 1980, with Cuban backing, as an umbrella organization of five groups: Central American Workers' Revolutionary Party, People's Revolutionary Army, Farabundo Martí Popular Liberation Forces, Armed Forces of National Resistance, and the Communist Party of El Salvador's Armed Forces of Liberation. These groups carried out bombings, assassinations, economic sabotage, and arson, in both rural and urban operations, during the early years of the conflict.

Struggle between the FMLN, paramilitary groups working with government sponsorship or permission, and the military resulted in a negative balance of trade for El Salvador in the 1980s. Escalating military expenditures continued to generate budget deficits until the 1990s, when peace agreements and a change in government in the nation began a process of stabilization and an end to most violent activities by the FMLN. Fighting between government forces and the FMLN during the 1980s caused thousands of civilian deaths, indicating that both the FMLN and government forces were guilty of terrorism.

The FMLN received direct support from Cuba and for a time from the Sandinistas in Nicaragua, where it maintained an office. But all of its operations took place in El Salvador, with occasional limited activity in neighboring Honduras. The umbrella group reached a peace agreement with the government of El Salvador on December 31, 1991, which remains in effect.

Reference: National Memorial Institute for the Prevention of Terrorism (MIPT). "Farabundo Martí National Liberation Front." Available online. URL: http://www.tkb.org/Group.jsp?groupID=228. Accessed February 15, 2006.

FARC *See* REVOLUTIONARY ARMED FORCES OF COLOMBIA.

al-Fatah

Led by YASIR ARAFAT, Fatah joined the PALESTINE LIBERATION ORGANIZATION in 1968, seizing a leadership role in this organization in 1969. Its commanders were expelled from Jordan after events such as BLACK SEPTEMBER in 1970 and continuing violent confrontations with Jordanian forces from 1970 to 1971. Israel's invasion of Lebanon in 1982 led to the group's scattering into several countries in the Middle East, including Tunisia, Algeria, Yemen, and Iraq, among others.

Fatah offered training during the 1960s and 1970s to a wide range of European, Middle Eastern, Asian, and African terrorist and insurgent groups. This was made possible, in part, by its close, long-standing political and financial ties to Saudi Arabia, Kuwait, and other Persian Gulf states. Its members received weapons, explosives, and training from the former U.S.S.R. and other former communist regimes in eastern Europe. The People's Republic of China and North Korea also reportedly provided some weapons to this group.

Al-Fatah carried out numerous acts of international terrorism in western Europe and the Middle East in the 1970s but now operates primarily though groups that serve as its military and intelligence wings, including but not limited to the HAWARI SPECIAL OPERATIONS GROUP and the AL-AQSA MARTYRS' BRIGADE. Through these wings, it has been linked to terrorist attacks against Israeli and foreign civilians in Israel and the occupied territories. In January 2006, Fatah lost its majority in the Palestinian parliament to HAMAS.

Reference: National Memorial Institute for the Prevention of Terrorism (MIPT). "Al-Fatah." Available online. URL: http://www.tkb.org/Group.jsp?groupID=128. Accessed February 15, 2006.

fedayeen

An Arabic term for "self-sacrificers" the fedayeen were one of the earliest experiences the Israeli state had with terrorism. Egyptian fedayeen during the 1950s used the Gaza Strip as a base to attack Israeli civilian settlements across the border in the Negev. The attacks helped provoke the military campaign by Israel at the end of October and beginning of November 1956 against Egypt that resulted in Israel's brief occupation of the Gaza Strip and the Sinai. The fedayeen bases in Gaza were destroyed, and fedayeen attacks were stopped.

Federal Bureau of Investigation (FBI)

The FBI is the largest investigative agency in the U.S. federal government, responsible for conducting investigations where federal interest is concerned. It gathers facts and reports the results to the attorney general of the United States and his/her assistants in Washington, D.C., and to the U.S. attorneys' offices in the federal judicial districts of the nation. Headquartered in Washington, D.C., it also maintains field offices in large cities throughout the United States and liaison posts in several major foreign cities to facilitate the exchange of information with foreign agencies on matters relating to international crimes, including those types of terrorism regarded as international crimes.

The FBI's Counterterrorism Threat Assessment and Warning Unit, in the National Security Division, investigates terrorists in the United States, as well as conducting investigations of international terrorism, under guidelines set forth by the attorney general. There is no single law specifically making terrorism a crime, so its investigations, arrests, and convictions are made under existing criminal statutes.

The *Code of Federal Regulations* contains the definition of terrorism used by the FBI, describing terrorism as "the unlawful use of force and violence against persons or property to intimidate or coerce a government, the civilian population, or any segment thereof, in furtherance of political or social objectives" (28 C.F.R. Section 0.85). The FBI states that terrorism is either domestic or international, depending upon the origin, base of operations, and objectives of the terrorist (organization). Domestic terrorism is, by FBI definition, the unlawful use, or threatened use, of force or violence by a group or individual based and operating entirely within the United States or Puerto Rico without foreign direction committed against persons or property to intimidate or coerce a government, the civilian population, or any segment thereof in furtherance of political or social objectives. International terrorism, on the other hand, involves "violent acts or acts dangerous to human life that are a violation of the criminal laws of the United States or any state, or that would be a criminal violation if committed within the jurisdiction of the United States or any state." These acts of international terrorism "appear intended to intimidate or coerce a civilian population, influence the policy of a government by intimidation or coercion, or affect the conduct of a government by assassination or kidnapping." These acts constitute *international* terrorism in terms of the means by which they are accomplished, the persons they appear intended to coerce or intimidate, or the locale in which their perpetrators operate or seek asylum, according to the FBI.

The FBI divides terrorist-related activity into three categories: terrorist incident, suspected terrorist incident, and terrorism prevention. The first category is based on the definition of terrorism already stated. A *suspected* terrorist incident is defined as a possible act of terrorism to which responsibility cannot be attributed at the time to a known or suspected terrorist group or individual. A terrorism *prevention* is "a documented instance in which a violent act by a known or suspected terrorist group or individual with the means and a proven propensity for violence is successfully interdicted through investigative activity."

In the wake of the events of 9/11, the Federal Bureau of Investigation suffered considerable public condemnation for failing to detect and prevent the actions of the 19 individuals who entered the United States to carry out those acts. Evidence surfaced suggesting that information was ignored about both individuals and potential terrorist plots. The 9/11 COMMISSION REPORT indicated serious intelligence gaps and errors, some of which fell within the purview of this agency, with the result that, in June 2002, the FBI's official top priority became counterterrorism. The USA PATRIOT Act granted the FBI increased powers, especially in wiretapping and monitoring of internet activity. One of the most controversial provisions of the act is the so-called sneak and peek provision, which grants the FBI powers to search a house while the residents are away and does not require it to notify the residents for several weeks afterward. Under the PATRIOT Act's provisions, the FBI also resumed inquiring into the library records of those whom it suspected of terrorism, a practice not utilized since the 1970s.

Effective July 2005, the FBI's counterterrorism duties were consolidated in the new National Security Service, an organizational structure similar to the United Kingdom's MI5 (domestic intelligence) service.

See also MONTANA FREEMEN; 9/11 COMMISSION REPORT; WACO, TEXAS, INCIDENT; WORLD TRADE CENTER BOMBINGS.

References: Federal Bureau of Investigation. Available online. URL: http://www.fbi.gov. Accessed March 9, 2006; Powers, Richard Gid. *Broken: The Troubled Past and Uncertain Future of the FBI* (New York: Simon & Schuster, 2004).

female genital mutilation (FGM)

While most Westerners are appalled at the practice of female genital mutilation, it is a widespread practice throughout the African continent and most frequently in countries with a strong Islamic presence. Islam, though, does not require FGM. The practice apparently predates Islam at least in most places. In some areas, the practice is known as female genital cutting. In some African countries, FGM affects as many as 50% to more than 90% of the female population. The percentages, however, are only estimates furnished by Amnesty International. It's impossible to be entirely accurate. Approximately 6,000 women undergo the practice each day.

FGM is viewed as an important rite of passage to womanhood, and most who accept the practice do so with that understanding. In recent years, there has been growing evidence of resistance to FGM, in part due to the efforts of UNICEF. Entire villages have renounced and abandoned the practice. There is an economic incentive for those who perform the procedure since they are relatively well paid for their services. In Senegal, the rate of FGM decreased appreciably during the 1990s in great part because of Tostan, a nongovernmental organization that is funded by UNICEF. Pointing out the health risks for women are an important part of the Tostan program. Occasionally, Tostan encountered hostility from both men and women who were irritated by this challenge to a long-standing tradition considered part of village culture.

Another influence to blunting FGM is also at work. The isolation between villages is gradually being lessened as a result of better communication technology and transportation. Those who do not practice FGM are having an impact on those who do. None of this means that FGM will end soon. There remains substantial resistance to eliminating the practice. African governments themselves will have to make a greater effort to educate their citizenries. UNICEF reported in 2005 that an estimated 3 million girls undergo this procedure in sub-Saharan Africa and the Middle East. Cultural norms continue to resist the public outcry for reform.

Reference: World Health Organization. "Female Genital Mutilation." Available online. URL: http://www.who.int/topics/female_genital_mutilation/en. Accessed March 6, 2006.

15 May Organization

Emerging in 1979 from the remnants of Wadi Haddad's POPULAR FRONT FOR THE LIBERATION OF PALESTINE—Special Operations Group (PFLP-SOG), this organization was led by Muhammad al-Umari, known throughout the Palestinian world as Abu Ibrahim, or the "bomb man." This group was never a part of the PALESTINE LIBERATION ORGANIZATION (PLO) and reportedly disbanded in the mid-1980s when several key members joined Hawari's Special Operations Group of FATAH.

15 May Organization claimed credit for several bombings during the early 1980s, however, including hotel bombings in London, El Al's Rome and Istanbul offices, and Israeli embassies in Athens and Vienna. They also launched an attempted bombing of a Pan Am airliner in Rio de Janeiro and a successful bombing on board a Pan Am flight from Tokyo to Honolulu. This last attack killed a Japanese teenager, and its perpetrator, Mohammed Rashid, was convicted and imprisoned in Greece.

During the early 1980s, the group probably received logistical and financial support from Iraq until around 1984 and had its headquarters, reportedly, in Baghdad. Abu Ibrahim was believed to be in Iraq at the time of the U.S.-led invasion in 2003.

Reference: National Memorial Institute for the Prevention of Terrorism (MIPT). "May 15 Organization for the Liberation of Palestine." Available online. URL: http://www.tkb.org/Group.jsp?groupID=155. Accessed February 15, 2006.

Fighting Communist Cells

This group, originating in Belgium in the late 1970s, carried out acts of violence primarily against targets associated with the North Atlantic Treaty Organization (NATO), or with nuclear weapons sites. Most of its activities were carried out in conjunction with other left-wing groups in Europe, including but not limited to the RED ARMY FACTION (RAF) from Germany, the RED BRIGADES from Italy, ACTION DIRECT (AD) from France, and the ETA from Spain.

When two Americans were killed in a bomb blast at a U.S. air base in Frankfurt, West Germany, in August 1985, this attack and a subsequent bombing at a U.S. antiaircraft missile site were claimed by the RAF and the AD. These two groups used explosives stolen from a Belgian quarry, suggesting a connection with the Fighting Communist Cells (FCC). The FCC also bombed NATO pipelines and defense-related companies during the 1980s.

First of October Antifascist Resistance Group (GRAPO)

GRAPO formed in 1975 as the armed wing of the Communist Party of Spain, during the Franco era, advocating the overthrow of the Franco government and demanding its replacement with a Marxist-Leninist regime. This group has been steadfastly anti–United States, seeking the removal of all U.S. military forces from Spanish territory. It has conducted several attacks against U.S. targets in its 28-year history

GRAPO has killed more than 90 people and injured more than 200 since its inception in the 1970s. Its operations have traditionally been designed, however, to cause material damage and to gain publicity rather than to inflict casualties. However, in May 2000, GRAPO killed two security guards during a failed armed robbery attempt of an armored truck carrying an estimated $2 million, and in June of the same year, members assassinated a Spanish policeman, perhaps in retaliation for the arrest of several GRAPO members in France.

This group has not mounted a successful terrorist attack in several years, having suffered major setbacks in the arrest of several of its leaders and the outlawing of its political wing in March 2003. With fewer than two-dozen activists remaining, after large-scale police arrests of members that crippled the organization, GRAPO is presumably in a lengthy rebuilding period.

Reference: National Memorial Institute for the Prevention of Terrorism (MIPT). "First of October Antifascist Resistance Group (GRAPO)." Available online. URL: http://www.tkb.org/Group.jsp?groupID=188. Accessed February 15, 2006.

Force 17 *See* HAWARI.

France, reign of terror in

During 1793–94, the French Revolution that had begun in 1789 went through its most extreme and bloodiest phase. It also coined the terms *terrorist* and *terrorism*. This period is known as the *régime de la terreur.* By 1793, the radical Jacobins, led by Maximilien Robespierre, had seized control of the revolutionary regime. The passing of the Law of Suspects in September 1793 in effect launched the Terror. A total of 400,000 people (2% of France's total population) were targeted as suspects. The number included thousands of children. This law provided the Committee of General Security and the Revolutionary Tribunal with the authority to arrest and execute arbitrarily anyone suspected of treason.

During the Terror, about 40,000 people were sent to their deaths. In its last stages, the Jacobins began to turn on revolutionaries who were considered moderate. Finally, Robespierre himself went too far and frightened even members of the Committee of Public Safety, many of whom had supported him and the Terror. Robespierre and his closest collaborators were themselves deposed and executed on July 26, 1794.

The Terror had lasted less than a year but left a model for future imitators. It had begun as an attack on "enemies of the revolution" and grew into wholesale murder. There is little doubt that thousands of individuals lost their lives for reasons they probably did not comprehend. The original target of the attack was the French aristocratic class since it was understandably assumed that its members were opposed to the Revolution. Yet, in the end, the aristocrats formed a minority of those executed. The Terror chose its victims without respect to social rank, gender, or age. In other words, no one could feel secure, and this is the ultimate goal of a terrorist state.

Reference: Parry, A. *Terrorism from Robespierre to Arafat* (New York: Vanguard Press, 1976).

Franz Ferdinand, Archduke, assassination of

Archduke Franz Ferdinand and his wife were assassinated in July 1914 by a Serbian nationalist during a visit to Sarajevo, the capital of the Austrian province of Bosnia-Herzogovina. The archduke was the designated successor to the emperorship of the Austrian-Hungarian Empire. His murder is generally assumed by historians to have provoked World War I since Austria, with the support of Germany, mobilized its military against Serbia. That action in turn led to Russia mobilizing its military to support fellow Slavs in Serbia. Finally, Britain and France mobilized to counter a possible German hegemony on the European continent. One mobilization provoked others until governments seemed to lose control of events.

The sequence of descent into war was not foreseen by any of the participants. During 1914–18, a total of 9 million soldiers died in battles that were unprecedented for both their violent horror and the modern technology that enabled thousands to kill one another in a single day. All of this suggests the remarkable influence one terrorist can have on world history. A single terrorist act launched a world war that ultimately destroyed four empires and may have helped prepare the way for an even more lethal world war a generation later.

The lesson of this particular assassination is that terrorism cannot be underestimated. It may have unintended or unanticipated consequences that are completely unforeseen by both the terrorists themselves and the governments that attempt to subdue them.

See also CYCLICAL NATURE OF TERRORISM.

References: Kahler, Miles. "Rumors of War: The 1914 Analogy." *Foreign Affairs* 58, no. 2 (1979–80): 374–396; Van Evera, Stephen. "The Cult of the Offensive and the Origins of the First World War." *International Security* 9 (1984): 58–107.

Free Aceh Movement (Gerakin Aceh Merdeka, or GAM)

Aceh, in the northern tip of Sumatra, is one of Indonesia's most troubled areas, comparable to East Timor, which successfully seceded from the state near the turn of the new millennium. The Free Aceh Movement has been fighting for independence and the creation of an Islamic state, since the 1970s. Although the Indonesian government granted "special region" status for Aceh in 1959, recognizing the Islamic character of the population and its desire for autonomy and a greater role for

Islamic law, the desire for a separate state continued to flow.

Operational military status was put over Aceh in 1991, as separatist activity surged. The military, in its crackdown to "root out" the separatists, was accused of human rights abuses, including abductions, tortures, rapes, and mass killings. In early 1998, several caches of foreign arms were discovered, resulting in the arrest of suspected rebels, who were imprisoned and threatened with torture or shot and killed by police in "suspicious circumstances." Disappearances and extrajudicial executions of alleged political opponents also occurred during this period with alarming frequency.

The alleged state terrorism by the military on the citizens of Aceh diminished in 1999 with an announced troop pullout and an apology by the armed forces chief for "any excesses." Indonesia now classifies the Aceh Merkada as an "unauthorized agitation movement." In December 2004, as the region struggled to recover from the devastating effects of a tsunami, the Free Aceh Movement declared a cease-fire with the government in order to facilitate the movement of aid to the affected areas. The Indonesian government, in response to this offer to halt hostilities, removed the restrictions on northern Sumatra, allowing rescue efforts to reach that area. A delegation from GAM, in the first two months of the next year, met with a delegation from the Indonesian government to begin another round of peace talks.

The talks, held in Vantaa, Finland, and moderated by the former Finnish president, resulted in a peace agreement, ending the 30-year insurgency, announced on July 16, 2005. This agreement, signed in August 2005 by Indonesia's chief negotiator and the leader of GAM, committed both sides to an immediate halt of all hostilities. The Indonesian government agreed to withdraw all nonlocal military and police, and GAM agreed to disarm, both actions to be completed by the end of 2005.

The president of Indonesia issued a decree granting amnesty to almost 500 former GAM members living in exile in other countries and unconditionally set free some 1,400 members of the organization who had been jailed by the government for their actions in the insurgency. The government also agreed to help establish Aceh-based political parties, to organize a "truth and reconciliation commission," and to allow 70% of the income from local natural resources to stay within Aceh (in response to the contentious issue of the uneven distribution of income).

The leaders of the Free Aceh Movement, on December 27, 2005, announced that they had disbanded their military wing. A Monitoring Mission, from the European Union and Association of South East Asian Nations, is overseeing the process of disarmament of GAM and the reintegration into Indonesian society of GAM members.

References: National Memorial Institute for the Prevention of Terrorism (MIPT). "Free Aceh Movement (GAM)." Available online. URL: http://www.tkb.org/Group.jsp?groupID=3600. Accessed February 15, 2006; Schulze, Kirsten E. *The Free Aceh Movement (GAM): Anatomy of a Separatist Organization* (Washington, D.C.: East-West Center, 2004).

freedom of press

See GOALS OF MEDIA, IN TERRORIST EVENT.

freedom of speech

See GOALS OF MEDIA, IN TERRORIST EVENT.

Free Papua Movement (a.k.a. Organisasi Papua Merdeka [OPM])

Irian Jaya, the former Dutch New Guinea or West New Guinea, remained under Dutch control after Indonesia achieved independence in 1949. In Operation Trikora, Indonesian forces in 1961 took over West New Guinea, renaming it Irian Barat. By October of the following year, the Dutch transferred sovereignty to the United Nations Temporary Executive Authority, which was supported by a military observer force that oversaw the cease-fire, and in May of 1963, Indonesia was given full administrative control. Indonesia organized an Act of Free Choice in 1969, which integrated this largest and least-populated republic as Indonesia's 26th province, but the act involved little more than a token assent by a few handpicked people carefully schooled to say the right words in front of an audience, without the consent of even a substantial minority of the population.

As a result, opposition to Indonesia's control of this area continues, taking two distinct forms: those who favor a federation with Papua New Guinea and those who prefer independence as West Papua or "West Melanesia." The indigenous people of the region feel that they are being left behind economically by the flood of Indonesian immigrants coming in via the central government's sponsorship of a transmigration program. International critics of the government's policy in Irian Jaya have accused the Indonesian leadership of waging a form of demographic GENOCIDE.

The OPM, in response to Indonesia's efforts to exploit the natural resources, which are very rich, and to assimilate the Papuan and Melanesian populations into the national culture and administration, have waged low-level but committed guerrilla warfare, which peaked in the late 1970s with attacks on government outposts. In 1996, a group of foreigners was taken hostage in this province by the Free Papua Movement, although they were subsequently released. In early 1997, the movement took 26 people hostage in Mapunduma village, releasing several. Eleven Indonesians and foreigners were later released after a military operation five months later, but two hostages were killed during the release operation.

See also FREE ACEH MOVEMENT.

References: King, Peter. *West Papua and Indonesia since Suharto: Independence, Autonomy or Chaos?* (Sydney, Australia: University of South Wales Press, 2004); National Memorial Institute for the Prevention of Terrorism (MIPT). "Free Papua Movement (OPM)." Available online. URL: http://www.tkb.org/Group.jsp?groupID=4023. Accessed February 15, 2006.

Front du Libération du Québec (FLQ)

Quebec, an eastern province of Canada, has a population that is predominantly of French descent. The French-Canadian movement for national identity has asserted itself in terms of cultural and political struggle. Under the leadership of such men as Louis-Joseph Papineau (leader of the 1837 rebellion of French-Canadians), Louis Lafontaine, Henri Bourassa, and the abbé Lionel Grouix, the province developed as a "political home" for French-Canadians, and the government assumed responsibility for the defense of French culture.

The Front du Libération du Quibec was responsible for numerous acts of violence in the 1960s and 1970s. These included the assassination of the labor minister of Quebec, Pierre LaPorte, in 1970, and the kidnapping of a British envoy, James Cross, during the same year. The reaction by the Canadian government, led by Pierre Elliott Trudeau, resulted in the capture or scattering of most of the FLQ under an emergency law. Many members of the party were eventually "coopted" into the system by legal changes to protect the French character of the province. However, a referendum on Quebec independence was held in 1995, resulting in a loss for those in favor of seccession. Shortly thereafter, Rheal Mathieu, a former FLQ terrorist who had served jail time for murder as a result of an FLQ bombing, led a group who subsequently firebombed several Quebec companies that were incorporated with English names and also a church that served as the headquarters for an English-rights group. In 2001, Mathieu was convicted but only given 10 months of jail time.

See also CANADA AND THE FLQ.

Front for the Liberation of the Cabinda Enclave (FLEC)

Cabinda is a province within the state of Angola. The Front for the Liberation of the Cabinda Enclave (FLEC) is a nationalist movement devoted to the creation of an independent state of Cabinda, founded in 1963. Shortly after its founding, FLEC divided into three principle factions: "Front for the Liberation of the Cabinda Enclave—Renewed," "FLEC—Forces Amardas de Cabinda," and "Frente Democratica de Cabinda." These separate factions, or splinter groups, have their own military wings that seek to complement their different political goals.

The group, in all of its factions, bases its demand for independence from Angola on three premises. The first is geographic: Cabinda and Angola are noncontiguous. A thin strip of land belonging to the Democratic Republic of the Congo separates Cabinda from Angola. Second, some historical documents imply that Portugal, Angola's former colonizer, regarded Angola and Cabinda as separate states. Finally, and most important, Cabinda produces 60% of Angola's total oil output of approximately 700,000 barrels per day. Angola's oil accounts for 90% of its total export earnings, so the financial argument for Cabindan independence is strong. The Cabindan oil industry, however, is not sympathetic to the FLEC-R, since the group has too often engaged in the kidnapping of oil executives.

References: Hodges, Tony. *Angola from Afro-Stalinism to Petro-Diamond Capitalism.* (Bloomington: Indiana University Press, 2001); National Memorial Institute for the Prevention of Terrorism (MIPT). "Front for the Liberation of the Cabinda Enclave." Available online. URL: http://www.tkb.org/Group.jsp?groupID=118. Accessed February 15, 2006.

Fujimori, Alberto

See OPERATION CHAVÍN DE HUÁNTAR; SENDERO LUMINOSO.

G

al-Gama'at al-Islamiyya (a.k.a. al-Gama'a al-Islamiyya [GAI], Islamic Group [IG])

An indigenous Egyptian Islamic extremist group active since the late 1970s, the Islamic Group appears to be loosely organized, with no single easily identifiable operational leader. It has an external wing with supporters in several countries worldwide. Shaykh Umar Abd al-Rahman, the group's preeminent spiritual leader, was sentenced to life in prison in January 1996 for his involvement in the World Trade Center bombing of 1993. Although the group issued a cease-fire in March 1999, Rahman rescinded his support for this cease-fire in June 2000.

The group is now unofficially split into two factions: one led by Mustafa Hamza that supports the cease-fire, and one led by Rifa'I Taha Musa, who has called for a return for armed operations. Musa, who published a book in early 2001 in which he attempted to justify terrorist attacks that would cause mass casualties, disappeared several months after the publication of this book, and there is uncertainty as to his current location.

The Islamic Group carried out armed attacks against Egyptian security and other government officials, Coptic Christians, and Egyptian opponents of Islamic extremism. It began to launch attacks on tourists in Egypt in 1992, including but not limited to the attack at the Cairo National Antiquities Museum on September 18, 1997, involving a grenade attack on a tour bus, and an attack at Luxor on November 17, 1997, in what came to be called the Hatshepsut Temple massacre, in which 58 foreign tourists died. The group claimed responsibility for the attempt in June 1995 to assassinate President Hosni Mubarak in Addis Ababa, Ethiopia. At the time, the group stated as its goal the overthrow of President Mubarak's government and its replacement with an Islamic state.

The IG has not conducted an attack inside Egypt since August 1998. In March 2002, members of the group led by Hamza declared the use of violence misguided and renounced its future use, in response to which the Egyptian government released more than 900 former IG members from prison in 2003.

The declaration of renunciation of violence was not accepted by the other faction of IG, who are still dedicated to violent JIHAD. Potentially inspired by Musa or al-Rahman, the goal of overthrowing the Egyptian government and replacing it with an Islamic state remains.

With probably severally thousand hard-core members and another several thousand sympathizers, this group has operated mainly in the Al Minya, Asyu't, Qina, and Soha governorates of southern Egypt. Supporters, however, are also found in Cairo, Alexandria, and other urban locations in Egypt, particularly among unemployed graduates and students. While the Egyptian government believes that Iran, Sudan, and Afghan militant groups support the group, there is no definitive evidence of external aid given to this group. Cells and supporters give the group a worldwide presence, including in the United Kingdom, Afghanistan, Yemen, and various locations in Europe, and perhaps support from various Islamic nongovernmental organizations.

See also EGYPT, EXTREMIST ATTACKS.

Reference: National Memorial Institute for the Prevention of Terrorism (MIPT). "al-Gama'a al-Islamiyya (GAI)." Available online. URL: http://www.tkb.org/Group.jsp?groupID=3760. Accessed February 15, 2006.

Gandhi, Rajiv (1944–1991)

Born on August 20, 1944, in Bombay, India, Rajiv was the son of Feroze and Indira Gandhi. Although his mother, Indira, became prime minister in 1966, and his brother, Sanjay, was a vigorous political figure until his untimely death in a plane crash in 1980, Rajiv largely stayed out of politics until his brother's death. Instead, he completed an engineering degree at Cambridge University in 1965 and, three years later, he began piloting for Indian Airlines. Indira drafted him into a political career after Sanjay's death. In June 1981 he was elected to the lower house of Parliament in India, and in the same month he became a member of the national executive of the Youth Congress.

Rajiv was considered a nonabrasive person, one who usually consulted other party members and rarely made hasty decisions. When his mother was assassinated on October 31, 1984, Rajiv moved from being the leading general secretary of India's Congress (I) Party to prime minister. Later that same year, he led the Congress (I) Party to a landslide victory, and he undertook vigorous measures to reform the government bureaucracy and liberalize the economy.

Gandhi's attempts to discourage separatist movements in several provinces caused serious concern in Punjab, Kashmir, and Sri Lanka. In 1989, Rajiv resigned as prime minister, though he remained leader of the Congress (I) Party. While campaigning in Tamil Nadu for upcoming parliamentary elections in 1991, he was killed by a bomb carried by a woman who may have had ties with Tamil separatists.

See also LIBERATION TIGERS OF TAMIL EELAM.

general threat indicators

General threat indicators are used to determine whether, within the nation or state, conditions exist that might stimulate or provoke terrorism. Such indicators are extremely general and subsequently of little use in predicting the likelihood of a specific terrorist attack. Instead, they are used to assess the climate—political, ideological, religious, etc.—that might influence the willingness of a portion of the population to resort to terrorism. Politically, for example, the presence of an unpopular, repressive, or corrupt government is considered a positive indicator of the probability of terrorism. Similarly, an economic climate that includes extreme poverty and/or high unemployment is regarded as conducive to terrorism.

Observation of these indicators does not indicate that a nation or region possessing these conditions will necessarily have a large degree of terrorism. They simply mean that the presence of such conditions makes the likelihood of terrorism greater in such places than it might be in areas without similar political or economic climates. These are indicators only, not predictors of terrorism. For example, a geopolitical indicator that has been identified is the concentration of large foreign populations within a nation or region. Yet in some nations, most large cities have such concentrations without outbreaks of terrorism. However, in occupied territories or nations involved in border disputes, such populations have been useful indicators of the probability of terrorism.

generational differences among terrorists

During the last two decades of the 20th century, a generational difference between young militants and older leaders was observed in terrorist groups. The young militants appeared to be less likely to be involved in pickets and demonstrations before resorting to violence. They seemed more willing to throw bombs first and talk later (if at all) about their grievances and goals. This "do something now" mentality caused some difficulties and embarrassment to some of the older leaders of established movements. In the PALESTINE LIBERATION ORGANIZATION (PLO), for example, the 1990s witnessed a number of splits, frequently between older, more "institutionalized" members of the organization who were more willing to pursue an end to the violence with Israel and younger members who wanted to take violent action at once against the existing situation, as became evident in the second intifada, which derailed the peace talks in 2000. YASIR ARAFAT, in his attempts to make serious efforts toward securing a lasting peace as well as establishing a Palestinian state, could not always restrain the younger elements from acts of rock throwing, shootings, and even bombings by younger more militant members impatient with the slow process.

HAMAS, the fundamentalist and radical element seeking the establishment of an Islamic state and which is supported by Iran and active in the West Bank and Gaza, strongly rejected any such renunciation of terrorist tactics. The difficulties experienced by Arafat in governing Gaza during the last decade illustrates the deepening splits between the older leadership, willing to compromise in order to achieve a portion of that for which they fought, and the younger factions, willing to continue the struggle with violence and unwilling to settle for less than full success. Similar difficulties appear to plague the leadership of AL-QAEDA, as the chatrooms and billboards of the Internet reveal. Impatient young activists call for immediate action, while older leaders continue to suggest long-term planning of events and patience.

Geneva Convention on Treatment of Civilians during Times of War

The Geneva Convention on the treatment of civilians in times of war demands special protections for "persons taking no active part in the hostilities." Nonactive status does not imply that the person is good, virtuous, or even disinterested in the outcome of the conflict. A person need only be innocent of participation in the hostilities to be protected by the convention.

This means that membership in the civilian population of a nation against which a group is waging war is an insufficient reason for according a "guilty" status to a person, thereby removing those special protections. This means that a state carrying out acts of violence against civilians merely because they belong to a particular ethnic group is violating the laws of war, just as terrorist groups that target persons from a particular country or ethnic association are violating this same law.

What are, then, the special provisions in the Geneva Convention relating to the treatment of civilians? First of all, this convention states that such persons "shall in all circumstances be treated humanely." Article 3 of this document lists various actions that are prohibited "at any time and in any place whatsoever with respect to such persons." These prohibited acts include "violence to life and person, in particular murder of all kinds, mutilations, cruel treatment and torture; taking of hostages; and outrages upon the personal dignity, in particular humiliating and degrading treatment."

Furthermore, in Article 27, the Geneva Convention on Civilians emphasizes the degree of legal protection afforded to these noncombatants, stating:

> They are entitled, in all circumstances, to respect for their persons, their honor, their family rights, their religious convictions and practices, and their manners and customs . . . and shall at all times be treated humanely, and shall be protected especially against all acts of violence or threats thereof.

Article 33 of the Geneva Convention for the Protection of Civilian Persons (1949) provides that:

> No protected person may be punished for an offense he or she has not personally committed. Collective penalties and likewise all measures of intimidation or terrorism are prohibited.
>
> Pillage is prohibited.
>
> Reprisals against protected persons and their property are prohibited.

"Protected persons" in this convention are civilians who have the misfortune to be living in a combat zone or occupied territory. Not only does this convention specifically prohibit the use of terrorism against this civilian population, but it also, in Article 34, prohibits the taking of hostages of any sort. Such rules make it clear that the kidnapping or murder of any civilian, even during times of war, to exact punishment for an injustice real or imagined, is not legal, unless the victim was directly responsible for the injustice.

This prohibition against collective punishment applies to states as well as to revolutionary organizations. Control Council Law No. 10, used in the trials of war criminals before the Nuremberg Tribunals, makes this clear. Neither side in an armed conflict, whether involved in the "liberation" of a country or in the efforts of the state to maintain itself while under attack, may engage in warfare against the civilian population.

Terrorist acts against innocent persons by the state, as well as acts of terrorism by nonstate groups, are as illegal in times of war as they are in times of peace. The laws of war offer neither justification nor protection for the willful and wanton taking of innocent life. If terrorism by its very nature involves victimizing an innocent third party in order to achieve a political goal and to evoke a particular emotional response in an audience, then it seems reasonable to say that terrorism is illegal under the laws of war as set forth in the Geneva Convention.

While this convention was drafted with the protection of civilians in occupied territories in mind, Protocols I and II to the convention, drafted in 1976, extend these protections to civilians in nonoccupied territories. Article 46 of Protocol I codifies the customary international law doctrine that the civilian population as such, as well as individual citizens, may not be made the object of direct military attack. One significant provision in this article states that "Acts or threats of violence which have the primary object of spreading terror among the civilian population are prohibited."

This article goes on to prohibit indiscriminate attacks that are "of a nature to strike military objectives and civilians or civilian objectives without distinction." The Article further states:

> A bombardment that treats as a single military objective a number of clearly separated and distinct military objectives located within a city, town or village, or other area which has a concentration of civilians is considered to be indiscriminate and is therefore prohibited.

In terms of legal restraints on terrorism, this means that a state may not commit an attack on a city or town as a whole simply on the basis of information that insurgents or combatants may be making a base in that area. To do so would be to commit an act of terrorism under international law. This convention makes it clear that states as well as groups are prohibited from punishing the innocent in efforts to stop the insurgents in guerrilla warfare. To do so would be to commit acts of terrorism.

Article 50 of Protocol I codifies customary international law concerning what is called the RULE OF PROPORTIONALITY. This provision, along with other provisions in the article, means that those launching or planning to launch an attack are legally responsible for making sure that the military objectives that they expect to gain justify the minimal loss of civilian life that may occur.

There are two important points here. One is that the objective is assumed to be a military, never a civilian, target. The law makes it clear that, whereas legitimate attacks may be expected against military targets, there is no legal expectation or right to launch attacks against civilian targets. On the contrary, the civilians within the target zone are to be protected against the effects of that attack, as far as it is militarily possible.

The other point is that, while military reality makes note of the fact that some civilian injury may occur during an attack, the injury or deaths of civilians should be incidental to the operations, on a scale proportionate to the military objective sought. If civilian casualties are expected to be high, then the attack cannot be justified under international law.

Two other implications of these provisions are significant. One is that guerrilla or revolutionary groups that select predominantly civilian targets are in violation of international law, even if there is a military target which may also be hit. Thus, the fact that a cafi is frequented by members of an enemy military does not make it a legitimate target since there would be a great likelihood of many civilian casualties in such an attack. If the target area is populated predominantly with civilians, then it cannot be a justifiable military target.

The other policy that this provision evokes is that states may not strike civilian settlements, even if there are guerrilla soldiers taking refuge or making their headquarters in such settlements. To attack such places would mean inflicting unacceptably high levels of civilian casualties in proportion to the military objective sought. Thus, those who seek to destroy Palestinian revolutionaries may not, under international law, drop bombs on Palestinian refugee camps, since such camps have large civilian populations, including women and children, the sick, and the infirm.

It is true that those revolutionaries who make their headquarters in the midst of civilian encampments are deliberately placing those civilians at risk in the ensuing war. But this does not justify enemy attack of such settlements. The civilians have, for the most part, no choice but to be there, in their own homes or shelters. The state seeking to destroy the revolutionaries cannot take advantage of their vulnerable status to make war on the insurgents at a cost of countless civilian lives. Even when seeking to destroy an enemy who takes refuge among protected persons, a state may not deliberately wage war on those protected persons.

Reference: Jinks, Derek. *Rules of War: The Geneva Conventions in the Age of Terror* (Oxford: Oxford University Press, 2007).

genocide

Genocide is the systematic physical elimination of a community of people who have been designated by another community or, more frequently, by a government to be destroyed. The victim community is normally but not exclusively a minority of a national population. Its intended destruction can be based on ethnicity, religious affiliation, social class, or any combination of these features. Genocide is often a form of STATE TERRORISM. In the typical genocide experience no exceptions are considered. Age and gender are characteristics that are usually ignored.

Genocide often follows a government propaganda effort both to dehumanize and to demonize the victims. Executioners are more eager to kill defenseless people if they are convinced that they are subhuman or in some way undeserving of continued life. It is not uncommon for the victims to be portrayed as a cabal of evildoers intent on destroying their superiors as soon as an opportunity is available. The German government during 1933–45 increasingly viewed its own and neighboring Jewish communities in this light. Jews at first were discriminated against and finally were sent to death camps.

During the 1990s, the term *ethnic cleansing* became almost synonymous with genocide. Serbs in BOSNIA massacred thousands of Muslims. In Rwanda during the summer of 1994, a Hutu-dominated government encouraged and oversaw the slaughter of a half million Tutsis. Genocide is unlikely to occur when governments protect the rights of all of their citizens.

See also DARFUR; ETHNIC CLEANSING; OVERVIEW OF TERRORISM, BY REGION; STALIN, JOSEPH.

Reference: Gutman, Roy, ed. *Crimes of War: What the Public Should Know* (New York: W. W. Norton & Company, 1999).

Germany *See* GSG-9; HITLER, ADOLF; HOLOCAUST DENIAL; MUNICH MASSACRE OF ISRAELI ATHLETES; STATE TERRORISM.

globalization

The emerging global economy is frequently considered a threat to traditionalist mores and to religious orthodoxy. At the same time, globalization is often viewed in the developing regions as a conspiracy formulated and executed by the economic and military predominance of the West in general and of the United States in particular to sustain and enhance the submission and dependency of the rest of the planet. Much of the Islamic world—the Middle East, North Africa, and large areas of South Asia—is especially concerned with and fearful of globalization's impact. The understanding that modernization, accompanied by secularism and Americanization (sometimes referred to as "cocacolonization"), is destructive of divinely sanctioned values has become a basis for confrontation with those who are perceived as exemplifying and projecting sacrilege.

Globalization and its consequent social and cultural disruptions in many ways characterize and form the basis of much of the increasingly violent features of Islamic and other forms of terrorism. Extremist left-wing and some right-wing organizations in the West argue, for different reasons, that globalization has more destructive than productive qualities. Proponents of globalization argue that the phenomenon is both healthy and inevitable and has already been at work for centuries; it has merely become accelerated during the last few decades because of rapid advances in communications and technology. Because of its increasing pace, globalization has produced some economic dislocations, but the overall and long-term impact, according to its proponents, is greater general prosperity. Its critics in turn suggest that globalization wrecks societies by enabling the individual to pursue selfish and solely material objectives at the expense of the greater collective good. Women, for example, no longer submissive to and dependent upon their male relatives, descend into immorality as they enter the workplace, adopt family planning, and insist on full equality with men.

Because of the perceived threat to traditionalist values regarded as absolutist by religious radicals, much of the reaction to globalization has been violent. It has been observed that violence to events generally observed to be progressive, particularly in the form of suicide bombings, is an act of desperation by people who are convinced they are both victimized and in danger of losing all that they hold dear. However, the visceral reaction to globalization by Islamic radicals is also viewed by them as part of a continuing struggle between good and evil, between the Islamic and non-Islamic worlds, and between Muslim resistance to the heralds of globalization that include intervention by the American military in the Arab and Islamic homeland of Saudi Arabia and Iraq as well as the Israeli presence in Palestine.

There is no doubt that globalization can be disruptive of economies and lifestyles. The Industrial Revolution that began in Europe during the 17th and 18th centuries was also disruptive and, in fact, contributed to regime overthrow in several countries, most notably France during the 1790s. "Luddites" appeared in England during the 1600s to sabotage machines that put them out of work. Globalization, in addition to its disruptive qualities, has accelerated in unprecedented ways. So has terrorism, in some ways—a reaction to globalization.

References: Enzensberger, Hans Magnus. "The Radical Loser." Signandsight (December 1, 2005). Available online. URL: http://www.signandsight.com/features/493.html. Accessed March 6, 2006; Friedman, Thomas L. *The Lexus and the Olive Tree: Understanding Globalization* (New York: Farrar, Straus and Giroux, 2000); Gilpin, Robert. *The Challenge of Global Capitalism: The World Economy in the 21st Century* (Princeton, N.J.: Princeton University Press, 2002).

goals of government, concerning media in terrorist event

In democratic systems, journalists usually have substantial freedom to report news, including that involving terrorist events. But unlimited freedom of the press has led, at times, to an escalation of events and loss of life—results that neither the press nor the government desire. In many ways, the goals of the government in terrorist incidents are quite similar to those of the group carrying out the act of terror-violence.

Not all governments share the same goals with respect to the media in a terrorist event. Nevertheless, there are a few common goals that most governments have shared in the interactive relationship between terrorists, the media, and the government. Listed below are those most often found to be held by governments in this type of situation.

Publicity

Most governments know that the event will be publicized and therefore want the press to offer publicity designed to help the government to achieve its goal of ending the situation without loss of innocent lives. This means that publicity, from the government's perspective, should be carefully disseminated in a manner that will not endanger lives and that will help the public to understand the positive actions undertaken by the government to resolve the situation. This may not be compatible with the GOALS OF TERRORISTS, CONCERNING MEDIA, since from the terrorists' point of view, publicity should be used to spread fear, not reassurance, about the government's handling of the situation. The media are thus left with difficult choices about what news to release and how it should be worded.

Criminality of the Act

Law enforcement forces would prefer that the media portray the terrorists as the "bad guys" and usually try to achieve that goal by stressing the criminality of the act that is occurring. In contrast, the terrorists will seek to have the press convey the "justice" of the cause for which the act is being committed, rather than the serious breach of law being perpetrated. Because TERRORISM is, by legal definition, carried out against innocent victims, government authorities generally want the media to focus on the injustice of the actions being taken by the group or individual, and on the criminal nature of the offense, by highlighting the innocence of the victims. If the public can be made to view the persons carrying out the terrorist act as common criminals of a particularly nasty sort, then the government will be viewed as the "good guys," rescuing the victims and ending the violence. To achieve this goal of stressing the criminality of the act, the government clearly needs the cooperation of the media.

Denial of a Platform

It is certainly in the interest of most governments to prevent the terrorists from using the press as a "bully pulpit" for their propaganda, thereby denying them a platform to reach their audience. Not only can a platform be used to generate understanding and even sympathy for the cause of the group or individual carrying out the act but it can also be used to generate tangible support. The 1986 hijacking of TWA FLIGHT 847 in Beirut provides an excellent example of the dangers of allowing the media to publicize the terrorist's platform during a terrorist attack. The skyjackers reportedly offered the press tours of the plane for $1,000 and a session with the hostages for $12,500. Although few situations ever offer quite so open a platform, it is in most government's interest to separate the terrorist from the media as far as possible so that neither propaganda nor funds can be generated from the event.

Information and Cooperation

While for most government agencies the optimum solution would be exclusion of the media and other observers from the area in which the terrorist event occurs, this is seldom an option in democratic systems. Instead, governments may encourage a relationship based on information sharing and cooperation. They may have as their goal a willingness on the part of the media to share information that the media might have about the individuals involved and a commitment not to share information with the hostage-takers that might be of use to them. Thus, the media could be asked by a government to be discrete, careful not to reveal how successful operations were performed, and cautious about revealing information about an event that might provoke an observer into a subsequent act or enable a copycat operation (one in which a terrorist act is copied by an observer in a subsequent act). Cooperation may even, in some cases, be interpreted by the government as a willingness on the media's part to share disinformation—that is, inaccurate information designed to confuse—when such cooperation will help in resolving the threat in the terrorist action.

These are not, of course, the only goals sought by governments with respect to the media's involvement in terrorist events. Since the media are the link between the persons committing the terrorist act and their audience, the role of the media is crucial in the government's efforts to resolve the situation. Problems involving issues such as the potential for an AMPLIFICATION EFFECT, the RIGHT OF ACCESS of the media is fundamental to most democratic societies, and the legally thorny questions of CENSORSHIP and prior restraint are resolved by many governments on a case-by-case basis, with the conflicting goals of governments, terrorists, and media making clear decision patterns difficult.

References: Alexander, Yonah, and Robert Patter, *Terrorism and the Media: Delimma for Government, Journalism, and the Public* (Washington, D.C.: Brassey's, 1990); Alali, A. Odasno, and Kenoye K. Eke, "Terrorism, the News Media, and Democratic Political Order." *Current World Leaders* 39, no. 4 (August 1996): 64–72.

goals of media, in terrorist event

Terrorism has been called "propaganda by the deed." This particularly violent form of propaganda has captured the attention of millions of people and has made today's media a vital link between terrorists and their audience. It has also placed the media in the awkward position of being a weapon in the hands of either the terrorist or the law-enforcement agencies responding to the violence. Thus, the goals of the media, when confronted with terrorism today, are of vital importance in determining how the media shapes its role in what is an increasingly interactive, and potentially symbiotic, relationship.

Possible goals of the media that might impact this relationship have been explored by many researchers during the latter part of the 20th century. Listed below are some of those revealed in these studies. The list is not, of course, comprehensive, but it has consensus among most researchers as being shared by modern media.

Getting a "Scoop"

In a world with fast-breaking news, 24 hours a day, being the first to report the news—or getting a "scoop"—is a crucial goal. High-tech communications make it possible, and increase the pressure, to transmit news stories in "real time"—that is, as the event is actually happening. This leaves little option for editing or carefully evaluating the impact of such a news release on the situation. In such cases, this may mean that stopping to discuss the impact of their reporting with public safety officers, a goal discussed with respect to the law enforcement agencies involved in terrorist events, may be costly to the journalists, who stand to lose that "scoop" to a less scrupulous reporter.

Dramatic Presentation of News

The media, in this fierce competition for public attention, clearly needs to create a dramatic presentation of the event, as well as a timely one. During the hijacking of TWA FLIGHT 847 in June 1985, ABC broadcast extensive interviews with the hijackers and the hostages. Indeed, in one dramatic reel, a pistol was aimed at the pilot's head in a staged photo opportunity for the interviewers. The media argue that the intense scrutiny they give to each aspect of the event actually protects the hostages. This view assumes that the primary goal of the act is to communicate a cause, drawing support from this explication. If drama is needed to demonstrate the seriousness of the cause, however, then the lives of the hostages could be jeopardized by a media demand for drama. If killing a hostage, or a planeload of hostages, becomes the price of "drama," then the media may, in the pursuit of this goal, be held responsible for raising the stakes in the hostage situation.

Protection of Rights

Most news media have a strong commitment to the protection of the public's right to know about events as they occur, in democratic systems. Usually, this does not mean that the media see their role as being in opposition to law enforcement personnel. Most media seek to be professional and accurate, careful not to give out disinformation, playing as constructive a role as possible in the event. Freedom of speech is not, in most systems, an absolute and inviolable value; most democracies have experienced times when civil liberties, including free speech, have been curtailed in the interests of national security and public good. The conflict in these situations between the media and law enforcement is often between a commitment on the part of the media to unhindered public discourse and on the part of law enforcement to the need for public security.

The concept of CENSORSHIP of the press in most democracies is unacceptable. The idea of voluntary restraints by the press on itself is advocated, but it is difficult to establish in a form flexible yet effective enough to satisfy all concerned. If democracies give up free speech to stop terrorism, then regardless of the "success" of this effort, the government perceives the terrorists as winning, because the government and its citizens lose a fundamental part of their system. But an absolutely free press can cost lives. In the hijacking of TWA flight 847 in 1985, radio broadcasts alerted the hijackers aboard the Lufthansa jet that the captain of the plane was transmitting information to authorities on the ground. The hijackers then killed the captain. The press was free, and the cost was the pilot's life.

Personal Security

The Committee to Protect Journalists, based in New York City, noted that more than 400 journalists were murdered between 1992 and 2006 as a result of their work. In 1995 alone, according to this group's records, 45 were assassinated. In 2002, *Wall Street Journal* reporter Daniel Pearl was kidnapped and murdered in Karachi, Pakistan. Pearl was on his way to interview a terrorist leader when he was abducted by a Pakistani militant group. The militant group claimed Pearl was a CIA agent and sent the U.S. a list of demands for his release, including the freeing of all Pakistani terror detainees. Nine days later, Pearl's body was found outside Karachi. Thus, one of the goals of the media is increasingly a focus on personal security, an ability to be able to protect themselves both during and after terrorist operations. Journalists who interview terrorists are at risk, and those who fail to satisfy terrorists' goals of understanding and favorable publicity may be vulnerable to attack by the terrorists and their sympathizers.

The goals of the media in terrorist events are not always compatible with either the goals of the government or those of the terrorists. The media are increasingly confronted with the task of achieving their goals without becoming a tool of either the terrorists or the government, a free and responsible press that reports with integrity without endangering lives. This constitutes a formidable task.

Reference: Pert, Ralph F. *Terrorism, the Media, and the 21st Century* (Washington, D.C.: Congressional Research Service, 1998).

goals of terrorists, concerning media

In the view of many experts, terrorists have goals that the media can help them to achieve. A brief examination of these goals makes clear that most of these goals are not compatible with the GOALS OF GOVERNMENT, CONCERNING MEDIA IN TERRORIST EVENTS. This incompatibility creates a strain in democratic systems.

Publicity

Because TERRORISM is an act of theater and requires an audience, most terrorist groups welcome the opportunity to acquire free publicity. Getting information out to a large, even a global, audience about the cause for which the acts are being committed is a vital part of the act itself. Press coverage that makes the world aware of the "problem" that the individual or group is seeking to resolve is clearly advantageous. This publicity can offer both tactical (short-term) and strategic (long-term) gains for the operation itself and, in some cases, for the cause for which the terrorist act was committed.

Tactical gains in publicity are usually measured in terms of getting information concerning demands that must be met within a time frame to more than just the law enforcement officers at the scene. If the general public can be made aware of the demands and the consequences threatened for lack of fulfillment of the demands, then pressure may be put by a concerned public onto the legal officers to comply. Strategic gains can be achieved by increasing that large audience's awareness of the "justice" of the cause for which the acts are committed and the seriousness of the "problem" that the terrorists are trying to rectify.

Favorable Understanding of Cause

This is an important goal of most terrorists today. Everyone wants to be understood, and an individual or group that is clearly breaking important laws and norms of behavior has an intense desire for a favorable understanding, for their audience to understand why they are carrying out the acts. Sympathy for their suffering and for their cause can be generated by a press willing to convey their message. If terrorists live with images of their world that are unlike those of most of their audience, then it is crucial to them to convey to that audience the justice for which they struggle and the reasons that have driven them to carry out acts of terrorism.

Good relationships with the press are important for individuals and groups engaged in terrorist acts, and these relationships have been cultivated and nourished over a period of time by some of these individuals. While not all who commit terrorist acts have access to or longevity sufficient to build such friendly relations with the press, many individuals and groups carrying out terrorist acts do want the press to share with the public a positive understanding of why the incident is occurring. This leaves the media in the invidious position of trying to decide what is news to be reported and what is rhetoric from the terrorists' platform. The decision whether or not to broadcast or publish interviews with admitted terrorists forces journalists to define the thin line between being a bearer of news and a forum for propaganda.

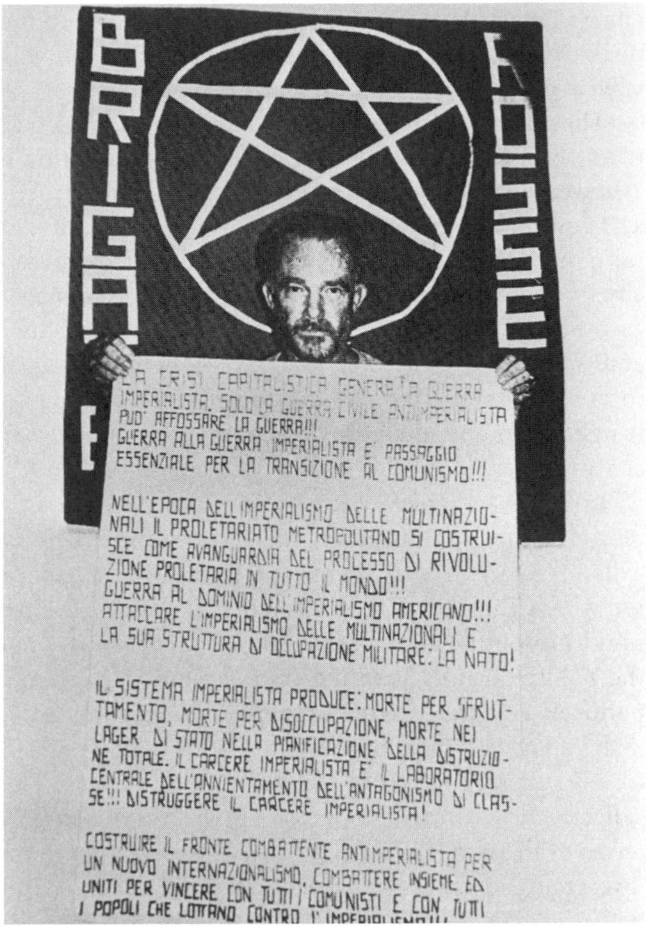

Kidnapped American general James L. Dozier, in front of a Red Brigades flag, carries a sign reading "The capitalist crisis leads to imperialistic war." (CORBIS)

Legitimacy and Identity

To recruit effectively, groups must convey legitimacy and identity, a clear sense of purpose to those who might be seeking similar political goals. Proving to be both committed and effective in kidnapping, bombing, assassination, and other dramatic terrorist events can be a very useful tool in the recruitment of new members and bases of support to a group's cause. Moreover, if the group needs funding for their operations, as most do, good publicity of a successful operation can be the key to drawing such support from nations and individuals who share a concern for the cause motivating the group.

When numerous groups exist that share a similar general "problem" focus, then a group may carry out bombings or assassinations simply to establish a separate and credible identity. Certainly in areas such as the Middle East this has been the case, as splinter groups commit acts of terrorism whose tactical objective seems to be establishing a separate identity.

Destabilizing the Enemy

A goal often cited by terrorist groups is that of causing damage by destabilizing the enemy—that is, generating a sense of unrest, enhancing a fear that the government is unable to offer security and stability to its people. Because terrorism is an act designed to create a mood of fear in an audience, the press can be seen by terrorists as a valuable tool in achieving this goal. If the media can be used to amplify the fear, to spread panic, and to make the population feel less secure, then the terrorists will have won an important goal.

Terrorism is a crime of theater. For it to be effective, the terrorists need to be able to communicate their actions and threats to their audience as quickly and dramatically as possible. Statistically, terrorist incidents worldwide are insignificant in terms of both the number of dead and injured and in the number of incidents reported annually. But mass media coverage of individual terrorist attacks can reach a vast audience, creating an impact far beyond that which the incident, in the absence of this medium, could be expected to effect. The goals of terrorists, then, with respect to the media focus on achieving this impact, is as positive a way as possible.

The media has, to varying extents in differing cultures, become a tool of modern terrorists, offering a "showcase" through which those carrying out terrorist acts can impress and threaten an audience, recruit and train new members, and support and coordinate an emerging network of followers. The role of the media as a showcase—which by definition offers structure and support with a clear display of items arranged to attract the attention of an audience—offers useful insights into one method of teaching terror in the 21st century.

In order to understand the use of the media as a teaching tool for terrorism today, it is important to examine at least two important facets: the audience for which the showcase is designed and the response sought from that audience. Clearly, all of those viewing the media do not share the same cultural, economic, political, religious, or demographic traits. Therefore, if the showcase is to be effective, it must be designed to have divergent appeals to differing audiences. The "effectiveness" of the showcase could be evaluated in terms of the responses sought and obtained from those divergent audiences. So it becomes necessary to clarify both the types of audiences targeted and the types of responses sought to assess the role of the media as a showcase by which terrorism is taught.

There is also one other perspective of the relationship between media and terrorism that must be a part of this analysis. Many terrorism scholars have identified a symbiotic relationship between terrorists seeking attention from an audience and news organizations, which seek dramatic stories to increase their readership and ratings. Clearly, terrorists seeking attention and the media searching for dramatic events can benefit from an association. The intimacy of the association and the degree to which each benefits will depend on a variety of factors, including the goals sought by each "organism" and the limitations of the systems in which both operate. Thus, a look at the role of the governments involved in shaping the way in which media can interact in the event, as well as an examination of the goals of the media and the terrorists, may help to clarify the relationship that exists between these dissimilar organisms.

A *showcase,* according to *Webster's Dictionary,* is a "glass-fronted cupboard, fitted with shelves, in which goods are set out on view for sale or objects for exhibition." If terrorists are intentionally using the media as a showcase, then, like any good vendor, they will be careful to display their causes, actions, and leaders in the best possible light, with the display designed to offer information in formats designed to evoke the desired response from their viewing audience.

Terrorism is a crime of theater. In order for terrorism to be effective, the terrorists need to be able to communicate their actions and threats to their audience as quickly and dramatically as possible. Statistically, terrorist incidents worldwide are insignificant—both in terms of the number of dead and injured and in terms of the number of incidents reported annually—compared to the number injured or killed in wars, famines, natural disasters, or even auto accidents. But massive media coverage of individual terrorist attacks reaches a vast audience, creating an impact far beyond that which the incident, in the absence of this media, could be expected to effect. Without intensive media coverage, it could be argued that few would know of terrorist actions, motivations, and actors. Hence, the showcase in which terrorism is displayed dramatically amplifies the effect of the single act of terrorism.

Theater is a form of showcase, in which not only the talents of the actors are illuminated but also those of the playwright, producer, director, sound and lighting experts, costume designer, and many others, whose effective techniques make the play a success. Since terrorism is a crime of theater, it is logical to assume that, in showcasing the terrorism, highlights will fall on the actors, the plot or cause for which all of the action occurs, those who produced/directed/wrote the script for the action, and the support staff who make all of the action flow.

Just as no theater or theater billboard can focus on all of these aspects simultaneously, terrorists using the media for a showcase for their acts must carefully select the items to be displayed, choices which will depend in large measure on the audiences (supporters/collaborators, enemies, the general public) to be drawn to the "play" and the response sought in that audience (fear, support, anxiety, excitement, etc.). Since all of the prospective audiences can have access to the display in the media, important decisions with regard to the display in the showcase rest on the type of audience targeted and the type of responses desired from those audiences. Showcasing demonstrably effective terrorist actions for an audience of potential supporters and/or collaborators has become an effective and essentially cost-free teaching technique for terrorists today.

There are at least three different audiences for which most terrorist media showcases are designed: current and potential supporters, the general public, and enemy publics. Each of these target audiences is offered a different view, designed to convey a different message and thus to evoke a different response. Let us briefly examine each of these potential audiences in terms of the showcase structure most often utilized.

Current and potential supporters are most often drawn to the media window of the Internet. Most active terrorist groups today have established their presence on the Internet, with hundreds of websites existing worldwide utilized by terrorists and their supporters. These websites use slogans to catch attention, often offering items for sale (such as T-shirts, badges, flags, and videos or audiocassettes). Frequently, the websites are designed to draw local supporters, providing information in a local language and giving information about the activities of a local cell as well as that of the larger organization. The website is therefore a recruiting tool as well as a basic educational link for local sympathizers and supporters.

The general public, including the international public—while they are not directly involved in a specific conflict—often have some interest in the issues involved and are actively sought as an audience in most terrorist events today. Terrorists will use the media to offer information about the cause for which the action is being taken, as well as historical background material about the organization and individuals involved in the cause, seeking to draw sympathetic understanding and even support from this audience.

It is also this audience, however, which must be made to fear the consequences of not changing the policy or system that is the target of the attack. If terrorism is defined by the creating of a mood of fear, this is the audience which must be made to feel that fear most intensely.

The third type of audience, the enemy public, includes not only the state but frequently the citizens of the state against which the terrorist act is being committed. While the enemy which is the target is not always clearly defined, at least one governing regime, or the policy of one regime, is usually a clear target, since terrorism by definition is seeking to cause some type of political/social change. The enemy public, then, is the audience that the terrorist showcase is intended to demoralize and humiliate as well as threaten, thereby weakening public support for the targeted regime by facilitating a change in public opinion.

Thus, terrorist events may be showcased in the media to impact at least three definable audiences. The critical difference is the type of reaction that the display is designed to evoke. These responses can be described as the goals of a terrorist group in its intentional interaction with the media. The extent to which that goal is achieved will depend in part on the goals of the media in this interaction. Remember that the relationship *can be* symbiotic and that the media can be a showcase for terrorist activity, but that neither of these may be the case. If the goals of media and terrorists converge and are compatible, the relationship may be symbiotic and an effective showcase may be achieved. If not, then the display may carry a different message from the intent of the terrorists, and the impact on the audience may not produce the desired effect.

References: Nacos, Brigitte. *Terrorism and the Media: From the Iran Hostage Crisis to the World Trade Center Bombing* (New York: Columbia University Press, 1994); Weimann, Gabriel. *Theatre of Terror: Mass Media and International Terrorism* (New York: Longman Publishing Group, 1993).

Goldstein, Baruch (1958–1994)

Goldstein was an Israeli army physician and West Bank settler who in 1994 shot several Muslims while they were in a Hebron mosque praying. He was eventually overcome and beaten to death by the survivors. Goldstein was known as a physician who so disliked Arabs that he did not want to attend them. The Israeli government and public officially condemned his actions. Many Israeli Jews announced that they were ashamed. Only a small extremist right-wing element of Israelis defended Goldstein.

Gray Wolves (Sivi Vukovi)

The "Gray Wolves" was the name of the 2nd Posavina brigade, a paramilitary unit from Serbia equipped by the Serbian Ministry of Internal Affairs, led by Slobodan Miljković. Miljković received the nickname "Lugar" after returning from Šamac (formerly Bosanski Šamac) in 1992 and was accused before the Hague Tribunal for crimes commited in that region. Terror and crimes in the region of Bosanski Samac were, according to the indictment, part of a wide and systematic campaign against the civilian population in that municipality. According to the 1991 census, this municipality had 33,000 inhabitants, of which 17,000 were Croats and Muslims. In 1995, less than 300 of them were still there.

On August 7, 1998, Miljković was murdered in Kragujevac by an employee of the Serbian Interior Ministry, Branislav Luković. The killing prompted speculation that the Serbian state security was beginning to order the assassination of people who could testify about the activities of the Serb authorities in Bosnia and Herzegovina during the war. Tatomir Leković, Miljković's lawyer, stated that his murder was "one more in a series of murders, individual liquidations which are carried out in the organization and under the watchful eye of the Serbian Interior Ministry and the state security service, in order to eliminate proof of the involvement of (Yugoslav president) Slobodan Milošević and his services in the war in Bosnia."

See also BOSNIA, GENOCIDE IN.

Grey Wolves

The National Movement Party (Milliyetçi Hareket Partisi, or MHP) was founded by Alparslan Türkeş in the 1960s, but banned, like all other parties, after the military coup in Turkey in 1980. In 1992, when it emerged again as the MHP, it supported the government's military approach regarding the insurgency by the KURDISTAN WORKERS' PARTY (PKK) in southeast Turkey and opposed any concessions to Kurdish separatists. MHP has as a central tenet the goal of the creation of the Turan, the Great Turkish Empire, to include the Turkish people in the countries of the former Soviet Union, and is therefore opposed to any Turkish separatist movement.

The Grey Wolves, the unofficial militant arm of the MHP, has been involved in street killings and gunbattles. Mehmet Ali Ağca, the Turkish gunman who shot and wounded Pope John Paul II in 1981, was a former Grey Wolf. The Grey Wolves have also been accused of assassinating the prominent Turkish Cypriot journalist Kutlu Adali on July 6, 1966, in response to his criticism of the Denktash regime and of Turkey's policies in Cyprus.

Great Eastern Islamic Raiders Front (IBDA-C)

The Great Eastern Islamic Raiders Front (IBDA-C) is a Sunni Salafist group supporting Islamic rule in Turkey, believing that Turkey's present secular leadership is not legal. For this reason, it has been known to cooperate with other opposition elements in Turkey to destabilize the national political structure. It advocates the establishment of a "pure" Islamic state to replace the "corrupt" secular regime that is cooperating with the West.

This group has been active since the mid-1970s, carrying out bombings and sabotage and attacking churches, charities, television transmitters, newspapers, pro-secular journalists, taverns, banks, clubs, and tobacco shops. In July 1993, it launched a firebomb attack on a hotel in Sivas, killing 37 people, and it was tied to an assassination attempt in 1994 on a Jewish businessman and an attack on a Greek Orthodox church in Istanbul. After the arrest of its founder, Salih Erdis, in 1998, the group seemed to quiet down, only to burst back in 2003 with a bombing in Istanbul that killed 24 people and injured many more.

Reference: National Memorial Institute for the Prevention of Terrorism (MIPT). Group Profile. "Islamic Great Eastern Raiders Front." Available online. URL: http://www.tkb.org/Group.jsp?groupID=56. Accessed February 15, 2006.

group dynamics, impact on terrorist of

The impact of a terrorist group upon the terrorist can be an important factor in the lethality of the actions carried out by the individual. If group dynamics help to shape terrorist thought and action, then its impact must certainly be understood in order to understand the contemporary terrorist.

Modern terrorists are, for the most part, individuals whose sense of reality is distorted. They operate under the assumption that they, and they alone, know the truth and are therefore the sole arbiters of what is right and what is wrong. They believe themselves to be moralists, to whom ordinary law does not apply, since the law in existence is created by immoral persons for immoral purposes.

They are not necessarily consistent in their logic. For example, they demand that governments who capture terrorists treat them as prisoners of war, as they are involved in a war against either a specific government or society in general. Yet they vehemently deny the state's right to treat them as war criminals for their indiscriminate killing of civilians. In other words, they invoke the laws of war only as far as it serves their purposes but reject any aspect of such laws that limits their ability to kill at will.

Two other points should be made with respect to understanding the contemporary terrorist. The first point is relatively simple and involves what seems like a truism. The less clear the political purpose that motivates terrorism, the greater its appeal is likely to be to unbalanced persons. A rational individual will be more likely to require a clear purpose for the commission of an extraordinary act. Thus an act whose motivation is unclear is more likely to appeal to an irrational mind.

Contemporary terrorism has significantly less clear political purpose than that of earlier centuries. Thus, it seems fair to say that a larger proportion of contemporary terrorists may well be unbalanced persons, the "crazies" described by Frederick Hacker.

The second point relates to what psychologists term group dynamics. If it is true that a terrorist's sense of reality is distorted, then the greater the association the terrorist enjoys with his group of fellow terrorists, the greater that distortion will be. The more an individual perceives his identity in terms of the group of fellow terrorists, the less will be his ability to see the world as it really is. For the terrorist who is a member of a close-knit organization, reality is defined by the group. Moreover, this group rejects the reality of laws as they currently exist, and morality, as it is defined by anyone except themselves.

Thus, conventional moral and legal constraints have little meaning to an individual who is deeply involved in a terrorist group. The group determines for itself what is moral and what is legal. An individual who has just joined the group may be able to perceive the difference between what the group declares to be morally or legally justified. The longer he or she remains with the group, or the stronger the identification with the norms of the group the individual adopts, the less able the individual becomes to see the difference between reality and "reality" as it is defined by the group.

The strength of the individual's acceptance of the group's definition of "reality" is particularly evident in situations in which terrorism has been a significant part of the culture for several generations. In Northern Ireland, for instance, many young people have grown up in a culture where democracy is part of everyday humdrum existence but also one in which recourse to violence is viewed as something existing on a superior plane, not only glorious but even a sacred duty.

Religion, as a Factor in Group Dynamics

Religions, as a rule, offer to some extent their own versions of "reality" as well as a promise of "reward" for conformity to the norms of that reality. The reward is usually promised for a future time, when the present "reality" has passed away. Thus the religious zealot committing an act of terrorism is assured by his/her religion and its leaders that his/her acts are acceptable to a higher morality than may currently exist. He/she is reinforced in the belief that what he/she is doing is right by the approval of fellow zealots. Further, the religious fanatic is assured of immortality and a suitable reward therein if he/she should die in the commission of the act of terrorism.

It would be difficult, perhaps impossible, to dissuade such a person from his/her beliefs by reasonable arguments. There is little that could be offered to such a person as an inducement for discontinuing the act of terrorism. What reward can compete with the promise of immortality, approval by one's peers, and religious sanctification?

The dynamics of some groups are much more powerful than those of others whose reward system and extensive spiritual support system is less organized or persuasive. Certain types of terrorists, thus, are much more difficult to deal with on a rational basis due to this ability of a group to distort reality.

References: Esposito, John L. *Unholy War: Terror in the Name of Islam* (New York: Oxford University Press, 2002); Juergensmeyer, Mark. *Terror in the Mind of God: The Global Rise of Religious Violence* (Berkeley: University of California Press, 2000).

GSG-9 (Grenzschutzgruppe 9)

GSG-9 was formed in 1973 after the massacre of Israeli athletes at the 1972 Munich Olympics. The inadequate response of the German police to actions of the BLACK SEPTEMBER group generated a determination of the part of the German government to create a response team capable of handling terrorist activity. Until this incident, German authorities had been reluctant to create an elite military unit of any sort, due in part to a desire to reassure its neighbors that it was no longer a threat to their security (after World War II). Thus, Germany had, until 1972, a very low-profile security system.

Given this low-profile security system, it was possible for members of Black September to penetrate the Olympic compound, kill two Israeli athletes, and take nine others hostage. The situation became a debacle when the on-site commander of the German police ordered his men to open fire on the terrorists as they were getting ready to board two helicopters in their escape at Fürstenfeldbrück military airfield. This led to an open gun battle, which, when the smoke had cleared, found all nine remaining hostages dead as well as all of the remaining terrorists.

After this disaster, German authorities were determined never to be caught unprepared again by such a terrorist action. The government created a counterterrorist unit, GSG-9, which was designed to be manned and controlled by the Federal Border Police Force (Bundesgrenzschutz), instead of the military. Operational only six months after the Munich massacre, GSG-9 is unique among counterterrorist forces in many respects.

GSG-9 makes no claim to be a "killer troop" or a "hit squad," terms used in conjunction with other elite counterterrorist forces. Instead, it makes a point of being less dependent on weapons than on the talents, discipline, and training of its men. As the ninth unit of the Border Police, it makes its headquarters at St. Augustin, just outside of Bonn, and it is formed very much along the same lines as the SAS, operating with five-person "sticks."

Within GSG-9, there is a headquarters unit, a communications and documentation unit, and three fighting units. Its three technical units deal with weapons, research, equipment, backup supply, and maintenance services. Each of its three strike forces has 30 people, comprising a Command Section and five Special Tactical Sections (which are composed of four people and an officer)—the five-person stick.

Selection for those interested in becoming GSG-9 members is demanding. All recruits must be volunteers and all must come from the Bundesgrenzschutz, according to the strict charter written for this unit. Members of the German army who seek to become a part of GSG-9 must first leave the military service and join the Border Police to become eligible. This is similar to the requirement that those seeking to join the SAS must give up their military rank, and start over as a private, in order to be eligible. Thus, each requires that its military recruits sacrifice their military rank in order to become a part of this elite counterterrorist unit.

The first 13 weeks of the 22-week-long training course is devoted to learning the fundamentals of counterterrorism and police operations, including a serious amount of academic study. This group differs from the Sayaret Mat'kal, the SAS, and Delta Force in its unique training in knowledge of the law, particularly as that law pertains to counterterrorism operations. Members of GSG-9 are more conscious of the law, and of their need to stay within its boundaries as far as possible, than are other similar strike forces.

This does not mean that GSG-9 does not train its personnel in active counterterrorism techniques. The last part of the 22-week training course is devoted to specialization of operator skills and advanced antiterrorist studies. In fact, Germany's elite force has one of the most sophisticated arsenals in the world. Because the deplorable marksmanship at Fürstenfeldbrück Airport demonstrated the need for training in this field, every person in GSG-9 is taught to be an expert marksman, proficient in the use of the Mausser 66 sniper's rifle, equipped with infrared sights and light intensifiers for night shooting. Like the SAS, they favor the Heckler and Koch MP5s for their routine work, but they are also armed with .357 Magnum revolvers.

An attrition rate of 80% is not uncommon for the volunteers seeking to join GSG-9. However, some graduates do excel, and some are sent to attend NATO's International Long Range Reconnaisance Patrol (LRRP) School located in Weingarten, Germany.

Because they are required to be able to reach any part of Germany within two hours, ready for action, units are supplied with Mercedes-Benz autos of special design and BO-105 helicopters. The units are trained to descend from hovering helicopters, via special ropes. The troopers enjoy the full support of the government when it comes to their equipment. As such, they are issued not one, but two complete sets of combat gear, one tailored to daytime operations and one for use at night. GSG-9 has its own aviation unit, known as Bundesgrenzschutz Grenzschutz-Fliegergruppe.

GSG-9 units spend a great deal of time studying the origins and tactics of known terrorists to determine how best to defeat them. Every member of a team learns such useful tricks as how to pick locks and how to handle airport equipment, to facilitate efforts to mount successful attacks against terrorists who have hijacked an airplane.

This elite force practices assault on hijacked airliners, training on mock-ups of aircraft and sometimes on aircraft on loan from Lufthansa. Such training stood them in good stead in MOGADISHU in 1977, when Zohair Akache's terrorist team hijacked a Lufthansa Boeing 737 with 82 passengers, in support of the Baader-Meinhof gang. GSG-9 successfully stormed the airliner and rescued all of the hostages without harm. An excellent example of careful planning and execution, in which no laws were broken and no unnecessary injuries to innocent persons occurred, with both hostages and plane recovered intact, this was a vindication of Germany's developing counterterrorism (CT) expertise.

Unlike many other CT units, GSG-9 members are not required to leave the unit after a set period of time or upon reaching a certain age. Instead, members are allowed to stay as long as they are able to maintain the group's high standards of performance. This policy has allowed the lessons learned by the senior operators to be passed down to newer members, so that mistakes need not be repeated by each successive year's recruits. Germany clearly takes its investment in this unit quite seriously, as it provides them with excellent equipment, a virtually unlimited supply of training munitions, and the flexibility to operate, within the law, without unnecessary bureaucratic interference.

GSG-9 has first access to one of the most sophisticated antiterrorist intelligence operations in existence today. In Weisbaden, a computer nicknamed the KOMMISSAR, controlled by the Federal Criminal Investigation Department (BKA), with an incredible database of information about known terrorists. By using this database, called PIOS (Personnen, Institutionen, Objekte, Sachen), GSG-9 has been able to work with TARGET SEARCH TEAMS to locate and arrest terrorist cells throughout Germany and much of Europe.

A brief look at several incidents give evidence of the challenges faced by this CT unit:

- In June 1994, German CT police attempted to apprehend RED ARMY FACTION leader Wolfgang Grams. Gunfire was exchanged, and Grams was killed (although later reports suggested that his death may not have occurred in the gun battle but after he was subdued by GSG-9 members). Retaliation for this arrest/shooting was carried out by an offshoot group, AIZ, which firebombed the home of a GSG-9 member. Since all personal information about the identities of GSG-9 members is classified top secret, the ability of AIZ to locate such a target indicates that the RAF/AIZ may have had an "inside" source of help.
- In July 1994, a KLM flight from Tunis to Amsterdam was hijacked by a single terrorist who demanded the release of Sheikh Omar Abdel Rahman, who was at that time being held in New York in connection with the WORLD TRADE CENTER BOMBINGS. GSG-9 managed to subdue the lone hijacker without firing a shot.

GSG-9 no longer carries out activities involving terrorist situations outside of German borders. Reclaiming, in some respects, its original role from which its name derived—Border Protection Group 9—GSG-9 operates internally today, carrying out roles similar to that of the FEDERAL BUREAU OF INVESTIGATION's Hostage Rescue Team, responding to terrorism only when it occurs within Germany's borders. Their Target Search Teams and their spectacular rescues offer excellent examples of counterterrorism successfully carried out within the borders of the law.

See also MUNICH MASSACRE OF ISRAELI ATHLETES.

Guatemala *See* OVERVIEW OF TERRORISM, BY REGION.

guerrilla warfare

Since the French Revolution, terrorism and guerrilla warfare have become increasingly difficult to separate clearly. Guerrilla warfare is, essentially, an insurrectionary armed protest, implemented by means of selective violence. To the extent that the violence remains "selective" and the choice of targets military rather than civilian, it is possible to distinguish between guerrilla warfare and terrorism.

The term *guerrilla,* meaning "little war" evolved from Spanish resistance to the invasions of Napoleon in 1808. This war on the Iberian Peninsula, in which Spanish "guerrillas" were aided in making increasingly successful attacks on French encampments by the British military, has become in some measure a prototype for the 20th-century wars of national liberation. In such contemporary struggles, indigenous vigilante groups are often supported openly (as were the Spanish) or covertly, by the military of other nations.

Ideology and nationalism combined with terror-violence in the INTERNAL MACEDONIAN REVOLUTIONARY ORGANIZATION (IMRO), a group that made its first appearance in 1893. For several years the IMRO waged guerrilla warfare, sometimes employing terrorist tactics, against the Turkish rulers of their region. As in the Iberian conflict, other nations both assisted and interfered in the struggle. Bombings and kidnappings, as well as the murder of civilians and officials, were frequent in this "little war." Violence escalated into the "Saint Elliah's Rebellion" in August 1903, which was dealt with ruthlessly by Turkish authorities. This struggle left thousands dead on both sides, at least 70,000 homeless, and 200 Macedonian villages in ashes.

Turkey's suppression of similar nationalist struggles on the part of its Armenian population in the early part of the 20th century helped to create Armenian groups willing to engage in terrorist activities for the remainder of the century. These activities, which include bombings and murder reminiscent of the IMRO, were directed less by nationalism than by a desire for revenge for the ruthless suppression of that earlier nationalism. In this case, savagely suppressed nationalism has spawned vengeful "terrorism" by individuals and groups whose demands are perhaps even harder to satisfy than were those of the nationalists of earlier decades.

Events in the 1990s in the former Yugoslavia give credence to the concept that repressed nationalism can, in a resurgent form, exact a bloody toll on innocent civilian populations. In the turbulent years before the outbreak of World War I, the Balkan states were engaged in a wide variety of revolutionary violence. Brigands, calling themselves Comitatus ("Committee Men"), covertly sponsored by Greece, Serbia, and Bulgaria (which was also involved in the IMRO struggles), roamed the countryside. In the worst, not the best, tradition of revolutionaries, these brigands terrorized their own countrymen, burning, murdering, and robbing all who stood in their way. The destruction and genocidal murders that took place in the Balkans in the 1990s parallel, and even exceed, this pattern.

World War I was triggered by a transnational assassination that had its roots in guerrilla warfare that led to revolutionary terrorism. A secret Serbian organization, popularly known as the BLACK HAND, was both an organization employed by the Serbian government as an unofficial instrument of national foreign policy and a lethal weapon of political protest against the Austro-Hungarian Empire. On June 28, 1914, a 19-year-old Serbian trained by the Black Hand murdered the heir to the imperial throne of that empire, Archduke FRANZ FERDINAND, in Sarajevo. This assassination was the catalyst for a series of events that, within a month's time, grew into a global conflagration. Revolutionary terror-violence triggered international devastation on a scale unprecedented at that time. Conflict in and around Sarajevo in the 1990s is partially explained, too, by this early pattern of guerrilla warfare that spawned revolutionary terror-violence. At least twice within the 20th century, revolutionary terror-violence has been unleashed by groups, governments, and militias against a civilian population. This type of violence makes reconciliation extremely difficult, if not impossible, to achieve. Memories of violence against women and children within families are hard to relinquish, and repetition of such violence within less than a century makes the creation of a sense of common identity (nationalism) and reconciliation between populations within that region perhaps an impossible goal.

Revolutions are not by definition terrorist events. Indeed, some have been successfully carried out without resorting to terrorist tactics. It is increasingly difficult, however, for an untrained and sparsely equipped indigenous army to wage a successful "guerrilla war" against a national standing army. With mounting frustration in the face of apparently insurmountable odds, it is increasingly easy to resort to terror-violence to achieve by psychological force what it is not possible to achieve by force of arms.

The evolution of revolutionary violence into terrorism is significant. It has long been a stumbling block in the creation of effective international law concerning terrorism. Revolutions have occurred throughout history without recourse to terror-violence; there needs to be an effort made to understand why such revolutions do not continue to occur without the use of terrorist tactics. Do they not occur, or can they not occur *successfully* without the use of terrorism?

As noted earlier, although rebellion cannot be separated from violence, certain types of violence have not been acceptable. Violence that is directed deliberately against innocent parties is destructive not only of law and legal systems but also of civilized society.

As the United Nations Secretariat, in its study of the nature and causes of terrorism, concluded, "The legitimacy of a cause does not in itself legitimize the use of certain forms of violence, especially against the innocent." Paragraph 10 of the Secretariat's study notes that this limit on the legitimate use of violence has long been recognized, even in the customary laws of war.

There are two points here worth noting. One is that the community of nations regards the limits on the legitimate use of violence as being of long standing, not the product of 20th-century governments seeking to prevent rebellions. Although many nations have come into being during this century through both rebellion and peaceful decolonization, the customary laws restraining the use of force were not created to harness this explosion of nationalism.

The second point is that the community of nations, not just in the Secretariat's report but in many documents and discussions, has agreed that there are in fact limits to the legitimate use of violence, regardless of the justice of the cause. Moreover, these limits are acknowledged to exist even in times of war. Indeed, it is from the laws of war that we obtain our clearest understanding of precisely what these limits on the use of violence are.

Therefore, a condemnation of "terrorism" is not a denunciation of revolutionaries or guerrillas. It is only a reiteration of the limits of violence that a civilized society is willing to permit. It does not in any sense preclude the right to revolution, which is a recognized and protected right under international law.

References: Beckett, I. F. *Modern Insurgencies and Counter-Insurgencies: Guerillas and Their Opponents since 1750* (Philadelphia: Taylor & Francis, 2001); Joes, Anthony James. *America and Guerilla Warfare* (Louisville: University Press of Kentucky, 2000).

Guzmán, Abimael

See SENDERO LUMINOSO.

H

Habbash, George *See* POPULAR FRONT FOR THE LIBERATION OF PALESTINE.

Haganah

Haganah is the Hebrew word for "defense." During the prestate period (roughly 1918–1948) in PALESTINE, the Jewish community determined by the early 1920s that some sort of armed military was necessary for security. By that time anti-Jewish riots in Palestine had begun to occur with disturbing frequency. The British, who controlled Palestine during this period, discouraged and often banned outright the acquisition of arms and weapon training within the Jewish community. Many Palestinian Jews, however, secretly acquired weapons from a variety of sources, including a few sympathetic British officers.

The Haganah became the predecessor of the IDF (Israel Defense Forces) or the Israeli army. Many of Haganah's officers, for example, quickly assumed high rank with the IDF in 1948 when Israeli statehood was declared. As the end of the British Mandate approached, the Haganah became bolder and attacked or occupied military positions as they were evacuated by the British. The Haganah also initiated retaliatory attacks on Arab marauders who had assaulted Jewish settlements. Many of the Haganah's officers as well as rank-and-file soldiers also gained experience during World War II when they served under British command, especially in North Africa. Some of its personnel even served as Allied spies in German-occupied Europe.

It is important to point out that the Haganah was intended to become the Israeli army from its beginnings. Other and smaller military units such as the IRGUN ZVAI LEUMI and the STERN GANG were disbanded after Israeli statehood became a fact. The first Israeli prime minister, David Ben-Gurion, insisted that the state's integrity would be compromised if military organizations were allowed to function independently of legal authority. Indeed, for a moment, there was even the possibility of conflict between the Haganah and Irgun. The potential was not resolved until the Israeli government successfully ordered Irgun's dissolution. Its leaders and members then went into politics and for much of Israel's early history functioned as the parliamentary opposition.

Reference: Slann, Martin. "Tolstoyan Pacifism and the Kibbutz Concept of *Haganah Azmit* [Self-defense]," *Reconstructionist* 44, no. 7 (November 1978): 13–21.

Haiti

Still one of the poorest countries in the Western Hemisphere, Haiti has been plagued by political violence for most of its history. For more than three decades, Haiti suffered under the dictatorship of François "Papa Doc" Duvalier, elected president in 1957. He organized a private military force, the Tontons Macoutes, to subdue his opponents through terrorist tactics. The elder Duvalier ruled as a dictator until his death in 1971, and he was succeeded by his son, Jean-Claude "Baby Doc" Duvalier.

Under Baby Doc's rule, Haiti's gross economic inequalities, political repression, and corrupt government continued until, in 1986, popular unrest became so strong that Jean-Claude went into exile. His regime was followed by military rule, which ended in 1990 when Jean-Bertrand Aristide was elected president. Most of his term was usurped by a military takeover, but he was able to return to office in 1994 and oversee the installation of a close associate to the presidency in 1996.

Aristide was reelected in 2000 but was expelled from office and left the country, with the assistance of the United States, after an uprising in 2004. In spite of the continued presence of United Nations troops, the cities in Haiti are rife with violence, with gunshots being exchanged throughout the night in some areas. Volunteers with agencies such as Doctors Without Borders have described Port-au-Prince and other cities as "war zones," with most of the casualties being women and children who are often treated in hospitals where bullets continue to pound the walls and come through the windows.

Reference: Diebert, Michael. *Note from the Last Testament: The Struggle for Haiti* (New York: Seven Stories Press, 2005).

Hamas

Hamas is an Arabic acronym for "resistance movement." More precisely, Hamas is a resistance organization to both the state of ISRAEL, which Hamas refers to as the Zionist Entity, and to the Israeli-Palestinian peace process, which Hamas argues is a betrayal of the Palestinian people. Hamas has referred to the Zionist ideology that calls for a Jewish state as racist and nationalist, which is determined to oppress the Palestinian people.

Hamas endorses the practice of martyrdom in which recruits (some as young as 13 years) are encouraged to sacrifice themselves in the effort to destroy the enemies of Islam. Successful martyrs are told to expect to enter Paradise immediately. Several Hamas members became suicide bombers during the middle 1990s by blowing themselves up in crowded Israeli buses. In 2001 a new and even more lethal series of Hamas suicide bombers helped to at least temporarily blunt the Israeli-Palestinian peace process.

Persuading Palestinians to support and become members of Hamas is facilitated by the economic and social conditions many regard as deplorable. The Israeli-Palestinian peace process has gone forward as living standards in the West Bank and Gaza Strip have deteriorated. Young Palestinians grow up entirely under an Israeli military occupation they find onerous and oppressive. Many of them regard the Palestinian Authority (PA) under YASIR ARAFAT to be corrupt. They also believe that PA negotiators have been too eager to compromise with Israel and have conceded too much territory. Much of the membership and leadership of Hamas assumes that Israel should not exist at all and consider the PA to be traitors to both Islam and the Palestinian cause. Thus, much of the violence perpetuated by Hamas is against the PA as well as against Israeli targets.

Hamas is fairly loosely structured, with some elements working clandestinely and others working openly through mosques and social service institutions to recruit members, raise money, organize activities, and distribute propaganda. It has also built support by investing some of the funds raised in social and economic development projects for the Palestinians in the occupied territories. Although it continues to receive some funding from Iran, it primarily relies for support on donations from Palestinian expatriates from around the world and private supporters in moderate Arab states.

Hamas (Harakat al-Muqawama al-Islamiyya) won 74 of 132 seats in the January 2006 Palestinian legislative election, making it the majority party of the Palestinian Legislative Council. After Hamas took control of the legislature, the Palestinian territories experienced a period of sharp internal conflicts, as the members of the PA, many of whom were members of Fatah, struggled with the transition of power. An elevator bomb attack on May 20 on the Palestinian intelligence chief by Hamas militants, preceded as it was by a threat on a Hamas radio channel to kill Abu Rajab, was unsuccessful, killing security guards but not Abu Rajab, who was rushed to a hospital in Cairo. The conflict between

Wearing hoods and bomb vests and carrying cut-outs of AK-47s, children parade at a Hamas rally in Gaza City. (CORBIS)

Fatah and antagonists in Hamas grew increasingly bloody, with more than two-dozen security personnel killed in the following month.

Israeli prime minister Ehud Olmert subsequently approved the shipment of small arms—reportedly hundreds of American-made M-16 rifles—from Jordan to President Mahmoud Abbas's Force 17 guards, in an effort to strengthen Abbas as he sought to cope with Hamas militants. The action may have had at least two unintended consequences: announcement by Israel of the arms sale depicted Abbas as an "Israeli collaborator" to the some of the Palestinians of Gaza, and the black-market purchase of the M-16s rose from $5,000 to $10,000, with arms dealers claiming that "Hamas [is] buying like crazy."

Militants tunneled under the Gaza/Israel border and attacked an army post on June 25, killing two soldiers and capturing a third. On Thursday June 29, Israeli forces rounded up dozens of Palestinian Cabinet ministers and lawmakers from Hamas, including the deputy prime minister, Nasser Shaer, in an effort to pressure the militants to release the captured Israeli soldier. The mayor of the West Bank town of Qalqiliya and his deputy were also detained, as members of Hamas. Israeli tanks and bulldozers moved into northern Gaza in the largest military operation in the year following its pullout of the territory. Artillery barrages and multiple air strikes occurred over the next two days, as Israel demanded the return of its soldier and the cessation of the firing of homemade rockets at Israeli communities around Gaza. Anger at support for Hamas from Syria led to the incursion of Israeli warplanes over Syrian airspace, buzzing the seaside home of Syrian president Bashar Assad.

Heavy shelling around Gaza's airport and Israeli missile attacks on alleged Hamas training camps and a rocket-building factory had less serious impact on the community than did the bombing of critical infrastructure, including roads, bridges, and the electric power plant and the water supply system. A humanitarian crisis emerged in Gaza, as the loss of transit, fresh food and water, and medical supplies crippled the territory. The Hamas-led government's information ministry warned of "epidemics and health disasters" because of damaged water pipes to central Gaza and the lack of power to pump water.

Israeli prime minister Olmert threatened harsher action to free the Israeli soldier, refused to negotiate with the militants, and rejected the demand for a "prisoner exchange"—freeing Palestinian prisoners held in Israeli jails in return for the Israeli soldier. He denied that there was a plan to reoccupy Gaza. Abbas, the Palestinian president, deplored the incursion into Gaza as a "crime against humanity." Efforts by Assad to persuade Hamas to free the soldier were ineffective.

References: National Memorial Institute for the Prevention of Terrorism (MIPT). Group Profile. "Hamas." Available online. URL: http://www.tkb.org/Group.jsp?groupID=49. Accessed February 15, 2006; Sela, Avraham. *The Palestinian Hamas* (New York: Columbia University Press, 2000).

Harakat al-Shuhada'a al-Islamiyah (a.k.a. Islamic Martyrs' Movement)

In May 1998, Abdallah Ahmad, spokesman for the Harakat al-Shuhada'a al-Islamiyah (Islamic Martyrs' Movement [IMM]) claimed responsibility for an assassination attempt that injured Mu'ammar al-Qadhafi and killed four of his guards. Although the Libyan government denied that any attack took place, Qadhafi canceled his planned trip to Egypt. The group reportedly used machine guns to open fire on Qadhafi's motorcade as it was crossing at the border between Libya and Egypt.

Known to be active in the al-Jabal al-Akhdar region along the caves on the Egyptian border, Harakat al-Shuhada'a al-Islamiyah has waged an ongoing, low-intensity conflict with the regime for several years. Clashes between Qadhafi's forces and the group have occurred there in the past, as the group has made use of the many caves in that region. Its members are thought to consist largely of Libyan veterans of the Afghan war who are unhappy with their limited economic opportunities and Qadhafi's rule. In 1997, Ahmad denied rumors that the Islamic Martyrs' Movement was planning to merge with the Libyan Militant Islamic Group (MIG), but he confirmed that the IMM's emir, Abu Shaltilah, had met with Abd al-Rahman al-Hattab, the MIG's emir, to discuss the possibility. Harakat al-Shuhada'a al-Islamiyah opposes the government of Mu'ammar al-Qadhafi, seeking to oust the Libyan leader in favor of an Islamic republic.

Reference: National Memorial Institute for the Prevention of Terrorism (MIPT). Group Profile. "Harakat al-Shuhada'a al-Islamiyah." Available online. URL: http://www.tkb.org/Group.jsp?groupID=3605. Accessed February 15, 2006.

Harakat ul-Jihad-i-Islami/Bangladesh (HUJI-B)

HUJI-B, led by Shauqat Osman, has sought to establish Islamic rule in Bangladesh. This group has links to the Pakistani militant groups Harakat ul-Jihadi-Islami (HUJI) and HARAKAT UL-MUJAHIDIN. The groups advocate similar objectives in Pakistan and in the disputed areas of Jammu and Kashmir.

Members of HUJI-B were accused of stabbing a senior Bangladesh journalist in November 2000. The group was suspected of responsibility in the July 2000 assassination attempt of Bangladesh's prime minister, Sheikh Hasina. It maintains at least six training camps in Bangladesh for its members and receives funding primarily from madrassas in Bangladesh, although its ties to militants in Pakistan may provide alternative sources of funding for the activities of its estimated several thousand members.

References: National Memorial Institute for the Prevention of Terrorism (MIPT). Group Profile. "Harakat ul-Jihad-i-Islami/Bangladesh (HUJI-B)." Available online. URL: http://www.tkb.org/Group.jsp?groupID=4404. Accessed February 15, 2006; Riaz, Ali. *God Willing: The Politics of Islamism in Bangladesh* (Lanham, Md.: Rowman & Littlefield Publishers, 2004).

Harakat ul-Mujahidin (HUM)

The Harakat ul-Mujahidin is, in many respects, a constantly shifting alliance/splintering of Muslims dedicated to both the linking of the state of Kashmir to Pakistan and to the struggle of Muslims in Afghanistan with first the Soviet Union and then the United States. It is made easier to understand by separately identifying the elements that have been, and in many cases continue to be, distinct parts of this coalescing group.

Harakat ul-Jihad-i-Islami

Harakat ul-Mujahidin emerged initially as the Harakat ul-Jihad-i-Islami (HUJI, or Movement of Islamic Holy War), a Sunni extremist group that followed the Deobandi tradition of Islam. HUJI was founded in 1980 in Afghanistan to fight in the JIHAD against the Soviet Union. The group was affiliated with the Jamiat Ulema-i-Islam Fazhur Rehman Jalili faction and the Deobandi school of Sunni Islam. Led by Qari Saifullah Akhtar and chief commander Amin Rabbani, HUJI was primarily composed of Pakistanis and foreign Islamists fighting for the "liberation" of the Indian regions of Jammu and Kashmir and for their accession into Pakistan.

Harakat ul-Mujahidin

Harakat ul-Mujahidin (HUM) split from the HUJI under the leadership of Fazhar Rehman Khalil, whose association with OSAMA BIN LADEN shifted the focus of the group's activities from Kashmir to Afghanistan. Khalil signed his fatwa in February 1998, calling for attacks on the United States and Western interests. HUM operated training camps in eastern AFGHANISTAN and suffered extreme casualties in the U.S. MISSILE STRIKES on Bin Laden–networked training camps in Khowst in August 1998. Fazhar Rehman Kahlil stated, after these attacks, that HUM would take revenge on the United States.

Khalil resigned as HUM emir in February 2000, turning the reins over to the popular Kashmiri commander (who was also his second in command) Farooq Kashmiri. Khalil then assumed the position of HUM secretary-general. HUM operated training camps in eastern Afghanistan until Coalition air strikes destroyed them during the fall of 2001. In 2003, HUM assumed the name Jamiat ul-Ansar (JUA) and was banned by Pakistan in November of that year.

This group conducted several operations against Indian troops and civilian targets in Kashmir. It has also been linked to the Kashmiri militant group al-Faran in the kidnapping of five Western tourists in Kashmir in July 1995. One of these tourists was killed in August of that year, and the remaining four were reportedly killed in December 1995. HUM was responsible for the hijacking of an Indian airliner on December 24, 1999, which resulted in the release of Masood Azhar, an important leader in the former Harakat ul-Ansar imprisoned by India in 1994, and of Ahmed Omar Sheik, who was convicted of the abduction/murder in early 2002 of U.S. journalist Daniel Pearl.

HUM lost a significant portion of its membership in defections to the JAISH-E-MOHAMMED (JEM) in 2000. Most of the activities of this group took place in Kashmir. While it was based in Muzaffarabad, Rawalpindi, and several other towns in Pakistan, it generally trained its members in Afghanistan and Pakistan and conducted most of its activities in Kashmir. It also received support in the form of donations from Saudi Arabia and other Persian Gulf and Islamic states. The sources of this group's military funding are not clear. However, in anticipation of asset seizures in 2001 by the Pakistani government, HUM withdrew funds from bank accounts and invested in legal businesses, such as commodity trading, real estate, and production of consumer goods. Its fund-raising in Pakistan was constrained when the government increased pressure on extremist groups and began freezing terrorist assets.

Harakat ul-Ansar

Hurakat ul-Ansar (HUA) was formed in October 1993 by the merging of the two groups described above—HUJI and HUM. An Islamic militant group based in Pakistan, Harakat ul-Ansar operates primarily in the disputed region of Kashmir. The HUA, in its merged form, has carried out a number of operations against Indian troops but has also attacked civilian targets in Kashmir. Through its merger with Harakat ul-Mujahidin, it has been linked to the kidnapping of five Western tourists in Kashmir in July 1995, all reportedly killed by the end of that year.

Pakistani intelligence reports that Harakat (all merged segments) commands at least 500 well-trained militants. However, most of the HUA commandos have gone underground since the U.S. administration labeled Harakat a terrorist group in 1997. Although this prompted Pakistani security agencies, which covertly have backed Muslim insurgents in Kashmir, to distance themselves from Harakat, Pakistan has not cracked down on the group's militant activities in Kashmir, concerned that there might be a backlash against Pakistan from Islamic fundamentalist groups. In fact, in the summer of 1994, Pakistan's Inter Services Intelligence organized 13 leading organizations into the United Jihad Council (Muttahida Jihad Council, or MJC) under Commander Manzur Shah, leader of Jamiat-ul-Mujahedin. The MJC includes Harakat ul-Ansar, HIZB UL-MUJAHIDIN, Jamiat ul-Mujahedin, AL-JIHAD, al-Barq, Ikwan-ul-Mussalmin, and Tariq-ul-Mujahideen.

The HUA trains its militants in Afghanistan, Pakistan, and parts of Kashmir, and its leadership reportedly worked, as did that of the groups which merged to form it in 1993, with Osama bin Laden. At least seven HUA members were killed and two dozen wounded during the 1998 U.S. attack on Bin Laden's training camps in Afghanistan, as were militant members of LAKSHAR-E-TAIBA and Hizb ul-Mujahidin. The HUA claims to be fighting not only in Kashmir but also in the Philippines, Bosnia, Tajikistan, and the Middle East.

While the HUA collects donations from sympathizers in Saudi Arabia and other Gulf and Islamic states, as well as from Pakistanis and Kashmiris, the precise sources and amounts of the group's military funding remain unknown.

References: Bose, Sumantra. *Kashmir: Roots of Conflict, Paths to Peace* (Cambridge, Mass.: Harvard University Press, 2005); National Memorial Institute for the Prevention of Terrorism (MIPT). Group Profile. "Harakat ul-Mujahidin (HUM)." Available online. URL: http://www.tkb.org/Group.jsp?groupID=50. Accessed February 15, 2006.

al-Hasan, ibn Sabbah (d. A.D. 1124)

The leader of an Islamic sect, Hasan is commonly believed to be the founder of the order known as the Assassins. Having studied theology in the Persian city of Rayy, he adopted the Nizari Isma'ili faith (one of the two divisions in the Shiite faith), became an active believer, and rose in the Isma'ili organizations. In 1076, he traveled to Egypt, returning to Iran about three years later. Upon his return, he traveled widely throughout the land, seeking to convert others to Isma'ili. In 1090, he and his converts took the great fortress of Alamut in Daylam, a province of the Seljuq Empire.

As the leader of a geographically dispersed region linked only by a shared faith, Hasan is believed to have given birth to an order known as the Assassins. After the last siege, he was able to live for many years a fairly aesthetic existence, writing many treatises upon his faith and imposing a puritanical regime on Alamut. For example, when one of his sons was accused of murder and the other of drunkenness, he had them both executed.

His treatises stressed in particular the need to accept absolute authority in matters of religious faith. It is interesting to note that this doctrine remains widely accepted by the contemporary sect of Naziris. Hasan died in 1124 in Daylam, Iran (Persia).

See also BROTHERHOOD OF ASSASSINS.

Hawari Group (a.k.a. Fatah Special Operations Group, Martyrs of Tal Al Za'atar, Amn Araissi, Force 17)

Formed as part of YASIR ARAFAT's FATAH apparatus, the Hawari Group was named for its leader, Colonel Abdallah Abd El Labib, who was commonly known as Colonel Hawari. The colonel died in an automobile accident in May 1991, en route from Baghdad to Jordan. The group has long-standing ties to Iraq, and its membership includes former members of the radical Palestinian 15 MAY ORGANIZATION.

The Hawari Group engaged in attacks in 1985 and 1986, primarily in Europe and often against Syrian targets, although it also targeted Americans. The April 1986 bombing of TWA flight 840 over Greece, which killed four people, was carried out by this group.

According to Israeli Defense Force (IDF) records, when Arafat signed the Oslo Accords and became the leader of the new Palestinian Authority (PA), the Hawari Group—or Force 17, as it was then called, after the death of its leader—became a part of the national security apparatus. In this role, according to IDF allegations, during the second INTIFADA, the group became responsible for a wide range of activities, including acquiring and securing arms shipments for Palestinian armed groups loyal to Arafat, as well as carrying out terror attacks or resisting incursions by Israeli military or police forces into PA territory.

According to records acquired by the IDF in 2002 during Operation Defensive Shield, when IDF forces besieged Arafat and Force 17 in his Muqat'ah compound in Ramallah, PA files recording the continued operations of Force 17 were found. The IDF alleges that the explosion that destroyed the Force 17 camp in Bethlehem in October 2000 was probably an "accident" caused by preparations of the group to prepare an explosive device. The capture of the six members of Force 17 in January 2001 by IDF forces, believed by the Israeli government to be responsible for the shooting deaths of at least seven Israelis in the Ramallah area, including Binyamin KAHANE and his wife, and the killing by gunfire from IDF helicopters of Masoud Ayad (a lieutenant colonel in Force 17) in February 2001 in Gaza, were justified by the Israeli government by documents secured during the Operation Defensive Shield raid in 2002.

heads of state, international law for the protection of

See DIPLOMATIC PERSONNEL AND HEADS OF STATE, AS TARGETS OF TERRORISM.

Hiroshima and Nagasaki, bombing of

A controversial political decision by President Harry Truman was taken after American scientists successfully tested a nuclear device in the New Mexico desert in July 1945. The atomic bombing of the two Japanese cities of Hiroshima and Nagasaki on August 6 and 9 was intended to end the war and avoid an anticipated 500,000 to 1 million American casualties that a land invasion of Japan would have cost. The bombings did end the war but produced a debate that is still revived from time to time.

The questions that characterize the debate have to do with whether the bombings were necessary. Perhaps Japan would have surrendered anyway or perhaps a demonstration of the power of the atomic bomb in an unpopulated area would have produced the desired result. There is no way to be sure, of course. The president never expressed any regrets or doubts. Moreover, the Japanese were warned that they would face prompt and utter destruction if they did not surrender.

The controversy also suggests that the United States visited nuclear terrorism on Japan. The question revolves around whether a state was committing a terrorist act against another state. The loss of life was horrifying, and most of the lives lost were civilian rather than military. But the counterargument is that even more lives would have been lost had the war continued.

Hisba

The institution of *hisba* in Islam is generally understood to involve efforts to ensure correct economic and commercial practices among the Muslim community. Among some societies today, the term has been attached to vigilante efforts by non-state actors to enforce Islamic law, or sharia, in a community. Two examples of the application of this term to terror-related activities suggest the diversity with which the institution of *hisba* is incorporated in secular states.

Nigeria

Islamic fundamentalists in northern Nigeria, in the Hausa-Fullani Islamic community, who have assumed the role of vigilantes, attempting by force to implement Islamic law, have called themselves *Hizba,* suggesting that they see themselves as implementing correct practices among the Muslim community in that region. The government of Nigeria has allowed this region to adopt sharia (Islamic law), permitting states from this region such as Kano to let the Hisba vigilantes reprimand, arrest, and even punish Nigerians who are accused of violating Islamic law.

This state-tolerated terrorism in Kano extends to allowing the Hisba to punish people for selling or drinking alcoholic beverages, soliciting sex (from a prostitute), and for having premarital sex. Since the sharia also dictates a segregation of people by gender, segregation of buses in northern Nigeria is also enforced by the Hisba, with the government's permission. In April 2001, a Hisba gang destroyed hotels in a Christian area of the city of Kano, justifying their violence on the suspicion that the hotel had been selling liquor.

The national leadership in Nigeria has been reluctant to interfere with the actions of the Hisba, since Nigeria has suffered genocidal ethnic conflict (the Biafran war) and is still suffering from considerable ethnic tensions between the Ibo, the Yaruba, and the Hausa-Fullani communities, which have been divided by religion for centuries. The Hisba are able to carry out state-tolerated terrorism in their efforts to enforce the Islamic law, as they understand it.

Pakistan

The parliament in Pakistan entertained a bill called the "Hisba bill" in summer 2005 that former Pakistani prime minister Benazir Bhutto called a bid to copy the policies of the Taliban regime in neighboring Afghanistan. Opponents of the bill claimed that it was designed to set up a moral brigade, a "Hisba," to deny citizens freedoms of choice and to allow the clergy to decide what is "virtuous." Bhutto stated bluntly that the bill was in violation of Islam, since it would encourage Muslims to spy on each other.

The Hisba bill, under consideration at this point but not implemented by the legislature, would also overturn legislation intended to eliminate "honor killings." These killings, called for by the Hisba, are carried out against women whose "honor" has been lost, often by rape but also by premarital sex. Murder of such women, by Hisba in fulfillment of their interpretation of Islam, creates a mood of fear generated by the violence against innocent victims, for social reasons and without legal trial or recourse, making such acts fit the criteria of terrorism. The implementation of such a bill would make the terrorism state-directed.

Reference: National Memorial Institute for the Prevention of Terrorism (MIPT). Group Profile. "Hisba." Available online. URL: http://www.tkb.org/Group.jsp?groupID=3606. Accessed February 15, 2006.

Hitler, Adolf (1889–1945)

A World War I veteran, Adolf Hitler was an early member of a small extremist political party that carried the acronym of Nazi. The party took power in Germany in 1933 and immediately pursued its agenda of rearmament and reversing the losses Germany suffered after World War I. The Germans in the early years of World War II occupied most of Europe, followed a policy of genocide against Jews and other selected victims, and permitted no opposition in or out of Germany to the regime.

Hitler's early political and then military successes won for him a popular base in Germany. He came to power legally, but his success contributed to an invincibility myth that he personally fostered and apparently believed himself. The intoxication of power eventually led to one military disaster after another. As it became increasingly obvious that Germany would lose World War II, Hitler and his closest collaborators denied reality.

The end came during the spring of 1945 after perhaps 60 million people had died. Hitler held on until literally the last week of the war before ending his life in a Berlin bunker. He had created a political movement, an incredibly brutal totalitarian regime that became synonymous with evil and caused the deaths of tens of millions.

Reference: Kershaw, Ian. *Hitler: 1889–1936, Hubris* and *Hitler: 1936–1945, Nemesis* (New York: W. W. Norton, 1999 and 2001).

Hizballah (Hezbollah) (a.k.a. Islamic Jihad, Islamic Jihad for the Liberation of Palestine, Organization of the Oppressed on Earth, Revolutionary Justice Organization, Party of God, Lebanese Hizballah)

This group, formed in 1982 in response to Israel's invasion of Lebanon, is a radical Shia organization with ideological inspiration drawn from the Iranian revolution and the teachings of the late Ayatollah Khomeini. Led by the Majlis al-Shura, or Consultative Council, Hizballah is dedicated to liberating Jerusalem from Israeli rule and to the establishment of Islamic rule in Lebanon. It has actively participated in Lebanon's political system since 1992 and has maintained close ties with Iran. Although Hizballah does not share Syria's secular orientation, the group has been a strong ally of Syria in the region.

Hizballah has a full-fledged military organization numbering in the thousands that was formed in Lebanon and operates in the southern part of the country close to Israel's northern border. Hizballah quickly occupied this area upon the Israeli military's and Southern Lebanese Militia's evacuation in May 2000. Its stated objective is the destruction of Israel.

From its inception, Hizballah received assistance from Iran and has apparently worked with Iran in joint projects, such as the assassination of Kurdish opposition leaders in Berlin in 1992. The relationship with Iran is a logical one, since Hizballah is composed entirely of Shia Muslims. Hizballah receives financial, training, weapons, explosives, political, diplomatic, and organizational support from Iran, with much of the training taking place in Lebanon's Bekka valley. It also receives diplomatic, political, and logistical support from Syria.

Hizballah considers itself at war with the United States and its allies and has been suspected of involvement in numerous terrorist attacks, including the suicide truck bombings of the U.S. embassy and U.S. marine barracks in Beirut in 1983 and the U.S. embassy annex in Beirut in 1984 and the hijacking in 1985 of TWA flight 847. Members of this group also attacked the Israeli embassy in Argentina in 1992 and the Israeli cultural center in Buenos Aires in 1994.

The Hizballah websites are sophisticated and offer chatrooms and propaganda efforts. Moreover, Hizballah also conducts a substantial outreach program to health clinics and schools in Shiite communities. The organization's television station, *al-Manar,* engages in inflammatory rhetoric and reporting in an effort to encourage the intifada, to promote Palestinian suicide operations, and to advocate "death to America."

Hizballah has hard- and soft-liners. A split developed during the 1990s when portions of Hizballah decided to offer candidates for the Lebanese parliament. Hard-liners regarded this activity as a disturbing feature of selling out and as contrary to the effort of jihad, or holy war, against enemies of Islam. In 2003, Hizballah established a presence in Iraq but initiated limited activities.

Hizballah's very success may have blunted its future prospects. Its murder of eight Israeli soldiers and kidnapping of two in July 2006 was branded as irresponsible and even provocative by several Arab governments, including Saudi Arabia (which feared an extension of Iranian radical Shiite influence). Hizballah succeeded in launching a total of around 2,500 rockets into Israel, causing severe dislocations in and flight from northern Israel. Hundreds of thousands of Israeli civilians fled the area for the relative safety of central and southern Israel. Dozens of Israeli civilians, including several of its Arab and Muslim citizens, became casualties.

Israel and Hizballah underestimated each other. Hizballah did not anticipate a ferocious response from Israel, which, it hoped, would agree to a prisoner exchange since Israel had incarcerated hundreds of Hizballah operatives. For its part, Israel did not expect an ability by Hizballah to experience at least partial success in resisting the best-trained and -equipped air force and army in the Middle East. As close observers had pointed out, Hizballah had six years after the Israeli departure from Lebanon in 2000 to "dig in" and build bunkers and tunnels able to withstand heavy aerial bombardment. And while the Israeli government enjoyed, at least initially, widespread support for its policy against Hizballah, this was still an organization that could counter by drawing support not only from Lebanon's substantial Shiite community but also from its Syrian and Iranian patrons. Early on it became clear that the Israeli objective to destroy or at least disarm Hizballah would not be achieved. On the other hand, the objective of Hizballah to terrorize and murder Israelis was also not achieved.

None of this prevented either side from claiming victory. Hizballah had become the only Arab army to stand up successfully to the Israelis. Many Arabs, both Sunni and Shiite and even some Christians, inside and outside of Lebanon, view Hizballah's confrontation with Israel as heroic.

References: Council on Foreign Relations. Terrorism: Questions and Answers. "Hezbollah." Available online. URL: http://cfrterrorism.org/groups/hezbollah.html. Accessed February 16, 2006; Palmer Harik, Judith. *Hezbollah: The Changing Face of Terrorism* (New York: I. B. Tauris Publishers, 2005).

Hizb-I Islami Gulbuddin (HIG)

Founded by Gulbuddin Hekmatyar as a faction of the Hizb-I Islami Party in 1977, HIG was one of the major mujahideen groups involved in the war against the Soviet Union in Afghanistan. From this foundation, it is unsurprising to note that HIG has long-established ties with OSAMA BIN LADEN. In the early 1990s, HIG leader Hekmatyar ran several training camps for terrorism in Afghanistan and pioneered the sending of mercenaries to other Islamic conflicts from these camps. When bin Laden fled Sudan in 1996, Hekmatyar offered him shelter in Afghanistan.

This group has staged fairly small attacks in Afghanistan, focused on forcing U.S. troops to withdraw from the country, the overthrow of the Afghan Transitional Administration, and the establishment of an Islamic state in Afghanistan. Its current strength is uncertain.

Reference: Overseas Security Advisory Council. Profiled Groups. "Hizb-I Islami Gulbuddin (HIG)." Available online. URL: http://www.osac.gov/Groups/group.cfm?contentID=1351. Accessed February 15, 2006.

Hizb ul-Mujahidin (HM)

The largest Kashmiri militant group, the HM was founded in 1989, officially to support the liberation of Jammu and Kashmir from India and the accession of these territories to Pakistan (although some cadres favor independence for the region). This group is the militant wing of Pakistan's largest Islamic political party, the Jamaat-e-Islami. The HM is focused at present on Indian security forces and politicians in Jammu and Kashmir and has conducted operations jointly with other Kashmiri militants.

The HM reportedly operated in Afghanistan during the mid-1990s and trained with the Afghan HIZB-I ISLAMI GULBUDDIN (HIG) in Afghanistan until the Taliban takeover. Its targets have been primarily Indian military personnel and structures in Kashmir, although it has occasionally struck at civilian targets in the region. Efforts to achieve peace in this region in 2005 include attempts to co-opt this group's political agenda.

Reference: National Memorial Institute for the Prevention of Terrorism (MIPT). Group Profile. "Hizbul Mujahideen (HM)." Available online. URL: http://www.tkb.org/Group.jsp?groupID=52. Accessed February 15, 2006.

Holocaust denial

A form of literary terrorism presented as serious scholarship that "refutes" the "myth" of the Jewish Holocaust during the World War II period. The denial can take several forms. One of the most pronounced is that the Holocaust was simply a ruse perpetrated by Zionists after World War II in an attempt to gain sympathy for the Jewish people and to establish Israel. Another is that Jews died in World War II but not to any greater degree than other peoples. They were not singled out for death camps. In fact, the existence of the death camps is also denied. In its most extreme form, the claim is offered that the Holocaust did not happen but should have since Jews caused World War II.

While not a physically violent form of terrorism, Holocaust denial attacks the historical record that has been confirmed by numerous reputable historians and hundreds of thousands of survivors and eyewitnesses as well as by the physical evidence located at the death camps at the end of the war in Europe. Holocaust deniers do have their followers, but their research methods and findings lack all plausible credibility in the scholarly community. Moreover, in several lawsuits the deniers have consistently been on the losing side. This form of literary terrorism attempts to rewrite history for ideological purposes. In doing so, both victims and honest scholarship are insulted.

Some European countries, such as Germany and Austria, have made Holocaust denial a crime punishable by law under "inciting racial hatred." Ernst Zündel, publisher of the Holocaust-denying pamphlets *The Hitler We Loved and Why* and *Did Six Million Really Die?,* was deported from Canada in 2005 back to his native Germany, where he is awaiting trial for Holocaust denial. In 2006, pro-Nazi writer David Irving was sentenced to three years in prison by an Austrian court for giving several speeches in which he denies the Holocaust ever took place. However, some contend that making this type of expression (no matter how hateful) an illegal act is a form of censorship and that the best way to deal with these people is to ignore rather than prosecute them.

Holocaust denial is also rampant in many Middle Eastern countries. In January 2006, the president of Iran, Mahmoud Ahmadinejad, issued invitations to a conference in Tehran to verify that the Holocaust never happened. It is unclear whether any nation will openly attend this meeting.

References: Lipstadt, Deborah. *Denying the Holocaust: The Growing Assault on Truth and Memory* (New York: Plume, 1993); ———. *History on Trial: My Day in Court with David Irving* (New York: HarperCollins, 2005).

Homeland Security, Department of

In June 2002, U.S. president George W. Bush proposed the creation of a Department of Homeland Security (DHS), the most significant transformation of the U.S. government in over a half-century, transforming and realigning the confusing patchwork of government activities into a single department whose primary mission was to protect the U.S. homeland. This new department was designed to help the men and women who daily protect the borders and secure the nation to do their jobs better with increased communication, coordination, and resources. Specifically, the Department of Homeland Security has three primary missions:

- Prevent terrorist attacks within the United States
- Reduce America's vulnerability to terrorism
- Minimize the damage from potential attacks and natural disasters

In order to accomplish these three goals, the department has focused on creating the new capabilities discussed in the July 2002 National Strategy for Homeland Security. This strategy points out that, in 2002, no one single government agency had homeland security as its primary mission. In fact, responsibilities for homeland security were dispersed among more than 100 different government organizations. The new DHS was designed to give state and local officials one primary contact instead of many, an important advantage when it comes to matters related to training, equipment, planning, exercises, and other critical homeland security needs. It was also intended to manage federal grant programs for enhancing the preparedness of firefighters, police, and emergency medical personnel. The DHS also was empowered to set standards for state and local preparedness activities and equipment.

The Department of Homeland Security initially had the following goals:

Awareness—Identify and understand threats, assess vulnerabilities, determine potential impacts, and disseminate timely information to homeland security partners and the American public

Prevention—Detect, deter, and mitigate threats to the homeland

Protection—Safeguard the people and their freedoms, critical infrastructure, property and the economy of the nation from acts of terrorism, natural disasters, or other emergencies

Response—Lead, manage, and coordinate the national response to acts of terrorism, natural disasters, or other emergencies

Recovery—Lead national, state, local, and private sector efforts to restore services and rebuild communities after acts of terrorism, natural disasters, or other emergencies

Service—Serve the public effectively by facilitating lawful trade, travel, and immigration

Organizational excellence—Value the most important resource, the people. Create a culture that promotes a common identity, innovation, mutual respect, accountability, and teamwork to achieve efficiencies, effectiveness, and operational synergies

A six-point agenda for the Department of Homeland Security was initiated to ensure that its policies, operations, and structures are aligned in the best way to address the potential threats—both present and future—that face the nation. The agenda was designed to serve as a guide for the department in the near term and to effect changes that will:

1. Increase overall preparedness, particularly for catastrophic events
2. Create better transportation security systems to move people and cargo more securely and efficiently
3. Strengthen border security and interior enforcement and reform immigration processes
4. Enhance information sharing with the country's partners
5. Improve DHS financial management, human resource development, procurement, and information technology
6. Realign the DHS organization to maximize mission performance

The Homeland Security Act of 2002 (HSA) provides certain flexibility for the secretary of homeland security to establish, consolidate, alter, or discontinue organizational units within the department. The mechanism for implementing these changes is a notification to Congress, required under section 872 of the HSA, allowing for the changes to take effect after 60 days. Currently, the organization includes functional departments in border and transportation security, emergency preparedness and response, information analysis and infrastructure protection, science and technology, management, Coast Guard, Secret Service, citizenship and immigration services, and inspector general.

Tom Ridge was appointed by President Bush as the first director of homeland security; he served in this post until early in 2005, On February 15, 2005, Michael Chertoff was sworn in as the second secretary of the Department of Homeland Security.

References: Council on Foreign Relations. Terrorism: Questions and Answers. "Department of Homeland Security." Available online. URL: http://cfrterrorism.org/security/dhs.html. Accessed February 16, 2006; Homeland Security. Available online. URL: http://www.dhs.gov/dhspublic. Accessed March 7, 2006; Freeman, Mike. "Security, and Event, Will Be Extraordinary." *New York Times* (December 1, 2001).

humiliation

The causes and sources of terrorism are numerous. Many, such as economic deprivation and ethnic discrimination, are tangible. Others are perceived or real injustices that are also intangible. A sense of humiliation is an important aspect that is difficult to measure but is often in ample evidence. Palestinian terrorists, for example, have frequently cited personal experiences of humiliation at the hands of Israeli soldiers who routinely searched them or their relatives at checkpoints. In addition to being a substantial inconvenience, the act of an involuntary physical search can be demeaning to any individual who feels the search is unjustified in the first place. It is possible that, in an effort to prevent terrorist activities, such behavior helps to create terrorists.

Islamic radicals, such as the AL-QAEDA leaders, have publicly cited episodes of humiliation that for them are unforgivable. The American military presence in the "land of the two holy cities" (Mecca and Medina) is considered intolerable and an affront to all of Islam. The Israeli acquisition of Jerusalem's Islamic holy places is another humiliation that cannot be ignored. For organizations such as al-Qaeda, the arrogance revealed by Americans and Israelis must be punished and destroyed.

Most terrorists believe that humiliation can only be eliminated when the dignity of those who are offended and exploited can be restored. Sayyid Qutb, for example, viewed the Crusades of the Middle Ages and current Islamic radicals view the current "New Crusaders," such as the Americans and their European allies, as interlopers on sacred Islamic lands. In Qutb's view, even the cold war was nothing more than a competition between two powers, the United States and the Soviet Union, to occupy and subdue Islamic lands and drain their wealth—in complete ignorance of or interest in the spiritual and cultural heritage of these lands.

Many terrorists see themselves as victims responding with the only means left to them, violence. In this sense, violence becomes a means by which humiliation is purged and overcome. Violence for the terrorist is not simply revenge for real or imagined wrongs; it is a rite of purification that ennobles the victim while overcoming the victim's feelings of subjection.

References: Fanon, Franz. *The Wretched of the Earth* (New York: Grove Press, 1963); Reich, Walter. *Origins of Terrorism: Psychologies, Ideologies, Theologies, States of Mind* (Princeton, N.J.: Woodrow Wilson Center Press, 1998).

Hur Brotherhood *See* BROTHERHOOD OF ASSASSINS.

Hussein, Saddam (1937–2006)

Saddam Hussein took power in Iraq in 1979 as president after serving as vice chairman of the Revolutionary Command Council. The Hussein regime was characterized by the brutal suppression of any opposition, which occasionally came from members of his own family. His power was so consolidated that, even after losing the first Gulf War to the United States in 1991, an international embargo, and the effective loss of the northern third of Iraq to United Nations jurisdiction, Hussein remained in control of the rest of the country. He also relentlessly pursued the building of a chemical and biological arsenal. Some observers believed he was intent on acquiring nuclear weapons as well. Hussein initiated an eight-year-long war with IRAN (1980–88) that cost hundreds of thousands of lives on both sides and achieved no lasting territorial gains for either country. He modeled his police state on that established in the Soviet Union by JOSEPH STALIN, his idol and one of the most murderous tyrants of the 20th century.

Hussein's regime was listed by the U.S. Department of State as a state sponsor of terrorism that emphasized American and Israeli targets. Ironically, two of Hussein's bitterest enemies were Syria and Iran, two other states on the list. Hussein's armed forces committed atrocities against civilian populations by using chemical weapons against the Kurds in the north and the Shiites in the south during various rebellions against the central government. The regime practiced complete denial of human rights. Even to joke about

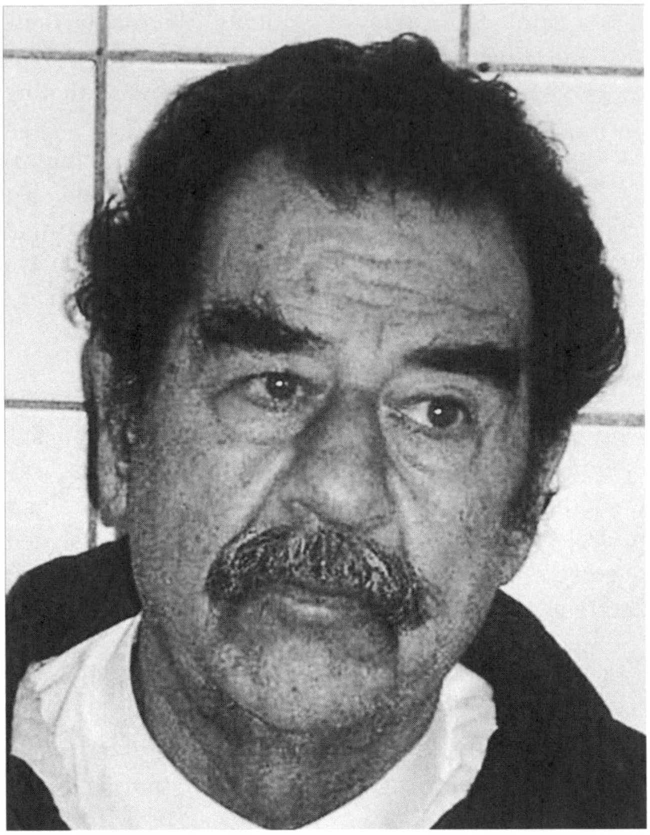

Iraqi dictator Saddam Hussein shortly after his capture in December 2003 (SGT. DAVID BENNETT/U.S. ARMY)

Saddam Hussein or his family members was a punishable offense if overheard by one of several government agencies that regularly spied on Iraqi citizens and one another. Hussein was fond of remarking that he knows when an individual is getting ready to become disloyal before the individual does.

Hussein sustained himself in power by catering to the military, especially the elite Republican Guard units that enjoyed better housing, food, and medical care than the great majority of Iraqis. He was genuinely popular in his hometown of Tikrit and its environs, in part because he took care to provide this critical area of supporters with a viable economic infrastructure. His antagonism toward the United States and refusal to comply with United Nations resolutions eventually precipitated an international crisis.

In March 2003, the George W. Bush administration presented the Iraqi regime with an ultimatum that insisted Hussein and his two sons, Uday and Qusay, leave Iraq within 48 hours. Bush also claimed that Hussein possessed or was building weapons of mass destruction. No evidence of this charge was forthcoming, but military forces headed by the United States and the United Kingdom, with token units provided by other countries such as Italy and Spain, invaded and occupied Iraq. Within a few weeks, the regime had dissolved, and Hussein as well as his top lieutenants became fugitives. Most were caught or, like Uday and Qusay, killed. Hussein himself was apprehended in December 2003. He was in a disheveled state but insisted that he remained the legal head of the Iraqi government. Along with seven others, Hussein was placed on trial in 2005 for the murder of several dozen civilians after an assassination attempt on Hussein nearly two decades ago. He complained in court about mistreatment and torture at the hands of American interrogators. The trial continued through 2006.

On November 4, 2006, Hussein and two codefendants were sentenced to death by hanging. The sentences were immediately appealed, but Hussein was executed on December 30, 2006.

References: Coughlin, Con. *Saddam: King of Terror* (New York: HarperCollins, 2002); Karsh, Efraim, and Isari Rauti. *Saddam Hussein: A Political Biography* (New York: Free Press, 1988); Senate Committee on Foreign Relations. *Iraq: Can Saddam Be Overthrown: Hearing before the Subcommittee on Near Eastern and South Asian Affairs,* 105th Congress, 2d session, March 2, 1998.

I

ideological mercenaries

While there is little doubt that such persons have existed throughout history and have caused a great deal of violence carrying out acts of terror for personal gain, even when they are ideologically drawn to the group or individual hiring them to commit the act, there was an increase in the number of such individuals toward the end of the 20th century. Although the legendary CARLOS "THE JACKAL" (a.k.a. Ilyich Ramírez Sánchez), was clearly one of the best known "terrorists for hire" of that time, he was not the only such mercenary. SABRI AL-BANNA (a.k.a. Abu Nidal) was another such, although, unlike Carlos, Abu Nidal remained at large at the end of the century while Carlos languished in a French prison. The unwillingness of so many nations to harbor Carlos, as his ideological commitment became less believable to leaders in the Middle East, and the intensity with which France sought him might indicate a diminishing political tolerance, and hence a reduced potential for action, for this type of terrorist.

images, held by terrorists

Individuals capable of carrying out terrorist acts have, according to several studies, frequently developed images of themselves, their enemies, and the struggle in which they are engaged. These images make it easier to justify to themselves actions that would otherwise be intolerable by ordinary norms of behavior.

Image of Enemy

One significant component of a terrorist belief system is the image of the enemy. Dehumanization of the enemy is a dominant theme. The enemy is viewed in depersonalized and monolithic terms, as capitalist, communist, bourgeois, or imperialist. It is not human beings whom the terrorist fights; rather, it is this dehumanized monolith.

As Franco Ferracuti and Francesco Bruno noted in their study of aggression in Italy, for many terrorists, "the enemy is nonhuman; not good enough. He is the enemy because he is not the hero and is not friendly to the hero." This rationalization is particularly prominent among right-wing terrorists, whether neofascist or vigilante. Like other right-wing theorists, such groups tend toward prejudicial stereotyping based on class or ethnic attributes. The "enemy" thus might be all journalists, lawyers, students, intellectuals, or professors, who are regarded by such terrorists as leftist or communist. It is easy to make war, even illegal "unthinkable" war, on an "inhuman" enemy. As long as that enemy does not have a face, a wife or child, a home, grieving parents or friends, the destruction of that enemy is a simple matter, requiring little or no justification beyond the enemy status.

Image of Struggle

Viewing the "enemy" in these terms also makes the image of the struggle in which the terrorists see themselves as engaged relatively simple. It is a struggle in which good and evil, black and white, are very obvious to the person carrying out the terrorist act. The "enemy" is often seen as much more powerful in its monolithic strength, with many alternatives for action from which to choose. The terrorists, on the other hand, perceive themselves as having no choice except to resort to terrorism in confronting this "monster," which becomes, in their view, a response to oppression, not a free choice on their parts, but a duty.

Image of Self

Also of interest in this belief system is the terrorists' images of themselves. Terrorists of both the left and right tend to think of themselves as belonging to an elite. Most left-wing revolutionary terrorists view themselves as victims, rather than aggressors, in the struggle. The struggle in which they are engaged is an obligation, a duty, not a voluntary choice, because they are the enlightened in a mass of unenlightened.

Like terrorists of the right, revolutionary terrorists seem to view themselves as above the prevailing morality, morally superior. Normal standards of behavior do not apply to them. They do not deem themselves in any sense bound by conventional laws or conventional morality, which they often regard as the corrupt and self-serving tool of the "enemy." It would be useless to condemn as "immoral" an action by a terrorist since it is likely that the person embracing terrorist tactics has already reached the belief that the morality that would condemn his/her action is inferior to his/her own morality.

Image of Nature of Conflict

This view of morality is integral to the terrorist view of the nature of the conflict in which they are engaged. Not only is this a "moral" struggle, in which good and evil are simplistically defined, but terrorists tend to define the struggle also in elaborately idealistic terms. Terrorists seldom see what they do as murder or the killing of innocent persons. Instead, they describe such actions as "executions" committed after "trials" of "traitors."

MENACHEM BEGIN offered insights into this legalistic rationalization. According to Martha Crenshaw in her study of ideological and psychological factors in international terrorism, Begin noted that in terrorist struggles, "What matters most necessary is the inner consciousness that makes what is 'legal' illegal and the 'illegal' legal and justified."

Images of Victims

Also of importance in understanding the belief system of terrorists is the image that terrorists have of the physical victims of the violence. If the victims are easily identifiable with the "enemy," then as representatives of the hostile forces, they can be despised and their destruction easily justified, even if such victims have committed no clear offense against the terrorist or his/her group. As Michael Collins, founder of the IRISH REPUBLICAN ARMY (IRA), noted with reference to the killing of 14 men suspected of being British intelligence agents, such persons were "undesirables . . . by whose destruction the very air is made sweeter." This remained true, according to Collins, even though not all of the 14 were guilty of the "sins" of which they were accused.

Innocent victims, persons whose only "crime" was in being in the wrong place at the wrong time, are generally dismissed as unimportant by-products of the struggle. "Fate," rather than the acts of people, is often blamed for the deaths of such persons.

Image of Millennium

This brings up one last important point about terrorist belief systems: the predominant theme of millennarianism. Personal redemption through violent means is a millenarian theme found in many terrorist belief systems. Violence is often viewed as being essential to the coming of the millennium, whose arrival may be hastened by the actions of believers willing to violate the rules of the old order in an effort to bring in the new order (often conceived of in terms of total liberation).

Such beliefs have led to a deliberate abandonment of restraints. Coupled with the tendency to divide the world into clear camps of good and evil, as noted earlier, this abandonment of restraints usually entails a strong conviction that no mercy can be shown to the evil that the "enemy" embodies. The terrorist is wrapped in an impenetrable cloak of belief in the absolute righteousness of his/her cause and the ultimate success that will inevitably come. If all violence brings the millennium closer, then no violence, regardless of its consequences, can be regarded as a failure. The terrorist always "wins" in this struggle.

References: Benesh, Peter. "Many Terrorists Are Seduced by Thoughts of Becoming a Martyr." *The Blade* (October 1995); Hoffman, Bruce. *Inside Terrorism* (New York: Columbia University Press, 1998); Jenkins, Brian M. *The Terrorist Mindset and Terrorist Decisionmaking: Two Areas of Ignorance* (Santa Monica, Calif.: Rand, 1999).

immigrants and terrorism

Many workers from East and South Asia as well as from the Middle East and Sub-Saharan Africa have been confronted by violence after their arrival in several European countries. Most of these workers have traveled hundreds or thousands of miles to accept menial jobs in the hope of securing a better economic future for the families they left home. However, several western and central European countries by the middle and late 1990s had double-digit unemployment rates. The rates are especially high among younger people in their late teens and early twenties.

Some of the unemployed (and without the necessary skills, the unemployable) have been attracted to extremist right-wing organizations that cast blame for misfortune on immigrants who take jobs away from the indigenous population. Foreign workers have been beaten up in eastern Germany where the unemployment rate is much higher than in the western part of the country. An element of racism is also present: the attackers are frequently "skinheads" who dress in black leather and shout Nazi slogans, most of which are illegal in Germany.

During the last six months of 2005, France was rocked with violence from immigrants who believed that French law and custom were responsible for their high rates of unemployment and homelessness. The burning of hundreds of vehicles daily resulted in a government-enforced curfew and stringent police action. Ironically, in this situation, the immigrant population was not the target of terrorist attack but may well have been influenced by radical groups to carry out attacks against the government, with little to no loss of life but considerable destruction of property and disruption of the economy.

India

See GANDHI, RAJIV; SIKH TERRORISM.

Indonesia

In 1965 and again in 1998, Indonesians turned violently against the country's Chinese minority. In 1965, a military coup led by Suharto toppled the Sukarno regime that had led the country since political independence and had developed close ties with the Peoples' Republic of China. In 1998, Suharto was overthrown amid accusations of corruption. In both years Indonesians of Chinese ancestry were singled out for persecution and even brutal murders. The Chinese minority comprises no more than 6% of the country's population of over 200 million. However, the Chinese control a disproportionate amount of the country's economy and have not been fully accepted by the majority as fully Indonesian. This puzzles many of the Chinese minority, especially those who have adopted Indonesian names and have converted to Islam, the country's prevailing religion.

It is clear that in both instances, the government did not do very much to protect the Chinese minority from mob violence. There is evidence that the government may have encouraged or sanctioned the violence. Chinese businesses were ransacked, and personal violence and death were visited on their owners. For all practical purposes, the situation of the Indonesian Chinese minority is an example of wanton state terror on a community of people whose ethnic background is distinct from the overall majority of citizens. The 1998 terror, which lasted for only a few murderous days, has been compared to the *Kristallnacht* experienced 60 years earlier by Germany's Jewish minority. The parallel is compelling. In each case, a defenseless and overwhelmingly law-abiding community was victimized by a terror that the state was expected to prevent or to have stopped after it had gotten under way. In each case, the state refrained from doing so. Possibly even worse, no national leader of any political persuasion denounced or condemned the terror.

The Jemaah Islamiya Organization (JI) was responsible for the bombing of the J. W. Marriott Hotel in Jakarta on August 5, 2003, and the Bali bombings on October 12, 2002. The Bali attack, which left more than 200 dead, was reportedly the final outcome of meetings in early 2002 in Thailand, where attacks in Singapore and against soft targets such as tourist spots were also considered. The capture in August 2003 of Indonesian Riduan bin Isomoddin (a.k.a. Hambali), JI leader and AL-QAEDA Southeast Asia operation chief, hurt the organization, but JI maintains the ability to target Western interests in the region. On October 1, 2005, a series of explosions in Bali killed 23 people, including the three bombers. Although the link has not

A Balinese man walks through the rubble at the site of the Bali nightclub that was destroyed by a bomb, 2002. (GETTY IMAGES)

been confirmed, the bombings have the earmarks of Jemaah Islamiya.

See also OVERVIEW OF TERRORISM, BY REGION.

Reference: BBC News. "Bali Terror Attacks." Available online. URL: http://news.bbc.co.uk/1/hi/in_depth/asia_pacific/2002/bali. Accessed February 24, 2006.

innocent person, as target under rules of war

While the laws that govern warfare today are complex, it is possible to find a number of fundamental rules that involve the establishment of minimum standards of behavior, even for parties engaged in hostilities. Of these particular rules of war, perhaps the most significant with respect to terrorism are those that affect the treatment of innocent persons.

This category of persons is an extremely important one for students of terrorism. It is crucial to establish a clear understanding of what is meant by the term *innocent*. Terrorists have claimed that "there is no such thing as an innocent person," yet the Geneva Conventions on the laws of warfare extend special protections to "persons taking no active part in the hostilities."

"Innocence," as it is used by the laws of war, has much the same meaning as that found in any expanded international dictionary definition of the term. In both cases, innocence signifies freedom from guilt for a particular act, even when the total character may be evil. It is in one sense a negative term, implying as it does something less than righteous, upright, or virtuous. Legally, it is used to specify a lack of guilt for a particular act/crime, denoting nonculpability.

Innocence is thus imputed to a thief found innocent of the crime of murder. By this logic, even a government official guilty only of indifference can still be said to be innocent of any crime committed by his government. That official, in other words, has been guilty of nothing that would justify his summary execution or injury by terrorists with a grievance with his government.

This concept of a lack of guilt for a specific act is appropriate in examining the random selection of "any Englishman" or "any Israeli" or "any member of a particular ethnic group" by terrorist groups or states as acceptable targets. If "innocent person" status can be removed only by guilt for a specific act or crime committed by the person (not by others of the same age group, nationality, race, religion, or other similar categories), then there can be no legal justification for such a random selection of targets.

International law neither recognizes nor punishes guilt by association. The records of the Nuremberg trials give credence to this point in terms of the efforts made to establish personal guilt for specific criminal acts (such as murder or torture), instead of prosecuting simply on the basis of membership in the Nazi Party or Hitler's SS troops. In refusing to punish all Germans or even all Nazi Party members for crimes against humanity and crimes of war, the precedent was established for differentiating between a person guilty of committing a crime during times of war and those who were innocent of actual wrongdoing.

The importance of this legal concept of innocence as an absence of guilt for a particular act cannot be overstated. The reason for its significance lies in the justification set forth by modern terrorists for their selection of victims. Many organizations that commit terrorist acts do so on the premise that they are legitimately engaged in seeking to overthrow an existing government or to change existing conditions radically and are thus engaged in warfare.

By accepting, for the moment, this claim to revolutionary action, it is logical to assume that the actions of these groups should still conform to the rules of warfare. Terrorists have rejected the laws of peace as too restrictive to their revolutionary efforts. If the acts are instead tested for legality according to the laws of war as these laws apply to "innocent persons," then the acts of terrorists against such persons are illegal, even during times of war, when much broader parameters for violent action are accepted.

See also GENEVA CONVENTION ON TREATMENT OF CIVILIANS DURING TIMES OF WAR; TERRORISM, WORKING DEFINITION OF.

References: *Convention Related to the Protection of Civilian Persons in Time of War,* U.S.T. 3516, T.I.A.S. No. 3365, 75, U.N.T.S. 287 (1949); Jinks, Derek. *The Rules of War: The Geneva Conventions in the Age of Terror* (Oxford: Oxford University Press, 2007); Huffman, Stanley. "International Law and the Control of Force." *International and Comparative Law Quarterly,* 32 (June 1995).

Internal Macedonian Revolutionary Organization (IMRO)

The IMRO was a secret revolutionary society that operated in the late 19th and early 20th centuries, seeking to make Macedonia an autonomous state. It later became an agent serving Bulgarian interests in Balkan politics in struggles against the Ottoman-Turkish Empire. Founded in 1893, its leaders adopted the slogan "Macedonia for the Macedonians" and carried out a concerted effort to win autonomy for Macedonia from the Ottoman Turks. The IMRO also sought to create a Balkan federation in which Macedonia would be an equal partner with all of the other Balkan states.

The IMRO carried out violent anti-Turkish activities in 1897, staging in 1903 a large but unsuccessful rebellion. After Macedonia was divided between the Turks and the Greeks in the Balkan Wars of 1912–13, the IMRO's bands committed terrorist acts to further Bulgarian foreign policy since this policy sought a redistribution of Macedonia. The IMRO's indiscriminate and unprincipled use of terror, however, alienated its supporters in both Macedonia and Bulgaria.

See also CYCLICAL NATURE OF TERRORISM.

internal terrorism

This form of STATE TERRORISM is practiced by a state against its own people and has produced some of the most flagrant violations of human rights that the world has ever known. No matter how chilling the atrocities committed by individuals or groups, these crimes pale into insignificance compared with the terror inflicted by a state on its own people. Since governments have a much greater array of powers, they are capable of inflicting a much greater degree of terror on their citizens.

A look at casualty figures gives some perspective on the magnitude of the harm states can inflict on their people, compared with the damage caused by nonstate terrorists. In the decade between 1968 and 1978, about 10,000 people were killed worldwide by terrorist groups. In just *one* of those years, 1976–77, the new military dictatorship in Argentina was responsible for almost that same number of deaths.

Levels of Internal State Terrorism

At least three levels of internal state terrorism have been identified as useful gradations in understanding the scope of terrorism practiced by the state. The first is intimidation, in which the government tries to anticipate and discourage opposition and dissent, frequently through control of the media and prolific use of police force. This form of state terrorism has existed in almost every nation-state at some point in its history, most often during times of war. Chile, Argentina, South Africa, and Uganda offered, at several points in the 20th century, excellent examples of this type of internal state terrorism. Coerced conversion, involving government efforts to create a complete change in a national lifestyle, is not unusual in the aftermath of a revolution, as the Soviet Union experienced in the early 20th century and Iran in the 1980s.

Nations in the 20th century have also practiced the third level of internal state terrorism, genocide, the deliberate extermination of an entire class, or the extermination of an entire ethnic or religious group of people, for ideological reasons, while the rest of the "civilized" world watched in horror, disbelief, or studied indifference. Nor was this destruction of innocent persons confined to Nazi Germany or Stalin's Soviet Union. Certain tribes in African nations were all but obliterated by rival tribal leaders who grasped the reins of government. Rwanda, in the mid-1990s, experienced at least one wave of this form of terror. Bosnia in the early 1990s was the scene of mass slaughter of people of one ethnic group by leaders of another. In Argentina, thousands of persons "disappeared" during an oppressive regime.

Examples of Internal Terrorism

State terrorism during the 20th and early 21st centuries was not confined to one nation, nor to one continent. While history is sprinkled with examples of gross state terrorism, such as that practiced by Nero or by the Jacobins during the French Revolution, many modern nations must share the "honors" as terrorist states today.

One of the nations that comes most readily to people's minds when one refers to a modern terrorist state is Nazi Germany (1933–45). ADOLF HITLER moved swiftly after he rose to power to create an authoritarian regime. He suspended all civil rights, eliminated the non-Nazi press, and banned all demonstrations. The Gestapo, his secret police, was given the power to arrest and even to execute any "suspicious person."

Under this regime, in the beginning, thousands of people were imprisoned, beaten, or tortured to death. But this did not end Hitler's terrorism of the remaining population. Instead, borrowing the idea of concentration camps from Russia, he created such camps in Germany and in occupied nations, and he gave the Gestapo the power to send anyone they wanted to these camps, without trial or hope of appeal.

These camps became the instruments for Hitler's "final solution" for ridding himself of all his "enemies." It is estimated that during his 12-year rule of terror, between 10 and 12 million people died. Some were gassed, others hung; some faced firing squads, and countless others died by other equally violent and vicious means. In 12 years, one state murdered between 10 and 12 million innocent people and was responsible, through the war that it initiated, for the deaths of countless more. It is a record of terror almost unparalleled in modern history, even by the most vicious terrorists.

But it is only "almost" unparalleled: the Soviet Union under JOSEPH STALIN was responsible for millions of deaths as well. Only estimates have been given for the number of people who fell victim to Stalin's totalitarian society. By the time of Stalin's death in 1953, scholars have estimated that between 40 and 50 million people were sent to Soviet jails or slave labor camps. Of these, somewhere between 15 and 25 million died there—by execution, hunger, or disease.

In some ways it is more difficult for the world to grasp the magnitude of terror inflicted by such regimes because the numbers are so large and the masses of individuals relatively "faceless." It is possible to identify with Alexander Solzhenitsyn in his description of the terrors of the "psychiatric-ward" prison in his book *The Gulag Archipelago,* but it is difficult to identify with the 25 million who died, unheralded, in the labor camps.

Dictators, as a whole, have found it easier to commit terrorism without world censure than have individuals, for state terrorism is committed, generally, in secret. The shadowy world of internal state terrorism is thus less susceptible to the pressures of world opinion than the activities of terrorist groups, who actively seek this spotlight of global attention.

Cambodia, under the rule of the KHMER ROUGE, illustrates this point. During its rule of less than four years, this systematic terrorism was responsible for more than 1 million deaths. When one notes that there were only about 7 million people in that land, the magnitude of the terror becomes evident. This regime committed genocide against its own people.

Africa has had its share of internal state terrorism, too. Colonial powers used terrorism, often in the form of summary imprisonment and execution, to suppress national liberation movements. But this was not the only form that terrorism has taken in Africa. Uganda, under IDI AMIN, was clearly a terrorist state. Between 1971 and 1979, over 100,000 Ugandans lost their lives to his terrorist acts.

Latin America continues to have regimes that practice terror on their people. At least five nations on this continent—Argentina, Bolivia, Chile, Paraguay, and Uruguay—have suffered under cruel and repressive regimes. In Uruguay, the terrorism instigated by the leftist TUPAC AMARU REVOLUTIONARY MOVEMENT (MRTA) has been repaid a hundredfold by the repressive military regime that came to power in the wake of the collapse of what was, at that time, South America's only democracy.

Argentina suffered under the yoke of a brutally repressive military regime, which finally ended in 1983. Leftist terrorism in that nation provoked a right-wing military-backed response so savage that it staggered the imagination. For a time the press reported the appearance of bodies in ditches and mutilated corpses on garbage heaps and in burned-out vehicles. People "disappeared" by the thousands, abducted by armed men claiming to be members of "security forces." Although the "disappearances" became less frequent as the nation moved toward democracy, the legacy of brutality continues to burden the government in its quest for legitimacy and acceptance.

SADDAM HUSSEIN's regime in Iraq was characterized by the brutal suppression of any opposition, including occasionally from members of his own family. He was able to hold onto power, even after losing the first Gulf War to the United States in 1991, an international embargo, and the effective loss of the northern third of Iraq to United Nations jurisdiction. He also relentlessly pursued the building of a chemical and biological arsenal. Some observers believed he was intent on acquiring nuclear weapons as well. Hussein initiated an eight-year-long war with Iran (1980–88) that cost hundreds of thousands of lives on both sides and achieved no lasting territorial gains for either country.

References: MacKey, Sandra. *The Reckoning: Iraq and the Legacy of Saddam Hussein* (New York: W. W. Norton & Co., 2003); Meredith, Martin. *The Fate of Africa: From the Hopes of Freedom to the Heart of Despair* (New York: Perseus Books, 2003); Overy, Richard. *The Dictators: Hitler's Germany, Stalin's Russia* (New York: W. W. Norton & Co., 2004); Short, Philip. *Pol Pot: Anatomy of a Nightmare* (New York: Holt Rinehart, 2005); Skidmore, Thomas E., and Peter H. Smith. *Modern Latin America* (New York: Oxford University Press, 2004).

International Criminal Court, and crimes of terrorism

The International Criminal Court (ICC), which began to emerge from draft convention to legal body at the end of the 20th century, would, according to the principles put in place in its initial draft code, be able to try individuals rather than merely states for crimes. The International Court of Justice (ICJ) in The Hague was created by states to replace the Permanent Court of Justice at the end of World War II. However, the only actors party to its rules and use are states, not individuals or groups. Thus, in the absence of laws making acts of state terrorism illegal, international law had little remedy for international terrorism. Moreover, even in areas in which law does exist to make illegal such terrorist acts as genocide or aircraft hijacking, no international court existed, prior to the creation of the ICC, to which an individual or state could be taken for committing such a crime. States could, by statute of the court, be taken to the ICJ only by consent, so that if a state committed acts of terror against its own people, it would have to agree to be taken to the ICJ willingly to be held legally accountable. Few, certainly, would ever agree to be tried for crimes against their own people.

As several situations during the last decade of the 20th century demonstrated, the need for a court to deal with such crimes was recognized. The genocide that occurred in Bosnia and Kosovo, as well as that occurring in Rwanda and Zaire, created an intense international awareness of the need for an international court capable of trying individuals involved in these heinous acts of terror. The effort to resolve the issue of responsibility for the explosion of the Pan Am plane over LOCKERBIE also focused attention on the need for an international tribunal with jurisdiction over such crimes. While in each of these cases an ad hoc tribunal was convened eventually, no permanent solution was established.

The ICC was established in 2002 as a permanent tribunal to prosecute individuals for war crimes, crimes against humanity, and genocide, but not specifically terrorism, and was structured to implement the code of law as it is defined by several international conventions and agreements. The primary agreement, detailing the structure of the court as well as the basic premises of law that would fall within its jurisdiction, was the Rome Statute, which, as noted, did not include the crime of "terrorism" in its criminal code.

The ICC has been called upon, however, to deal with acts taken by individuals whose states were involved in the war on terrorism in the context of the war in Iraq, initiated by the U.S.-led coalition in 2003. Nationals of the United States, which is not a party to the ICC statute, were not liable for prosecution by the court for any relevant crimes; but the United Kingdom, Australia, and Poland (U.S. allies in this invasion), were all parties to the Rome statute, making their nations liable for prosecution by the court. Under the statute, U.S. citizens could only be prosecuted by the ICC if the alleged crime took place in the territory of a state party to the statute or if the situation were referred to the ICC by the United Nations Security Council—an unlikely scenario, since the United States has veto power in this council.

In February 2006, the Office of the Prosecutor of the ICC reported that it had received more than 200 communications regarding war crimes allegedly committed during the invasion of Iraq that began in 2003. Responding to these communications, the chief prosecutor reminded those who had sent communications that the ICC could not consider the complaint concerning the legality of the invasion. Although the statute includes the crime of "aggression" as a war crime, Article 5(2) does not allow the ICC to exercise jurisdiction over the crime until a provision has been adopted that both defines "aggression" and the conditions under which the court may exercise jurisdiction concerning alleged acts of aggression.

Charges of torture and torture-deaths have also been raised in the communications sent to the court relating to the invasion of Iraq. None of these which involve American military or security forces are admissable before the ICC, since the United States is not a party to the ICC, but those relating to actions alleged to have occurred in British-controlled areas are within the purvue of the court. However, according to the prosecutor for the ICC, since the information concerning wilfull killing and inhumane treatment identified only between four and 11 victims, the statute does not permit an investigation by the ICC, as the number of victims is less than 20 persons. Although the killing and/or torture of any individual is certainly a crime, the ICC statute Article 8(1) limits involvement by the court until a "grave situation" is determined to exist, and, according to the prosecutor's office, the number of cases does not reach the "gravity" threshold of the statute at this point.

Reference: International Criminal Court. Available online. URL: http://www.icc-cpi.int/home.html. Accessed March 13, 2006.

international terrorist congress

A meeting of terrorists from all over the world to work out agendas and to organize cooperative efforts took place in Frankfurt, Germany, in 1986, reportedly attended by no less than 500 people. Meeting under the slogan, "The armed struggle as a strategic and tactical necessity in the fight for revolution," delegates proclaimed the U.S. armed forces in Europe to be the main enemy. At this congress, it was decided that the correct strategy was to kill individual soldiers in order to demoralize their colleagues and lower their collective capacity to kill.

Among those represented at this congress, or present as guests, were German, French, Belgian, Spanish, and Portuguese terrorists, as well as the PALESTINE LIBERATION ORGANIZATION (PLO), the POPULAR FRONT FOR THE LIBERATION OF PALESTINE (PFLP), the African National Congress, the IRISH REPUBLICAN ARMY (IRA), the TUPAC AMARU REVOLUTIONARY MOVEMENT (MRTA), the Italian RED BRIGADES (BR), and the BASQUE FATHERLAND AND LIBERTY (ETA). Most of the manifestos issued by this congress were basically Marxist-Leninist in style. The congress was financed largely by Libya.

Reference: Lacqueur, Walter. *The Age of Terrorism* (Boston/Toronto: Little, Brown, 1987).

Interpol

The International Criminal Police Organization, or Interpol, as it came to be known, is an organization that exists to facilitate the cooperation of the police forces of more than 125 countries in the struggle against international crime. The aims of Interpol are to promote the widest possible mutual assistance between all the police authorities of the affiliated nations within the limits of the laws existing in those countries and to establish and develop all institutions likely to contribute effectively to the prevention and suppression of ordinary crime.

Interpol's principal target is the international criminal, of which there are three main categories: those who operate in more than one country, such as smugglers, dealing mainly in gold and narcotics and other illicit drugs; criminals who do not travel at all but whose crimes affect other countries, such as counterfeiters of foreign bank notes; and criminals who commit a crime in one country and flee to another. While individuals or groups committing terrorist acts could fit into all three categories, depending upon the type of terrorist crime committed, until the 1990s Interpol was not permitted by its statutes to deal with the crime of terrorism. Cooperative international police efforts since that time to create a data bank, which includes known and suspected terrorists, increased the ability of law enforcement to track down and apprehend persons guilty of crimes fitting the description of international terrorism.

intifadas (Israeli-Palestinian conflict)

By 1987, the Palestinian Arabs of the Gaza Strip and the West Bank had experienced two consecutive decades of Israeli military occupation, beginning in 1967. An entire generation of Palestinians had grown up knowing nothing else except the Israeli presence. While many Palestinians were militant in their strong conviction that Israelis should evacuate the occupied territories, the intifada—uprising or "shaking off"—was in the beginning considerably less violent than the second intifada that began in 2000 and is still continuing. It was also more spontaneous. On December 9, 1987, an Israeli truck collided with two vans containing several Palestinian workers at a checkpoint in Gaza. Four of the Palestinians were killed, and their funerals inspired mass demonstrations in both Gaza and the West Bank.

The Israelis were taken by surprise at both the outbreak of the intifada and its durability. So was the PALESTINE LIBERATION ORGANIZATION (PLO) that was at this time headquartered several hundred miles away in Tunis. Israel closed schools and imposed a curfew on 200,000 Palestinians that was gradually extended to nearly all the Palestinians living in the occupied territories. These actions only increased popular support for the intifada. And Israel was also doing poorly in the area of public relations. By 1987, the news organization CNN was an increasingly visible presence everywhere in the world, and it covered the intifada from the start. The coverage by American and European electronic and print news outlets also encouraged Palestinian youths to turn out into the streets to throw stones and yell insults at Israeli soldiers. The scene of heavily armed Israeli troops confronting stone-throwing Palestinian children armed only with slingshots was disconcerting to many of Israel's allies and supporters.

The PLO had its own problems. While it supported the intifada, it did not control the uprising's participants or their agenda. New organizations were being formed in Gaza and the West Bank that included the Unified National Leadership Command, composed of elements of the PLO but with a strong degree of autonomy from the Tunis leadership. The command issued leaflets, called for demonstrations, most of which were only minimally violent, and overall defiance of the Israeli presence. More ominous for both the PLO and Israel was the emergence at this time of HAMAS, the Islamist organization that was not as hesitant as the mainstream Palestinian leadership in calling for violence against Israeli soldiers and the inhabitants of Israeli settlements in the territories and which urged and activated attacks on civilians within Israel itself.

By the early 1990s, the Israelis and the PLO had finally become convinced that neither could be destroyed by the other. Representatives of the Israeli government and the PLO began to meet secretly in Oslo. The negotiations were remarkable for the fact that they occurred at all. Years earlier, the Israeli parliament had passed a law that sanctioned prison terms for any Israeli caught meeting with PLO personnel. Palestinians who worked with or even were on friendly terms with Israelis were often murdered by the PLO as collaborators. Nevertheless, the Oslo talks ultimately resulted in mutual and public recognition. Some observers felt that both the Israelis and PLO were very concerned that there was a need to preempt the growing appeal of Hamas. Many young Palestinians were increasingly attracted to Hamas's militant stance and regarded the PLO as outmoded and portions of its leadership as corrupt. They believed that the mainstream political organizations over two decades of Israeli occupation had accomplished nothing. The Israelis had not yet evacuated any portion of the occupied territories. There was also a growing degree of weariness on the Israeli side with the military occupation. The political left in particular was uncomfortable with the numerous settlements and increasing Jewish population in the West Bank and Gaza. There is little doubt that this first intifada pushed the peace process along, at least for a short period of time.

The first intifada greatly decreased in intensity after the famous handshake between the Israeli prime minister, Yitzhak Rabin, and the chairman of the Palestine Liberation Organization, YASIR ARAFAT, during a ceremony hosted at the White House in September 1993 by President Bill Clinton. Each side recognized the other's legitimate existence, and the Israelis agreed to eventual Palestinian sovereignty over territories in the West Bank and Gaza.

The old difficulties, however, remained. Israelis remained split over whether to dismantle the settlements, while many Palestinians were reluctant to cede Israel's right to exist. The violence that was to come was hinted at by the assassination of Rabin in November 1995 by a Jewish extremist. His successor and partner in the peace process, Shimon Peres, was defeated the next year by Benjamin Netanyahu, the right-wing Likud leader and former Israeli ambassador to the United Nations, who believed that the Palestinian leadership could not be trusted and that Jewish settlements should not be dismantled. Netanyahu also refused to deal with Arafat, whom he believed to be a terrorist and murderer.

In 1999, Netanyahu was defeated by the opposition Labor candidate for prime minister, Ehud Barak. One issue that worked to Barak's advantage was his promise to withdraw Israeli soldiers from southern Lebanon, an area of about 400 square miles that the Israelis partially controlled for nearly two decades in order to block terrorist attacks into northern Israel. It had become a place where dozens of Israelis lost their lives over the long occupation. The promise was kept, and by the early months of 2000, all Israeli military personnel had been evacuated from southern Lebanon.

Barak then turned his attention to restarting a peace process with the Palestinian Authority that had become dormant under Netanyahu's government. He was encouraged in this effort by President Clinton, still hoping during his last months in office to finalize an Israeli-Palestinian agreement. Barak and Arafat were invited to Washington for talks. To the amazement of most Israelis, Barak offered Arafat nearly everything an Israeli prime minister could offer. Rabin had been assassinated for offering a lot less. The Palestinians would receive all of Gaza and as much as 95% of the West Bank. Barak even conceded the Arab parts of Jerusalem as long as Israelis could retain access to their holy places. To his and Clinton's consternation, Arafat refused the proposal, did not provide a counterproposal, and received the blame from Barak and Clinton for the unsuccessful meeting.

In the meantime, Ariel Sharon helped to precipitate the second intifada when he visited the area in Jerusalem's Old City in September 2000 that is the holiest place in Jerusalem, the Temple of Solomon, and the third-holiest place in Islam, the al-Aska mosque. He was accompanied by about a thousand bodyguards. His and their presence was considered by many Palestinian Muslims to be an intentional provocation. Sharon had a long and established reputation as being a hard-liner when it came to dealing with Arabs. Many Palestinians consider him the architect of or at least complicit in the 1982 massacres by Christian militia in the Sabra and Shatila refugee camps in southern Lebanon. Sharon was the Israeli defense minister at the time and responsible for the Israeli military forces in the area, but he did not act to prevent the Christian outrages against Muslim men, women, and children.

As the second intifada—usually referred to by its proponents as the "al-Aqsa Intifada" to encourage the display of religious passions—got underway during the fall of 2000, the violence increased on both sides. Hamas and ISLAMIC JIHAD both launched numerous suicide attacks against Israeli civilians. Neither age nor gender was a defense against the men and women who were recruited to achieve martyrdom by blowing themselves up in crowded restaurants and buses. In the 2001 elections, Sharon defeated Barak and assumed the prime ministership, an office he had pursued for decades, in great part as the result of the wholesale violence that was by then striking Israelis in their own cities. Sharon's policy of selective assassination of Palestinian extremist leaders in retaliation for terrorist attacks was widely supported by Israelis.

Sharon also authorized the construction of a 125-mile-long fence to separate Israel proper from the West Bank in order to blunt terrorist attacks originating from the West Bank. The fence was viewed by the Palestinians as inimical to the peace process and as a land grab, since an uncertain amount of the West Bank was scheduled to end up on the Israeli side. Ironically, the extremists on the Israeli side viewed the fence no less harshly, believing that Israel was giving up on settlements in the West Bank and ceding land to the Palestinians that should become part of Israel as it was in ancient times. The barrier was immediately denounced by both the Palestinian Authority and much of the rest of the world. The Palestinians were convinced of the Israeli desire to seize more land before any peace settlement could be arranged. Governments elsewhere argued that the existence of the barrier would be detrimental to any peace initiatives.

By the spring of 2003, the United States had made it clear that the Bush administration would not deal with

Arafat and urged the Palestinians to acquire new leadership. Arafat did not step aside as the president of the Palestinian Authority, but he acquiesced to the installation of a prime minister, Mahmoud Abbas, to negotiate with Israel and the United States. Abbas condemned the terrorism visited against Israelis and was able to persuade Hamas and Islamic Jihad to accept a temporary (and tenuous) three-month cease-fire. As of July 2006, the second intifada is not over, and may only be in the midst of a brief interruption.

In one sense, of course, the intifada(s) began at least as far back as 1929, when there were Arab riots against the Jewish community in Palestine, and they have continued intermittently ever since. However one interprets the history of the intifadas, though, there is no doubt that, with each new expression of violence, they have become increasingly lethal. The intifada that began in 2000 is the most violent of all, with a high death toll on both sides mounting almost weekly. This intifada has inspired the Israeli government's controversial decision to construct a security barrier between Israel proper and the West Bank, mostly, but not exclusively, along the Green Line, the de facto border between Israel and the West Bank. By the summer months of 2004, however, the intifada was nearly four years old. Many Palestinians were convinced that thousands of lives had been lost, with little achieved and a depressed economy and greater misery than before the intifada began. Some even blamed the Palestinian Authority for a lack of concern with the plight of the average Palestinian and argued that they were better off when the Israelis were in full control. By 2005, the Israelis had been able to effectively interdict or thwart suicide attacks on civilian targets.

The construction of the security fence between Israel and much of the Palestinian community seriously blunted the ability of Hamas to furnish suicide bombers who were capable of penetrating Israeli cities and towns to detonate themselves. Ironically, though, Hamas itself must have begun to doubt the wisdom of its own violence after the 2006 elections that resulted in its control of the government. The intifada that began in 2000 had to be curtailed in order for Hamas to at least gain the appearance of international respectability and financial assistance. This is not to say that Hamas stopped its violence; in July 2006 it killed several Israeli soldiers and kidnapped one. In turn, the Israelis arrested and incarcerated several Hamas members of the Palestine Authority's Legislative Council and members of the PA's cabinet. The intifada that commenced in 2000 was not necessarily over by 2006, but it had definitely crested and would require a new agenda for it to be resumed. Clearly, it was not achieving its goals.

References: Beitler, Ruth M. *The Path to Mass Rebellion: An Analysis of the Two Intifadas* (Lanham, Md.: Rowman & Littlefield Publishers, 2004). Cleveland, William. *Palestine and the Arab-Israeli Conflict: A History with Documents* (New York: Bedford Books, 2004).

Iran

Iran has the largest population, about 80 million in 2006, of any country in the Middle East. The largest ethnic group in Iran is Persian, comprising about 51% of the population; the second is the Kurdish community. The population has increased approximately 50% since the 1979 revolution ended the monarchy and brought to power a new regime dominated by Shiite clerics. Nearly 90% of Iranians are Shiite, making it the largest Shiite country in the world (about 15% of Muslims are Shiites).

Prior to the revolution, Iran had been considered a close political and military ally of the United States. Led by the AYATOLLAH RUHOLLAH KHOMEINI (1902–89), the clerics departed from this policy and regularly condemned the United States as the "Great Satan" (Israel was simultaneously condemned as the "Little Satan"). Between November 4, 1979, and January 21, 1981, Iran held approximately 50 American diplomatic personnel hostage in violation of international law. During 1980–88, Iran and Iraq fought a war that cost each country thousands of casualties but changed little else.

According to the U.S. Department of State, the Iranian government has also supported international terrorism. Iran remains included on the U.S. list of countries that actively support terrorism. This support has been linked to attacks on American personnel and installations, including the WORLD TRADE CENTER BOMBING in New York City. Iran has also provided assistance to the HIZBALLAH organization's operations in southern Lebanon on Israel's northern border. Both Iran and Hizballah have consistently opposed the Israeli-Palestinian peace process.

According to the U.S. State Department Report, Iran remains an active state sponsor of terrorism. Its Islamic Revolutionary Guard Corps and Ministry of Intelligence and Security have allegedly been involved in the planning and support of terrorist acts and exhort a variety of groups to use terrorism in pursuit of their goals. Supreme Leader Khamenei in 2004 praised Palestinian terrorist operations, and Iran provided Hizballah and Palestinian groups, including HAMAS, the Palestinian Islamic Jihad, the AL-AQSA MARTYRS' BRIGADE, and the POPULAR FRONT FOR THE LIBERATION OF PALESTINE–GENERAL COMMAND, with funding, safe haven, training, and weapons. Iran provided an unmanned aerial vehicle that Lebanese Hizballah sent into Israeli airspace on November 7, 2004. Iran's support for groups and individuals engaging in terrorist violence in Iraq remains an issue of concern, as Iraq's fragile new democracy emerges.

References: Harris, David. *The Crisis: The President, the Prophet, and the Shah* (New York: Little, Brown & Co., 2004); Pollack, Kenneth M. *The Persian Puzzle: The Conflict between Iran and America* (New York: Random House, 2004); Timmerman, Kenneth R. *Countdown to Crisis: The Coming Nuclear Showdown with Iran* (New York: Crown Publishing Group, 2005).

Iraq

About the size of California, Iraq had a population of 26 million people in 2006. The ethnic majority are Arab, at about 75–80% of the total population, and the rest are KURDS, Iraqi Turkmen, and others. Most Iraqis are Shiite Muslims (60%), while the Sunni make up about 35% of the population and are mostly Arabs and Kurds. Iraq is a country in the Middle East that historically has been known as Mesopotamia, the site of the Sumerian culture, the world's first civilization. The Islamic faith made its way into the region around the 7th century B.C.E., and the city of Baghdad became the capital of a great Islamic empire, the Abassid caliphate. In the 13th century this area became part of the Ottoman Empire, until the empire's expiration at the end of World War I, when the British took over the area under a mandate from the League of Nations.

In 1932, Iraq acquired its independence from Great Britain. The British continued to exercise influence until at least 1958, when the Hashemite monarchy they had installed was deposed in a coup. A succession of Arab nationalist leaders followed. SADDAM HUSSEIN took full control of the state in 1979. For several years before, he had, as vice chairman, become the most powerful figure in the country. After he became president, Hussein's security apparatus brutally suppressed any possible or actual opposition.

One Iraqi soldier stands guard as another digs for buried weapons, 2005. (DEPARTMENT OF DEFENSE)

Iraq has over 100 billion barrels of oil reserves. It also possesses an abundant agricultural base, especially the alluvial plain between the Tigris and Euphrates Rivers. Iraq should be a prosperous country. However, during Saddam Hussein's reign, the country was continuously either at war or preparing for one. During 1980–1988 Iraq fought a war with Iran that resulted in a standstill. In 1990 Iraq invaded and occupied Kuwait only to be ejected in 1991 by a military coalition led by the United States. When not fighting outside powers, the Iraqi army regularly attacked the Kurdish community in the northern third of the country and the Shi'ites in the southern third. Iraq was an example of a state terror apparatus that completely and ruthlessly applied all instruments of oppression. Saddam Hussein's presence was everywhere in pictures as large as buildings. Most of his closest aides were family relations.

For nearly a quarter of a century the Iraqi regime was determined to establish the country as a major military presence in the Persian Gulf region. In addition to the attempt to acquire or manufacture nuclear weapons, Hussein built up an arsenal of chemical weapons and used such weapons on rebellious Kurds before the creation of the no-fly zone in the north. These horrific weapons were indiscriminately applied to whole villages and murdered men, women, and children, for the most part noncombatants. The Iraqis also played, with some measure of success, a cat-and-mouse game with United Nations weapons inspectors by moving out of sight banned weapons and even the installations that house them.

In January 2002, President George W. Bush denounced Iraq, Iran, and North Korea as an "axis of evil." Iraq was singled out by President Bush for possessing "weapons of mass destruction" and for harboring terrorists. President Bush urged the UN to pass a resolution that would declare Iraq in material breach of earlier UN sanctions against Iraq for possessing illegal chemical, biological, or nuclear weapons. The Iraqi government denied that it possessed any weapons banned by the UN or was harboring terrorists. UN weapons inspectors spent the next several months searching for such weapons, but their findings were "inconclusive." The membership of the UN was divided over the next course of action. A group of nations led by France, Germany, and Russia called for further inspections, while the United States, Britain, and others called for use of force in disarming Iraq.

In March 2003, U.S. president George W. Bush delivered an ultimatum to Saddam Hussein in a public address to the American people. Hussein was informed that he and his sons had to leave Iraq within 48 hours or face forcible removal from power. No one, of course, expected Hussein to leave Iraq voluntarily. Instead, he announced that Iraq would resist any American-led initiative and invited other Arab and Islamic countries to join Iraq in resisting American imperialism. Joined principally by the British and other countries that agreed to furnish token amounts of troops, the United States invaded Iraq and within a few weeks occupied the entire country.

While Saddam Hussein's government quickly disintegrated, Saddam—as well as his sons Uday and Qusay—went underground. Over the next several months, they became the most hunted men in the country. Uday and Qusay were found and killed in a firefight with American forces. Saddam, however, continued to elude his pursuers until December 2003, when he was found in a spiderhole in a disheveled state. Saddam was imprisoned and finally brought to trial at the end of 2005. Sentenced to death by an Iraqi tribunal, Saddam Hussein was hanged on December 30, 2006.

Since the end of Saddam's autocracy, Iraq has been plagued by almost daily terrorist attacks that do not distinguish between civilians and military personnel. The attacks included roadside bombings and targeted assassinations of government and judicial officials including lawyers assigned to defend Saddam Hussein in court. Most top Iraqi and American personnel work and live in the "Green Zone," a three-square-mile security area in the center of Baghdad. Most of the attacks have been perpetrated by Sunni insurgents, many of whom are members of the former regime. There is some evidence to suggest that outsiders are infiltrating Iraq from Syria, Iran, and Saudi Arabia and that some of them are al-Qaeda operatives.

Iraq, through all of this, may be making some progress toward the goal of democratization. During 2005, a new constitution was approved and an interim government installed. On December 15, 2005, a national vote elected a permanent government, though sectarian violence continues apace.

References: Keegan, John. *The Iraq War* (New York: Knopf Publishing Group, 2005); Tripp, Charles. *A History of Iraq* (New York: Cambridge University Press, 2000).

Irgun Zvai Leumi

The Irgun was established during the 1930s and remained active during the prestate years in Palestine. It competed with and was often condemned by the mainstream Jewish community political structure as well as the HAGANAH, the Jewish self-defense organization. The Irgun was also an ideological rival in the sense that it believed the Jewish people must not be hesitant to protect their security regardless of whether the methods for doing so are respectful of international law. The Irgun's leaders and membership were convinced that Jews would continue to be victimized.

For nearly all of its history, the Irgun was led by MENACHEM BEGIN (1913–92), later prime minister of Israel (1977–83). Begin was a disciple of Zev Jabotinsky (1880–1940), who warned European Jews of the emerging holocaust that was about to befall them. The Holocaust during World War II convinced the Irgun of the necessity to apply strong measures to secure an

A Republican poster in support of the Provisional Irish Republican Army, 1974 (CAIN)

independent Jewish state. The Irgun leadership consistently denied that the organization was a terrorist group though it was condemned as one by the British Mandate authorities. It was responsible for blowing up the KING DAVID HOTEL in Jerusalem in 1947. The Irgun argued that the hotel was a legitimate military target because it housed high-ranking British military officers. However, numerous British, Jewish, and Arab civilians who were also employed in the hotel lost their lives.

The Irgun is a somewhat unusual terrorist organization in that it quickly transformed itself into a viable political party, the current-day Likud, that scrupulously adhered to electoral rules and eventually took power in 1977 after nearly three decades of opposition. It was also fortunate in the sense that the British apparently did not employ all of the power at their disposal in Palestine to eradicate it. However, the official Israeli authority that succeeded the British refused to accept the Irgun's status as a military organization and successfully ordered it to be dissolved.

Reference: Begin, Menachem. *The Revolt,* rev. ed. (New York: Dell, 1977).

Irish Northern Aid *See* NORAID.

Irish Republican Army (IRA)

The IRA was an unofficial semimilitary organization based in the Republic of Ireland that sought complete Irish independence from the United Kingdom. It strove, along with numerous successor organizations, for the unification of the Republic of Ireland with Northern Ireland, which had remained a part of the United Kingdom by choice when Ireland became an independent state.

The IRA was itself a successor organization, growing out of the Irish Volunteers, a militant nationalist organization that was started in 1913. While the SINN FÉIN sought at the political level to achieve an independent republic of Ireland, the IRA's purpose was to make British rule in Ireland untenable by using an armed force. While these two groups have sought a common goal of independence and later unification, their means to that end have differed radically, and they operated independently, with the IRA seldom recognizing any form of political control.

By engaging in a form of GUERRILLA WARFARE, the IRA used tactics such as ambushes, raids, and sabotage to force the British to negotiate a political settlement. This settlement was unacceptable to many within the IRA, however, since it provided for the creation of an Irish Free State with dominion status within the British Empire. The IRA split into two factions: one supporting the peace settlement; the other, which came to be called the Irregulars, opposing it. The Irregulars lost the ensuing civil war, but they did not surrender their weapons or disband. Instead, they began carrying out occasional acts of violence, which resulted in its being declared illegal by the Irish Free State in 1931.

When the Irish Free State withdrew from the British Commonwealth and became a republic in 1948, the IRA refocused its efforts toward the unification of the predominantly Protestant Northern Ireland provinces, which had remained a part of the United Kingdom. Violence by the IRA was sporadic until the late 1960s, when Catholics in Northern Ireland began to demonstrate against discrimination in voting, housing, and employment by the dominant Protestant majority. A split in the IRA occurred after a Sinn Féin conference held in Dublin in 1969 between the "official" and the "provisional" wings of the organization. The former sought a union of all Irish and Northern Ireland Catholics and Protestants in an Irish republic. The latter, called the Provos, were committed to the use of terror tactics to force British withdrawal of troops from Northern Ireland so that Northern Ireland could be united with the rest of Ireland. The Provos's activities resulted in the deaths of many Ulster (Northern Ireland) Protestant civilians and British troops. One of the most publicized attacks was the assassination of Lord Mountbatten in 1979.

Activities by the successor groups to the IRA continued the use of terrorism, generating similar acts from militant Protestant groups, making peace difficult to achieve throughout the end of the century.

Continuity Irish Republican Army (CIRA; a.k.a. Continuity Army Council)

The Continuity IRA (CIRA) is a radical splinter group, formed in 1994 as the clandestine armed wing of the Republican Sinn Féin (RSF), a political organization dedicated to the reunification of Ireland. The RSF formed after the Irish Republican Army (IRA) announced a cease-fire in September 1994.

This group has been involved in bombings, assassinations, kidnappings, extortion, and robberies. Its targets have included British military, Northern Irish security guards, and Northern Irish Loyalist paramilitary groups. It also launched bomb attacks against predominantly Protestant towns in Northern Ireland. Unlike the Provisional IRA (PIRA), the CIRA has not observed the cease-fire, continuing its bombing campaign in 2003 with a series of low-level improvised explosive device attacks. In June 2003, one senior CIRA member was arrested, and two powerful Real IRA (RIRA) bombs were seized in a raid. More than 10 CIRA members have been convicted of criminal charges, and others are awaiting trial. Active recruiting efforts continue, in response to effective police countermeasures, which have reduced the group's strength. There is no established presence or capability of the CIRA to launch attacks on the United Kingdom mainland.

Although there are fewer than 50 hard-core activists in this group, it reportedly receives limited support from IRA hard-liners who are dissatisfied with the IRA cease-fire and from other republican sympathizers, particularly from supporters in the Balkans working in cooperation with the Real IRA. The CIRA is suspected of receiving funds and arms from sympathizers within the United States as well.

In 2004, the U.S. government declared the CIRA to be a foreign terrorist organization, unlike the PIRA or the RIRA. The CIRA continues to abstain from participation with the ongoing peace talks.

Irish National Liberation Army (INLA; a.k.a. People's Liberation Army, People's Republican Army, Catholic Reaction Force)

Formed in 1975 as the military wing of the Irish Republican Socialist Party, which split from the official Irish Republican Army because of the official IRA's cease-fire in 1972, the Irish National Liberation Army (INLA) was responsible for some of the most notorious killings of "the Troubles," including the bombing of the Ballykelly pub in 1982, which killed 17 people. Internal feuding within the INLA has been frequent and bloody, in spite of the cease-fire which it announced in 1998.

This group was active in Belfast and the border areas of Northern Ireland, carrying out bombings, assassinations, kidnappings, hijackings, extortion, and robberies. Occasionally, the INLA provided advanced warning to police about forthcoming attacks against targets, which included British military, Northern Ireland security forces, and Loyalist paramilitary groups. Its willingness to disarm in the peace efforts of the early 21st century remains unclear.

Provisional Irish Republican Army (PIRA; The Provos)

The Provisional IRA has observed a cease-fire since 1997. However, extreme hard-line elements have occasionally broken away from the PIRA and refused to accept the cease-fire. The PIRA has consistently sustained a membership of several hundred activists. It is difficult to be sure how many sympathizers the group has, but they probably number in the several thousand within the Northern Irish Catholic community.

The Provisional IRA has, unlike the CIRA and the RIRA, participated in both the peace talks currently underway in Northern Ireland and the decommissioning of weaponry. While there remains concern about the culmination of the decommissioning, the participation of this group has been beneficial.

Real Irish Republican Army (RIRA; Real IRA)

The Real IRA (RIRA) came into existence as a result of the 1997 peace process, spearheaded in part by Sinn Féin (the political wing of the IRA) and vigorously supported by the IRA. Many high-ranking members of the IRA were unhappy with these talks, which they believed would not result in the eventual reunification of the Six Counties, (Antrim, Armagh, Down, Fermanagh, Londonderry, and Tyrone) of Northern Ireland to the Republic of Ireland. The original IRA had been attempting reunification of the northern counties after Home Rule (limited legislative autonomy) was established in 26 counties of Ireland, with the exception of the six northern counties that elected to remain under British rule. After 80 years of intermittent violence, a cease-fire was arranged and a tentative agreement, the Good Friday Agreement, came into effect. The RIRA's stated goal is the disruption of the peace talks in the hope that British troops will eventually leave Northern Ireland.

Michael "Mickey" McKevitt, a former quartermaster general of the Provisional IRA, founded the RIRA. It opposed the September 1997 Mitchell principles of democracy and non-violence which the IRA had agreed to through their political wing, Sinn Féin, as well as the alteration of the republic's constitution, specifically Articles 2 and 3, which laid claim to Northern Ireland as a territory. The RIRA is generally considered to be the militant wing of the 32-County Sovereignty Movement, which is a political pressure group that pushes for the reunification of the Six Counties to the rest of the republic, as well as the expulsion of all British troops from Ireland.

Unlike the splinter group Continuity IRA, which split off in the 1980s, the RIRA was composed of very experienced members who brought to the group a wealth of information and expertise on fighting a guerrilla war; in particular, several of the IRA's top bomb experts joined. At first, the RIRA had difficulties with secrecy; in the first half of 1998, they were heavily infiltrated by informers, which led to several high-profile arrests, including the founder, Michael McKevitt. The RIRA's membership numbers somewhere between 100 and 250, with about 40 members currently imprisoned, including their founder, McKevitt. The men and women who did join had one thing in common: They were violently opposed to any peace settlement that did not include the timely reintegration of Northern Ireland with the Republic of Ireland and a complete withdrawal of all British personnel (especially British military) from Ireland. Between the dissident members' implacable refusal to allow the northern counties to remain a part of Great Britain and the experience they bring to the RIRA, it becomes clear that these individuals are likely to use extreme violence to achieve their goals.

The RIRA uses dynastic, focused random, and random terror tactics. Their main method of attack is the use of car bombs, generally targeting places where Protestants gather. This use of random terrorism to achieve their goals is nothing new, as the IRA had been doing it for decades. The RIRA will simply place a bomb in heavily populated social gathering areas, such as cafés or shopping centers, and kill as many Protestant civilians as they can. However, the RIRA also targets members of the Protestant political elite and other high-ranking members of Northern Ireland's Protestant citizenry, attempting to assassinate them; essentially, using dynastic terrorism. Still, the most common type of terrorism the RIRA uses is focused random terrorism, targeting areas where the enemy (British military or the Royal Ulster Constabulary [RUC]) gather, even if there are innocent civilians there as well.

A great deal of the RIRA's funding comes from sympathizers in Northern Ireland and the Republic of Ireland, as well as disenchanted members of the IRA who decided to stay within that organization even though they may be disappointed with some of its decisions (regarding the peace efforts, or lack thereof). Robberies of banks and armored cars are also a significant way of making money. While a good deal of money is raised from both the sympathizers and the various robberies, the RIRA also swells their coffers through their interaction and control of both the drug and prostitution trades within Northern Ireland, the republic, and to a lesser degree, England.

RIRA strikes are varied; they most often use bombs to attack British soldiers, Protestant civilians, and members of the RUC or its successor, the Police Service of Northern Ireland. One of the most notable attacks close to the commencement of the RIRA as a group includes the infamous bombing of the Armagh Town Center. The RIRA called to inform a news organization of the bombs' location; when the police directed the people away from that location, they actually moved them directly into the blast radius of where the bomb was actually positioned. When detonated, the blast killed 29 civilians and injured more than 100.

This attack generated outrage not only from Northern Ireland and the United Kingdom but also from the Republic of Ireland. Several Catholic civilians were killed in the attack. Because of the near-universal outrage, the group declared a unilateral cease-fire in the middle of the winter of 1998. This cease-fire lasted less than two years before the group began an even more prolific bombing campaign. A civilian construction worker was killed in County Kerry when a bomb placed in a lunch pail detonated in 2002, and the group began to target sites in England itself. A taxi-car bomb hit the BBC Television Centre in West London, primarily because the BBC ran a documentary on the Armagh bombing, displaying the names, pictures, and other details about those suspected to have been involved. They also attacked the headquarters of MI6 (Military Intelligence section 6, Britain's version of the U.S. Central Intelligence Agency) with an RPG. In December 2004, Belfast was hit with 15 different firebomb attacks on various properties. This increase in successful attacks may indicate a growing support for the group, possibly because of the repeated failures to revive the peace effort. As Irish Catholics in Northern Ireland see their chance at freedom swiftly departing, they willingly give more moral and financial support to the actions of the RIRA, as well as make it easier for the group to recruit new members.

Members of the RIRA believe that they are fighting against a vastly superior military force that has been and continues to be an occupying force. They view themselves as self-sacrificing freedom fighters who simply desire their nation to be whole again; their desire is not the eradication of all Englishmen or the destruction of the United Kingdom.

The peace process initiated in the 1990s sought to create autonomy in measure to the troubled Ulster area, with shared government between the parties involved in decades of conflict.

On July 19, 1997, the IRA declared a cease-fire, effective July 20. At the end of August, the secretary of state for Northern Ireland announced that the cease-fire was being observed, allowing Sinn Féin, the political party closely identified with the IRA, entry into negotiations on Northern Ireland's political future. In 2002, the IRA restated its commitment to the peace process and apologized to the families of noncombatants who had been killed or injured by the IRA during its struggles.

The IRA had, in the past, received aid from various groups and countries, including training and weapons from Libya and the Palestine Liberation Organization and funding, arms, and other support from sympathizers in the United States. It has also been linked in operations with ETA and the Revolutionary Armed Forces of Colombia (FARC). Three suspected IRA members were arrested in Colombia on charges of assisting the FARC in improving its explosives capabilities in August 2002. The IRA's refusal in late 2004 to allow photographic documentation of its decommissioning process was an obstacle to progress in implementing the Belfast Agreement and stalled the peace talks. The group has disposed of light, medium, and heavy weapons, ammunition, and explosives in three rounds of decommissioning. However, the group is believed to retain the ability to conduct paramilitary operations with the equipment it still possesses. The IRA's extensive criminal activities allegedly provide the group and the political party Sinn Féin with millions of dollars each year. The IRA was implicated in two significant robberies in 2004, one involving about $50 million. On July 28, 2005, the Irish Republican Army made a formal announcement to end its violent campaign and promised a complete decommissioning of all weapons.

References: Coogan, Tim Pat. *The IRA* (New York: Palgrave Macmillan, 2001); Council on Foreign Relations. Terrorism: Questions and Answers. "Irish Republican Army." Available online. URL: http://cfrterrorism.org/groups/ira.html. Accessed February 16, 2006.

E.C.

Islamic Army of Aden (IAA; a.k.a. Aden Abyan Islamic Army, Aden Islamic Army)

Emerging publicly in mid-1998, the Islamic Army of Aden (IAA) issued a series of communiqués expressing support for OSAMA BIN LADEN and advocating the overthrow of the Yemeni government. These communiqués also called for operations against the United States and other Western interests in Yemen.

The IAA has engaged in bombings and kidnappings in pursuit of these goals. This group was responsible for the kidnapping of 16 British, American, and Australian tourists near Mudiyah in southern Yemen in 1998 and for the bombing of the British embassy in Sanaa in October 2000. It was believed to be responsible for the attack in June 2003 on a medical assistance convoy in the Abyan governorate. The Yemeni authorities responded with a raid on a suspected IAA facility, which resulted in the deaths of several individuals and the capture of others, including the group's leader, Khalid al-Nabi al-Yazidi. He was reportedly released from prison in mid-October 2003.

Reference: National Memorial Institute for the Prevention of Terrorism (MIPT). "Aden Abyan Islamic Army." Available online. URL: http://www.tkb.org/Group.jsp?groupID=4. Accessed February 15, 2006.

Islamic Jihad

See EGYPTIAN ISLAMIC JIHAD.

Islamic Movement of Uzbekistan (IMU)

This group is a coalition of Islamic militants from Uzbekistan and other Central Asian states opposed to Uzbekistani president Islom Karimov's secular regime. Its original goal was to establish an Islamic state in Uzbekistan, although propaganda suggests that it has become anti-Western and anti-Israeli.

The IMU is believed to be responsible for five car bombs in Tashkent in February 1999. It instigated two hostage crises in Kyrgystan in the fall of that year, including a two-and-one-half-month crisis in which IMU militants kidnapped four Japanese and eight Kyrgystanis.

The IMU primarily targeted internal Uzbekistani interests before October 2001, but following the ATTACKS ON AMERICA and the subsequent U.S.-led "war on terror," initiated with attacks in Afghanistan, the movement began to carry out attacks on U.S. and Coalition soldiers in Afghanistan and Pakistan. The IMU was responsible for explosions in the Kyrgyzstan capital, Bishkek, in December 2002 and in Osh in May 2003 that killed eight people and for an explosion in November 2004 (again in the southern Kyrgyzstan city of Osh) that killed one police officer and one of the IMU's own members. Kyrgyzstan security forces disrupted an IMU cell in Kyrgyzstan that was trying to bomb the U.S. embassy and a nearby hotel in Bishkek.

The current strength of the group is unknown, but militant supporters probably number in the thousands. Most of these militants are believed to be in Afghanistan in the winter, although some may remain in Tajikistan. Its areas of operation include Afghanistan, Pakistan, Uzbekistan, Tajikistan, Kyrgyzstan, Kazakhstan, and Iran, but the IMU has cells scattered throughout South Asia.

The IMU receives support from other Islamic extremist groups in central and South Asia and individuals and patron states in the Middle East. IMU leadership broadcast statements over Iranian radio.

Reference: National Memorial Institute for the Prevention of Terrorism (MIPT). "Islamic Movement of Uzbekistan." Available online. URL: http://www.tkb.org/Group.jsp?groupID=4075. Accessed February 15, 2006.

Israel

After winning its political independence during the 1948–1949 war with its Arab neighbors, Israel became the first Jewish state in nearly 1,900 years. It also became the first and so far the only full-fledged democracy in the Middle East. Arab governments refused to accept Israel's legitimacy and fought several more wars. Israel endured, and during 1977–79, Egypt made peace and extended diplomatic recognition. Jordan did the same 15 years later.

The absence of major wars did not resolve the Palestinian refugee problems created in the late 1940s when many Palestinians were displaced by Jewish settlers, many of whom were themselves refugees from several European countries. A fifth of Israel's citizenry, however, consists of the descendants of Palestinian Arabs who remained in the country and have full citizenship. Like Israel's Jews, the country's Arabs are divided along religious and ideological lines. One Arab community, the Druse, actively supports Israel and serves in the military. An electorate of less than 4 million normally provides a dozen parties in a 120-member parliament.

Israel remains a modern society in a region where traditionalism prevails. The country has a strong economy with a technological emphasis. Its population is diverse. Immigrants from a hundred countries have moved to Israel. Several languages are widely spoken, though only Hebrew, Arabic, and English are official. There is constant tension between religious and secular Jews over such issues as observance of dietary laws. Israel along with the United States is the target of choice of numerous terrorist organizations. Since many of these have their origins in the Middle East and receive support from various governments, Israelis consider themselves to be on the front line of the terrorist threat. Israel has a strong counterterrorism program and does not hesitate to retaliate against the personnel and installations of suspected terrorist organizations.

During 2000 and 2001, the second intifada, an uprising among Palestinians in Gaza and the West Bank, unleashed numerous terrorist attacks against Israel. The attacks were compounded by Islamic radical organizations furnishing suicide bombers in Israeli population centers. Moreover, the fact that public opinion polls revealed 70% of Palestinians in support of the Islamic suicide bombers' causing havoc among Israelis convinced many Israelis that the peace process was dead and the country was under siege once more by Arabs sworn to the Jewish state's destruction. The national mood regressed to the mindset that Israel is alone and must do all that is necessary to guarantee its national security and survival.

Israel employed a variety of military operations in its counterterrorism efforts, some of which have been characterized by international experts as "terrorism," in that civilians were often killed or injured. Israeli forces launched frequent raids throughout the West Bank and Gaza, conducted targeted killings of suspected Palestinian terrorists, destroyed homes—including those of families of suicide bombers—imposed strict and widespread closures and curfews in Palestinian areas, and worked intensely to build an extensive SECURITY BARRIER in the West Bank. Attacks by Palestinian groups in response to these measures continue to be intense, as the cycle of violence continues.

Ariel Sharon, in 2005, completed a significant step in the long-delayed withdrawal of Israeli forces and settlers from the Gaza Strip. However, his subsequent effort to form a new political party, followed by his severe stroke, and hampered by the victory of HAMAS in the 2006 Palestinian elections have made the prospects for further steps in the peace process for this country very tenuous.

The Sharon era ended in early January 2006, with the prime minister's stroke that left him incapable of discharging his responsibilities. His handpicked successor, Ehud Olmert, a former mayor of Jerusalem, became acting prime minister until national elections were held several weeks later in March. Olmert's new Kadima (Hebrew for "forward") Party, originally established by Sharon, received the plurality of votes and parliamentary seats needed to form a new government. Olmert became the official prime minister and successfully invited leaders of the rival Labor Party to join a broad-based coalition government.

The Olmert government, unusual for most Israeli regimes, provided both a prime minister and defense minister (from the dovish Labor Party) who lacked a military background. The previous two governments, for example, headed by Ehud Barak (1999–2001) and Ariel Sharon (2001–06) both had prime ministers who had spent most of their careers as high-ranking military officers. Barak and Sharon, very different in political outlook, had both participated in several wars, with Sharon going all the way back to the Israeli War of Independence in 1948–49.

Olmert was soon tested by Israel's enemies. In July, both Hamas in the Gaza Strip and HIZBALLAH on Lebanon's southern border that is contiguous with Israel's northern border attacked and killed Israeli soldiers and kidnapped others. By mid-July 2006, Israel was fighting a two-front war. The most serious fighting occurred in and around the border regions between Israel and Lebanon. Hizballah underestimated the anger of the Israeli government and its determination to punish the group for its provocations. Israel, however, underestimated Hizballah and its military abilities. Hizballah had managed, with the assistance of the Iranian and Syrian governments, to secure and store about 13,000 rockets that had the ability to attack northern Israel civilian communities, including Israel's third-largest city, Haifa. As many as 3,000 rockets fell on Israel. The damage was not substantial, but the violence disrupted the economy and caused several hundred thousand Israelis to leave their homes.

The Israeli-Hizballah conflict lasted 34 days before a tenuous cease-fire was put into place under the auspices of the United Nations and the Lebanese government, neither of which had the resources to control, let alone disarm, Hizballah. Hizballah was early on criticized by several Arab governments for antagonizing Israel, but Israel was roundly condemned for attacking by land and air civilian homes where the Israelis claimed Hizballah hid personnel and weapons. Hundreds of thousands of Lebanese fled the southern part of the country.

This conflict revealed a new and frightening dimension for the capability of a terrorist organization that is supported by one or more governments. Hizballah operatives were well trained and well equipped and inflicted losses on Israeli forces. Hizballah was even able to attack an Israeli warship. There is little doubt that terrorism had become both more lethal and more capable of murdering people in large numbers.

Reference: Sprinzak, Ehud, and Larry Diamond, eds., *Israeli Democracy under Stress* (Boulder, Colo.: Lynne Reinner, 2000).

Italy, legal initiatives against terrorism in

Italy has experimented with a legal response to terrorism, with considerable success. In June 1983, Italians voted for the first time in more than a decade without an array of urban guerrilla groups holding the nation's political system at gunpoint. Long regarded as the Western European country most vulnerable during the upsurge of terrorism in the 1970s, many of Italy's politicians and media experts hoped that their country was finally beginning to emerge from its terrorist nightmare.

The man credited with a large share of Italy's success in its war on internal terrorism was Interior Minister Virginio Rognoni, who assumed his office in the wake of the kidnap-murder of former prime minister

Aldo Moro. At the time in which he took office, the RED BRIGADES (BR) terrorists appeared to be acting with impugnity.

Statistics issued by the Interior Ministry indicated that, in 1978, there were 2,498 terrorist attacks within Italy. Between 1968 and 1982, 403 people were killed in terrorist incidents in Italy, and another 1,347 were injured. These people came from all walks of life. One out of every four victims was a police officer. Apart from politicians such as Moro, businesspeople and journalists were favorite targets. But the bulk of the dead and injured were ordinary citizens unlucky enough to be on a train or in a piazza when it was blown up.

After 1980, a significant drop occurred in Italy's internal terrorist activity, apparently a result of a combination of legal initiatives and coordinated police efforts. Nearly 2,000 convicted urban guerrillas, including most of the leading members of the Red Brigades, were imprisoned. The Italians gave the task of hunting down these persons to a portly general of the Carabinieri named Carlo Alberto Della Chiesa. Armed with about 150 carefully chosen men, his antiterrorist cadre, he was responsible only to Minister of the Interior Rognoni and to the prime minister. With his support, the government enacted a number of decrees: strengthening sentences for convicted terrorists, widening police powers (allowing police to hold suspects longer for questioning and to search without a warrant), and making abetting terrorism a crime. Increased powers were also given to the police in matters of detention, interrogation, and wiretapping.

Rognoni, during this increased police activity, began to exploit what he perceived as a growing disillusionment with the efficacy of terrorism as a problem-solving instrument. He helped to have enacted, in 1982, a law that promised "repentant" terrorists lighter sentences if they confessed. Beset by gathering doubts about the utility of terrorist tactics, large numbers of the *brigandisti* began to "confess." One of the most prominent of the *penititi* was Patrizio Peci, a former Red Brigades commander from Turin. He noted that, while he had been driven to become an urban guerrilla by police harassment for bombing attacks (which were later discovered to have been committed by neofascists), he no longer believed that the Red Brigades could create a better society in Italy using terrorism.

Terrorism was not eliminated in Italy by these legal initiatives. Both left- and right-wing terror continue to destroy individuals and property. Right-wing terror was responsible, for example, in 1981 for an explosion in the Bologna train station that killed 85 people. But for a time, terrorism was significantly reduced by this legal and police-intensive approach. During 1980, for example, deaths from terrorism occurred every three days on the average; but in the first six months of 1983, in the wake of the government's police and legislative initiatives, only one terrorist-related death was reported. The judicious blending of strong police investigative and arrest action, coupled with the offer of a government pardon for "penitent" transgressors, proved a potent and effective mixture. By closing many of the places to hide while holding open a friendly government door to the possibility for a pardon, Italy made serious efforts to resocialize a large number of its disaffected youth without unnecessary violence.

See also RED ARMY FACTION.

al-Ittihaad al-Islami (AIAI)

Following the collapse of the Siad Barre regime in Somalia, al-Ittihad al-Islami became the largest militant Islamic organization in that nation. Its stated aims, to establish an Islamic regime in Somalia and to force the secession of the Ogaden region of Ethiopia, have been essentially abandoned, although some elements of the AIAI have maintained ties to AL-QAEDA. The AIAI is believed to be responsible for a series of bombing attackes in Addis Ababa in 1996 and 1997 and for the kidnapping of several relief workers in the same area in 1998. With roughly 2,000 members at present, of whom only a small percentage are believed to be militant, the group clearly sustained significant losses at the hands of the Ethiopian military. Membership is difficult to determine, as the group now operates in small cells that do not share leadership. Funds from Middle East financiers and Somali citizens who have immigrated to the West continue to support this group. It is believed to have received training in the camps in Afghanistan in the past, as well as weapons funneled through Sudan and Eritrea, although neither of these options may be available to the group at present.

Reference: National Memorial Institute for the Prevention of Terrorism (MIPT). "al-Ittihaad al-Islami (AIAI)." Available online. URL: http://www.tkb.org/Group.jsp?groupID=4329. Accessed February 15, 2006.

J

Jaish-e-Mohammed (JEM; a.k.a. Army of Mohammed)

JEM is an Islamist group based in Pakistan that rapidly expanded in size and capability in 2000 after Maulana Masood Azhar, a former ultrafundamentalist Harakat ul-Ansar (HUA) leader, announced its formation in February of that year. The HUA, which had by this time become known as the HARAKAT UL-MUJAHIDIN (HUM), passed on to JEM its goal of uniting Kashmir with Pakistan. JEM is politically aligned with the radical, pro-Taliban political party Jamiat-i Ulema-i Islam (JUI-F).

Azhar, JEM's leader, was released from Indian prison in December 1999 in exchange for 155 hijacked Indian Airlines hostages in Afghanistan. The HUA in 1994 kidnapped U.S. and British nationals in New Delhi, and in July 1995 participated in the kidnappings of Westerners in Kashmir. Each of these kidnappings were part of an effort to free Azhar. Upon his release, Azhar organized large rallies and recruitment drives across Pakistan. In July 2000, a JEM rocket-grenade attack failed to injure the chief minister at his office in Srinagar, India, but wounded four other persons. In December 2000 JEM militants launched grenade attacks at a bus stop in Kupwara, India, which injured 24 persons. Similar attacks at a marketplace in Chadoura, India, injured 16 people. JEM activists also planted two bombs, killing 21 people, in Qamarwari and Srinagar, both in India, in 2000. Azhar was placed under house arrest when Pakistan President General Pervez Musharraf banned the group in December 2002. Another JEM leader, Sheikh Omar Saeed, was released from prison in 1999 after having served a five-year prison sentence for the 1994 kidnapping of an American and three Britons in India. In 2003 Saeed was convicted and sentenced to death in Pakistan for masterminding the 2002 murder of American journalist Daniel Pearl.

JEM appears to have several hundred armed supporters, primarily in Asad Kashmir, Pakistan, and in India's southern Kashmir and Doda regions. Upon Azhar's release from prison, about three-quarters of the HUM members defected to the new JEM organization, particularly a large number of the urban Kashmiri youth. Supporters were mostly Pakistani and Kashmiris, but some Afghans and Arab veterans of the Afghan war also support the group, as does the Taliban. OSAMA BIN LADEN is also suspected of giving funding to JEM.

See also OVERVIEW OF TERRORISM, BY REGION.

Jamaat al-Fuqra (JF)

This Islamic sect seeks to purify Islam through violence. It was created by Pakistani cleric Sheikh Mubarak Ali Gilani, who established the organization in the early 1980s when he visited the United States. Members of the group are described as Islamic extremists who breed hatred toward their perceived enemies of their faith. In fact, in one his treatises, published by the Quranic Open University in the United States, Gilani told his followers that their foremost duty was to wage JIHAD against "oppressors of Muslims." This was published in the United States in the 1980s, long before OSAMA BIN LADEN issued his own call to jihad against the United States. Gilani, also known as the sixth sultan Ul-Faqr, is the leader of JF and has established its headquarters in Hancock, New York.

Although the JF is headquartered on the eastern seaboard, investigations by law enforcement in Colorado in the 1980s found that it was composed of approximately 30 different *Jamaats,* or communities, which were more or less mobile, and which, according to recent studies, still exist today. Investigators of the JF also found several covert paramilitary training compounds operated by this group, one of which was located in a mountainous area near Buena Vista, Colorado, prior to the Colorado prosecutions of JF members in the mid-1990s. These *Jamaats* in the United States have, over the years, drawn many Muslims from converts, some from prisons, and others from local communities, with the result that the JF is believed today to have from 1,000 to 3,000 members in the United States.

While Gilani lived in Lahore, Pakistan, most of the cells of his organization were located in North America. JF members purchased isolated rural properties in North America to live as a community, practice their faith, and insulate themselves from Western culture, which they perceive as being a corrupting influence on Islam. There are perhaps half a dozen JF residential compounds in rural hamlets across the United States, each of which shelters hundreds of cadres. JF members have at times traveled for paramilitary and survivalist training, under Gilani's supervision.

The exact number of JF members is not known, since both Gulani and the members themselves deny that the organization exists. Individuals selected to live on JF premises agree to abide by the law and discipline of the JF and are taught to carefully conceal their identity. Cadres are reportedly well versed in the use of aliases, and the structure of JF is concealed behind front outfits. It appears to consist of a network of safe houses and cells.

These cells, unsurprisingly, have been responsible for many violent acts, since the JF teaches its members to regard all those who do not follow the tenets of Islam explicitly as enemies of Islam, including Muslims as well as non-Muslims. They also teach that violence is a significant and vital aspect of their quest to purify Islam. Targets of JF attacks—which have ranged from firebombing to assassination—have included Muslims who, from their perspective, are heretics in their failure to follow the Koran; Hindus; and a wide range of other individuals and groups regarded by the JF as "enemies of Islam."

Native Americans, individually and in groups, were early targets of JF attacks in the 1980s, as were many other ethnic groups. Stephen Paster, a leading JF member, was convicted of planting a pipe bomb at a Portland hotel owned by followers of the Bhagwan Rajneesh cult and was suspected but not charged in two other bombings in Seattle. After his arrest in Colorado in July 1983, Paster served four years of a 20-year prison sentence for the Portland bombing. Paster is reported to be working at Gilani's base in Lahore, Pakistan, where, according to intelligence sources, he provides explosives training to JF cadres.

The JF is suspected of involvement in a wide range of crimes, but few members are serving prison sentences. For instance, two JF cadres are alleged to have killed Mozaffar Ahmad, a leader of the minority Ahmadiyyah sect in Canton, Michigan, but both suspects supposedly died in a fire they set at the Ahmadiyyah mosque in Detroit, so there has been no trial or conviction. The JF is also suspected to have been involved in the killing of three Indians on August 1, 1984, in a suburb of Tacoma, Washington, and a series of fire bombings of Hindu and Hare Krishna temples in Seattle, Denver, Philadelphia, and Kansas City. Given the lack of firm membership roles and carefully structured secrecy of the organization, the connections remain "suspect" at this point.

However, federal investigators have found disturbing evidence of criminal intent at several communes. In 1989, during a search of a storage locker in Colorado Springs, a large cache of armaments and documents with multiple links to the JF were discovered by U.S. investigators, including semiautomatic firearms, explosives, pipe bombs, bomb components, and several fully operational bombs. Some of the seized documents included maps and lists, with details of potential

JF targets and victims in Los Angeles, Arizona, and Colorado—oil and gas installations, electrical facilities, the U.S. Air Force Academy at Colorado Springs, other military sites, and people of Jewish or Hindu ethnicity in at least 12 U.S. states.

JF cadre efforts in 1991 to bomb an Indian cinema and a Hindu temple near Toronto were not successful, and five members were arrested at the Niagara Falls border crossing when U.S. Customs agents searched their cars and found plans of the interiors of the targets and a description of timed explosives. Although a Canadian jury convicted the three American JF members of conspiracy to commit mischief and endanger life, the fourth suspect, who had come to Canada from Pakistan shortly before the planned bombing, fled to Pakistan.

The links of Jamaat ul-Fuqra cadres to serious terrorist attacks in the United States are evident in the 1993 WORLD TRADE CENTER BOMBING. One of the persons convicted in this bombing, Clement Rodney Hampton-el, was a JF member, and the JF was subsequently linked in congressional testimony to the planning of the 1993 bombing. The JF, in recent years, has in fact served as a support network for a number of groups involved in terrorist activity, including groups operating in Pakistan and in the Indian state of Jammu and Kashmir. Sheikh Gilani maintains links with Islamist groups such as the HAMAS and HIZBALLAH, providing, through the JF, both moral and material assistance to these groups. Since Gilani has allegedly admitted to receiving hundreds of thousands of dollars a year in donations from America, the material support of the JF to such groups may be substantial.

The recruitment of members to groups engaged in terrorism has roots, with the JF, in its links to the Quranic Open University. This institution, with which Gulani maintained strong ties, portrayed itself as a religious and charitable educational institution dedicated to studying the Quran. It also provided prolific recruiting grounds of young Muslims for the JF communes. Gilani, in an interview in 2002, claimed that the government of Pakistan had requested him to "mobilize" his university students to the cause of Kashmir in the United Sates by holding rallies and "informing the public." To this end, he established the Kashmir-American Friendship Society in 1993—the same year that at least one member of the JF was involved in the World Trade Center bombing.

The JF is alleged to be linked to many other terrorist acts. There have been media reports of JF links with Richard Reid, a Briton accused of trying to use explosives in his shoes to blow up a Paris-to-Miami jetliner on December 22, 2001. Reid reportedly trained at one of Gilani's Pakistani camps. In addition, raids by police on a house in Virginia linked to the JF in December 2001 resulted in two people being arrested for possession of illegal weapons. There were additional problems in 2001, when suspected JF members were arrested and convicted on weapons charges. One of those convicted, Vincente Pierre, is the owner of a Virginia compound that reportedly served as a JF base.

The JF is also linked to money-laundering schemes in the United States. In 1993, Colorado law-enforcement agencies convicted five JF cadres for defrauding the Colorado government of approximately $350,000 through bogus workers' compensation claims. Prosecuting agencies stated that the money was laundered through Professional Security International (PSI), a JF security firm, and Muslims of the Americas, another of JF's links in the 1990s. A portion of the funds was tracked through PSI to JF couriers traveling to Pakistan.

The links between the laundering of money, the purchase of weapons, and the training of recruits was evident in the 1993 Colorado raid. The Colorado commune spread across 101 acres, and police recovered bombs, weapons, and plans for terrorist attacks in their raid. Investigations revealed that two other communes in New York and California have shooting ranges and that a small Muslim community on an 1,800-acre commune in the Sierra Mountains in California also reportedly has an airstrip.

Gilani is also under investigation for his links to terrorist activity. He was temporarily in Pakistani custody for the abduction of U.S. journalist Daniel Pearl, since Gilani is reportedly the person whom Pearl was attempting to meet in the days before Pearl disappeared in Karachi. Upon his arrest in Rawalpindi on January 30, 2002, and transfer to Karachi for questioning, Gilani denied any link to the abduction. Gilani is currently under investigation for his alleged links to the al-Qaeda terror network of Osama bin Laden and for laundering money in transit between the United States and Pakistan.

The Jamaat ul-Fuqra remains the focus of probes by U.S. authorities for charges ranging from links with terrorist groups to laundering money into Pakistan.

Reference: South Asia Intelligence Review. "Jammat ul-Fuqra." Available online. URL: http://www.satp.org/

satporgtp/countries/pakistan/terroristoutfits/jamaat-ul-fuqra.htm. Accessed March 13, 2006.

Jamiat ul-Mujahedin (JUM)

The Jamiat ul-Mujahedin (JUM) was the first breakaway faction of the HIZB UL-MUJAHIDIN (HM), emerging out of a personality clash between Master Ahsan Dar, at that time the leader of the HM, and Hilal Ahmed Mir. Mir opposed the move to transform the Hizb into Jamaat-e-Islami's armed wing. JUM officially formed in 1990 with Sheikh Abdul Basit as its chief, with primarily Kashmiris as members.

The Jamiat ul-Mujahedin has a militaristic command structure, with a commander in chief as well as vice commander in chief who commands four divisional commanders. Each divisional commander in turn commands the various district commanders and area commanders. JUM publishes a monthly magazine, *Mahaz-e-Kashmi*, that systematically describes the terrorist operations in which the group has engaged.

While JUM is unlike other terrorist organizations that draw support along sectarian lines in that it has attempted to recruit members from all sects, it has not been able to grow significantly. It played a significant role in the early years of militancy in Jammu and Kashmir but has not been able to maintain its momentum. Although the cadre strength of this group is currently reported to be in the hundreds, many of its cadres languish in prison. Several JUM leaders were killed in a series of encounters after 1996, leaving its cadre disorganized.

With a purported expertise in grenade attacks and the use of explosives, JUM has been linked to a variety of acts of terror. In 1991, JUM was allegedly involved in the killing of Mohammed Sayeed, joint director in the Information Department. It is also suspected to have been involved in the killing of a human rights activist in December 1992. JUM was also reportedly responsible for the Badami Bagh cantonment blast in March 1993 in which 29 persons were killed. A cadre of the Jamiat-ul-Mujahedin, who was part of a suicide squad that infiltrated into the army battalion headquarters at Beerwah in Budgam district and launched an attack on forces inside the camp on September 12, 2000, was subsequently killed in the encounter. With the arrests of JUM terrorist Muzzafar Mirza and his associates in Srinagar and of Nissar Ahmad Gandroo in Kolkata on January 10, 2001, the police foiled the group's plans to launch terrorist attacks on the eve of Republic Day.

The group's use of non-discriminate weapons such as grenades and explosives injured civilians, causing JUM to lose popular support in Kashmir during the mid- to late 1990s, since many other larger and more powerful insurgent groups were more careful to not target Kashmiri locals. On January 3, 1997, a bomb concealed in a rickshaw detonated near the chief minister's residence and wounded 10 guards on duty, also killing four civilians. JUM claimed responsibility for this attack and countless others that killed civilians, damaging its image further and diminishing its level of popular support.

In 2002, in response to the ATTACKS ON AMERICA in September 2001, India passed the Prevention of Terrorism Act (POTA), banning groups like JUM. Subsequently, JUM opposed the All Parties Hurriyat Conference (APHC), a large conglomerate of terrorist organizations that included its former parent organization the HM. JUM leaders claimed that the APHC had no right to represent the interests of insurgents in Jammu and Kashmir to the world. When the Indian government invited the APHC to peace talks on January 22, 2004, to try to end the struggle over the region, JUM threatened to kill members of the APHC, particularly the leader of the APHC who, by JUM standards, had "sold out" Kashmir. The HM attended the peace talks, announcing on January 24, 2004, that it would call for a three-month cease-fire and hold talks with the Indian government. JUM denounced the HM leadership, claiming that the leaders had been "bought" by the Indian government.

The Indian government rejected the claim by JUM to be responsible for the shooting down of a MiG-21 fighter plane near Srinagar in December 2002. According to the Indian air force, the claim was not credible.

JUM's insistence that jihad is the only way to reclaim Kashmir remains a factor in the diminishing membership and role of this group. Its uncompromising position on the role of aggression against India has caused other terrorist outfits in Kashmir to distance themselves from this group, since most view JUM goals as impractical and unrealistic. Several hundred members still claim an allegiance to the group, and it continues to conduct operations against Indian armed forces in Kashmir and Jammu.

Reference: National Memorial Institute for the Prevention of Terrorism (MIPT). "Jamiat ul-Mujahedin (JUM)." Available online. URL: http://www.tkb.org/Group.jsp?groupID=3617. Accessed February 15, 2006.

Janjaweed *See* DARFUR.

Japan, attack in Tokyo subway

In March 1995, on a Monday morning before a Tuesday holiday celebrating the first day of spring, a chemical weapon of mass destruction originally concocted in Nazi Germany was placed simultaneously in five subway cars at morning rush hour in Tokyo. Ten people died as a result of this attack, and thousands more were injured.

Interviews with victims after the attack indicate the following sequence of events:

A man, wearing big sunglasses and a surgical mask, boarded the eight-car B711T train on Tokyo's Hibiya line when it originated at 8 A.M. at the Nakameguro station. Since it was hay-fever season, a lot of people in Tokyo were wearing masks, so this attracted no special attention. The Hibiya train was less crowded than usual since there was a holiday the next day. The man easily found a seat and began fiddling with a foot-long rectangular object wrapped in newspapers. At the next stop, he set the package on the floor and left the train.

An Irishman in Tokyo to train Japanese jockeys boarded the train at the next station and noticed the moist spot on the wrapping of the object and an unpleasant odor. Others noticed the smell as well, and, by the Kamiyacho station, 11 minutes after the strange man had boarded, passengers panicked. Most began to run off the train, but not all were successful in leaving in time. Several dozen people collapsed on the platform or were on their knees unable to stand. Those who could walk staggered up three flights of stairs to reach fresh air. Some vomited; others were temporarily blinded or lost their voices.

Within half an hour, similar scenes had unfolded at five other subway stops on three lines. Police arrived within minutes, administered first aid, and rushed thousands to hospitals where an antidote was administered by doctors who suspected what had happened, based on visible symptoms. But for some, it was too late. The deadly nerve gas, sarin, claimed 10 lives that morning. Two days later, Japanese national police deployed 2,500 troops to the doors of AUM SHINRIKYO. At the main compound in Kamikuishiki, 110 miles west of Tokyo, the police made a dramatic discovery: a warehouse with vast quantities of toxic chemicals, among them many of the constituent ingredients of sarin. As investigators raided the headquarters and hideaways of this cult, they emerged with ton after ton of these chemicals—sodium cyanide, sodium flouride, phosphorus trichloride, isopropyl alcohol—some benign, but others deadly, and still others that, if mixed together, might create something deadlier still.

This was the first large-scale terrorist attack by a civilian group using a toxic chemical agent against innocent civilians. It became the focus of governments worldwide involved in assessing the potential for attacks by terrorists using chemical weapons of mass destruction in transportation systems, including subways, buses, trains, and planes.

See also AUM SHINRIKYO; PHYSICAL SECURITY.

Japanese Red Army (JRA; Anti-Imperialist International Brigade [AIIB])

The Japanese Red Army (JRA) was an international terrorist group, with an anarchist philosophy, which formed around 1970. It broke away from the Japanese Communist League–Red Army Faction, a coalition of anarchists with ties to Germany. Led by Fusako Shigenobu, it was headquartered in the Syrian-controlled area of Lebanon's Bekáa valley.

Initially, its stated goals were to overthrow the existing Japanese government and the monarchy. It was also committed to the fomenting of world revolution against all governments, hence its anarchistic, international focus.

The organizational structure of the JRA is not clear, but it appears to exercise control, or at least have ties to, the Anti-Imperialist International Brigade, from which it had earlier broken. It may also have had links to the Antiwar Democratic Front, an openly leftist political organization in Japan. After the arrest in November 1987 of Osamu Maruoka, a leader of the JRA, it became evident that the JRA might have organized cells in Asian cities such as Manila and Singapore. The JRA has maintained since its beginning close and long-standing relations with various Palestinian groups engaged in terrorism, all of which are based and operate outside of Japan. It was clearly an internationally focused organization.

During the 1970s, the JRA carried out a series of attacks around the world. Perhaps the most widely recognized of these operations was the massacre at LOD AIRPORT in Israel in 1972. The JRA was also responsible for the hijacking of two Japanese airliners and the attempted takeover of the U.S. embassy in Kuala Lumpur, Malaysia.

The JRA underwent severe factional infighting that led in 1972 to its militants executing 14 of their fellow members. The organization remained quite small, but it continued to undertake terrorist acts intermittently up until the end of the 20th century. Evidence of continued activity by the JRA surfaced in 1988 with the capture of JRA operative Yu Kikumura, who was arrested with explosives on the New Jersey Turnpike. Kikumura was apparently planning an attack to coincide with the bombing of a USO club in Naples, a suspected JRA operation that killed five, including a U.S. servicewoman. Kikumura was convicted of these charges and served a lengthy prison sentence in the United States. In March 1995, another JRA activist, Akita Yukiko, was arrested in Romania and subsequently deported to Japan to face trial.

Tsutomu Shirosaki, captured in 1996, is also jailed in the United States. In 2000, Lebanon deported to Japan four members it arrested in 1997, but granted a fifth operative, Kozo Okamoto, political asylum.

Longtime leader Shigenobu was arrested in November 2000 and faced charges of terrorism and passport fraud. After her arrest, Shigenobu announced that she intended to pursue her goals using a legitimate political party rather than revolutionary violence, and the group announced that it would disband in April 2001. The United States has removed the JRA from its current listing of FTOs, as it is no longer an organization with structure and leadership committed to the carrying out of terrorist acts.

References: Combs, Cindy. *Terrorism in the Twenty-First Century* (Upper Saddle River, N.J.: Prentice Hall, 2000); Segaller, Stephen. *Invisible Armies: Terrorism in the 1990s* (New York: Harcourt, Brace, Jovanovich, 1987).

Jewish Defense League

The Jewish Defense League (JDL) was founded in 1968 by Rabbi Meir Kahane in New York City, with a professed goal of protecting Orthodox Jewish neighborhoods in NYC and of protesting against anti-Semitism. Kahane, shortly after founding the group, migrated to ISRAEL and established the KACH Party in 1971. He remained the group's official leader until 1985.

Described in congressional testimony by the FEDERAL BUREAU OF INVESTIGATION (FBI) as a "violent" and "extremist" group, the JDL has vowed "no sanctuary for those who threaten or attack Jewish individuals or institutions." The FBI, in its *Terrorism 2000/2001* report, identified the JDL as a right-wing terrorist group, based on its involvement in several bombing and arson incidents during the previous decade. During the 1980s, the JDL repeatedly attacked Soviet institutions, gradually widening their attacks to include institutions of other states viewed as "anti-Semitic" by the group's leadership.

Two members of the JDL were arrested in 2001 for their involvement in a plot to bomb the office of a Lebanese-American congressman from Orange County, California, and a mosque in Culver City, California. Irving Rubin, a former leader of this group, committed suicide in prison while awaiting trial on the charges, and Earl Krugel pled guilty to the charges regarding this plot in January 2003. Krugel, 60, faced 10 to 20 years in prison under terms of a plea agreement; if convicted at trial, he could have faced life without possibility of parole.

JDL member Dr. Baruch Goldstein shot and killed 29 Muslims worshipping in the Mosque of Abraham (or al-Ibrihimi Mosque) at the site of the Cave of the Patriarchs in the West Bank town of Hebron on February 25, 1994. Baruch's membership in the JDL drew attention once again to this group, although there is no specific evidence of collaboration by this group in this incident.

According to FBI reports, this organization was the secondmost active terrorist terrorist group in the United States for roughly two decades, second only to the Puerto Rican separatist group Armed Forces of National Liberation.

Reference: Anti-Defamation League. Backgrounder: The Jewish Defense League. Available online. URL: http://www.adl.org/extremism/jdl_chron.asp. Accessed March 20, 2006.

jihad

Originally this term referred to the inner struggle each Muslim faces in the attempt to come to peace with one's self. Many religious Muslims prefer this interpretation to the one commonly asserted by and accepted in the West that Islam views itself in a struggle with and under siege by infidels. Islam, like other major religions, is not monolithic, and important terminology and issues of doctrine may be interpreted in a variety of ways.

The interpretations of the legitimate targets of a jihad are varied. OSAMA BIN LADEN, for example, does "not differentiate between those dressed in military uniforms and civilians; they are all targets. . . ." Some Islamic scholars, however, argue that bin Laden is wrong and that Islamic sharia (holy law) protects civilians. In any case, they argue, only the head of an Islamic state, something bin Laden is not, can legitimately conduct a jihad. Others suggest that a jihad can occur after its intended target is at least offered the opportunity to convert to Islam and that, in any event, a jihad is a last resort.

In Islam, spreading the faith "by the sword" helps to describe the growth of Islam in its earliest stages. This method, however, does not distinguish Islam from Christianity, its greatest and most durable competitor. Most of the growth in each religion is due to a natural increase rather than forced or voluntary conversions. It is important to remember that a jihad has acquired a political purpose in the hands of governments and Islamic radical organizations. These have made a point of encouraging and in some cases announcing that they have declared and are fighting a jihad with the West in general and the United States and Israel in particular.

Martyrdom is viewed by radical Islamists as justified and warranted in a jihad. Islamic scholars, though, have pointed out that Islamic law prohibits suicide. Clearly, there is a debate raging here. Radical elements believe they are already engaged in a jihad with the West because of what they regard as the West's cultural invasion and economic exploitation of traditionally Islamic lands. The jihad cannot end until the West is thoroughly defeated and Israel eliminated.

Reference: Cook, David. *Understanding Jihad* (Berkeley: University of California Press, 2005).

Jihad Group *See* EGYPTIAN ISLAMIC JIHAD.

Julius Caesar, assassination of

Caesar was murdered on March 15, 44 B.C., the famous Ides of March celebrated in countless movies based more or less on Shakespeare's play. Political assassination is a terrorist act against a government official, but in this case, the assassination was coordinated and carried out by other government officials. A large number of Roman senators desired to restore the Roman Republic. They viewed Caesar as one more in a series of military dictators and resented his close association with Cleopatra, the Egyptian queen whose own political ambitions threatened to challenge Roman supremacy in the eastern Mediterranean. At the time of his death, Caesar was politically unchallenged since he had eliminated all of his political opponents. Caesar is said to have been preparing to consolidate his military victories and may have considered becoming king.

On the day of his murder, Caesar traveled to the Senate where he was attacked by several of its members wielding knives. One of them, Brutus, apparently was the last to plunge his blade into Caesar's body. The closeness in age of the two argue against Brutus being Caesar's son. Like most political assassinations, this one was based on a combination of altruism and perceived self-interest. Caesar's popularity with the Roman masses frightened many senators who saw him as a successful demagogue. They viewed their own positions as being in jeopardy.

Caesar's death achieved in fact what his murderers feared. Within a few years Caesar's successors, his grand nephew Octavian and Marc Antony, destroyed the republican armies and then fought each other. In the end Octavian established the Roman Empire and the republic was never restored. The assassination of a high public official can lead to any number of unintended consequences that are unpredictable. However, it is unlikely that an assassin considers all the possibilities or even cares to do so.

K

Kach/Kahane Chai

Kach is a political organization that advocates the restoration of the biblical state of Israel. For several years, Kach functioned in Israel as a political party that drew enough public support at election time to enable its founder, Rabbi Meir Kahane, to take a seat in the Israeli parliament. Kahane was assassinated in the United States in 1990, and the movement was transformed into Kahane Chai (Hebrew for "Kahane lives") by his son and successor, Binyamin. It was declared by the U.S. government to be a terrorist organization at that time.

The Israeli government declared Kahane Chai a terrorist organization in March 1994 under the 1948 Terrorism Law. This followed the group's statement of support for Dr. Baruch Goldstein's murder of dozens of Islamic worshippers in the al-Ibrahimi Mosque in Israel in February 1994. Palestinian gunmen killed Binyamin Kahane and his wife in a drive-by shooting in December 2000 in the West Bank.

The group has organized protests against the Israeli government and has harassed and threatened Palestinians in Hebron and the West Bank. Kach vowed revenge for the death of Binyamin and his wife. It is suspected of involvement in a number of low-level attacks since the start of the al-Aqsa INTIFADA in 2000. Known Kach sympathizers were vocal and active in opposition to the 2005 withdrawal of Israeli settlers and forces from the Gaza Strip. Kahane Chai formally disbanded after being declared a terrorist group, but it continues to exist today as an active organization, advocating the transformation and expansion of Israel into a purely Jewish state with its ancient boundaries. It operates and recruits in some Jewish settlements in the West Bank as well as inside Israel. Its most obvious stronghold is in Qiryat Arba, a religious Jewish community of about 500 within Hebron, a West Bank Arab city of 100,000. It now calls itself the Kahane Movement and terms itself an advisory group for those who also oppose Jewish settlement withdrawal from the Occupied Territories.

The size of Kahane Chai's membership is uncertain. It continues to receive financial support from sympathizers in the United States and several western European countries.

Reference: National Memorial Institute for the Prevention of Terrorism (MIPT). "KACH." Available online. URL: http://www.tkb.org/Group.jsp?groupID=61. Accessed February 15, 2006.

Khaled, Leila (1936–)

During the late 1960s, Leila Khaled was a famous and, for a limited time, successful airplane hijacker. Her last known hijacking attempt failed. In September 1970, she attempted, with an associate, to take over a flight from Amsterdam to London of the Israeli national carrier, El Al. By this time, though, El Al had become one of the most secure international airlines. Antihijacking measures included the presence of armed sky marshals and bulletproof lockable doors that divided the cockpit from the passenger cabin. Israeli security agents now had become passengers on every flight. Khaled's colleague was shot to death after attempting to blow up the plane with a hand grenade. Khaled herself was wounded and subdued. She was detained by British authorities and eventually released. To the disgust of the Israelis, the British were anxious to cut a deal with the POPULAR FRONT FOR THE LIBERATION OF PALESTINE (PFLP) after it had masterminded three simultaneous hijackings to get the now desperate passengers released (they were being held in 100°F heat in the Syrian desert). Khaled then disappeared from public view, married, and had a family. She was never placed on trial.

Reference: BBC. UK Confidential. "Transcripts: The Guerilla's Story." January 1, 2001. Available online. URL: http://news.bbc.co.uk/1/hi/in_depth/uk/2000/uk_confidential/1090986.stm. Accessed March 15, 2006.

Khmer Rouge (Party of Democratic Kampuchea)

A radical communist movement that came to power in Cambodia in 1975 after 12 years of GUERRILLA WARFARE. The Khmer Rouge's leader, Pol Pot (1925–98), immediately initiated a reign of terror against the Cambodian nation of 7 million people. By the time he was driven from power in 1979, a fourth of that number were dead. Most of these died in horrific circumstances. The Khmer Rouge emptied Cambodia's cities, determined to turn the country into a pristine agricultural society. Physicians, teachers, journalists, and engineers

A woman looks at the skulls on display at the Choeung Ek killing fields memorial. (GETTY IMAGES)

were summarily executed in an irrational attempt to purify the society and rid it of any foreign influence that could threaten the sanctity of the revolution. Not even the sick and infirm were spared. At least 20,000 hospital patients were thrown out of their beds and forced to join the exodus to the countryside where Cambodians began dying by the thousands from starvation and disease.

The Khmer Rouge also attempted with a good deal of success to destroy ethnic minorities in Cambodia, including the Chinese and Vietnamese communities. Vietnamese were considered the historic enemies of Cambodia. By 1978, Vietnam invaded Cambodia and was able to dislodge the Khmer Rouge from power during the early months of 1979. However, the Khmer Rouge continued its resistance and attempted to recover power for many more years. The Cambodian government during the 1990s granted amnesty to those Khmer Rouge fighters who would give up their arms. The organization finally disintegrated; Pol Pot and others of its surviving leaders were arrested. In 1998, Pol Pot died in captivity, probably of complications from malaria.

By 1999, the remnants of the Khmer Rouge either surrendered or disbanded. However, only two of Pol Pot's 10 former lieutenants have been convicted of crimes and sent to prison. In 2005, the United Nations and the Cambodian government agreed to setting up a tribunal that will try remaining Khmer Rouge leaders. Thirty Cambodian and UN judges were sworn in in July 2006, and trials were expected to start in 2007.

References: BBC. Asia-Pacific. "Khmer Rouge Court Gets Go-ahead." April 30, 2005. Available online. URL: http://news.bbc.co.uk/1/hi/world/asia-pacific/4500391.stm. Accessed March 15, 2006; Kiernan, Ben. *How Pol Pot Came to Power: Colonialism, Nationalism, and Communism in Cambodia, 1930–1975* (New Haven, Conn.: Yale University Press, 2004); Short, Philip. *Pol Pot: Anatomy of a Nightmare* (New York: Holt Rinehart, 2005).

Khomeini, Ayatollah Ruhollah (1902–1989)

The ayatollah spent a good part of his life in exile from his native land of IRAN. He was exiled to Turkey in 1963, to IRAQ the next year, and finally to France in 1978 because of his implacable opposition to the reforms initiated by Reza Shah Pahlavi. The ayatollah was convinced that the shah's regime was straying from Islamic orthodoxy by pursuing the reforms and in becoming too closely allied to and identified with Western secularism. After the shah was overthrown in 1979, the ayatollah returned to Iran to establish the country's Islamic Republic, a regime that has since applied the Qu'ran to most aspects of daily life. Khomeini was instrumental in reversing Iran's close ties with the United States and Israel. A policy of hostility was substituted that included his eventual support for the seizure of the American embassy and personnel during 1979–81. This was an act considered by the international community to be in violation of international law and by many to be an act of political terrorism as well. The Khomeini regime also encouraged martyrdom during the eight-year-long conflict with Iraq, a fact that helps to account for the tremendous casualties suffered by Iran.

Several months before his death, Khomeini issued a fatwa, which called for the death of author Salman Rushdie because of his book *The Satanic Verses* and its alleged blasphemy against the prophet Muhammad. Despite Khomeini's death, the fatwa is currently still in effect.

Reference: Milani, Mohsen M. *Making of Iran's Islamic Revolution: From Monarchy to Islamic Republic* (New York: Perseus Publishing, 1994).

Kim Jong Il (1941–)

Kim has the dubious honor of presiding over what is probably the world's most centrally planned economy in the People's Republic of (North) Korea, a position he inherited at the time of his father's death in 1994. This was the first time in history that a family political transition occurred in a communist country. There is little evidence in recent years that Kim's regime sponsored terrorist activities outside of North Korea, but Kim apparently has a long history of kidnapping movie stars from South Korea. (Kim also enjoys surfing the Net and watching satellite television, two leisure activities expressly denied to most of the country's population.) Kim's domestic policies have caused a disaster for his people. North Korea throughout most of the 1990s experienced widespread starvation as it increasingly became isolated both politically and economically.

Kim has apparently authorized occasional attacks on the Republic of (South) Korea. Technically, the two Koreas have been in a state of war since 1950, though

Kim Jong-Il (GETTY IMAGES)

the visit of the South Korean president to the north in June 2000 may be the beginning of a peace process. The suppression of human rights in North Korea has been especially severe. No criticism of or political opposition to Kim, the "dear, glorious leader" according to government pronouncements, is officially permitted or tolerated.

See also OVERVIEW OF TERRORISM: NORTH KOREA.

References: BBC. Asia-Pacific. "Profile: Kim Jong-Il." July 31, 2003. Available online. URL: http://news.bbc.co.uk/2/hi/asia-pacific/1907197.stm. Accessed March 15, 2006.; Becker, Jasper. *Rogue Regime: Kim Jong Il and the Looming Threat of North Korea* (New York: Oxford University Press, 2004).

King David Hotel, bombing of

Located in central Jerusalem, the King David Hotel has long been one of Israel's premier establishments. As the prestate period was winding down, the British made the hotel an important symbol of its presence in Palestine. Because the hotel housed several British administrative offices and some military personnel, it was considered a legitimate target by Jewish resistance groups. At first both the HAGANAH and the IRGUN ZVAI LEUMI cooperated in planning to bomb the hotel. The Haganah, however, withdrew its cooperation because its more moderate leadership believed that destroying the hotel would invite extremely harsh retribution.

The Irgun was convinced of the opposite. It felt that the British public was already weary of the seemingly never-ending fighting and was growing more and more convinced that Britain would only sacrifice more lives in a meaningless effort to keep the peace in Palestine. Bombing the hotel would, in its opinion, hasten the British departure and the arrival of an independent Jewish state.

On July 22, 1946, an Irgun team, dressed as waiters, rolled seven milk churns full of dynamite and TNT into the empty Regency Grill of the King David Hotel in Jerusalem. At 12:37 P.M., the TNT in the milk cans exploded, creating pressure so great that it burst the hearts, lungs, and livers of the clerks working on the floors above.

Thurston Clarke gives a gruesome description of the fate of the people in the King David Hotel at that time:

> In that split second after 12:37, thirteen of those who had been alive at 12:36 disappeared without a trace. The clothes, bracelets, cufflinks, and wallets which might have identified them exploded into dust and smoke. Others were turned to charcoal, melted into chairs and desks or exploded into countless fragments. The face of a Jewish typist was ripped from her skull, blown out of a window, and smeared onto the pavement below. Miraculously it was recognizable, a two-foot-long distorted death mask topped with tufts of hair.
>
> Blocks of stones, tables and desks crushed heads and snapped necks. Coat racks became deadly arrows that flew across rooms, piercing chests. Filing cabinets pinned people to walls, suffocating them. Chandeliers and ceiling fans crashed to the floor, impaling and decapitating those underneath.

Ninety-one people died in that bomb blast. Of these, 28 were British, 41 were Arabs, and 17 were Jewish. Another 46 were injured.

The person who commanded this attack stated bluntly:

> There is no longer any armistice between the Jewish people and the British administration of Eretz Israel

> which hands our brothers over to Hitler. Our people are at war with this regime—war to the end.

While many in Britain wanted revenge, the Irgun may have been correct in its assessment. The British government began seeking a way to exit and more and more sought assistance from the United States and the United Nations. Less than two years later it ended its mandate and evacuated its personnel from Palestine.

It is interesting to note that the leader in this attack, the man responsible for the destruction of 91 lives, was MENACHEM BEGIN, who later served during 1977–1983 as prime minister of ISRAEL. The Irgun fighter who acted to destroy the hotel is the same man who, working with President Carter of the United States and President Anwar Sadat of EGYPT, made significant efforts to move Israel on the road to peace with its Arab neighbors, signing the famous Camp David Accords, bringing a measure of peace between Israel and Egypt, breaking the cycle of violence between Israel and at least one of its neighbors.

This incident illustrates how difficult the line between "patriot" and "terrorist" is to maintain clearly. Individual acts may be "terrorism"; individuals need not be unilaterally "terrorists." Thus, to define terrorism may be possible, but to define terrorists may not.

See also CYCLICAL NATURE OF TERRORISM.

References: Bell, J. Bowyer. *Terror out of Zion: Irgun Zvai Leumi, LEHI, and the Palestine Underground, 1929–1949* (New York: Simon & Schuster, 1987), pp. 168–175; Clarke, Thurston. *By Blood and Fire: The Attack on the King David Hotel* (New York: Putnam, 1981); Metzer, Milton. *The Terrorists* (New York: Harper & Row, 1983).

Kommissar, the

In Weisbaden, a computer nicknamed "the Kommissar" plays a vital role in Germany's battle against terrorism. It is controlled by the Federal Criminal Investigation Department (the BKA). During the 1980s and 1990s, it experienced an enormous growth in the federal resources put at its disposal.

The heart of the computer system is an index of information called PIOS (Personnen, Institutionen, Objekte, Sachen), in which is stored every clue (such as addresses, contracts, movements) about known and suspected terrorists. Every address found in a suspect's possession, every telephone number, and the name of any person who writes to him or her in prison is stored in this system. Information about every object found at the scene of a terrorist attack or in an place where terrorists have been becomes a part of this computer's data banks.

This information has been effectively used by another German intelligence investigative tool—a special unit of investigators operating in small teams on *Zielahnungen* (TARGET SEARCH TEAMS). These searches are instituted, according to German officials, for the apprehension of terrorists wanted under an arrest warrant, with priority given to a "hard core" of about 15 violent offenders. The Kommissar is used by the search teams as a base of information from which the search can be focused, and it is thus a key tool in counterterrorism efforts by Germany.

See also GSG-9.

Kongra-Gel *See* KURDISTAN WORKERS' PARTY.

Ku Klux Klan

The Ku Klux Klan was founded in 1866 by several Confederate Civil War veterans. It has seen several cycles of growth stemming from periods of rapid social and political change, such as the Civil Rights movement in the 1960s. It has also seen cycles of collapse as a result of corrupt or ineffectual leadership.

The majority of the Ku Klux Klan's beliefs are based on the ideology of the CHRISTIAN IDENTITY MOVEMENT (CIM). In fact, The KKK has traditionally been the CIM's largest movement. Members of the CIM believe that Anglo-Saxon, Celtic, Scandinavian, Germanic, and associated cultures are the racial descendants of the tribes of Israel and that the Jews are the descendants of Satan. The KKK and the CIM believe in the end of the world and the Second Coming of Christ. However, before the Second Coming, this belief system posits the need for a "cleansing process" in which the white race needs to rid the world of the forces of evil, which are the Jews and the nonwhites. Christian Identity followers believe that they are chosen by God to wage the battle during Armageddon, and they will be the last line of defense for the white Christian race. As one leader of Christian Identity stated, "We are going to build the Kingdom of our God on this continent if we have to turn it into a Bosnia first!"

The KKK, as a Christian Identity group, distorts many biblical texts in order to justify its hatred of

A Ku Klux Klan member salutes during an American Nazi Party rally, 2004. (GETTY IMAGES)

blacks, Jews, homosexuals, abortion providers, and communists. Followers believe that they are the descendants of Adam's son Abel, thus they are God's chosen people. In their mind-set, Jews are descendants of Cain, and nonwhites are subhuman. In fact, many of these members refer to nonwhites as the "mud races" and believe they should be exterminated.

Most of the Ku Klux Klan's incidents of violence and terror were prevalent during periods of rapid social change, such as the period of reconstruction after the Civil War and the Civil Rights movement in the 1960s. A belief that they were under attack and had to protect their way of life motivated many members to commit acts of intimidation, murder, torture, and terrorism and to justify these acts as "self-defense." In the 1860s, former slaves, Northern teachers, judges, and politicians were the intended targets of terrorism by Klan members in response to the extension of rights to Southern blacks (through the Anti-Defamation League). During this time, Klansmen also began waging guerrilla warfare against a government that they felt was corrupt and depriving them of their white rights. In the early 1900s, with the revival of the Klan, lynchings and vigilantism were the main acts perpetrated by members.

With the rise of the Civil Rights movement in the 1960s, more incidents of terrorism occurred in the forms of cross and church burnings and murders. Several incidents of Klan murders have occurred in the 21st century. Recently, there have been a series of cross burnings outside of black churches in Durham, North Carolina. Police officials have found KKK recruitment fliers at the sites of these terror incidents. Also, members of the Christian Knights were accused of burning two black churches in June 1995. The majority of the Klan's violent activities have diminished to rallies and meetings today. However, sporadic incidents of violence and terror continue to be linked to Klansmen.

The Ku Klux Klan has three headquarters in the United States. The Imperial Klans of America (IKA) is headquartered in Powderly, Kentucky. This splinter group of disgruntled members of the KKK is the largest of the remaining Klan. The IKA has about 20 cells spread throughout the United States and chapters in seven foreign countries. The American Knights of the Ku Klux Klan is headquartered in Butler, Indiana, and the Knights of the White Kamelia is in Jasper, Texas. Today there are a few thousand members of the Ku Klux Klan organized into just over 100 cells. Many of these members are connected with other militia groups, including but not limited to the ARYAN NATIONS, the National Alliance, and many other groups affiliated with Christian Identity.

Unlike many of the world's terrorist organizations, the KKK does not receive funding from states or other organizations. The KKK receives some funding from membership dues and the sales of Klan paraphernalia. The majority of members hold regular jobs and simply donate a great deal of their earnings to the Klan organization. Klan members tend to be lower- and working-class Caucasians.

One of the general goals of the Ku Klux Klan is racial separation. As the Grand Dragon of the KKK, Christian Knights, stated, "The Klan is not for violence. . . . It's for racial separation, but the government is conspiring with the blacks and others to mingle the races and trample on individual rights." The U.S. government is therefore one of the Klan's main enemies, since it refuses to grant the Klan's "white rights": the right to be separated from nonwhites.

The Klan is currently fragmented into hundreds of independent groups. Most of their activities consist of public rallies and protests, with recruitment through mass mailings, leaflets, and the Internet. Although most of the new Klan groups are independent, several are still affiliated with the Imperial Klans, American Knights, and the Knights of the White Kamelia. It has been suggested that several Klan groups are currently linking with al-Qaeda–based cells, which share their hatred of the U.S. government.

References: MacLean, Nancy. *Behind the Mask of Chivalry: The Making of the Second Ku Klux Klan* (New York: Oxford University Press, 1994); Ridgeway, James. *Blood in the Face: The Ku Klux Klan, Aryan Nations, Nazi Skinheads and the Rise of a New White Culture* (New York: Thunder's Mouth Press, 1995).

L. A. B.

Kurdistan Workers' Party (PKK)

The struggle for an independent Kurdistan affected the countries of Turkey, Iraq, Iran, Syria, and areas of the former Soviet Union, all areas of heavy Kurdish concentration. Countless numbers of groups emerged during this struggle, sharing the specific aim of protecting Kurdish rights and, at times, attempting Kurdish independence, using various operational methods to achieve their goals. This resulted in the rise of a wide spectrum of organizations ranging from terrorists to political advocates.

It was in this context that the Kurdistan Workers' Party (PKK) emerged in Turkey in the early 1970s. Indicative of the environment in which the self-proclaimed Marxist Party was born, there continue to be heated debates as to exactly what type of organization the PKK truly is. Members of the group consider themselves to be revolutionaries. Many governments, including those of Turkey and the United States, consider the group a terrorist organization. Even parts of the Kurdish population regard the PKK with hostile ambivalence. Many Kurds do not support such militant behavior as the group exhibits and consider that the PKK made matters even worse for the Kurdish population in some instances. Also, many Kurds lost loved ones at the hands of the PKK because the group deemed them to be "state collaborators," justifying Kurdish civilians as targets of violence just like the Turkish government. This PKK tactic contributed to a great distrust of the group by many of their own people.

Each country that contains a heavy Kurdish concentration offers a vastly different experience. Turkey is a significant player in the overall Kurdish question because the state was the successor of the Ottoman Empire, the former imperial ruler of the area called Kurdistan (as the five pieces of independent countries that comprise the areas of Kurdish concentration are often designated). The Ottoman Empire did not allow for any independence movements or opposition against imperial exploitation. What the Ottomans did do, however, was to allow the Kurds to exist autonomously with their own language, religion, and cultural characteristics relatively intact. This trend began to change, though, at the beginning of the 20th century when Turkish nationalist forces took control of the Ottoman administration right before the empire was dismantled after World War I. This resulted in the installation of a widespread ethnic cleansing program in the country. The policy of "Turkification," the banning of all other languages and cultures other than Turkish, became an important state goal.

The "Turkification" policy of banning any language other than Turkish stood in opposition to the Treaty of Lausanne (July 24, 1923), which founded the Republic of Turkey. This official international document did not deny the Kurd's right of existence. Paragraph 39 even provided for the free social use of a minority's language. This stands in contrast to the ban of all non-Turkish languages that exists even today and is one of the most contested issues between the Kurds and the Turkish government.

The history of the Kurdish Workers' Party begins in the 1960s, emerging from a Turkish leftist movement. Many of the groups were revolutionary, either following the Marxist-Leninist or Maoist approach. These first extremists did not, however, separately advocate the liberation of the Kurds from Turkey as a whole. Realizing there was no group to satisfy the main objective of Kurdish liberation, political science student Abdullah Oçalan started the first phase of the PKK's existence (1970–78), by creating his own ideology and party platform. It was during this first phase that the basis for Kurd-on-Kurd violence was established, stemming from the development of sharp criticism of the continuing exploitation of the Kurds by Turkish imperialism and the Kurdish elements that cooperated within that system. This led to the PKK targeting its own people, causing division within its ranks.

The second phase in PKK history was the most difficult and violent, as well as the most memorable period of PKK and Turkish relations. Due to a crackdown on political activity because of a Turkish military coup on September 12, 1980, the PKK was forced out of Turkey and began training politically and militarily in other Middle Eastern states, such as Syria, and also working with Palestinian radicals. This network flourished for the PKK, enabling the group to improve steadily its support network of Turkish Kurds abroad.

This bloody period of PKK-Turkish relations culminated in the 1990s. The PKK until this point was blamed for including civilians and Kurdish villagers in the scope of violence against the Turkish government. These accusations, which came from around the world, resulted in a significant change in PKK policy. In a 1990 party congress, the group pledged to cease all activities that could compromise innocents and to increase the focus on military targets. Also during this conference, the party declared a general amnesty, available for one year, for any Kurd who refused to collaborate further with the Turkish state. These particular modifications marked the beginning of a distinct change in the party's orientation, moving toward a more political rather than a separatist organization.

Besides the need to soften their image to their fellow Kurds and the international community, other factors necessitated the PKK's change in doctrine. The most important one was the collapse of the Soviet Union. Originating as a socialist organization, the PKK depended on influence and support from the communist superpower. This support came in the past in direct forms such as weapon provisions or indirectly from the support the PKK received from Syria, a well-known Soviet ally. All this vital international support quickly dried up at the conclusion of the cold war.

After finding themselves without historical allies in Syria and the former Soviet Union, and especially with the PKK leader Oçalan expelled from Syria, his host country of 18 years, late in 1998, the PKK found it necessary to reexamine its strategies yet again. The group found it convenient to do so by way of propaganda, presenting themselves as the true socialist entity unlike what the former Soviet Union had become. In doing so, the PKK made themselves more marketable, especially at its Fifth Congress (January 8–27, 1995), by complaining about the lack of individual and economic rights that existed in the former Soviet Union. Even though the PKK lost that valuable ally, the group did find itself with new possibilities in the face of the eradication of the stagnant socialism in the former Soviet Union. The PKK's new definition of socialism was revolutionary in itself, stating in its party program, "Socialism means the free orientation of the relationship between people and the society. Socialism is in opposition to all forms of authority, which are separated from social reality and which seek to oppress or exploit."

It was during this last round of ideological changes that the PKK distanced itself from overt terrorist activity and made gestures in an effort to be considered a legitimate political entity. On several occasions since 1994, the PKK has offered a cease-fire in exchange for a dialogue for the purpose of solving the conflict within Turkey's borders. These efforts, many made by Oçalan himself to Western leaders, were ignored due to Turkey's refusal to negotiate with the group.

The PKK's attempts for legitimacy were further strengthened in 1994 when the organization issued a "Declaration of Intent." This document formally decreed that the PKK was to abide by all humanitarian laws and rules of war as set forth in the Geneva Convention and pursuant protocols. Trying to make the PKK seem more like a legitimate entity, the declaration explicitly described who were legitimate and legal targets of attacks, including certain Turkish authorities and Kurdish persons who were proven to be village guards.

The "Declaration of Intent" was followed by another attempt to show the PKK's desire to peacefully settle the decades-long conflict with Turkey. In September 1999, with Oçalan already in Turkish captivity, his brother Osman declared that the PKK was following Oçalan's call to disarm forever. The organization followed by announcing that the word "Kurdistan" would be dropped from references with regard to the PKK's doctrine and objectives, a concession to the Turkish government, which declared the use of the term "Kurdistan" to be a crime.

When the chairman of the group, Abdullah Oçalan, was captured by Turkish authorities in Kenya in early 1999, he was sentenced to death. Oçalan's subsequent order for members to refrain from violence was endorsed by a PKK Congress in January 2000, when members approved Oçalan's initiative and claimed that the group would subsequently use only political means to achieve its goal of improved rights for Kurds in Turkey. The PKK changed its name to the Kurdistan Freedom and Democracy Congress (KADEK) and proclaimed its commitment to nonviolence in its support of Kurdish rights. However, a PKK/KADEK spokesman stated that its armed wing, the People's Defense Force, would not disband or surrender its weapons, for reasons of self-defense.

In late 2003, the PKK sought to engineer another political face-lift, renaming itself Kongra-Gel and promoting its peaceful intentions while continuing to conduct attacks in "self-defense" and to refuse to disarm. After five years, the group's hard-line militant wing, the People's Defense Force, renounced its self-imposed cease-fire on June 1, 2004. During the cease-fire, the group had divided into two factions: politically minded reformists and hard-liners who advocated a return to violence. The hard-liners took control of the group in February 2004.

References: McKiernan, Kevin. *The Kurds: A People in Search of Their Homeland* (New York: St. Martin's Press, 2006); Natali, Denise. *Kurds and the State: Evolving National Identity in Iraq, Turkey and Iran* (Syracuse, N.Y.: Syracuse University Press, 2005).

M.G.

Kurds

The Kurds are a Middle Eastern people whose origins can be traced back at least a millennium and whose total numbers range between 20 and 25 million. The great preponderance of Kurds are Sunni Muslims. The Kurds are not Arabs, and most of them do not live in Arab lands. The Kurds have never established an independent state, though separatist movements have functioned in the three countries where most of the Kurdish community is located—IRAN, IRAQ, and Turkey. Nearly all Kurds live in the contiguous areas of eastern Turkey, western Iran, and northern Iraq. They are either engaged in conflict with their respective governments or disengaged in periods of lull between conflicts.

None of these three states is willing to cede any territory to the Kurdish community to establish a sovereign "Kurdistan." A price is being paid for not doing so, however. Turkey has been denied membership in the European Union in great part because of its war against Kurdish insurgents. Iran and Iraq are already regarded by much of the international community as having governments that treat their Kurdish populations inhumanely. In Iraq, the government, under SADDAM HUSSEIN in order to destroy its own Kurdish citizens, has used chemical weapons.

It is not uncommon for Kurds to fight among themselves as well. Tribal loyalties sometimes take precedence over unity. Kurds have also been manipulated by outside powers. In northern Iraq during the Persian Gulf conflict (1990–1991), Kurds became the victims of state terror when they rebelled against the central government in Baghdad. The Iraqi Kurds had understood that the United States would support them in their attempt to secede from the central government's control. They suffered terrible losses at the hands of the Iraqi army.

It is not uncommon for Kurds to fight among themselves as well. Tribal loyalties sometimes take precedence over unity. Kurds have also been manipulated by outside powers. In northern Iraq during the Persian Gulf conflict (1990–91) Kurds became the victims of state terror when they rebelled against Saddam Hussein's government in Baghdad. The Iraqi Kurds had understood that the United States would support them in their attempt to secede from the central government's control. However, they suffered terrible losses at the hands of the Iraqi army.

Kurdish forces aided the U.S.-led invasion of Iraq in 2003, joining with U.S. and British forces to seize the traditionally Kurdish cities of Kirkuk and Mosul.

Although Kurds were given a limited veto over constitutional changes in the subsequent interim Iraqi constitution (2004), many Iraqi Shiites found this unacceptable. Kurdish leaders were wary, as a result, of political developments as the United States ceded sovereignty to a new Iraqi government.

In Turkey, where the government has suppressed Kurdish culture, fighting erupted in the mid-1980s, mainly in southeast Turkey, between government forces and guerrillas of the KURDISTAN WORKERS' PARTY (PKK), which was established in 1984 and has engaged in terrorist attacks. The PKK announced in February 2000 that it would end its attacks, but the arrest the same month of the Kurdish mayors of Diyarbakir and other towns on charges of aiding the rebels threatened to revive the unrest. Reforms passed in 2002 and 2003 to facilitate Turkish entrance in the European Union included ending bans on private education in Kurdish and on giving children Kurdish names. In 2004, following Turkish actions against it, the PKK—renamed Kongra-Gel—said that it would end the cease-fire. There were also clashes between the Kurds of Turkey and Iraq in the 1990s and Kurdish unrest in Syria in 2004.

Reference: McDowall, David. *A Modern History of the Kurds* (New York: I. B. Tauris, 2004).

L

Lashkar-e-Tayyiba (LT; a.k.a. Army of the Righteous)

The LT is the armed wing of the Pakistani-based religious organization, Markaz-ud-Dawa-wal-Irshad (MDI), a Sunni anti–United States missionary organization formed in 1989. A Pakistani group with ties to HAMAS and HIZBALLAH, the Lashkar-e-Tayyiba operates primarily in Kashmir, an area the Lashkar refers to as "occupied Kashmir." Lashkar currently has an unknown number of activists, probably numbering in the thousands. Since 1993, Lashkar has conducted numerous operations against both Indian military and civilian targets in Kashmir. The organization has basically two goals—to remove all remnants of Indian rule in Kashmir and to convert Pakistan into an Islamic society.

It considers the Indian military to be corrupt and demonstrates this observation by arguing that most of its weapons have been purchased from corrupt Indian military officers. Lashkar considers itself a high-tech organization and uses the Internet to attract followers. It has had better success in efforts to attract well-educated youths to its ranks than most Islamic extremist organizations. Lashkar has few age restrictions and accepts recruits as young as eight years old to prepare for jihad. Training for recruits is extensive. It has its own Secret Intelligence and Analysis Wing (SRAJ). While Lashkar sympathizes with organizations such as Hamas and Hizballah in their animosity toward Israel and the United States, the organization has restricted its own energies toward removing India from Kashmir by extreme militant means. In this sense, Lashkar regards its own struggle and objectives as local rather global.

While the LT is one of the three largest and best-trained groups fighting in Kashmir against India, it is not formally connected to a political party. Its leader is MDI chief Professor Hafiz Mohammed Saeed. Under his leadership, the LT has carried out a number of violent operations against Indian troops and civilian targets in Kashmir. It is suspected of being responsible for eight separate attacks in August 2000 that killed nearly 100 people. Militants in the LT are also suspected of kidnapping six persons in Akhala, India, in November 2000 and of killing five of them.

Information indicates that there are several hundred members of the LT in Azad Kashmir, Pakistan, and in India's southern Kashmir and Doda regions. Almost all LT cadres are foreigners, mostly Pakistanis from seminaries across the country and Afghan veterans of the Afghan wars. Based in Muridke, near Lahore, and Muzaffarabad, LT members are trained in mobile training camps across Pakistan-administered Kashmir and

Afghanistan, in the use of assault rifles, light and heavy machine guns, mortars, explosives, and rocket-propelled grenades.

Reference: National Memorial Institute for the Prevention of Terrorism (MIPT). "Lashkar-e-Taibia (LT)." Available online. URL: http://www.tkb.org/Group.jsp?groupID=66. Accessed February 15, 2006.

Lebanon

Lebanon is a relatively small country somewhat less than the size of Connecticut, but it is one of the most heterogeneous states in the Middle East. It is in many ways a collection of the main Islamic sects, Sunnis and Shiites, as well as a variety of Christian denominations that include Greek Orthodox and Greek Catholic communities. There are a total of five Muslim and 11 Christian officially recognized organizations. Based on the country's last census, taken in 1932, seats in the national parliament as well as the top offices of president and prime minister are distributed according to sectarian demographic strength.

In part because of its geographical location—borders with ISRAEL and Syria, two stronger states hostile to one another—and because of traditional conflict between and mutual distrust of the largest communities, Christian, Sunni, Shiite, and Druse, Lebanon has in recent decades been a violent society. In addition, 400,000 Palestinian refugees in the southern part of the country have been an excellent recruiting ground for terrorist organizations intent on attacking Israel. The Lebanese government has not admitted these refugees to citizenship and apparently has no intention of doing so, regarding them almost as a state within a state. Syria has also considered Lebanon as part of historic Syria. The Lebanese government has consistently taken great care not to take any actions that could irritate the Syrian government. Between 20,000 and 30,000 Syrian soldiers have been permanently stationed in Lebanon over the last few decades.

Lebanon has been both a base for and a victim of terrorist outrages. Several of the sectarian communities have committed outrages against one another. The government is not in complete control of the country. The civil war of 1975–90 is long over, but sectarian politics are still the rule.

Lebanon's Christian militia, during its civil struggle, was guilty of the massacre in 1982 of hundreds of Palestinian refugees at two camps, Sabra and Shatilla, which were supposed to be under the guard of ARIEL SHARON and his troops at that time. The massacre resulted in the forced resignation of Sharon from the Israeli military and continues to feed Palestinian hatred and fear of Israel, which in turn has led to continued attacks across Jordan's southern border against Israel. The withdrawal of Israeli troops in 2000 from the "security buffer" Israel had retained in southern Jordan to help prevent such attacks led to a short period of calm between Israel and Jordan.

In the past, the country played host to the JAPANESE RED ARMY and remains host to numerous groups engaged in terrorism, including HIZBALLAH, the Palestinian Islamic Jihad, the POPULAR FRONT FOR THE LIBERATION OF PALESTINE–GENERAL COMMAND, the ABU NIDAL ORGANIZATION, and HAMAS. The government has, however, moved legally against Sunni extremist groups, including those similar in ideology to AL-QAEDA. Syria's withdrawal of troops from the Bakáa valley in 2004–05 and the continuing political struggle between these two countries, which has cost the lives of several important political and media leaders by assassination, has made unclear the level of government support for the control of these groups within its borders.

On July 12, 2006, Hizballah seized two Israeli soldiers in a cross-border attack at Shtula, killing eight Israeli soldiers. Israel declared the attack to be an act of war and immediately struck back by bombing roads, bridges, power stations, and Hizballah posts in southern Lebanon, vowing to continue attacks until Hizballah disarmed. Hizballah's offer to exchange the two captured Israeli soldiers for prisoners held by Israel was rejected by Israel at that point.

The following day, Israel imposed a naval blockade on Lebanon and bombed Beirut's international airport, roads, and bridges. Hizballah continued to rain rockets onto northern Israel, killing two people. On July 14, Israel bombed Hizballah headquarters and a radio station in the Shiite community in Beirut and continued to destroy more roads and bridges, effectively sealing Lebanon off from the outside world in an effort to prevent Syria or Iran from getting aid to Hizballah and to deter Hizballah from escaping into Syria to regroup. That same day, Hizballah rockets landed in Haifa and other northern Israeli communities. Hizballah leader Hasan Nasrallah declared "open war" on Israel.

During the following weeks, the violence continued to escalate, with Israeli air strikes hitting targets in Beirut's primary Christian enclave, while its warplanes battered southern Lebanon, with civilian casualties mounting. Hundreds of thousands of Lebanese were displaced by the fighting and the bombings, creating a humanitarian crisis for the Lebanese government, which appealed to the international community for assistance. As thousands of tourists and non-Lebanese citizens sought to flee the embattled country, disaster assistance agencies were overwhelmed with the demands for help.

Fouad Siniora, the Lebanese prime minister elected in the early days of 2006, called for a cease-fire and urgent humanitarian aid. He offered in August to deploy 15,000 Lebanese troops to the southern part of his country to stabilize the region and to hasten the withdrawal of Israeli forces. Israel has demanded that Hizballah be disarmed before its withdrawal and that there be a competent international peacekeeping force in place, with Lebanese forces, to ensure the end of Hizballah attacks. Hizballah continued rocket attacks on the Israeli port city of Haifa and demonstrated its possession of longer-range rockets potentially capable of reaching Tel Aviv, with rockets landing near Nazareth on July 17.

United Nations involvement in the crisis was initially limited. On July 25, Israeli air strikes hit a United Nations post in Khiyam, Lebanon, killing four UN observers. Israeli prime minister Ehud Olmert expressed deep regret over the deaths of UN observers. Israeli media reported a government plan for a 1.2-mile "security zone" in southern Lebanon. The UN Security Council was unable to take action on the situation, due to division over the extent of Israel's "right to defend itself," strongly advocated by the United States, and the actions of a nonstate actor, Hizballah, supported by Syria and Iran. Calls by the UN on July 29 for a three-day cease-fire were accepted by Hizballah and rejected by Israel. The Israeli air strike the following day on Qana in southern Lebanon, which killed at least 50 civilians, mostly children, drew condemnation from UN ambassadors but no further action.

The humanitarian crisis deepened, and the political situation fractured further with the call on July 27 by al-Qaeda's number-two leader, Ayman al-Zawahiri, for Muslims to unite in a "holy war" against Israel and to join in the fighting in Lebanon and Gaza until "Islam reigns from Spain to Iraq." Al-Jazeerah news reported a taped message from al-Zawahiri, the first from al-Qaeda since Israel began its offensive against Hizballah militants in southern Lebanon.

By early August, Israel had expanded its ground offensive in Lebanon, thrusting its troops deeper into Lebanon and receiving authorization from the prime minister and his cabinet to push 13 miles into Lebanon, to the Litani River, in efforts to strike at Hizballah and to stop its rocket attacks on Israel. Israel at this point had approximately 10,000 troops in Lebanon, and it was unclear how many more would be committed to this expanded offensive.

At least 1,005 people in Lebanon and 160 Israelis were killed in the conflict sparked when Hizballah seized two Israeli soldiers in a cross-border raid on July 12. The United Nations Security Council sought to craft a resolution that would bring an end to the fighting as quickly as possible, balancing the need for Israeli security from Hizballah attacks with the exploding humanitarian crisis and climbing death toll. On August 11, the United Nations Security Council approved Security Council Resolution 1701, which called for an end to the hostilities. The resolution was approved by the Lebanese government on August 12 and by the Israeli government the next day, although smaller attacks from both Hizballah and Israel still continued.

References: Council on Foreign Relations. Background Q&A. "Terrorist Havens: Lebanon." Available online. URL: http://cfrterrorism.org/publications/9516.html. Accessed February 16, 2006; Fisk, Robert. *Pity the Nation: The Abduction of Lebanon* (New York: Avalon Publishing Group, 2002).

Liberation Tigers of Tamil Eelam (LTTE)

Founded in 1976 with a goal of establishing an independent Tamil State, the LTTE is the most powerful Tamil group in Sri Lanka. It began to engage in armed conflict with the Sri Lankan government in 1983, using a guerrilla strategy that has included terrorist tactics. The Tamil Tigers, as they are often called, have integrated a battlefield insurgent strategy with a terrorist campaign, targeting not only key government personnel in the more rural areas but also senior Sri Lankan political and military leaders in Colombo.

While political assassinations and bombings have been a common tactic, the Tigers have not targeted Western tourists. This may be due to the fact that much of the funding, military supplies, and cells of sympathizers are from this region, making attacks on these tourists a counterproductive move.

The exact strength of the LTTE is not known. As noted, there is significant overseas support involving fund-raising, weapons acquisition, and propaganda

Buddhist monks take part in a street demonstration in Sri Lanka to protest against the Tamil Tigers, 2005. (GETTY IMAGES)

activities, indicating a widespread support structure. Within Sri Lanka, there are about 8,000 to 10,000 armed members involved in the violent struggle, of whom there are between 3,000 and 6,000 trained fighters. With this strength, the Tigers control most of the northern and eastern coastal areas of Sri Lanka. From the Tigers' headquarters in the Jaffina Peninsula, LTTE leader Velupillai Prabhakaran used the internal support network to establish a comprehensive pattern of checkpoints and informants to keep tabs on any outsiders who enter the LTTE's area of control.

Most of the LTTE attacks have followed a typical insurgent strategy. Vulnerable government facilities are targeted, attacked, and the LTTE troops withdrawn quickly before government reinforcement can arrive.

The Tigers enjoy a widespread network of support by overt, legitimate organizations that operate in other countries. These support organizations include the World Tamil Association (WTA), the World Tamil Movement (WTM), the Federation of Associations of Canadian Tamils (FACT), the Ellahan Force, and the Sangillan Force. Many of these organizations support Tamil separatism (the goal of the Tigers) by lobbying foreign governments and the United Nations. These international contacts are also useful to the Tigers in procuring weapons, communications, and bomb-making equipment. The large Tamil communities in North America, Europe, and Asia are also sources of funding for the Tigers. Information indicated that some Tamil communities in Europe engaged in drug smuggling in the 1980s. Activities undertaken by drug couriers, moving narcotics through Europe, have historically served as a source of revenue for the Tamils.

The LTTE has successfully carried out assassinations of both Indian and Sri Lankan leaders, including the heads of state of both countries: former Indian prime minister Rajiv Gandhi in 1991, and Sri Lankan president Ranasinghe Premadasa in 1993. In 1999, the group was responsible for the assassination of Neelan Thiruchelvam, a Sri Lankan member of parliament, and two suicide bombings in Colombo that wounded Sri Lankan president Chandrika Kumaratunga. The following year, the LTTE killed Sri Lankan industry minister C. V. Gooneratne.

The last significant attack clearly linked to, or claimed by, the LTTE, however, was in July 2001, when a suicide bomb exploded at the international airport, killing 14 people. The following year, leaders of the LTTE signed a permanent cease-fire with the government, and by December of that year, the group had begun a process of decommissioning its weapons. Although in December 2002 the government and the rebels agreed to share power, the next two years still had several violent incidents allegedly linked to the LTTE.

The LTTE is currently observing a cease-fire agreement with the Sri Lankan government. In the wake of the devastation caused by the tsunami in December 2004, which killed more than 30,000 people, efforts to recover and rebuild much of the LTTE-controlled area have generated a spirit of cooperation and a willingness to abide by the cease-fire agreement.

The August 2005 assassination of Sri Lankan foreign minister Lakshman Kadirgamar—with which the Tamil Tigers are suspected to have been involved, though they deny any involvement—raised doubts about the reality of this peace.

Reference: Council on Foreign Relations. Background Q&A. "Terrorist Havens: Lebanon." Available online. URL: http://www.cfr.org/publication/9242/liberation_tigers_of_tamil_eelam_sri_lanka_separatists.html. Accessed February 16, 2006.

Libya, state-supported terrorism by

Under the leadership of General MU'AMMAR QADHAFI, Libya dispersed large amounts of aid during the 1970s and 1980s to various groups engaged in terrorist activities. That this dispersal appeared to depend greatly on whim, and consequently caused a great deal of frustration among terrorists dependent upon Qadhafi's support, does not detract from the substantial contributions he has made to the financing of terrorism worldwide.

Qadhafi supported Palestinian groups, including the POPULAR FRONT FOR THE LIBERATION OF PALESTINE (PFLP) and the POPULAR FRONT FOR THE LIBERATION OF PALESTINE–GENERAL COMMAND with donations of as much as $100 million a year. He also assisted the IRISH REPUBLICAN ARMY (IRA), the BASQUE FATHERLAND AND LIBERTY (ETA), the RED ARMY FACTION (RAF)/Baader-Meinhof gang, the JAPANESE RED ARMY, the RED BRIGADES (BR), the TUPAC AMARU REVOLUTIONARY MOVEMENT (MRTA), and the Moros (in the Philippines).

Libya's assistance was not confined to the financing of the terrorist operation itself. Israeli intelligence suggested that Qadhafi paid a $5 billion bonus to the BLACK SEPTEMBER terrorists who were responsible for the MUNICH MASSACRE OF ISRAELI ATHLETES in 1972. Western intelligence also believed that Qadhafi paid CARLOS "THE JACKAL" a large bonus, around $2 billion, for his role in the seizure of OPEC oil ministers in Vienna in December 1975.

Bonuses were given for success, such as that paid to Carlos, and for "injury or death on the job." By the 1990s, these significantly decreased in amount. Qadhafi reportedly paid only between $10,000 and $30,000 to the families of terrorists killed in action in the late 1980s, down considerably from the $100,000 reportedly paid to a terrorist injured in the OPEC incident in 1972.

So Qadhafi gave money to support terrorist groups and furnished monetary incentives for participating in terrorist events. Other leaders throughout history have supported dissident groups and provided for the survivors of their military or quasi-military activities.

However, Qadhafi took his support of terrorists to great lengths. When the United States carried out air raids on Libya on April 15, 1986, Qadhafi was furious. He offered to buy an American hostage in Lebanon so that he could have him killed. On April 17, Peter Kilburn, a 62-year-old librarian at the American University in Beirut who had been kidnapped on December 3, 1984, was "executed" after Qadhafi paid $1 million to the group holding him. He paid $1 million to be able to kill an elderly librarian in order to "punish" the United States for its bombing attack.

Declining oil revenues, due in part to UN sanctions, diminished Libya's role in financing terrorism.

In six years, Libya's oil-dependent income fell from $22 billion to about $5.5 billion, seriously reducing the state's ability to bankroll terrorism. Although Libya remained, in spite of this loss, involved in the training of terrorists, Qadhafi's role as "godfather" of terrorism decreased dramatically during the last decade of the 20th century, making it difficult to predict his role for the 21st century.

Libya's role decreased, but did not end, with the turn of the millennium. This became obvious when, after having been expelled from both Iraq and Syria, Abu Nidal, the Palestinian leader who planned the *ACHILLE LAURO* hijacking, was given refuge in Tripoli. Western sources feared that, under Libya's protection, Nidal would repay Qadhafi by striking at more American targets.

Libya also developed a strong "connection" to Central and South America through its ties to Nicaragua. The Sandinista government of Nicaragua was, until the early 1990s, the "Libyan connection" in this region, supplying arms, training, and logistical support to revolutionary groups in that region.

In 1986, Daniel Ortega wrote to Libya's leader, "My brother, given the brutal terrorist action launched by the U.S. government against the people of the Libyan Arab Jamahiriyah, I wish to send sentiments and solidarity from the FSLN National Directorate and the Nicaraguan people and government."

This was not the first time these leaders pledged friendship and support. Long before they came to power in 1979, Sandinista leaders had been training in PALESTINE LIBERATION ORGANIZATION (PLO) camps in Libya and Lebanon. When the Sandinistas finally seized power, Qadhafi promised political and financial aid, promises that he kept over the years.

In the early years of their rule, the Sandinistas received a $100 million "loan" from Libya. In 1983, Brazilian authorities inspecting four Libyan planes bound for Nicaragua discovered that crates marked "medical supplies" actually contained some 84 tons of military equipment. This "military assistance" included missiles, bombs, cannons, and two unassembled fighter planes.

In Managua, leaders from Germany's Red Army Faction/Baader-Meinhof gang, Spain's ETA, Colombia's M19, Peru's SENDERO LUMINOSO, and El Salvador's FMLN met with Libya and the PLO. Through Nicaragua, Libya was able to funnel arms to many of these groups.

M19's attack on Colombia's supreme court, in which more than 100 were killed, was carried out with arms supplied, through Nicaragua, by Libya. Many of the guns captured in that raid were linked to Libya, some of which reached M19 through conduits in Vietnam, Cuba, and Nicaragua.

Nicaragua's Libyan connection highlighted the continuing spiral of terror funded by Qadhafi. Libya supported a revolutionary terrorist group with money and arms, and when it had managed to seize control of Nicaragua, Libya used that government as a conduit to funnel arms and support to other terrorist groups engaged in similar struggles throughout Central and South America.

The peaceful end of the Sandinista regime, through democratic elections, brought to an end this "Libyan connection." Since Libya's profile in supporting terrorist groups similarly declined in the latter part of the 1990s, this transition has left several groups without a sponsor or support system. Some began to link up with the illicit drug cartels in Colombia, providing "security" for drug lords and the shipment of their goods. This diminished, to some degree, the revolutionary focus of such groups, and such operational switches helped to fill the gap left by the loss of Libyan patronage.

Libya's support for acts of terrorism continued to cause economic and political penalties during the 1990s, following the bombing of Pan Am flight 103 in 1988 over Scotland. The UN Security Council passed Resolution 731, which demanded that Libya take steps to end its state-sponsored terrorism, including extraditing two Libyan intelligence agents indicted by the United States and the United Kingdom for their role in that bombing. The resolution also required that Libya accept responsibility for the bombing, disclose all evidence related to it, pay appropriate compensation, satisfy French demands regarding Libya's alleged role in bombing UTA flight 772 in 1989, and cease all forms of terrorism.

In 1992, the UN Security Council adopted Resolution 748, imposing an arms and civil aviation embargo on Libya. This resolution demanded that Libyan Arab Airlines offices be closed and required that all states reduce Libya's diplomatic presence abroad. When these measures failed to elicit full compliance from Libya, the Security Council adopted Resolution 883 in 1993, imposing a limited assets freeze and oil technology embargo on Libya and strengthening existing sanctions against that nation.

In 1999, Libya surrendered the two suspects accused of the bombing of Pan Am flight 103 over Lockerbie, Scotland, in 1988, to a court in The Hague, presided over by international jurists. On January 31, 2001, the court found Abdel Baset Ali Mohamed al-

Megrahi guilty of murder, concluding that he caused an explosive device to detonate on board the airplane, resulting in the murder of the flight's 259 passengers and crew as well as 11 residents of Lockerbie, Scotland. The judges found that he acted "in furtherance of the purposes of . . . Libyan Intelligence Services." The other defendant, Al-Amin Khalifa Fhimah, was acquitted based on a lack of sufficient evidence of "proof beyond a reasonable doubt."

In 1999, Libya paid compensation for the death of a British policewoman, a move that preceded the reopening of the British embassy in Tripoli. The policewoman was killed and 11 demonstrators were wounded when gunmen in the Libyan People's Bureau in London fired on a peaceful anti-Qadhafi demonstration outside their building. Libya also paid damages to the families of victims in the bombing of UTA flight 771. Six Libyans had been convicted in absentia in that case.

In the wake of UN intervention in the Lockerbie case, in fact, the regime in Libya largely avoided open association with acts of terrorism and terrorist groups. While Qadhafi offered public support for radical Palestinian groups opposed to the PLO's Gaza-Jericho accord with Israel in 1993, and openly threatened to support extremist Islamic groups in neighboring Algeria and Tunisia, the level of practical open support by Libya for terrorism decreased substantially.

Instead, Libya played a high-profile role in negotiating the release of a group of foreign hostages seized in the Philippines by the Abu Sayyaf Group, reportedly in exchange for a ransom payment. The hostages included citizens of France, Germany, Malaysia, South Africa, Finland, the Philippines, and Lebanon. Libya also expelled the Abu Nidal Organization and distanced itself from Palestinian groups engaged in terrorism against Israel, although it maintained contact with groups such as the Palestine Islamic Jihad and the PFLP-GC.

In the wake of the September 11 attacks on the United States, Libya was vehement about its noninvolvement and condemned the actions. Clearly, Libya is seeking to redefine itself with regard to the soubriquet of "state sponsor of terrorism." In 2004, Libya joined the international community in condemning terrorism, and sanctions were lifted against its economy as it began to rebuild relations damaged by its long-term role as a state-supporter for terrorism.

References: Council on Foreign Relations. Background Q&A. "State Sponsors: Libya." Available online. URL: http://www.cfr.org/publication/9363/state_sponsors.html. Accessed February 16, 2006; Simons, Geoff. *Libya and the West: From Independence to Lockerbie* (New York: I. B. Tauris, 2003).

Libyan Islamic Fighting Group (LIFG; a.k.a. al-Jama'a al Islamiyyah al-Muqatilah; Fighting Islamic Group; Libyan Fighting Group; Libyan Islamic Group)

The exact date of the formation of the LIFG is not clear, although it issued a formal declaration of existence in October 1995. The origins of this group can be traced with some accuracy to an Islamic fundamentalist organization established clandestinely in Libya in 1982 that had ties with Islamic movements in the region, especially in Afghanistan, to which many of the Libyan organizations were drawn. In the fight against the Soviet-supported regime in the 1980s in Afghanistan, the Libyan jihadists networked with those of other nations and honed their fighting skills.

As these fighters returned home after the collapse of the Soviet regime, they found a country suffering from soaring unemployment, shortages of goods, and other socioeconomic problems engendered by economic mismanagement, the falling price of oil, and the sanctions imposed on Libya by the United Nations for its support of terrorism. This unsettled populace was receptive to the radical brand of Islam espoused by fledgling groups such as the Muslim Brotherhood and the Islamic Gathering and to the militant brand of Islamic radicalism brought home by returning mujahideen from Afghanistan. The initial LIFG was comprised primarily of these returning Afghan war veterans, who advocated bringing all of the smaller militant groups together to create a more united front against the current Libyan regime.

The Libyan Islamic Fighting Group was dedicated to two goals: the overthrow of the current Libyan government led by Mu'ammar al-Qadhafi and the furtherance of the international jihadist campaign of which the returning veterans had been a part in Afghanistan. Believing that Qadhafi and his government were "un-Islamic" and should therefore be overthrown, LIFG members attempted, but failed, to assassinate Qadhafi in 1994. Led by Abu Abdallah al-Sadeq, the LIFG planned this assassination attempt, which occurred in Derna. The LIFG continued to believe that Qadhafi was un-Islamic and needed to be removed from his position of leadership in Libya, trying again to achieve that objective by a grenade assault on Qadhafi during his visit to the desert town of Brak in 1996. This second failed attempt did not injure Qadhafi but killed several of his bodyguards.

The formal declaration of existence was issued by the group after a violent effort to free comrades detained in a prison in Benghazi in September 1995. The battle of LIFG forces and prison security left dozens dead on both sides, after weeks of intense fighting. In March of the following year, several dozen of the Islamist detainees escaped from the prison near Benghazi and fled into the mountains in the northeast of Libya, with security forces in pursuit. Subsequent fighting, which included the murder of eight policemen at a training center near Derna, resulted in a nationwide arrest effort and a major ground and air assault on LIFG bases by the Libyan government forces. The second failed attempt to assassinate Qadhafi spun out of this massive crackdown, and martial law was imposed on the Derna region.

The Libyan Islamic Fighting Group's second objective, contributing to the international jihadist campaign, has become increasingly central to LIFG's activities, and the LIFG has significant ties with AL-QAEDA as well as with extreme Islamic groups in Egypt and Algeria. Analysts suggest that certain LIFG senior leaders maintain positions in al-Qaeda's senior command structure, and LIFG is suspected of being one of the terrorist entities that provided materials for the May 2003 suicide bombings in Casablanca.

The LIFG is divided into three subunits: a consultative committee, a judicial committee, and an information bureau. The consultative committee, the Majlis Shura, is the ruling body and must, according to its charter, have a quorum of seven members to make legally binding decisions. Normally, there are up to 15 members in the consultative committee, so its quorum is only one less than 50% of its membership.

The judicial committee (al-Lajnah al-Shar'iyyah) is responsible for all judicial issues and for the education and training of LIFG members. This committee is responsible for issued judicial writings and issues messages and articles concerning the "proper conduct" of Libyan society, from the point of view of radical Islam. With these diverse tasks, it is divided into three branches: research and study, propaganda and guidance, and judicial matters.

The third committee, the information bureau, publishes open letters to the Libyan people, often calling on the nation to devote itself to the Islamic faith. This committee, currently led by Omar Rashid, is also fervent in its efforts to clarify for Libyans the nature of the struggle between Islamists and the regime of Qadhafi, and hence the need for the first goal—the elimination of Qadhafi and his regime. This committee stresses that the struggle is not a personal one, or a tribal/ethnic one, but a struggle between "real" Islam and the heretics, implicitly led by Qadhafi himself.

While the exact membership of this group is not known, it is roughly estimated to have around 300 members/supporters. Most of its support is believed to be from private donations by individuals, various Islamic nongovernmental organizations, and occasional criminal acts. The short declaration issued by the group in May 2005, in response to the story of the abuse of the Quran in the American detainee camp in Guantánamo Bay, Cuba, was less strident than most issued by Islamist groups, lacking even a call to fight the United States.

Reference: National Memorial Institute for the Prevention of Terrorism (MIPT). "Libyan Islamic Fighting Group (LIFG)." Available online. URL: http://www.tkb.org/Group.jsp?groupID=4400. Accessed February 15, 2006.

Lockerbie, bombing of Pan Am flight 103

On December 21, 1988, Pan Am flight 103 from Frankfurt to New York, via London, exploded over the Scottish town of Lockerbie. All 259 passengers and crew were killed, as were 11 residents of Lockerbie. Three years later, an investigation into the tragedy concluded, with the Lord Advocate, Scotland's chief law officer, obtaining a warrant for the arrest of two Libyans, Abdel Baset Ali Mohamed al-Megrahi and Al-Amin Khalifa Fhimah. The charges against them included conspiracy, murder, and contravention of the Aviation Security Act of 1982. An indictment in the United States was also issued at this time, citing similar accusations.

The U.S., U.K., and French governments issued in December 1991 a joint statement calling on the Libyan government to surrender the suspects for trial. Libya, concerned that these men would not receive a fair trial in Scotland, refused to hand the men over. Instead, Libya said that it would bring the two to trial in Libya, and, using only the evidence provided for them by the United States and Scotland, acquitted them of the charges. This action satisfied at least the letter of the Montreal CONVENTIONS ON AERIAL HIJACKING, which requires a nation either to extradite or to prosecute individuals of acts or threats of violence aboard aircraft.

In January 1992, the UN Security Council in Resolution 731 ordered Libya to surrender the Lockerbie suspects. At this point, Libya offered instead to hand the suspects over to the Arab League. The UN Security Council's Resolution 748, passed on March 31, 1992, gave Libya 15 days to hand over the suspects or face a worldwide ban on air travel and arms sales and the closure of Libyan Arab Airline offices. Fifteen days later, this embargo took effect. By December of the following year, sanctions were imposed, including a freezing of Libyan assets in foreign banks and an embargo on oil industry-related equipment.

The argument over where the men would be tried spanned more than seven years. Finally, in 1997, when Libya stated that it did not object to Scottish law or Scottish judges, but believed that its nationals could not receive a fair trial in Britain, alternative solutions became possible. The following year, an agreement was reached to hand the two suspects over for trial by a Scottish judge in a neutral country, which the United States and the United Kingdom concurred would be the Netherlands, home of the World Court. Another year passed in wrangling over the technical and legal details of this trial, including disagreement over where the men would serve the prison time if found guilty and the security of the men in prison during that time.

More than a decade after the explosion that claimed 259 lives, a trial of the two suspects took place in the Netherlands. The court acquitted one defendant for lack of clear evidence and sentenced the other to significant prison time, though perhaps not sufficient to satisfy those who lost loved ones in the bombing. International law, efforts by several presidents of African nations, including Mubarak of EGYPT, Kabila of the Democratic Republic of Congo, Museveni of Uganda, and many others, and UN Security Council sanctions and resolutions combined to resolve this difficult case of aerial terrorism. Many of the legal issues raised by this case impact new legal efforts on terrorism, particularly those relating to the treatment of terrorism as an international crime, together with issues of universal jurisdiction.

Reference: BBC. World. "Libyan Guilty of Lockerbie Bombing." January 31, 2001. Available online. URL: http://news.bbc.co.uk/1/hi/world/1144893.stm. Accessed March 16, 2006.

Lod Airport attack

This terrorist attack was organized by the POPULAR FRONT FOR THE LIBERATION OF PALESTINE (PFLP), under the leadership of George Habbash. Working with the PFLP, three members of the JAPANESE RED ARMY went to Tel Aviv airport in May 1973. After arriving, they took automatic weapons and grenades from their baggage and opened fire, killing 23 travelers and wounding 76 others. Two of the three terrorists were killed during the attack, Kozo Okamoto, the lone survivor, was convicted in an Israeli court in 1972 but was released during a prisoner exchange in 1985 with the PFLP and fled to Libya. Eventually, he reunited with other members of the JRA in Lebanon. Because of his actions against Israel, the Lebanese government granted Okamoto asylum in 1999.

London terror attacks, July 7, 2005

The 2005 annual G-8 economic summit was scheduled to begin on July 7 in Gleneagles (near Edinburgh), Scotland. The focus of the summit was an emphasis on economic and technical assistance to African countries. Attention quickly switched to bombings in London targeted at concentrations of civilian population movements during the morning commute to work. The immediate conclusion was that the attacks were the work of AL-QAEDA. Indeed, the Organization of Qaeda't al-Jihad in Europe claimed credit for the bombings. Its statement posted after the attacks provided support for the assumption: "Rejoice the nation of Islam, rejoice the nation of Arabs, the time of revenge has come for the crusaders' Zionist British government. As retaliation for the massacres which the British commit in Iraq and Afghanistan, the mujahideen have successfully done it this time in London." A warning followed that was issued to Denmark and Italy indicating that they could be next since both countries retained military units in Iraq. However, it is not yet clear whether this or any other organization executed the attacks.

Within a week following the attacks, the British determined that four Muslim men, ranging in ages from 18 to 30, had each detonated a bomb killing himself and innocent victims. Many Britons were especially disturbed that the bombers were British citizens who had grown up or been born in Britain. None of them had exhibited any discernible streaks of radicalism. Nor did any of them appear to be any more religiously observant than most of their counterparts. They all

This London underground train was damaged in the terrorist bombing of July 7, 2005. (GETTY IMAGES)

belonged to middle-class families and lived in relatively stable environments. The oldest one, Mohammed Sidique Khan, was married and had a baby daughter. The youngest, Hasib Hussain, had gone to Saudi Arabia on a hajj (a pilgrimage taken by religious Muslims at least once during a lifetime) and returned visibly more religious. Forensic evidence tied the suspects to the particular scene of detonation. The three subway bombers purchased roundtrip tickets, a fact that led to speculation that they may have been unaware they were going to die with their victims.

Surveillance tapes, ubiquitous in London (the average Londoner is taped 300 times daily), suggest that the four bombers met with an apparent coordinator before embarking on their tasks. British authorities remain involved in an effort to determine the identity and location of this person.

The United Kingdom's population of 60.5 million includes 1.6 million Muslims (only a minority of whom are Arabs) or around 2.7% of the total, a smaller number and proportion than counterpart communities in France and Germany, though most are concentrated in London. Security experts estimate between 600 and 3,000 people living in Britain are alumni of the training camps run in Afghanistan by Osama bin Laden. Of course, authorities were also originally uncertain whether the culprits were British citizens or from abroad. Britain has one of the most lenient policies on asylum in Europe. Radicals from North Africa and the Middle East have for many years taken up residence there and have unwittingly provoked jokes about Britain's capital city, "Londonistan."

The London attacks instantly reminded commentators of the 9/11 terrorist event in the United States and the March 11, 2004, train attacks in Madrid, Spain. In each of these cases, the targets were concentrations of population, with efforts designed to kill and injure as many people as possible. London had not experienced this level of devastation since World War II aerial bombing blitzes during 1940–41 and the rocket attacks during 1944–45. Even the IRISH REPUBLICAN ARMY (IRA) had, during its many years of terrorist attacks, restricted its activities to bombing targets that were often devoid of people.

It was at first believed that the attacks in London were not conducted by suicide bombers. Speculation suggested that the bombs were activated by timers. The MADRID BOMBINGS were set off by cell phones. However, the loss of life in Madrid was much greater: 191 people killed by 10 bombs that destroyed four commuter trains during rush hour. Three of the four London explosions occurred in subways within one minute of each other. A fourth explosion occurred an hour later in a double-decker bus. A total of 52 people, including the bombers, were killed while riding the trains and bus, and more than 700 were injured. There was speculation that this last bomb exploded prematurely while one of the bombers was traveling to an intended target. This theory, however, remains unsubstantiated.

Why it was London that was attacked is another controversial issue. Few were surprised that the attack came; officials had for many months publicly warned that it was a question of "when" rather than "if" London would be attacked. The United Kingdom had the second-largest military force in Iraq allied with the United States. It had consistently supported the United States in the war on terror since 9/11. London's mayor, Ken Livingston, blamed Western imperialism in the Middle East as the provocation for the attacks. The claim was rejected by the British government. Prime Minister Tony Blair countered Livingston's argument, pointing out that Western military expeditions were not in Afghanistan or Iraq before the 9/11 attacks.

Reference: BBC. In Depth. "London Attacks." Available online. URL: http://news.bbc.co.uk/2/hi/in_depth/uk/2005/london_explosions.stm. Accessed March 16, 2006.

Lord's Resistance Army (LRA)

This group, formed in 1992, is based in Uganda and Sudan and is committed to the destabilization and overthrow of the government of Uganda. Led by Joseph Kony, the group espouses an extremist form of Christianity, focusing on creating a Ugandan theocracy. The Uganda Democratic Christian Army, a resistance movement, was the precursor to this group but did not share the LRA's willingness to achieve this state by rampant brutality. Rape, torture, and murder have become the group's hallmarks in northern Uganda, according to organizations, such as Human Rights Watch, that report the actions of this group to the United Nations.

About 80% of the members of the LRA are children who have been kidnapped and co-opted into service with the group. Human Rights Watch reports that children as young as eight years old have been kidnapped, tortured, raped, virtually enslaved, and even murdered by the LRA in the name of "the Holy Spirit." The group has attacked homes and schools in northern Uganda, targeting children for use as soldiers.

No one is certain precisely how many children have been abducted by this group, but reliable estimates suggest that at least 3,000–5,000 children have escaped from rebel captivity. An equal number are believed to be still in captivity, and an unknown number of abducted children are dead. Children who are captured are forced to take part in combat, carry heavy loads, act as personal servants to the rebels, and, in the case of girls, serve as "wives" to rebel commanders. They undergo a brutal initiation into rebel life, being forced to participate in acts of extreme violence, often being compelled to help beat or hack to death fellow child captives who have attempted to escape. LRA leaders march their child captives to base camps in neighboring southern Sudan, marches that claim the lives of many of the children.

Accounts from children who have escaped paint a harrowing picture of the violence and brutality to which these "child soldiers" are subjected. The words of Susan, who was 16 when she escaped, vividly depict the horrors of her experience:

> One boy tried to escape [from the rebels], but he was caught. . . . His hands were tied, and then they made us, the other new captives, kill him with a stick. I felt sick. . . . I refused to kill him [but] they pointed a gun at me, so I had to do it. The boy was asking me, "Why are you doing this?" I said I had no choice. After we killed him, they made us smear his blood on our arms. . . . They said we had to do this so we would not fear death and so we would not try to escape. I still dream about the boy [whom] I killed. I see him in my dreams, and he is talking to me and saying I killed him for nothing, and I am crying.

The Lord's Resistance Army receives military assistance and other support from the Sudanese government, which aids the Lord's Resistance Army in return for assistance in fighting the rebel Sudan People's Liberation Army (SPLA) and also possibly in retaliation for Ugandan government support of the SPLA.

In 2002, the Sudanese government reversed its longstanding policy of support for the LRA, cooperating instead in efforts to eliminate the group's sanctuaries. However, the LRA continues to perpetrate its brutal attacks within both northern and eastern Uganda. Talks between the LRA and the Ugandan government generated an 18-day truce between the two in February 2005. This truce has been complicated, though, by the INTERNATIONAL CRIMINAL COURT's investigation into the conflict. In July and September 2005, the ICC issued warrants for the arrest of Joseph Kony and several of his commanders on charges of crimes against humanity and war crimes. In June 2006, INTERPOL issued several arrest warrants or "red notices" on the ICC's behalf, but reports from the Human Rights Watch organization make it clear that the government of southern Sudan is ignoring the arrest warrants and continues to harbor wanted members of the LRA. The LRA stated that it would never surrender unless granted immunity from prosecution. Peace talks resumed in July 2006 between the LRA and the Ugandan government, and a ceasefire was declared on August 26, 2006. As a result, many members of the LRA have migrated to southern Sudan, but peace talks were still ongoing.

References: BBC. Africa. "Uganda Drops Peace Talks Deadline." Available online. URL: http://news.bbc.co.uk/2/hi/africa/5337888.stm. Accessed December 4, 2006. National Memorial Institute for the Prevention of Terrorism (MIPT). "Lord's Resistance Army (LRA)." Available online. URL: http://www.tkb.org/Group.jsp?groupID=3513. Accessed February 15, 2006.

Loyalist Volunteer Force (LVF)

This extremist group formed in 1996 as a faction of the mainstream loyalist Ulster Volunteer Force (UVF), but it did not emerge publicly until February 1997. Membership consisted largely of UVF hard-liners who sought to prevent a political settlement with Irish nationalists in NORTHERN IRELAND. Their activities included attacks on Catholic politicians, civilians, and Protestant politicians who endorsed the Northern Ireland peace process. Mark "Swinger" Fulton led the group after the assassination in December 1997 of LVF founder Billy "King Rat" Wright.

Bombings, kidnappings, and close-quarter shooting attacks characterized the efforts of this group to prevent political settlement of the dispute. The bombs often contained Powergel commercial explosives, an ingredient typical of many loyalist groups' explosives. Their attacks have been vicious and often directed deliberately toward civilians who were innocent victims. LVF terrorists killed an 18-year-old Catholic girl in July 1997 because she had a Protestant boyfriend. Following Billy Wright's assassination, Catholic civilians were often murdered who had no political or terrorist affiliations.

While most of its activities have occurred in Northern Ireland, the LVF has also conducted successful attacks against Irish targets in border towns on the Irish side of the border. It receives no external aid. The press in the United Kingdom suggests that there exist approximately 250 LVF activists, but this is an unconfirmed number.

The LVF observed the cease-fire after May 15, 1998. In October 2001, the British government ruled that the LVF had broken the cease-fire it declared in 1998, after linking the group to the murder of a journalist. According to the Independent International Commission on Decommissioning, the LVF decommissioned a small amount of weapons in December 1998, but it has not repeated this gesture. Loyalist violence broke out during the summer of 2005 due to a bloody feud between the LVF and the UFV. In October 2005, the LVF announced it was standing down on the heels of the Irish Republican Army's announcement to do the same. However, the Independent Monitoring Commission still considers the LVF to be active in criminal enterprise.

See also IRISH REPUBLICAN ARMY.

Reference: National Memorial Institute for the Prevention of Terrorism (MIPT). "Loyalist Volunteer Force (LVF)" Available online. URL: http://www.tkb.org/Group.jsp?groupID=68. Accessed February 15, 2006.

M

Madrid train bombings

On March 11, 2004, the Abu Hafs al-Masri Brigade detonated 10 bombs in four different locations on Madrid's train line. Casualties numbered 191 killed and more than 1,800 others injured. Three of the bombs detonated in a train that was pulling into the Atocha station, a busy hub for the commuter train line and the metro rail. It is not clear how many fatalities occurred at each location, but this was the most serious of the bomb sites. The bombs were left in backpacks and detonated by cell phones.

Initially, the Spanish government blamed the separatist group BASQUE FATHERLAND AND LIBERTY (ETA) for the attacks, but later the Abu Hafs al-Masri Brigade claimed responsibility on behalf of AL-QAEDA. By the end of March 2004, authorities had arrested over 20 people in connection with the attack. The suspects hailed from Morocco, India, Syria, and Spain.

In their claim of responsibility, the Abu Hafs al-Masri Brigade said that Spain was targeted because of their cooperation with the United States in the war in Iraq. At least in part in response to the attacks, the ruling Spanish party was defeated in elections (which took place four days after the incident), and the new prime minister vowed to remove Spanish troops from combat in Iraq.

On April 3, as the police were closing in on four suspects, including Serjame ben Abdelmajid Fakhet, who they believe was the ringleader in this incident, the suspects blew themselves up in their apartment in Madrid. This blast also killed a police officer. One suspect managed to escape the apartment explosion, as he was taking out the trash at the time of the raid. Abdelmajid Bouchar escaped to Serbia, where he hid out until he was captured in August 2005.

Reference: BBC. In Depth. "Madrid Train Attacks." Available online. URL: http://news.bbc.co.uk/2/hi/in_depth/europe/2004/madrid_train_attacks.stm. Accessed March 16, 2006.

Manson, Charles (1934–)

On August 9, 1969, a housekeeper reported for work at film director Roman Polanski's home in the Hollywood hills and found five bodies, slashed and bloodied. Slain were Polanski's young wife, actress Sharon Tate, who was eight and one-half months pregnant; her friend Abigail Folger, the heiress to the Folger coffee fortune; and Folger's boyfriend, Voytek Frykowski; Jay Sebring, a well-known hairstylist, who, according

Rescue workers search through the wreckage of a commuter train after it was devastated by a bomb blast in Madrid, Spain, 2004. (Getty Images)

to news reports, lived in Hollywood's "fast lane," and Steve Parent, a young man who was apparently simply in the wrong place at the wrong time, were also among the dead. The victims had been beaten and stabbed dozens of times, and the word "PIG" was written in blood on the front door.

The following night, Leno LaBianca, the owner of a chain of grocery stores, and his wife, Rosemary, were found beaten and stabbed in their home east of Beverly Hills. Written in blood were the mysterious words: "Death to Pigs Rise" and (misspelled) "Healter Skelter." Charles Manson and three of his "acolytes" were convicted after a nine-month trial, with a fifth accomplice convicted later. Although all were sentenced to death for the bizarre murders, their sentences were commuted to life in prison. Vincent Buglosi, who prosecuted in the Manson case, noted that, "Manson has become the metaphor for evil." The terror he produced by his crimes remained vivid several decades later for those who watched the appalling footage of the crime scene.

Charles Manson remained in prison through December 2005, having been repeatedly denied parole. Four members of his "family" were also sentenced to life imprisonment for this attack. Other members of his "family" are also serving jail terms for related crimes; among them, Lynette "Squeaky" Fromme, who attempted to assassinate then-president Gerald Ford.

Reference: Bugliosi, Vincent. *Helter Skelter: The True Story of the Manson Murders* (New York: W. W. Norton & Co., 1994).

Manuel Rodríguez Patriotic Front (FPMR)

Originally founded in 1983 as the armed wing of the Chilean Communist Party, this organization was named for the hero of Chile's war of independence against Spain. The group splintered in the late 1980s, and one faction became a political party in 1991. The dissident wing, the FPMR/D, was Chile's only remaining active terrorist group at the end of the 20th century.

The FPMR/D attacked civilians and international targets, including businesspeople and churches. In 1993, this group bombed two McDonald's restaurants and attempted to bomb a Kentucky Fried Chicken restaurant. Successful counterterrorist operations by the government significantly undercut the organization in the following years. However, the group staged a successful escape from prison, using a helicopter, for several of its members/supporters, in December 1996.

It had, at last report, between 50 and 100 members. The FPMR/D apparently had no source of foreign support.

Martyrs of Tal al-Za'atar *See* HAWARI GROUP.

media *See* GOALS OF MEDIA, IN TERRORIST EVENT.

Meir, Golda (1898–1978)

Golda Meir grew up in Milwaukee, Wisconsin, before migrating to PALESTINE in 1921. She joined a kibbutz and immediately became involved in the politics of a small Jewish community in Palestine. While not particularly religious, Meir was a fervent Zionist—as were her contemporaries David Ben-Gurion and other leaders of Israel's founding generation. She quickly demonstrated important diplomatic skills. Meir became the first Israeli ambassador to the Soviet Union in 1949, a posting that was followed by a long tenure as Israeli foreign minister (1956–65). Meir retired from public life in 1965, though she remained politically active and personally popular.

Meir was recalled after the sudden death of Israeli prime minister Levi Eshkol in 1969. There was a widespread endorsement of her candidacy for the prime ministership. Throughout this time and until the end of her life, Meir refused to acknowledge that there was any such thing as a Palestinian national identity.

Meir's prime ministership (1969–74) was marred by two events that impacted her entire country. One of these, of course, was the Yom Kippur War that began on October 6, 1973, and lasted into the first weeks of 1974. Like most of the rest of the Israeli political leadership, Meir had underestimated the ability of the Arab side to launch a military attack that was, at least in its initial stages, successful. Israel experienced an intelligence failure that placed the country in mortal danger and eventually forced the Meir government to step aside. She was succeeded by Yitzhak Rabin.

More than a year before the war, 11 Israeli athletes were murdered by Palestinian terrorists during the 1972 Summer Olympics in Munich. Five Palestinian terrorists were also killed during a shoot-out with German police at the Munich airport. Meir and her cabinet authorized the targeting of those Palestinians they designated as having responsibility for planning the attack. MOSSAD agents eventually tracked down and assassinated those men.

The revenge killings were very important in helping set the later Israeli policy of "focused preventive acts" (translated from the Hebrew for selective assassination). From Munich on, all terrorists who attacked Israeli personnel in or outside of Israel were put on notice that planning and otherwise assisting and coordinating in any attack made them as culpable as those who actually carried out the attack itself. Successive Israeli governments have continued to endorse and practice this policy. In fact, there has even been an expansion of the policy. During Meir's time, the policy was not made public and was applied only rarely. By the time of the Ariel Sharon government (2001–06), the policy was both public and frequently implemented.

See also MUNICH MASSACRE OF ISRAELI ATHLETES; ZIONISM.

Memorandum of Understanding of Hijacking of Aircraft and Vessels and Other Offenses

This was one of the antihijacking agreements concluded in the 1970s. It was signed by the United States and Cuba on February 15, 1973. It was denounced by Cuba in October 1976, after more than five years of interstate cooperation between these countries in the effort to end the hijacking of airplanes. Many planes that were hijacked after the denunciation were nevertheless returned promptly to the country of origin, although the prosecution of the hijackers was somewhat less successful.

Reference: 24 U.S.T. 737, T.I.A.S. No. 7579 (1973).

Middle East *See* OVERVIEW OF TERRORISM, BY REGION.

Middle Eastern news outlets

Newspaper, television, and Internet networks sharing a similar name have become, in differing degrees, important in the context of terrorism in the Middle East. Although the television station, Al Jazeera, is arguably the best known, each has contributed different news inputs in the emerging world of media, the Middle East, and terrorism.

Al Jazeera

Founded through a grant from the emir of Qatar for US $150 million, this television station now rivals the British Broadcasting Corporation (BBC) in worldwide audiences, with an estimated 50 million viewers. Although it continues to be subsidized by the emir each year (about $30 million in 2004), about 40% of its income is now from advertising and the sale of footage. According to the Russian newspaper *Pravda,* Al Jazeera received $20,000 per minute for OSAMA BIN LADEN's speech in 2004.

The channel began broadcasting in 1996 but did not experience extensive growth until the turn of the century, although its strong documentary on the Lebanese civil war in 2000–01 significantly increased its ratings. Its broadcasts in late 2001, however, after the ATTACKS ON AMERICA, of video statements by AL-QAEDA leaders gave it worldwide popularity. Al Jazeera's interviews with leaders in the Middle East and other footage are now being rebroadcast in the U.S. British, and other Western media outlets, such as the BBC and CNN, and the network is considered fairly mainstream, though often more controversial than most.

Its role in SHOWCASING TERRORISM, which it has neither sought nor denied, continues to significantly affect its market. Al Jazeera carried tapes of bin Laden, with full transcripts and video, both after the 9/11 attacks and in November 2004. The killing of hostages in Iraq on video for broadcast reached most of the Arab world as well as much of Europe and the West. The tapes of the messages or killings were sent to Al Jazeera and were generally aired, unedited, in order to protect the interests of "authenticity." In the United States, video footage from this network is largely limited to vignettes showing the hostages pleading for mercy.

Increasing Western opposition to the station's willingness to air messages from al-Qaeda and other terrorist leaders led to pressure on the government of Qatar. On January 30, 2005, the Qatari government was reported in the *New York Times* to be under pressure from the U.S. president and was "speeding up plans to sell the station." Relations with the United States continued to deteriorate, culminating in November 2005 with the leak of a memo from 10 Downing Street that stated that President Bush had considered bombing Al Jazeera's Doha headquarters in April of the previous year, when U.S. Marines were engaged in an assault on Fallujah, Iraq. Since the station's Kabul office had been bombed in 2001 by the United States, and a missile had hit its office in Baghdad in 2003 during the U.S.-led invasion—in both cases, in spite of Al Jazeera's providing to the United States the locations of their offices prior to the attacks—the station remains concerned about its future safety. It also declares itself to still be an independent news agency.

Al-Jazirah

Al-Jazirah Corporation was founded by Sheikh Abdullah bin Mohammed bin Khamis in April 1960, beginning as a monthly magazine and later, in 1972, evolving into a daily newspaper. The newspaper is now published in three editions, covering news from around the world. Its head office is located in the city of Riyadh, the capital of the kingdom of Saudi Arabia. Its circulation has doubled in recent years, now that it is available in other Arab and European countries, with an average daily circulation of around 100,000 copies.

Al-Jazeerah

This nonprofit U.S.-based news and research publication was founded in 2001 and is not affiliated in any way with the Qatar-based news station. Edited by Dr. Hassan el-Najjar, an associate professor at Dalton State College in Georgia, this educational publication seeks to "promote peace in the world, between Palestinians and Israelis and between the U.S. and the Arab and Muslim worlds." It also describes itself as an "independent U.S. news and research publication, not related to any government in the world."

This news agency contains primarily press releases from various sources, as well as editorials by various authors, primarily on topics related to the Middle East, with special focus on the issues involving Palestine and Iraq.

References: BBC. Middle East. "Al-Jazeera and Bin Laden." November 14, 2002. Available online. URL: http://news.bbc.co.uk/2/hi/middle_east/2460705.stm. Accessed March 20, 2006; Lynch, Marc. *Voices of the New Arab Republic: Iraq, al-Jazeera, and Middle East Politics Today* (New York: Columbia University Press, 2006).

millennial movements

As the third millennium approached, governments, particularly in the United States and western Europe, tracked groups motivated by a belief that the end of the world was at hand. Since an apocalyptic battle was an essential part of this belief for many in these movements, the probability of terrorism seemed high. While there were, in most countries, no specific threats, the governments alerted law enforcement agencies, as they often do, about the potential significance of the impending date for terrorist attacks.

In the United States, the FEDERAL BUREAU OF INVESTIGATION (FBI) distributed a 40-page research report entitled *Project Megiddo,* analyzing "the potential for extremist criminal activity in the United States by individuals or domestic groups who attach special significance to the year 2000." The report was named after an ancient battleground in Israel cited in the Bible's New Testament as the site of a millennial battle between the forces of good and evil. It examines the ideologies that advocate or call for violent action beginning in the year 2000. According to this report, such ideologies motivate violent white supremacists who seek to initiate a race war; apocalyptic cults that anticipate a violent Armageddon; radical elements of civilian militia groups who fear that the United Nations will initiate an armed takeover of the United States in an effort to create a one-world government; and other individuals and groups that promote violent millennial agendas.

The action of an individual, also in the United States, demonstrated the threat of terrorism based on racism and religious fervor as the millennium approached. Buford Furrow, Jr., shot and killed a Filipino-American mail carrier and wounded four children and a woman at a Jewish community center in California in the summer of 1999. He had ties to anti-Semitic hate groups such as the ARYAN NATIONS and the CHRISTIAN IDENTITY MOVEMENT, both of which consider whites a superior race and the latter of which prophesies an eminent race war and an end to the world.

One apocalytic religious group that had clashed with the U.S. government with dire results was the Branch Davidians in WACO, TEXAS. The Davidian sect had a long history of apocalytic beliefs—sub-sects of this religion were often created due to differing predictions of the apocalyse, as well as disbanded when the predictions did not come true. In 1993, the Branch Davidians were holed up in their Waco compound as the FBI tried to serve an arrest warrant for their leader, Vernon Howell, a.k.a. David Koresh. Rumor had it that the Davidians had stockpiled weapons and supplies in case of a "siege" by government agents. Defectors from the group claimed that Koresh would demand that his followers be willing to die—by suicide if necessary—in the "final showdown" that was due to come between the church and the government. Koresh even changed the name of the compound from Mount Carmel to Ranch Apocalypse. In a final tragic irony, Koresh's apocalytic predictions came true, but not in the Branch Davidians' favor. The standoff eventually turned to violence when shooting began and the compound caught fire, killing 75 Davidians while only nine escaped.

As experts have since pointed out, many of these "millenial groups," such as the Branch Davidians, are not violent when left alone. However, as was the case with the Davidians, when challenged by outsiders the situation only seemed to reenforce the "us v. them" mentality already prevalent in the group, with potentially fatal results. Since the Waco incident, there have not been any violent clashes with apocalyptic groups. Experts speculate that when the year 2000 (or "Y2K") passed without any apparent signs of the end of the world, many of these apocalyptic groups disbanded.

References: Kaplan, Jeffrey. *Radical Religion in America: Millenarian Movements from the Far Right to the Children of Noah* (Syracuse, N.Y.: Syracuse University Press, 1997); Lamy, Philip. *Millennium Rage: Survivalists, White Supremacists and the Doomsday Prophecy* (New York: Da Capo Press, 1996); PBS. "Apocalypse!" Available online. URL: http://www.pbs.org/wgbh/pages/frontline/shows/apocalypse. Accessed March 17, 2006; Scarritt, James, and Jeffrey Kaplan. *Millenial Violence: Past, Present and Future* (Philadelphia: Taylor & Francis Co., 2002).

Mogadishu, GSG-9 hostage rescue in

Germany's newly created GSG-9, with only about 180 total personnel who had undergone a few years of counterterrorism training, was nevertheless one of the best units of its kind in the world in 1977. It was confronted early in its career with a challenging hostage-rescue operation involving an airline hijacking, which tested the group's ability to operate successfully within the law without engendering loss of life.

In September/October 1977, shortly after the unit was formed, the RED ARMY FACTION (RAF) took hostage German businessman Hans-Martin Schleyer. The RAF immediately demanded the release of 11 of their comrades-in-arms who were being held in prison in West Germany. In spite of attempts by the German government to find a nation willing to take the terrorists, a whole month passed without resolution of the situation. At last, on October 13, French authorities reported that a Lufthansa airplane had been hijacked en route from the Balearic Islands to Germany. The Boeing 737 jet, with 85 passengers and five crew members on board, had been hijacked by an individual calling himself "Captain Mahmoud" (later identified as known terrorist Zohair Youssef Akache) and forced to change course toward Rome.

Landing in Rome, the plane refueled after the hijackers threatened to blow up the plane with all on board. It flew to Cyprus, where Mahmoud demanded another refueling, and a new problem arose. Word about the hijacking had spread, and many governments publicly resolved not to allow flight LH 181 to land on their territory. Indeed, in Beirut, the runways were physically blocked with equipment to prevent an unauthorized landing. The pilot eventually landed in Dubai, despite government denial of landing privileges.

At Dubai, the crew was able to communicate with ground officials, telling them that there were in fact four terrorists aboard. The long ordeal began to have an effect on terrorists as well as hostages, to the extent that later that same day, Mahmoud killed the pilot. He also postponed his original deadline (for the release of the 11 held in prison in Germany) from 4 P.M. to 2:45 A.M. the next day, as he accepted a promise from the West German minister of state (who was acting as chief negotiator). Having changed the deadline, Mahmoud ordered the plane to be flown to Mogadishu, Somalia, where it landed on October 17.

One of GSG-9's 30-person groups had been following the aircraft since its landing in Cyprus, in a modified Lufthansa 707. This group was airborne soon after the German government learned of the plane's destination of Mogadishu, having flown from Bonn to Cyprus to Ankara and back to Germany before learning of its final destination. A second 30-person unit, including commander Ulrich Wegener, had flown in the meantime from Germany to Dubai so as to be in a better position to attempt hostage rescue operations. The Somali government was cooperative, and it permitted Wegener's group to land and also set up a security perimeter of Somali commandos around the airport before their arrival. This enabled the GSG-9 unit to receive vital intelligence about the plane from the security forces. GSG-9 deployed sniper and reconnaissance teams and prepared to carry out an immediate assault on the plane, if the need for such an event arose. Such an action did not prove necessary, and, with the arrival of the second GSG-9 unit, planning for the hostage rescue began with intensity.

As the night progressed, officials concluded that, since Mahmoud was growing increasingly unstable and had already demonstrated a willingness to execute hostages (e.g., the pilot), a rescue operation would be necessary. At 11:15 P.M., sections of the assault team began a covert approach to the plane, accompanied by two SAS men who were skilled in the use of "flash-bang" grenades. In an attempt to draw at least some of the terrorists to the cockpit (to establish their location), Somali commandos at 2:05 A.M. lit a bright signal fire a few hundred feet in front of the plane. GSG-9 reconnaissance reported that Mahmoud and another terrorist had gone to the cockpit and appeared confused by the fire.

Simultaneously, GSG-9 commandos made entry through the airplane's doors, using special rubber-coated ladders to muffle the sound of their approach. The emergency doors were blown open at 2:07 A.M. with explosive charges. The two SAS men, who had managed to get undetected onto the plane's wings, tossed their grenades inside, and the GSG-9 teams entered the plane, ordering the hostages to get down. In just a few seconds, three of the terrorists were killed and the fourth severely wounded, with all of the hostages retrieved unharmed and one GSG-9 man slightly wounded. The operation was officially over by 2:12 A.M. on October 18.

Three days later, the body of Schleyer, the German businessman who was kidnapped about a month earlier, was recovered.

Reference: B. Taillon, J. Paul de. *Hijacking and Hostages: Government Responses to Terrorism* (Westport, Conn.: Praeger Publishers, 2002).

Montana Freemen

The Montana Freemen is the name taken by a right-wing extremist group located in eastern Montana. In March 1996, the U.S. FEDERAL BUREAU OF INVESTIGATION (FBI) initiated a siege of the Clark Ranch near Jordan, Montana, headquarters of the Freemen, for outstanding warrants. The siege ended peacefully with no gunfire or loss of life.

The Clark Ranch is also known as the Justus Township to Freemen members and is considered by them to be their sovereign territory. The Freemen's doctrine comprises a mixture of legal maxims drawn from the British Magna Carta, the U.S. Constitution (including the first 10 amendments), and biblical law (the parts of which emphasize the sovereignty of its members). From this doctrine, Freemen state that the U.S. government has no authority to govern and that federal laws and tax codes are not binding on them.

Led by LeRoy Schweitzer, the group instructs its people how to manipulate the U.S. tax codes to make an (illegal) profit. Liens against the federal government were accepted as collateral to purchase money orders, and debtors printed fake money orders. Money order amounts were written larger than the amount owed and the overpayment was returned to the sender. In addition to money fraud, Freemen members also threatened and harassed local government officials.

Local government agents and law enforcement officials of Garfield County asked the FBI to assume investigation of this group and to detain Freemen members, primarily because these actions would require a large amount of resources. In late March 1996, FBI agents lured Schweitzer and other members out from the Justus Township/Clark Ranch and placed them under arrest. The remaining members barricaded themselves inside the ranch and refused to surrender. The FBI encircled the Freemen enclave and prepared to wait, deciding not to use force, as in the WACO and Ruby Ridge incidents. Mediators, including Bo Gritz and Gerry Spence, were called in but provided few results. Electricity and water was shut off and all cellular-phone use was blocked. After several weeks of negotiations, the remaining Freemen members surrendered on June 13, 1996, and they were taken into federal custody.

See also POSSE COMITATUS.

References: National Memorial Institute for the Prevention of Terrorism (MIPT). "Montana Freemen." Available online. URL: http://www.tkb.org/Group.jsp?groupID=3406. Accessed February 15, 2006; The Rick A. Ross Institute. "Freemen." Available online. URL: http://www.rickross.com/groups/freemen.html. Accessed March 17, 2006.

T.L.

Morazanist Patriotic Front (Frente Patriótico Morazanista [FPM])

This group first appeared in the late 1980s, making attacks in protest of the intervention of the United States in Honduran economic and political affairs. The FPM claimed responsibility for the bombing of Peace Corps offices in December 1988, a bus bombing that wounded three U.S. servicemen in February 1989, an attack on a U.S. convoy in April of that same year, and a grenade attack that wounded seven U.S. soldiers in La Ceiba in July 1989. Its last claimed attack was on a bus in March 1990 that wounded seven U.S. servicemen. It has not engaged in terrorist activity in Honduras in recent years but is suspected of links to gang violence generated by Hondurans deported from the west coast of the United States in the early part of the 21st century.

Reference: National Memorial Institute for the Prevention of Terrorism (MIPT). "Morazanist Patriotic Front (FPM)." Available online. URL: http://www.tkb.org/Group.jsp?groupID=4132. Accessed February 15, 2006.

Mossad

The Israeli Institute for Intelligence and Special Operations is referred to as Mossad (institution). It was established early in Israel's history, within months after independence was declared on May 14, 1948. It was formally authorized by the first Israeli prime minister, David Ben-Gurion, on December 13, 1949. Originally under the auspices of the Israel's foreign ministry, Mossad's director (whose identity was a state secret until 1996) began reporting directly to the prime minister in 1951. Mossad eventually adopted a verse from the Book of Proverbs as its motto: "Where No counsel is, the people fell, but in the multitude of counselors there is safety" (Proverbs XI/14).

Mossad is generally regarded as one of the top intelligence agencies in the world, though it has made occasional mistakes that included the assassination of people who were mistaken for terrorists. It gained notoriety for its capture in 1960 of Adolf Eichmann, the long-wanted German war criminal, and its ability to smuggle Eichmann out of Argentina, his adopted country, to Israel for trial and eventual execution in 1962. After the murder of Israeli athletes during the 1972 Olympics in Munich, Mossad agents tracked down and killed several Palestinian terrorists who planned the attack.

Most of Mossad's activities have to do with covert intelligence gathering; developing and maintaining diplomatic and secret relations; preventing the development and procurement of non-conventional weapons by countries hostile to Israel; preventing terrorist attacks against Israeli targets abroad; bringing Jews to Israel from countries that obstruct their migration; producing and analyzing strategic, political, and operational intelligence; and planning and executing special operations beyond Israel's borders.

Mossad is also the subject of much fiction. After 9/11, some of the European and Arab press formulated the possibility that Mossad and the Central Intelligence Agency combined forces to attack targets in the United States and blame Arab Muslims for the attacks. Almost as macabre, but this time apparently accurate, is the notion that Mossad helped to establish HAMAS during the late 1980s in an effort to counterbalance the Palestine Liberation Organization. If true, the ploy worked only too well. More recently, Mossad has been linked to the creation of fake al-Qaeda cells in Jordan, again without any substantive documentation.

Mossad has shared intelligence with their American counterparts and even worked with the Vatican after the attempted assassination of John Paul II in 1980. It is an effective organization, though it probably has fewer than 1,500 operatives and staff personnel. Mossad has almost certainly engaged in "focused preventive acts," a euphemism for the assassination of top-tier terrorist organization leaders.

See also MUNICH MASSACRE OF ISRAELI ATHLETES.

References: Katz, Samuel M. *The Hunt for the Engineer: The Inside Story of How Israel's Counterterrorist Forces Tracked and Killed the Hamas Master Bomber* (New York: Lyons Press, 2002); Thomas, Gordon. *Gideon's Spies: The Secret History of the Mossad* (New York: Thomas Dunne Books, 1999).

Mujahideen-e-Khalq Organization (MEK or MKO; The National Liberation Army of Iran [NLA, the militant wing of the MEK], the People's Mujahideen of Iran [PMOI], National Council of Resistance [NCR])

College-educated children of Iranian merchants formed this group in the 1960s seeking to counter what they perceived as excessive Western influence in the shah's regime. Their philosophy was an interesting mixture of Marxism and the teachings of Islam. It became one of the largest and most active armed Iranian dissident groups in the world. It has not only focused its activities against Western targets but has also focused on attacking the interests of the clerical regime of Iran at home and abroad.

During the 1970s, the MEK staged attacks inside Iran, killing several U.S. military personnel and civilians working on defense projects in Teheran. The MEK supported the takeover in 1979 of the U.S. embassy in Teheran. The MEK leaders were forced by Iranian security forces to flee to France in the 1980s. Most had resettled in Iraq by 1987. Consequently, the group did not launch, in the 1980s, terrorist operations in Iran on the scale of those mounted by the MEK in the 1970s.

However, in the 1990s, the group began to claim credit for an increasing number of operations inside and outside of Iran. In 1992, it began conducting attacks on Iranian embassies in 13 different countries, carrying out large-scale operations overseas with relatively little difficulty. In June 1998, MEK was responsible for three explosions in Teheran that resulted in the deaths of three people. In August of the same year, the MEK assassinated Asadollah Lajevardi, the former director of the Evin Prison. In April 1999, an MEK operative killed, in Teheran, Brigadier General Ali Sayyad Shirazi, the deputy joint chief of staff of Iran's armed forces.

Most of the fighters comprising the MEK are organized in the MEK's National Liberation Army (its militant wing). With several thousand of these fighters based in Iraq, the MEK also has an extensive overseas support network. The aforementioned front organizations serve as important sources of funds, soliciting contributions from expatriate Iranian communities.

In April 2000, the MEK attempted to assassinate the commander of the Nasr Headquarters, Tehran's interagency board responsible for coordinating policies on Iraq. The normal pace of anti-Iranian operations increased during "Operation Great Bahman" in February 2000, when the group launched a dozen attacks against Iran. During 2000 and 2001, the MEK was involved regularly in mortar attacks and hit-and-run raids on Iranian military and law-enforcement units and government buildings near the Iran-Iraq border. After Coalition aircraft bombed MEK bases at the outset of the U.S.-led invasion of Iraq in 2003, the MEK leadership ordered its members not to resist the Coalition forces, and a formal cease-fire agreement was reached in May 2003.

Reference: National Memorial Institute for the Prevention of Terrorism (MIPT). "Mujahedin-e-Khalq (MEK)." Available online. URL: http://www.tkb.org/

Group.jsp?groupID=3632. Accessed February 15, 2006.

Munich massacre of Israeli athletes

The 1972 XX World Olympiad was held in Munich. The German authorities were anxious to display a "new Germany" to the world to demonstrate the extent to which Germany had distanced itself from the genocidal Nazi regime that ended in 1945. Eight Palestinians, members of the BLACK SEPTEMBER group, were able to enter the Olympic compound during the early-morning hours of September 5. Most of them had grown up in Lebanon's refugee camps and had been trained in Libya. Of the Israeli delegation that was attacked, two members were killed outright, two escaped, and nine were taken prisoner. The Palestinians demanded the release of 234 prisoners from Israeli prisons and two, Andreas Baader and Ulrike Meinhof, from German prisons.

The Germans were aghast at the prospect of Jews again being killed on German soil. The foreign minister, Hans-Dietrich Genscher, offered himself up in exchange for the release of the hostages. He pleaded that the Palestinians were in danger of reminding the world of what happened to Jews who came under the Nazi control, not quite understanding that Palestinians had no compunction about killing Jews. The Germans also offered the Palestinians money if they would release the hostages and go away.

Finally, the Germans and Palestinians agreed that both the terrorists and the hostages would be flown to Egypt. The Germans set a trap at the airport that resulted in disaster. Fifteen Munich police officers disguised themselves as Lufthansa workers and opened fire on the Palestinians. For two hours gunfire was exchanged. In the end the terrorists either shot their captives or blew them up in a helicopter with a hand grenade. All nine of the remaining Israeli hostages were killed. Five of the terrorists were killed in the shooting with German police. The three who survived were arrested and eventually released, to the chagrin of the Israeli government, which then tracked each of them down and assassinated two of them. One of the terrorists remains at large.

One of the eight Palestinian terrorists in the Black September group stands on the balcony of the Olympic village during the standoff after they kidnapped nine members of the Israeli Olympic team, 1972. (GETTY IMAGES)

References: Bar-Zohar, Michael. *Massacre in Munich: The Manhunt for the Killers behind the 1972 Olympics Massacre* (New York: Lyons Press, 2005); Klein, Aaron J. *Striking Back: The Munich Olympics Massacre and Israel's Deadly Response* (New York: Random House, 2005).

N

narco-terrorism

Narco-terrorism is the alliance between drug producers and an insurgent group carrying out terrorist acts. Several Latin American nations offer an example of this. In countries like Peru or Colombia, this has involved the cocaine syndicate (coca growers and drug traffickers) and groups such as SENDERO LUMINOSO (in Peru) and the REVOLUTIONARY ARMED FORCES OF COLOMBIA (FARC). While the ultimate ends sought by each group is usually different, the alliance offers them immediate benefits. The stability and the legitimacy of the governments in these countries, however, is seriously sabotaged by these alliances.

The members of these alliances—the coca growers, drug traffickers, and terrorist groups—often share common goals. These include, but are not limited to, the destabilization of the government, the creation of discipline (for market purposes) among growers, and liberation from the meddling of the police and military. Mutual needs make the pursuit of these goals beneficial in some respects to all involved.

Farmers in most drug-producing countries encounter hostility from the traffickers, who often threaten death if a crop is not produced on time. They cannot turn to the government for protection, since it is illegal for them to produce the coca crop. The government is usually trying to shut down the whole coca production, often by destroying crops. This puts the farmers at risk and hurts the drug trade (hence, the traffickers) as well. Thus, the traffickers need strong support to fight back against the government in its attempts to stop the drug trade. The traffickers do not generally have military resources adequate for their own protection from the government.

The terrorist group then provides coca growers with support against governmental activities directed against coca, support against exploitation by traffickers for the coca crop, negotiation with the traffickers for better prices for the coca, and an outlet for animosity toward the government. Unsurprisingly, these support efforts lead growers to provide the groups with many "willing" people (sometimes recruited without their real consent) to help the group in its activities, and territories to "control" that the government cannot actually govern.

The terrorist groups usually provide local traffickers, through their acts of terrorist violence, with discipline among the growers, protection from the police and military, and the promise of further government destabilization. In return, traffickers supply the groups with money, arms, and a network of support.

Narco-terrorism is a growing movement in several parts of the world, involving lucrative crops of coca,

A member of the U.S. Coast Guard stands guard over 11.5 tons of cocaine before a press conference. (COAST GUARD)

opium poppies (for making heroin), and other expensive and addictive drugs.

After 9/11 and the U.S. invasion of Afghanistan, the opium poppy that was once banned by the ruling Taliban was now being planted again by farmers desparate for income in the war-ravaged economy. Concern grew that some of the profit from this lucrative crop was being diverted to Taliban, AL-QAEDA, and other terrorist groups. In 2005, the U.S. and the Afghan government joined forces to extradite Baz Mohammad, who was charged with being a Taliban-linked narco-terrorist and conspiring to import more than $25 million worth of heroin from Afghanistan into the United States. Mohammad was on the list of a dozen or so major drug traffickers that have been targeted by the United States thus far as a result of the "Kingpin Act." South American individuals and organizations such as FARC and the UNITED SELF-DEFENSE FORCES OF COLOMBIA (AUC) are also on the Kingpin list. This act allows the United States to go after drug traffickers if they represent a threat to the national security, foreign policy, or economy of the United States. However, these actions by the United States and other countries have not stemmed the tide of drugs coming out of Afghanistan. It is not even clear if al-Qaeda or any other terrorist organization receives a significant amount of money from the drug trade. In the 9/11 COMMISSION REPORT, it was stated that no reliable evidence could be found linking drug money to al-Qaeda.

See also COLOMBIA AND NARCO-TERRORISM.

Reference: U.S. Department of the Treasury. Office of Foreign Assets Control. Counter Narcotics Trafficking Sanctions. Available online. URL: http://www.treasury.gov/offices/enforcement/ofac/programs/narco/narco.shtml. Accessed March 17, 2006.

Narodnaya Volya *See* CYCLICAL NATURE OF TERRORISM.

National Army for the Liberation of Uganda *See* ALLIED DEMOCRATIC FORCES.

National Liberation Army (Ejército de Liberación Nacional [ELN])—Colombia

This anti-U.S. insurgent group was formed in 1965. While it was structured at first to conduct an insurgent war against the Colombian government, its military capabilities have declined over time. It has instead engaged in kidnapping, hijacking, bombing, and extortion. The ELN annually conducts hundreds of kidnappings for ransom, often targeting foreign employees of large corporations, particularly those in the petroleum industry. Indeed, this industry has been attacked by the ELN in several forms, including assaults on the power infrastructure as well as on the pipelines and the electric distribution network.

In late 1999, the ELN began a dialogue with Colombian officials, following a campaign of mass kidnappings, each involving at least one citizen of the United States. The purpose of the kidnappings was apparently to demonstrate to Colombian authorities the strength of the ELN and its continuing viability so as to make credible its demands that the Colombian government negotiate with the ELN as it has done with FARC.

With between 3,000 to 6,000 members engaged in its struggle, the ELN remains based mostly in the rural and mountainous regions of Colombia. It also has an unknown number of active supporters in its anti-U.S. efforts. The only external aid known to be available to this group is the occasional medical care supplied by Cuba and the political consultation offered periodically by the Castro regime.

In May 2004, Colombian president Álvaro Uribe proposed a renewal of peace talks, but these talks did not begin until 2005. The ELN has begun to be involved in the talks but has not agreed to either disarmament or a full cease-fire.

Reference: National Memorial Institute for the Prevention of Terrorism (MIPT). "National Liberation Army (Colombia)." Available online. URL: http://www.tkb.org/Group.jsp?groupID=218. Accessed February 15, 2006.

Naval Special Warfare Development Group *See* SEAL TEAM SIX.

Nazi Germany, state terrorism in

One of the most extremist and violent regimes in modern history came to power in Germany in January 1933, and it became a subsequent model for the "terror state." The Nazi (an abbreviation of National Socialist German Workers' Party) success came about as the result of economic depression, successful political demagoguery, and intrigue within the German political establishment, many of whose members were opposed to the Nazi leader, ADOLF HITLER, but thought he could be controlled or moderated. Upon coming to power, the Nazis launched a state terror that for a brief time controlled most of the European continent. They used to full advantage the apparatus of a modern industrial state to indoctrinate millions of people into an ideology characterized by racism and anti-Semitism. An entire culture was dedicated to demonstrating the racial superiority of Germans and to inculcating their right to rule Europe.

The Nazi pursuit of a foreign policy that featured military aggression and enslavement of conquered nations led to World War II. During the conflict, the Nazis sought out and received cooperation from other Europeans who accepted the German preference for ethnic cleansing. The Nazis were eventually defeated and removed from power in May 1945. Their legacy was a memorable one: tens of millions of people had lost their lives in the war. The Nazis built death camps. At least 12 million people, mostly civilians, were murdered, starved, or left to perish from disease.

Since the Nazi era, thousands of volumes have been researched and published on how such an experience could occur in a country that had been considered one of the more civilized cultures in the world. Germany itself has conducted a long period of soul-searching. Nazi Germany is identified with the Stalinist period in the Soviet Union, a regime that also embodies one of the fullest expressions of state terror in history.

See also ETHNIC CLEANSING; HITLER, ADOLF; STATE TERRORISM.

Reference: Burleigh, Michael. *The Third Reich: A New History* (New York: Hill & Wang, 2000).

neo-Nazis

There are several neo-Nazi organizations in North America and Germany. One of the most visible neo-Nazi group in the United Nations is the ARYAN NATIONS, sometimes referred to as the Aryan Nations and the Church of Jesus Christ Christian, formerly led by Pastor Richard Butler, and located, until early 2001, in Hayden Lake, Idaho. Another is the White Aryan Resistance, led by Tom Metzger. Neo-Nazi groups in Germany have mostly appeared in the eastern part of the country where unemployment, around 17% during most of the 1990s, has created an atmosphere of resentment and desperation. Neo-Nazis are also closely associated with skinheads and other white supremacists. The general belief system consists of emphases on racial superiority of whites and anti-Semitism.

Democracies deal with the antidemocratic stance of neo-Nazis in a variety of ways. In Germany the memories of the Nazi regime of 1933–45 remain a haunting part of the country's political culture. The Nazi salute and other symbols associated with this regime are banned by law. (This is in contrast to the United States where the First Amendment protects the expression of views and symbols even if they are obnoxious to the majority of the citizenry.) Nevertheless, during the last years of the 20th and beginning of the 21st centuries, numerous crimes, including several that led to the deaths of immigrants to Germany, were associated with right-wing extremists. Most of the violence occurred in eastern Germany.

Neo-Nazi groups are increasingly characterized by a sophistication that takes full advantage of modern technology, which includes websites. There are even rock bands that record lyrics that are blatantly racist and include an advocacy of violence against nonwhites. Neo-Nazi group activities are being countered by lawsuits that often successfully result in depleting the resources of the organizations.

According the information collected by the Anti-Defamation League, there are more than 100 racist/skinhead groups that have emerged since the beginning of the new century. Since these new neo-Nazi groups are, like many other modern hate groups, leaderless movements, and consequently very fluid, some of the emerging groups have not survived for very long, although some of those which dissolve have reemerged in new forms and locations. Nor are these groups of a uniform size: They may vary in membership from less than 10 to more than 100.

The current neo-Nazi groups are not consistently engaged in terrorism, although their rhetoric continues to include strong advocacy for violent actions. The crimes committed by these racist groups are not all considered terrorism but have included several significant terrorist events, including attempted murder and arson. In 2005, a member of a neo-Nazi group was convicted of planning to firebomb a synagogue in Oklahoma City.

The death of William Pierce, the head of the neo-Nazi group the National Alliance, in July 2002, provided a rallying point for hate groups in the United States. Pierce was the author of the book about a hypothetical race war, *The* TURNER DIARIES, whose significance was enhanced by its cited impact on the perpetrator of the OKLAHOMA CITY BOMBING, Timothy McVeigh. Pierce worked, during the last few years of his life, to "professionalize" the National Alliance operations, increasing its national staff and enhancing its propaganda campaigns. His death at his West Virginia compound became a rallying point for U.S. neo-Nazi groups.

References: Anti-Defamation League. Racist Skinhead Project. Available online. URL: http://www.adl.org/racist_skinheads. Accessed March 20, 2006; Goodrick-Clarke, Nicholas. *Black Sun: Aryan Cults, Esoteric Nazism and the Politics of Identity* (New York: New York University Press, 2003).

networking, of groups

As an example of the networking of international terrorists to create an interconnected system linking groups with common goals, the incident at LOD AIRPORT excels. In this event, Japanese members of the JAPANESE RED ARMY (JRA) killed Puerto Ricans on behalf of Palestinian Arabs who sought to punish Israelis.

Cooperation between terrorist groups with, if not a common cause, at least a shared hatred has occurred frequently. Anti-NATO sentiment, for example, drew several European groups into cooperative action. A communiqué on January 15, 1986, declared that the RED ARMY FACTION (RAF) of West Germany and ACTION DIRECT (AD) of France would together attack the multinational structures of NATO. Shortly thereafter, assassins killed the general in charge of French arms sales and a West German defense industrialist. On August 8, 1985, two Americans were killed in a bomb blast at a U.S. air base in Frankfurt, West Germany. The RAF and AD claimed joint responsibility for this attack. This attack was followed by the bombing of a U.S. antiaircraft missile site.

These French and German terrorists used explosives stolen from a Belgian quarry, suggesting a connection with Belgium's FIGHTING COMMUNIST CELLS. This latter group bombed NATO pipelines and defense-related companies. Portuguese and Greek terrorists have also attacked NATO targets in their homelands, although evidence of collaboration in these countries is less clear.

In 1975, French police learned that the international terrorist known as CARLOS "THE JACKAL" was running a clearinghouse for terrorist movements. His clients included the TUPAC AMARU REVOLUTIONARY MOVEMENT (MRTA), the FRONT DU LIBÉRATION DU QUÉBEC, the IRISH REPUBLICAN ARMY (IRA), the Baader-Meinhof gang from West Germany, Yugoslavia's Croatian separatists, the Turkish People's Liberation Army, and various Palestinian groups.

An INTERNATIONAL TERRORIST CONGRESS took place in Frankfurt, Germany, in 1986, reportedly attended by no less than 500 people. Meeting under the slogan, "The armed struggle as a strategic and tactical necessity in the fight for revolution," the congress proclaimed the U.S. armed forces in Europe to be the main enemy. Among those represented at this congress, or present as guests, were German, French, Belgian, Spanish, and Portuguese terrorists, as well as the PALESTINE LIBERATION ORGANIZATION (PLO), the POPULAR FRONT FOR THE LIBERATION OF PALESTINE (PFLP), the African National Congress, the Irish Republican Army, the TUPAMAROS, the Italian RED BRIGADES (BR) and BASQUE FATHERLAND AND LIBERTY (ETA).

Reports that surfaced in May 1987 tell of Iranian Ayatollah Khomeini making the following offer to Nicaragua: Teheran would raise its $100 million in annual economic and military aid by 50% if Nicaragua would help recruit Latin American immigrants in the United States to join Iranian expatriates in forming joint terror squads. The mission of these squads: to strike back if the Americans made any attack on Iran.

While there is some evidence that attempts at coordinating activities have been made by various terrorist groups, concrete proof of shared strategies suggesting a "terrorist conspiracy" perhaps manipulated by a common hand is insufficient. One prominent expert, James Adams, suggested instead that terrorist groups act more like a multinational corporation, whose different divisions are sprinkled around the world and all of whom act in an essentially independent manner.

This analogy between different divisions in a multinational corporation and terrorist groups is more credible than that of a "conspiracy," based on the fragmentary and often subjective nature of the evidence brought forth as "proof" of a true "conspiracy" among terrorist groups. The cooperation in terms of strategic planning that has been authenticated to date between terrorist groups has been

1. ad hoc, focused on the planning of just one particular operation between groups whose other contacts remain fragmentary; and/or
2. bombastic, consisting primarily in the issuing of declarations by "congresses" or transient alliances between groups briefly united against a perceived common target.

However, contact between various terrorist groups does exist and has been documented. Thomas L. Friedman, writing for the *New York Times* (April 27, 1987) briefly details this loose-linked network. Western intelligence indicates that, between 1970 and 1984, 28 meetings involving different terrorist groups have been held around the world. While these meetings were generally called to discuss cooperation rather than coordination or revolutionary activities, it is difficult to establish precisely what plans and agreements have emerged from these contacts.

With the 21st century and the advent of the information age, terrorism is clearly taking on a new dimension in terms of networks. Described as "netwar," an asymmetric mode of conflict and crime at societal levels, this type of networking involves measures short of conventional war carried out by "protagonists" using network forms organization and related strategies and information-age technologies to carry out attacks. The individuals involved in a "netwar" usually connect in small groups that communicate and coordinate their activities/attacks but generally lack an organized central command authority.

Networks of terror groups, similar to the structures emerging in the world of business, generally organize in one of three types: chains, hubs (or stars), or all-channel. Chain networks are organized much like an organization of smugglers, where goods, information, and even people are passed along a line of separate contacts, from one end of the chain to the other. In contrast, hub or star networks are similar to the structure of a drug cartel, with actors and cells tied to a central cell or actor that controls communication and coordinates action. In the all-channel network, however, each small group or cell is connected to every other group in a collaborative effort but without a central command cell.

It is perhaps easier to understand the differences in these network structures by attaching each to a famil-

Types of Terrorist Networks

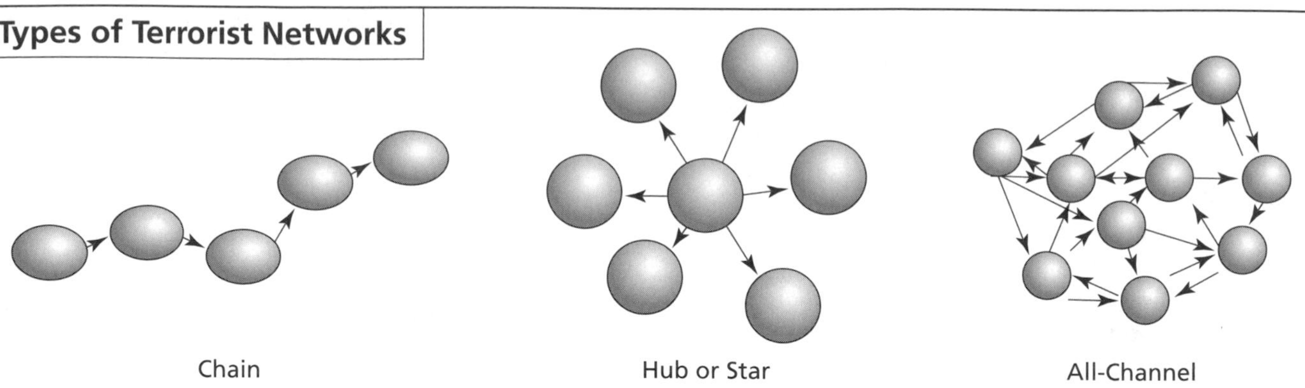

iar organization. Chain networks are common to most smuggling rings, where contraband items or individuals are passed up or down the chain. Law enforcement can break the chain of such an operation by simply capturing or killing one of the links, presumably crippling the operation of the network. Organized criminal syndicates often operate as hub or star networks, with a central command (one individual or a small command cadre) whose capture or destruction is essential to law enforcement seeking to disable the network. All-channel networks are leaderless movements, with no clear beginning, no clear end, and no central authority, a pattern similar to many insurgencies today.

The structure of AL-QAEDA today is believed to be an all-channel network, with cells in many different countries that share information, resources, common targets, and even personnel but not a command structure. Initially, the United States believed that OSAMA BIN LADEN was at the center of this organization and thus that his capture or death would disrupt and ultimately destroy the organization. However, the action of multiple cells of this organization, sometimes in concert and others without apparent coordination, with bin Laden in hiding and perhaps very ill, suggests that the organization is today an all-channel network, with much interaction but no formal leadership cadre such as the one that did exist for a time under bin Laden's hands, prior to the 9/11 attacks.

References: Howard, Russell D. and Reid L. Sawyer, eds. *Terrorism and Counterterrorism: Understanding the New Security Environment* (Guilford, Conn.: McGraw-Hill, 2003); Sageman, Marc. *Understanding Terror Networks* (Philadelphia: University of Pennsylvania Press, 2004).

New People's Army (NPA)

A Maoist group formed in December 1969, the NPA is the military wing of the Communist Party of the Philippines. Its initial aim was the overthrow of the Philippine government through protracted GUERRILLA WARFARE. While the NPA was primarily a rural-based guerrilla-based group, it had an active urban infrastructure. It used city-based assassination squads called "sparrow units" from this urban infrastructure. Most of the NPA's funding derived from contributions from supporters and "revolutionary taxes" extorted from local businesses.

The NPA primarily targeted Philippine security forces, corrupt politicians, and drug traffickers. It opposed any U.S. military presence in the Philippines and attacked U.S. military interests, before the U.S. base closures in 1992. In 1999, press reports indicated that the NPA would target U.S. troops participating in joint military exercises under the Visiting Forces Agreement and U.S. embassy personnel.

With an estimated strength of between 6,000 and 8,000, it was much larger than most other groups accused of committing terrorist acts. The NPA operated in rural Luzon, Visayas, and parts of Mindanao, with cells in Manila and other metropolitan centers. It received no external aid. The NPA was declared by the U.S. government to be a foreign terrorist Organization in 2003. Its founder, José María Sison lives in exile in the Netherlands.

Reference: National Memorial Institute for the Prevention of Terrorism (MIPT). "New People's Army (NPA)." Available online. URL: http://www.tkb.org/Group.jsp?groupID=203. Accessed February 15, 2006.

The 9/11 Commission Report

In the wake of the ATTACK ON AMERICA on September 11, 2001, a commission in the United States was appointed to investigate and report on the events and the prelude to these events. In 2004, the 9/11 Commission Report was presented to the president of the United States, the U.S. Congress, and the American people. Ten commissioners—five Republicans and five Democrats chosen by elected national leaders—came together to present this report without dissent. Their conclusion: The nation was unprepared.

More than 2,600 people died at the World Trade Center, 125 died at the Pentagon, and 256 died on the four planes. The death toll surpassed that at Pearl Harbor in December 1941.

This immeasurable pain was inflicted by 19 young Arabs acting at the behest of Islamic extremists headquartered in Afghanistan. Some had been in the United States for more than a year, mixing with the rest of the population. Though four had training as pilots, most were not well educated. Most spoke English poorly, some hardly at all. In groups of four or five, carrying with them only small knives, box cutters, and cans of Mace or pepper spray, they had hijacked the four planes and turned them into deadly guided missiles.

The commission concluded that the 9/11 attacks were a shock but that they should not have come as a surprise. Instead, they found that Islamic extremists had given plenty of warning that they meant to kill Americans indiscriminately and in large numbers. Although OSAMA BIN LADEN himself did not emerge as a signal threat until the late 1990s, the threat of Islamic terrorism grew over the decade.

According to the report, in February 1993, a group led by RAMZI YOUSEF tried to bring down the World Trade Center with a truck bomb. The terrorists killed six and wounded a thousand. Plans by Omar Abdel Rahman and others to blow up the Holland and Lincoln tunnels and other New York City landmarks were frustrated when the plotters were arrested. In October 1993, Somali tribesmen shot down U.S. helicopters, killing 18 and wounding 73 in an incident that came to be known as "Black Hawk down." Years later, it was learned that those Somali tribesmen had received help from AL-QAEDA.

In early 1995, police in Manila uncovered a plot by Ramzi Yousef to blow up a dozen U.S. airliners while they were flying over the Pacific. In November 1995, a car bomb exploded outside the office of the U.S. program manager for the Saudi National Guard in Riyadh, killing five Americans and two others. In June 1996, a truck bomb demolished the Khobar Towers apartment complex in Dhahran, Saudi Arabia, killing 19 U.S. servicemen and wounding hundreds. The attack was carried out primarily by Saudi HIZBALLAH, an organization that had received help from the government of IRAN.

Until 1997, the U.S. intelligence community viewed bin Laden as a financier of terrorism, not as a terrorist leader. In February 1998, bin Laden and four others issued a self-styled fatwa, publicly declaring that it was God's decree that every Muslim should try his or her utmost to kill any American, military or civilian, anywhere in the world, because of American "occupation" of Islam's holy places and aggression against Muslims.

In August 1998, bin-Laden's group, al-Qaeda, carried out near-simultaneous truck-bomb attacks on the U.S. embassies in Nairobi, Kenya, and Dar es Salaam, Tanzania. The attacks killed 224 people, including 12 Americans, and wounded thousands more.

In December 1999, Jordanian police foiled a plot to bomb hotels and other sites frequented by American tourists, and a U.S. Customs agent arrested Ahmed Ressam at the U.S.-Canadian border as he was smuggling in explosives intended for an attack on Los Angeles International Airport. In October 2000, an al-Qaeda team in Aden, Yemen, used a motorboat filled with explosives to blow a hole in the side of a destroyer, the USS *Cole*, killing 17 American sailors and almost sinking the vessel.

The 9/11 attacks on the World Trade Center and the Pentagon were far more elaborate, precise, and destructive than any of these earlier assaults. But by September 2001, the executive branch of the U.S. government, the Congress, the news media, and the American public had received clear warning that Islamic terrorists meant to kill Americans in high numbers.

Osama bin Laden built over the course of a decade a dynamic and lethal organization. He built an infrastructure and organization in Afghanistan that could attract, train, and use recruits against ever more ambitious targets. He rallied new zealots and new money with each demonstration of al-Qaeda's capability. He had forged a close alliance with the Taliban, a regime providing sanctuary for al-Qaeda.

By September 11, 2001, al-Qaeda possessed, according to the 9/11 Commission Report:

- Leaders able to evaluate, approve, and supervise the planning and direction of a major operation;

- A personnel system that could recruit candidates, indoctrinate them, vet them, and give them the necessary training;
- Communications sufficient to enable planning and direction of operatives and those who would be helping them;
- An intelligence effort to gather required information and form assessments of enemy strengths and weaknesses;
- The ability to move people great distances; and
- The ability to raise and move the money necessary to finance an attack.

During 2000, U.S. president Bill Clinton and his advisers renewed diplomatic efforts to get bin Laden expelled from Afghanistan. They also renewed secret efforts with some of the Taliban's opponents—the Northern Alliance—to get enough intelligence to attack bin Laden directly. Diplomatic efforts centered on the new military government in Pakistan, and they did not succeed. The efforts with the Northern Alliance revived an inconclusive and secret debate about whether the United States should take sides in Afghanistan's civil war and support the Taliban's enemies. The CIA also produced a plan to improve intelligence collection on al-Qaeda, including the use of a small, unmanned airplane with a video camera, known as the *Predator.*

After the October 2000 attack on the USS *Cole,* evidence accumulated that it had been launched by al-Qaeda operatives, but without confirmation that bin Laden had given the order. The Taliban had earlier been warned that it would be held responsible for another bin Laden attack on the United States. The CIA described its findings as a "preliminary judgment"; President Clinton and his chief advisers told the U.S. public they were waiting for a conclusion before deciding whether to take military action. The military alternatives remained unappealing to them.

The transition to the new Bush administration in late 2000 and early 2001 took place with the *Cole* issue still pending. President George W. Bush and his chief advisers accepted that al-Qaeda was responsible for the attack on the *Cole* but did not like the options available for a response. As a result, the commission concluded, bin Laden's inference may well have been that attacks, at least at the level of the *Cole,* were risk-free.

The 9/11 Commission Report noted that the Bush administration began developing a new strategy with the stated goal of eliminating the al-Qaeda threat within three to five years. During the spring and summer of 2001, U.S. intelligence agencies received a stream of warnings that al-Qaeda planned, as one report put it, "something very, very, very big." Director of Central Intelligence George Tenet told the commission, "The system was blinking red."

Although bin Laden was determined to strike in the United States, as President Clinton was told and President Bush was reminded in a presidential daily brief article given to him in August 2001, the specific threat information pointed overseas. Numerous precautions were taken overseas. Domestic agencies were not effectively mobilized. The threat did not receive national media attention comparable to the millennium alert.

While the United States continued disruption efforts around the world, its emerging strategy to eliminate the al-Qaeda threat was to include an enlarged covert action program in Afghanistan, as well as diplomatic strategies for Afghanistan and Pakistan. The process culminated during the summer of 2001 in a draft presidential directive and arguments about the *Predator* aircraft, which was soon to be deployed with a missile of its own, so that it might be used to attempt to kill bin Laden or his chief lieutenants. At a September 4 meeting, President Bush's chief advisers approved the draft directive of the strategy and endorsed the concept of arming the *Predator.* This directive on the al-Qaeda strategy was awaiting President Bush's signature on September 11, 2001.

According to the 9/11 Commission Report, September 11, 2001, began with the 19 hijackers getting through a security checkpoint system that they had evidently analyzed and knew how to defeat. They took over the four flights, taking advantage of air crews and cockpits that were not prepared for the contingency of a suicide hijacking. The defense of U.S. airspace depended on close interaction between two federal agencies: the Federal Aviation Administration (FAA) and the North American Air Defense Command (NORAD). Existing protocols on 9/11 were, according to the report, unsuited in every respect for an attack in which hijacked planes were used as weapons.

The military was unprepared for the transformation of commercial aircraft into weapons of mass destruction. A shoot-down authorization was not communicated to the NORAD air-defense sector until 28 minutes after United 93 had crashed in Pennsylvania. Planes were scrambled, but ineffectively, as they did not know where to go or what targets they were to intercept. When the shoot-down order was finally given, it was not communicated to the pilots. In short, while leaders in Washington believed that the fighters circling above them had been instructed to "take out" hostile aircraft, the only orders actually conveyed to the pilots were to "ID type and tail."

Like the national defense, the emergency response on 9/11 was necessarily improvised. In New York City, the Fire Department of New York, the New York Police Department, the Port Authority of New York and New Jersey, the building employees, and the occupants of the buildings did their best to cope with the effects of almost unimaginable events—unfolding furiously over 102 minutes. Casualties were nearly 100% at and above the impact zones and were very high among first responders who stayed in danger as they tried to save lives. Despite weaknesses in preparations for disaster, failure to achieve a unified incident command, and inadequate communications among responding agencies, all but approximately 100 of the thousands of civilians who worked below the impact zone escaped, often with help from the emergency responders.

At the Pentagon, while there were also problems of command and control, the emergency response was generally effective. The Incident Command System, a formalized management structure for emergency response in place in the National Capital Region, overcame the inherent complications of a response across local, state, and federal jurisdictions.

The commission identified specific points of vulnerability in the plot and opportunities to disrupt it. Operational failures—opportunities that were not or could not be exploited by the organizations and systems of that time—included

- Not watchlisting future hijackers Hazmi and Mihdhar, not trailing them after they traveled to Bangkok, and not informing the FBI about one future hijacker's U.S. visa or his companion's travel to the United States;
- Not sharing information linking individuals in the *Cole* attack to Mihdhar;
- Not taking adequate steps in time to find Mihdhar or Hazmi in the United States;
- Not linking the arrest of Zacarias Moussaoui, described as interested in flight training for the purpose of using an airplane in a terrorist act, to the heightened indications of attack;
- Not discovering false statements on visa applications;
- Not recognizing passports manipulated in a fraudulent manner;
- Not expanding no-fly lists to include names from terrorist watchlists;
- Not searching airline passengers identified by the computer-based CAPPS screening system; and
- Not hardening aircraft cockpit doors or taking other measures to prepare for the possibility of suicide hijackings.

Across the government, the commission found that there were failures of imagination, policy, capabilities, and management. Each failure, according to the report, cost the United States in its ability to anticipate and respond to the attacks on 9/11. They included:

Failure of imagination—The commission concluded that leaders in the United States did not understand the gravity of the threat. The terrorist danger from bin Laden and al-Qaeda was not a major topic for policy debate among the public, the media, or in the Congress. Indeed, it barely came up during the 2000 presidential campaign. Al-Qaeda's new brand of terrorism presented challenges to U.S. governmental institutions that they were not well designed to meet. There was uncertainty among the leaders as to whether this was just a new and especially venomous version of the ordinary terrorist threat the United States had lived with for decades, or it was indeed radically new, posing a threat beyond any yet experienced. As late as September 4, 2001, Richard Clarke, the White House staffer long responsible for counterterrorism policy coordination, asserted that the government had not yet made up its mind how to answer the question: "Is al-Qaeda a big deal?"

Failure of policy—Terrorism was not the overriding national security concern for the U.S. government under either the Clinton or the pre-9/11 Bush administration. The policy challenges were linked to the failure of imagination. Officials in both the Clinton and Bush administrations regarded a full U.S. invasion of Afghanistan as practically inconceivable before 9/11.

Failure of capabilities—Before 9/11, the United States tried to solve the al-Qaeda problem with the capabilities it had used in the last stages of the cold war and its immediate aftermath. These capabilities were insufficient. Little was done to expand or reform them. The CIA had minimal capacity to conduct paramilitary operations with its own personnel, and it did not seek a large-scale expansion of these capabilities before 9/11. The CIA also needed to improve its capability to collect intelligence from human agents. At no point before 9/11 was the Department of Defense fully engaged in the mission of countering al-Qaeda, even though this was perhaps the most dangerous foreign enemy threatening the United States. America's homeland defenders faced outward. NORAD itself was barely able to retain any alert bases. Its planning scenarios occasionally considered the danger of hijacked aircraft being guided to American targets, but only aircraft that were coming from overseas.

The most serious weaknesses in agency capabilities were in the domestic arena. The FBI did not have the capability to link the collective knowledge of agents in the field to national priorities. Other domestic agencies deferred to the FBI.

FAA capabilities were weak. Any serious examination of the possibility of a suicide hijacking could have suggested changes to fix glaring vulnerabilities—expanding no-fly lists, searching passengers identified by the CAPPS screening system, deploying federal air marshals domestically, hardening cockpit doors, alerting air crews to a different kind of hijacking possibility than they had been trained to expect. Yet the FAA did not adjust either its own training or training with NORAD to take account of threats other than those experienced in the past.

Failure of management—The missed opportunities to thwart the 9/11 plot were also symptoms of a broader inability to adapt the way government manages problems to the new challenges of the 21st century. Action officers should have been able to draw on all available knowledge about al-Qaeda in the government. Management should have ensured that information was shared and duties were clearly assigned across agencies, and across the foreign-domestic divide.

The 9/11 Commission Report also identified several specific problems, including but not limited to unsuccessful diplomacy, a lack of military options, problems with the intelligence community, problems with the FBI, permeable borders and immigration controls, permeable aviation security, financing, an improvised homeland security (with serious communication problems), emergency response (which lacked equipment and coordination), and a Congress unable to act swiftly. The commission concluded that although since 9/11 the United States and its allies have killed or captured a majority of al-Qaeda's leadership; toppled the Taliban, which gave al-Qaeda sanctuary in Afghanistan; and severely damaged the organization, terrorist attacks continue. The problem, according to the report, is that al-Qaeda represents an ideological movement, not a finite group of people: "It initiates and inspires, even if it no longer directs. In this way it has transformed itself into a decentralized force. Osama bin Laden may be limited in his ability to organize major attacks from his hideouts. Yet killing or capturing him, while extremely important, would not end terror. His message of inspiration to a new generation of terrorists would continue."

Thus, although because of offensive actions against al-Qaeda since 9/11, and defensive actions to improve homeland security, the commission concluded that the United States is safer today, it also noted that the United States is not "safe." Instead, the report contained several recommendations that the Commissioners believed could make America safer and more secure. These recommendations are divided into two basic parts: what to do and how to do it.

The global strategy includes three dimensions: (1) attack terrorists and their organizations, (2) prevent the continued growth of Islamic terrorism, and (3) protect against and prepare for terrorist attacks. This would include efforts to root out sanctuaries; strengthen long-term U.S. and international commitments to the future of Pakistan and Afghanistan; and confront problems with Saudi Arabia in the open and build a relationship beyond oil, a relationship that both sides can defend to their citizens and includes a shared commitment to reform. It would also require measures to communicate and defend American ideals in the Islamic world, while offering an agenda of opportunity that includes support for public education and economic openness, developing a comprehensive coalition strategy against Islamic terrorism, using a flexible contact group of leading coalition governments and fashioning a common coalition approach on issues such as the treatment of captured terrorists and devoting a maximum effort to the parallel task of countering the proliferation of weapons of mass destruction.

In order to achieve the third dimension, protecting against and preparing for terrorist attacks, the 9/11 Commission Report includes several detailed suggestions, including

- Targeting terrorist travel, an intelligence and security strategy that the 9/11 story showed could be at least as powerful as the effort devoted to terror finance;
- Addressing problems of screening people with biometric identifiers across agencies and governments, including U.S. border and transportation systems, by designing a comprehensive screening system that addresses common problems and sets common standards. As standards spread, this necessary and ambitious effort could dramatically strengthen the world's ability to intercept individuals who could pose catastrophic threats;
- Quickly completing a biometric entry-exit screening system, one that also speeds qualified travelers;
- Setting standards for the issuance of birth certificates and sources of identification, such as drivers' licenses;
- Developing strategies for neglected parts of the transportation security system. Since 9/11, about 90% of the nation's $5 billion annual investment in transportation security has gone to aviation;
- In aviation, preventing arguments about a new computerized profiling system from delaying vital improvements in the "no-fly" and "automatic selectee" lists. Also, giving priority to the improvement of checkpoint screening;
- Determining, with leadership from the president, guidelines for gathering and sharing information in the new security systems that are needed, guidelines that integrate safeguards for privacy and other essential liberties;
- Underscoring that as government power necessarily expands in certain ways, the burden of retaining such powers remains on the executive to demonstrate the value of such powers and ensure adequate supervision of how they are used, including a new board to oversee the implementation of the guidelines needed for gathering and sharing information in these new security systems;
- Basing federal funding for emergency preparedness solely on risks and vulnerabilities, putting New York City and Washington, D.C., at the top of the current list. Such assistance should not remain a program for general revenue sharing or pork-barrel spending; and
- Making homeland security funding contingent on the adoption of an incident command system to strengthen teamwork in a crisis, including a regional approach. Allocate more radio spectrum and improve connectivity for public safety communications and encourage widespread adoption of newly developed standards for private-sector emergency preparedness—since the private sector controls 85% of the nation's critical infrastructure.

The title page of the 9/11 Commission Report (DEPARTMENT OF HOMELAND SECURITY)

The report calls for unity of effort in five areas, beginning with unity of effort on the challenge of counterterrorism itself:

- Unifying strategic intelligence and operational planning against Islamic terrorists across the foreign-domestic divide with a National Counterterrorism Center;
- Unifying the intelligence community with a new National Intelligence Director;
- Unifying the many participants in the counterterrorism effort and their knowledge in a network-

based information-sharing system that transcends traditional governmental boundaries;
- Unifying and strengthening congressional oversight to improve quality and accountability; and
- Strengthening the FBI and homeland defenders.

Some, but not all, of the 9/11 Commission Report's recommendations have been implemented since its publication.

Reference: *The 9/11 Commission Report: Final Report of the National Commission on Terrorist Attacks upon the United States.* New York: W. W. Norton & Company, Inc. 2004.

NORAID

Irish Northern Aid—generally known as NORAID—was established by Michael Flannery, a former IRISH REPUBLICAN ARMY (IRA) member living in New York, in 1969. Its purpose was to facilitate the giving of assistance to the IRA. Headquarters were established at 273 East 194th Street, in the Bronx, New York City.

Conflicting reports are offered about the importance of NORAID for the IRA (now known as the Provisional IRA or PIRA after the 1969 split in the IRA leadership) during the last three decades of the 20th century. Certainly in the early 1970s, NORAID could be termed crucial to the PIRA's survival since it supplied over 50% of the cash used by the PIRA. By the end of the 20th century, however, the PIRA received less than $200,000 of their estimated $7,000,000 budget from NORAID.

NORAID during the late 1980s no longer supplied only cash to the PIRA. Instead, cash raised at traditional annual "dinners" was frequently used to purchase arms, which were then smuggled to Ireland. Since each dinner was expected to raise between $20,000 and $30,000, and such dinners were held in cities throughout the United States during the 1980s, the supply of arms that could be purchased and smuggled was substantial.

Following the murder of 79-year-old Lord Mountbatten and other members of his family, including his 14-year-old grandson, by the IRA in 1979, U.S. intelligence agencies, including the FBI, began to cooperate with the British in attempting to stem the flow of arms from NORAID to the IRA. Although initial successes in this effort were few, by 1984, the cooperation yielded significant results. In early September of that year, an 80-foot trawler, registered in Ipswich, Massachusetts, left Boston bound for Ireland. In its cargo were rockets, grenades made in Korea, 100 German automatic rifles, 51 pistols and revolvers, shotguns, and a .50 caliber heavy machine gun. A CIA surveillance satellite tracked the trawler to its rendezvous with an Irish trawler. A report on this cargo and its transfer was made to the Irish government, which subsequently seized the ship and confiscated its $500,000 cargo of illegal arms.

NORAID was crippled in the last two decades of the 20th century by more than the stepped-up scrutiny and cooperation between intelligence services of the United States and Britain. Court challenges to NORAID members in the United States, based on claims for injuries incurred by victims of the weapons purchased by NORAID money, substantially drained NORAID coffers, making the donation of cash and the purchase of arms difficult, if not completely impossible. Moreover, the peace process, begun in the mid-1990s, helped to make the transfer of this type of aid to the IRA much less politically acceptable in the United States.

See also NETWORKING OF GROUPS; STATE TERRORISM.

Reference: Adams, James. *The Financing of Terrorism* (New York: Simon & Schuster, 1986).

Northern Ireland

The five northwestern counties that share an island with the Republic of Ireland. Economically, Northern Ireland is the poorest region of the United Kingdom with the smallest population. Approximately 900,000 Protestants and 600,000 Catholics inhabit the region. Protestants generally desire to remain within the United Kingdom's jurisdiction, while Catholics tend to prefer that the region join the Republic of Ireland. The latter argue that Ireland was mistakenly partitioned in 1922 by the British government. Northern Ireland since the late 1960s has suffered from a "Time of Troubles" in which terrorist acts by Catholic and Protestant militants against one another have cost hundreds of lives.

Terrorism in Northern Ireland has an old lineage. The region is a residue of the Protestant-Catholic rivalry that can be traced back at least three centuries. During most of that time, rivalries in addition to those based on religion have marked differences between Catholics and Protestants. Catholics have felt significant economic and political discrimination since Protestants for the most part have controlled the courts and police and Protestants enjoyed standards of living that were consistently higher.

In Northern Ireland, Republican and Loyalist paramilitary organizations have shifted their activity from political action to criminal racketeering in recent years. This shift began during the 1994 cease-fires of the PIRA, the UDA, and the UVF and accelerated since the beginning of the Good Friday Agreement in 1998. Two relatively small "dissident" Republican paramilitaries, the Continuity Irish Republican Army (CIRA) and the Real Irish Republican Army (RIRA) are not observing the cease-fire, and both continue to advocate the use of violence to support their goal of uniting the northern and southern parts of Ireland. The activities of the Loyalist paramilitaries take place almost exclusively in Northern Ireland, but the Republican paramilitaries also carry out actions in the Republic of Ireland.

See also IRISH REPUBLICAN ARMY.

Reference: Tonge, Jonathan. *Northern Ireland: Conflict and Change* (New York: Pearson Education, 2002).

Northern Ireland Act (Emergency Provisions)

See UNITED KINGDOM ANTI-TERROR LEGISLATION.

novation

Novation is a fairly simple, uncomplicated process. Legally, it refers to the substitution of a new indebtedness or obligation, creditor or debtor, for an existing one. When applied to the creation of laws applying to the crime of TERRORISM, it has offered an avenue by which old law (on PIRACY of the sea) could be applied to newer forms of the same crime. In other words, aerial hijackers would assume the legal "indebtedness" of sea pirates under international law. Thus, it would not be necessary to create new international law to deal with what is, in many respects, a very old form of criminal activity.

November 17

See REVOLUTIONARY ORGANIZATION NOVEMBER 17.

nuclear terrorism

One of the worst nightmares of security officials tasked with protecting a population against terrorism is the possibility of a nuclear device being detonated in a populated area by a terrorist organization that may or may not be sponsored by a "rogue state." IRAN, IRAQ, LIBYA, and North Korea are all known either to have sought to purchase nuclear weapons or to manufacture their own. The first three remain determined enemies of both the United States and ISRAEL and have sworn the destruction of the latter. Israel in 1980 even successfully launched an apparently preemptive attack on an Iraqi nuclear reactor near Baghdad.

Terrorist organizations are not uniformly interested in acquiring or using nuclear weapons. However, there is little doubt that some are actively considering their acquisition. Others that are not may instead be pursuing bacteriological or chemical weapon systems, hardly an improvement. Moreover, many terrorists argue that the United States is (thus far) the only nuclear terrorist in the history of the world to have dropped two atomic bombs on civilian populations (Hiroshima and Nagasaki, Japan, during World War II).

Nuclear terrorism in the 21st century constitutes probably a greater possibility than it did in the 20th. The general and comforting notion that "terrorists want a lot of people watching, not a lot of people dead" is not without important exceptions. Throughout the 1990s, terrorist incidences tended to decline compared with the decade of the 1980s. At the same time, however, they were becoming more lethal because civilians were being increasingly targeted. More powerful explosives are being used by terrorists and, of course, a nuclear bomb is the ultimate explosive.

The use of nuclear devices by terrorists was a threat ridiculed in the 1980s by most analysts studying terrorist trends, but by the end of the 1990s, they were regarded by those same analysts as a distinct threat. With the demise of the Soviet Union, a great deal of enriched fissionable material became "unaccounted for," apparently smuggled from country to country, evading most international control mechanisms. Since the amount of such material needed to make a bomb is not large (about 15 pounds of enriched plutonium or about 30 pounds of enriched uranium would be enough to make a sizeable nuclear weapon), the potential for the construction of such bombs escalated considerably. Moreover, these bombs can be built by advanced students in the field, using readily available information. A highly qualified nuclear engineer is no longer essential to its successful construction.

In 1997, Russian president Boris Yeltsin's former security adviser, General Lebed, informed the world that, during the 1970s, a considerable number of "luggage nukes" (small nuclear devices built in the form of a suitcase and easily transportable by a single person) were produced by the Soviet military industry. He further declared that a number of these weapons were "unaccounted for" following the breakup of the Soviet Union. This claim has been both confirmed and denied by Russian experts, but none have denied that such weapons had indeed been made.

Terrorism experts during the 1970s and 1980s suggested that terrorists would not use nuclear weapons, even if they were available, since the cost in terms of both money and scientific expertise would be prohibitive. But a "luggage nuke" would not necessarily be too expensive or difficult to secure, given the number that may have made it onto the black market of arms sales throughout the world in the 1990s. Small, easily transportable "luggage nukes," potentially available after the demise of the Soviet Union, make these arguments against their potential use less valid.

Another argument raised against the use of nuclear weapons by terrorists concerns the potential adverse effect of the use of a weapon of mass destruction (WMD). Even democracies, which tend toward underreaction to acts of terrorist violence, since identification of the perpetrator is often not completely clear, might instead overreact to an attack with a WMD. Terrorist acts are designed to create a mood of fear, not a demand for retaliation, in its targeted audience. The use of nuclear weapons was believed to be potentially counterproductive in terms of the projected reaction of the audience.

Yet the possible use of "luggage nukes" may alter the projected reluctance to use of such weapons by terrorists. Such a weapon, relatively small in size but capable of producing an enormous "bang" (with potentially dramatic psychological impact), may become an attractive option for terrorists. It has been estimated that, if the van used by the terrorists involved in the WORLD TRADE CENTER BOMBINGS in New York had been filled with nuclear material instead of ammonium nitrate, the explosion would probably have been large enough to destroy lower Manhattan. Such a bomb could thus destroy a state's center of power, political or economic, in a fairly focused fashion.

This latter point is crucial in analysis of the potential for nuclear terrorism. Other weapons of mass destruction, biological and chemical, are either less focused territorially and unpredictable or are limited by environmental conditions, making the more focused and controllable nuclear weapons psychologically more appealing to terrorists as "cleaner" and hence more easily justified.

Effective defense against the use of nuclear weapons has been based on the ability to deter such use by the threat of a WMD. But this assumes that the perpetrator and/or its sponsoring state could be determined without undue delay, so that such a threat would be credible. With the influx on the black market of "luggage nukes," which may pass through many hands before use, such a response may not continue to be a sufficient deterrent. There exists the possibility that a small group of domestic terrorists may obtain such a weapon without the sponsorship of another state, making response with a comparable WMD an unlikely deterrent. As terrorism expert Walter Laqueur noted in his book *The New Terrorism:*

> Given the amount of fissionable material that is available, the voluminous literature on nuclear weaponry, and military and state budgets in which hundreds of millions of dollars is a paltry sum, the chance that a terrorist group will come into possession of a nuclear device is significant.

Although initial concerns over the acquisition of nuclear bombs by terrorists has diminished to some degree, new concerns arose over the possibility that terrorists could instead use nuclear material to create a different type of weapon: a "dirty bomb." Speculation about a possible al-Qaeda nuclear threat mounted after then–attorney general John Ashcroft announced the arrest of Abdullah al-Mujahir, a U.S. citizen and former Chicago street-gang member, for allegedly conspiring with al-Qaeda to detonate a dirty bomb inside the United States.

Public understanding of this new potential threat is often flawed, since the precise nature of the weapon remains speculative, in the absence of a genuine attack with such a weapon. A dirty bomb, according to the U.S. Department of Homeland Security, is a conventional explosive salted with radioactive isotopes in order to spew out that nuclear material and contaminate a wide area. The military usefulness of such devices remain in dispute. The explosive, such as TNT, in such a bomb may be more dangerous than the nuclear material, and its destructive power would depend on the size of the conventional bomb, as well as the volume and nature of the nuclear material.

Dirty bombs, or radiation dispersal devises (RDD), are what an organization (or a state) might choose to make if it is unable to create a real nuclear bomb, the destructive capabilities of which are essentially marginal by comparison. A dirty bomb is far easier to make and is fundamentally a weapon of terror, since a bomb that kills people and sets off Geiger counters would certainly terrify any city. It would be unlikely to kill, as would a substantial nuclear bomb, 100,000 people, but it would obviously create the mood of fear and terror sought by terrorists and accomplish at least in part the terrorist goal of destabilizing the city's government.

While concern continues to grow about the potential for disruption by the detonation of such a weapon, there are few examples to sustain the reality of the threat. In 1996, rebels from CHECHNYA planted, but did not detonate, an RDD in Moscow's Izmailovo Park. The RDD consisted of dynamite and cesium-137 removed from cancer-treating equipment. Reporters, tipped off by the rebels about the bomb's location, passed information to the national authorities, and the bomb was defused. Clearly, the potential for damage was real, but the intent to cause such destruction was not in the rebels.

In the United States, José Padilla, an American citizen of Puerto Rican descent, was arrested in 2002 and charged (among other things) with the intent to detonate a dirty bomb in the United States. He was labeled an "enemy combatant," but when an indictment was issued three years later, there was no mention of this alleged intent to use a dirty bomb, indicating a lack of prosecutable evidence of such an intent.

Nuclear weapons, then, remain a plausible but not necessarily an imminent threat from terrorist groups today. While the likelihood of such a group acquiring a functioning nuclear bomb is only modertate, concern over the possible use of radioactive materials to create dirty bombs is escalating.

See also BIOLOGICAL AND CHEMICAL ATTACKS; CHEMICAL WEAPONS.

References: Allison, Graham. *Nuclear Terrorism: The Ultimate Preventable Catastrophe* (New York: Henry Holt & Company, 2005); Laqueur, Walter. *The New Terrorism: Fanaticism and the Weapons of Mass Destruction* (New York: Oxford University Press, 1999); Stern, Jessica. *The Ultimate Terrorists* (Cambridge, Mass.: Harvard University Press, 1999).

Nuremberg Trials

At the end of World War II in 1945, most of the surviving German Nazi leaders were captured by the Allies who occupied Germany that spring. They were placed on trial the next year for crimes against humanity. The Nazi regime, during its 12 years in power (1933–45), authorized and encouraged a remarkable degree of brutality toward its enemies and entire communities of people it considered unfit to live because they were considered racially inferior (Slavs), perceived as intent on the destruction of the Nordic race (Jews), or otherwise were socially undesirable (communists, homosexuals, and Roma). Concentration camps were established that for years sustained an industry of genocide in which inmates were starved, experimented upon, gassed, or simply worked to death. Perhaps as many as 12 million men, women, and children perished. In addition, tens of millions of others in areas occupied by the Germans and their allies were also murdered en masse. Russian prisoners of war died by the hundreds of thousands in camps that were totally inadequate to care for them under the rules of the Geneva Convention on the Treatment of Prisoners of War.

The Germans had been warned while the war was still in progress that they would be held responsible for their violations of human rights. However, even after it was increasingly evident that Germany would lose the war, the systematic murder of millions of defenseless civilians was still energetically pursued. In fact, the regime authorized an accelerated program of death to ensure that those perceived as enemies of Germany would not live to see its military defeat. Gas chambers and crematoriums were kept at full operation until literally the last days of the war. Concentration camp guards, when about to be overrun by the Western or Soviet military units, force-marched prisoners further into Germany's interior to prevent their liberation. The resources required by Germany's relentless genocidal activities doubtlessly detracted from its war effort because of the personnel and equipment needed to manage a huge system of camps, a rail system for deportation to the camps, and the bureaucracy to oversee the efficient destruction of millions of lives. German behavior during the war was one of the most horrendous examples of state terror in history.

Most of the Nazis on trial at Nuremberg argued that the tribunal, composed of judges from France, the Soviet Union, the United Kingdom, and the United States, had no jurisdiction in Germany and no authority to pass judgment on them. In one sense, this defense had an element of merit. After all, there was little if any precedent to place on trial the political and military leadership of a country that had just lost a major conflict. There had been discussions in the aftermath of World War I about bringing to trial the kaiser and other high-ranking officials of the German state for war crimes, but no trials were ever held. The defendants argued that the trial was simply for show and that the victors were simply exercising revenge on those who had lost the conflict.

Nuremberg established an important legal precedent that has since been pursued against heads of government who tolerate or implement brutal crimes against their own and/or other peoples. Serbian leader Slobodan Milošević and Iraqi president Saddam Hussein are the most recent examples of once powerful leaders who created and sustained a regime of terror, engaged in ethnic cleansing, and had individuals murdered sometimes on a whim. Nor are their underlings immune from prosecution. As Nuremberg demonstrated, a state terror apparatus that kills hundreds of thousands or tens of millions of people requires the active cooperation of countless police—military, bureaucratic, and judicial personnel—who may be called to account for their actions.

Legally, the Nuremberg trials highlighted the critical need to create treaties and agreements documenting the legal standards of behavior that the Germans were being accused of violating. Unfortunately, international laws at that time did not include treaties making genocide illegal. Legal principles and case law could be cited to create the basis for criminal trials here, but most of the treaties focused on human rights violations, the treatment of prisoners of war, and of civilians during times of war, as well the treaty making genocide an international crime, created after World War II, much of it in response to the horrors described at the Nuremberg trials. State terrorism has become internationally illegal in large measure as a result of these trials.

References: Persico, Joseph. *Nuremberg: Infamy on Trial* (New York: Penguin Books, 1995); Tusa, Anna, and John Tusa. *The Nuremberg Trials* (New York: Cooper Square Publishers, 2003).

O

Oklahoma City bombing (1995)

On April 19, 1995, the United States experienced its worst act of internal terrorism ever recorded. At 9:02 A.M., a truck bomb exploded in front of the Alfred P. Murrah Federal Building in Oklahoma City, Oklahoma. The blast ripped away one-third of the building, killing 168 people and injuring 503 more. Many of those killed or injured were, in legal terms, INNOCENT PERSONS, women and children from a day-care center, clerks, and typists who were simply "in the wrong place at the wrong time." Moreover, the resulting shock wave damaged over 300 surrounding structures. The 4,800-pound ammonium nitrate and nitromethane charge, stored in 55-gallon drums, was arranged in a conical form inside the truck to generate the maximum amount of blast force. Immediately following the explosion, federal, state, and local emergency officials descended on the scene.

Early in the investigation, local law enforcement discovered the rear axle of the truck that was used to carry the explosives to the Murrah Federal Building. This rear axle proved to be the essential piece of information for FEDERAL BUREAU OF INVESTIGATION (FBI) officials. By using the vehicle identification number (VIN) on the axle, investigators found that the truck was owned by the Ryder Truck Corporation in Miami, Florida. It had been last rented in Junction City, Kansas. Agents quickly arrived in Junction City, and the first FBI sketches of the two men that rented the truck put a visible face on the suspects.

Around 10:30 A.M. the same day, an Oklahoma Highway Patrol officer pulled over a yellow 1977 Mercury Marquis near Perry, Oklahoma, for driving without a license plate. Officer Charles Hangar noticed that in addition to driving without a license plate, the driver had a concealed .45-caliber Glock pistol. The driver, Timothy J. McVeigh, was arrested and charged with driving without a license plate, no insurance, and carrying a concealed weapon.

After seeing the sketches of the two suspects, Officer Charles Hangar realized that the man he had arrested a week earlier fit the drawing of the suspects. The FBI had narrowly avoided having their prime suspect escape. McVeigh was taken by the FBI just before being released for bond, and he was officially charged with the attack on the Murrah Federal Building on April 25, 1995. Fellow suspect Terry L. Nichols voluntarily turned himself in to authorities in Herrington, Kansas. Subsequent searches for evidence were executed at the farm home of James Nichols, Terry Nichols's brother, at the home address of Timothy McVeigh in Decker, Michigan, and at Terry Nichols's residence in Herrington, Kansas.

Aftermath of the Oklahoma City bombing (DEPARTMENT OF DEFENSE)

McVeigh and Nichols had met during army basic training in Fort Benning, Georgia. Together they were stationed at Fort Riley, Kansas, along with Michael Fortier, who became the government's main informant, turning state's evidence against his former friends. Timothy McVeigh had an excellent record in the army and served in the Gulf War, where he was awarded a Bronze Star. After being discharged, McVeigh became in some respects a drifter, traveling across the United States. Terry Nichols's reason for discharge is less clear. Their shared view of government injustices apparently helped to solidify their friendship.

The attack on the Murrah federal building happened exactly two years after the fiery ending of the WACO, TEXAS, INCIDENT. Both McVeigh and Nichols were supporters of groups that thought that the U.S. government had abused its power in ways that led to the death of 78 Branch Davidians. McVeigh traveled to Waco during the standoff to voice his discontent. This, combined with other incidents such as the standoff at Ruby Ridge, were in McVeigh's mind proof of government infringement on the rights of U.S. individuals. Many experts in domestic terrorism believe that the federal law enforcement offices in the Murrah Federal Building were the target of McVeigh's attack as a form of retribution for these earlier incidents.

Timothy McVeigh stood trial and was sentenced to death by lethal injection for the Oklahoma City bombing. His accomplice Terry Nichols was sentenced to life for his part in the act. In response to the attack, the federal government took several steps to avoid further acts of terrorism. Defensive design techniques were incorporated into existing federal structures, as well as being incorporated into plans for new federal buildings. Barriers were erected to keep vehicles a safer distance from buildings, and better surveillance systems were instituted. Measures were also taken by the U.S. Congress to permit hiring of more agents to work on counterterrorism and domestic terrorism threats. The Oklahoma City bombing was the first substantial act of domestic terrorism and served as a reminder that terrorism could be carried out on U.S. citizens on U.S. soil by their fellow citizens.

As a result of this incident, several important changes occurred in this country. A significant piece of anti-terror legislation was passed: the Antiterrorism and Effective Death Penalty Act of 1996. The site of the building was cleared and became part of the National Park Service, with a memorial to those who died, including chairs to represent the victims. In 2001, the Oklahoma City National Memorial Center dedicated a museum for the bombing, with graphic pictures and statements. Thousands travel each year to visit the site and to remember the victims of this attack. The center is also home to the National Memorial Institute for the Prevention of Terrorism (MIPT), a nonprofit group dedicated to the research and study of terrorism.

Timothy McVeigh was executed by lethal injection in June 2001.

References: CNN. Oklahoma City Tragedy. Available online. URL: http://www.cnn.com/US/OKC. Accessed March 21, 2006; National Memorial Institute for the Prevention of Terrorism (MIPT). "Oklahoma City Bombing Conspirators." Available online. URL: http://www.tkb.org/Group.jsp?groupID=3740. Accessed February 15, 2006.

T.L.

Okrana

See CYCLICAL NATURE OF TERRORISM.

Omega 7

Omega 7 was a violent Puerto Rican independence faction operating during the 1960s and 1970s in the United States. It carried out a variety of violent acts, including the placing of bombs in New York's crowded airports and the attempted murder of U.S. officials. As Puerto Rico struggled with the issue of integration into the U.S. federal system as a full state or independence as a separate nation-state, Omega 7 sought to convince the U.S. citizenry and its government to make Puerto Rico independent.

OPEC, kidnapping in Vienna

See CARLOS "THE JACKAL."

operational security

Operational security has as its primary objective the denial of opportunity to terrorists to collect any information on either the facility or its activities that might enable them to predict those activities. To be able to predict those activities would make it possible for terrorists to penetrate the facility or the activity and disrupt or destroy it. By denying that information to terrorists, organizations can significantly decrease the risk of a group or an individual successfully carrying out an attack.

Prediction of operational activities normally relies on discerning patterns of behavior. For this reason, operational security analysis tries to identify those patterns, studying also the way in which the patterns are communicated to personnel. Emphasis is placed on making such patterns less predictable, randomizing activities as far as possible (without creating chaos within the organization). Repeated activities too often create in the minds of employees responsible for security a numbness, a lack of alertness to small differences that may be vital to security. The arrival of a particular car at the same time every morning, the use of a van of a specific model and color delivering goods at the same place and time—these routines can deaden the alertness of personnel to such factors as the driver's identity or the presence of an unauthorized person in the vehicle. Such a failure to notice, and to carry through a thorough security check each day, can prove calamitous to the organization's security.

The training of personnel in operational security measures is important. Organizations focusing on operational security as a preventive tool for terrorism attempt to train personnel in the recognition of intelligence-gathering activities so that they can more easily identify individuals who appear to be engaged in this type of activity. Another major focus of operational security efforts involves the screening of employees and casual but regular contacts (e.g., vendors), since these individuals can be strong tools working against a breach of security or a threat to the operation of the organization.

Organizations seeking to build operational security as a tool against terrorist attack focus on a variety of critical techniques, including keeping a low profile within the community, so that the organization does not become an attractive target provoking publicity for terrorists. These organizations also concentrate on improving security of communications, making it less possible for penetration of the flow of commands or patterns of communication. Finally, most organizations seeking to build operational security attempt to develop counterintelligence capabilities within both management and security-related personnel so that the organization need not always struggle defensively against terrorism but can take proactive measures.

Operational security alone, however, is insufficient to deter terrorism. Personal security and physical security are vital areas of equal concern.

See also AIRPORT SECURITY; PERSONAL SECURITY; PHYSICAL SECURITY.

Operation Chavín de Huántar

On December 17, 1996, rebels from the TUPAC AMARU REVOLUTIONARY MOVEMENT (MRTA) seized the Japanese embassy residence in Lima, Peru, during a festive cocktail reception. Demanding the release of 400 of their comrades who were in Peru's prison at the time, the 14 Tupac Amaru guerrillas gradually released hundreds of the hostages, retaining only 72 for the entire siege. Alberto Fujimori, Peru's president, saw little chance for resolving the situation peacefully since he was determined not to release the prisoners. But he gave the negotiators an opportunity to try. Attempting to alleviate the tension, he arranged the safe passage to Cuba for the rebels if they wished (which they did not choose to accept as most wanted to remain in Peru). He also appointed Archbishop Luis Cipriani to be the special negotiator.

The 72 hostages who were held for the whole 126-day siege included senior Peruvian officials, Fujimori's brother Pedro, foreign diplomats, and the Japanese ambassador. Britain, Germany, Israel, and the United States all offered to help in the rescue attempt but were all officially turned down. Fujimori, however, was under intense pressure to resolve the situation as quickly and peacefully as possible.

However, he resisted all calls for a quick solution, choosing instead to allow time for his military and intelligence units to create and implement Operation Chavín de Huántar (named in honor of a pre-Incan archaeological site that was honeycombed with underground passages). What evolved was a highly successful rescue mission using 140 Peruvian special forces troops and professional miners. During the seemingly endless weeks of the standoff, while negotiations continued, the professional miners were brought into the area near the residence to build large, ventilated, and lighted tunnels through which the troops could reach the inside of the compound.

The outstanding success of the operation (with only one of the 72 hostages being killed) can be attributed to split-second timing, well-planned diversions, and superb intelligence. During the months of time that elapsed between the start of the incident and its conclusion, listening devices of all sorts were smuggled into the residence. Some were hidden in a guitar and thermos bottle that the Red Cross workers were given to deliver; others were placed in buttons on clothing brought to the hostages as changes of clothes were needed. During the final four days, intelligence agents posed as doctors and were allowed to enter the compound and "check on the health" of the hostages, implanting while they were there matchstick-sized two-way microphones that helped intelligence officers on the outside to communicate with the military and police commanders being held among the hostages within.

With this intelligence access, those planning the operation were able to monitor the movements of the guerrillas and hostages each day, noting patterns of behavior. This information made a carefully timed assault possible since the intelligence officers were able to learn that the Tupac Amaru guards played a game of soccer at about 3 P.M. in the ground-floor living room each day. They also found, using audio and visual sensors to confirm the pattern, that, prior to this game, the 14 guards stacked their rifles in a corner of the room.

Since the building plans were readily available to government forces, the special forces team had plenty of time to train on mock-ups of the building. Construction of the tunnels, if detected by the hostage-takers, could have triggered a violent battle and possibly a massacre of the hostages. To prevent this, Peru's leaders used blaring martial music, played day and night outside of the embassy compound, to mask the noise. This diversion also served to deny rest to the hostage-takers, demoralizing or at least weakening their resistance and stamina. To add further confusion to the rebels when the assault began and to give another strategic advantage to the rescue teams, the tunnels were built to offer as many as six different accesses to the compound.

At 3:10 P.M., the listening devices indicated that the afternoon soccer game had begun, with at least half of the guards participating. By 3:17, the hostages, who were being held upstairs during the game, as usual, alerted by a hidden receiver held by a military officer who was among the hostages, moved a desk to block the second-floor entrance and took cover. Three minutes later, nine pounds of explosives were detonated in the tunnel directly under the reception room, where the soccer game was in progress. This explosion killed four of the eight guards and opened a hole through which troops began to pour.

The patience exercised by the Peruvian government in talking with the terrorists through extensive negotiations, using the time to gather intelligence, build tunnels, and repeatedly practice the assault, was amply rewarded when the hostages were successfully rescued with the loss of only one hostage's life. Peru presented to the international community an example of the value of careful intelligence and planning in such hostage-rescue situations. The rescue efforts broke no laws, wasted no civilian or innocent lives (except for the one who was shot by a guard as the attack began), and made use of plenty of time to plan a successful final act. Patience and careful planning, based on timely intelligence information, were keys to the success of Operation Chavín de Huántar.

Operation Dark Winter

Operation Dark Winter was the code name for a senior-level bioterrorist attack simulation executed on June 22–23, 2001. It was intended to carry out a mock version of a covert and prevalent smallpox attack on the United States. The Center for Strategic and International Studies, the Johns Hopkins Center for Civilian

Bio-defense Studies, the ANSER Institute for Homeland Security, and the Oklahoma City National Memorial Institute for the Prevention Terrorism hosted the senior-level war game to examine the national security, intergovernmental, and information challenges of a biological attack on the American homeland. This exercise outlined a fictional scenario in which Iraq has launched a covert bioterrorism attack with smallpox against shopping malls in three U.S. states—Oklahoma, Pennsylvania, and Georgia. Fictional TV stations showed footage of a mother in tears, pleading for vaccine, while being pushed back by riot police. During the 13 days of the game, the disease spread to 25 states and 15 other countries. Fourteen participants and 60 observers witnessed terrorism/warfare in slow motion.

Dark Winter was intended to evaluate the weaknesses of a national emergency response during an attack with biological weapons against the American population. The simulation was exclusively anticipated to set up defensive procedures and response measures by triggering governmental and public alertness on the scale and magnitude of such a threat posed by chemical and biological weapons.

Dark Winter's simulated scenario implicated a contained smallpox attack that gets out of control. This would create a situation in which the National Security Council would not be capable of determining the origin of the attack, nor would it be in a position to implement emergency strategies to contain the spreading virus. This failure to deliver swift countermeasures to contain the virus and therefore to keep pace with the disease's rate of spread would cause a new disastrous eventuality in which enormous civilian fatalities would overwhelm America's emergency response capabilities.

The simulation was used to evaluate the U.S. healthcare infrastructure and its ability to cope with such a threat. The event also intended to tackle the widespread panic that would surface and which would likely result in mass social breakdown and mob violence. Exploits would also include the many difficulties that the media would face when providing American citizens with the crucial information concerning safety measures.

Reference: Hopkins Tanne, Janice. "Preventing "Dark Winter"—The Public Health System's Role in Strengthening National Security." *Carnegie Reporter* (Spring 2002) Available online. URL: http://www.carnegie.org/reporter/04/preventing. Accessed March 21, 2006.

S.B.

Operation Eagle's Claw

The problems with U.S. counterterrorism forces are obvious and brought on by the lack of cohesive command illustrated by the abortive attempt to send a strike team into Iran to free Americans held hostage in the U.S. embassy in Tehran in 1979. Operation Eagle's Claw, as this mission was called, was characterized by a confusion of command, insufficient training, and critical equipment failure.

Cloaked in so much secrecy that even some of the military officers involved were not told the aim of the mission for which they were preparing, this operation became a model for what can go wrong in a strike force maneuver. In addition to too much secrecy, there were too many chiefs and there was not enough cooperation between military units. An army officer, Major General James Vaught, was in overall command, Colonel James Kyle of the Air Force had responsibility for fixed-wing aircraft, while Colonel Charles Pitman of the U.S. Marines also had command responsibility, and Colonel Beckwith controlled Delta Force unit.

The Delta Force squad lacked sufficient training and experience for such an operation. It had been created less than five years earlier by Colonel Beckwith, and its training program was incomplete and not designed for the type of situation that evolved. It was underfunded and ill equipped to handle the hostage raid, having trained primarily in GUERRILLA WARFARE and low-intensity conflict. None of the hostages were rescued, as the embassy in Teheran was never reached by the rescue units. Several of the members of the units carrying out the rescue attempt died in a fiery crash of planes over the desert rendevous point. The attempt was an embarrassing failure for the United States.

Reference: Farber, David. *Taken Hostage: The Iran Hostage Crisis* (Princeton, N.J.: Princeton University Press, 2004).

Operation Enduring Freedom

The aftermath of the September 11, 2001, terrorist attacks in New York City and Washington, D.C., included an overwhelming endorsement of support for the American government to plan and execute a military response. Once the Taliban regime in Afghanistan refused to hand over or detain OSAMA BIN LADEN and his chief aides, the response became virtually unanimous. The United States from the outset insisted that it was conducting a war against terror-

U.S. Marines assigned to 3rd Battalion, 6th Marines, patrol a mountain ridge along the Wusbin Valley, located in the Surobi district of Afghanistan, 2004. (DEPARTMENT OF DEFENSE)

ism, not Islam. It also maintained that AL-QAEDA, the organization headed and funded by bin Laden, was an occupying force in Afghanistan composed of Muslim militants from Saudi Arabia, Pakistan, and Chechnya. The United States therefore sought to present itself as Afghanistan's liberator, attempting to work with indigenous resistance groups, such as the Northern Alliance, to vanquish a common enemy.

The assistance of longtime allies, including the United Kingdom, and Islamic countries on Afghanistan's borders, especially Pakistan, was sought. Several of Afghanistan's neighbors feared the extremism of the Taliban and took advantage of the opportunity to end the regime's existence. By early October 2001, the United States began an offensive over and within Afghanistan that gradually increased in intensity over the next two months. In addition, the United States offered a $25 million reward for information that would enable American military forces to capture bin Laden. Considering the amount of personnel and weapons involved, Operation Enduring Freedom is likely the most expensive counterterrorism activity in history.

From the beginning the operation pursued several primary goals simultaneously. Among them were the following:

1. The removal of the Taliban from power;
2. The destruction of the terrorist base camps operated by al-Qaeda, the terrorist network that is operational in dozens of countries but had a major concentration of its personnel and equipment in Afghanistan; and
3. The capture or death of Osama bin Laden and his main lieutenants.

The operation was initiated by an air war against the Taliban and al-Qaeda that included dropping 15,000-pound bombs on suspected installations. The Taliban were routed, and many al-Qaeda terrorists were either killed or captured, their network effectively smashed in Afghanistan at least. However, Osama bin Laden has eluded capture thus far.

There is no intention of occupying part or all of Afghanistan beyond the time required to complete military operations. Mindful of history—Afghan tribes fought tenaciously against foreign invaders such as Alexander the Great, the British in the 19th century, and the Russians in the 20th—the United States is helping to establish an indigenous civil government in the country. The installation of newly elected president Hamid Karzai and the ratification of a new constitution have changed the political landscape of this country, which is now an active participant in the U.S.-led war on terrorism. It has not, however, eliminated the attacks on civilian as well as military targets in Afghanistan; indeed, a new type of terrorism for this country began to emerge in 2004: suicide bombing. While this type of attack has become increasingly common in Israel and Iraq, it had not occurred in Afghanistan until very recently. Vehicle bombings continue to occur, such as the attacks in June 2003 in Kabul, in which a taxi rigged with explosives rammed into a bus carrying German peacekeepers of the International Security Assistance Force, killing five German peacekeepers and injuring 29 others. For these and other similar attacks, no one claimed responsibility.

The American administration has repeatedly advised that Operation Enduring Freedom will not be a quick conflict and warned that the time required to accomplish its goals may take months or even years. Throughout its history the country has been divided into ethnic and tribal alliances that are constantly shifting. Many suspect that the United States may have to continue to play a significant role in mediating the divisions and providing support to reconstruct a country and economy that has been devastated by seemingly endless warfare.

Reference: BBC. South Asia. "Country Profile: Afghanistan." December 21, 2005. Available online. URL: http://news.bbc.co.uk/1/hi/world/south_asia/country_profiles/1162668.stm. Accessed March 22, 2006.

Operation Infinite Reach

On August 20, 1998, the United States carried out a cruise missile attack on seven targets in Afghanistan and Sudan, launching from ships in the Red Sea and the Arabian Sea. The attacks were in response to the bombing attacks earlier that month on the U.S. embassies in Tanzania and Kenya that killed 224 people and injured 5,000 others. U.S. intelligence sources indicated that the embassy attacks were engineered by OSAMA BIN LADEN, a wealthy ex-Saudi who had been connected with a number of other terrorist attacks around the world. Bin Laden was believed to have established, with the consent of the ruling Taliban in Afghanistan, training camps for terrorists in that country, presumably at the locations bombed. Six of the sites targeted were about 95 miles south of Kabul, near the Afghani-Pakistani border. Twenty-seven people were killed in the attack on these six sites.

The seventh site was a pharmaceutical plant in Khartoum, the capital of Sudan. The United States justified the attack on the Al-Shifa pharmaceutical factory on the links it claimed existed between this plant and bin Laden. While there were few casualties as a result of this strike, international opinion on the legality of such an attack was unfavorable. Although some U.S. allies indicated an understanding of the reasons for the attack, this unilateral action of aggression, without UN consent or discussion by the Security Council, violated most of the precepts of law governing the actions of states.

Although the government of Sudan demanded an apology from the U.S. administration, none has been given, as the U.S. government alleges that the plant had ties to chemical weapons production. Approximately 75 cruise missiles were launched by the United States into Afghanistan, targeting what it believed to be AL-QAEDA's training camps and killing about 20 people. Dozens of people were reported to have been wounded in the missile attacks on Sudan's pharmaceutical plant, but none killed.

In September 2001, following an ATTACK ON AMERICA launched by bin Laden operating from his al-Qaeda network in Afghanistan, the United States again attacked Afghanistan, in Operation Infinite Justice. This attack was initiated by a U.S.-led coalition that included the United Kingdom, Germany, other NATO allies as well as nations within the Middle East. This attack, described by the coalition as a "war on terrorism," resulted in the toppling of the Taliban rule in Afghanistan and the dislocation of millions of people to refugee camps to escape the bombing raids as well as the harsh Taliban rule. Operation Infinite Justice was changed to OPERATION ENDURING FREEDOM on September 25, 2001.

Operation Nimrod

On May 5, 1980, Britain's 22nd SPECIAL PROJECTS TEAM-SPECIAL AIR SERVICE (SAS), supported by special police units, carried out Operation Nimrod, an assault on the Iranian embassy in the heart of downtown London. As thousands watched, black-clad SAS members swung down from ropes and burst into the building through the windows. Wearing gas masks, the assault force moved from room to room, throwing stun grenades mixed with CS gas. As they moved through the building, they identified the terrorists, shot them with their Heckler and Koch MP5s or Browning automatic pistols, and bundled the hostages out of the burning building.

During this operation, Britain worked hard to maintain the speed and secrecy that have become the hallmark of SAS operations. The assault team wore hoods, which served to hide their identities as well as to frighten the terrorists. When the incident was over, the unit handed authority back to the police and quietly made their way back to the St. John's Wood barracks for a small celebration before returning to their permanent station at Bradbury Lines in Hereford.

Reference: Talor, Peter. "Six days That Shook Britain." *Guardian Unlimited.* July 24, 2002. Available online. URL: http://www.guardian.co.uk/Archive/Article/0,4273,4467433,00.html. Accessed March 21, 2006.

Orange Volunteers (OV)

This extremist Irish Protestant group is comprised largely of disgruntled Loyalist hard-liners who split from groups observing the cease-fire in 1998. OV sought to prevent a political settlement with Irish nationalists by attacking Catholic civilian interests in Northern Ireland.

The OV was involved in bombings, arson, beatings, and possibly robberies of Catholic civilians and property. With about 20 hard-core members, many of whom were experienced in terrorist tactics and bomb making, its operations have been confined to Northern Ireland, and it received no external aid in support of its efforts.

The Orange Volunteers declared a cease-fire in 2000 and are no longer an active organization. They have not been included on the United States's foreign terrorist organization list for several years.

See also LOYALIST VOLUNTEER FORCE.

Reference: National Memorial Institute for the Prevention of Terrorism (MIPT). "Orange Volunteers (OV)." Available online. URL: http://www.tkb.org/Group.jsp?groupID=79. Accessed February 15, 2006.

Orly Group

See ARMENIAN SECRET ARMY FOR THE LIBERATION OF ARMENIA.

Oslo Accords

The second INTIFADA that began in 1987 caught YASIR ARAFAT and his lieutenants by surprise. They had been chased out of Jordan in 1970 by King Hussein and out of Lebanon in 1982 by the Israelis. They were geographically hundreds of miles away from Palestine in Tunis. In the meantime, an entire generation had grown up in the West Bank and Gaza under the Israeli occupation that began in 1967. Arafat feared, not without reason, that he could lose control of the Palestinian resistance movement to a generation that regarded him and his colleagues as absentee leaders out of touch with the reality on the ground. On November 15, 1988, Arafat announced that he recognized ISRAEL, but no immediate follow-up ensued. However, the decision that prompted Arafat's announcement—the acceptance of Security Council Resolutions 242 and 338—by the Palestine National Council by a 5:1 margin was a remarkable breakthrough that accepted Israel's existence and even renounced terrorism. Israelis remained convinced that Arafat was not sincere and that, in any case, he was untrustworthy.

Within a few years, however, both Israel and Arafat recognized that it was in their mutual interests to deal directly with one another. Secret meetings in Oslo were preceded by secret meetings in Madrid in 1991. The Madrid talks included representatives from other Arab regimes as well as the Palestinians and Israelis. These meetings did not achieve any significant outcomes but did lead, at least indirectly, to continued talks between Israeli and Palestinian representatives. A new left-of-center government led by the Labor Party came to power in Israel in 1992. Yitzhak Rabin became prime minister, and his frequent political rival as well as collaborator, Shimon Peres, was named foreign minister.

In many ways, Peres was the architect of Oslo, usually in the background, but always directing the Israeli side. He was instrumental in persuading Rabin to proceed with and become an advocate of direct negotiations with individuals he had long considered architects of violence against Israelis. Rabin had deemed Arafat for decades as nothing more than a terrorist. But Rabin was also a pragmatist. He understood that the Arafat camp was increasingly nervous about rival organizations such as HAMAS and might become more reasonable in their demands on Israel. The Palestinian counterparts were, of course, responsible to Arafat who, from Tunis, was constantly informed and supervised his representatives.

The deliberations began and remained, for some time, in an atmosphere of suspicion and even dislike. Each side regarded the other as untrustworthy and with blood on its hands. Each felt awkward sitting at the same table across from one another. Whether Oslo ultimately achieved lasting or progressive results is an endless debate. However, Oslo was successful in getting each side to regard the other as human, no small achievement for the time and circumstances. After all, the negotiators at Oslo belonged to a generation that had grown up in a political environment that was hardly conducive to cooperation and compromise. Eventually, individual members of both negotiating teams took a personal interest in one another to the point of discussing their respective families.

Reference: Savir, Uri. *The Process: 1,100 Days That Changed the Middle East* (New York: Random House, 1998).

Ottawa Ministerial Declaration on Countering Terrorism

The heads of state and governments of the seven most industrialized Western nations and Russia met in December 1995 in Ottawa, Canada. They discussed counterterrorism by collective effort and issued the Ottawa Ministerial Declaration on Countering Terrorism. This declaration notes that these nations were determined as a group to provide leadership to the international community on the problem of TERRORISM, using both bilateral and multilateral instruments and other measures to counter terrorism. The nations agreed to continue to work out specific, cooperative measures to "deter, prevent, and investigate terrorist acts and to bring terrorists to justice." They pledged to strengthen the sharing of intelligence and information on terrorism and to promote mutual legal assistance, particularly on the issue of extradition.

overview of terrorism, by region

The overviews of terrorism offered here are focused on terrorism committed by groups, rather than state terrorism, and are accurate for conditions at the turn of the 21st century. State terrorism is not omitted completely, but since most overt state terrorism had ceased by this point in time, it is only mentioned in historic context.

AFRICA

Continuing civil war and ethnic violence in parts of Africa, as well as the ensuing human disaster relief needs, continue to overshadow individual incidents of terrorism in this region. The presence of a small number of AL-QAEDA operatives in East Africa and increasing anti-American and anti-Western rhetoric from Islamic radicals, as well as continuing fund-raising activities by Hizballah, continue to be a source of concern. During the late 1990s, the number of specific terrorist attacks remained relatively consistent, about 10 per year. The range of violence in these attacks varied considerably. The U.S. embassy bombings in Kenya and Tanzania in 1998, for instance, caused hundreds of civilian casualties and massive damage, while the most violent attack in 1999 involved an attack by Rwandan Hutu rebels killing several tourists in March. Deaths by GENOCIDE in Rwanda, Burundi, and Zaire (later known as the Democratic Republic of the Congo) in the early and mid-1990s numbered in the hundreds of thousands, in a conflict difficult to separate into separate incidents of terrorism, being instead a period of almost continuous terrorism/genocide.

Many African countries have taken cooperative efforts against terrorism, including making significant efforts to sign and ratify the 12 international conventions and protocols relating to terrorism. In October 2004, the African Union opened the African Center for the Study and Research of Terrorism in Algiers. Several nations have also formed national counterterrorism centers, including Nigeria, Kenya, and South Africa. The Sahel countries of Mauritania, Mali, Niger, and Chad have begun to devote more resources to improve their counterterrorism capabilities, including participation in the U.S.-sponsored Pan-Sahel Initiative, a program designed to assist those nations in protecting their borders, combating terrorism, and enhancing regional stability.

Angola

Angola gradually began to rebuild in 2002 when its 27-year civil war ended with the death of one of the leaders of the insurgency. When Portugal granted Angola independence in 1975, fighting broke out between the Popular Movement for the Liberation of Angola (MPLA), led by José Eduardo dos Santos, and the National Union for the Total Independence of Angola (UNITA), led by Jonas Savimbi. Peace was almost achieved in 1992 when Angola held national elections, but UNITA renewed fighting when it was beaten by the MPLA at the polls.

Army officers are seen in a drill during joint anti-terrorism exercises with officers from Kenya, Uganda, and Tanzania, 2005. (GETTY IMAGES)

At least 4 million people were displaced, and almost 1.5 million died in the war that spanned a quarter of a century. The death of UNITA's leader, Savimbi, in 2002 ended UNITA's insurgency, simultaneously strengthening the MPLA's hold on power. MPLA's leader, dos Santos, pledged to hold legislative elections in 2006.

Chad
In October 2004, the government of Chad helped to negotiate the turnover from a Chadian rebel group to the Algerian government of captured SALAFIST GROUP FOR CALL AND COMBAT (GSPC) leader Amari Saifi (a.k.a. Abderazak al-Para). Al-Para headed a faction of the GSPC responsible for the kidnapping of 32 European tourists in Algeria in the summer of 2003. Al-Para took the captives to Mali, whose government was instrumental in securing their release.

Djibouti
Djibouti has taken a strong stand against international terrorist organizations. The government has increased its efforts to train security forces, secure borders, and expand its capacity for maritime interdiction. It has also closed down terrorist-linked financial institutions and has shared information of possible terrorist activity in the region.

Ethiopia
Ethiopia, in resolving to some extent its long struggle with the people of Eritrea for independence, began to experience a diminishing of its problems with guerrilla attacks. Ogaden National Liberation Front rebels continued to kidnap foreign aid workers, as well as staff workers from Somalia and the Ethiopian government, but some were released without violence. To counter the threat from elements of the Somalia-based AL-ITTIHAAD AL-ISLAMI (AIAI) and other groups, the government has increased its military efforts to control its border with Somalia. It has also developed and installed improved security systems for its international airport at Addis Ababa, improved its capabilities for tracking terrorists and terrorist supporters, and introduced more secure passport technology with anti-tampering features.

Kenya
The government of Kenya brought to trial seven terror suspects in 2004—arrested in November 2003 on charges related to the Kikambala hotel bombing and attempted shooting down of an Israeli airliner in November 2002, the 1998 U.S. embassy bombings, and a subsequent plot to attack the U.S. embassy in 2003. Four of the individuals were charged with killing 15 people in the bombing of a beachfront hotel north of Mombasa in 2002. In January 2004, the government established the National Counter Terrorism Center and a National Security Advisory Committee to oversee the operations of the center.

Liberia
Although the United Liberation Movement for Democracy in Liberia continued to be active, engaging in hostage-taking through the end of the 1990s, all hostages were reportedly released unharmed. No acts of terrorism beyond these troubled this state through the end of the century.

Morocco
In Casablanca on May 16, 2003, one of five near-simultaneous bombs exploded at the Casa de España restaurant–nightclub, killing approximately 42 people, including three Spaniards and one Italian. According to press reports, about 14 people, ages 18–22, took part in the five attacks, which also injured at least 100.

The group al-Sirat al Mustaqim, which has links with al-Qaeda, claimed responsibility for the attacks.

Nigeria

Ethnic violence flared across this nation, with several changes in government as the turmoil reached a boiling point. Bloody feuds broke out among various indigenous groups battling for access to and control of limited local resources. Poverty-stricken Nigerians across the nation, particularly in the oil-producing southern regions, demanded a larger share of the nation's oil wealth. Violence against oil firms took the form of kidnapping of oil workers with demands for ransom on behalf of the village, ethnic group, or larger community represented by the angry groups carrying out the attacks. Most of the hostages were released unharmed, usually within days. Government efforts to repress this violence sometimes took the form of state terrorism.

In late December 2003, early January 2004, and again in September 2004, a group calling itself the "Taleban" raided police stations in the northeastern states of Yobe and Borno, reportedly taking several police officers hostage, stealing weapons, and killing at least seven civilians. Nigerian forces quickly responded to both attacks and claimed to have killed or captured dozens of Taleban members in the aftermath of the attacks.

Rwanda

Conflict between Hutu and Tutsi in this country led into an explosion of genocide, killing hundreds of thousands and displacing millions. Attacks with machetes, guns, and grenades continued to cost the lives of aid workers, UN personnel, and ministers, even after the explosion of violence gradually ended in the mid-1990s. Hundreds of thousands of people displaced by the violence fled to neighboring Zaire, where refugee camps filled to overflowing became the focus of a revolution in Zaire that eventually led to the overthrow of Mobutu Sese Seko. The ethnic conflict sparked in Rwanda, by overflowing into Zaire, continued to spark violent conflict throughout central Africa for years.

During the first five years of the 21st century, an armed force including former soldiers and supporters of the previous government that orchestrated the genocide in 1994—the Democratic Forces for the Liberation of Rwanda (FDLR; known as the Army for the Liberation of Rwanda [ALIR] until 2001)—continued to operate in Rwanda and the Democratic Republic of the Congo. An ALIR unit was responsible for the kidnapping and murder of nine persons in Bwindi Park in 1999. By 2005, three suspects were arrested with U.S. assistance and await trial.

Sierra Leone

During the latter part of the 1990s, this country experienced serious insurgency violence. The Revolutionary United Front (RUF) mounted an offensive on the capital in January 1999, taking captive several foreign missionaries during the siege of Freetown. A peace agreement was signed in July of that year, but violence continued to flare sporadically as the government and rebels fought for control of the countryside. Both government and rebel forces committed acts of terrorism against the civilian population during the struggle for control.

Somalia

The famine that devastated much of Somalia during the early 1990s resulted in UN/U.S. intervention to bring food aid. War between rival clans for control of the resources being brought in erupted into violence that claimed the lives of several soldiers responsible for the food distribution and resulted in a pullback of UN resources and personnel. For much of the remaining decade, control of Somalia remained unresolved among these rival clans. In 1999, in Elayo village in the self-declared Republic of Somaliland, some 20 unidentified gunmen kidnapped UN and European aid workers, all of whom were released very shortly after the attack, unharmed. Violence diminished, but the primary issues (food resources and control) remain unresolved.

Members of the Somalia-based AL-ITTIHAAD AL-ISLAMI (AIAI) continue to carry out terrorist acts, primarily in Ethiopia. This group, whose stated goal is to create an Islamic state in Somalia, has become highly factionalized and diffuse, but it continues to pose a threat to countries in the region. Some members maintain ties with al-Qaeda.

Sudan

The ongoing violence in DARFUR, and the unwillingness of the government to accept responsibility for, or to effectively restrain and punish, the Janjaweed whose attacks on non-Arab citizens provoked United Nations condemnation for genocide, continues to mar Sudan's efforts to counter terrorism. The government has increased cooperation with Ugandan authorities to diminish the capabilities of the Lord's Resistance Army

(LRA), a Ugandan group that has terrorized civilians in northern Uganda and claims to seek an overthrow of the current Ugandan government.

In March 2004, a new HAMAS representative arrived in Khartoum. According to press reports, he was received by the Sudanese government in an official capacity, although the government later closed a Hamas office in the capital.

South Africa

With the end of apartheid government in this country, the focus of violence shifted somewhat. The black townships remained subject to acts of violence, but not by government officials. Problems with drugs, poverty, and gangs caused violent attacks throughout regions of the state during the 1990s. Even opponents of these problems carried out violent acts in their attempts to end the problems. Islamic militants associated with QIBLA and PEOPLE AGAINST GANGSTERISM AND DRUGS conducted bombings and other acts of domestic terrorism in Cape Town, including a firebombing of a Kentucky Fried Chicken in 1999. Two years earlier, the Boere Aanvals Troepe claimed responsibility for a bombing attack on a mosque in Rustenburg, which injured a Sudanese citizen and one South African. Ethnic violence continued, in many forms, but violence no longer took the form of state violence.

Two South Africans were arrested in Pakistan in July 2004 as part of the Pakistani government's efforts against al-Qaeda. In March of that year, the South African government organized a four-week multinational Anti-Terrorism Training Program in Pretoria, bringing together police from South Africa and 11 other African countries to teach methods of combating terrorism.

Tanzania

After the bombing in 1998 of the U.S. embassy in Dar es Salaam, Tanzania worked with U.S. authorities to bring the bombing suspects to trial. Rashid Sweleh Hemed, on trial in Tanzania in late 2003 for his role in the embassy attacks, was acquitted by the High Court following the government's appeal of his initial acquittal earlier in the year. A Tanzanian suspected of involvement with the 1998 bombing, Ahmed Khalfan Ghailani, was arrested in July 2004 in Pakistan. Although the government approved in late 2002 a comprehensive Prevention of Terrorism Act, this act has not yet been enforced, owing perhaps to the lack of implementing regulations for the law.

Uganda

The state of Uganda survived the state terrorism instituted by IDI AMIN for more than a decade. During the last two decades of the 20th century, levels of state terrorism seriously diminished. Nevertheless, this country suffered during the latter part of the 1990s from ethnic violence and terrorism as the Hutu conflict in Rwanda spilled over into Zaire and then into neighboring Uganda. Rwandan rebels carried out attacks, from bases suspected to be in the Democratic Republic of Congo, killing and kidnapping many civilians in acts of terrorism. On March 1, 1999, these rebels attacked three tourist camps in the Bwindi National Forest, kidnapping 14 tourists, including three U.S. citizens, six British nationals, three New Zealanders, one Australian, and one Canadian. Eight were killed before the rest were released the next day.

The government of Uganda has fought the LORD'S RESISTANCE ARMY (LRA) since the 1990s. The LRA has carried out acts of extreme brutality against innocent civilians, including the kidnapping of children for use as soldiers and sex slaves. In February 2004, the LRA attacked the Barlonyo refugee camp near Lira, Uganda, killing nearly 200 people. In spite of amnesty offers and limited cease-fire agreements by the government, the LRA continues to carry out attacks in northern and eastern Uganda.

Zambia

Violence troubled Zambia toward the end of the 1990s, though no group emerged to claim responsibility for the attacks. In 1999 alone, at least 16 bombs exploded across Lusaka in February, at the Angolan embassy, near major water pipes, around powerlines, and in parks and residential areas, killing one and injuring two. Lacking claims for responsibility, it is difficult to classify the violence in this country as terrorism, since no clear political motive emerged.

EAST ASIA AND PACIFIC OVERVIEW

Incidents of terrorism in East Asia increased as the 20th century neared its end. The dreadful "killing fields" in Cambodia, in which more than 1 million, perhaps as many as 2 million people died under the hands of POL POT and the KHMER ROUGE, came to an end, but the violence in that country continued to spill over through the 1990s. In the Philippines, successive turnovers in government after Marcos's departure, and continued separatist efforts as well as Islamic militants continued to claim lives in terrorist attacks.

Southeast Asia continues to be an attractive theater of operations for groups such as Jemaah Islamiya (JI) and the ABU SAYYAF GROUP (ASG). In February 2004, the Philippines suffered the worst terrorist attack in its history when a bomb planted by the ASG sank Superferry 14, killing approximately 130 passengers. In September of the same year, a car bomb was detonated in front of the Australian embassy in INDONESIA, reportedly killing 10 and wounding nearly 200. JI claimed responsibility for the attack.

In South Asia, many factions from the civil war in Afghanistan remained involved in terrorism, sponsoring training camps in areas under their control. The Taliban, emerging from the Afghan conflict with Russia as the strongest power, and thus the governing group, provided safe haven for international terrorists, particularly OSAMA BIN LADEN and his network. In Sri Lanka, the government continued its prolonged conflict with the LIBERATION TIGERS OF TAMIL EELAM (LTTE).

The Association of Southeast Asian Nations (ASEAN) and the Asia-Pacific Economic Cooperation forum (APEC) strengthened and expanded cooperation in regional efforts to combat international terrorism and other transnational crimes. Lack of specific anti-terrorism legislation, however, continues to be a challenge to comprehensive law-enforcement efforts in several countries in the region.

Cambodia

While the genocide of the Pol Pot regime ceased before the end of the century, enduring violence by the Khmer Rouge continued to plague the country. Defections by the Khmer Rouge to the government and the split of the group into pro–and anti–Pol Pot factions made the organization less of a threat, but hard-liners based in the Khmer Rouge stronghold at Anlong Veng continued to launch GUERRILLA WARFARE attacks on government troops in several provinces. Ethnic Vietnamese civilians in Cambodia were also the victims of violent attacks, as were workers from other countries employed in companies operating in Cambodia.

In November 2003, authorities arrested seven members of the Cambodian Freedom Fighters (CFF), an antigovernment group, for allegedly plotting a terrorist act in Koh Kong, a southwestern town. Subsequently, in April 2004, a bomb detonated at a ferry at Koh Kong, slightly injuring several people; five persons allegedly belonging to the CFF were arrested. However, the court in October of that year dropped all charges in these cases. Some of those accused claimed that they were coerced into confessions of crimes that they did not commit.

In May 2003, four supporters of Jemaah Islamiya (JI) were arrested by Cambodian authorities for using an Islamic school run by the Saudi Arabia–based nongovernmental organization Umm al-Qura as a front for channeling terrorist money into Cambodia from Saudi Arabia. Three of those arrested (one Cambodian and two Thai) were convicted in December 2004 and sentenced to life imprisonment. The court acquitted the fourth defendant, an Egyptian. During the trial, the court also convicted in absentia JI chief of operations Hambali and two others of attempted murder for terrorist purposes for their involvement in planning terrorist attacks on the U.S. and U.K. embassies in Phnom Penh.

China

While the government of the People's Republic of China has been accused by many of its own people of state terrorism, documented evidence of such incidents is sporadic. The events in Beijing in the early 1990s involving government violence in response to student-led protests were recorded for a world audience by CNN news network, but most incidents of state terrorism are less verifiable. However, separatist movements in China persist, some of which have resorted to terrorist tactics. Uygur separatists, part of the Chinese Muslim ethnic minority group concentrated in the Xinjiang Uighur Autonomous Region in far-western China, have continued a campaign of violence. In 1997, Uygur separatists carried out a series of bus bombings in Urumqi that killed nine persons and wounded 74. Rioting by this group in February caused about 200 deaths, and a pipe bombing of a bus in Beijing in March by members of these separatists killed three persons and injured eight. The Chinese government executed several people involved in these acts.

Indonesia

Separatists groups have, during the latter part of the 20th century, carried out violent attacks in Indonesia. In East Timor, attacks, including bombings, left civilians dead and eventually led to a concerted effort on the part of these people to be free of Indonesian rule. In the wake of the toppling of the long-standing government by financial crisis and charges of fraud and embezzlement, the government that emerged sought an end to the continuous ethnic conflict and allowed East Timor to vote to secede. However, the military who had long held positions of authority and wealth in the area were allowed by the government to engage in a campaign of terror to prevent this vote. The ethnic violence that accompanied this effort to establish a separate state had not completely subsided by the end of the 20th century, and Indonesia continued to face similar separatist efforts in other parts of its ethnically diverse and scattered island populations.

The Jemaah Islamiya Organization (JI) was responsible for numerous high-profile bombings, including the bombing of the J. W. Marriott Hotel in Jakarta on August 5, 2003, and the Bali bombings on October 12, 2002. Members of the group were also implicated in the September 9, 2004, attack outside the Australian embassy in Jakarta. The Bali attack left more than 200 dead. The capture in 2003 of JI's operations chief, Tiruan bin Isomoddin (a.k.a. Hambali) damaged the organization, but has not stopped its efforts to target Western interests in Indonesia.

Japan

Its actions in World War II, particularly those taken against the Chinese, brought charges of terrorism against Japan in the latter part of the 20th century. The charge of the use of biological agents against a civilian population in China, by the dropping of wheat infected with various diseased insects, has not yet been resolved. Japan's actions in Korea, particularly against the female population, is also the subject for much debate in the literature on the use of terrorism in warfare. However, Japan was the only nation in that century to ever experience an open attack with a weapon of mass destruction—two atomic bombs—targeted against two areas of heavy civilian population, Hiroshima and Nagasaki.

At least two groups have practiced terrorism in Japan or are comprised of Japanese citizens but operate outside of the country. The JAPANESE RED ARMY, an anarchist group whose activities took place primarily outside of Japanese territory toward the end of the century, had largely fled the country and were in hiding or under arrest by 2000. Several members of the JRA were arrested in 1997. Five were convicted in Lebanon and sent to prison for three years. Another member, Jun Nishikawa, was captured in Bolivia and deported to Japan, where he was indicted for his role in the 1977 hijacking of a Japanese Airlines flight. Tsutomu Shirosaki was captured in 1996 and brought to the United States to stand trial for offenses arising from a rocket attack against the U.S. embassy in Jakarta, Indonesia, in 1986. Longtime leader Shigenobu was arrested in November 2000 and faced charges of terrorism and passport fraud.

In March 1995, members of the AUM SHINRIKYO sect attacked Tokyo's subway with sarin nerve gas. The leader of this sect, Shoko Asahara, was arrested and charged with this attack and 16 other charges for actions carried out by his group, ranging from kidnapping and murder to illegal production of drugs and weapons. The sect continued, even after the arrest of Asahara and other members, to exist, operate, and even recruit new members in Japan. Asahara was sentenced to death in February 2004, but appeals are still pending.

Laos

Efforts to implement the counterterrorism provisions of multilateral agreements were undertaken after the events of 2001 but have been hampered by weak enforcement procedures. Laos lacks specific counterterrorism laws, although the Office of the Prosecutor General has drafted amendments to existing criminal laws, under which acts of terrorism fall.

A group calling itself the Free Democratic People's Government of Laos claimed responsibility for several small bombings that resulted in one death and numerous injuries in 2004. This group also claimed credit for several explosions in Vientiane designed to disrupt the ASEAN summit in late November of that year.

Malaysia

Malaysia has taken a leading role in the war on terror, facilitating regional cooperation through its Southeast Asia Regional Center for Counter Terrorism (SEARCCT). This center, established in 2003, focuses primarily on training for regional authorities in law enforcement, banking, and other sectors.

The ABU SAYYAF GROUP (ASG) continues to be active in Malaysia, however. In October 2004, an armed group kidnapped six persons—three Indonesians, two Filipinos, and a Malaysian—from a resort area. One of the kidnap victims escaped, and five were found executed on October 29 in Languyan, Philippines. The ASG was believed to be responsible.

North Korea

North Korea is not known to have sponsored any terrorist act since the bombing of a Korean Airlines flight in 1987. Four JAPANESE RED ARMY members remain in the Democratic People's Republic of Korea following their involvement in a jet hijacking in 1970. In January

2002, President George W. Bush declared North Korea to be a part of an "Axis of Evil" along with Iran and Iraq. Shortly thereafter, North Korea withdrew from the Nuclear Non-Proliferation Treaty and announced it would restart its Yongbyon nuclear plant, which could be used to make weapons-grade plutonium. Concern grew in international circles that North Korea could sell weapons-grade plutonium—or even a working nuclear bomb—to a terrorist group or nation. Tensions increased when North Korea declared it had conducted it first successful explosion of a small nuclear device in October 2006. A small tremor was detected in the region, but many experts had doubts that the test was successful, as it was only a small explosion. The test was immediately denounced by the United Nations, which approved sanctions against North Korea. Kim Jong Il threatened to declare war on the United States if these sanctions were enforced and informed China that North Korea planned to conduct three more nuclear tests. China, which is North Korea's largest trading partner, has been called on to apply pressure to North Korea to halt the tests and return to peaceful negotiations.

Philippines

The Philippine government, after the end of the U.S. lease on the two primary military bases in that country and the disengagement of the substantial U.S. military presence as the bases were evacuated, had a resurgence of separatist violence in several regions. Gradual success from peace talks has attended government efforts to assimilate some of these groups into its own forces. The Moro National Liberation Front (MNLF) signed a peace agreement in 1996, and the government began to integrate the former MNLF rebels into the Philippine military, but negotiations had not yet produced a similar result with other groups, including the ABU SAYYAF GROUP (ASG), the NEW PEOPLE'S ARMY (NPA), or the ALEX BONCAYAO BRIGADE. Muslim rebels in the southern Philippines continued to conduct kidnappings, usually for ransom. In March 2003, a bomb hidden in a backpack exploded in a crowded airline terminal in Davao, killing 21 persons and injuring 146 others. The Moro Islamic Liberation Front claimed responsibility. A similar attack in April of that year, also in Davao but this time on a crowded passenger wharf, killed 16 people and injured 55 others. This attack was carried out, however, by members of Jemaah Islamiya (JI), a regional group with ties to al-Qaeda.

The Philippines experienced the worst terrorist attacks in its history when a bomb planted by the ASG sank Superferry 14 in Manila Bay, killing approximately 130 passengers in February 2004. In December of that year, a bomb exploded in a crowded market in General Santos City, Mindanao, killing a reported 17. No group claimed responsibility for this attack.

Philippine authorities have had a number of successes against terrorists in recent years. Seven ASG members believed responsible for the Superferry bombing were arrested in March 2004, and six ASG members were killed in April by a military unit on Basilan Island. Two of the NPA's leaders were captured without bloodshed in June, and a court in August of the same year sentenced 17 ASG members to death, although four were convicted in absentia (having escaped from jail).

Singapore

Although neither domestic nor international terrorist attacks in Singapore have been prevalent in recent years, the authorities of this country continue to press their investigation of the regional terrorist group Jemaah Islamiya (JI), detaining JI members who have plotted to carry out attacks in Singapore. Recognizing piracy as an emerging terrorist threat in its region, Singapore joined Indonesia and Malaysia in initiating coordinated patrols in the Strait of Malacca. As part of an initiative of Japan, Singapore joined 15 other countries in a regional Cooperation Agreement on Combating Piracy and Armed Robbery against Ships in Asia in 2004. The agreement established a center in Singapore to coordinate information exchange on maritime piracy.

SOUTH ASIA OVERVIEW

South Asia continues to be a major theater of global terrorism, although partner countries in this region achieved notable successes in the war on terrorism. While Afghanistan ratified a new constitution and had its first popularly elected president in 2004, insurgent and terrorist elements continue to target international organizations and nongovernmental organizations, the new government, and Afghan civilians, with increasing numbers of suicide bombings (an action quite rare in the country until 2005.) Activities of al-Qaeda, the Liberation Tigers of Tamil Eelam (LTTE), and a variety of groups involved in the conflict over Kashmir have kept the incidence of terrorism high in this region.

While the cease-fires initiated between the government of Sri Lanka and the LTTE, and between Indian and Pakistani elements over the status of Kashmir, sporadically halted the violence, the impact of natural disasters in this region may have had greater impact on the diminishing number of terrorist incidents in some countries. Certainly the tsunami in December 2004 reduced for a time both the ability and the interest of the LTTE in carrying out terrorist attacks in Sri Lanka; and the earthquake in Pakistan in 2005 diverted governmental resources toward disaster relief rather than efforts to find elements of al-Qaeda. Both of these disasters also reduced the level of conflict in Kashmir, as both the people and the states sought to aid and recover from these non-terrorist incidents.

Afghanistan

From the intense guerrilla warfare supported clandestinely by the United States against the Soviet-supported government of the country during the heat of the cold war, to the withdrawal of Soviet troops and support, into the continuing struggle for power by the factions who had fought the communist government, Afghanistan has suffered from both state and group terrorism for several decades. As the 20th century came to an end, Islamic extremists from around the world—including a large number of Egyptians, Algerians, Palestinians, and Saudis—continued to use Afghanistan as a training ground and home base from which to operate. The Taliban, emerging as the strongest force controlling the majority of the territory, facilitated the operation of training and indoctrination facilities for non-Afghans in the territories they controlled. Several Afghani factions also provided logistic support, free passage, and sometimes passports to members of various terrorist groups. These individuals, in turn, were involved in attacks in Bosnia, Kosovo, Chechnya, Tajikistan, Kashmir, the Philippines, Lebanon, and other parts of the Middle East.

Terrorist financier OSAMA BIN LADEN relocated from Jalalabad to the Taliban's capital of Kandahar in early 1997, establishing a new base of operations. In Decem-

U.S. Army soldiers enter a building believed to be storing illegal weapons during a combat raid in Zurmat, Afghanistan, 2004. (U.S. DEPARTMENT OF DEFENSE)

ber of 1999, Jordanian authorities arrested members of a cell linked to bin Laden's AL-QAEDA organization—some of whom had undergone explosives and weapons training in Afghanistan—and were planning terrorist operations against Western tourists visiting holy sites in Jordan over the millennium holiday. Also in that month, the Taliban permitted hijacked Indian Airlines flight 814 to land at Kandahar airport after refusing it permission to land the previous day. The hijacking, which began on December 25, ended on the 31st when the Indian government released from prison three individuals linked to Kashmiri militant groups in return for the release of the passengers aboard the aircraft. The hijackers, who had murdered one of the Indian passengers during the course of the incident, were allowed to go free.

In September 2001, an ATTACK ON AMERICA was launched by bin Laden from his base in Afghanistan. Demands that the Taliban turn bin Laden over to U.S. forces for trial were rejected, and in response, the United States launched a "war on terrorism." Attacks were launched by a U.S.-led coalition against al-Qaeda bases as well as Taliban strongholds in Kabul and other cities, with bombing raids and the deployment of special forces units. The Northern Alliance, which had been fighting the Taliban for control of Afghanistan, recaptured Kabul after U.S. bombing cleared Taliban forces from the area. With the crumbling of the Taliban rule in Afghanistan, the strength of al-Qaeda and bin Laden became difficult to gauge, but reports of the extent of his network in other countries suggested the probability of future terrorism from this group, if not from the same leader.

The installation of a newly elected president and the ratification of a new constitution have changed the political landscape of this country, which is now an active participant in the U.S.-led war on terrorism. It has not, however, eliminated the attacks on civilian as well as military targets in Afghanistan; indeed, a new type of terrorism for this country began to emerge in 2004: suicide bombing. While this type of attack has become increasingly common in Israel and Iraq, it had not occurred in Afghanistan until very recently. Vehicle bombings continue to occur, such as the attacks in June 2003 in Kabul, in which a taxi rigged with explosives rammed into a bus carrying German peacekeepers of the International Security Assistance Force, killing five German peacekeepers and injuring 29 others. For these and other similar attacks, no one claimed responsibility.

Bangladesh

This country's long tradition of inclusive, moderate Islam is increasingly under attack from extremist elements. Endemic corruption and poverty also contribute to the increasing loss of stability and widespread frustration, providing an increasingly attractive breeding ground for terrorist groups. In May 2004, the British High Commissioner and more than 70 others were injured in a grenade attack in Sylbet; in August of the same year, about 20 Awami League supporters were killed and another 200 injured during an attack on the party's opposition rally in Dhaka.

India

Having survived the assassinations of two prime ministers—one, Indira Gandhi, while still in that office, and one, her son, Rajiv Gandhi, who was assassinated a short time after he left that position—India continued to deal with serious levels of violence and terror, particularly in the region of Kashmir. Kashmiri militant groups continued to attack civilian as well as government and military targets in India-held Kashmir and throughout the country. Militant groups were held responsible for the bombing of a passenger train traveling from Kashmir to New Delhi in 1999, killing 13 people and wounding 50. The number of bombings appeared to be diminishing, however, since 1997 recorded more than 25 bombing attacks in New Delhi alone, primarily in the marketplaces and buses of Old Delhi, which killed 10 and left more than 200 injured. The attacks appeared to be aimed at spreading fear among the public rather than causing casualties. Almost 100 bombings of a similar nature took place in the rest of the country in 1997.

The Indian cabinet ratified the international convention for the suppression of terrorist bombings in 1999. It continued to assert that Pakistan provided support for the Kashmiri militants, a charge that Pakistan continued to deny.

In 2003, violence escalated, beginning with a hand grenade explosion at a bus station in January in Kulgam, Kashmir, injuring 40 persons. In February, a landmine planted near a busy marketplace in Varmul, Kashmir, exploded, killing six persons and injuring three others. Bombs in March killed a student in the Doda District of Kashmir, two persons in a candy store, and four at a bus stop in Rajouri, Kashmir. Attacks throughout the year, at cricket matches, the famous Mughal Garden, bus stations, dairy yards, courthouses, homes, poultry stores, crowded markets, community kitchens, banks, parks, and many other sites were largely unclaimed by any group, although most were attributed to Kashmiri separatists.

Separatists continued to stage hundreds of attacks on people and property in 2004, especially in Jammu and Kashmir, in the northeastern states, and the "Naxalite belt" in eastern India. More than 500 civilians were killed in the attacks in the northeastern states by insurgent and terrorist groups. Foreign organizations, such as LASHKAR-E-TAYYIBA (LT) and JAISH-E-MOHAMMED (JEM), operating through groups in India, claimed responsibility for attacks on prominent Indian politicians and for killing the uncle of a prominent Kashmiri religious and political leader.

Nepal

The Maoist insurgency, active in Nepal since 1996, continues to be the focus of most anti-terrorism attention by the Nepalese government. In 2004 alone, this insurgence was responsible for the deaths of at least 383 civilians and 214 government security forces, although the total of victims by this element may be as high as 831 victims during that year. The violence appears cyclical, however, as the government of Nepal claims to have killed more than 1,555 members of this insurgent group during that same year and to have arrested thousands.

Pakistan

Pakistan had a tumultuous exercise in attempted democracy during the latter part of the 20th century. With alternately elected governments and military coups, violence and terrorism have become in many respects a normal part of life for much of the country. It remained one of only three countries that maintained formal diplomatic relations with Afghanistan's Taliban, a position that left the government defending itself against charges of lending support to training camps for terrorists. Pakistan has also been accused of allowing militant groups, including those from Kashmir, to obtain weapons as well as training and of allowing certain madrassas (religious schools) in Islamabad to serve as conduits for terrorists.

Pakistan's long-standing struggle with India over control of Kashmir contributed to the tendency of the government to allow Kashmiri extremist groups, such as the HARAKAT UL-MUJAHIDIN (HUM), to operate in Pakistan. Pakistani officials from both Prime Minister Nawaz Sharif's government and, after his removal by the military, General Pervez Musharraf's regime, publicly stated that Pakistan provided diplomatic, political, and moral support for "freedom fighters"—including the HUM—in Kashmir but denied providing the militants training or materiel.

After the two nearly successful assassination attempts against President Musharraf in December 2003, AL-QAEDA declared the government of Pakistan to be one of its main enemies and called for its overthrow. In the government's subsequent pursuit of this organization and other groups, it has killed or captured over 600 since September 2001. In 2004, Pakistan captured al-Qaeda communications expert and Heathrow bomb-plot suspect Naeem Noor Khan in July; arrested Ahmed Khalfan Ghailani, a suspect of the 1998 U.S. embassy bombings; killed Daniel Pearl murder-suspect Amjad Farooqi; detained the head of Harakat ul-Mujahidin for several months; and arranged for the extradition of the head of HARAKAT UL-JIHAD-I-ISLAMI.

Sri Lanka

The separatist group LIBERATION TIGERS OF TAMIL EELAM (LTTE) maintained a high level of violence during the last decade of the 20th century. Attacks on numerous civilian as well as government, police, and military targets made Sri Lanka the victim of substantial domestic terrorism. LTTE activity focused on the continuing war in the northern part of the country. The Sri Lankan military's attempts to open and secure a ground supply route for its troops through LTTE-held territory resulted in intense battles that caused thousands of casualties on both sides. Most of the attacks by the LTTE were against domestic rather than foreign targets, as its conflict remained primarily an internal insurgency against the Sri Lankan government. The bombing assassination of a moderate Tamil politician in 1999, however, indicated somewhat random terror tactics, as 34 innocent bystanders were also killed.

Although there is currently still a cease-fire in place between the government and the LTTE, violations of the agreement continue to occur, and a significant faction led by eastern military commander Karuna has been engaged in a lethal struggle for power. The LTTE is also still notorious for its cadre of suicide bombers, the Black Tigers.

EUROPE AND EURASIA OVERVIEW

After the violent breakup of the former Yugoslavia in the early part of the 1990s, much of Europe experience spillover terrorism from this turbulent region. Peace talks in NORTHERN IRELAND helped to reduce the violence carried out by the IRA, but both Catholic and Protestant splinter groups continued to carry out violent attacks, often in efforts to derail the peace process. While most European countries still experienced terrorist attacks throughout the decade, many of the groups carrying out such attacks that emerged during the 1960s and remained active until the early 1980s began to disintegrate, often replaced by right-wing groups.

Terrorist activity and the presence of terrorist support networks in Europe remain a source of concern. Major terrorist events occurred in this region in 2004 and 2005, with hundreds dying or injured in mass transit attacks in Spain and the United Kingdom. The Netherlands was shaken in 2004 by the assassination of a prominent film director by a Dutch-born Moroccan dual national.

Central Asia, or Eurasia, became separate states with records of terrorism at the beginning of the 1990s, with the breakup of the Union of Soviet Socialist Republics. The state terrorism that had been in place for most of the history of the U.S.S.R. has been well documented. But terrorism by groups as well as governments continued to plague the states in the region. The Russian conflict in Chechnya was the focus of much of the violence, including explosions on Moscow subways, a suicide bomber outside a Moscow metro station, and the seizure of about 1,200 hostages, most of whom were schoolchildren, at a school in BESLAN that left at least 331 people dead and hundreds injured. Uzbekistan also suffered suicide bomber attacks in March and April of 2004.

European nations, and much of Eurasia, are active participants in a variety of multilateral organizations involved in counterterrorist efforts. Members of the Organization for Security and Cooperation in Europe have committed themselves to becoming parties to the 12 United Nations terrorism conventions and protocols. Switzerland cohosted the sixth Counterterrorism Conference for Eurasian states in Zurich in December 2004, providing participants an opportunity to describe and identify components of their national programs to respond to a bioterrorism attack.

Albania

Albania's problems with terrorism have been primarily in the form of terrorists from other nations penetrating their borders to carry out terrorist acts against individuals living within their system. A lack of resources, porous borders since the collapse of the communist system, and high crime rates have provided an environment conducive to the conduct of terrorist activity. In 2004, the government froze the assets of terrorist financiers, curtailed the activities of suspect Islamic nongovernmental organizations, and detained or expelled individuals suspected of having links to terrorism or attempting to foment religious intolerance.

Armenia

Individuals, rather than organized groups, have been the primary agents of violence since the conflict with Azerbaijan over the region of Nagorno-Karabach was resolved in the mid-1990s. In October 1999, five gunmen opened fire on a Parliament session, killing eight government leaders, including the prime minister and the speaker of the National Assembly. The killers claimed to be protesting the responsibility of government officials for dire social and economic conditions in Armenia since the collapse of the Soviet Union, and they surrendered later to authorities. They were sentenced to life in prison in December 2003. Armenia is a party to six of the 12 UN conventions and protocols on terrorism and has signed a seventh.

Austria

Like Albania, Austria has suffered primarily from international rather than domestic terrorism. As with many west European countries, Austria suffered a Kurdish backlash in the aftermath of the arrest in 1999 of Kurdistan Workers' Party (PKK) leader Abdullah Oçalan in Kenya. Most of these protests, however disruptive, were peaceful rather than violent, and therefore not terrorist events. A deadly letter-bomb campaign from 1993 to 1997 carried out by Franz Fuchs that killed four members of the Roma minority in Burgenland Province and injured 15 others ended with the sentencing of the terrorist to life imprisonment. A suspected member of the German RED ARMY FACTION (RAF) was killed in a shootout in Vienna in 1999. Terrorist Horst Ludwig-Mayer's accomplice, Andrea Klump, was arrested and extradited to Germany for trial, in which she was charged with complicity in an attack against the chairman of Deutsche Bank and involvement in an attack against a NATO installation in Spain in 1988.

Along with its European allies, Austria made serious efforts after 2001 to tighten financial oversight of suspected terrorist financing. In 2004, the government increased surveillance of suspected Afghan extremists entering Austria to seek asylum and of the Egyptian al-Jamaah al-Islamiyah movement.

Azerbaijan

This predominantly Muslim state, after the conclusion of its conflict with Armenia, did not face any serious threat from international terrorism. It has, however, served as a logistic hub for international mujahideen with ties to terrorist groups seeking to move men, money, and materiel throughout the Caucasus. Having acceded to all 12 international conventions and protocols relating to terrorism, the government in 2004 increased its border controls to prevent foreign terrorists from operating within its borders and took steps to combat terrorist financing. Members of Jaysullah, an indigenous group responsible for terrorist acts, were arrested in 2000 and tried in 2001 for plotting to attack the U.S. embassy in Baku.

Belgium

Belgium, too, has experienced little threat of terrorism from indigenous terrorist groups. Instead, organizations such as the ARMED ISLAMIC GROUP (GIA), an Algerian group, and the Turkish group DHKP/C were arrested by Belgian police for alleged acts committed in other countries. In 1999, Belgian police raided a DHKP/C safe house and arrested six individuals believed to be involved in planning and support activities for that group. During the raid, police seized false documents, detonators, small-caliber weapons, and ammunition.

The GIA threatened a "blood bath" in Belgium if authorities did not released imprisoned group members. Belgium refused to comply, instead convicting eight of 10 suspects charged with criminal conspiracy related to possible terrorist activities. The courts also upheld the sentencing of 18 others convicted in the 2003 terrorist trial, actually extending the sentences of some of the defendants, including Tarek Maroufi and Nizar Trabelsi (a Tunisian national and al-Qaeda associate). Criminal investigations of over 20 other suspects continue, including possible links to the March 2004 MADRID bombing and the November murder of Dutch filmmaker Theo van Gogh.

In Brussels on June 4, 2003, letters containing the nerve agent adamsite were sent to the U.S., British, and Saudi embassies; the government of Prime Minister Guy Verhofstadt, the Court of Brussels; a Belgian ministry; the Oostende airport; and the Antwerp port authority. Belgian police suspected a 45-year-old Iraqi political refugee opposed to the U.S. war in Iraq. Following a police search of his residence and confiscation of a document and a plastic bag containing some powder, the Iraqi was charged with premeditated assault.

Bosnia and Herzegovina

Hundreds of thousands of civilians were killed in Bosnia and Croatia in the wars that were fought as Yugoslavia disintegrated. Terrorism exploded throughout the region in the form of "ethnic cleansing," as tens of thousands of women were raped, some of them more than a hundred times, while their sons and husbands were beaten and tortured. Millions lost their homes as the Serbian military in Bosnia advanced, expelling non-Serbian civilians from towns and villages to create ethnically pure enclaves for Serbs. Led by Ratko Mladić, a war criminal sought by the War Crimes Tribunal before which Serbian leader Slobodan Milošović was brought, Serbian troops shelled particular villages with fewer Serbs and more Muslim populations.

Ethnic cleansing created more than 2 million refugees and displaced persons from the former Yugoslavia. Serbs were by far the most successful "cleansers," although all sides adopted this method in the course of war. Record ethnic-cleansing operations include Serbian Operation Horseshoe against the Muslim population in Kosovo and Croatian Operation Storm against the Serb population in Krajina.

Having experienced, unthinkable acts of genocide during the tumultuous disintegration of the former state of Yugoslavia, the government of Bosnia and Herzegovina (BiH) has become a strong partner in the global war on terrorism. The country's ethnic divisions, its complex government structure, and its weak central institutions continue to complicate its efforts against terrorism. However, in 2004, the BiH government took significant steps in apprehending suspects and shutting down nongovernmental organizations and bank accounts tied to terrorist-linked organizations, disrupting the operations of al-Furqan (a.k.a. Sirat Istikamet), al-Haramain and al-Masjed al-Aqsa Charity Foundation, and Taibah International, organizations listed by the UN 1267 Committee as having direct links with AL-QAEDA. The activities of foreign Islamic extremists who remain in Bosnia as a legacy of the 1992–95 war remain a serious concern.

France

The place from which the term *terror* with respect to state terror was generated, France experienced in the latter part of the 20th century relatively little indigenous terror. France's indigenous group, ACTION DIRECT, dissolved by the end of the 1980s. After avoiding most of the violence troubling other western European states during the 1960s through the 1980s from Middle Eastern groups, as well as from groups like ETA in neighboring Spain, France began in the 1990s to experience serious terrorist attacks from some of these groups. Its perceived role as a safe haven for those "independence fighters" fleeing persecution had led France to allow the PALESTINE LIBERATION ORGANIZATION and other Middle East groups to have open refuge and to allow ETA members fleeing capture in Spain to flee across France's southern border to safety.

This changed when Paris began to be a target for attack by terrorist groups in the late 1980s and early 1990s. By the end of that decade, France had initiated aggressive efforts to detain and prosecute individuals from a variety of groups suspected of supporting or carrying out terrorist acts. The Armed Islamic Group's attack on the Paris metro, and the Libyan sponsorship of a bombing of UTA flight 772 over Niger, as well as numerous other violent acts, fueled France's determination to seek greater security against terrorism by cooperative efforts. It worked with Spain to track down ETA members suspected of terrorism taking refuge in or launching attacks from France. In 1999, France arrested some of ETA's most experienced cadre and seized large weapons and explosives caches.

In April 2004, French authorities shut down a cell of the Moroccan Islamic Combatant Group (GICM). In July of that year, the government took custody of four former detainees of Guantánamo Bay and charged them with terrorist conspiracy. The arrest in October by French and Spanish authorities of two top ETA leaders and the seizure of arms and materiel caches was a significant cooperative effort. However, France has not designated HAMAS-affiliated charities as conducting terrorism financing, and it opposed designating Lebanese HIZBALLAH as a terrorist organization.

Georgia

Separatist violence in Abkhazia (a predominantly Muslim area) and Osetia escalated during the first few years of Georgia's existence as a separate state in 1991. By the end of the decade, most of the violent insurrection had been subdued, often by force. Kidnapping of officials near Abkhazia for ransom and assassination attempts on Georgian officials (including an attempt on President Eduard Shevardnadze) continued, but most terrorist attacks against civilian populations had ceased.

Georgia is still used to a limited degree as a terrorist transit state, although much less so since the government crackdown on the Pankisi Gorge in late 2002. Counterterrorism operations increased in late 2004 in Pankisi, in the wake of the BESLAN terrorist attack in September 2004 in Russia.

Germany

Like France, Germany has experienced serious state terrorism, especially during the NAZI regime from 1933 to 1945. It also had an indigenous group during the 1960s that, while violent, carried out few terrorist acts, in that few if any civilian casualties resulted from the attacks of the Baader-Meinhof Gang before the arrest of many of its members, including Ulrike Meinhof. The RED ARMY FACTION (RAF) that succeeded this early gang, however, was much more violent, carrying out attacks against NATO as well as government and industrial targets. The RAF officially disbanded in March 1998, and there were no known indications of renewed activity.

Right-wing NEO-NAZIS attacked foreigners during the 1990s, particularly after the collapse of the Berlin Wall. This xenophobic violence targeted, as had the Nazis, a particular group—in this case, those who were not German by birth—for crimes of violence, including murder.

GSG-9, the German unit designated to carry out counterterrorism efforts, has been remarkably effective against international terrorism but less so against right-wing hate groups. German counterterrorism focused on the use of the law rather than the use of force, in most cases. In December 2004, the interior minister announced the establishment of a Berlin-based Information and Analysis Center that would bring together all agencies involved in Germany's fight against terrorism. The German Federal Criminal Office also established an Office for International Coordination to improve counterterrorism collaboration with foreign law-enforcement authorities.

In 2002, the German Interior Ministry banned the al-Aqsa Foundation on the grounds of providing financial support to HAMAS. It also banned the extremist Islamic association Hizb ut-Tahrir from activities within the country and seized the association's assets. Efforts to convict purported members of the "Hamburg cell" of AL-QAEDA that had formed around 9/11 suicide pilot Mohammed Atta were less successful, ending in rulings that were either overturned or ended in acquittal.

Greece

REVOLUTIONARY ORGANIZATION 17 NOVEMBER carried out a wide variety of terrorist acts against Greek, U.S., and other foreign interests for several decades. Rocket attacks, bombings, assassinations, incendiary devices, and drive-by shootings have been used by this group—and others with whom it has networked—with little ability on the part of Greek authorities to successfully curb its activities.

Greece hosted the 2004 Olympics without incident. In October of that year, a Greek court sentenced four of five accused members of the indigenous Peoples' Revolutionary Struggle (ELA) to approximately 25 years of imprisonment, the maximum allowed under Greek law, for bombings and attempted murder, possession of firearms/explosives, and involvement in the 1994 assassination of a police officer. Another court announced that the appeals process for members of the 17 November group, convicted in December 2003 of hundreds of crimes over the years, would begin in December 2005. Anarchists and domestic groups continue to conduct numerous small-scale attacks, most involving gas canisters or other crude improvised explosive devices against perceived establishment and imperialist targets, such as banks, U.S. fastfood restaurants, courts, and personal vehicles.

Italy

Italy dealt for more than three decades with an indigenous terrorist group known as the RED BRIGADES (BR), but the capacity of this group for action seriously diminished by the end of the century. The group was responsible in its early career for the death of Prime Minister Aldo Moro, and individuals who claimed to be members were responsible for the murder in 1999 of Italy's labor minister. A leftist group, the Anti-Imperialist Territorial Nuclei, that formed in 1995 and was believed to be allied with former Red Brigades members held demonstrations and issued public threats against U.S. interests in Italy, but did not commit terrorist acts.

Italy's support of the U.S.-led war in IRAQ generated a different wave of terror in this country. In 2004, Italian authorities arrested more than 60 persons suspected of planning or providing support to terrorist activity, both internationally and internally, including many AL-QAEDA sympathizers and recruiters supporting anti-coalition activities in Iraq. Many were also suspected of having ties to ANSAR AL-ISLAM and other al-Qaeda–linked organizations. Included among those arrested was Rabei Osman Sayed Ahmed, who was suspected of involvement in the March MADRID bombings. In April 2004, Italy also coordinated with four of its European neighbors in the arrests of multiple suspects believed to have ties to the Turkish DHKP/C.

The new Red Brigades–Communist Combatant Party, an offshoot of the original BR, presented a diminished threat in recent years. The sentencing in June 2004 of the BR's presumed leader, Desdemona Lioce, to a lifetime in prisons following the killing of one police officer and the wounding of a second during a train shootout in 2003, further dismantled this organization's capabilities for action.

Kyrgyzstan

Kyrgyzstan experienced international terrorism at the turn of the century when the ISLAMIC MOVEMENT OF UZBEKISTAN (IMU) crossed into Kyrgyzstan twice and carried out a two-and-one-half-month hostage crisis, holding four Kyrgyzstanis hostage in the first attempt. These were released without violence, but the militants returned later the same month (August 1999) and seized 13 hostages. Since Kyrgyzstan had no experience with counterterrorism, and the terrain was mountainous and difficult to assault, the militants held out until winter forced their retreat to Tajikistan, where release of the hostages was negotiated. The IMU had demanded money, safe passage, and a prisoner exchange.

Following the July 30, 2004, suicide bombings in Tashkent, Uzbekistan, the government of Kazakhstan actively sought and prosecuted individuals involved in extremist groups targeting Western interests in the region. It also joined with Belarus, China, Kyrgyzstan, Tajikistan, and Russia in the Eurasia Group, a regional anti–money laundering organization. The government announced in November 2004 that its security agencies had detained leaders and accomplices of the Islamic Jihad Group.

The Netherlands

In November 2004, the Netherlands was shaken by the murder of prominent Dutch film director Theo van Gogh. Since the murder was carried out by a Dutch Moroccan acting out of radical Islamic convictions, this action prompted a national debate on the need to strengthen counterterrorism laws. The government had already blocked the accounts and financial transactions of a HAMAS fund-raiser, the al-Aqsa Foundation, and AL-QAEDA–affiliated Benevolence International Nederland and frozen the assets of the Dutch branch of al-Haramain.

Portugal

In response to the March MADRID train bombings, Portugal increased security for the June–July EURO 2004 soccer tournament. The games went forward without incident, but authorities later revealed that the government had apprehended 10 suspected terrorists, primarily Moroccan nationals. The suspected terrorists were deported to both Morocco and the Netherlands. One was later linked to the terror cell that carried out the murder of Dutch filmmaker Theo van Gogh.

Russia

After experiencing various forms of state terrorism under first the czars and then the subsequent communist system, particularly under JOSEPH STALIN, from the beginning of the century, Russia at the close of the century was relatively free of this type of terrorism but beginning to have to deal with terrorism by groups and individuals. Insurgency, taking the form of GUERRILLA WARFARE, took place in CHECHNYA during the middle of the 1990s. Russia was accused by Chechens of committing acts of state terrorism against their people during the conflict, which continued to simmer without complete resolution as the century ended. While bombing attacks continued to occur in Moscow as well as a few other Russian cities, Chechen rebels did not claim responsibility for any of them, although Russian authorities attributed most of these attacks to the rebels. Support for Chechen militant activity from foreign mujahideen, including OSAMA BIN LADEN, caused concern for Russia and for Chechnya's neighbors, who feared a spillover of violence.

Russia continues to experience terrorist violence. On February 6, 2004, suicide bombers blew up a Moscow subway train, killing at least 41 and injuring more than 100. In May of that year, Chechen president Akhmed Kadyrov was assassinated during Victory Day celebrations in a Grozny stadium, and in June, armed militants seized a Ministry of Interior building in Ingushetia, killing at least 92 people. On August 24, suicide bombers simultaneously brought down two Russian airliners, killing 88 passengers and crew, while on the 31st, a female suicide bomber killed at least eight persons and wounded more than 50 others when she detonated explosives outside a Moscow subway station.

A woman walks by a memorial to the victims of the Beslan school siege, Russia, 2004. (GETTY IMAGES)

The most shocking display of violence during that year, however, occurred in September, when terrorists seized approximately 1,200 hostages, more than half of them children, at a school in BESLAN, North Osetia. According to official reports after the fierce gun battle between the hostage-takers and security forces, 331 people were killed, 172 of them children, though many believe that the number of deaths was much higher. Hundreds of others were wounded.

Spain

ETA, Spain's indigenous group seeking independence for its region, continued to carry out violent attacks, with intermittent cease-fire agreements with the Spanish government, through the end of the century. Spain's other domestic terrorist group, the First October Anti-Fascist Resistance Group (GRAPO), was largely inactive by 1999.

On the morning of March 11, 2004, terrorists detonated bombs on commuter trains in MADRID, including five near Atocha, the city's biggest train station, killing 191 and wounding hundreds of others. Extremists associated with the Moroccan Islamic Combatant Group (GICM), most of them North Africa residents of Spain, carried out the attacks.

Spain, initially an active supporter of the U.S.-led war in Iraq, found itself increasingly a target of radical Islamic organizations and arrested scores of individuals with possible links to AL-QAEDA since the events of September 11, 2001. Spanish police have also worked intensely with French authorities to eliminate domestic groups such as ETA, arresting more than 70 individuals in 2004 for association or membership in ETA and dismantling several ETA operational cells, dealing serious blows to ETA's logistic, recruitment, and operational capabilities. In March 2006, ETA leadership announced a permanent cease-fire.

Switzerland

Switzerland continued to experience primarily spillovers from terrorist events. Swiss authorities, for example, arrested a Red Brigades activist and his accomplice in 1999 on charges of suspected violations of the war materiels law. Switzerland also was caught in the backlash of Kurdish anger concerning the apprehension of Kurdistan Workers' Party (PKK) leader Oçalan, with Kurds storming the Greek consulate in Zurich—taking hostage a policeman and the building's owner—as well as the Greek embassy in Bern. All hostages were released, and the incidents ended peacefully. However, PKK sympathizers carried out several arson attacks against Turkish-owned businesses in Basel, including the torching of two trucks from Turkey.

Tajikistan

Like Kyrgyzstan, Tajikistan has had terrorism as a new state only in the incursion of the International Movement of Uzbekistan (IMU) into its territory. The IMU's use of Tajikistan as a staging ground for its incursion into Kyrgyzstan in 1999, leaving from bases in Tajikistan to capture hostages and returning to Tajikistan with their central Asian and Japanese hostages, caused the Tajikistani government to request that the militants leave, when the incident was resolved with the release of the hostages.

Tajikistan also has experienced violence in the clashes of Tajik warlords Rizvon and Bahrom Sodirov, whose militant followers resorted to kidnapping employees of international organizations in 1996 and 1997. Personnel from the UN and the International Committee of the Red Cross (ICRC), Russian journalists, and the Tajik security minister were kidnapped in 1997. After the government met the demands for safe transport to Afghanistan, weapons and ammunition, the hostages were released. A violent shootout in November of that year ended another hostage incident by this group, with one hostage killed.

Tajikistan is a cofounder of the Eurasia Group, established in 2004 with Russia, Kazakhstan, Kyrgyzstan, China, and Belarus to serve as a regional anti–money laundering organization.

Turkey

Under the Ottoman Empire, Turkey's turmoil included internal clashes with ethnic groups, including the Armenians, Kurds, Serbs, and a host of others. By the end of the 20th century, some of the principle actors involved in internal terrorism were, according to Turkish authorities, the KURDISTAN WORKERS' PARTY (PKK), the REVOLUTIONARY PEOPLE'S LIBERATION PARTY/FRONT (DHKP/C), and several Islamic militant groups. Turkish counterterrorist operations have apprehended Oçalan, leader of the PKK, and more than a hundred DHKP/C members and supporters, confiscating numerous weapons, ammunition, bombs, and bomb-making materials. Attempted bombings against U.S., Russian, and NATO interests in Turkey continue, as well as attempts to use light antitank weapons against diplomatic facilities.

In the summer of 2004, PKK/KADEK/Kongra-Gel renounced its self-proclaimed cease-fire and threatened to renew its struggle in both the southeast and in Turkey's western cities. This group maintains approximately 500 armed militants in Turkey and an estimated 3,000 to 3,500 armed militants in northern Iraq, according to Turkish government sources. A new group, calling itself the Kurdistan Liberation Hawks (TAK) used pro-PKK/KADEK/Kongra-Gel media sources in Germany to claim responsibility for several attacks on civilian targets in 2004, including two Istanbul hotels, the governor of Van province, and a music festival in Mersin. Several civilians, including international tourists, were killed and dozens wounded in these attacks.

Turkmenistan

Following the November 25, 2002, attack on President Saparmurat Niyazov's motorcade, the government of Turkmenistan made significant changes in its antiterrorism laws. While these laws were intended to ensure the survival of the Niyazov government, they have also created serious infringements on civil liberties and violations of human rights.

United Kingdom

The majority of the terrorist violence experienced by the U.K. has been generated by the struggle in NORTHERN IRELAND. The IRISH REPUBLICAN ARMY, and many subsequent splinter groups, has carried out bombing attacks, assassination attempts, arson, and a wide range of other tactics against the U.K., seeking to force the U.K. to withdraw its troops and its interests from the northern provinces, facilitating a fully united, and predominantly Catholic, Republic of Ireland. The renewed efforts in the 1990s toward peace in that region were troubled by violence from both Protestant and Catholic extremists who objected, for opposing reasons, to the solutions being offered at the peace table.

Republican and Loyalist paramilitary organizations have increasingly shifted their activity from political actions to criminal racketeering. This shift began with the 1994 cease-fires of the Provisional Irish Republican Army (PIRA), the Ulster Defense Association (UDA), and the Ulster Volunteer Force (UVF) and has accelerated since the signing of the Good Friday Agreement in 1998. The Continuity Irish Republican Army (CIRA) and the Real Irish Republican Army (RIRA)—two relatively small dissident Republican paramilitaries—have not observed this cease-fire and continue to advocate the use of armed violence to secure their goal of uniting northern and southern Ireland.

The United Kingdom's active support of the U.S.-led war in Iraq appears to have stimulated another group of dissidents. The 2005 LONDON BOMBINGS, carried out by individuals from the Middle East living in Britain who opposed Britain's role in the conflict, gave dramatic evidence of this new form of terrorist threat on British soil.

Uzbekistan

The ISLAMIC MOVEMENT OF UZBEKISTAN (IMU) began carrying out acts unprecedented in a former Soviet Republic. Car bombs killing innocent people and wounding hundreds of others and kidnappings at home and abroad led to serious international efforts to curtail the activities of this group by the turn of the century. It remained active, however, and has provoked calls for JIHAD by Islamic extremists in neighboring countries, including Tajikistan.

In June 2004, the Shanghai Cooperation Organization (SCO) Regional Antiterrorism Center was established in Tashkent. The SCO membership includes China, Kazakhstan, Kyrgyzstan, Russia, Tajikistan, and Uzbekistan. The IMU continued to carry out terrorist attacks in Uzbekistan in 2004, including several bomb attacks in March, April, and July, but Uzbek courts in August and September convicted more than 80 individuals for involvement in the spring attacks.

WESTERN HEMISPHERE OVERVIEW

Historically, terrorism in the Western Hemisphere has been carried out by groups seeking political change and by criminal organizations seeking to intimidate society and government to allow them to operate unrestricted. This has meant that most terrorist groups have been primarily domestic, attacking predominantly internally rather than externally. Groups engaged in terrorism in the region have become increasingly active in illicit transnational activities, however, including the drug trade, arms trafficking, money laundering, contraband smuggling, and document and currency fraud. The preponderance of "soft" targets—in the tourism industry, the large American expatriate communities, thriving aviation sector, and busy ports—give ample opportunities for terrorist attacks.

Although by the end of the 20th century much of Latin America was free of terrorist attack, several countries within that region have had active groups carrying out acts of terrorism. Mercosur (the Southern Cone common market) interior and justice ministers signed agreements on a number of initiatives to fight crime in the Southern Cone region, with particular emphasis being given to the need to cooperate in preventing terrorist activity. NARCO-TERRORISM remained a destabilizing influence in several countries. The attacks of September 11, 2001, in the United States and the bombings of the Israeli embassy in Buenos Aires in 1992 and the Argentine-Jewish Cultural Center in 1994 were stark reminders of the continued dangers of terrorism in this hemisphere.

Argentina

In spite of the fact that Argentina's 1853 constitution placed strong emphasis on protecting individuals from abuse by authority, repressive military rule made this a difficult tradition to maintain. In 1930, the military deposed President Hipólito Yrigoyen, beginning a trend of regimes. After five military coups and 30 out of 46 years spent under military rule, the 1976 military coup that overthrew President Isabel Perón was hardly remarkable in itself, but the "dirty war" carried out during the next seven years remains a dark period of state terrorism tarnishing Argentina's history.

General Juan Domingo Perón became president of Argentina twice, in 1946–55 and again briefly from 1973 to 1974. Perón's advocacy of social justice and a "third way" between capitalism and socialism generated animosity among both the military and the Catholic bishops, leading to his ouster and flight into exile in 1955. In exile, he remained a powerful political figure and "Peronism" continued to make the country difficult to govern for a succession of anti-Peronist military regimes. The Peronist movement splintered into several factions, several of which were violent and carried out terrorist activities.

To combat the activities of the opposition groups, the Argentine government resorted to the use of death squads as a form of counterterrorism. The Argentine Anti-Communist Alliance (AAA, or Triple A) was the most notorious of the death squads during this time. The Triple A was established under the government of Isabel Perón, who became president upon the death of her husband Juan in 1975. Her social security minister, José López Rega, created the Triple A, and his close relationship with Isabel Perón gave him the freedom to carry out operations under the Social Welfare Ministry. About 200 of the security forces were recruited to carry out special tasks, including terrorism against opposition political groups and any individuals thought to have leftist ideas or contacts. These individuals included journalists, actors, singers, socialists, academicians, and many university professors. During what came to be called Black September in 1975, these individuals were given 72 hours to leave the country, following a warning by Triple A.

In 1976, a new military junta, comprised of three commanders of the military (army, navy, and air force), took control of the government. General Jorge Rafael Videla was the leader of the coup and president of Argentina from 1976 to 1981. Under his direction, the government issued a Process of National Reorganization (PRN) that sought to eliminate all opposition. Together with General Robert Viola, who succeeded him as president in 1981, Videla developed a myth of necessary counterterrorism and security, which later became known throughout the world as a "dirty war." Exaggerating the violence of the Peronist-left, Videla called for increases in counterterrorism in the form of secret police, death squads, and censorship of the media and the universities. Although the Montoneros, a group whose members were drawn from the Peronist-left, had engaged in acts of violence and terrorism, they were all but extinct by the time Videla came to office. Yet this group became the focus of the Videla government's counterterrorism and the basis for his claim that a civil war was occurring that required strong government action in the subsequent dirty war.

While it is impossible to be certain of the exact number of deaths generated in this state terrorism, which included extrajudicial killings, abductions, and torture executed by the military regime from 1976 to 1983, at least 30,000 people were killed and another 9,000 "disappeared" during that time. The *desaparecidos,* or "disappeared ones," include those who, after being kidnapped by secret police or military units, were never traced. Secret police and military units maintained secret lists of names of those targeted for abduction, torture, and murder. Clandestine places of detention were known as "holes," and many of those taken to these secret camps were tortured for information. Most were eventually killed and their bodies disposed of secretly.

Victims of this period of state terrorism included trade unionists, artists, teachers, human rights activists, politicians, Jews, and all of their respective relatives. Virtually no one was safe, and the intense mood of fear generated by this state terrorism lingered long after the "war" ended. One well-documented example of this state terrorism was known as the Night of the Pencils. High school students decided to protest for lower bus fares, specifically a half-rate fare, already in existence for younger children. The government labeled these protests "subversion in the schools" and ordered the death of those who participated. More than 20 students were kidnapped from two schools.

Only three of the 15 children seized in La Plata survived. One of them was 16-year-old Pablo Dias, who described how his captives blindfolded him, put him in front of a mock firing squad, asked questions, stripped him, tied him down, and began to burn his lips. His captors subjected him to electric torture in his mouth and on his genitals. They pulled out one of his toenails with tweezers, an action that became almost a signature of the army torture. He was beaten with clubs and fists, and kicked repeatedly. He related that his friend Claudia, who was also kidnapped, had been raped at the detention camp. The ordeal lasted from September to December of 1976.

Scholar Martin Andersen in his book *Dossier Secreto: Argentina's Desparecidos and the Myth of the "Dirty Wars"* noted that in the dirty wars, the Argentine military practiced a forged disappearance of people that was modeled on the tactics of Hitler's night-and-fog decrees, a systematic, massive, and clandestine operation. The government built 340 secret camps in which the victims were housed and prepared mass graves for their burial. Prisoners in these camps were, like those in Nazi concentration camps, lined up or made to kneel in front of large, previously dug graves, blindfolded, and gagged. Although some were put in the grave alive, they were then doused with oil and burned with tires to cover the smell. Indeed, disposal of bodies became an exercise in creativity, and many were dumped in rivers or even in the South Atlantic from airplanes or ships. According to Andersen, detainees were usually tortured to the maximum extent before being killed. Torture methods used by the military were intended to produce pain, a breakdown of resistance, fear and humiliation, a strong sense of imminent death, and weakness. Anyone who escaped or survived these camps was changed forever by the terrorism endured.

Nine of the top officials responsible for these acts of violence and mass terror were eventually brought to trial under the rule of President Raúl Alfonsín. Two of them, Videla and Viola, were sentenced to life imprisonment, with the others also receiving substantial prison terms. In 1990, however, President Carlos Menem issued pardons to every official involved in the dirty war, intending to help Argentina move forward. None were ever indicted in an international forum for crimes against humanity.

In recent years, Argentina suffered from international terrorism carried out, apparently, by HIZBALLAH, against Israeli targets in Buenos Aires. Investigation of the bombings of the Israeli embassy in 1992 and the Argentine-Israeli Community Center in 1994 led the Argentine Supreme Court to rule in 1999 that Hizballah leader Imad Mughniyah was responsible for the first attack.

In September 2004, a three-judge panel acquitted all 22 Argentine defendants charged in connection with the 1994 attack on the community center, in which at least 85 people were killed. An Argentine criminal court judge reconfirmed the validity of international arrest warrants against 12 Iranian nationals, including one Lebanese official believed to head Hizballah's terrorist wing.

There were no significant acts of international terrorism in Argentina in 2004. No group claimed responsibility for the small explosive devices set to detonate after hours at three foreign banks in November, which killed one security guard and injured one policeman.

Brazil

Argentina, Brazil, and Paraguay struggled with illicit activities of individuals linked to Islamic terrorist groups in the triborder region. Efforts to cooperate actively in promoting regional counterterrorism consolidated between these governments in 1999, as this region became clearly the focal point for Islamic extremism in Latin America.

In 2002, at the invitation of these three countries, the United States joined them in a consultative mechanism—the "Three Plus One" Group on Triborder Area Security—to strengthen the capabilities to fight cross-border crime and thwart money laundering and terrorist fund-raising activities. The United States articulated the concern that HIZBALLAH and HAMAS may raise funds among the sizable Muslim communities in the region and that the high incidence of illicit activity could tempt terrorist groups to establish safe havens in this largely uncontrolled triborder area. The United States remains concerned about the possible use of Brazilian territory for transit by terrorists using established illegal migrant smuggling groups or for fund-raising for terrorist groups.

Chile

The Manuel Rodríguez Patriotic Front (Frente Patriótico Manuel Rodríguez [FPMR]) that emerged in the 1980s continued to be active in this country through the end of the century. While many members of this group were eventually captured by the government, four escaped in December 1996. One was tracked, through cooperative intelligence efforts, to Switzerland, where he was detained pending extradition. Chile believed that the other three had taken refuge in Cuba, where members of the FPMR had taken refuge in the past.

This group and several other domestic groups continue to be responsible for terrorist attacks in Chile, firebombing a McDonald's restraurant and planting and detonating low-powered explosives outside banks, ATM machines, a subway, and a restroom in the Brazilian consulate in Santiago in 2004. However, these attacks resulted in no reported deaths or injuries.

Colombia

Insurgent and paramilitary groups posed a significant threat to the country's peace and security and to the security of innocent civilians caught up in the conflict. In spite of efforts to foster a peace process by the government during the 1990s, Colombia's two largest guerrilla groups, the REVOLUTIONARY ARMED FORCES OF COLOMBIA (FARC) and the NATIONAL LIBERATION ARMY (ELN), did not significantly moderate their terrorist attacks. The ELN carried out high-profile kidnappings, the hijacking of aircraft, and bombings. FARC also continued to kidnap, and often kill, candidates and local office holders, attacking and bombing security and civilians locales. The two groups carried out a campaign of murder and intimidation, as well as working with the drug cartels in NARCO-TERRORISM, which impacted many of its neighbors, particularly the United States.

The UNITED SELF-DEFENSE FORCES OF COLOMBIA (AUC) has also become involved in significant foreign narcotics trafficking. These three organizations, FARC, the ELN, and the AUC continue to conduct terrorist acts, including car bombings, kidnappings, political murders, the indiscriminate use of land mines, and attacks on critical infrastructure, including water, oil, gas, electricity, public recreation areas, and modes of

Police investigate a bicycle bombing in front of a police precinct in Bogotá, Colombia, 2002. (GETTY IMAGES)

transportation. Paramilitaries continue to displace forcibly civilians who reside along drug and weapons transit corridors or who are suspected of being guerrilla sympathizers.

Although kidnappings have declined, Colombia still suffers from the world's highest kidnapping rate (more than 1,500 in 2004). It also has experienced links with terrorists from other nations. On December 16, 2004, the Bogotá Appeals Court reversed an earlier decision to acquit three IRISH REPUBLICAN ARMY (IRA) members of providing support for FARC, sentencing them to 17 years in prison and ordering their recapture. This case emerged from Interpol information suggesting a three-way link between FARC, the IRA, and ETA, information emerging from a study of the networking of terrorism.

The use of areas along Colombia's porous borders by FARC, the ELN, and the AUC to find logistical support and havens, as well as to transship arms and drugs, continues to pose serious problems. The situation on the Venezuelan side of the Colombian border, which all three groups exploit, remains particularly challenging.

Cuba

Cuba, under the leadership of Fidel Castro, provided a safe haven to terrorists wanted by other nations during most of the last three decades of the 20th century. It also offered training camps for groups engaged in terrorism, as well as serving as a conduit for weapons for many groups. Cuba was accused by the United States of sponsoring terrorism in Latin America by its encouragement and support for various insurgent groups in the region.

Ecuador

Ecuador continues to aggressively campaign to prevent Colombia's NARCO-TERRORISM from spreading to Ecuador. Government efforts, led by its armed forces, disrupted several Colombian narco-terrorist encampments in Ecuador in 2004, conducting large-scale operations in Sucumbíos province near the Ecuador border, capturing several Revolutionary Armed Forces of Colombia (FARC) members. Since 2003, Ecuadoran armed forces have interdicted thousands of gallons of smuggled petroleum ether, a precursor used in Colombian cocaine laboratories. FARC continues to utilize Ecuador for resupply, rest, and recuperation, in spite of Ecuador's growing willingness to cooperate with Colombian authorities in capturing FARC members.

Panama

Panama's primary terrorism concern is incursions by Colombian narco-terrorists into Panama's remote Darien region. Following the murder of four Panamanians by narco-terrorists in 2003, the government entered into a border security cooperation agreement with Colombia. Although Panama also has a significantly increasing Muslim population, with a recent influx of South Asian immigrants, there has been no credible evidence of ties between this community and the Muslim extremist groups in the Middle East.

Paraguay

Paraguay's indigenous revolutionary group, the Tupamaros, named for Túpac Amaru, a Peruvian rebel Indian leader who was burned at the stake in the 18th century, began a nationalist movement in 1962. It was led in the beginning by Raúl Sendic, born in 1925 in the Flores province of Uruguay in an upper-middle-class family. Sendic became unhappy with his law studies and dropped out of school, heading to the northern part of Uruguay to work among poor sugar beet laborers. In 1962, he went to Cuba for a few months, returning to organize the sugar plantation laborers in their first march on the capital, Montevideo. As support grew for Sendic and the sugar beet laborers, the Tupamaros movement was launched.

The Tupamaros protested against what they considered to be a democratic, quasi-welfare state, viewing it as an attempt to destroy the political soul of the masses with economic incentives. Over the next few years, their activities ranged from the hijacking of trucks carrying food (which they subsequently distributed to needy people) to bank robbery and kidnapping for ransom. Seeing themselves as the "Robin Hood" of their country, they robbed banks and corporations, then distributed the money to the poor. Kidnapping was another profitable method of financing their activities, and their victims included a Brazilian consul, a U.S. adviser to the Uruguayan police (whom they later killed), and the British ambassador to Uruguay. They also assassinated leading figures, including the chief of the civil defense forces.

These activities alone would not constitute terrorism, perhaps. However, the targets for the kidnapping were frequently foreign diplomats or employees of foreign companies, whose only "crime" was their presence in Uruguay. Assassinations of police officers were so common that some police officers refused, in fear, to wear their uniforms to work.

Convinced that the Tupamaros constituted a threat to democracy in Uruguay, President Óscar Gestido banned the Socialist Party in 1967, and the government declared an internal war against the Tupamaros. By 1972, more than 4,000 Tupamaros sympathizers had been arrested, and the government passed the Law of State Security, suspending the normal time period allowed for the holding of suspects. It also permitted military trials of suspected Tupamaros supporters. Free press and free speech were also suspended by the government in order to curb the media coverage of the Tupamaros.

The desire to drive out "foreign" influence and to forcibly redistribute wealth served, in the case of the Tupamaros, as the justification for its acts of terror-violence. In response, the government declared a state of "war" to exist, making it difficult to justify the killing of those innocent persons by the group, since the consequences for much of the population were actions of state terrorism. The cycle of violence generated by terrorist acts by a group spiraled out of control, and hence the justification for the terrorism by the revolutionaries diminished in credibility.

In spite of the current government's increased vigilance against extremists seeking to raise funds among Paraguay's Muslim community for terrorist activities outside of Paraguay, there is no credible evidence of operational Islamic terrorist cells in this country. It remains a committed member of the "Three Plus One" group, working with the United States to combat terrorism in the region.

Peru

Audiences around the world watched with anxiety, then relief, on April 22, 1997, as Peruvian military forces, in what was called OPERATION CHAVÍN DE HUÁNTAR, stormed the residence of the Japanese ambassador in Lima, ending the hostage crisis initiated by the TÚPAC AMARU REVOLUTIONARY MOVEMENT (MRTA), which had begun in December 1996. With the resolution of this crisis, terrorist activity in Peru diminished considerably, compared to previous years. Terrorist incidents by the SENDERO LUMINOSO (SL) and MRTA had generated in Peru a fairly high level of violence. Government counterterrorism efforts had caused the level of violence to fluctuate considerably, as the groups regrouped and often emerged once again as potent forces. Only a few active members of the SL remained at large by the close of 1999, however. Peruvian authorities arrested and prosecuted several of the remaining active members, including principal regional committee leader Óscar Alberto Ramírez (a.k.a. Feliciano), who had headed the decimated group since the capture in 1992 of its founder and leader Abimael Guzmán.

Armed terrorist incidents fell to 40 in 2004, down from 100 in 2003. While reports suggest that the SL is trying to rebuild support in the universities where it exercised considerable influence in the 1980s, the Peruvian government continues to arrest suspected SL members and leaders, including alleged key leader Gabino Mendoza. It also successfully extradited from Spain suspected SL leader Adolfo Olaechea in 2003 and brought him to trial in 2005. The MRTA has not conducted a significant terrorist attack since the December 1996 hostage siege at the Japanese ambassador's residence in Lima.

Peru's president has repeatedly extended a state of emergency, which suspends some civil liberties and gives the armed forces authority to "maintain order," for successive periods of up to 60 days in parts of Peru where SL is believed to still have members.

Uruguay

There continue to be no significant terrorist incidents in Uruguay. The government has occasionally assisted in monitoring the possibility of extremists raising funds for terrorist groups from Muslim communities in the Triborder area and along Uruguay's northern frontier with Brazil.

Venezuela

The 1,400-mile border that Venezuela shares with Colombia continues to be used by the REVOLUTIONARY ARMED FORCES OF COLOMBIA (FARC), the NATIONAL LIBERATION ARMY (ELN), and the UNITED SELF-DEFENSE FORCES OF COLOMBIA (AUC) as a safe area to conduct cross-border incursions, transship arms and drugs, rest, and secure logistical supplies, as well as commit kidnappings and extortion for profit. Weapons and ammunition flow from Venezuelan suppliers and intermediaries into the hands of these three groups. It is unclear whether the government has taken action to stem this flow.

NEAR EAST AND NORTH AFRICA

One of the most tumultuous regions on the planet, the Near East and North Africa have various political and geographical definitions. For most purposes, the area consists of western Asian countries and North Africa. While most of the region's inhabitants are Muslims, there are substantial Christian (Egypt, Iraq, and Lebanon) and Jewish (Israel) communities.

While the Middle East is often associated with the export of terrorism, there is as much reason to believe that the area is just as often victimized by terrorism. The electronic and print media frequently emphasize the Arab-Israeli conflict, but there are ongoing conflicts elsewhere in the Middle East. These generally take the form of separatist movements (*see* KURDS) and religious struggles. The latter is a familiar feature in Egypt and Algeria, where radical Islamic groups have attacked government installations and personnel thought to be less than vigilant in protecting Muslim values.

The Middle East is a culturally and ethnically diverse region with an ancient history. With the possible exception of Israel, it has until recently demonstrated a noticeable lack of hospitality for the process of democratization. In recent years, several of the smaller Persian Gulf states have created political institutions that provide for free elections and restraints on royal prerogatives.

Algeria

From colonial rule, to military dictatorship, to a fluctuating elected/coup leadership pattern, Algeria is no stranger to violence. The violence perpetrated by both the ARMED ISLAMIC GROUP (GIA) and the government in its counterterrorism response has taken the lives of hundreds of innocent civilians. Massacres of villages and bombing attacks carried out both in Algeria and in other countries in the region continued for the last decade of the 20th century with undiminished intensity on the part of the GIA, although the government has offered amnesty to other groups and invited the GIA to surrender and accept a similar offer.

In 1998, a splinter group of the GIA, the SALAFIST GROUP FOR CALL AND COMBAT (GSPC), eclipsed the GIA, and is currently the most effective and largest armed group inside Algeria. The GSPC seeks to overthrow the Algerian government with the goal of establishing an Islamic regime and, unlike the GIA, has pledged to avoid attacks on civilians inside Algeria. Instead, it attacks Algerian government and military targets, primarily in rural areas. In August 2004, the GSPC carried out an ambush on a military convoy in which 40 members of the security forces were killed. In June of the same year, the group exploded a device outside the El-Hamma electric power generating facility in central Algiers, causing no casualties but knocking out 210 MW of generating capacity for several months.

Government forces significantly weakened the GSPC in 2004 by capturing or killing several leaders, including the leader Nabil Sahraoui and one of his top lieutenants, Abbi Abdelaziz. However, in late 2003, the GSPC leader issued a communiqué announcing the group's support of a number of jihadist causes and movements, including support of AL-QAEDA. According to press reports, some GSPC members in Europe and the Middle East maintain contact with other North African extremists sympathetic to al-Qaeda.

Bahrain

Bahrain's primary link to terrorism is its role in blocking the financing of terror groups. In 2004, it announced that it had frozen $18 million in terrorist-linked funds. It has no indigenous terrorist groups.

Egypt

AL-GAMA'AT AL-ISLAMIYYA, currently this country's most active terrorist group, has reduced its level of violence in the last few years of the century. The assassination of ANWAR SADAT, followed two decades later by the attempted assassination of Hosni Mubarak, indicate that Egypt in the past century has suffered from terrorism carried out by extremist groups and individuals. The bombings in Cairo carried out by al-Gama'at in 1997 offered evidence that this violence continues. The peace agreement reached with Israel in the 1970s has led to anger within its own citizens as the peace talks in the 1990s began to unravel.

Rifa'i Taha Musa, who led the faction of al-Gama'at al-Islamiyya (IG) that opposed the 1997 cease-fire, published a book in early 2001 attempting to justify terrorist attacks that cause mass casualties. Musa disappeared several months after this publication. In March 2002, leaders of the group in Egypt declared the use of violence "misguided" and renounced its future use, a declaration that prompted denunciations by much of the group's leadership abroad. The Egyptian government continued to release IG members from prison each year.

Egypt was the victim of serious terrorist attacks in 2004. On October 7, 2004, terrorists attacked tourist targets in Taba and Nuweiba on the Sinai Peninsula in three separate but coordinated actions. Thirty-four people were killed, including Egyptians, Israelis, Italians, a Russian, and an American-Israeli dual national, and more than 140 were injured. Three weeks later, the minister of the interior announced that the government had identified nine individuals responsible for the attacks. By 2005, all but two of these individuals had been killed or captured. The government asserted that the nine perpetrators were not part of a wider conspiracy and did not receive assistance from international terrorist organizations.

Iran

According to a U.S. State Department report, Iran remains an active state sponsor of terrorism. Its Islamic Revolutionary Guard Corps and Ministry of Intelligence and Security have allegedly been involved in the planning and support of terrorist acts and exhort a variety of groups to use terrorism in pursuit of their goals. Supreme Leader Khamenei in 2004 praised Palestinian terrorist operations, and Iran provided HIZBALLAH and Palestinian groups—including HAMAS, the Palestinian Islamic Jihad, the AL-AQSA MARTYRS' BRIGADE, and the POPULAR FRONT FOR THE LIBERATION OF PALESTINE–GENERAL COMMAND—with funding, safe haven, training, and weapons. Iran provided an unmanned aerial vehicle that Lebanese Hizballah sent into Israeli airspace on November 7, 2004.

Iran's support for groups and individuals engaging in terrorist violence in Iraq remains an issue of concern, as Iraq's fragile new democracy emerges.

Iraq

In the wake of the U.S.-led war in Iraq in 2003, this country has become the central battleground in the global war on terror. Former elements of the regime as well as foreign fighters and Islamic extremists conduct terrorist attacks on civilians but also fight as insurgents in attacking coalition and Iraqi security forces. Terrorist attacks against a variety of targets mingled with insurgent attacks against the emerging Iraqi government make it difficult to determine the exact level of "terrorism" occurring in this country at this time.

Jordanian-born Abu Musab AL-ZARQAWI and his organization, Jama'at al-Tawhid wa'al-Jihad, emerged in 2004 to play a leading role in terrorist activities in Iraq. In October of that year, Zarqawi announced the merger of his group and BIN LADEN's AL-QAEDA organization, and in December, bin Laden endorsed Zarqawi as his official emissary in Iraq. Zarqawi claimed credit for the March 2004 simultaneous bomb attacks in Baghdad and Karbala that killed over 180 pilgrims as they celebrated the Shia festival of Ashura, and for the suicide attack on the offices of the leader of the Supreme Council for the Islamic Revolution in Iraq, which killed 15 and wounded over 50. These attacks were, according to Zarqawi, part of a sectarian war in Iraq, focusing on creating a rift between Shia and Sunnis through attacks on the Iraqi Shia.

In August 2004, the Kurdish group Ansar al-Sunna claimed responsibility for the kidnapping and murder of 12 Nepalese construction workers. This group is believed to be an offshoot of the ANSAR AL-ISLAM group founded in Iraq in September 2001. Al-Sunna claimed responsibility for bomb attacks on the offices of two Kurdish political parties in Irbil that killed 109 Iraqi citizens. PKK/KADEK/KONGRA-GEL also maintains an estimated 3,000 armed militants in northern Iraq, according to Turkish government sources, although no terrorist incidents by this group in Iraq have been reported.

See also IRAQ; SADDAM HUSSEIN.

Israel, the West Bank, and Gaza

For six decades, ISRAEL has struggled to secure its right to govern its land and the people who live in it. But it has had to do so through force, maintaining its existence through the occupation of additional lands. Born, in part, of a desperate need to leave a Europe engaged in war and a Holocaust that killed millions of Jews, Israel is still torn by violence and terror, caught in a cycle of violence that has abated from time to time but not ended.

On July 22, 1946, an Irgun team, dressed as waiters, rolled seven milk churns full of dynamite and TNT into the empty Regency Grill of the King David Hotel in Jerusalem. At 12:37, the TNT in the milk churns exploded. Ninety-one people died in that bomb blast. Of these, 28 were British, 41 were Arab, and 17 were Jewish. Another 46 were injured.

The perpetrator of this atrocity was Menachem Begin, who in the 1970s served as prime minister of Israel. The Irgun leader who plotted to destroy the hotel was the same man who, working with President Jimmy Carter of the United States and President ANWAR SADAT of Egypt, made significant efforts to move Israel on the road to peace with its Arab neighbors, signing the famous Camp David Accords and bringing a measure of peace between Israel and Egypt.

Ironically, the "right of self-determination" that the Palestinians seek to exercise today is the same one for which the Hagganah fought against the British occupying forces in the 1930s and 1940s. Just as the Jewish Irgun and its radical offshoot, the Stern Gang, used terror tactics to force out an occupying power, the Palestinians have resorted to terrorist acts to rid

A U.S. Army soldier provides perimeter security during a reconnaissance patrol at the sight of an insurgent attack near Taji, Iraq, 2006. (DEPARTMENT OF DEFENSE)

themselves of what they perceive to be an "occupying power."

The assassination in late 1995 of Yitzhak Rabin, prime minister of Israel, by a Jewish student seeking to derail this withdrawal of Israel from the occupied territories, clearly illustrates both the continuing cycle of violence and the hazards of seeking to end it, as Rabin tried to do by making a significant step toward peace in the signing of the OSLO ACCORDS. Violent actions taken since the signing of the accords and the assassination of Rabin have also made it clear that some factions of Palestinians do not want "independence" in the West Bank or the Gaza Strip. They want to return to, and to claim, their "homeland" of PALESTINE, including the land that is today Israel. It will be difficult to satisfy their right to self-determination without infringing upon Israel's right to exist. Just as the Jewish people rejected other offers of homelands made by the British before the Balfour Declaration in the early 1900s, insisting on their right to return to the homeland of their theological ancestors, Palestinians have found it difficult to accept alternatives that fall short of a return of their homeland, which encompasses what is now Israel.

Individuals and groups engaged in terrorism continue to conduct a large number of assaults in Israel, the West Bank, and Gaza Strip. The first INTIFADA was relatively nonviolent and culminated in the Oslo Accords, but the second intifada was quite violent, with numerous suicide bombings and many deaths. HAMAS, PALESTINIAN ISLAMIC JIHAD, the AL-AQSA MARTYRS' BRIGADE, and the POPULAR FRONT FOR THE LIBERATION OF PALESTINE have been responsible for most of the attacks, which included SUICIDE BOMBINGS, shootings, and mortar and rocket firings against civilian and military targets.

Israel employed a variety of military operations in its counterterrorism efforts, some of which have been characterized by international experts as terrorism, in that civilians were often killed or injured. Israeli forces launched frequent raids throughout the West Bank and Gaza, conducted targeted killings of suspected Palestinian terrorists, destroyed homes—including those of families of suicide bombers—imposed strict and widespread closures and curfews in Palestinian areas, and worked intensely to build an extensive SECURITY BARRIER in the West Bank. Attacks by Palestinian groups in response to these measures continue to be intense, as the cycle of violence continues.

Ariel Sharon, in 2005, completed a significant step in the long-delayed withdrawal of Israeli forces and settlers from the Gaza Strip. However, his subsequent effort to form a new political party, followed by his severe stroke, and hampered by the victory of Hamas in the 2006 Palestinian elections have made the prospects for further steps in the peace process for this country very tenuous.

The Sharon era ended in early January 2006, with the prime minister's stroke that left him incapable of discharging his responsibilities. His handpicked successor, Ehud Olmert, a former mayor of Jerusalem, was elected prime minister. In July 2006, both Hamas in the Gaza Strip and HIZBALLAH on Lebanon's southern border that is contiguous with Israel's northern border attacked and killed Israeli soldiers and kidnapped others. By mid-July 2006, Israel was fighting a two-front war. The most serious fighting occurred in and around the border regions between Israel and Lebanon. By mid-August, the United Nations managed to get both Israel and Hizballah to agree to a cease-fire.

Jordan

Jordan, with a largely Palestinian population, has been both a victim and a facilitator of terrorist violence in this area. The Palestinians who initially fled Israel into Jordan in the 1967 war were subsequently driven out of Jordan after they used their Jordanian refuge to continue to launch attacks against Israel. This forced expulsion generated the name for the group Black September (since the event occurred in September); this group carried out the MUNICH MASSACRE OF ISRAELI ATHLETES in 1972, triggering the formation of Israeli hit squads to track down and kill those responsible, feeding this cycle of violence.

In recent years, Jordan has sought to curb the actions of Hamas and Hizballah and to prevent organizations such as AL-QAEDA from using Jordan as a safe haven. It has strongly supported the peace process, making peace with Israel in the 1990s, 20 years after Egypt. Jordan has also pursued the network of fugitive Jordanian terrorist Abu Musab al-Zarqawi, believed to be responsible for numerous plots and attacks in Jordan and Iraq. The most serious of these attacks occurred in 2005, with a bombing of the hotel in Amman used by the United States in connection with its war efforts in Iraq.

Border security continues to be a serious concern of Jordanian officials. The government continues to interdict weapons and potential infiltrators at its borders with Syria, Israel, and Iraq.

Lebanon

Having experienced a long and debilitating civil war from 1975 to 1990 that left it with far less control than is customary over much of its territory, Lebanon still struggles to deal with terrorist groups using its territory for bases or training camps. Refugee camps in its southern region, filled with Palestinians who have lived there for sometimes more than one generation, have been hotbeds of anti-Israeli activity. HIZBALLAH fighters have networked in these camps, using them as a cover for the launching of missiles into Israel. This group, supported in part by Syria, has established training camps in Lebanon's Bekáa valley and has allowed groups from around the world to use these camps as well.

In 1982, Lebanon's Christian militia, during its civil struggle, was guilty of the massacre of hundreds of Palestinian refugees at two camps, Sabra and Shatilla, that were supposed to be under the guard of ARIEL SHARON and his troops at that time. The massacre resulted in the forced resignation of Sharon from the Israeli military and continues to feed Palestinian hatred and fear of Israel, which in turn has led to continued attacks across Lebanon's southern border against Israel. Israeli troops withdrew from the security buffer it had retained in southern Lebanon in 2000, only to see Syria fill the void.

Lebanon remains host to numerous groups engaged in terrorism, including Hizballah, the Palestinian Islamic Jihad, the POPULAR FRONT FOR THE LIBERATION OF PALESTINE–GENERAL COMMAND, the ABU NIDAL ORGANIZATION, and HAMAS. The government has, however, moved legally against Sunni extremist groups, including those similar in ideology to AL-QAEDA. Syria's withdrawal of troops from the Bekáa valley in 2004–05 and the continuing political struggle between these two countries, which cost the lives of several important political and media leaders by assassination, have made it unclear how much government support there is for the control of these groups within its borders.

In July 2006, conflict started anew between Israel and Lebanon. In recent years, Hizballah had greatly increased its influence in Lebanon, particularly in the south. On July 12, a group of Hizballah fighters captured two Israeli soldiers and killed three others during a cross-border raid. Israel responded with air strikes across Lebanon, followed by a ground invasion. Hizballah launched thousands of rockets into Israel and fought a guerrilla warfare campaign against the Israeli army. On August 12, the United Nations was able to get Israel and Lebanon to agree to a cease-fire, with the understanding that a UN peacekeeping force would occupy southern Lebanon. The conflict has seen over a thousand people killed, mostly Lebanese civilians, damaged Lebanese infrastructure, and displaced about 1 million Lebanese and 500,000 Israelis.

Libya

Long a sponsor of groups engaged in "freedom struggles" against Western systems and a foe of Israel, Libya has allowed its territory to be used for training camps for terrorists. Under the leadership of MU'AMMAR AL-QADHAFI, terrorism has been sponsored, as in the payment given to a Lebanese group for the killing of American hostage Peter Kilburn, a librarian at the American University in Beirut. It has also been supported by supplies of arms, money, intelligence information, and a variety of other state support tactics.

Libya, while also an oil state, has been less obvious in its support for terrorism since 1985, when linkage to a terrorist act in West Germany evoked a bombing attack on Tripoli by the United States. Libya's support for acts of terrorism continued to cause economic and political penalties during the 1990s, following the bombing of Pan Am flight 103 in 1988 over Lockerbie, Scotland. The UN Security Council passed Resolution 731, which demanded that Libya take steps to end its state-sponsored terrorism, including extraditing two Libyan intelligence agents indicted by the United States and the United Kingdom for their role in that bombing. The resolution also required that Libya accept responsibility for the bombing, disclose all evidence related to it, pay appropriate compensation, satisfy French demands regarding Libya's alleged role in the bombing of UTA flight 772 in 1989, and cease all forms of terrorism.

In 1992, the UN Security Council adopted Resolution 748, imposing an arms and civil aviation embargo on Libya. This resolution demanded that Libyan Arab Airlines offices be closed and required that all states reduce Libya's diplomatic presence abroad. When these measures failed to elicit full compliance from Libya, the Security Council adopted Resolution 883 in 1993, imposing a limited assets freeze and oil technology embargo on Libya and strengthening existing sanctions against that nation.

In 1999, Libya surrendered the two suspects accused of the bombing of Pan Am flight 103 over Lockerbie, Scotland, to a court in The Hague, presided over by international jurists. On January 31, 2001, the court found Abdel Baset Ali Mohamed al-Megrahi guilty of murder, concluding that he caused an explosive device to detonate on board the airplane, resulting in the murder of the flight's 259 passengers and crew as well as 11 residents of Lockerbie. The judges found that he acted "in furtherance of the purposes of . . . Libyan Intelligence Services." The other defendant, Al-Amin Khalifa Fhimah, was acquitted based on a lack of sufficient evidence of "proof beyond a reasonable doubt."

In 1999, Libya paid compensation for the death of a British policewoman, a move that preceded the reopening of the British embassy in Tripoli. The policewoman was killed and 11 demonstrators wounded when gunmen in the Libyan People's Bureau in London fired on a peaceful anti-Qadhafi demonstration outside their building. Libya also paid damages to the families of victims in the bombing of UTA flight 771. Six Libyans had been convicted in absentia in that case.

In the wake of UN intervention in the Lockerbie case, in fact, the regime in Libya largely avoided open association with acts of terrorism and terrorist groups. While Qadhafi offered public support for radical Palestinian groups opposed to the PLO's Gaza-Jericho accord with Israel in 1993, and openly threatened to support extremist Islamic groups in neighboring Algeria and Tunisia, the level of practical open support by Libya for terrorism decreased substantially.

Instead, Libya played a high-profile role in negotiating the release of a group of foreign hostages seized in the Philippines by the Abu Sayyaf Group, reportedly in exchange for a ransom payment. The hostages included citizens of France, Germany, Malaysia, South Africa, Finland, the Philippines, and Lebanon. Libya also expelled the Abu Nidal Organization and distanced itself from Palestinian groups engaged in terrorism against Israel, although it maintained contact with groups such as the Palestinian Islamic Jihad and the Popular Front for the Liberation of Palestine–General Command.

In the wake of the September 11 attacks on the United States, Libya was vehement about its noninvolvement and condemned the terrorist actions. Clearly, Libya is seeking to redefine itself with regard to the sobriquet of "state sponsor of terrorism." In 2004, Libya joined the international community in condemning terrorism, and sanctions were lifted against its economy as it began to rebuild relations damaged by its long-term role as a state-supporter for terrorism.

Morocco

Suicide bombers from the Salafiya Jihadiya group killed 42 and wounded about 100 others on May 16, 2003, in Casablanca. In response, the government arrested several thousand people, prosecuted about 1,200, and sentenced about 900 for various terrorism-related crimes. The AL-QAEDA–affiliated Moroccan Islamic Combatant Group (GICM) continues to pose a threat in Morocco as well as in Europe. Moroccan extremists associated with the GICM were among those implicated in the March 11 MADRID bombings in 2004.

Saudi Arabia

This country, site of some of Islam's holiest shrines, has been the field on which some violent acts have occurred, but it has no indigenous terrorist group. The fact that OSAMA BIN LADEN was originally a Saudi citizen, although that citizenship was revoked after he began his terrorist acts, has changed Saudi Arabia's perspective and its role in counterterrorism. Saudi forces have launched dozens of security sweeps throughout the country, dismantling several AL-QAEDA cells.

As custodian of the two holy mosques in Mecca and Medina, the Saudi government has worked to delegitimize the inappropriate use of Islam to justify terrorist attacks. In June 2004, the Grand Mufti Shaykh Abd al-Aziz Al al-Shaykh issued a fatwa condemning terrorist acts and calling on citizens to report "saboteurs and anyone planning or preparing to carry out terrorist acts to the concerned authorities."

Syria

Former Syrian president Hafiz al-Asad long sought to become the dominant power broker in the Middle East, and until the fall of 1986, he came close to achieving that objective. Until that time, Assad masked his support for terrorists beneath a cloak of state secrecy. By distancing himself from the terrorists, he managed to preserve deniability; and when it seemed strategically expedient, he renewed his credit with the West by intervening on behalf of Western hostages.

Assad's secure power base at home and close ties with Moscow made diplomats hesitant to criticize him openly. In the absence of evidence to the contrary, some observers have even assumed that he was a "helpful partner" in Mideast negotiations concerning Lebanon.

Evidence of his duplicity eventually came to light, particularly after the demise of the Soviet Union. Former secretary of state George Schultz noted that Syrian Nezar Hindawi's unsuccessful attempt to blow up an El Al jetliner in London provided "clear evidence" of Syrian involvement in terrorism. Ariel Merari, director of the Tel Aviv University Project on Terrorism, suggested that "there is no doubt that the general policy of sponsoring terrorist activity in western Europe is done with Assad's approval and probably his initiative." The same report suggested that "Qadhafi is an erratic bumbler compared with Assad, a hard-eyed strategist who uses terror as an essential tool of statecraft."

Assad's preferred tool of persuasion was terror. During the early 1980s, he began exporting his deadly product by increasingly indirect means. The CIA made public evidence that the Syrian intelligence services gave logistical support to the individuals who bombed the U.S. Marine barracks in Lebanon. After the attack, the National Security Agency also intercepted messages showing payments were sent through Damascus to an Iranian-sponsored group responsible for the bombing.

In 1986, *U.S. News & World Report* published what it called a "bill of particulars" concerning Syria's links to terrorist events in the early 1980s. Since these events were also noted in the U.S. State Department's annual report on global terrorism, there is little reason to doubt the link to terrorism that the "bill" implies belongs to Syria. This bill included incidents such as the bombing attack in September 1986 in Paris that killed 10 persons and injured more that 160 people, carried out by an obscure Mideast group, thought to be a cover for the Syria-linked Lebanese Armed Revolutionary Faction; and another incident in the same month in Istanbul, which killed 22 and wounded three, when terrorists from the Syrian-backed ABU NIDAL ORGANIZATION opened fire on Jewish worshippers at a synagogue. (Abu Nidal himself, architect of the Rome and Vienna airport massacres, lived at the time in a heavily guarded apartment building on the outskirts of Damascus.)

There were five bases near Damascus and at least 20 other Syrian-controlled camps where instruction in the techniques of terrorism was provided. Yarmouk, near Damascus, was the camp most often used for advanced terrorist training. Skills acquired at these camps were tested in Lebanon's Bekáa valley, which Syria controlled.

General Mohammed Khouli, at one time the head of the Syrian Air Force (which was Assad's personal intelligence service and base of power), directed most of these training operations. One of his deputies, Colonel Haitham Sayeed, was also the intelligence coordinator for Abu Nidal. Khouli and Sayeed, according to Western intelligence agents, directed the Hindawi case.

Yet Assad managed to maintain relatively cordial relations with Western nations. Part of his ability to continue to be acceptable (or at least be difficult to condemn) lay in the care with which he distanced himself from actual terrorist attacks. He also won approval by helping in hostage crises. Indeed, he became a master at the strategy of helping groups to take hostages with one hand and gaining favor with the West by aiding in their release with the other hand.

Unlike Libya's Qadhafi, Assad seemed to prefer secrecy to the spotlight of international attention in the drama of terrorist involvement. Assad relied on sporadic, preferably untraceable attacks, that allowed him to avoid retribution. Qadhafi, in the 1980s, treated terrorism like a banner to be waved before the troops.

Assad had no wish to make himself an obvious target for retribution in a terrorist incident, as Qadhafi had done. He did not underestimate the desire for revenge of a nation whose citizens have been attacked, and he clearly did not wish to make himself or his country a tempting target. He preferred to wage a hit-and-run war, in which it was hard to find the guys wearing the black hats. He was, at heart, a pragmatic politician, a survivor.

The end of the cold war at the beginning of the 1990s changed Syria's position significantly. Without the Soviet Union as an ally, capable of support and willing to protect, Assad became even more determined not to be directly involved in planning or executing terrorist attacks. His death near the end of the 1990s did not immediately change Syria's role as a "quiet" supporter of terrorism.

Syria continued to provide safe haven and support for several groups that engage in terrorist attacks. Ahmad Jabril's Popular Front for the Liberation of Palestine–General Command (PFLP-GC) and the Palestinian Islamic Jihad (PIJ) and George Habbash's Popular Front for the Liberation of Palestine (PFLP) have maintained their headquarters in Damascus. The Syrian government allowed HAMAS to open a new main office in Damascus in March 2000, while Hamas continued to seek permission to reestablish its headquarters in Jordan. Syria also granted to several groups practicing terrorism—including Hamas, the PFLP-GC, and the PIJ—basing privileges or refuge in areas of Lebanon's Bekáa valley under Syrian control, privileges which remained in place through the end of the 20th century.

Upon Hafez al-Assad's death in 2000, his son, Bashar, was swiftly elected president after the parliament, led by the Baath party, which had been the ruling party throughout his father's reign, quickly voted to lower the minimum age for presidential candidates from 40 to 34 (Bashar's age at that time). Although moderate reform efforts, dubbed the "Damascus Spring," began with Bashar's rule, the security apparatus of Hafez al-Assad's state did not loosen control to any degree. A major crisis confronted Bashar in February 2005, with the assassination of Lebanese prime minister Rafik Hariri. Although Syria had been very slowly removing its troops from Lebanon since 2000, according to Bashar's orders, it was forced to complete this pullout rapidly after a UN investigation of the assassination led to accusations of Syrian involvement. His security minister, Ghazi Kanaan, allegedly committed suicide while being investigated by the UN, although Bashar denied any involvement in the murder.

Bashar's leadership was also challenged in 2006, as Hamas attacked Israel on the Gaza border, killing two soldiers and capturing another, provoking prolonged Israeli counterattacks in Gaza. Although he met with other Arab leaders and reportedly sought to negotiate a prisoner exchange of Palestinians in Israeli jails for the captured soldier, his ability and in some respects his desire to control the actions of this group were unclear. In the ensuing conflict generated by the attack of Hizballah on Israeli forces in northern Israel in the summer of 2006, Assad's unwillingness and/or inability to curtail the acts of either Hamas or Hizballah became evident.

It should be noted that, in the wake of the Gulf War, Syria began to distance itself from its role as a sponsor of terrorism. Seeking to improve its relations with the Western nations, Syria moved away from obvious links with various Middle Eastern groups engaging in terrorism. Whether this move was permanent or only a feint designed to deflect Western criticism remains unclear. The situation in Lebanon has not yet stabilized, and the known terrorist groups have not yet been forced to leave that country to seek sanctuary and assistance elsewhere. The Middle East peace process tests Syria's willingness to cooperate in the control of violence against Israel by refusing to provide shelter and assistance to such groups.

Tunisia

Tunisia's active stance against terrorism has been reinforced by its own experience with international terrorism. In April 2002, a suicide truck bomb detonated outside the el-Ghriba synagogue on the island of Djerba, killing at least 20.

Yemen

Although Yeman has expanded security cooperation with other Arab countries, signing a number of international antiterrorist conventions, it remained a sanctuary for many terrorist groups. HAMAS and the Palestinian Islamic Jihad had official representatives in Yemen, and sympathizers or members of many other groups engaged in terrorism—including Egypt's AL-GAMA'AT AL-ISLAMIYYA, Algeria's GIA, and several others—reside in the country. In 2001, Yemen was the scene of a spectacular bombing attack on the USS *Cole,* a U.S. military ship in its harbor, suspected to have been carried out by agents connected to OSAMA BIN LADEN.

Reference: *Country Reports on Terrorism.* April 2005. U.S. Department of State Office of the Coordinator for Counterterrorism.

P

Palestine

This is a place that can be defined only with some difficulty. A form of the term *Palestine* was in use when the area was a province of the Roman Empire. There is an uncertain possibility that Palestine is a derivation of the ancient country of Philistinia, the old nemesis of the Israelite kingdom. The term *Palestine* endured during Ottoman times and lasted into the British Mandate during 1922–48.

In the early 20th century Palestine geographically consisted of what is currently the state of ISRAEL, the Gaza Strip and the West Bank, and the Hashemite Kingdom of Jordan. The British Mandate, however, was restricted to the territory west of the Jordan River when Jordan became an independent country in 1922. In 1947, the United Nations authorized the partition of the mandate's territory into Arab and Jewish states. The resulting war enabled Israel to assume control of about three-fourths of the total amount of territory.

An independent Palestinian state is generally expected to consist of most of the West Bank and the Gaza Strip. The Palestinian people are therefore resentful of what they view as a disproportionate partition in which they are expected to accept a much smaller territorial settlement than the one envisioned in the 1947 partition plan. The Palestinians also insist that East Jerusalem, under Israeli jurisdiction since 1967, is their natural capital and that it must be retrieved in any final peace settlement.

The conflict over Palestinian boundaries has frequently resulted in expressions of political terrorism. Some of the terrorism has religious features and motivations that suggest the spiritual association that parts of Palestine, mostly but not restricted to Jerusalem and its environs, hold for Christians (who form nearly 1/12 of Palestine's population) as well as Jews and Muslims.

Demographic pressures are adding to an already complicated economic and political situation. In the territory that comprises Israel, the West Bank, and Gaza—an area that collectively is less than the size of the U.S. state of Georgia—live more than 4 million Arabs and 5 million Jews. The Arab population in this region is one of the fastest growing in the world and by 2020 may exceed the Jewish one. Military occupation by Israel of Arab communities is therefore expected to become less and less tenable. Moreover, an increasingly desperate Arab youth population can be expected to be attracted to extremist movements if their career and financial aspirations are blunted by political and military considerations.

With the Israeli withdrawal of settlements from the Gaza Strip in 2005, authority for governance over this

A Palestinian throws a stone at an Israeli armored vehicle in the northern West Bank, 2006. (GETTY IMAGES)

territory was to be ceded by Israel to the Palestinians. However, continuing violence in Gaza made the transition less than complete, and the subsequent electoral success in 2006 of HAMAS made it even less likely that a new "state" of Palestine would emerge immediately. The erection by Israel of a SECURITY BARRIER that, according to an advisory opinion of the International Court of Justice, breaches international law since it does not follow the "Green Line" of the pre-1967 borders, has also made the creation of a state of Palestine more difficult. Both the territory and the population of a Palestinian state remain undefined under present conditions.

Reference: Shlaim, Avi. *The Iron Wall: Israel and the Arab World* (New York and London: W. W. Norton, 2001).

Palestine Liberation Front (PLF)

The PLF began as a breakaway group from the POPULAR FRONT FOR THE LIBERATION OF PALESTINE–GENERAL COMMAND sometime during the middle 1970s. It is pro–PALESTINE LIBERATION ORGANIZATION (PLO) and was led by Muhammad Abbas (a.k.a. Abu Abbas), a former member of the PLO Executive Committee who was captured by the U.S. forces in Baghdad in April 2003. The PLF has committed attacks against Israel by using hang gliders with mixed success. Its most notorious activity was the 1985 hijacking of the Italian cruise ship, the *ACHILLE LAURO*. An American citizen, Leon Klinghoffer, was murdered in this attack.

Before the *Achille Lauro* attack, the PLF had been based in Tunisia. The Tunisian authorities encouraged the PLF to leave; moreover, the Israelis were believed to have the capability to pursue the PLF there. The PLF moved to IRAQ where it received support from the SADDAM HUSSEIN regime. Iraq furnished nearly all of the PLF's support, though at one point, the PLF did receive support from LIBYA.

After the *Achille Lauro* episode, the American government offered a reward for the apprehension of Muhammad Abbas, who retaliated by offering a reward for the capture of then-president Ronald Reagan. The PLF's strength is unknown, but it is probably composed of a hard-core of a few hundred personnel at the most.

Abu Abbas died of natural causes in April 2004 while in U.S. custody in Iraq. Current leadership and membership of the relatively small PLF appears to be based in Lebanon and the Palestinian territories. The PLF became more active after the start of the al-Aqsa INTIFADA, and several PLF members were arrested by Israeli authorities for planning attacks in Israel and the West Bank.

Reference: National Memorial Institute for the Prevention of Terrorism (MIPT). "Palestine Liberation Front." Available online. URL: http://www.tkb.org/Group.jsp?groupID=157. Accessed February 15, 2006.

Palestine Liberation Organization (PLO)

The PLO was established in 1964 originally as an appendage of the Arab League. By 1969, though, it had become a more or less independent organization as various Palestinian resistance groups, including Fatah, the movement headed by YASIR ARAFAT and the one that tended to dominate the PLO. By the 1970s, the PLO had become an opponent that Israel had to take seriously. The PLO was capable of launching strikes against Israel's civilian population. The PLO not only launched operations against Israel. It became almost a de facto government of the hundreds of thousands of Palestinian refugees who were confined to camps in countries along Israel's borders. The PLO provided both an institutional expression of nationalism and served as a quasi-government, in delivering public services to the refugees.

For much of its history and in the eyes of most Western countries as well as Israel, the PLO was linked to political terrorism. By the late 1980s the PLO had begun to refashion its image. On December 14, 1988, Arafat held a press conference in Switzerland in which he renounced terrorism and accepted Israel's right to exist. A few years later, Arafat's representatives held secret talks in Oslo, Norway, to work out an agreement that would enable Israel to withdraw from parts of the West Bank. The PLO at this point dominated the Palestinian Authority, the political structure that was put in place wherever Israeli authority was withdrawn in Gaza and the West Bank.

The PLO has consistently been an umbrella organization rather than a homogeneous one. Various hardline factions within the PLO still oppose the peace process and argue that Arafat conceded too much to Israel, including its recognition of Israel's existence. This "rejectionist camp" within the PLO is composed of such groups as the Popular Front for the Liberation of Palestine, which remains ideologically leftist. Recently there has been support by Islamic radicals who perceive themselves to be engaged in a relentless struggle to destroy Israel completely. The rejectionist camp adheres to the notion of armed struggle as the only means by which Israel can be dislodged from the West Bank and Gaza.

For much of its existence, the PLO has also operated as a state without territory. Under Arafat's leadership, the PLO tried with some success to be considered by Arab regimes as an evolving Palestinian government and therefore a co-equal in the Arab community. This role had certain advantages, such as providing Arafat a role as the de facto head of state who could deal with other governments. There exists a disadvantage, though, in that the PLO might also come into conflict with the foreign policies of governments it worked with to secure assistance from. For example, the Syrians have often viewed the PLO and Arafat as obstacles to their desire to expand Syrian influence in Lebanon, where both the PLO and Syria had a strong presence. It was in the refugee camps of southern Lebanon that the PLO developed the reputation of being a "state within a state."

The PLO must also contend with rival organizations such as HAMAS and HIZBALLAH. In addition, the PLO may not be at all in tune with the Palestinian people. The first intifada that occurred in 1987 surprised the PLO leadership, most of whom were at the time hundreds of miles away in Tunis. The second intifada of 2000–01 was not completely under the PLO's control either, given the fact that much of the violence was being coordinated by such organizations as ISLAMIC JIHAD.

When Yasir Arafat led the PLO into the peace agreement at Oslo with Israel, the organization renounced terrorism and merged into a political entity, the Palestine Authority (PA), with Arafat as its elected leader. Militant factions of the PLO still existed, but under other names and without the sanction of the PLO leadership who became part of the new political organization. In the early summer of 1993, Arafat, as PA head of government, shook hands with Israeli prime minister Yitzhak Rabin at the White House. The peace process seemed finally underway. The expectation was widespread that the peace process would eventually lead to an independent Palestinian state, governed by the PA.

The optimism that Oslo inspired did not last. Both Israelis and Palestinians had significant numbers of those within their ranks who condemned any negotiation with the other side. Rabin was assassinated in 1995 by a Jewish religious fanatic. Rabin's immediate successor was his foreign minister, Shimon Peres, one of the primary architects of Oslo. Peres, however, was defeated in the 1996 elections by Benjamin Netanyahu, a hard-liner who did not trust Arafat or the newly formed PA and was suspicious of the benefits of any Israeli withdrawals from the territories.

The peace process stalled and eventually broke down completely. Arafat had another opportunity with Ehud Barak, a Rabin protégé who defeated Netanyahu in the 1999 elections. With the encouragement and support of the Clinton administration, Barak offered to Arafat between 95% and 97% of the West Bank, most of East Jerusalem, and all of the Gaza Strip. Arafat refused the offer without providing a counteroffer. The outgoing American president, Bill Clinton, publicly blamed Arafat for the failure of the negotiations. In the 2001 elections, Barak lost in a landslide, unusual for Israeli elections, to Ariel Sharon, the former Israeli general who led the 1982 invasion of Lebanon to destroy the PLO and who expressed regret that he had not killed Arafat in Beirut when he had the opportunity.

The Sharon government gradually reduced Arafat's position to one of powerlessness. The Israeli Defense

Forces almost completely destroyed the Palestine Authority's compound in Ramallah where Arafat lived and worked, and Arafat was understandably afraid to leave the compound for fear the Israelis would not allow him to return. During the Sharon regime, Arafat was basically reduced to house arrest, though he still met with his cabinet and gave interviews to the media. He remained a popular figure with rank-and-file Palestinians because of the defiance shown to Israel's policies and despite the fact that meaningful accomplishments were rare after Oslo. The economy and standard of living of Palestinians steadily deteriorated because of the Israeli reluctance to allow Palestinian workers into Israel, the corruption of PA officials, and President Arafat's refusal or inability to blunt or stop terrorist attacks on Israeli targets that invite retaliatory strikes.

By the summer of 2004, different Palestinian factions began to attack one another in great part because of the rampant corruption, nepotism, and cronyism that seemed characteristic of Arafat's political style. The appointment of a cousin as chief of security in the Gaza Strip was, for many, the last straw. After Palestinians, apparently members of the AL-AQSA MARTYRS' BRIGADE, attacked and burned down a security installation in Gaza, Arafat withdrew the appointment of his cousin. Arafat's second prime minister in only two years, Ahmed Queria, threatened to resign because of an inability to exert control over Palestinian security forces, but Arafat refused to accept the resignation, and Queria was persuaded to stay on at least as the prime minister of a caretaker government. The episode was symptomatic of the increasingly restive members of the Palestinian Authority who were growing weary of the institutionalized corruption that had become pervasive.

With Israeli withdrawal imminent, the strong possibility of a civil war between Islamists in Gaza, such as Hamas, and secular nationalists began to evolve. Arafat's health problems by 2004, when he turned 75, worsened, and by October, he was in a serious quandary as well as seriously ill. He needed to go where he could secure necessary medical treatment, but he had not left his Ramallah compound since 2002 and was afraid to do so because of his conviction that the Israelis would not allow him to return. By November 2004, his health had deteriorated seriously, and he was evacuated to Paris for treatment at a military hospital. The Israeli government guaranteed that he would be allowed to return following recovery.

Reports began to go out in early November that Arafat's condition was critical, and on November 4, a report circulated that he had died, but this report was denied by the hospital where he was receiving his medical treatment. Yasir Arafat was declared dead on November 11, 2004, after he went into a coma and while he was on life support. Mahmoud Abbas, having been elected chairman of the PLA on November 11, was in January of 2005, elected president of Palestine, replacing Arafat as leader of the Palestinians.

Elections for the legislative arm of the PA were held again in early 2006, and Palestinian displeasure with the PA under the old Palestine Liberation Organization leadership was evident in the emergence of the political wing of Hamas as the dominant political party. With this political shift, the PLO as the leadership of the Palestinians in the occupied territories of the West Bank and the Gaza Strip came to an end, leaving Israel and its Western allies confronted again with the question of whether to recognize an organization engaging regularly in terrorism (Hamas) as a legitimate political entity.

Reference: Rubin, Barry. *Revolution until Victory? The Politics and History of the PLO* (Cambridge, Mass.: Harvard University Press, 1994).

Palestinian Islamic Jihad (PIJ)

A militant extremist organization of Palestinians opposed to both the occupation of the Gaza Strip and West Bank by ISRAEL and to the existence of Israel itself. It was established in the Gaza Strip among the most desperate elements in the Israeli-occupied territories. The PIJ is inspired by religious doctrine rather than political ideology. It does not advocate a democratic regime but desires to establish a Palestinian state based upon adherence to Islamic principles.

Israel and the United States, because of its support of Israeli interests, are the primary targets in what the PIJ sees as a holy war against the enemies of Islam. In addition, moderate, pro-Western, and secularized Arab governments have also been targeted. The PIJ considers these regimes as tainted with impurities as a result of their association with Western governments and readiness to compromise or establish normal relations with Israel. The PIJ receives support from both Syria, where it is based, and IRAN.

The PIJ has sponsored suicide bombings against Israeli targets and threatened to do the same against the United States. Its numbers are uncertain but most likely include a hard-core of a few hundred members. The PIJ is opposed to the Israeli-Palestinian peace process and considers the Palestinian Authority to be a betrayal of the Palestinian people.

The group maintained operations in 2004, claiming numerous attacks against Israeli interests. The PIJ continues to direct attacks against Israelis mainly inside Israel and the territories, although U.S. citizens have died in attacks by the PIJ as well.

Reference: National Memorial Institute for the Prevention of Terrorism (MIPT). "Palestinian Islamic Jihad." Available online. URL: http://www.tkb.org/Group.jsp?groupID=82. Accessed February 15, 2006.

Pan Am flight 103 bombing *See* LOCKERBIE, BOMBING OF PAN AM FLIGHT 103.

Party of Democratic Kampuchea *See* KHMER ROUGE (PARTY OF DEMOCRATIC KAMPUCHEA).

pathological terrorists

Some persons kill and terrorize for the sheer joy of terrorizing, not for any "cause" or belief. CHARLES MANSON was perhaps such an individual. Those who commit serial murders are of much the same cast. David Berkowitz, the New York City killer who murdered six young people and wounded seven with a .44-caliber Charter Arms Bulldog revolver, called "Son of Sam" because he said he received "commands" from a man named Sam who lived 6,000 years ago and spoke to him through a dog, was a pathological terrorist.

Berkowitz was in many ways the epitome of this type of killer in the United States during the 1970s: a serial killer, who did indeed create a mood of fear in his audience, committed acts of violence against innocent people but was not necessarily a terrorist in that he often had no political motive. He fit the profile of crazies described by Frederick Hacker, someone whose motive is difficult to understand and hence is called, often inappropriately, a terrorist.

During the 1970s, this type of "terrorist" came in many forms. In addition to 24-year-old Berkowitz, who took instruction from a dog as to whom to kill, there was Ted Bundy, the handsome one-time law student who crossed the country to charm and then murder between 36 and 100 young women, and John Wayne Gacy, a contractor who performed as a clown at children's parties but who also sexually abused and then murdered 33 young men and boys, burying most of them under his house. There was also Jeffrey Dahmer, an ex-chocolate factory worker who lured his victims from bars, bus stops, and shopping malls, then killed them and ate their flesh. The fear and horror generated by these serial killers were real, as was the violence committed and the innocence of the victims. But the motive in most such cases was unclear, and hence the label of "terrorist" cannot always be appropriately applied.

See also CRIMINALS, CRUSADERS, AND CRAZIES, AS TERRORIST TYPES.

People against Gangsterism and Drugs (PAGAD)

This organization was formed in 1996 as a community anticrime group focused on fighting drugs and violence in the Cape Flats section of Cape Town, South Africa. However, by early 1998, PAGAD had also become antigovernment and anti-Western. PAGAD and its Islamic ally QIBLA view the South African government as a threat to Islamic values. Much of its political activity is intended to promote greater political voice for South African Muslims. The group is led by Abdus Salaam Ebrahim.

PAGAD's Gun Force (G-Force) operates in small cells and is believed to be responsible for carrying out acts of terrorism. Specifically, it is suspected of conducting recurring bouts of urban terrorism, in the form of bomb attacks, in Cape Town since 1998, including nine bombings in 2000. Targets for these bombs have included South African authorities, moderate Muslims, synagogues, gay nightclubs, tourist attractions, and Western restaurants. PAGAD is believed to have orchestrated the bombing on August 25, 1998, of the Cape Town Planet Hollywood.

In 2000, a magistrate presiding over a case involving PAGAD members was slain in a drive-by shooting. PAGAD leader Abdus Salaam Ebrahim was convicted in 2002 for public violence and was sentenced to seven years in prison. Since that time, PAGAD has been less active in the Cape Town Muslim community.

Reference: National Memorial Institute for the Prevention of Terrorism (MIPT). "People against Gangsterism and Drugs (PAGAD).” Available online. URL: http://www.tkb.org/Group.jsp?groupID=4194. Accessed February 15, 2006.

personal security

The issue of personal security for persons at risk from terrorist attack, by virtue of the position they hold in a government, corporation, or social system, involves minimizing the likelihood of successful access to the person. Most governments, and many large multinational corporations, provide security forces, and often security training, to improve the personal security of these prospective targets.

For those most likely to be targets of terrorist attacks, such as heads of state, ambassadors, and heads of large corporations, significant effort is usually made to create counteractive procedures for terrorist attacks. These include, but are not limited to:

1. Special protection for high-threat individuals. In the United States, this involves the use of the Secret Service to provide special protection for the president and other high-ranking members of the government.
2. Development of individual crisis management files. Since information about individuals and groups that pose potential threats to the person being protected is essential, creating files that organize the documents related to each potential crisis, and proposed resolution of such event, is vital to establish a managed response to terrorism.
3. Special antiterrorism devices for some individuals. This can include the wearing of bulletproof vests, travel in specially armored vehicles, scanners designed to detect the presence of weapons, and many other such devices.
4. Randomization of travel routes. Since a successful terrorist attack would depend to some degree on an ability to predict routes of entry and exit, as well as schedules of travel, persuading or requiring the person at risk to randomize his/her travel route to and from the office can be a very useful tool in counterterror action.
5. Maintenance of a low profile. While most high-ranking government officials cannot and will not maintain a low profile, and few leaders of business are willing to be less “visible” to the general public, personal security can be enhanced by an effort to make one less easily identifiable as the desired target. Thus, riding inside of a car instead of in an open-topped vehicle, wearing casual clothes instead of business attire or dress uniform, entering by the back door instead of up the front steps are examples of measures suggested by security forces for those in need of personal security.
6. Alerting law enforcement agencies about possible threats perceived. This entails reporting threatening calls or letters, encounters, or relevant information about individuals or groups posing a threat of terrorist attack on the individual.

In developing personal security measures to meet these potential attacks, the individuals or groups responsible for providing such security usually set up periodic training for all personnel involved in this personal security process. Consideration is given to the level of risk for different individuals. This involves not only the rank or position of the individual but also their current location and the credibility of the threats made against them. Thus, while an ambassador might not have a high level of risk in one country, in another the risk might be quite high; and a general in the military might have a very low risk factor on his home base but a much higher risk level in certain countries at particular times. Thus, this risk analysis is a constantly changing dynamic.

Evaluation is also made, with respect to personal security, of the different types of threats that could be posed. Letter bombs, assassination attempts, bombs in vehicles, poison—clearly the attack could take a wide variety of forms. Assessment then must include the vulnerability to many different types of attack, and security planned for as many as possible, depending on the credibility of the threat posed.

Finally, personnel responsible for the personal security are encouraged to be constantly aware of the pre-incident PHASE OF A TERRORIST INCIDENT. During this phase, reconnaissance of the target is effected. If personnel are aware that individuals or groups may be investigating them while they are planning an attack, then that awareness may offer insight into an attack before it can occur.

Personal security, while vital, is impossible to effect completely. A determined terrorist can, in most cases, breach this security in an attack, particularly if the individual is willing to die for his/her cause, simply because few people can have complete personal security in effect 24-hours each day, every day of the year. Taking measures to improve personal security lessens, while not preventing, the likelihood of a successful terrorist attack on the target.

Examining the actions taken to provide personal security to high-value targets during the attacks on September 11, 2001, in the United States offers insights into the application of the guidelines suggested here.

At the time when the second plane crashed into the south tower, President George W. Bush was meeting with second-graders in an elementary school in Sarasota, Florida. After being briefed on the unfolding situation by his National Security Advisor Condoleezza Rice and his chief of staff Andrew Card, the president concluded his talk with the children while *Air Force One* was rechecked by bomb-sniffing dogs and another fighter escort was added to his entourage. Aboard *Air Force One,* Bush was in his office in the front of the plane consulting over the phone with his vice president, Dick Cheney; Rice; the FBI director Robert Mueller; and his wife, Laura, back in Washington, D.C. About 45 minutes into the flight, a decision was made to fly to Offut Air Force Base in Nebraska, site of the nation's nuclear command and one of the most secure military installations in the country. After a brief touchdown at Barksdale Air Force Base outside of Shreveport, Louisiana, for a brief press conference, with full military security, the president was taken to Offut, where he remained for almost 24 hours.

Enhanced personal security for Vice President Cheney was also a priority at this time. Within two minutes of the crash of the plane into the Pentagon, a "credible threat" forced the evacuation of the White House, and eventually State, Justice, and all of the federal office buildings. Vice President Cheney was in his West Wing office when the Secret Service agents burst in and physically rushed him out of the room. They hurried him into a bunker on the White House grounds, along with the National Security staff and other administration officials, Mrs. Cheney, and Mrs. Bush.

While the gridlock in evacuation of office workers and other civilians from the Washington, D.C., area indicated that the plans for such an evacuation needed serious work, the actions to secure the personal safety of the chief of state and his closest advisers were executed with efficiency and precision. Senator Robert Byrd, the Senate's president pro tempore and fourth in line to the presidency, was put in a chauffeured car and driven to a safe house, as were House Speaker Dennis Hastert and other congressional leaders. The government's leadership was moved, as quickly and efficiently as possible, to more secure quarters until the situation was clarified, and the personal safety of these officials was made a priority by their staff.

Reference: Schneier Bruce. *Beyond Fear: Thinking Sensibly about Security in an Uncertain World* (New York: Springer Verlag, 2003).

Peru *See* OPERATION CHAVÍN DE HUÁNTAR; OVERVIEW OF TERRORISM, BY REGION; SENDERO LUMINOSO; TÚPAC AMARU REVOLUTIONARY MOVEMENT.

phases of a terrorist incident

Study of modern terrorist incidents has indicated that most incidents evolve according to a sequence entailing from three to five different stages. Most terrorist incidents first entail a preincident phase, in which the group or individual planning the act engages in reconnaissance and often a rehearsal of the event. Having assessed the training topics and chosen tactics of terrorists, it is also useful to note the patterns that have emerged in modern terrorist incidents. Much of what was taught in the training camps is clearly used in the structuring of an incident itself, at least by well-trained operatives.

Since it is clear that some organizations, such as al-Qaeda, have very intelligent and organized lieutenants orchestrating the training of operatives, it should not be surprising to find that modern, well-planned terrorist incidents often have five discernible phases, which for the purpose of this study will be called: pre-incident, initiation, negotiation, termination, and post-incident. Each of these stages deserves attention, for each offers both insights into the sophistication of the group carrying out the operation and indicators that might be useful to law-enforcement personnel seeking to prevent or resolve such incidents.

In the pre-incident phase, the individuals or groups planning the incident will generally carry out two important functions: intelligence gathering and rehearsal of the event. At this point, nothing illegal has yet occurred. Members of the group are gathering information about the target, making plans for the attack, and often rehearsing the event before it is initiated. At this stage, training in clandestine travel and intelligence gathering becomes useful, as does training in evaluation of security systems and access routes.

Five Phases of a Terrorist Event

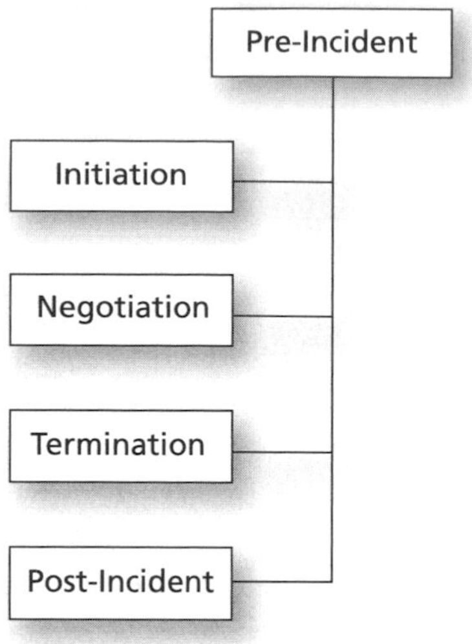

This phase differs from the others in one critical respect: No law has yet been openly violated, and therefore surveillance and intervention by law enforcement is difficult to justify. Unless the intelligence gathering and rehearsal offer sufficient evidence for an investigation—for example, there is information about the group or plot *before* the incident, or the individuals are careless and/or ill-trained in their intelligence-gathering efforts—intervention by law enforcement at this point is difficult. This issue will be pursued in more depth in the discussion later about U.S. efforts to expand law-enforcement capabilities in this area, particularly with the so-called USA PATRIOT ACT.

Phase two, the initiation phase, entails exactly what it suggests: the beginning of the implementation of the incident. This involves moving the individuals involved to the location(s) necessary for the event, as well as any equipment needed. During this phase, a diversion is also planned, by the more well-organized groups, to draw the attention of law enforcement and the media away from the intended target. Thus, those seeking to protect the public from the planned attack may have to be able to discern between the real target and the diversion, during this initiation stage.

The third phase, negotiation, does not occur in every terrorist incident. If there is only the placing of a bomb or the driving of a truck filled with explosives to a desired target, there may well be no negotiation phase, since there is nothing to discuss about the act. This phase occurs when an individual or group has a demand (or a list of demands) to communicate and is willing to talk to someone in authority about meeting those demands. Generally, this involves either the taking and negotiated release of hostages and/or the threatened detonation of a bomb or other weapon capable of mass destruction. During this phase, the training that members of the group have received in the making of explosives, and in the framing of demands for ransom or release of prisoners, can significantly impact the flow of events.

What often appears to be the final stage, called here the termination phase, is not actually the end of the event in most cases today. This phase simply involves either the escape, surrender/capture, or death of the individuals involved in the incident. Here, planning for a backdoor escape, a diversion to draw some of the attention away to allow this escape, or a demand that includes safe passage for the perpetrators, often depends on the quality of training and experience the terrorists have.

It is important to note here that for law enforcement, the primary focus is usually on the safety of the hostages, not the capture or killing of the criminals. If the event is handled by a military authority, however, the focus is most often on the capture or death of the individuals responsible. Thus, the success of this phase may depend on the nature of the enforcement officials seeking to end the incident.

The final phase is in many respects the most important, and, unfortunately, the least understood. In the post-incident phase, the remaining members of the group that planned the attack will regroup to *learn* from the mistakes as well as the successes of the incident. By studying what went right and what went wrong in the event, groups learn how law enforcement met the challenges and can then plan how to exploit the weakness of those protecting the public. The group members, in fact, do what military forces do in their debriefing after an incident.

The important point here is that terrorists learn from mistakes, and from successes, and use those lessons in the next plans. While they may be copycat perpetrators who will repeat the group's initial mistakes, the perpetrators, if they are well organized and trained, will not repeat their errors. Thus, if security forces only copy the attacks made by groups in planning security, they will miss a critical point, since no future attack by that group will be just like the one that occurred. Instead, the next incident will reflect the learning curve of the group from its post-incident evaluation.

Reference: Bolz, Frank, Jr. *The Counterterrorism Handbook: Tactics, Procedures and Techniques, Third Edition* (Boca Raton, Fla.: CRC Press, 2005).

physical security

One vital aspect of counterterrorist efforts made by governments, corporations, and other organizations involves strengthening the physical security of the threatened facility. Physical security has as its objective the hardening of the target against which an attack may be made. Although there is no "master plan" for successful physical security measures against terrorist attacks, there are a few conditions and countermeasures that have begun to be accepted by governments and businesses engaged in this effort.

Both of these communities, increasingly aware that security against terrorism must extend beyond the level of normal crime prevention, are focusing on extraordinary physical security measures. Physical security, confronted by terrorists who are not "common" criminals but who instead possess too often a willingness to sacrifice innocent lives and to die in their attacks, has begun to evolve into complex patterns in the 21st century.

To determine what, if any, extraordinary security measures are needed to protect against a terrorist attack, government and business communities have employed a number of relatively ordinary tactics. A physical security survey, by professionals who are aware of the dangers in a particular area or to a particular business or region, is standard procedure. This approach has, in recent years, begun to include the use of penetration teams whose job it is to discover "holes" in security systems through which other teams, such as terrorist attack teams, could possibly penetrate and sabotage or destroy the target.

The penetration team, or the organization conducting the physical security survey, can suggest the use of certain devices that have proven to be effective in guarding against attack or sabotage. For example, a wide variety of intrusion detection devices are on the market today. Alternatively, an evaluation could emphasize the importance of such factors as lighting, access control, or physical security and access control codes. Advice might include precluding use of surreptitious approaches by increased lighting in entryways, fences, hallways, and other points of access. Greater access control is often recommended since physical security measures usually focus on access control, including the limitation of the number of individuals cleared to work in the facility as a whole or in a specific and sensitive part of the operation. One of the most common recommendations regarding enhanced physical security is that security and access codes be changed fairly frequently to make penetration more difficult. The use of guards, or even specially trained counterterrorist guards, is another increasingly attractive physical security option advised by assessment teams.

Examining the problems, and the new demands, of physical security in the wake of the events of 9/11 offers useful insights into the strengths—and weaknesses—that still exist in the United States, in spite of massive efforts by the new Department of Homeland Security to improve security. Some experts suggest that commercial aviation was used as the "weapon" in the attacks of 9/11 precisely because of convenient flaws that existed within the security system of this industry. A quick look at a few of these weaknesses will illuminate the logic of this claim.

Ease of Access to the Cockpit

Since none of the 9/11 pilots had the pilots or copilots informing air-traffic controllers that they were being hijacked, and since the planes were turned into "missiles" flown deliberately into facilities on the ground, it seems reasonable to assume that the terrorists were able to take over the cockpits. This was probably done in one of three patterns: by stealth, by the use of sudden overwhelming force, or by creating a disturbance that drew one of the crew to exit the cockpit and thereby gave access to the flight deck for the hijackers.

Taking the cockpit by stealth would require access to a key to the cockpit of the plane. Unfortunately, prior to 9/11, every flight attendant was required by the standards of the Federal Aviation Authority (FAA) to carry such a key at all times. On American flight 11 (the first plane to fly into the World Trade Center on that day), one of the flight attendants reported that two flight attendants had been stabbed. The second plane to fly into the WTC, United flight 175, also reported that one flight attendant had been stabbed, and two had been killed. Since each of these attendants had a key to the cockpit, it is reasonable to assume that the terrorists were able to take the cockpit by stealth.

As one expert noted, prior to the events of 9/11, "a normal-sized man with a karate kick or a shoulder shove could have broken down a cockpit door without too much exertion." Numerous examples of this weakness were reported by news agencies, including attacks

An officer with a bomb-sniffing dog patrols in front of the U.S. District Court of Virginia, 2006. (GETTY IMAGES)

by a passenger on a Boeing 747-400 British Airways flight from London to Nairobi in December 2000 and by a young couple on a flight in February 2001 from Miami to New York. In these, as in so many other cases, the passengers were able to breach the cockpit by force—and neither incident involved a large or well-trained attacker.

Finally, it was possible to take the cockpit by creating a distracting disturbance in the passenger area. This security weakness was possible because pilots were instructed, in the event of a disruptive incident in the passenger cabin, to intervene personally by leaving the cockpit and confronting the disruptive passenger. This instruction may have led to access for the terrorists on 9/11. After the United flight crashed into the WTC, the operations center in Chicago sent an electronic text message to the airliners (including United flight 93) that read: beware, cockpit intrusion. This message could have been interpreted by the flight crew as an air rage incident, requiring that the pilot exit the cabin to confront the problem. The pilots responded to confirm receipt of the message, and a few minutes later, the plane was taken over by four terrorists. The policy of having the pilot exit the cockpit to confront may have facilitated the seizure of the aircraft.

Inadequate Screening Processes

As noted earlier, the screening process for passengers and luggage prior to the events of 9/11 was seriously flawed. Perhaps the most obvious evidence of the flaws in this process lies in the handling of at least half of the 19 hijackers. Consider the following:

- Nine of the hijackers were selected for special security screenings on the morning of 9/11.
- Of these, six were chosen for extra security by a computerized screening system.
- Two others were singled out because of irregularities in their documents.
- One was listed on ticket documents as the travel companion to one who had questionable identification.

Yet they were all, in the end, allowed to board their flights, since on 9/11, FAA security regulations required that passengers selected for further screening were only required to have their *checked* baggage further evaluated for possible weapons. Since only one or two of the terrorists actually checked any luggage, there would be no reason for the security process in place at that time to detect the weapons in the carry-on luggage of the terrorists. Clearly, the process needed refining.

While airport security clearly had flaws prior to these attacks, this demonstration of the dreadful consequences of airline hijacking dramatized the issue and forced the government and the industry to rapidly reassess and reorganize to reassure the public. The attacks, as noted earlier, caused airports across the country to be shut down, in an effort to prevent further hijackings. It took several days before the airports could be fully reopened. In the meantime, thousands of passengers were stranded at airports to which their flights had been diverted when the closings were ordered.

Moreover, the United States learned that the 9/11 hijackers cased airports in the weeks prior to the attacks, taking test runs on flights to identify weaknesses within the system.

Confronted with the task of both reassuring the public that it was safe to fly and immediately taking effective measures to ensure (as far as possible) that such hijackings did not occur again, the government and industry took several rapid steps to achieve both goals, at least in part. These included

1. Banning curb-side check-in of luggage
2. Severely limiting the use of e-ticketing
3. Restricting access to areas beyond the security scanning checkpoints to ticketed passengers only
4. Assigning members of the National Guard to offer visible security at the checkpoints

Not all of these initial steps remained permanent or even universally applied at all airports, but they represented a significant effort to improve airport security and the public's perception of that security. At some airports, scrutiny of handbags and carry-on luggage was intense and resulted in the confiscation of fingernail files, pocket knives, letter openers, and a variety of other potential "weapons." Since those who carried out the hijackings in September did not use guns, apparently, or other conventional weapons for which baggage-handlers had been trained to scan, this represented a serious change in the perception of dangerous personal items on the part of airport personnel.

Moreover, new potential threats continued to emerge, challenging previous patterns of security operations at airports. The potential of explosives in shoes became evident with the attempt of an individual to "light" what appeared to be a fuse attached to his shoes on a flight from Paris. Subsequently, airports at several major points around the country began to require passengers to submit to a scanning of their shoes for explosives.

The fact that the people who seized control of the airplanes were not initiating a conventional "hijacking" situation also demonstrated a need to change security patterns. Pilots had been trained to cooperate, if possible, with hijackers, in efforts to get them to let the plane land in order to offer opportunities for negotiation or hostage-rescue operations. The cockpits of the planes were seldom equipped with locking systems that would prevent such a takeover of the plane by skilled pilots. Thus, the pilots' training had to be revised, and mechanisms have now been added to most passenger planes that enable the cockpit to be secured from the inside against passengers, if necessary.

Moreover, physical security is still not completely effective. Weapons experts have testified before Congress about the possibility of smuggling guns through metal detectors, by carrying them on certain spots on the body. Nor are metal detectors, on which much airline physical security relies, effective at all heights. Although some airports now have technology to detect explosive materials, it is expensive and therefore will not be used in all airports. Training in the search for explosive materials, too, is not yet effective. A gentleman whose shoes showed evidence of explosive materials was stopped in January 2002 at the San Francisco airport and then allowed to walk away before security personnel could check it out, resulting in a shutdown of flights for several hours as airport security tried to locate the individual, without success.

There was not a system, until after the events in September, in place to x-ray checked baggage on domestic flights, according to the FAA. The argument was made that the volume of such baggage is too high and that many weapons which are forbidden in carry-on baggage (for which the current detectors are designed) are still permitted on checked baggage. After those events, a program to match luggage with passenger flight manifests has been instituted, but only for the first check-in point. Unless all checked baggage is tested for weapons/explosives, then a person could still get a bomb into a plane in checked luggage if his/her flight had at least one stop where the passenger could disembark, leaving the luggage (and the bomb) on the next leg of the flight. The argument against the more comprehensive scanning and baggage-matching scheme continues to be that it is too expensive, in terms of time and money, but the Transportation Safety Administration is beginning to draft and implement rules to make more comprehensive scanning and matching mandatory.

Physical security is dependent upon other types of security, including OPERATIONAL SECURITY and PERSONAL SECURITY. Fortress walls, barbed fences, and barred gates are not, in modern times, either reasonable or sufficient protection against determined terrorists. Such overt physical security measures are, moreover, very unpopular measures for governments (who want to be viewed as accessible to their constituents) and businesses (who need to foster good public relations images). A combination of all of these aspects of security, tailored to the situation and specific needs, is sought by both types of agencies.

piracy, as a form of terrorism

The term "crimes against humanity" that was used to describe war crimes at Nuremberg did not originate with laws of war but with laws of peace. The term was used in international legal writings to describe acts of piracy. The English jurist, Sir Edward Coke, during the reign of James I, described pirates as *hostis humanis generis,* meaning "common enemies of mankind."

National case law confirms this view of piracy as an international crime. The U.S. Supreme Court, in the case of *U.S. v. Smith* (1820), went on record through Mr. Justice Joseph Story as declaring piracy to be "an offense against the law of nations" and a pirate to be "an enemy of the human race." Judge John Bassett Moore of the World Court reaffirmed this assessment in his opinion in the famous *Lotus* case (1927).

In fact, from the Paris Declaration of 1856 to the Geneva Convention of 1958, the proliferation of treaties dealing with aspects of terror-violence on the high seas has helped to codify international law with regard to piracy. Piracy—of the sea—is one of the first and most universally recognized "international crimes." The following definition of piracy is contained in article 101 of the 1982 United Nations Convention on the Law of the Sea (UNCLOS):

> Piracy consists of any of the following acts:
> (a) any illegal acts of violence or detention, or any act of depredation, committed for private ends by the crew or the passengers of a private ship or a private aircraft, and directed—
> (i) on the high seas, against another ship or aircraft, or against persons or property on board such ship or aircraft
> (ii) against a ship, aircraft, persons or property in a place outside the jurisdiction of any State;
> (b) any act of voluntary participation in the operation of a ship or of an aircraft with knowledge of facts making it a pirate ship or aircraft;
> (c) any act of inciting or of intentionally facilitating an act described in subparagraph (a) or (b).

Nations have not been so willing to deal, through international law, with modern SKYJACKING, which some legal experts have termed "air piracy." Robert Friedlander suggested that the legal status of aerial hijackers could become the same as sea pirates through the process of NOVATION wherein the former would be presumed to stand in the shoes of the latter. This provides a way to bring perpetrators of the modern crime of skyjacking under the existing legal restrictions and penalties imposed on crimes of a similar nature, such

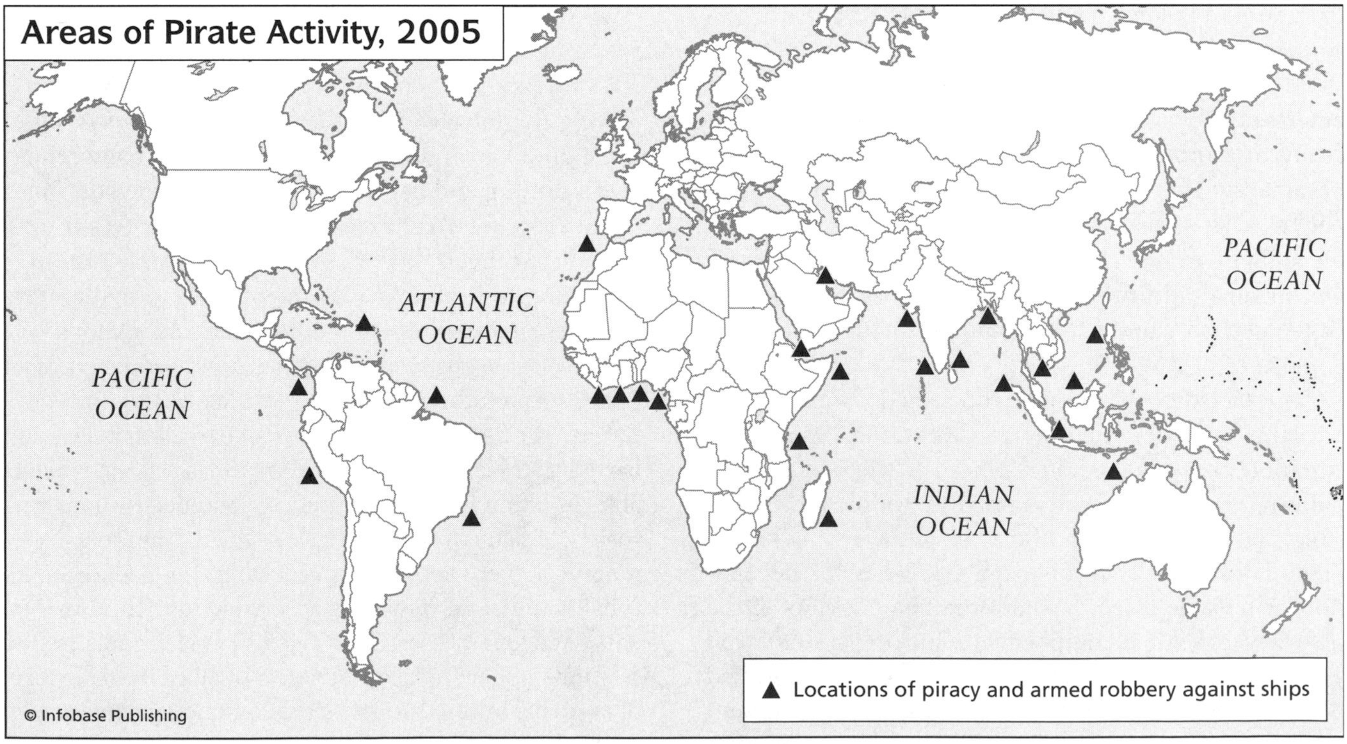

as sea piracy, which were more common at an earlier date.

The Convention for the Suppression of Unlawful Seizure of Aircraft, signed at The Hague on December 16, 1970, offers a definition for the actions that may constitute the offense of skyjacking. Article 1 states that any person commits an offense who on board an aircraft in flight:

1. Unlawfully, by force or threat thereof, or by any other means of intimidation, seizes, or exercises control of, that aircraft, or attempts to perform any such act; or,
2. Is an accomplice of a person who performs or attempts to perform any such act.

Modern acts of piracy continue to occur, including the seizure of ships and planes. Three conventions dealing with skyjacking have been enacted, supplementing those in existence concerning piracy of the sea. The hijacking of the *ACHILLE LAURO* brought to international attention the potential for the latter crime in modern times, while the numerous seizures and/or destruction of aircraft prompted the enaction of the three new conventions on this newer form of piracy. Moreover, in the intense shipping areas near the South China Sea, piracy has emerged again as both a large enterprise by wealthy groups and a small-scale endeavor by desperate individuals whose poverty has driven them to this extreme. Other piracy hotspots are Bangladesh, Nigeria, and Somalia. In September 2005, a cruise ship carrying 302 passengers sailing off the coast of Somalia successfully evaded gunmen in speedboats that opened fire on the terrified passengers. Somalia alone had 19 incidents of piracy during 2005 in its coastal waters. The International Maritime Bureau (IMB) reported that in a nine-month period during 2005, worldwide pirates boarded 141 ships, of which 15 were fired upon and 11 were hijacked.

See also LOCKERBIE, BOMBING OF PAN AM FLIGHT 103; TWA FLIGHT 847.

References: Burnett, John S. *Dangerous Waters: Modern Piracy and Terror on the High Seas* (New York: Penguin Group, 2003); Luft, Gal, and Anne Korin. "Terrorism Goes to Sea." *Foreign Affairs* (November/December 2004). Institute for the Analysis of Global Security. Available online. URL: http://www.iags.org/fa2004.html. Accessed March 22, 2006; United Nations. International Maritime Organization. "Piracy and Armed Robbery against Ships." Available online. URL: http://www.imo.org/home.asp. Accessed March 28, 2006.

plastic weapons

The development, during the latter years of the 20th century, of plastic weapons, particularly handguns, is potentially a security nightmare. Cost-efficient, undetectable, with a potentially long life span, a plastic weapon would be in many ways an ideal weapon. It cannot be discovered in ordinary metal detectors, because of the absence of metal. Plastics and ceramics can also be used to make knives as sharp as the metal version but invisible to metal detectors.

Fear of where this new technology could lead prompted the U.S. government to pass the 1988 Undetectable Firearms Act, which supposedly banned the sale and manufacture of plastic guns. However, as a concession to gun makers to get the bill passed, any plastic gun that had over a certain amount of metal was still considered legal. Since there was no working firearm on the market that was made from 100% plastic—so-called "plastic" guns such as the Glock pistol have always had some metal parts—the law in effect accomplished nothing. In addition, many weapons experts point out that there is no firearm that is invisible to metal detectors (at least from known gun manufacturers), and in any case the ammunition would also have to be made of a nonmetallic substance to pass. Yet spy organizations such as the CIA and Great Britian's MI6 are known to have developed firearms (as well as other weapons) for their own agents that (in theory) could pass ordinary airport screening methods. However, as a result of the September 11, 2001, ATTACK ON AMERICA—in which the hijackers were able to use simple box-cutters to accomplish their goals—AIRPORT SECURITY has increased the accuracy of its searches by using special X-ray "scatter" machines that can detect hidden objects regardless of substance or method of concealment.

Pol Pot

See KHMER ROUGE (PARTY OF DEMOCRATIC KAMPUCHEA).

Popular Front for the Liberation of Palestine (PFLP)

Founded in 1967 in the immediate aftermath of the Six-Day War by George Habbash, a pediatrician. The PFLP is ideologically based on Marxist-Leninism and has been a hard-line opponent of ISRAEL. In 1993 the PFLP announced its opposition to the just-concluded Declaration of Principles between Israel and the Palestinian Authority. It also suspended its relationship with the PALESTINE LIBERATION ORGANIZATION (PLO), the umbrella organization for most Palestinian groups resisting Israel. The PFLP does cooperate with Fatah, YASIR ARAFAT's organization, in an effort to maintain the national unity of Palestinians.

The PFLP has been consistently and adamantly opposed to negotiations between Palestinian representatives and Israel. It has committed several terrorist attacks against Israeli targets but also against Arab targets that display a perspective of moderation and compromise toward Israel. The PFLP has received assistance from the Syrian government and has been successful in recruiting activists from refugee camps in LEBANON. The current strength of the PFLP is under 1,000 personnel. It has operated in the Occupied Territories of the West Bank and in Israel itself.

During the 1970s, and 1980s, the PFLP was considerably more active than during the 1990s. This decline may have to do with Habbash's own questionable health.

The PFLP stepped up its operational activity since the start of the second INTIFADA, highlighted by at least two suicide bombings since 2003, multiple joint operations with other Palestinian groups, and the assassination of the Israeli tourism minister in 2001 to avenge Israel's killing of the PFLP secretary-general earlier that year.

References: Alexander, Yonah. *Palestinian Secular Terrorism* (Ardsley, N.Y.: Transnational Publishers, 2003); National Memorial Institute for the Prevention of Terrorism (MIPT). "Popular Front for the Liberation of Palestine (PFLP)." Available online. URL: http://www.tkb.org/Group.jsp?groupID=85. Accessed February 15, 2006.

Popular Front for the Liberation of Palestine–General Command (PFLP-GC)

This group comprises a splinter organization that separated from the POPULAR FRONT FOR THE LIBERATION OF PALESTINE (PFLP) in 1968 soon after the PFLP was formed. However, the PFLP-GC does not see itself as a rival to the PFLP. Rather, the PFLP-GC prefers to emphasize the military aspect of the struggle with ISRAEL and let other Palestinian groups deal with political questions. It is one of the more militant Palestinian resistance groups and has close ties to and receives support from both Syria and IRAN. The PFLP-GC is one of the more imaginative groups and has attacked Israelis with the use of hot-air balloons and motorized hang gliders. Its leader, Ahmad Jabril, is Syrian, not Palestinian. Most of its strength, however, is Palestinian and numbers in the several hundreds.

The PFLP-GC has rejected the peace process between Israel and the Palestinian Authority. Like the PFLP, it regards Israel as an illegitimate political entity that should not be negotiated with. The PFLP-GC has long been headquartered in Damascus and is strongly influenced by Syrian policies toward Israel.

References: Alexander, Yonah. *Palestinian Secular Terrorism* (Ardsley, N.Y.: Transnational Publishers, 2003); National Memorial Institute for the Prevention of Terrorism (MIPT). "Popular Front for the Liberation of Palestine–General Command (PFLP-GC)." Available online. URL: http://www.tkb.org/Group.jsp?groupID=148. Accessed February 15, 2006.

Posse Comitatus

The term is Latin for "power to the country" and originated during medieval times in England. There and in the western United States during the 19th century, posses were assembled by local or county sheriffs to capture criminals and bring them to trial. The current version established chapters during the 1980s in the midwestern and western states. Its basic ideology considers the federal government under Jewish control and the Federal Reserve Bank the creature of the "international Jewish banking conspiracy." Posse Comitatus does not recognize any authority higher than county sheriffs.

The Posse's members have been involved in counterfeiting and arms dealing. One of its heroes and principal martyrs is Gordon Wendell Kahl (1920–83). Kahl, a World War II veteran, was arrested for income tax evasion, convicted, and served time. He was released on probation but continued to refuse to pay taxes. In a shoot-out with U.S. marshals, Kahl shot and killed two law enforcement officers and wounded two others. After several months, Kahl was tracked down and killed by state and federal law officers. The shootout inspired Posse memberships and became the impetus for a successful movie based on Kahl's career.

Posse Comitatus is somewhat less active than it was in the 1980s. However, it has gradually become an umbrella organization for a variety of NEO-NAZI and anti-Semitic groups. All of them share a relentless hatred of the federal government, which they believe is undermining the original intent of the U.S. Constitution and has fallen under the influence or outright control of anti-Christian and Satanic forces.

References: Kusher, Harvey W. *Terrorism in America: A Structured Approach to Understanding the Terrorist Threat* (Springfield, Ill.: Charles C. Thomas Publisher, 1998), 64–68; National Memorial Institute for the Prevention of Terrorism (MIPT). "Sheriff's Posse Comitatus." Available online. URL: http://www.tkb.org/Group.jsp?groupID=110. Accessed February 15, 2006.

Prevention of Terrorism Act (Temporary Provisions) *See* UNITED KINGDOM ANTI-TERROR LEGISLATION.

privateers *See* PIRACY, AS A FORM OF TERRORISM.

Provisional Irish Republican Army (PIRA) *See* IRISH REPUBLICAN ARMY.

Q

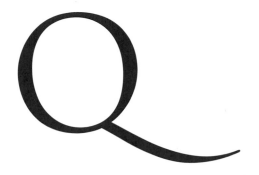

al-Qadhafi, Mu'ammar (1942–)
Mu'ammar al-Qadhafi is a Libyan army colonel who took power in September 1969 as the head of the Revolutionary Command Council of Libya after ending the country's monarchy. After Castro, Qadhafi is the longest-serving dictator. His hero and model was Gamal Abdul Nasser (1918–70), who came to power in Egypt in similar circumstances. Like Nasser, Qadhafi has taken in the past a hard line against the United States and ISRAEL. Qadhafi has been linked to several terrorist groups that targeted American personnel and installations, groups that he supported and financed. However, relations with the United States have improved since Libya agreed in 2003 to dismantle its clandestine nuclear weapons under international inspection.

During his more than three decades in power, Qadhafi has supported different organizations associated with terrorist activities, including the IRISH REPUBLICAN ARMY (in great part because of their shared dislike of British government policies) and the BAADER-MEINHOF gang. He has selectively supported Palestinian groups, including at one point the PALESTINE LIBERATION ORGANIZATION (PLO), that are opposed to peace with Israel. Support from Qadhafi takes the form of money, logistics, training camps, and refuge. (He has harbored individual terrorists, including CARLOS "THE JACKAL" at one time.) Israelis strongly and, apparently from the evidence thus far discovered, accurately suspected Qadhafi of involvement with and support of the terrorists who perpetrated the 1972 Munich Olympics massacre of Israeli athletes.

In April 1986, the United States launched an air attack on Libya in retaliation for this support of anti-American terrorism. Many observers, both American and Libyan, believe that Qadhafi himself was a target. His regime was also linked with the terrorist bombing of Pan Am flight 103 in 1988. The Lockerbie trial began in 2000 and ended in 2001, resulting in one guilty and one nonguilty verdict. In 2003, Libya reached a $2.7 billion settlement with families of the victims of the Pan Am bombing.

During his career, Qadhafi has not enjoyed the best of relations with most other Arab regimes. The late Egyptian president Anwar Sadat is reputed to have called Qadhafi "crazy." Qadhafi resented the remark and unsuccessfully attempted to have Sadat assassinated. His regime has been resented and feared by the more conservative governments that neighbor or are in close proximity to Libya in North Africa. During the 1980s, Qadhafi attempted to invade Chad, a country on its southern border. Libyan forces were quickly routed by Chad forces, generally considered inferior by military experts. Qadhafi authored the *Green Book,* a collection of observations based on Islamic teachings that prescribes proper daily behavior on the part of Muslims. However, most of Libya's Muslim population does not subscribe to a fundamentalist interpretation of Islamic law. An attempt by the terror group Libyan Islamic Fighting Force to assassinate Qadhafi in 1998 led to a crackdown on Islamic fundamentalist groups.

Reference: Simons, Geoff. *Libya and the West: From Independence to Lockerbie* (New York: I. B. Tauris, 2003).

al-Qaeda

Al-Qaeda is a multinational organization, with members from many countries and with a global presence. Senior leaders of this group are also the senior leaders of other terrorist organizations, such as the Egyptian AL-GAMA'AT AL-ISLAMIYYA and the EGYPTIAN ISLAMIC JIHAD. As leaders of this networked group, al-Qaeda's leaders seek a global radicalization of existing Islamic groups and the establishment of radical Islamic groups where none currently exist.

This group was established by OSAMA BIN LADEN in the late 1980s, bringing together Arabs who fought together in Afghanistan against the Soviet invasion. During this struggle against the Soviet-supported regime, bin Laden used this group to finance, recruit, transport, and train Sunni Islamic extremists for the Afghan resistance forces. Its goal, since the end of the struggle in Afghanistan against the Soviets, has been to unite all Muslims and to establish a government that follows the rule of the caliphs. Bin Laden has stated that the only way to establish the caliphate is by force. To this end, al-Qaeda works with allied Islamic extremist groups to overthrow regimes it deems "non-Islamic," to drive Western influence from Muslim countries, and ultimately to abolish state boundaries.

The long-term goal of establishing a pan-Islamic caliphate throughout the world is reflected in the statement issued by the group under the banner of "The World Islamic Front for Jihad against the Jews and Crusaders" in February 1998, which stated that it was the duty of all Muslims to kill citizens of the United States, both civilian and military, as well as their allies everywhere. Having merged with the Egyptian Islamic Jihad in June 2001, al-Qaeda continues to train, finance, and provide logistical support to groups that support these goals today.

With the strength of several thousand members, this group has carried out a number of spectacular bombing and assassination attempts. It claims to have shot down U.S. helicopters and killed U.S. servicemen in Somalia in 1993, during the food-relief effort supported by the U.S. military. It also claims to have been responsible for three bombings focused on U.S. troop presence in Aden, Yemen, in December 1992.

This group is believed to have been responsible in August 1998 for the bombings of the U.S. embassies in Nairobi, Kenya, and Dar es Salaam, Tanzania. These bombings claimed the lives of at least 301 people and injured more than 5,000 others. Al-Qaeda also directed the October 12, 2000, attack on the USS *Cole* in the port of Aden that killed 17 U.S. Navy members and injured another 39.

On September 11, 2001, this group was responsible for the ATTACK ON AMERICA, when 19 al-Qaeda suicide attackers hijacked four U.S. commercial jets. Two of these jets were crashed into the World Trade Center in New York City, one into the Pentagon near Washington, D.C., and a fourth into a field in Pennsylvania, leaving about 3,000 individuals dead or missing. Since bin Laden and his key lieutenants in al-Qaeda maintained training camps in Afghanistan, this terrorist attack resulted in the U.S. bombing attacks in Afghanistan in the area of those camps following the embassy bombings.

This did not end the ability of the al-Qaeda network to carry out terrorist attacks. In 2002, al-Qaeda operatives launched a firebombing of a synagogue in Tunisia on April 11 that killed 19 and injured 22 innocent people. On October 6 of that year, the group carried out a suicide attack on the MV *Limburg* off the coast of Yemen on October 6, killing one and injuring four. Another bombing attack, this time at a hotel in Mombasa, Kenya, killing 15 and injuring 40, was also carried out by al-Qaeda, as was, purportedly, the bombing of a nightclub in Bali, Indonesia, on October 12 that killed about 180 people.

Bombing attacks supported by this group continued in 2003, usually targeting American and/or Jewish citizens. On May 12, three expatriate housing complexes in Riyadh, Saudi Arabia, were bombed, killing 20 and injuring 139. The bombings on May 16 in Casablanca, Morocco, of a Jewish center, restaurant, nightclub, and hotel that took the lives of 41 and injured more than 100 others was supported by al-Qaeda operatives, as was the bombing of the J. W. Marriott Hotel in Jakarta, Indonesia, in August that killed 17 and injured 137.

Al-Qaeda also carried out bombings of two synagogues in Istanbul, Turkey, in November that killed 23 and had another 200 casualties and the bombings in Istanbul of the British consulate and the HSBC Bank in that same month that killed 27 and injured 455 civilians. Clearly, al-Qaeda has a global network and continues to carry out lethal bombing attacks on a wide range of targets.

Al-Qaeda was also linked a number of planned, but unsuccessful, terrorist operations, including the assassination of the pope during his visit to Manila in late 1994, a plan to kill U.S. president Clinton during his visit to the Philippines in early 1995, plans to bomb in midair a dozen U.S. trans-Pacific planes in 1995, and to set off a bomb at Los Angeles International Airport in 1999. It also plotted to carry out terrorist attacks against U.S. and Israeli tourists visiting Jordan for millennial celebrations in late 1999, but Jordanian authorities thwarted these plans. In December 2001, a suspected al-Qaeda associate, Richard Calvin Reid attempted to ignite a shoe bomb on a transatlantic flight from Paris to Miami, without success. All of these operations were either disrupted by authorities or not carried out.

Al-Qaeda probably still has several thousand members and associates, although the arrests of senior level al-Qaeda operatives certainly interrupted some terrorist plots. It has cells worldwide and is reinforced by its ties to Sunni extremist networks. Although its base and training camps in Afghanistan were targeted for destruction by the bombings of that country and the subsequent removal of the Taliban from power by coalition forces in late 2001, it remains a powerful force. Its network of small cells stretches across South Asia, the Middle East, Europe, Africa, and more recently Central and South America, and it continues to carry out attacks, as the train bombing in MADRID in 2004 made clear.

Al-Qaeda has also produced material that is being used by other groups for training members. An al-Qaeda training manual was recovered from sites in Afghanistan, and much of it has made its way onto the Internet. The detail of training procedures in this manual reflects access to CIA and Special Forces training materials, as well as a strong desire to train in the use of nonconventional weapons, particularly biological and chemical weapons.

Osama bin Laden could not have carried out the attacks of September 11, 2001, without widespread help from a network of talented and committed lieutenants. These men were sought intensely by the United States following the attacks in 2001, since their participation was believed to be crucial to the attack's success. They include:

Ayman Zawahiri—Widely believed to be bin Laden's deputy and personal physician, Zawahiri was the leader of the Egyptian Islamic Jihad, the group blamed for the assassination of President Anwar Sadat in 1981, and a member of the *Shura,* a body of al-Qaeda that includes members of other terrorist groups. Zawahiri, a surgeon, was sought by the U.S. military in Iraq in 2004, where it was believed that he continued to coordinate attacks against U.S. military in that country. "Al-Zawahiri's experience is much broader that even bin Laden's," according to Dia'a Rashwan, one of Egypt's top experts on militants. "His name has come up in nearly every case involving Muslim extremists since the 1970s."

Muhammad Atef—Thought to be responsible for carrying out the detailed mechanics of the plan to hijack four aircraft simultaneously on September 11, Atef is also believed to be responsible for planning the 1998 bombings of U.S. embassies in Kenya and Tanzania. Responsibility for these attacks was claimed by the Islamic Army for the Liberation of Holy Sites, led by Sobhi al-Sitta, also a bin Laden lieutenant. Atef operated his own military training camps in Afghanistan, where he apparently trained members of the Islamic Army group.

Mustafa Ahmad—Ahmad, as Osama's "money man," financed the hijackers while they were in the United States. In fact, he was in the United Arab Emirates before the 9/11 attacks, waiting for the hijackers to return their unused U.S. dollars to him there.

Abu Zoubeida—This Palestinian was responsible for overseeing al-Qaeda's training camps. He is thought to have masterminded the "millennium bombings," including a plot to blow up the Los Angeles airport on New Year's Eve in 1999.

Saif al-Adel—This man, described by the Federal Bureau of Investigation as one of the most dangerous al-Qaeda leaders, was responsible for training elite terrorist recruits in handling explosives. Several of the September 11 hijackers were reportedly schooled by al-Adel in Afghanistan.

Bin Laden, son of a billionaire Saudi family but no longer a Saudi citizen, is believed to have inherited about $300 million, which he used to finance

These Afghan al-Qaeda members were captured from a battle in the Tora Bora mountains, 2001. (CORBIS)

the group. Al-Qaeda also served as a focal point for a loose network of umbrella organizations, including many Sunni Islamic extremist groups, such as factions of the Egyptian Islamic Jihad, al-Gama'at al-Islamiyya, and the Harakat ul-Mujahidin. Al-Qaeda also maintains financially profitable businesses, collects donations from like-minded supporters, and illicitly siphons funds from donations from legitimate Muslim charitable organizations. Global efforts to halt or disrupt the flow of funds to terrorist groups after the attack on America have been impeded, in part, by the use of Hawala as a method of funds transfer and by the primarily charitable nature of many of the Muslim organizations that have been accused of illicitly allowing funds to flow to al-Qaeda.

See also AFGHANISTAN, U.S. BOMBING IN; JIHAD; MADRID TRAIN BOMBINGS.

References: National Memorial Institute for the Prevention of Terrorism (MIPT). "Al-Qaeda." Available online. URL: http://www.tkb.org/Group.jsp?groupID=6. Accessed February 15, 2006; Phares, Walid. *Future Jihad: Terrorist Strategies against America* (New York: Palgrave Macmillan, 2005); Vidino, Lorenzo. *Al Qaeda in Europe: The New Battleground of International Jihad* (Buffalo, N.Y.: Prometheus Books, 2005).

Qibla (Muslims against Global Oppression [MAGO]; Muslims against Illegitimate Leaders [MAIL])

Qibla was a small South African Islamic extremist group led by Achmad Cassiem, who was inspired by Iran's Ayatollah Khomeini. Cassiem founded Qibla in the 1980s, seeking to establish an Islamic state in South Africa. Later, in 1996, PEOPLE AGAINST GANGSTERISM AND DRUGS (PAGAD) was founded as a community anticrime group fighting drug lords in Cape Town's Cape Flats section. PAGAD shared Qibla's anti-Western stance as well as some members and leadership. Though each group was distinct, the media often treated them as one. Both have used front names (MAGO and MAIL) when launching anti-Western campaigns.

Both Qibla and PAGAD routinely protested U.S. policies toward the Muslim world, and they used radio stations to promote their message and mobilize Muslims. PAGAD was suspected of the car bombing on January 1, 1999, of the Victoria and Alfred Waterfront in Cape Town and the firebombing of a U.S.-affiliated restaurant on January 8 of the same year. PAGAD was also believed to have masterminded the bombing on August 25, 1999, of the Cape Town Planet Hollywood.

Qibla was estimated to have about 250 members. However, with at least 50 gunmen among its membership and given the size of the demonstrations organized by its leaders, PAGAD appeared to have considerably more adherents than Qibla. Both operated mainly in Cape Town, which is South Africa's foremost tourist venue. Both also probably had ties to Islamic extremists in other nations.

Other community-based organizations that are modeled on PAGAD are believed to be heavily penetrated by the more secretive Qibla organization, which uses this penetration to marshal support for its Islamic revolutionary aims. The radical ideology of Qibla may make some individuals vulnerable to recruitment to terrorism at a later date.

Quebec Liberation Front

See FRONT DU LIBÉRATION DU QUÉBEC.

Qutb, Sayyid (1906–1966)

Qutb was an Egyptian who joined the Muslim Brotherhood at an early age. As a youth, he was at first attracted by secular modernism and then repelled by it. After a visit to the United States during 1948–51, Qutb decided that the West, especially America, was completely corrupt and that Islam and the West were diametrically opposed, both culturally and morally. He considered the United States racist as well and was horrified at the freedom of action exhibited by women who, he maintained, wore clothes to accentuate their sexual charms rather than modest attire to hide them. Moreover, he believed that the denial of Islamic values could only be ended when the governments and societies that perpetuate them were destroyed. In significant ways, Qutb anticipated OSAMA BIN LADEN with his call to destroy the *jahili*, or non-Islamic cultures, that are essentially pagan and/or opposed to the message of Islam. Qutb was in the United States during the years immediately following the creation of Israel. The Jewish state's popularity among Americans became another source of his displeasure with American society.

Qutb became a prolific writer, publishing more than two-dozen books. His works generally provided arguments on behalf of Islam as the spiritual alternative to materialism and moral decadence. He was offended by the American emphasis on individualism and was convinced that this was a vice rather than a virtue. He also did not completely understand American history. For some reason, Qutb was convinced that the Inidan wars were still going on in the middle of the 20th century.

Anti-Semitism is an important ingredient of Qutb's philosophy. He considers Jews to be murderers and thieves. His consideration of Christians is almost as harsh. Qutb, several decades before bin Laden, used the term *Crusaders* to describe the Christian regimes he considered antithetical to and at war with the Islamic world. He originally decided that it would be enough for Muslims to be isolated from the non-Islamic world. He eventually came to the conclusion that separation alone was insufficient because the non-Islamic world was in conflict with Islam, and the conflict was perpetual. It could only end when Islam was triumphant.

Qutb was convinced that only violence would succeed in taking power from the *jahili* regimes. No other means could work since apostate and infidel regimes would not voluntarily give up power nor do they possess the ability to willingly accept and follow divine law. These regimes therefore had to be totally destroyed. Qutb did not see any reason for compromise or flexibility since Islam cannot interact positively with those hostile to its value system.

References: Lewis, Bernard. *The Crisis of Islam: Holy War and Unholy Terror* (New York: Random House, 2004); Musallam, Adnan A. *From Secularism to Jihad: Sayyid Qutb and the Foundations of Radical Islamism* (Westport, Conn.: Greenwood Press, 2005).

R

Rabin, Yitzhak (1923–1995)

Rabin was the Israeli prime minister during 1974–77 and 1993–95. In between those two terms, he had also served as defense minister under his political rival Shimon Peres. Rabin had pursued a military career. He steadily gained prominence and steadily rose in rank beginning with Israel's Independence War in 1948–49. Rabin was chief of staff during the Six-Day War in June 1967 where he shared with Moshe Dayan, then defense minister, credit for military victory. After finishing his military career, Rabin served as Israel's ambassador to the United States.

Rabin's first term as prime minister ended abruptly in 1977 because of a minor scandal involving his wife, who was accused of maintaining an illegal bank account in the United States. When he returned to the prime minister post in 1993, his foreign minister, Peres, urged negotiation between Israel and the PALESTINE LIBERATION ORGANIZATION (PLO), then regarded by many Israelis as a terrorist organization. In September of that year, Rabin, Peres, and YASIR ARAFAT, head of the PLO, signed documents at the White House under the auspices of President Bill Clinton that were designed to end a half century of strife and violence. Most Israelis supported Rabin in great part because they were confident that his military experience would not allow territorial withdrawals by Israel from Palestinian territory to jeopardize national security.

Extreme religious zealots, however, considered Rabin to be a traitor to Judaism. A few even advocated his murder. A young university student, YIGAL AMIR, from a very religious background, shot Rabin in November 1995 after the prime minister had attended a rally of supporters. This assassination of a head of government was an unprecedented tragedy for Israel. It unmistakably demonstrated the large and growing rift between the religious and the predominantly secular communities within Israel's Jewish population. To an extent that will never be fully known, the peace process itself was impacted in adverse ways.

Reference: Rabin, Yitzhak. *The Rabin Memoirs* (London: Weidenfeld and Nicolson, 1979).

racism and terrorism *See* WILMINGTON COUP AND MASSACRE OF 1898.

Rajneesh, Bhagwan Shree (1931–1990)

The leader of a cult in Oregon, this individual was responsible for the poisoning by salmonella of residents in The Dalles, Oregon. This use of a biological weapon by followers of Rajneesh injured 751 people who visited at least one of two restaurants in that small town in which the salmonella was placed. This is one of the few openly documented occurrences of a BIOLOGICAL ATTACK by a dissident group in the United States in the last century.

random terror

Random terror involves the placing of explosives where people gather (e.g., post offices, cafés, railroads, subways) to damage or destroy whatever and whomever happens to be there. Many groups engage in this tactic, leaving bombs in public places, apparently from a philosophy that one member of the targeted community blown to bits is pretty much like any other and thus that it is immaterial who is actually there when the explosion occurs.

This type of terrorism is generally carried out by individuals or groups, rather than political leaders. The targets of this type of terror are simply people who were "in the wrong place at the wrong time." Bombs placed in markets, cafés, grocery stores, and other such public gathering places are nonselective weapons, hence the term "random terror." The bomb that destroyed the Pan Am flight over LOCKERBIE was an example of random terror; the passengers and crew were simply on the wrong plane at the wrong time, from the perspective of the perpetrators.

In the same context, the July 7, 2005, LONDON TERROR ATTACKS and the MADRID TRAIN BOMBINGS were also acts of random terror. The buses and subways chosen for the attacks were gathering places, and the weapons used were non-selective, injuring and killing people who were simply in the wrong place at the wrong time.

rape, as a tactic of warfare

During the early 1990s, the Balkans again erupted in warfare. Local Serb militia in the former Yugoslavian republic of BOSNIA battled Muslims for control of the region. During this period, several massacres of Muslim men by Serb soldiers occurred. Serbs also victimized large groups of young Muslim women. The women were placed in detention centers where they were systematically raped by the soldiers. Those women who became pregnant were not released until enough time passed to make it medically inadvisable to abort the pregnancies. Apparently, the Serb strategy was to destroy morale as well as humiliate the Muslim women and their relatives. Rape, of course, occurs in all wars, although this may be the first time it was adopted as a weapon designed to terrorize an entire community.

According to Dr. Jennifer Leaning, a professor of international health at Harvard University, in 2004 the Janjaweed, a government-linked militia in Sudan, killed men in the villages they attacked and then raped the women. This "act of war" generated critical problems in the refugee camps, where the children are the first to die from high levels of malnutrition, diarrhea, dehydration, and measles. Rape as a tactic of war is, in this country, devastating future generations as well as the female victims.

References: Allen, Beverly. *Rape Warfare: The Hidden Genocide in Bosnia-Herzegovina and Croatia* (Minneapolis: University of Minnesota Press, 1996); Gutman, Roy. *Crimes of War: What the Public Should Know* (New York: W. W. Norton & Company, 1999).

Real Irish Republican Army (RIRA) *See* IRISH REPUBLICAN ARMY.

Red Army Faction (RAF; Baader-Meinhof Gang, German Rote Armee Fraktion, Baader-Meinhof Gruppe)

Founded in 1968 by Andreas Baader (1943–77) and Ulrike Meinhof (1943–76), this left-wing group often bears their name in popular history. From its early years, its members supported themselves by robberies of banks and other businesses, and they engaged in terrorist bombings and arson. Much of their activity was directed against West German corporations and businesses, and the U.S. and West German military installations. The RAF also engaged in kidnappings and assassinations of prominent political and business figures, but always in West Germany.

By the mid-1970s, however, they had become internationalist and occasionally allied with Palestinian groups engaged in terrorism. Two RAF guerrillas, Wilfred B'o'se and Brigitte Kuhkmann, took part in a Palestinian hijacking of an Air France jetliner in 1976, which led to the Israeli raid on the ENTEBBE airport in Uganda. Both of the Germans were killed.

While the group had included at least 22 core members in the early 1970s, most from upper-income families and possessing at least several years of university study, the majority had been jailed by the summer of 1972. Ulrike Meinhof was jailed that summer and hanged herself in her cell in 1976. Andreas Baader, escaping one imprisonment in 1970, was arrested again in 1976. An attempt to force his release by hijacking a Lufthansa plane, landing eventually in MOGADISHU, failed after West Germany's special forces team stormed the plane and freed the hostages. Baader and two other RAF members were found shot in their cells the next day, October 18, 1977, presumably suicides.

The RAF continued its terrorist activities and created a number of splinter groups, focusing its activities outside of Germany after the German use of TARGET SEARCH TEAMS made continuing to operate in Germany extremely difficult. Instead, it began to network regularly with other left-wing groups carrying out acts of violence. Two members of the RAF, Hans-Joachim Klein and Gabriele Krocher-Tiedemann, were recruited by CARLOS "THE JACKAL" to assist in the raid on the Vienna OPEC conference in 1975.

In July 1984, West German police found documents indicating that the RAF planned to internationalize their struggle further by uniting with other terrorist groups in attacks on the "representatives of repression," specifically NATO allies. Linking up with French and Belgian radicals, they participated in the assassination of prominent members of Europe's defense establishment and set off explosives at such targets as a U.S. air base, military pipelines, and a variety of other NATO installations. A Berlin nightclub filled with off-duty soldiers and German civilians was bombed in 1984, allegedly by this terrorist alliance.

The networking of the RAF with other European groups took concrete form in 1981, when Italian RED BRIGADES (BR), the RAF, and members of other left-wing groups met in Paris. From this meeting, the order went out to kidnap James L. Dozier, a U.S. Army brigadier general stationed in Rome. From being an indigenous group engaging in occasional acts of terrorism, operating primarily on their own home soil in Germany for essentially nationalistic purposes, the RAF began to focus its attention and activities against an international enemy: NATO.

After the collapse of communism in East Germany in 1989–90, it was found that many fugitive members of the RAF had been given sanctuary in East Germany by the Stasi, the secret police. Reunification of Germany has made the RAF an ANARCHIST group, not focused or operating against any one state but against all governments and in cooperation with many other groups involved in antistate struggles. In 1998, a news agency received a message supposedly signed by the RAF that declared "the RAF is now history."

References: National Memorial Institute for the Prevention of Terrorism (MIPT). "Red Army Faction." Available online. URL: http://www.tkb.org/Group.jsp?groupID=163. Accessed February 15, 2006; Varon, Jeremy. *Bringing the War Home: The Weather Underground, the Red Army Faction and Revolutionary Violence in the Sixties and Seventies* (Berkeley: University of California Press, 2004).

Red Brigades (BR)

This extreme left-wing secret organization formed in 1969 in ITALY, in an effort to create a revolutionary state through armed struggle, based on Marxist-Leninist principles. It also sought to separate Italy from its Western alliance, NATO.

The reputed founder of the BR was Renato Curcio (b. 1945), who first set up a leftist think group at the University of Trento in 1967 committed to the study of such figures as Karl Marx, Mao Zedong, and Che Guevara. After his marriage to a fellow radical, Margherita Cagol, he moved with her to Milan and began gathering a corps of zealots. The Red Brigade was officially declared to exist in November 1970 by this group, and this proclamation was highlighted by the firebombing of various factories and warehouses in Milan. The following year the group devoted its activities to kidnappings and in 1974 began its first murders, including the chief inspector of Turin's antiterrorist squad.

The original group concentrated on assassination and kidnapping of Italian government and private-sector targets, including the murder of former prime minister Aldo Moro in 1978. It also kidnapped U.S. Army brigadier general James Dozier in 1981, who was held captive for 42 days before Italian police rescued him unharmed from a hideout in Padua. The BR also claimed responsibility for the murder of Leamon Hunt, U.S. chief of the Sinai Multinational Force and Observer Group, in 1984.

In spite of serious police efforts, involving the arrest and jailing of hundreds of alleged terrorists during the mid-to-late 1970s, the random murders continued. Statistics issued by the Interior Ministry in Italy indicate that, in 1978, there were 2,498 terrorist attacks within Italy. But by the mid-1980s the group had begun to be largely inactive, as Italian and French authorities arrested many of their members and, in Italy, offered the option of "repentance" and reconciliation within the system.

While most of the activities carried out by the Red Brigade were staged in Italy, it did network extensively with other European left-wing groups in carrying out violent acts of terror. Some of its members have supplied safe houses and technical support for other groups seeking to hit NATO targets in Italy. The New Red Brigades have claimed responsibility for a few random attacks, but the group was again shut down by police in 2003 and early 2004 by arrests of its leadership. This group is now thought to have fewer than 50 members.

References: Drake, Richard. *The Aldo Moro Murder Case* (Cambridge, Mass.: Harvard University Press, 1995); National Memorial Institute for the Prevention of Terrorism (MIPT). "Red Brigades." Available online. URL: http://www.tkb.org/Group.jsp?groupID=92. Accessed February 15, 2006.

Red Hand Defenders (RHD)

This extremist group is composed primarily of Protestant hard-liners from loyalist groups observing a cease-fire in Northern Ireland. The RHD's goal is to prevent a political settlement with Irish nationalists, and it carries out attacks on Catholic civilian interests in Northern Ireland. The group was responsible for numerous pipe bombings and arson attacks on such civilian targets as homes, churches, and private businesses, causing outrage in the republican community and provoking retaliation by the IRISH REPUBLICAN ARMY (IRA). RHD claimed responsibility for the car-bombing murder on March 15, 1999, of Rosemary Nelson, a prominent Catholic nationalist lawyer and human rights campaigner in Northern Ireland. The group was quiet in 2000, however, following a damaging security crackdown in late 1999 following this bombing attack. The RHD is a small group, with only about 20 members, but some of these members have considerable experience in terrorist tactics, particularly in bomb making.

In January 2002, the group announced that all staff at Catholic schools in Belfast and Catholic postal workers legitimate targets. In spite of calls in February of that year by the ULSTER DEFENSE ASSOCIATION (UDA), the Ulster Freedom Fighters (UFF), and LOYALIST VOLUNTEER FORCES (LVF) to announce its disbandment, the RHD continues to make threats and issue claims of responsibility for attacks. It is believed to be a cover name often used by militant members of the banned UDA and LVF and was designated a foreign terrorist organization by the United States in December 2001.

In January 2002, the RDH bombed the home of a prison official in northern Belfast. Two more times that year, this group claimed responsibility for attacks: the murder of a Catholic postman and that of a Catholic teenager. These attacks were later claimed by the UDA-UFF, as the lines of distinction between these groups blurred with shifting membership.

In early 2003, this group claimed responsibility for killing two UDA members in what was described as Loyalist intern-group warfare. The RDH also claimed responsibility for a bomb that was left in the offices of Republican Sinn Féin in West Belfast. This bomb was defused and never detonated.

Reference: National Memorial Institute for the Prevention of Terrorism (MIPT). "Red Hand Defenders." Available online. URL: http://www.tkb.org/Group.jsp?groupID=93. Accessed February 15, 2006.

religion, as a factor in group dynamics

In the case of the individual who commits terrorism as a member of a fanatic religious group, the impact of religion on the dynamics of the group is significant. Religions, as a rule, offer to some extent their own versions of "reality" as well as a promise of "reward" for conformity to the norms of that reality. The reward is usually promised for a future time, when the present reality has passed away.

Thus the religious zealot committing an act of terrorism is assured by his/her religion and its leaders that his/her acts are acceptable to a higher morality than may currently exist. He/she is reinforced in the belief that what he/she is doing is "right" by the approval of fellow zealots. Further, the religious fanatic is assured of immortality and a suitable reward after death in the event he/she should die in the commission of the act of terrorism.

It would be difficult if not impossible to persuade such a person to discard his/her beliefs by reasonable arguments. There is little that could be offered to such a person as an inducement for discontinuing the act of terrorism. What reward can compete with the promise of immortality, approval by one's peers, and religious sanctification?

Obviously, the dynamics of some groups are much more powerful than those of others whose reward system and extensive spiritual support system is less organized or persuasive. Certain types of terrorists, thus, are much more difficult to deal with on a rational basis due to the impact of religion on the ability of the group to distort reality.

See also ARYAN NATIONS; CHRISTIAN IDENTITY MOVEMENT; CHRISTIAN MILITIA; HAMAS; HIZBALLAH; IRGUN; ISLAMIC JIHAD; AL-QAEDA; RIGHT-WING TERRORISM.

References: Bergen, Peter. *Holy War, Inc.: Inside the Secret World of Osama bin Laden* (New York: Free Press, 2001); Juergensmeyer, Mark. *Terror in the Mind of God: The Global Rise of Religious Violence* (Berkeley: University of California Press, 2003); Stern, Jessica. *Terror in the Name of God: Why Religious Militants Kill* (New York: HarperCollins Publishers, 2004).

Revolutionary Armed Forces of Colombia (FARC)

This organization is the oldest, largest, most capable, and best-equipped insurgency in Colombia, which has been troubled by a surfeit of such groups. Established in 1964 as a "military wing" of the Colombian Communist Party, FARC has been structured along military lines. Although most of its supporters are drawn from rural areas of Colombia, it has several active urban fronts.

FARC has been an anti-American organization since its formation and has attacked a variety of U.S. citizens and interests. Its tactics have included terrorist bombings, murders, kidnappings, extortion, hijackings of civilians, and also armed insurgent attacks against Colombian political, military, and economic targets.

Financial support for the activities carried out by FARC derives from several sources. Foreign citizens are often the targets of FARC kidnapping for ransom. Substantial documentation exists to indicate that FARC has been involved in narcotics trafficking, principally through the provision of armed protection for the drugs in production and transit. This latter has been an extremely lucrative source of income.

In March 1999, FARC murdered three Indian rights activists on Venezuelan territory, whom they had kidnapped in Colombia. Throughout that year, the group continued its bombing campaign against the oil pipelines. Indeed, FARC has an expanding presence and base for operations in Venezuela, Panama, Ecuador, and Brazil, although Colombia remains its primary area of operation. It continues to receive occasional medical help and political consultations from Cuba, although this has diminished since the end of the cold war.

In January 2000, FARC began a new, nonviolent operation. It entered into peace negotiations with the Colombian government. The talks are slow-moving, but the prospect of an end to violence by this group is at least a tangible possibility. This is significant, since FARC has about 8,000 to 12,000 armed combatants and an unknown number of supporters, thus making its capability for prolonged violence a serious factor in Colombia's future.

However, in February 2003, FARC captured and held three U.S. contractors and killed one other American when their plane crashed in Florencia. On December 31, 2004, FARC leader Simón Trinidad, the highest-ranking FARC leader ever captured, was extradited to the United States on drug charges. In December 2004, a Colombian appeals court declared three members of the IRISH REPUBLICAN ARMY—arrested in 2001 as they left the former FARC-controlled demilitarized zone—guilty of providing advanced explosives training to FARC.

References: Dudley, Steven. *Walking Ghosts: Murder and Guerilla Politics in Colombia* (Philadelphia: Taylor and Francis, 2003); National Memorial Institute for the Prevention of Terrorism (MIPT). "Revolutionary Armed Forces of Colombia." Available online. URL: http://www.tkb.org/Group.jsp?groupID=96. Accessed February 15, 2006.

Revolutionary Organization 17 November (November 17, 17N)

Not a particularly well-known terrorist organization outside of Greece, November 17 is a durable, lethal, and successful group. For more than a quarter century, it has eluded authorities despite rewards for information that total $7 million. A Greek journalist has referred to November 17 as "Europe's Last Red Terrorists."

November 17 appeared soon after (November 17, 1973) the colonels' junta in Greece ended the country's constitutional monarchy and draws its name from the student uprising that protested the military junta that replaced the monarchy. The group tends to target American and British diplomats because of the two countries' support that kept the colonels in power for several years. Turkish diplomats are also likely targets, probably because of the long-standing antagonism between Greece and Turkey. A total of 22 victims, the most recent being a British diplomat assasinated in June 2000, have been attributed to November 17.

November 17 is committed to the removal of U.S. bases in Greece; to the removal of the Turkish military presence from Cyprus; and to the severing of Greek ties to NATO and the European Union (EU). Throughout its career, it has been vocally anti-Greek establishment, anti–United States, anti-Turkey, and anti-NATO. Most of the initial attacks carried out by November 17 were assassinations of senior U.S. officials and Greek public figures. During the 1980s, its tactics expanded to include bombings of these targets. From 1990 into the 21st century, the targets that this group has selected for bombings have expanded to include EU facilities and foreign firms investing in Greece. It has added rocket attacks to its arsenal and made bombing attacks in early 2000, indicating that it continues to be an active force in Greece.

The group, which is still active, maintains its base of operations in Greece, primarily Athens. While it may have networked with other Greek terrorist groups and perhaps with other antiestablishment groups outside of Greece, it has no known base for external aid, and its operatives have not participated in external attacks with other groups. It has, however, provided local logistical support for other groups seeking to attack Greek authority as well as EU or NATO representatives.

Little is known about the current size and organization of November 17. The organization is extremely secretive, but it also apparently enjoys some degree of popular support among sectors of Greek society. It does have a pronounced and extreme left-wing ideology that is contemptuous of free-market political democracy. The Greek political establishment and police have received extremely few offers of help from rank-and-file Greeks. This difficulty has provided Greece with some degree of embarrassment. The government made serious efforts to bring November 17 under control—if not to eliminate it altogether—with the concerns raised by the 2004 Olympic Games in Athens.

A failed bombing attempt in June 2002 led police to the first-ever arrest of a 17N member, Savvas Xyros (Xiros). Documents in Xyros's apartment led police to the arrest of 18 other suspects. Greek police stated that all core members of 17N are currently in custody. Xyros, however, claimed that 10 members of 17N remain at large. An unknown individual or group claiming to be 17N issued a statement insisting that the group is still active and threatening to take hostages with which to bargain for the release of its imprisoned members.

The trial of the imprisoned members began in March of 2003. Some suspects confessed to participating in assassinations; others admitted to limited participation; and many, including the group's alleged leader Alexandros Giotopoulos, have insisted that they are innocent of all charges. In December of 2003, all but four of the 19 defendants were convicted. Several, including Giotopoulos, were sentenced to life in prison. 17N has been inactive since the arrest of its only known members, but some believe that the new group REVOLUTIONARY PEOPLE'S STRUGGLE is composed of members of 17N still at large.

References: Kassimeris, George. *Europe's Last Red Terrorists: The Revolutionary Organization 17 November* (New York: New York University Press, 2001); National Memorial Institute for the Prevention of Terrorism (MIPT). "Revolutionary Organization 17 November (RO-N17)." Available online. URL: http://www.tkb.org/Group.jsp?groupID=101. Accessed February 15, 2006.

Revolutionary People's Liberation Party/Front (DHKP/C)

See DEVRIMCI SOL (REVOLUTIONARY LEFT).

Revolutionary People's Struggle (ELA)

Developing from opposition to the military junta that governed Greece from 1967 to 1974, the ELA came into existence in 1971. It is a self-described revolutionary, anticapitalist, and anti-imperialist group. It has openly and frequently declared its opposition to what it perceives as "imperialist domination, exploitation, and oppression." Like the REVOLUTIONARY ORGANIZATION 17 NOVEMBER, the Revolutionary People's Struggle is adamantly anti-American, and it seeks the removal of U.S. military forces from Greece.

Since its inception, the ELA has conducted bombings against Greek government and economic targets as well as U.S. military and business facilities. In 1986, the group increased its attacks on Greek government and commercial interests. A raid by Greek police on an ELA safe house in 1990 revealed a weapons cache and evidence of direct contacts with other Greek groups engaged in terrorism, including 1 May and Revolutionary Solidarity. In 1991, the ELA and 1 May claimed joint responsibility for more than 20 bombings. Greek police records indicated an established link between the ELA and Revolutionary Organization 17 November.

The ELA has not claimed responsibility for a terrorist attack since January 1995. However, ELA members may still be active and undertaking operations in the name of other Greek terrorist groups.

Reference: National Memorial Institute for the Prevention of Terrorism (MIPT). "Revolutionary People's Struggle." Available online. URL: http://www.tkb.org/Group.jsp?groupID=102. Accessed February 15, 2006.

revolutionary taxes *See* TERRORISM, FINANCING OF.

Revolutionary United Front (RUF)

The RUF is an effective guerrilla force, loosely organized and flexible, with brutal discipline. Its aim is to topple the government of Sierra Leone and to retain control of the lucrative diamond-producing regions of the country. The group funds itself largely through the extraction and sale of diamonds obtained in areas of Sierra Leone that the RUF controls. Using a blend of guerrilla, criminal, and terrorist tactics, it has fought the government, intimidated the civilian population, and kept United Nation peacekeeping units in check. Its tactics have included murder, torture, and mutilation.

In 2000, the RUF held hundreds of UN peacekeepers hostage until their release was negotiated, in part by the RUF's chief sponsor, Liberian president Charles Taylor. The group was also accused of attacks in Guinea, carried out for President Taylor. UN experts reported that Liberia's president provided support and leadership to the RUF, and that Libya, Gambia, and Burkina Faso served as conduits for weapons and other materiel for the group.

In May 2001, disarmament of RUF rebels began, and by January 2002, the war was officially declared over. One of the group's founders, Foday Sankoh, died in prison in July 2003 while awaiting trial on charges of war crimes. This was essentially the end of the RUF.

Reference: National Memorial Institute for the Prevention of Terrorism (MIPT). "Revolutionary United Front (RUF)." Available online. URL: http://www.tkb.org/Group.jsp?groupID=4247. Accessed February 15, 2006.

ricin

Ricin is a biotoxin found in the bean of the castor plant, *Ricinis communis,* and it is one of the most toxic and easily produced plant toxins. Originally cultivated in ancient Egypt as a lubricant and a laxative, castor beans are today used to produce castor oil, which is a brake and hydraulic fuel constituent found throughout the world. Ricin can, ironically, be made from the waste left over from processing castor beans.

Since it is both highly toxic and easily produced, ricin was studied and developed by the United States during both world wars in the 20th century. Unfortunately, these same characteristics have made ricin an attractive weapon of interest to radical individuals, groups, and governments in recent years as well.

Like anthrax, ricin may cause toxic reactions in people from three possible routes of exposure: inhalation, injection, and oral ingestion (the least toxic method). Inhaling ricin would, according some experts, produce symptoms within eight hours and, depending on the dose, death within 36–72 hours. There is, unfortunately, no known vaccine for ricin, and no antidote to the poison to counter it. While ricin poisoning is not contagious (it cannot be spread from person to person from casual contact), it has already been used as a weapon in recent history. In 1978, Georgi Markov, a Bulgarian writer and journalist who was living in London, died after he was attacked by a man with an umbrella that had been fixed to inject a poison ricin pellet under Markov's skin. Reports indicate, too, that ricin was used in the Iran-Iraq conflict in the 1980s. Quantities of ricin were reportedly found in caves in Afghanistan used by al-Qaeda prior to the 2001 attacks, and information about ricin appears in the so-called *Jihad Encyclopedia* discovered after 9/11. Ricin is more lethal than sarin, which was used in the Tokyo subway attack.

References: Centers for Disease Control and Prevention. Emergency Preparedness & Response. "Facts about Ricin." Available online. URL: http://www.bt.cdc.gov/agent/ricin/facts.asp. Accessed February 16, 2006; Mangold, Tom, and Jeff Goldberg. *Plague War: The Terrifying Reality of Biological Warfare* (New York: St. Martin's Press, 2001).

right of access, of media to terrorist events in the United States

Members of the media often claim to have an unlimited right to have access to, and the right to report, all news, including that relating to terrorist events. Those responsible for hostage rescue contend that such rights should not be regarded as unlimited and should never be exercised in ways that might endanger lives. The legal issues inherent in these contrasting viewpoints were explored extensively during the late 1970s and early 1980s. As T. K. Fitzpatrick succinctly noted in his article "The Semantics of Terror," "The media must not be the dupes of the radical scriptwriters, nor should they be the mouthpiece of government. There is a mean. Law enforcement and the media cannot be locked in combat."

The U.S. Supreme Court during Warren Burger's tenure as Chief Justice did not regard the media's right to access as superior to that of the general public. Abraham Miller, in his book *Terrorism, the Media, and the Law,* offered a useful review of U.S. case law decisions involving the issue of the right of access of the press to terrorist events—that is, the right of the press to get close to the events as they occur. He noted that, in the *Pell* decision, the Court stated that when the public is excluded from the scene of a crime or disaster, then the media may also be excluded, without violating the First Amendment to the U.S. Constitution.

Miller's study suggests that the U.S. Supreme Court, under Burger, viewed access by the media to a site where news is being made (as in a terrorist incident) as constituting not a First Amendment right but a privilege to be granted, or revoked, at the discretion of the law enforcement agency entrusted with ending the breach in the law. Even access to the perimeter between the tactical squad and the public (frequently established by law enforcement units in hostage-taking and siege situations for the purpose of permitting access for the media) is not a right guaranteed to the media by the Constitution but is instead a privilege accorded at the discretion of the government law enforcement agency in charge of the situation. Miller concludes with the observation:

> Access to the site where news is being made cannot be claimed by the press if the general public is also being excluded. Press access, largely a privilege under the most sanguine of circumstances, can be revoked, and where the situation is fraught with imminent danger of people being injured or killed, the media's claim to special access rings especially hollow.

An earlier study by Miller and Juanita Jones reached similar conclusions about the legality of excluding the press from certain areas during hostage situations, particularly those in which law enforcement procedures require secrecy in order to save lives. However, this study also noted that the Supreme Court did not allow blanket denial of access through a set of preconditions. U.S. case law, according to this study, did not support a total or standard ban on news access to terrorist events; only the circumstances surrounding each event could legally justify limitation of access. Differences have arisen over the type of restrictions and the body empowered to impose them. Most recent research focused on three alternatives: government-directed censorship, self-censorship by the media itself, and restraints imposed by a special commission. All three options have difficulties, and the first two have been seriously discussed for more than two decades.

See also CENSORSHIP, OF MEDIA CONCERNING TERRORIST INCIDENTS; GOALS OF GOVERNMENT, CONCERNING MEDIA IN TERRORIST EVENT; GOALS OF MEDIA, IN TERRORIST EVENT; GOALS OF TERRORIST, CONCERNING MEDIA.

References: Alali A. Odasno, and Kenoye K. Eke, "Terrorism, the News Media, and Democratic Political Order." *Current World Leaders* 39, no. 4 (August 1996); Finn, John E."Media Coverage of Political Terrorism and the First Amendment: Reconciling the Public's Right to Know with Public Order." *Violence and Terrorism: 98/99* (New York: Dushkin/McGraw-Hill, 1998); Miller, Abraham. *Terrorism, the Media and the Law* (New York: Transnational Publishers, 1982).

right of self-determination

One of the ingredients in the formulation of the rules that govern civilized society today that is new is the right of self-determination. The United Nations Charter, written in 1945, states that people have a right to determine for themselves the form of state under which they choose to live. Since that time, nations and legal scholars have been trying to work out just which "people" have this "right" and how extensive a justification this right confers on individuals engaged in wars of self-determination.

The answers to these and related questions are not readily obtainable. As Robert Friedlander noted:

> (A)ccording to United Nations practice, a "people" is any group that august organization wishes to liberate from "colonial and racist regimes." Thus, the Puerto Ricans are a people but the Kurds are not; the Namibians are a people and possess their own state but the population of East Timor (or what remains of it) is without identity and without hope.

Obviously, this right is not clearly defined by the concepts essential to it. Nor is it clear just how fundamental or extensive this "right to self-determination" is. It is unclear, for example, whether the right to self-determination is more fundamental than the right to life. If not, then the pursuit of self-determination cannot intentionally jeopardize any person's right to life. It is also unclear whether the right to self-determination supercedes the right of a state to try to protect itself and to provide a safe and stable system of government for its citizens.

No people seeking to exercise their right of self-determination do so in a vacuum. Their actions in the course of their struggle necessarily have an effect, often a negative one, on other persons within their community. As in any other armed struggle, there must remain limits within which their right to pursue self-determination must operate in order to limit the adverse effects of such a course of action on the rights of others.

The problem that this newly articulated right of self-determination has created in terms of the limitation of armed warfare is important. This right is readily conferred upon, or claimed by, many groups who do not enjoy, and probably can never gain, majority support among the indigenous population of their state. This means that many groups of disaffected persons may claim this right who have no hope of ever waging even a successful guerrilla war against an established state. The argument has been made that these groups therefore cannot reasonably be held to conventional rules of warfare, for to hold them to those rules is to condemn them to inevitable failure.

Faced with the overwhelming odds in favor of the well-established and well-armed state, many of the peoples seeking to exercise their right of self-determination have been increasingly willing to use less conventional methods and means of waging war. Lacking large popular support from the indigenous population, facing a state whose trained army and weaponry make conventional resistance a mockery, such groups are increasingly willing to use "unthinkable" weapons, such as terrorism, to achieve their "right."

The difficulties facing such groups seeking self-determination are very real, but the problems that they create are also formidable. What happens, for example, if two peoples claim that their right to self-determination gives them the right to occupy and control the same piece of land? Who decides which group's "right" should prevail? Should it be decided based upon which group can establish control or on which has the better legal claim to the land? Again, who or what is to make such a determination?

This is not a hypothetical situation. There exist such dilemmas in the world. The rival claims of the Palestinians and the Israelis to the same land have provoked decades of bloodshed and bitter fighting. Each people in this struggle claim a historic right to the land.

For more than four decades, ISRAEL managed to secure its right to determine its own form of government and to exercise control over its own people in the land of PALESTINE. But it has had to do so through force and to maintain, through the end of the 20th century, its existence through occupation of additional land. Peace is seldom achieved, in the long term, through occupation, and Israel began the difficult process of pulling out of those occupied lands. But there are Jewish settlers who have lived in those lands for decades, whose identity and security as a people is threatened by the withdrawal, and whose right to self-determination may well be lost in the peace process. As long as there exists within, or near, the borders of this troubled land a people whose right to self-determination remains unsatisfied, terrorist acts may well continue to be a threat to peace in the region.

The assassination in late 1995 of YITHZAK RABIN, prime minister of Israel, by a Jewish student seeking to derail this withdrawal of Israel from the Occupied Territories, makes this threat very clear. Certainly, the satisfaction of the Palestinians' right to self-determination will be difficult to achieve in any way that is acceptable to all of the people of Israel. One Israeli military officer noted that even children, born and raised in Palestinian refugee camps, will state that they are from Jaffa and other coastal cities (of what used to be Palestine). Since this land is now an integral part of Israel, there seems to be little likelihood that the aspirations of those Palestinian adults who have fostered this sense of "belonging" to old homelands can ever be satisfied.

Violent actions taken during the peace process begun in 1993 have made it clear that some Palestinians do not want "independence" in the West Bank or the Gaza Strip. They want to return to, and continue to claim, their "homeland" of Palestine, including the land that is today Israel. It would appear to be impossible to satisfy their "right to self-determination" without infringing upon Israel's "right to exist." Just as the Jewish people rejected other offers of homelands around the turn of the century, insisting on their right to return to the homeland of their theological ancestors, Palestinians have found it difficult to accept alternatives that fall short of a return of their homeland.

On whose side does "right" rest in this conflict? The "right of self-determination" that the Palestinians seek to exercise is the same one for which the HAGANAH fought against the British occupying forces in the 1930s and 1940s. Just as the Jewish IRGUN ZVAI LEUMI and its radical offshoot, the STERN GANG, used terror tactics to force out an occupying power, the Palestinians have resorted to terrorist acts to rid themselves of what they perceive to be "occupying powers."

This right to self-determination is, by its very lack of clarity, a dangerous justification for unlawful violence. Since neither the "peoples" nor the extent of the "right" itself appear to have any specific legal limitations, the exercise of such rights can lead to vicious spirals of violence, as rival peoples seek to claim their rights within an international system whose state of flux lends credence to first one, and then the other's, rights.

right-wing extremism in Germany

The right-wing movement in Germany came under close international scrutiny in the summer of 2000. A number of incidents throughout the year, culminating in an arson attack on a synagogue in D|sseldorf, led German leaders to reinvigorate the discussion about the presence of right-wing extremism in German society. Although authorities later disclaimed the arson attack as being linked to the right-wing movement, they are concerned about the relative increase in right-wing-related crime. A key element to this is the increase of attacks on foreigners. This is of particular importance as the European Union discusses its enlargement in Eastern Europe and its immigration policies. If Germany perceives that its society will be subject to a deluge of immigrants with EU expansion, antiforeigner sentiment and racism will only increase. Several immediate trends emerge from examination of the current state of the German right-wing movement: a concentration of violent right-wing activists in former East Germany, the increase in bomb-making materials found in raids against extremists, and the increased use of the Internet as an organizational tool.

According to the Bundesamt für Verfassungsschutz (BfV, the Federal Office for the Protection of the Constitution), the total number of right-wing extremists in Germany in 2000, both organized and unorganized, is 50,900. More than 70% of this number is represented in membership of the three right-wing German parties: 9,700 are violent extremists; 85% of these members are considered skinheads; and roughly 2,200 are estimated to be in neo-Nazi organizations. This total number has declined slightly from a total of 51,400 in 1999, primarily due to membership losses in one of the three parties. What has increased from 1999 is the number of violent extremists, up from 9,000 in 1999.

The number of criminal offenses with proven or suspect right-extremist links recorded by the Federal Office of Criminal Police (BKA) for 2000 reached 15,951, a 58% increase from 1999. Of these offenses, 999 were considered violent, an increase from 746 in 1999. Sixty-four percent of these were directed toward foreigners. By August 2000, 240 violent attacks had taken place in former East Germany, and 270, in former West Germany. It is estimated that two-thirds of the perpetrators are youth and adolescents, nearly 95% male, and only one-fifth unemployed, the rest in school or learning a vocation. What is striking is the concentration of crimes in the East: 2.21 crimes per 100,000 residents vs. 0.95 in the West. The number of actual deaths from right-wing extremism is disputed. The official number is 26 during the last decade; however, a joint investigation by Germany's newspapers the *Frankfurter Rundschau* and the *Berlin Tagespiegel* argues that nearly 100 deaths related to right-wing extremism occurred during the same time period.

The three main parties of the right in Germany are the Republikaners (REP), Deutsche Volksunion (DVU), and the Nationaldemokratische Partei Deutschlands (NPD). The REP had approximately 14,000 members in 16 state associations in 1999, but membership dropped to 13,000 in 2000. They are not represented in any of the country's state governments. The REP is considered the most moderate of the right-wing parties in Germany. Dr. Rolf Schlierer is the party leader and has tried to maintain a more mainstream front; however, the party is experiencing internal conflict over this position, with others in the party wanting to pursue a more radical approach. Their stronghold is Baden-Württemberg, where they received 4.4% of the vote in 2000, down from 9.1% in 1996. Their members have typically been predominantly males who have limited education. Experts predict that the turmoil over the party platform will cause the REP to lose more members.

The DVU is a further step right in the organized parties. It is the largest right-wing party in Germany with 17,000 members and is considered the strongest in terms of financial means and human resources. Dr. Gerhard Frey dominates the DVU through his position as party leader and through his financial support. This makes the DVU a "personal party," heavily dependent on its leader for existence. The DVU is represented in the state governments of Brandenburg, Bremen, and Saxony-Anhalt. Its platform is heavily nationalistic, with an emphasis on anti-Semitic and antiforeigner sentiment. It has its own publication, the *National Zeitung*. The DVU's ideology is also antidemocratic but does not go far enough to challenge the democratic institutions and, in fact, uses the democratic process to further its cause.

The most extreme of all the recognized parties is the Nationaldemokratische Partei Deutschlands (NPD). The party, which numbered 25,000 in the 1960s, dropped to 3,500 by 1996, but its membership grew again to 6,500 members in 2000. Its strategy is threefold: "Kampf um die Strasse" (fight to win the streets), "Kampf um die Köpfe" (fight to win the minds), and "Kampf um die Parliamente" (fight to win the parliament). Their platform is a "German socialism" with anticapitalist elements. This also includes a definition of German society that is based on biological elements. The party has a youth organization, the Junge Nationaldemokraten, which has openly mobilized skinheads and neo-Nazis in 50 demonstrations. Although the NPD has had a poor showing at elections, the German government and both houses of parliament, the Bundesrat and the Bundestag, have asked the Federal Constitutional Court to consider banning the NPD as a party. They argue that the NPD's collaboration with the neo-Nazis, as well as their political "fight to win the streets" and other elements of their ideology, make the party clearly undemocratic and unconstitutional. This ruling is still pending.

The neo-Nazi scene in Germany emerged with the decline of the NPD in the 1960s. As previously mentioned, neo-Nazis in Germany are currently estimated at approximately 2,200. This number has not increased from 1999. What is important to note is that roughly half of the known neo-Nazis are found in the former East Germany, which itself contains only 20% of Germany's entire population, approximately 17 million people out of 80 million. This dense presence, along with the concentration of skinheads in East Germany, causes concern among Germany's officials and scholars about the acceptance of violence and disillusionment with democracy in the former East Germany.

The neo-Nazi movement is organized into roughly 150 independent "brotherhoods" (Kameradschaften) with five to 20 members, usually men between 18 and 25 years old. The brotherhoods are prominent in Baden-Württemberg, Berlin, Brandenberg, Hamburg, Niedersachsen, Mecklenburg-Vorpommern, and Saxony-Anhalt. Since neo-Nazi demonstrations are forbidden in Germany, members have been using their alliance with the NPD to gain official permission for demonstrations. This worries the authorities, since it gives the neo-Nazis a way to organize on a national level. Previously, it was relatively difficult for the brotherhoods to work together openly.

German riot police arrest ultra right-wing skinheads after the confiscation of guns and banned Nazi symbols. (CORBIS)

This link with the NPD and the growing number of violent extremists is a critical issue. Of Germany's right-wing extremists, 85% are considered to belong to the subculture of skinheads. Like the neo-Nazis, it is estimated that over half of the violent extremists live in former East Germany. They usually have no precise ideology but are virulently antiforeigner. There is some crossover between skinheads and neo-Nazis. In 2000 the Federal Ministry of the Interior banned the German branch of a prominent international neo-Nazi skinhead organization, Blood and Honour, and its youth organization, White Youth, arguing that they reject Germany's constitutional order. There are two other active skinhead organizations: the Hammerskins and the Skingirl Freundeskreis Deutschland, a female organization.

Youth usually come into contact with skinhead movements through concerts of certain music groups. Bands such as Die Härte promote racism, anti-Semitism, and nationalism in their music. However, the number of concerts has dropped in recent years and authorities have moved in to break up others.

A new aspect to Germany's right-wing extremism is the use of the Internet to promote it. Certain groups use MP3 software to allow listeners to download their music, thus reaching a broader audience. This use of the Internet is not limited to extremist music groups; the BfV found 800 German websites containing far-right views in 2000, some also using music to entice readers, especially young people. The BfV believes that neo-Nazis are using these sites on the Internet to coordinate their activities nationwide. It is not easy to prosecute the authors of the sites that have criminal content, such as murder hit lists, since many use a foreign, usually American, provider.

Another developing phenomenon that is also found on the Internet is information on bomb making and weapons. Weapons have also been part of the neo-Nazi scene, but authorities now fear that they are being used more for terrorist activities. The bombing in 1998 of a Jewish grave in Berlin and in 1999 of an exhibition in Saarbrücken about the Wehrmacht's role in World War II highlight this problem.

Finally, another major issue is whether violent racism is merely a problem of the former East Germany. There is a clear trend of a growing presence of violent extremists in the former East Germany and crimes associated with right-wing extremism. Only 2% of the 9% of total foreigners live in East Germany, but nearly half of the violent extremists and neo-Nazis can be found there. Eastern Germany poses a particular problem with its economic crises, weakness in democratic institutions, and historical lack of discussion about the Nazi era. Furthermore, a vicious circle emerges. There are already significant acceptance issues between the West and the East; right-wing violence allows the West to be even more critical of the East, which then can fuel the kind of general discontent that gives rise to violent extremism. However, there are a significant number of attacks in the West. As a recent report of the Council of Europe noted, right-wing extremism cannot be dismissed simply as an "eastern phenomenon," since violent attacks also occur in the western part of the country. Instead, it attributes part of the ongoing problem in Germany to an overall reluctance in German society to discuss the problem of anti-Semitism and racism. Since the bombings in 2000, German authorities have begun an aggressive campaign throughout the country to mobilize the citizenry against right-wing extremism.

In 2003, the two houses of the German legislature, the Bundestag and the Bundesrat, jointly attempted to ban the National Democratic Party (NDP) in a trial before the highest court in Germany (the only institution that has the power to ban parties, if it considers them unconstitutional). The case, however, was thrown out of court when it was revealed that a large part of the leadership of the NDP were actually undercover agents sent by the German secret services, making it difficult for the court to determine genuine party decisions and those controlled by the secret services. Horst Mahler, a former member of the RED ARMY FACTION, defended the NDP in court.

References: Brinks, Jan Herman. *Children of a New Fatherland: Germany's Post War Right-Wing Politics* (New York: St. Martin's Press, 1999); Lee, McGowan. *The Radical Right in Germany: 1870 to the Present* (New York: Longman, 2002).

right-wing terrorism

One trend noted by researchers of terrorism is that the last two decades of the 20th century experienced a surge in right-wing terrorism, that is, terrorism carried out by militant, reactionary, and fundamentalist individuals and groups. In contrast, terrorism by individuals and groups in the 1960s and 1970s was described as left-wing, involving struggles against governments and social systems, carried out in efforts to force liberal social changes. The activities of such organizations as the NEO-NAZI youth groups against refugees from Eastern Europe in Germany in the 1990s provided grim evidence of the existence of such right-wing groups willing to resort to violence.

Activities in the United States by groups such as the ARYAN NATIONS and the CHRISTIAN IDENTITY MOVEMENT also offered insights into the growth of right-wing terror. Certainly the OKLAHOMA CITY BOMBING in 1995 generated concern about the potential for violence by right-wing militia groups in this country.

This right-wing terrorism has wide-ranging geographical dimensions, a diversity of causes its adherents espouse, and overlapping agendas among its member groups. There are right-wing groups from Idaho to California, Arizona to North Carolina, Georgia to Michigan, Texas to Canada. Almost every state has at least one such group, and most have several. These groups share motivations that span a broad spectrum: antifederalism, sedition, racial hatred, and religious hatred. Most have masked these unpleasant sounding motives under a rather transparent veneer of religious precepts.

Literature from these groups indicate that they are bound together by a number of factors. These include a shared hostility to any form of government above the county level and even an advocacy of the overthrow of the U.S. government (or the Zionist Occupation Government, as some of them call it). Vilification of Jews and nonwhites as children of Satan is coupled with an obsession with achieving the religious and racial purification of the United States and a belief in a conspiracy theory of powerful Jewish interests controlling the government, banks, and the media.

These facets of right-wing ideology give interesting insights in light of the material discussed earlier concerning the images that terrorists have of their world, their victims, and themselves. To view the "enemy" as "children of Satan" is to dehumanize them, as terrorists must in order to kill. To view the struggle of the group as an effort to "purify" the nation is to view it as a battle between good and evil, as terrorists must. The view of a coming racial war fits the millennial view that terrorists maintain. A warrior fighting in a cause to purify a state from the children of Satan will have little problem in justifying the use of lethal force.

Thus, right-wing terrorism in the United States is widespread, intricately linked by many overlapping memberships, and bound together in a political and religious doctrine that defines the world in terms that make the use of violence not just acceptable but necessary. Since many of the members of these groups are skilled in the use of weapons and utilize survival training in camps throughout the country, planning for an "inevitable" racial war, the impact of these groups may well be formidable in the 21st century.

See also ARMED MILITIAS IN THE UNITED STATES; IMAGES, HELD BY TERRORISTS.

References: Merkl, Peter H., and Leonard Weinberg. *Right-Wing Extremism in the Twenty-First Century* (Philadelphia, Penn.: Taylor & Francis, 2003); Snow, Robert L. *Terrorists Among Us* (New York: Perseus Publishing, 2002).

Ruby Ridge

Ruby Ridge is a small ridge located in the panhandle region of northern Idaho. This remote area of wilderness became the spotlight of federal law enforcement in August 1992. On August 21 and 22 of that year, U.S. marshal William Degan, Vicki Weaver, and her son Sam died as a result of a lingering standoff between federal law-enforcement officials and Vicki's husband, Randy Weaver.

Randy Weaver was a fundamentalist Christian who had moved his family from Iowa to give his children a better upbringing away from government interaction. Weaver had first come to the attention of the Bureau of Alcohol, Tobacco and Firearms (ATF) in 1986. Undercover agents met Weaver at an Aryan Nations Congress meeting. As a result of this encounter and subsequent meetings, Weaver sold undercover ATF agents two illegally sawed-off shotguns in 1989. This became the genesis of the Ruby Ridge standoff.

ATF agents wanted Weaver to become an informant; however, when he refused, he was arrested for illegal arms trafficking. When Weaver did not appear for his scheduled court date on February 19, 1991, a warrant was issued for his arrest. United States Marshals (USM) began an investigation and surveillance of the Weaver property, located at Ruby Ridge, that extended over 17 months. The plan was to capture Weaver while he was away from the residence due to concerns about a 300-meter kill zone erected by the Weavers around their home. On August 21, 1992, the Weavers' dog detected a three-man USM reconnaissance team patrolling the Weaver property. This alerted Sam Weaver and Kevin Harris, who were monitoring the area. A firefight broke out between the two groups, and Sam Weaver and Marshal William Degan were killed, along with the Weavers' dog.

Following the surveillance incident, the USM called in the Federal Bureau of Investigation (FBI). The FBI immediately set up a perimeter around the Weaver house and brought in its Hostage Rescue Team (HRT). An HRT sniper fired two shots the first day. The first shot injured Randy Weaver outside his home; the second shot, fired through the front door, wounded Kevin Harris and killed Vicki Weaver. A week later the Weaver household surrendered to authorities, ending the Ruby Ridge standoff.

Randy Weaver was taken into custody and tried in federal court. He was acquitted on all charges, except for failing to appear in court. The bloody standoff also raised serious questions regarding the legality of some federal law-enforcement activities. The greatest question concerned the FBI's policy on the use of deadly force. The policy of shooting any adult with a weapon by the HRT regardless of activity garnered extreme criticism, because of constitutional violations. A congressional investigation found both Randy Weaver and federal law-enforcement agencies responsible. Weaver could have easily avoided the incident by appearing in court. Federal agencies were culpable due to a lack of leadership responsibility, bad intelligence techniques resulting from accepting another agency's intelligence without rechecking any questionable material, and the inability of an agency to perform an adequate self-investigation. Accordingly, the FBI punished numerous agents and set a uniform policy on the use of deadly force, which has been accepted by other federal law-enforcement agencies.

This incident coupled with the WACO, TEXAS, INCIDENT at the Branch Davidian compound in 1993 was evidence to many right-wing groups of government abuses and religious persecution. Ruby Ridge has been cited by terrorism experts as one of the main reasons behind the OKLAHOMA CITY BOMBING of the Alfred P. Murrah Federal Building by Timothy McVeigh in 1995.

References: Crothers, Lane. *Rage on the Right: The American Militia Movement from Ruby Ridge to Homeland Security* (Lanham, Md.: Rowman & Littlefield Publishers, 2003).

T. L.

Eric Rudolph (1966–)

By the time of his arrest on May 31, 2003, Eric Rudolph had almost become a folk hero in some parts of North Carolina and beyond. In reality, he was a terrorist who, in several attacks, murdered three people and injured around 150. Rudolph lived in Florida until he was 15. At that age, his father died, and his mother moved the family to North Carolina. He went to college for one year and then enlisted in the U.S. Army in 1987. He was discharged in 1989, apparently for smoking marijuana.

Rudolph had early on drifted into political and religious extremism. He also accepted the racist teachings of Christian Identity that emphasize the notion of white Christians as the chosen people while other races and Jews are considered inferior and degenerate. Rudolph, however, later disavowed many of the teachings of Christian Identity and considered himself a Catholic.

The 1996 Summer Olympics, hosted by Atlanta, was marred by Rudolph's attempts to "force the cancellations of the Games" by a bombing attack that killed one person and wounded 111 others. Early the next year, Rudolph bombed an abortion clinic in an Atlanta suburb as well as a gay and lesbian nightclub that injured five people. In 1998, he bombed an abortion clinic in Birmingham, Alabama, that killed a police officer and severely injured a clinic nurse. He spent the next five years running from the law.

For several years, Rudolf was a fugitive and was successful in staying a step ahead of the authorities pursuing him. By 1998, Rudolph had become one of the FBI's 10 most-wanted fugitives. The FBI also offered a $1 million reward for information that would lead to his arrest. For five years, between 1998 and 2003, Rudolph eluded capture despite being hunted by professional law-enforcement officers as well as others interested in securing the reward for his apprehension. He was finally reported to the authorities when observed scavenging for food in a garbage can behind a convenience store. Though he had been pursued relentlessly for five years, Rudolph had never left the area of the Carolinas and

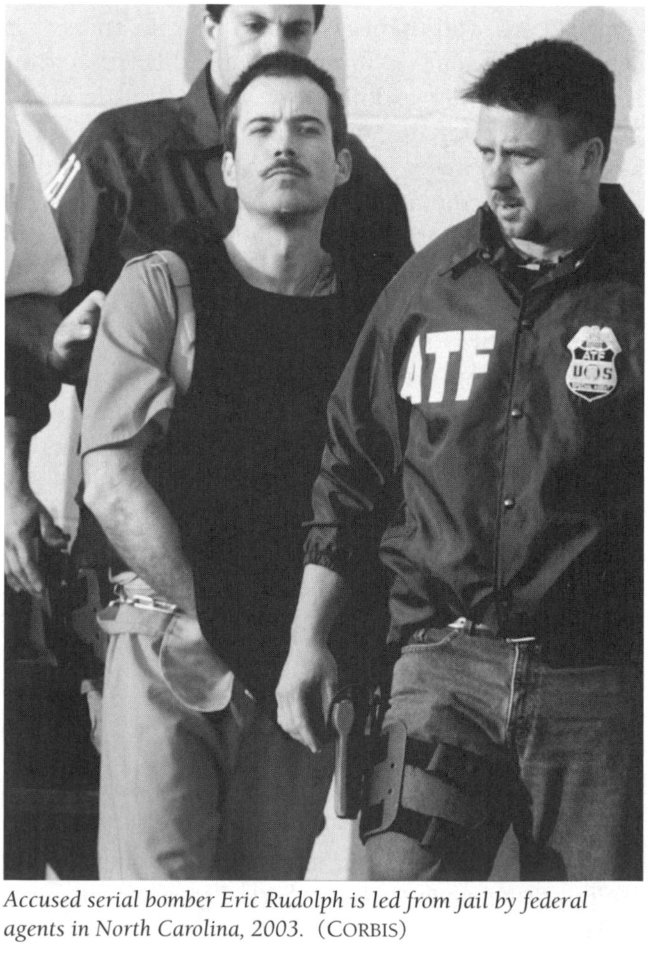

Accused serial bomber Eric Rudolph is led from jail by federal agents in North Carolina, 2003. (CORBIS)

Georgia, seemed in reasonably good physical shape, and was wearing relatively new clothes and shoes. These facts confirmed for many observers that Rudolph had been at least occasionally fed, clothed, and sheltered by numerous sympathizers, the only way to explain how he was able to avoid arrest for so many years. If any of this is true, Rudolph is keeping any information about his protectors to himself. What is factual is the praise Rudolph received and continues to receive from extremist "chatter" that refers to him as a hero.

In some respects, Rudolph comes across as an incomplete or even confused terrorist. He was unwilling to die for his beliefs and pled guilty to his crimes as part of a deal with the Department of Justice to serve four consecutive life terms. At the same time, though, he stated that he did not recognize the authority of the government to judge or imprison him. As a right-wing extremist, Rudolph was assumed to be anti-Semitic; yet his defense was conducted by a Jewish lawyer.

See also ANTIABORTION CLINIC ATTACKS; ARMY OF GOD.

Reference: Schuster, Henry, and Charles Stone. *Hunting Eric Rudolph* (New York: Penguin Group, 2005).

rule of proportionality

Article 50 of Protocol I of the GENEVA CONVENTION ON THE TREATMENT OF CIVILIANS DURING TIMES OF WAR attempts to make clear the precautions that a state and a revolutionary army must make in conducting an attack. This article codifies customary international law concerning what is called the rule of proportionality. Generally speaking, this refers to the need for the loss of civilian life to be minimal compared to the military advantage gained. It states specifically that those who plan or decide upon an attack must:

> Refrain from deciding to launch any attack which may be expected to cause incidental loss of civilian life . . . which would be excessive in relation to the concrete and direct military advantage anticipated.

In simple terms, this provision, along with other provisions in the article, means that those launching or planning to launch an attack are legally responsible for making sure that the military objectives that they expect to gain justify the minimal loss of civilian life that may occur. This provision is extremely practical. It recognizes a basic fact of life during war: There are inevitably civilians on and around military targets who will no doubt be injured or killed during an attack on those targets.

This rule was recently debated when ISRAEL was accused by the United Nations of "disproportionate use of force" in airstrikes by the Israeli military during the 2006 offensive against HIZBALLAH in Lebanon. Some legal scholars argued that Israel's response to the abduction of its soldiers was excessive, resulting in the unnecessary suffering of civilians. Israel countered that it was acting in self-defense and that the kidnapping of its soldiers was an act of war.

Reference: Council on Foreign Relations. "Israel and the Doctrine of Proportionality." Available online. URL: http://www.cfr.org/publication/11115/. Accessed December 5, 2006.

Rushdie, Salman (1947–)

Salman Rushdie is a well-known novelist who was condemned by the Iranian government for authoring and publishing his work *Satanic Verses*, which was declared to be blasphemous. Several months before his death, AYATOLLAH KHOMEINI issued a fatwa, or religious decree, advocating Rushdie's assassination by any Muslim willing to take on the task. A $2.5 million award is available to the successful assassin. Rushdie, a British citizen and a Muslim, has received the protection of the British government ever since. He has made several public appearances but remains in hiding most of the time. The decree has not been rescinded since Khomeini's death though the Iranian president, Mohammad Khatemi, stated in 1998 that "[the] Rushdie matter [was] completely finished."

In early 2005, Khomeini's fatwa against Rushdie was reaffirmed by Iran's spiritual leader, Ayatollah Ali Khamenei, in a message to Muslim pilgrims making the annual pilgrimage to Mecca. Iran has rejected requests to withdraw the fatwa on the basis that only the person who issued it may withdraw it, under Islamic law. The fatwa, however, has not been lifted by either the Iranian government or by the clerics whose foundation has financed the award for Rushdie's murder.

Reference: BBC. Middle East. "Iran Adamant over Rushdie Fatwa." February 12, 2005. Available online. URL: http://news.bbc.co.uk/2/hi/middle_east/4260599.stm. Accessed March 24, 2006.

S

Sabra and Shatila

On September 16, 1982, a massacre took place in Beruit at the Sabra and Shatila refugee camps. Lebanese Christian militia—in retaliation for the assassination of their leader—attacked the unarmed refugee camps, killing hundreds of innocent civilians. Israeli forces (allies to the Lebanese militia) stood nearby and did not intervene. The incident is considered one of the most horrific in the Arab-Israeli conflict.

In 1982, Ariel Sharon was the Israeli minister of defense, in a government dominated by the right-of-center political coalition, the Likud, led by Menachem Begin. The Likud and its allies won its first parliamentary majority in 1977, and Begin became prime minister. His choice of Sharon was controversial. By this time, Begin had concluded a peace treaty and exchanged diplomatic recognition with Egypt, and Israeli forces had been withdrawn from most of the Sinai. The PALESTINE LIBERATION ORGANIZATION (PLO) did not accept the Israeli-Egyptian peace process and continued its operations against Israeli targets from bases in southern Lebanon. The Israelis had also made overtures to the Lebanese government. The Palestinians living in Lebanon, mostly in refugee camps, had become a state within a state. The PLO had a great deal more control over the camps than did the host government. Moreover, the Palestinian refugees were now more than a 10th of the total population in Lebanon. They did not hold citizenship and lived at a subsistence level in camps sustained by United Nations relief organizations. The camps, though, contained around 400,000 Palestinians, including large numbers of disaffected and impoverished youths with no future prospects, an excellent recruiting ground for the PLO's campaign of terror against Israeli towns and collective settlements across the southern Lebanese border.

Sharon determined to end the menace once and for all by invading Lebanon in June 1982. He assumed it would be possible to dislodge the PLO from its bases and disarm its militants. The occupation of much of Lebanon and Beirut by Israeli military forces was a tactical success. It was not, however, the victory the Israelis would have preferred. Sharon was able to force the PLO out of Lebanon and into exile in Tunis for the next decade. This event, however, did not end terrorist attacks on Israelis, since other and even more radical organizations, including HIZBALLAH, began to fill the vacuum.

The newly elected Lebanese president, Bachir Gemayel, was assassinated on September 14. Gemayal, a Maronite Christian, had cooperated with Israelis to contain extremist forces, including the PLO, in

Lebanon. Two days later, Phalangist militia (the military arm of the Maronite Christian party of the same name) was allowed by the Israelis, and specifically encouraged by Sharon, to enter two Palestinian refugee camps near Beirut, Sabra and Shatila, ostensibly to locate PLO operatives and transfer them to Israeli authority. The Phalangists, apparently seeking revenge for the murder of their leader, handed over no one to the Israelis, but instead engaged in wholesale murder of defenseless civilians. Several hundred Palestinians were killed, though the true number will probably never be known.

The world community condemned the murders as an act of genocide. Israel was excoriated for allowing it to occur. Israeli forces certainly controlled access to the camps and could have intervened. Sharon was condemned as a war criminal by many even in Israel itself. Hundreds of thousands of Israelis demonstrated against the government and demanded Sharon's resignation. He was hounded into leaving the ministerial post he had long coveted. Sharon was relegated to the political wilderness and few anticipated his remarkable political comeback that would occur nearly two decades later. Israel established a Commission of Inquiry, chaired by a former Supreme Court justice. The commission held that Israel did not participate in the massacre but could have taken steps to prevent or stop it. It recommended that Sharon never hold political office again.

Tragically, Sabra and Shatila were not an isolated event. In 1976, Phalangists had massacred other Palestinians and the PLO had massacred Maronites, in separate instances. Neither Israel nor the PLO could fully control the civil war in Lebanon that lasted 15 years (1975–90) and cost 100,000 lives.

Reference: BBC. Middle East. "Flashback: Sabra and Shatila Massacres." January 24, 2002. Available online. URL: http://news.bbc.co.uk/2/hi/middle_east/1779713.stm. Accessed on March 24, 2006.

Sadat, Anwar (1918–1981)

Anwar Sadat was the last surviving colleague of the organization created by Gamal Abdul Nasser, the Egyptian Free Officers. The Free Officers, mostly colonels, took power in a successful coup in July 1952 that ended the corrupt monarchy of King Farouk. Sadat, during World War II, worked actively for a period against the British in an effort to aid the Germans in removing Britain from the Middle East. Sadat's nationalism was further intensified after the Egyptian defeat during the first Arab-Israeli war in 1948–49.

While he was always loyal to Nasser, there is little evidence that Sadat was consistently a member of the inner circle of power. Even during the coup, Sadat, apparently uninformed of the coup's immanence, went to a movie. As one of the coup's members after another fell away, Sadat remained. Shortly before his death in 1970, Nasser made Sadat his vice president. When he took power, Sadat was widely underestimated. Nevertheless, he acted quickly to consolidate his rule. In 1972, he expelled the Soviet military advisers whom Nasser had brought in. The next year Sadat attacked ISRAEL in a surprise attack on the Israeli military in the Sinai, which achieved enough of a victory for him to be referred to as the "hero of the crossing," although Israeli forces recovered and even landed troops in Egypt proper. His most daring move came in 1977 when Sadat flew to Israel and began the peace process.

Sadat was able to retrieve the Sinai Desert from Israel in exchange for diplomatic recognition, the demilitarization of the Sinai, and modest trade relations. He shared with MENACHEM BEGIN, the Israeli prime minister, the Nobel Peace Prize. Sadat, however, also irritated Islamic fundamentalists in Egypt who had long plotted against his life and assassinated him in 1981. He had, however, changed the nature of the Arab-Israeli conflict and ended its most serious hostility.

Reference: el-Sadat, Anwar. *In Search of Identity: An Autobiography* (London: Collins, 1978).

Saint Elliah's Rebellion *See* INTERNAL MACEDONIAN REVOLUTIONARY ORGANIZATION.

Salafist Group for Call and Combat

In 1998, a splinter group of the ARMED ISLAMIC GROUP (GIA), the Salafist Group for Call and Combat (GSPC), eclipsed the GIA and is currently the most effective and largest armed group inside Algeria. The GSPC seeks to overthrow the Algerian government with the goal of establishing an Islamic regime, and, unlike the GIA, has pledged to avoid attacks on civilians inside Algeria. Instead, it attacks Algerian government and military targets, primarily in rural areas. In August 2004, the GSPC carried out an ambush on a military convoy in which 40 members of the security forces were killed. In

June of the same year, the group exploded a device outside the El-Hamma electric power-generating facility in central Algiers, causing no casualties but knocking out 210 MW of generating capacity for several months.

Government forces significantly weakened the GSPC in 2004 by capturing or killing several leaders, including the leader Nabil Sahraoui and one of his top lieutenants, Abbi Abdelaziz, seriously weakening the organization. However, in late 2003, the GSPC leader issued a communiqué announcing the group's support of a number of jihadist causes and movements, including AL-QAEDA. According to press reports, some GSPC members in Europe and the Middle East maintain contact with other North African extremists sympathetic to al-Qaeda.

There are several hundred fighters still active in this group, with an unknown number of facilitators outside of Algeria. Algerian expatriates and GSPC members abroad, many of whom reside in western Europe, continue to provide financial and logistical support for this group. The GSPC has also engaged in kidnap for ransom.

Reference: National Memorial Institute for the Prevention of Terrorism (MIPT). "Salafist Group for Call and Combat (GSPC)." Available online. URL: http://www.tkb.org/Group.jsp?groupID=3777. Accessed February 15, 2006.

Sánchez, Ilyich Ramírez *See* CARLOS "THE JACKAL."

SAS *See* SPECIAL PROJECTS TEAM-SPECIAL AIR SERVICE (SAS).

Sayaret Mat'kal (General Staff Reconaissance Unit 269)

Founded nearly a decade after Israel's establishment in 1948, the Sayaret Mat'kal was one of the state's early elite antiterrorist military formations. The entrance process is severe, and only a tiny percentage of applicants are admitted to the training program. The Sayeret Mat'kal specializes in hostage-rescue operations in Israel. However, the unit also engages in foreign activities and is understood to have been involved in the 1976 ENTEBBE operation. Sayeret Mat'kal frequently cooperates with other Israeli counterterrorist organizations, such as Sayeret Tzanhanim, the elite paratrooper unit.

During the early 1970s Sayeret Mat'kal carried out several successful operations against BLACK SEPTEMBER, the group responsible for the MUNICH MASSACRE OF ISRAELI ATHLETES, that included hostage-rescue efforts and the assassination of several of its leaders in Beirut. Abu Jihad, one of the closest of YASIR ARAFAT's deputies and considered a leading terrorist by Israeli authorities, was assassinated in Tunis in 1988 by members of Sayeret Mat'kal. The former Israeli prime minister, Ehud Barak, was a Sayeret Mat'kal officer and was apparently involved in several counterterrorist activities.

In Israel, the Talmudic injunction, "If someone comes to kill you, rise and kill him first," has become the slogan of the Sayaret Mat'kal. This specialized Israeli antiterrorist strike force is so secretive that the Israelis rarely even mention it by name. It is this unit that has been responsible not only for the raids into Beirut to murder Palestinian leaders but also for the Entebbe rescue operation in June 1976.

It is this unit that has both successfully thwarted terrorist attacks and, in its zeal to "strike before being struck" and to punish terrorists, has also been guilty of the murder of innocent persons. When Prime Minister GOLDA MEIR unleashed "hit teams" the day after the Munich massacre, with orders to roam the world seeking out and summarily executing those responsible for the attack, the results were neither entirely legal nor wholly desirable.

One of these "hit teams" assassinated the wrong man. At Lillehammer, Norway, in 1973, an innocent Moroccan waiter was gunned down by a hit team in front of his pregnant Norwegian wife. The team had mistaken the waiter for the architect of the Munich massacre, Ali Hassan Salameh. International indignation forced Israel to restrain the hit squads temporarily. This was, however, only a brief setback in Israel's use of strike forces in its war on terrorism. In January 1979, one of Israel's hit teams succeeded in blowing up Salameh with a radio-controlled car bomb in Beirut. This bomb also killed his four bodyguards and five innocent people who happened to be passing by at the time. The Israeli hit team may also have been responsible for the assassination in Tunis on April 16, 1988, of Khalil al-Wazir, the PALESTINE LIBERATION ORGANIZATION's mastermind of terrorist strategy against Israel.

One of the ironies of Israel's response to this incident is that, as an excusatory footnote to their (unofficial) admission of regret at the loss of innocent lives,

Israel has suggested that these people were just "in the wrong place at the wrong time." This has unfortunate echoes of the "justification" offered by terrorists of harm to innocent people caused by their bombs.

The innocent persons killed, like Susan Wareham, a British woman working as a secretary for a construction company in Beirut, committed only the mistake of being too near Salameh's car when it exploded. While counterterrorist attacks like this may not deliberately take innocent life, they are undoubtedly culpable of a wanton disregard for the safety of innocent persons. Callous, uncaring, or deliberate disregard for the safety of innocent persons—the difference may be in the degree of disregard for the sanctity of human life. The net result for the innocent bystander is unhappily the same.

Not all of Israel's counterattacks on terrorism have been so counterproductive. Indeed, the Sayaret Mat'kal is one of the best-trained and well-equipped special forces unit in operation today, with an impressive record of successful missions as well.

This unit is not part of the regular army and reports only to the chief of intelligence. Its members do, however, wear uniforms. This unit does not rely on trained volunteers but instead draws on raw recruits from the Kelet (the recruit depot). Usually an officer of the Sayaret Mat'kal will go to the Kelet to select about 15 to 20 recruits to form a team.

This team does much of its training in enemy territory, where the bullets are as real as the enemy. Recruits who survive this basic training become permanent members of a squad. Such squads are trained in the use of the .22 Baretta pistol as well as the Uzi, the Israeli-invented machine pistol and the Kalashnikov, the Russian assault rifle.

The Sayaret Mat'kal conducted a raid inside Lebanon, in December of 1968, that was described as an attempt to force the Lebanese to prevent Palestinian terrorists from mounting their attacks from LEBANON. Earlier that year, the Palestinians had carried out a successful hijacking, taking over an El Al airliner en route from Rome to Tel Aviv. They had also attacked another El Al plane at Athens airport in Greece, damaging it with automatic fire and grenades. Israeli intelligence reports showed that both terrorist incidents originated in Beirut.

So a commando raid, carried out by the Sayaret Mat'kal, was launched against Beirut International Airport. Thirteen Arab aircraft, including nine jetliners, were destroyed. There were no casualties since all of the airplanes were cleared of passengers and crew first.

While the raid was a tactical success, its long-term effects were less rewarding. President Charles De Gaulle of France condemned the raid as a violation of the sovereignty of a nation-state and used it as a reason for cutting off all arms shipments to Israel. This cutoff came at a time when the Israeli Defense Forces were relying heavily on French equipment. Moreover, the other major supplier of Israeli arms, the United States, expressed its displeasure over the raid but stopped short of cutting off arms shipments.

Furthermore, the Palestinians acquired both publicity and a certain amount of public sympathy for their cause. Finally, the airline company that owned and operated the planes, Middle East Airlines, was able to purchase a whole new fleet of jetliners with the insurance money from the destroyed planes.

Other assault operations were equally "successful" but had perhaps less negative impacts. It was the Sayaret Mat'kal that in 1972 successfully ended the hijacking of a Sabena Boeing 707 jetliner, flight 517 from Brussels to Tel Aviv. When four members of the Black September Palestinian group hijacked the plane and forced it to land at LOD AIRPORT, they announced that they intended to blow up the plane, with its 90 passengers and 10 crew members, unless the Israeli government met their demands for the release of over 300 Arab prisoners.

The Sayaret Mat'kal assault force succeeded in storming the plane and freeing the passengers and crew members. While one passenger was killed, and two of the hijackers, this minimal loss of life became the standard for similar feats, such as that carried out by Germany's GSG-9 at Mogadishu.

When the Palestinians struck again, it was at the Olympic Games in Munich, only months after the Lod Airport rescue. Israeli athletes were the target, and the Sayaret Mat'kal was excluded from the attempts to free those hostages.

Sayaret Mat'kal's activities are difficult to monitor because of the secrecy that cloaks them. What can be safely assumed, however, is that the unit continues to be very much involved in Israel's counterterrorist program. Its activities were revived during the second intifadah that began in the fall of 2000 when peace talks between Israel and the Palestinian Authority broke down. The Israeli government has always justified the assassination activities of its special military units, which it says target especially brutal terrorists.

school site analysis

Typically, Americans do not include violence that occurs in a nation's schools within the scope of terrorism; however, schools are often the focal point of many communities and their children are the essence of a society. This makes them potential targets for domestic terrorism. Although research suggests that the number of violent acts occurring in schools is decreasing across the United States, the level of intensity of these acts is increasing and becoming more complex in nature. School-based terrorist incidents do not seem to discriminate between small and large communities. Furthermore, the media tends to highlight the element of fear that is produced when a violent act is committed in a school environment. As a result of strong media attention, communities demand that school officials create safe school prevention strategies aimed at curbing the potential for violence. Often, schools and the communities they reside in are ill prepared to combat and prevent terrorist acts from occurring. Partnerships between public safety professionals, school officials, and various members of the community are strongly encouraged to facilitate a collaborative, comprehensive approach to prevent terrorism from plaguing a community's schools. This can be accomplished by conducting a school site analysis.

School site analysis is a risk-reducing opportunity that binds, as well as encourages, all disciplines of public safety and school administrative staff to discuss how to interface with one another during any type of emergency event and specifically during terrorist acts. It is imperative for both groups involved in the analysis to understand one another's protocols and response capabilities to effectively manage any natural, technological, or human-made emergency incident that can directly or indirectly affect a school. General discussion topics that should take place during the analysis include, but are not limited to, proper evacuation protocols, bomb threat management techniques, crime prevention strategies, structural and nonstructural mitigation components, emergency notification issues, responder staging areas, and, most importantly, terrorist intrusion that may potentially result in mass violence.

In the event of a terrorist intrusion, it is important for school staff and students to be alerted to the potential threat in order to minimize and prevent further aggression that may lead to violence. Proper notification procedures essential during terrorist intrusions can be accomplished through the use of uniformly plain language. Using plain-language codes will eliminate confusion during a terrorist intrusion by aiding staff, substitute teachers, visitors, students, and public safety officials in instant recognition of the terroristic situation at hand. During the school site analysis, it should be determined if plain-language codes are currently in place and if they can be quickly announced throughout the interior and exterior areas of the school facility and campus.

Should a lockdown be initiated due to a terrorist act in progress, the following procedures are recommended for teachers:

- Make sure all students are out of the hallways and bathroom areas. If outside the facility, seek immediate cover and do not reenter the building unless instructed to do so by law enforcement officials or administrative staff.
- Teachers should secure their doors (if possible), making sure that the interior door window is unobstructed to allow for clear visibility into the hallway. NOTE: In most cases, public safety will prefer that classroom windows remain clear and unobstructed to aid response efforts and in building clearance efforts.
- Exterior windows should remain locked with blinds open to ensure that public safety has a clear line of sight into the classroom.
- Students should be instructed to seek a cover position out of sight from the main classroom door window. If possible, students should be placed near a reinforced concrete/brick wall.
- Teachers should not attempt to contact the office except in cases of medical emergencies.
- Teachers should not open any door during a lockdown unless a predetermined all-clear code is announced to them by public safety. This code should remain confidential between school staff and public safety officials.

Restricting school facility access is another factor to be considered during the site analysis. In order to monitor the ingress and egress of all students and visitors effectively, schools should secure all exterior doors and funnel people through an entrance located adjacent to the central office area if possible. This will increase school administrative staff's ability to recognize potentially threatening individuals as they enter the facility. Central office staff must have good visibility of the exterior pedestrian approach area located by the monitored entrance. On a daily basis it is recommended that teachers keep their individual classroom doors locked during instructional times. This will aid a safe school environment should an intruder enter the building through an exterior door without being observed.

Often, first responders are not familiar with school facilities and need to be provided with any site-specific information that can aid their efforts. A crucial area to be discussed during the site analysis is the development of detailed floor plans of the school facility and informative campus site plans. In order to assist public safety's response efforts, floor plans must provide vital facility information such as alarm panel stations, cable/satellite cutoff points, interior roof access, and critical utility shutoff points. Furthermore, all rooms must be visibly numbered and should correctly correspond to the floor plan that is provided to public safety. Public safety responders are encouraged to photograph critical areas within the school (i.e., roof access, shut panels, various classrooms, cafeteria, entrances and exits, and central office area). In addition to interior labels, exterior labeling of a school is also crucial. Hallways and classrooms should be labeled on the exterior of the building to assist public safety with response efforts. All exterior labeling should be reflective to increase visibility.

In conjunction with the development of the floor plan, a site plan should also be considered. Site plans encompass critical exterior areas that should be taken into consideration when responding to a terrorist event. Areas that should be marked on a site plan include, but are not limited to, gas mains, propane tanks, fire hydrants, campus access roads, possible landing zones, and heating and air-conditioning unit cutoff points.

This element of counterterrorism became, in the United States, a critical focus following incidents at elementary, middle, and high schools during the 1990s. Several states, led by efforts in Georgia, have instituted counterterrorism techniques, particularly focused on schools, in their emergency management personnel and planning.

B. L. and S. H.

SEAL Team Six (U.S. Naval Special Warfare Development Group [NSWDG]), a.k.a. Dev Group [DEVGRU])

Formed in 1980, with headquarters in Dam Neck, Virginia, the Naval Special Warfare Development Group, formerly known as SEAL Team Six, is responsible for U.S. counterterrorist operations in the maritime environment. While the origins of this unit can be traced to the aftermath of the failed 1980 attempt to rescue American hostages from the embassy in Teheran, Iran, the SEALs had already initiated counterterrorism (CT) training, including all 12 platoons in SEAL Team One on the West Coast. However, on the East Coast, parts of SEAL Team Two had also formed a dedicated two-platoon group, known as MOB Six (Mobility Six) in preparation for a maritime scenario that might require a CT response. Since only one group was needed for this type of operation, MOB Six was demobilized and SEAL Team Six (a name selected primarily to confuse Soviet intelligence as to the number of SEAL teams in operation) was formally created in October 1980. A large number of members of MOB Six, including the former MOB commander, were asked to join the new team. Based on the prior experience these operators possessed, with aggressive leadership and an accelerated training program, SEAL Team Six was declared mission ready only six months later.

SEAL Team Six was trained both in the United States and abroad, on military as well as civilian facilities. Joint training exercises and exchange programs with more experienced international teams, including Germany's GSG-9, the United Kingdom's Special Boat Squadron, and France's combat divers. Throughout the training process, emphasis was placed on realism, in accordance with the "Train as you fight, fight as you train" philosophy predominant in most of the world's CT and special operations units.

During the first decade of its existence, SEAL Team Six participated in several operations, overt and covert. In 1985, Six was responsible for the rescue and evacuation of Governor, Sir Paul Scoon from Grenada during Operation Urgent Fury. Four SEALs were lost in this operation during helicopter insertion offshore. The unit also took part in Operation Just Cause as part of Task Force White, which included SEAL Team Two, where their primary task, working with Delta Force, was the location and securing of Panamanian strongman Manuel Noriega in 1989. In 1991, SEAL Team Six reportedly recovered Haitian president Jean-Bertrand Aristide under cover of darkness following the coup that deposed him.

During the 1990s, Six was revamped and renamed. The U.S. government now refers to this unit as the Naval Special Warfare Development Group (NSWDG) and has charged it with overseeing development of NSW tactics, equipment, and techniques. While the unit is under the direct command of Naval Special Warfare Groups, it is also a component of Joint Special

Operations Command (JSOC) based at Pope Air Force Base, North Carolina, along with other CT units such as Delta Force based at Fort Bragg, North Carolina, and the 160th Special Operations Aviation Regiment (SOAR).

Information about the new NSWDG is less easily verified. It is believed that this group trains frequently with the 160th SOAR, especially in support of ship assaults, which often make use of the small MH-6 "Little Bird," operated exclusively by the 160th. Organization and manpower of NSWDG is classified, but estimates indicate that the group now has approximately 200 operators, which are broken down by teams in a similar pattern as that used by the SAS and Delta Force. There are reportedly four such teams currently in the group: assault units Red, Blue, and Gold and a special boat unit, Gray. There is also an administrative and testing section, which has approximately 300 personnel, responsible for the actual testing and development of new Naval Special Warfare equipment, including weapons. Operators in the NSWDG reportedly fire an average of 2,500 to 3,000 rounds per week in training. This group is one of a very small number of U.S. units authorized to conduct preemptive actions against terrorists and terrorist facilities. DEVGRU members have seen action in conflicts such as the 1991 Persian Gulf War, Bosnia in 1996, and are most likely still participating in current actions in Afghanistan and Iraq.

See also SPECIAL OPERATIONS UNITS OF THE UNITED STATES GOVERNMENT.

Reference: http://www.terrorism.com.

Navy SEALs prepare to launch one of the team's SEAL Delivery Vehicles (SDVs) from the back of the Los Angeles–class attack submarine USS Philadelphia. (U.S. NAVY)

Security Barrier, Israeli

The barrier is often referred to by its critics as a wall and sometimes as a new Berlin Wall. Parts of the barrier are walls while other parts are chain-linked fences. In 2003, Israel began construction of a 425-mile barrier to protect its national security. The progress of the barrier has been criticized by many governments outside of Israel as destructive of any hope to revive the peace process with the Palestinians. For their part, the Palestinians consider the barrier a "land grab" for more territory that should be part of a Palestinian state once it is created. The barrier occasionally goes deeply into the West Bank to enhance Israeli security as well as to annex settlements created in the West Bank since the 1967 conflict. Most Israelis accept and even encourage the government's rationale that only by constructing the barrier can terrorist attacks on civilians on Israel's side of the Green Line be stopped.

Many Israelis however, have objected to their government's decision to build the barrier. These are basically divided into two camps: 1.) religious and hard-line Israelis who believe that in building the barrier, the Israelite heartland of Judea and Samaria, center of the ancient kingdom, is being unilaterally surrendered when this land should belong to Israel in perpetuity; 2.) moderate Israelis who view the barrier as a permanent obstacle to any settlement with the Palestinians.

In July 2004, the International Court of Justice, in a 14-1 ruling, issued an advisory opinion that indicated the barrier was illegal and should be dismantled. Israel responded that it would not comply with the opinion. However, several weeks earlier, the Israeli Supreme Court ordered the government to reroute or remove a total of 32 miles of the barrier in order to ease the difficulties imposed by the barrier on West Bank Palestinians. The barrier, when finished, will include about 80% of the Jews who have settled in the West Bank and perhaps 1% of the Arabs who live there. It seems likely that the barrier will remain, at least in some form, even if there is an Israeli-Palestinian peace arrangement and even if the government is eventually more moderate.

Israeli Jews of nearly all political persuasions see in the barrier a response to the increasingly discussed one-state solution or a binational state that would eventually provide Arabs with a numerical majority because of their higher birthrate. If Israel and the West Bank region became unified under one jurisdiction, Arab Christians and Muslims would probably outnumber Jews by 2012 if those 1.3 million Israeli Arabs are included in the calculations. A binational state is anathema to most Israeli Jews because of the widespread desire to retain the Jewish character of Israel.

The barrier may also be a response by the Sharon government to the most extreme elements in his own party who have called for the expulsion of Arabs from the West Bank, many of whom live in West Bank settlements. These elements consider Arabs there to be interlopers who brought Islam to the area 14 centuries ago. What is clear about the barrier is the admission, at least from the Israeli side, that there is no realistic hope in attempting to resuscitate the peace process with the Palestinian Authority. The Israelis have determined to act unilaterally. The decisions to evacuate the Gaza Strip settlements and to construct the barrier are both part of a strategy to disengage from a population and regime the government considers unreasonable at best and pathologically violent at worst.

References: Netanyahu, Benjamin "Why Israel Needs a Fence." *New York Times*, July 13, 2004; Rabkin, Jeremy. "Lawfare," *The Wall Street Journal*, July 13, 2004, p. A14.

Sendero Luminoso

This is a Spanish term for "Shining Path." The organization first appeared during the 1960s in Peru. Between 1980 and 2000, approximately 30,000 civilians and military personnel died in violent incidents that involved the Sendero Luminoso. The organization was formed by a former university professor of philosophy, Abimael Guzmán. Guzmán was captured by the Peruvian military in 1992 and has since been confined to prison.

Sendero Luminoso's guiding ideology is an extreme form of Marxist doctrine. In some sense, the organization may be likened to the KHMER ROUGE (PARTY OF DEMOCRATIC KAMPUCHEA) in that its goals include the destruction of existing political, economic, and social institutions and their replacement with a communal and peasant society. It has also been consistently opposed to any foreign presence in Peru whether in the form of outside governmental or corporate influence. Numerous diplomatic missions were attacked by the Sendero Luminoso because they represented foreign interests.

The ideology also suggests that Peru's overall culture be transformed to the one that prevailed before the arrival of Europeans in the early 16th century. In other words, a regression to an agricultural and pastoral lifestyle that supposedly prevailed during the times of the Inca Empire is considered by the Sendero Luminoso to be a viable ideological goal. During the administration of Peruvian president Alberto Fujimori (1990–2000), the Sendero Luminoso's influence in rural regions was decidedly lessened. Guzmán's successor, Oscar Alberto Ramírez Durand, was captured in 1999.

Shaldag

A Hebrew term that means "kingfisher." Shaldag is an elite Israeli army unit that appeared at the end of 2000 in lethal form. Shaldag is composed of some of the best snipers in the Israeli military. The unit was formed to assassinate Palestinian operatives considered to be especially brutal terrorists. Shaldag and its activities are controversial among both Israelis and Palestinians. The Israeli government has consistently defended the assassination policy as "effective, precise, and just." Shaldag members have targeted not only Palestinians who commit terrorist acts against Israelis but also Palestinians who have murdered other Palestinians considered to be collaborators with the Israelis. Shaldag employs state-of-the-art technology to track its targets. For example, drones that can fly up to a mile high have been employed to follow a possible target and relay the target's movements with a live video feed.

Shaldag has a long lineage. After Palestinian terrorists murdered seven Israeli athletes at the 1972 Munich Olympics, Israeli hit squads located and murdered all of them with one exception. Even before that, Israeli agents made serious efforts to find surviving Nazi war criminals. With the notable exception of Adolf Eichmann, however, Israel was unable to locate, let alone arrest, any of these perpetrators of mass murder. The Palestinian leadership is especially disconcerted by Shaldag because the Israelis have not hesitated to target anyone whom they consider to be a justified target, regardless of how highly placed. A senior official in the Palestinian Ministry of Health, for instance, was shot to death in retaliation for the murder the same day of Benjamin Kahane, an Israeli extremist, and his wife.

References: Rees, Matt. "The Work of Assassins." *Time* (January 15, 2001): 36–39; Richburg, Keith R. "Israel's Assassination Policy." *Washington Post National Weekly Edition* (January 15–21, 2001): 14.

Sharon, Ariel (1929–)

Ariel Sharon became prime minister of Israel in 2001 at the age of 73, the oldest person ever elected to the office; he was reelected in 2003. He had long sought the office but, by the early 1990s, had been discounted as warrior turned politician out of step with the times. He had consistently opposed the Oslo Accords and, as a result, had restricted his political appeal to the Israeli right. Sharon's elevation to the Israeli head of government was in great part the result of the breakdown of the peace process in 2000 between the preceding government of Ehud Barak and Arafat's Palestinian Authority. It was also the result of the beginning of a new INTIFADA that many Israelis as well as Palestinians believed Sharon helped provoke by his visit to the Temple Mount in September 2000, accompanied by approximately 1,000 armed bodyguards.

Sharon had made his name as a clever and daring soldier. He had fought in all the Israeli conflicts with the Arabs since the War of Independence in 1948. For most of the 1950s, he was the founder and first commander of Unit 101, an elite commando unit charged with pursuing reprisal attacks against Arab terrorist organizations, at that time based primarily in the Gaza Strip. During the Six-Day War in 1967, Sharon commanded an armored division. He was credited at the time for his tactical successes. He was also criticized for insubordination, a criticism that was not new in his military career and would appear in the future. As a commander during the Yom Kippur War in 1973, Sharon exhibited a substantial amount of military daring by moving IDF forces under his command into Egypt proper while the main Egyptian army was engaged in the Sinai. The maneuver was well received in Israel and some began referring to Sharon as "king of Israel." Sharon desired to march to Cairo but was restrained, despite his strong protests, by the Israeli government. Yet it is widely accepted that the presence of Israeli military units in African Egypt helped to turn the tide to the Israelis' favor.

Immediately after the conflict, Sharon pursued a political career and became a member of parliament in 1974 with the LIKUD Party. He crossed party lines in 1976 to become a primary adviser of the Labor government's prime minister, Yitzhak Rabin. In the 1977 elections, he created his own party—which only won two seats. The new prime minister, MENACHEM BEGIN, appointed Sharon minister of agriculture. Sharon then began to pursue his ambition to create and sustain settlements in the West Bank. The process had been underway for several years, but Sharon accelerated the construction of existing and new settlements. Between 1977 and 1981, Sharon claims to have established a total of 64 settlements in occupied territories.

Likud won the 1981 parliamentary elections, and Sharon was appointed to the ministry he had long sought, defense. Sharon turned his attention to Lebanon for at least two reasons he felt were compelling: 1.) the sizable Christian Maronite community in Lebanon had the potential of becoming an ally of Israel. In some respects, it already was since from the time of Rabin's premiership (1974–77) and probably earlier Israel had furnished military aid to the Christian Phalange Party to combat rival Druse and Islamic factions; 2.) southern Lebanon was partially controlled by the PALESTINE LIBERATION ORGANIZATION (PLO) that was the de facto government for the 400,000 Palestinian refugees who lived in areas adjacent to Israel's northern border and who provided recruits for the PLO's terrorist attacks on Israel's towns. The Phalange was very apprehensive about having a large number of foreign refugees who had no loyalty to the Lebanese government the Phalange then dominated. Sharon was convinced that by invading Lebanon and with the assistance of the Christian Phalange it would be feasible to end the PLO's domination of the south, free northern Israel from terrorism, and guarantee a regime that was friendly to Israel. He was able to dislodge the PLO from Lebanon and force Arafat into exile in Tunis.

Sharon's military career came to an ignominious end soon after the 1982 Israeli invasion of Lebanon and the massacre of Palestinian Muslims by Lebanese Christian militia in the SABRA AND SHATILA refugee camps. Sharon was widely believed to have allowed the militia to enter the camps fully aware of what their presence might lead to. He neither restrained the militia nor ordered Israeli forces to end the violence when word reached him of the militia's depredations.

However, Sharon's political career was not over, it was only interrupted. He was now tainted and thoroughly identified with the extremist elements on the Israeli right. Sharon spent several years in the political wilderness but did not give up on his quest for the ultimate prize of the Israeli prime ministership. His visit to the Temple Mount in September 2000 was in one way an announcement of his candidacy for the job in the next national election and developed into a successful political strategy.

After being active on the Israeli military and political scene for a half century, Sharon was elected prime minister in February 2001. He became the country's fifth prime minister in eight years. The circumstances of Sharon's election were unprecedented. It was the result of the largest landslide and of the lowest voter turnout in Israeli political history. Most Israeli Arab voters boycotted the election.

Both Israeli and Palestinian Arabs considered Sharon an extremist who was brutally unfair in his view of the Arab world. They as well as some Israeli Jews held him responsible for the 1982 massacres of Palestinians in the Sabra and Shatila refugee camps in southern Lebanon by local Christian militia. As defense minister, Sharon had masterminded the invasion of Lebanon promising a brief conflict that went on until his predecessor withdrew Israel's military presence in 2000. A government inquiry into Sharon's role determined that while he did not order the militia into the camps, he was aware of their presence and responsible for what went on inside of them. Sharon later served as minister of housing (1990–92). In that capacity, he encouraged the building of permanent Israeli settlements in the West Bank. He had been consistently opposed to and critical of the Israeli-Palestinian peace process, arguing that Israel had already made excessive concessions to the Palestinians and received very little in return.

This attitude seriously impacted his ability to deal effectively with YASIR ARAFAT and with Arafat's successor, Abbas. While Sharon eventually orchestrated a pullout of the Gaza Strip by both Jewish settlers and the military, he also began construction of the so-called SECURITY BARRIER around parts of the West Bank, an action criticized by many but also applauded by many Israelis in that territory.

In 2005, Sharon began to try to form a new coalition, as his pullout of Gaza had angered many within his own party, making further pullouts in the West Bank impossible to negotiate. However, he suffered a stroke in the fall of 2005 and remained in a coma as the country prepared for new elections in 2006. The victory of HAMAS in the Palestinian elections in January 2006 made the future of Sharon's leadership even more uncertain.

Reference: Kimmerling, Baruch. *Politicide: Ariel Sharon's War against the Palestinians* (London and New York: Verso, 2003).

Shigenobu, Fusako (1945–)

Fusako Shigenobu was leader of the JAPANESE RED ARMY, an international terrorist group formed around 1970 after breaking away from the Japanese Communist League–Red Army Faction. Under her leadership, the JRA conducted a number of attacks around the world, including the massacre in 1972 at Lod Airport in Israel and an attempt to take over the U.S. embassy in Kuala Lumpur.

Fusako Shigenobu was arrested in November of 2000, and while imprisoned, she announced she was disbanding the Japanese Red Army, and said she would continue her fight through legal means. In February 2006 she was convicted of kidnapping and attempted murder over a 1974 attack on the French embassy in The Hague, for which she received a jail sentence of 20 years. Terrorism experts believe Shigenobu's declaration to be genuine, and the U.S. State Department removed the JRA from the list of designated foreign terrorist organizations in 2001.

Sikh terrorism

Sikh terrorism is sponsored by expatriate and Indian Sikh groups who want to carve out an independent Sikh state called Khalistan (Land of the Pure) from Indian territory. Sikh violence outside India, which erupted following the 1984 Indian army's assault on the Golden Temple (Sikhism's holiest shrine), has decreased since the early 1990s. Militant cells of Sikhs have been active internationally, and there is evidence that Sikh extremists receive funds from Sikh communities in other countries. The list of "active" Sikh groups includes, but is not limited to, BABBAR KHALSA, Azad Khalistan Babbar Khalsa Force, Khalistan Liberation Front, Khalistan Commando Force, and Khalistan National Army. Most of these groups operate under umbrella organizations, such as the Second Panthic committee.

Sikh attacks in India have been mounted against Indian government officials and facilities, other Sikhs, and Hindus. Their tactics have included assassination, bombing, and kidnapping. Perhaps the most spectacular acts of terrorism carried out by Sikh extremists were the two bombings that occurred on the same day in June 1985. The first bomb exploded in Tokyo's Narita Airport as the luggage was being transferred to Air India flight 182, killing two Japanese baggage-handlers. The second suitcase carrying a bomb was safely transferred to the Air India plane, which exploded over the Irish Sea, killing 329 passengers and crew. The bombs were planted by Sikhs on an Air India flight from Vancouver, Canada.

In 1991, Sikh terrorists tried to assassinate the Indian ambassador to Romania. The man had once been India's senior police officer in Punjab (from 1986–89). Sikhs also kidnapped and held the Romanian chargé d'affaires in New Delhi for seven weeks. In January 1993, Indian police arrested Sikhs in New Delhi as they were making plans to detonate a bomb to disrupt Indian Republic Day, and in September of that year, Sikh militants tried to assassinate the Sikh chief of the ruling Congress Party's youth wing, using a bomb.

However, attacks by Sikhs in India, including kidnappings, assassinations, and remote-controlled bombings, have significantly decreased since mid-1992. This is partly because Indian security forces have killed or captured a large number of senior Sikh leaders of militant cells. The total number of civilian deaths in the Punjab area also declined since reaching a record high of 3,300 civilian deaths in 1991. Reports attribute this decline to efforts by the Indian army, paramilitary forces, and police against extremist groups.

One of the most active Sikh terrorists, Talwinder Singh Parmar, the alleged mastermind of the 22 June 1985 midair explosion of Air India flight 182 *Kanishka,* off the Irish coast, was killed in Punjab in 1992. On October 27, 2000, Ajaib Singh Bagri and Ripudaman Singh Malik, two BABBAR KHALSA International terrorists, were arrested by Canadian police for their involvement in the explosion of Air India flight 182. They were placed on trial for the 329 deaths that resulted from that explosion but were subsequently acquitted of these charges on March 16, 2005. The investigation and prosecution of the accused was the costliest in Canadian history, estimated at about $130 million.

In 1991, Inderjit Singh Reyat was convicted in the Narita bombing case. Police presented evidence linking components of the bomb remains found in Tokyo with items Reyat had purchased in the preceding weeks, including a Sanyo stereo tuner that police believe housed the Narita bomb. Reyat served 10 years for manslaughter in the deaths of the two baggage-handlers at the Tokyo airport. He insisted he was innocent. Then on February 10, 2003, in a dramatic turn of events, Reyat changed his story. He pleaded guilty to one count of manslaughter and a charge of aiding in the construction of a bomb. All other charges against him—including the murder of 329 people—were stayed, and he was sentenced to five years in jail for his role.

The current strength of Sikh militant groups is unknown. Sikh militant cells remain active internationally, and extremists continue to gather funds from overseas Sikh communities. In fact, Sikh expatriates have formed a variety of international organizations that lobby for the Sikh cause in other parts of the world, such as the World Sikh Organization and the International Sikh Youth Federation. None of these organizations has endorsed or been connected to Sikh terrorist actions.

Reference: Mahmood, Cynthia K. *Fighting for Faith and Nation: Dialogues with Sikh Militants* (Philadelphia: University of Pennsylvania Press, 1996).

Sinn Féin

Sinn Féin, "We Alone," is a nationalist political party in the Republic of Ireland, which professes a socialist, anticapitalist ideology. While it has not been electorally significant in the last half of the 20th century in the republic, it has played a role of some importance in Irish political life. Part of its strength lies in its relationship with the IRISH REPUBLICAN ARMY (IRA), and later the Provisional Irish Republican Army (PIRA), of which Sinn Féin is sometimes described as the political wing.

The party's primary significance since the 1920s has been its activism over the question of Irish unification and its links to the IRA and the PIRA. Many members of the IRA belong to Sinn Féin, and both Sinn Féin and the IRA split into "official" and "provisional" wings over the tactics to be used in pursuit of unification.

In the peace process as it was restarted in the 1990s to bring a measure of peace to the troubled provinces of Northern Ireland, where terrorist violence by both the PIRA and by Protestant groups like the ULSTER DEFENSE ASSOCIATION have made life very difficult for most of its citizens, Sinn Féin and Gerry Adams, one of its leaders, have been significant players.

Sinn Féin today is the largest nationalist political party in Northern Ireland, having displaced the previously dominant nationalist Social Democratic and Labour Party in national elections in 2005. It had, in 2005, five Northern Ireland Members of Parliament (MPs) of the 18 Northern Ireland MPs and 24 Members of the Legislative Assembly (MLAs) of the Northern Ireland Assembly membership of 108, making it the joint second-largest, behind the Democratic Unionist Party (which had 33 seats). It is a much smaller political force in the Republic of Ireland, where in 2005 it had five Teachta Dálas (out of 166) in Dáil Éireann and no members of the Republic's Seanad Éireann (senate). Sinn Féin had, in 2005, two Members of the European Parliament (MEP) out of 16 Irish MEPs, one from either side of the Irish border; one out of three in Northern Ireland and one out of 13 in the Republic.

Although Sinn Féin had two ministers in the suspended Executive Committee (cabinet) of the Northern Ireland Assembly, it has never sat in the cabinet in the Republic. In 2005, the unionist parties indicated that they would not serve in the government with Sinn Féin until its relationship with the PIRA was terminated.

On July 28, 2005, the leadership of the Irish Republican Army announced that it authorized completion of the process to put arms verifiably beyond use. This step brought Sinn Féin closer to full acceptance by unionists as an active participant in the governance of Northern Ireland.

Reference: Feeney, Brian. *Sinn Féin: A Hundred Turbulent Years* (Madison: University of Wisconsin Press, 2003).

Six-Day War

June 5–11, 1967, were critical days for the Israeli-Arab conflict in general and the Israeli-Palestinian conflict in particular. While Israelis refer to the war as the Six-Day War, Arab opponents call it the June 1967 War. Whichever appellation is used, the war was an event that has greatly determined Middle Eastern political history and will likely continue to do so for decades to come. The conflict literally changed the map of the Middle East and unleashed developments neither side could foresee or predict. Israel felt provoked into a preemptive strike against its most immediate and implacable foes, Egypt and Syria. The government of Prime Minister Levi Eshkol pleaded with Jordan to remain neutral, but King Hussein decided he could not remain aloof while other Arab states were attacked. To some, the weeks preceding the Six-Day War were reminiscent of the events that preceded World War I. Governments felt they could not back down from facing their foes, while few could fully or even partially anticipate the full consequences of the conflict. The Egyptian and Syrian regimes apparently believed their own propaganda and determined that the Israeli military could be beaten and the Jewish state's existence eliminated once and for all. They were also trapped by it. Regimes that do not follow through on threats and ultimatums frequently lose credibility and popular support.

Before hostilities commenced, the Israelis understood that their strategic situation was tenuous. Eighteen years after establishing its independence during the first Arab-Israeli war in 1948–49, Israel's Arab neighbors still refused to recognize the Jewish state and repeated the mantra that Israel would not be negotiated with because it was illegitimate and an entity of aggression against the Arab and Islamic world. Instead, the Arabs insisted that Israel must be destroyed and the plight of the Palestinian Arabs redeemed by restoring them to the homes taken from them two decades earlier by Israeli transgressors.

Israel achieved a remarkable military success on all three fronts. It quickly overran and occupied the Golan Heights in the north; the Gaza Strip and Sinai desert in the south; East Jerusalem, including the Old City, site of the Second Temple destroyed in 70 C.E.; and the West Bank in the east. The Israel Defense Forces (IDF) victory was so complete that the Soviet Union threatened to intervene militarily on behalf of Egypt and Syria, two Arab countries it had long supported. The IDF reached the Suez Canal and then stopped, mindful of American pressures and Soviet hostility. In the meantime, Israel found itself in control of territory that was beyond the original mandated area of Palestine as well as several times its own territorial size.

Soon after the war, Israel enlarged and then annexed East Jerusalem to Israel proper; some years later, it also annexed the Golan Heights. No other country has recognized the legality of the annexations. Israel's conquests created a national debate that is still going over what to do with the newly acquired territories and their Arab populations. In fact, many Palestinians view the continued Israeli presence as a phenomenon that was to their advantage. They may have lost the military conflict but are confident of winning the demographic war. The Palestinian birthrate is one of the highest in the world. In this theory, Israel will eventually have to withdraw since it will be untenable to control an Arab population that within a few decades will be larger than the Jewish one.

The war changed the political constellation of the Middle East. Israel became and remained the strongest military power in the region. Its enemies, however, refused to make peace with the Jewish state and consistently vowed to renew the war (which Egypt and Syria did six years later). Israel now occupied territory that was many times larger than its own and assumed responsibility for a large and fast-growing population that was alienated from it by language, culture, and religion. It became the only democracy in the world to militarily occupy a people that clearly resented its presence. The war also helped to initiate a renewed phenomenon of international terrorism. At the same time, however, Israel established itself once and for all as a force with which to be reckoned. While most of its Arab neighbors remained publicly sworn to its destruction, the reality of Israel as a permanent fixture in the region was finally becoming realized if not accepted.

At the same time, though, Palestinian Arabs and their supporters realized that the frontline Arab states (those having contiguous borders with Israel) were either incapable or uninterested in eliminating Israel and allowing Palestinians to pursue their own political destiny. This atmosphere became an almost textbook example of some root causes of terrorism—dispossession, impoverishment, political desperation, and lack of empathy with victims of injustice. Many Palestinians turned to violence to make the world aware of their ignominy. The violence gradually escalated from occasional raids on Israeli agricultural settlements and towns from Gaza and the West Bank to airplane hijackings to the massacre of Israeli athletes at the 1972 Olympics to suicide bombings. It was even expanded to include targets of anyone considered sympathetic to or supportive of Israel. Thus, American and European Jews were viewed as legitimate targets. The United States was thought of as Israel's main supporter and, therefore, an enemy of the Palestinian cause. During the 1990–91 Persian Gulf War, Palestinians sided with SADDAM HUSSEIN. Israelis observed West Bank and Gaza Palestinians cheering when Iraq Scud missiles were launched on Israeli civilian targets. After the September 11, 2001, attacks by AL-QAEDA on the United States, adult Palestinians passed out sweets to children.

See also ARAFAT, YASIR; AL-FATAH; HAMAS; INTIFADAS; MUNICH MASSACRE OF ISRAELI ATHLETES; PALESTINE LIBERATION ORGANIZATION; SUICIDE BOMBINGS.

Reference: Oren, Michael. *Six Days of War: June 1967 and the Making of the Modern Middle East* (Oxford and New York: Oxford University Press, 2002).

skyjacking, international law and

Three major agreements on aircraft hijacking have evolved in recent years, as well as a number of smaller agreements between nations concerned with this crime. A short review of these agreements sheds some light on the state of the law with regard to this modern form of piracy.

One of the more successful antihijacking agreements in recent years has been the Memorandum of Understanding on Hijacking of Aircraft and Vessels and Other Offenses signed between the United States and Cuba on February 15, 1973. In spite of a denunciation of the agreement by Cuba in October 1976, there has been an impressive record of interstate cooperation in combating aerial hijacking between the two countries. Many of the hijacking attempts that have occurred between the United States and Cuba since 1978 have resulted in the prompt return of the hijacked aircraft and the somewhat less prompt seizure for prosecution of the hijackers.

However, treaties of a broader nature have met with less success. Three issues that need to be addressed in any successful hijacking convention have not been adequately resolved. These are the problems of determining who has jurisdiction, establishing a prosecutable offense, and providing for prompt processing of extradition requests.

The Convention on Offenses and Certain Other Acts Committed on Board Aircraft, signed in Tokyo on September 14, 1963, provided a general basis for the establishment of jurisdiction, that is, legal authority to exercise control. The hijacking of an aircraft is an act that often takes place in flight en route between countries. Such planes are often registered to yet another country and carry citizens of many countries. So a decision as to who has the right to bring a hijacker to justice is often a difficult one.

Article Three of the Tokyo Convention provides that the state of registration is the one that has the first and primary right to exercise jurisdiction. But this convention does not place on any signatory nation the responsibility to ensure that all alleged offenders will be prosecuted. Thus, a nation may accept jurisdiction and then refuse or neglect to bring the offenders to justice.

The subsequent Convention for the Suppression of Unlawful Seizure of Aircraft, signed at The Hague on December 16, 1970, deals more specifically with the issues of extradition and prosecution. This convention obliges contracting states to make the offense of unlawful seizure of aircraft punishable by severe penalties. Although not as explicit as the later convention drawn up at Montreal, this convention does provide an important legal framework for prosecution of an offense, reasonably and clearly defined in legal terms that are directly applicable in the legal systems of many states (meaning that the states are thus not given the sticky political task of creating laws to make such acts a legal offense).

Under this convention, jurisdiction for aerial hijacking was extended. Three states were given the legal responsibility for jurisdiction, in the following order of precedence: (1) the state of registration; (2) the state of first landing; and (3) the state in which the lessee has its principal place of business or permanent residence. This convention requires each contracting state to take measures to establish jurisdiction if the offender is within its territory and is not to be extradited.

This convention also addresses the issue of prosecution, obligating each contracting state either to extradite—that is, to send the person to another state seeking to prosecute—an alleged offender or to submit the case "without exception whatsoever to its competent authorities for the purpose of prosecution." While it does not create an absolute obligation to extradite, the convention states that the offense referred to is deemed to be included as an extraditable offense in any existing extradition treaties between contracting states and is to be included in every future extradition treaty concluded between such states.

The Convention for the Suppression of Unlawful Acts against the Safety of Civil Aviation signed in Montreal on September 23, 1971, adds more detail to the description of the offenses affecting aircraft and air navigation. It makes illegal:

1. Acts of violence against a person on board an aircraft in flight if that act is likely to endanger the safety of that aircraft; or
2. Destruction of an aircraft in service or damage to such an aircraft that renders it incapable of flight or that is likely to endanger its safety in flight; or
3. Placing or causing to be placed onto an aircraft in service, by any means whatsoever, a device or substance that is likely to destroy that aircraft, or to cause damage to it that is likely to endanger its safety in flight; or
4. Destruction or damage of air navigation facilities or interference with their operation, if any such act is likely to endanger the safety of the aircraft in flight; or
5. Communication of information that is known to be false, thereby endangering the safety of the aircraft in flight.

In spite of these efforts to specify the crime and to establish procedures for deciding who has jurisdiction over the crime, there remain large gaps in international legal efforts to deal with skyjacking today. There is little to compel a contracting state to honor its paper commitment to extradite or punish a terrorist who has hijacked a plane. This has become painfully evident in recent years, as the pressure and threats from powerful terrorist organizations have forced several Western nations to evade their responsibilities under these conventions. There are no sanctions or enforcement procedures in any of these conventions; they are, in effect, "gentlemen's agreements," dependent for their enforcement on the integrity of the contracting states.

Efforts to achieve an independent enforcement convention during the International Civil Aviation Organization Extraordinary Assembly in September 1973 ended in failure. Several proposals were made at that assembly with the aim of broadening the effectiveness of international control over interference with aircraft. A new multilateral convention was proposed, establishing an international commission with the power to investigate alleged violations of the enforcement provisions of the Tokyo, Hague, and Montreal Conventions. It provided for sanctions against states that refuse to comply with the commission's recommendations. (One of the contemplated sanctions was the collective suspension of flights to and from such a state.) None of the proposals were passed by the assembly.

See also UNITED NATIONS, RESPONSE TO TERRORISM.

References: United Nations. War on Drugs and Crime. "Convention on Offenses and Certain Other Acts Committed on Board Aircraft." Available online. URL: http://www.unodc.org/unodc/terrorism_convention_aircraft.html. Accessed March 27, 2006; ———. "Convention on the Suppression of Unlawful Seizure of Aircraft" Available online. URL: http://www.unodc.org/unodc/terrorism_convention_aircraft_seizure.html. Accessed March 27, 2006; ———. "Convention for the Supression of Unlawful Acts against the Safety of Civil Aviation" Available online. URL: http://www.unodc.org/unodc/terrorism_convention_civil_aviation.html. Accessed March 27, 2006.

Spain

See BASQUE FATHERLAND AND LIBERTY (ETA); OVERVIEW OF TERRORISM, BY REGION.

Special Operations units of the United States government

American counterterrorist forces are based in the United States, far from the Middle East, where the current "war on terrorism" is focused. The Joint Special Operations Agency, headed by a two-star general, is charged with preparing guidelines and plans to guide counterterrorist forces during their formation, training, and operations. But this agency has no command authority over the forces.

The U.S. Special Operations Command (USSOCOM) was established by the Department of Defense, under congressional orders, on June 1, 1987, as a single command for all of the special operations units. This command is located at MacDill Air Force Base, Florida, and commands the following units: the Special Operations Command (SOCOM) unit based at Fort Bragg, North Carolina; the Naval Warfare Special Operations Command, and the Joint Special Operations Command. The Air Force Special Operations Command is located at Hurlbert Field, Florida. At present, the U.S. Army maintains the highest number of special operations units, with three distinct parts. The air force and the navy each have one unit, and the marines also have one unit, arguably the largest special op unit, dedicated to amphibious beachfront assaults. The U.S. Navy's SEAL teams are under the command of the Naval Special Warfare Groups, headquartered in San Diego, California.

A brief look at some of these units will help make understanding the whole collection a little easier. It may also make clear the problems faced in successful use of such forces.

Special Forces, U.S. Army

The Joint special Operations Command (JSOC) and the U.S. Army Special Operations Command (USASOC) are both headquartered at Fort Bragg, North Carolina, under SOCOM. The JSOC is a multiservice/interdepartmental command, with antiterrorism as its primary job. It includes a command staff that oversees the training and operations of the army's Delta Force, the navy's SEAL Team Six, and, in times of national emergency, the FBI's Hostage Rescue Team.

The USASOC has more that 25,000 personnel and includes the U.S. Army Special Forces Command (SFC), the 75th Ranger Regiment, the 180th Special Operations Aviation Regiment (SOAR), the JFK Special Warfare Center and School, the U.S. Army Civil Affairs and Psychological Operations Command, the U.S. Army Special Operations Support Command, and various chemical reconnaissance units. Each of these "communities" has special roles and missions. For example, SOAR, often referred to as the "Nightstalkers" is the most secret and technologically advanced unit in the USASOC, while the SFC is home of the more widely known Green Berets and is regarded as the "brains" portion of the USASOC. The Rangers are referred to as the "muscle" of SOCOM.

The SFC has the highest operations tempo of any community within SOCOM, since the average special forces soldier generally spends more than half of every year in the field. These are the "trained professionals" who, with high levels of technical, cultural, and combat skills, work together to solve problems. In this sense, they are more like a Peace Corps team with guns than a counterterror unit. Yet they continue to be used in areas where terrorism is a serious threat, as in Iraq and Afghanistan during the early part of the war on terrorism.

While a special forces unit has three types of teams (A, B, and C), the latter two teams are generally not deployable, since they consist of staff and support personnel. Usually, an A-Team consists of 12 men, including a captain, a warrant officer, and 10 men who all are at least sergeants. All candidates for such a team must pass a very rigorous training course, much like the SAS. This training includes a "selection" session, with intense physical and mental training, and a qualification class (or Q-School). The 25-week process creates candidates who are experts in a variety of tasks, including but not limited to land navigation, basic weapons and demolition, water navigation, intelligence, and reconnaissance. Upon completing Q-School successfully, the candidate then as a team member must continue training in his chosen area of specialty, which can take from six to 56 weeks to complete.

1st Special Forces Operational Detachment–Delta (Delta Force), U.S. Army

Delta Force was commissioned under the command of Colonel Charles Beckwith on November 19, 1977, to be primarily a hostage-rescue and counterterrorism force. Most of its people are drawn from the Ranger units or the special forces units by a desire to serve in this very secret unit. Like the British Special Air Service (SAS), Delta Force is built on a premise of the critical need for secrecy, and its training is in many ways similar to that of the SAS.

Very little public information is available about this unit, except in very general terms. It is designed to be able to rapidly resolve hostage or hijacking incidents involving U.S. citizens abroad or on planes traveling beyond U.S. territory. Consequently, its members have a wide range of skills, from repelling (as the SAS did in London) to parachuting (into hostile territory) to rapid repair of a wide range of vehicles. Most of the training is altered regularly to be certain the men are able to respond to current world situations.

Ranger, U.S. Army

Drawn usually from the Airborne Infantry units, candidates for Ranger units must be extremely physically fit initially, since training involves intense physical challenges. The first stage involves successful completion of the Ranger Indoctrination Program (RIP), a three-week course of physical and mental training, including building strengths in swimming, land navigation, and endurance, as well as classroom instruction.

Three U.S. Army Rangers participate in a training exercise. (DEPARTMENT OF DEFENSE)

If one successfully completes RIP, the next nine weeks have four phases, each of which presents a different type of challenge. The first phase is another week of RIP, designed to facilitate the "weeding out" of those not completely motivated or physically able to continue. The second phase of training takes place in the swamps and forests near Eglin Air Force base in Florida, where the candidates stay continuously wet, continuously moving, and continuously hungry.

During the third phase of Ranger training, candidates operate in a mountainous terrain near Fort Drum, New York, again with little sleep or food, learning to repel down cliffs and to navigate through difficult valleys. Finally, the training groups are sent to the desert near Dugway, Utah, to learn how to navigate without many discernable landmarks and to conduct patrols and ambushes without cover or concealment. The objective for such a multifaceted form of training is to create a highly mobile infantry unit that is able to deploy anywhere in the world quickly and to lead the ground forces that will be deployed to follow, through any terrain.

Air Force Special Operations Command

AFSOC is based at Eglin Air Force Base in Florida. While the Air Force Special Operations Command units cover four different types of mission areas, only one is usually associated with counterterrorism: the Special Operations Forces Mobility. This unit consists of numerous fixed- and rotary-winged aircraft, with the pilots and support crews used to insert and recover soldiers of other special ops units of every service branch. AFSOC has units located strategically throughout the world that are ready to deploy with little advance warning to facilitate counterterrorism efforts by the other branches.

Naval Special Warfare Command

Although it has units stationed around the world, NAVSPECWARCOM has its home base in Coronado, California. A part of the Naval Special Warfare Groups, the SEALs (Sea, Air and Land) are made up of highly trained and intensely motivated seamen who have successfully completed 25 weeks of difficult training. If the volunteer candidates make it through the first five weeks of Basic Underwater Demolition training (the "toughening up" phase), they must then spend a week pushed to the limits of their physical endurance (called "hell week" by the men). Those who successfully complete this phase will then spend the next 19 weeks learning to navigate great distances underwater; becoming proficient at underwater demolition, reconnaissance, and navigation; and learning a variety of other skills essential for combat diving, including how to enter and exit a wide range of vehicles to carry out operations at sea.

These seamen also receive jungle, desert, and arctic training, as well as training at Fort Benning and the U.S. Army Parachute School. The final five weeks of their training is in simulations in which they are required to use their new skills to resolve real-world situations they might encounter.

Clearly, the United States has a wide range of military units that could be utilized in counterterrorism efforts. The problems with U.S. counterterrorism forces are equally obvious, particularly those brought on by the lack of cohesive command illustrated by the abortive attempt to send a strike team into Iran to free Americans held hostage in the U.S. embassy in Tehran. OPERATION EAGLE'S CLAW, as this mission was called, was characterized by a confusion of command, insufficient training, and critical equipment failure.

Cloaked in so much secrecy that even some of the military officers involved were not told the aim of the mission for which they were preparing, this operation became a model for what can go wrong in a strike force maneuver. In addition to too much secrecy, there were too many "chiefs" and not enough cooperation between military units. An army officer, Major General James Vaught, was in overall command; Colonel James Kyle of the air force had responsibility for fixed-wing aircraft, while Colonel Charles Pitman of the marines also had command responsibility and Colonel Beckwith controlled the Delta Force unit.

The Delta Force squad lacked sufficient training and experience for such an operation. It had been created by Colonel Beckwith in 1987, only two years earlier, and its training program was incomplete and not designed for the type of situation that evolved. Delta Force was underfunded and ill-equipped to handle the hostage raid, having trained primarily in guerrilla warfare and low-intensity conflict.

The United States has taken steps to create a command unit in which to vest coordination for this specialized training and command. However, within the armed services there remain strong rivalries, making it difficult for one branch to create and receive support needed for each of these separate specialized units. Although in the wake of Operation Eagle's Claw's disaster, there was a call for the establishment of a new special counterterrorism unit to be set up, with personnel drawn from all of the armed services, there was little immediate success in creating such a unit. The Delta Force unit, according to government reports, has been deployed several times, other than the highly publicized Operation Eagle's Claw fiasco and the *ACHILLE LAURO* incident. It was, for instance, sent to Venezuela to advise the armed forces there on ways to retake a hijacked aircraft. It was sent on a similar mission to Oman, to prepare to retake a hijacked plane in nearby Kuwait. At the time of the T.W.A. hijacking, Delta Force was deployed to the Mediterranean. But in each of these cases, its activities stopped short of assault; it simply made preparations for, or advised in preparations for, the assault.

Some have argued that this has had a detrimental effect on the morale of the individuals in Delta Force. To be always preparing and never doing counterterrorist activities is infinitely frustrating, as the men in GSG-9 and the SAS could attest. But the United States has been reluctant to field a strike force against the terrorists, until a "war" on terrorism was declared in 2001. The role that Delta Force plays in this war will remain secret for the foreseeable future, and hence its effectiveness at present is impossible to gauge.

Since it did not have many indigenous groups actively engaging in domestic terrorism until the 1990s, unlike Germany and Great Britain who were challenged by events in the 1970s to create units to deal with terrorism domestically, the United States was able to focus its attention on training its special forces to operate overseas. Emphasis was placed less on secrecy of identity than of rapid-response capabilities and combat training. If coordination of command problems can be surmounted, these forces may develop into units as efficient and respected as the SAS and GSG-9.

New Units and New Technologies

In the wake of the Operation Eagle's Claw debacle, the Pentagon began to establish the closest thing this nation has ever had to a secret army. Small, specially trained units were developed that were designed to operate much more covertly than some of the older military units, such as the Navy Seals. In addition to being given rather exotic code names, such as Yellow Fruit and Seaspray, these units were armed with newer, more sophisticated types of equipment. These included such items as the small, high-tech helicopters with which Task Force 160, operating out of Fort Campbell, train.

These new units were also given more sophisticated communications gear. This includes, for example, the one-man satellite-communications radios and dishes.

More important than these technological "toys," however, was the creation of the Intelligence Support Activity, a far-ranging intelligence organization that gave the army, for the first time, the ability to engage in full-fledged espionage, fielding its own agents. Through this organization, for the first time, the strike forces were able to gather the information they needed to plan their counterterrorist activities. They were no longer dependent upon the CIA or other intelligence services for vital data, which was too often not available or kept classified at a critical juncture in the planning process. Indeed, their intelligence and reconnaissance efforts in the early stages of the "war on terrorism" in 2001 facilitated U.S. military response options at this critical juncture.

Even with these innovations, however, these units have had difficulty in rising above the bureaucratic infighting and bungling which has for so long plagued U.S. strike forces. Seaspray, Yellow Fruit, and the ISA became involved in clandestine operations in Central America, which seriously impaired their credibility with Congress and within the military and intelligence communities of the United States. The struggle in Afghanistan and the war on terror offer U.S. special forces units contrasting opportunities for success. Actions by such units in Africa, particularly in Djibouti and Ethiopia, in helping communities to build wells and schools have received less global attention but have perhaps generated more long-term success in this "war" than the more widely known acts to stabilize regions of Afghanistan.

References: Robinson, Linda. *Masters of Chaos: The Secret History of the Special Forces* (New York: Perseus Publishing, 2005); Waugh, Billy, and Tim Keown. *Hunting the Jackal* (New York: HarperCollins Publishers, 2005).

Special Projects Team–Special Air Service (SAS; Counter Revolutionary Warfare Squadron [CRW])

The British Special Air Service (SAS) was founded in 1942, and the unit has been headquartered in Hereford, United Kingdom. It is perhaps the best-known special operations group in existence today, and the Special Projects (SP) team of the SAS is an equally well-known counterterrorist organization. The SP team, normally comprised of 80 personnel, is divided into four troops of 16 people each. However, the SP squadron is not a permanent entity since all SAS squadrons are rotated through duty in the Counterrevolutionary Warfare section. These CRW duty training cycles usually last six months. Thus, all SAS operatives are considered counterterrorist qualified, and refresher training is constant. In this, the SAS is unique among special operations groups.

The Special Projects unit is normally broken down into 65-person Red and Blue Teams, each of which has snipers and EOD-trained experts. Team members' proficiency in firearms, already very good, is refined for close-quarters battle in the "Killing House." The basic course lasts for six weeks, during which troopers may fire more than 2,000 rounds of ammunition. Their firearms proficiency is further developed during a squadron's SP duty.

These training exercises are incredibly intense and often have added elements of realism, by using live personnel as hostages during room-clearing operations. SAS counterterrorist and hostage rescue training is helped by cooperation from the highest members of the U.K. government, many of whom (including the prime minister) take part in actual training exercises. Contributing to the skill of the SAS is also the Operations Research Unit, which develops unique equipment for use by the SP team, such as the widely used stun ("flash-bang") grenade, specialized ladders for train and airplane assaults, night vision goggles, and audio-video equipment.

There are a number of organizations worldwide that also use the SAS name, such as the New Zealand SAS and the Australian SAS. The Special Boat Service (SBS) is also a special-operations group deployed by the United Kingdom that has trained to some extent with the SAS, particularly relating to the possibility of a situation that might require use of the personnel and skills of both, such as the simultaneous hijacking of two or more oil rigs in the North Sea. While each SAS squadron maintains its own Boat Troop, there does exist a high degree of respect and cooperation between the SAS and the SBS. A bomb scare on the ocean liner *Queen Elizabeth II* offered one opportunity for the two groups to deploy together successfully.

The SAS is the most sought-after exchange partner in the world of counterterrorism. Their people have trained troopers from many different organizations and states, including, but not limited to, the U.S. Delta Force, the FBI's Hostage Rescue Team, France's GIGN, Germany's GSG-9, Spain's GEO, the Royal Dutch Marines, and the SAS groups from Australia and New Zealand. In return, these organizations have let British SAS members train alongside their own units in a reciprocal swap of information. The result of these exchanges is that, worldwide, there has been an increase in counterterrorist skills to higher and higher levels. The SAS, though, has continued to improve its skills, looking always for "a better way of doing things." In fact, at least one or two SAS personnel have been present at every major counterterrorist operation involving a friendly country in the recent past, sometimes in an advisory role, but also as part of an effort by the SAS to learn from each operation elements of both success and failure. This information, culled from these experiences, is of course brought back to Hereford, where it is both shared with other team members and applied in training exercises.

Until the 1990s, there was one exception to this cooperative exchange of personnel and information, rooted in a fundamental distrust that the British had of the Israelis, another of the world's best at counterterrorist operations. For a long time, the SAS refused to engage in any sort of training or exchange program in this field with ISRAEL. However, this is no longer the case, and the two programs now enjoy a low-key but positive relationship.

The SAS has engaged in antiterrorist operations at home in the United Kingdom, most notably in Northern Ireland. Unlike its counterparts in the United States, the SAS can legally respond to domestic terrorist threats, as they did successfully in OPERATION NIMROD in London on May 5, 1980. They have also, however, worked for British interests overseas in counterterrorism activities in countries such as LIBYA and, more recently, AFGHANISTAN and IRAQ. Such exercises are not publicized since speed and secrecy are the key components vital to SAS success in their operations.

specific threat indicators

Specific threat indicators are used by those seeking to assess the degree of terrorism threatened against an individual, facility, or institution. They are used to evaluate the vulnerability of a particular target to terrorism, not the likelihood of terrorism in a nation or neighborhood. These indicators include such things as the history of attacks on similar targets, the publicity value of the target, the target's access to infiltration, the target's counterterrorist and communications capabilities, the tactical attractiveness of the target, and the availability of the police or other security personnel. Some of these indicators are essentially judgment calls, such as the determination as to whether the industry involves a "sensitive" installation, which is generally used to refer to a nuclear, chemical, or biological facility. Other indicators are very easily quantified, such as the population density in the immediate area.

See also GENERAL THREAT INDICATORS.

Reference: Combs, Cindy. *Terrorism in the Twenty-First Century* (Upper Saddle River, N.J.: Prentice Hall, 2000).

spillover events, terrorist violence and

The report on terrorism produced each year by the U.S. Department of State has demonstrated statistical evidence of the phenomenon that it terms "spillover" of terrorism. This occurs when the roots or causes of terrorism lie in one region but the terrorist attacks occur in different regions. The record in 1987, for instance, detailed the spillover of Middle East terrorism into other states during that year. The State Department records indicated that 50 such spillover events occurred that year. Of these, 43 took place in Western Europe. Altogether, spillover events occurred in 16 different countries. Sixteen nations became victims, in a variety of different ways, of one or more terrorist attacks when the real targets of the event were far away. Such nations watch their citizens and cities become enmeshed in violent struggles over which they may have little direct control.

Movements toward peace in areas like NORTHERN IRELAND and the MIDDLE EAST made violent spillover events in the United States and Europe, as individuals and groups dissatisfied with the peace process exported their anger to other nations. The ATTACK ON AMERICA and the bombings of transportation systems in LONDON and MADRID indicated that this type of spillover is in fact quite likely.

Stalin, Joseph (1879–1953)

Joseph Stalin was probably one of the most successful mass murderers of all time. Stalin was originally intended by his mother to become a priest in the Russian Orthodox Church. Instead, he joined the extreme communist movement of Bolsheviks led by V. I. Lenin.

Joseph Stalin (right) with Viacheslav Molotov (LIBRARY OF CONGRESS)

He led bank robberies to support Bolshevik revolutionary activities. After the Bolsheviks took control of Russia at the end of 1917, Stalin quickly moved as party general secretary to acquire and consolidate power through the party and state bureaucracies. After Lenin's death in 1924, Stalin was locked in a power struggle with Leon Trotsky, the leader of the Red Army during the Russian civil war of 1918–22. By 1929, Trotsky had been outmaneuvered and exiled from the Soviet Union. An agent of Stalin assassinated Trotsky in Mexico City in 1940.

During the three decades of his autocracy, Stalin remained paranoid and conducted purges of Communist Party members, high-ranking military officers, and anyone he deemed not sympathetic to his view of the Soviet state. He governed with the full implementation of state terror, which included persuading children to inform on disloyal parents. The 1941–45 war with Germany interrupted the process and, for a brief time, a foreign enemy killed more Soviet citizens than Stalin did. The numbers will never be accurately known, but it seems safe to say that Stalin was responsible for the deaths of as many as 20 million people. They died from planned famines, execution, exposure to Siberian winters, and torture by the secret police.

There is evidence that Stalin was planning a new purge when he died in March 1953. Despite his remarkable brutality, Stalin is still fondly remembered by millions of Russians as the leader who defeated the German invasion, made the Soviet Union into a modern industrial and nuclear state with superpower status, and was a global rival to the United States. Many are convinced that Russia enjoyed international respect during these years and has been in decline since the end of the Stalinist regime.

Reference: Conquest, Robert. *The Great Terror, a Reassessment* (New York: Oxford University Press, 1990).

state-sponsored terrorism

Terrorism has been an instrument of foreign policy used by states, often in a kind of irregular warfare. State-sponsored terrorism is characterized by more involvement by the state in the terrorist activity, sometimes as direct as decision making and control of the group's activities. In state-supported terrorism, in contrast, the state usually aids or abets existing terrorist groups that have varying degrees of independence. In both types of terrorism, the state utilizes the groups engaged in terrorist acts to enhance state goals in other countries.

Unlike the internal coercive diplomacy with which states may seek to enhance these goals, clandestine operations are, by their very nature, conducted in secrecy and, consequently, they are very difficult to discern. There is thus little verifiable data that can be used to study the phenomenon of state-sponsorship of terrorism. Such terrorism is primarily used to produce fear and chaos within potentially unfriendly or hostile states. It is often designed to demonstrate weaknesses and vulnerabilities of opposing governments in an effort to make such adversaries more willing to bargain or cooperate.

CENTRAL INTELLIGENCE AGENCY efforts in Chile in the early 1970s took this form. Not only was this agency involved in clandestine efforts to remove Salvador Allende from office, but it was also authorized to spend at least $7 million to destabilize Chilean society, including the financing of opposition groups and right-wing terrorist paramilitary units. Similar support was given by the United States to the Contras in Nicaragua, who fought in opposition to the Sandinista regime. Some states in the Middle East have chosen to sponsor Palestinian groups and individuals engaged in terrorist acts as a less risky method of redressing Palestinian grievances—less risky than provoking another war with Israel.

The governments of some states support international terrorism by providing arms, training, asylum, diplomatic facilities, financial backing, logistic, and/or other support to those carrying out terrorist activities. During the cold-war years (1946–90), the list of states sponsoring terrorism was extensive and subject to prejudice, since both the United States and the Soviet Union sponsored groups within a host of countries. Most of these groups engaged primarily in legitimate guerrilla warfare, but many often had members who participated in attacks on civilian populations that met the definition of terrorism.

There was a marked decline in state-sponsored terrorism in the last decade of the 20th century. A broad range of bilateral and multilateral sanctions enacted by states has served to discourage state sponsors of terrorism from continuing support for international acts of terrorism. The political and economic costs of being an open sponsor of terrorism became too high for most states to absorb. Most of the states who remain designated by the U.S. Department of State as "sponsors" of terrorism offer only safe haven rather than training, weapons, or logistical support.

Iraq, as it transitioned to democracy, ceased to support terrorism and its designation as a state sponsor of terrorism was removed in October 2004 by the United States. State sponsors of terrorism impede the efforts of the international community to fight terrorism, providing a critical infrastructure for terrorist groups. Without state sponsors, terrorist groups would have a much more difficult time obtaining funds, weapons, materials, and secure areas to plan and conduct operations. Some states engaged in sponsorship of terrorism also have the capacity to manufacture weapons of mass destruction, which could fall into the hands of the groups that they sponsor.

States still listed by the United States as sponsors of terrorism included, in 2005, Cuba, Iran, Libya, North Korea, Sudan, and Syria. These countries, although some have taken steps to improve cooperation with global counterterrorism efforts in some areas, continue the actions that led them to be designated as state sponsors of terrorism. Cuba, for example, continued to provide limited support to designated foreign terrorist organizations and was a safe haven for terrorists, through 2005. Libya, in contrast, curtailed its support for international terrorism in 2004 and succeeded in convincing the international community, including the United States, to remove the economic sanctions in place against it because of its sponsorship of terrorism in the past. State sponsors of terrorism have found it difficult to completely break all ties with former terrorist groups and to convince the international community of their desire to be partners in global counterterrorism efforts.

While no international list of states sponsoring terrorism exists, the United States still maintains an overview of this phenomenon in its *Country Reports on Terrorism* (formerly *Patterns of Global Terrorism*) report published annually. Although not all states involved in this type of activity are necessarily included in this list, it provides insights into this continuing form of terrorism. The material provided here is drawn from that report.

Afghanistan

In September 2001, an ATTACK ON AMERICA was launched by OSAMA BIN LADEN from his base in Afghanistan, making Afghanistan the premier state sponsor of international terrorism for that year. Demands that the Taliban turn bin Laden over to U.S. forces for trial were rejected, and in response, the United States launched a war on terrorism. Attacks were launched by a U.S.-led coalition against the AL-QAEDA bases as well as Taliban strongholds in Kabul and other cities, with bombing raids and the deployment of special forces units. The Northern Alliance, who had been fighting the Taliban for control of Afghanistan, recaptured Kabul after U.S. bombing cleared Taliban forces from the area. With the crumbling of the Taliban rule in Afghanistan, the strength of al-Qaeda and bin Laden became difficult to gauge, but reports of the extent of his network in other countries suggested the probability of future terrorism from this group, if not from the same leader, and without the support of the Afghan state.

The installation of a newly elected president and the ratification of a new constitution changed the political landscape of this country, which is now an active participant in the U.S.-led war on terrorism. It did not, however, eliminate the attacks on civilian as well as military targets in Afghanistan; instead, a new type of terrorism for this country began to emerge in 2004: suicide bombing. While this type of attack has become increasingly common in Israel and Iraq, it had not occurred in Afghanistan until very recently. Vehicle bombings continue to occur, such as the attacks in June 2003 in Kabul, in which a taxi rigged with explosives rammed into a bus carrying German peacekeepers of the International Security Assistance Force, killing five German peacekeepers and injuring 29 others. For these and other similar—and continuing—attacks, no one claimed responsibility.

Cuba

While during much of the latter part of the 20th century Cuba provided significant levels of funding, military training, arms, and guidance to various revolutionary groups around the world, after the collapse of its prime sponsor—the Soviet Union—in 1989, Havana scaled back dramatically its support to international terrorists.

The Cuban government continues to maintain in international forums that acts by legitimate national liberation movements cannot be defined as terrorism. It has sought to characterize as "legitimate national liberation movements" a number of groups that internationally target innocent civilians to advance their political, social, or religious agendas.

In 2004, Cuba continued to provide limited support to U.S.-designated foreign terrorist organizations. It offered safe haven to individual terrorists but no longer provided weapons, training, or funds for most of the groups with which it worked closely for four decades. The Cuban government refuses to turn over suspected terrorists to countries that have charged them with terrorist acts, alleging that the charges are "political" and that the government would not provide a fair trial. The government permitted various ETA members to reside in Cuba, in spite of a November 2003 public request from the Spanish government to deny them sanctuary, and it provided safe haven and some degree of support to members of the Colombian FARC and ELN groups.

Iran

Tehran continued to support groups such as Lebanese Hizballah, HAMAS, PALESTINIAN ISLAMIC JIHAD (PIJ), and the KURDISTAN WORKERS' PARTY (PKK) and to fund and train other groups engaged in terrorism. With the accession of President Mohammad Khatami, a moderate, Iran's public statements concerning terrorism became less supportive, including public condemnation of terrorist attacks by Algerian and Egyptian groups in 1997. However, Iran carried out at least 13 assassinations in 1997, most of them in northern Iraq, targeting members of Iran's main opposition groups, including the Kurdish Democratic Party of Iran (KDPI) and the MUJAHIDEEN-E-KHALQ (MEK).

In Germany, an Iranian was found guilty of the murder in 1992 of Iranian dissidents, including the secretary-general of the KDPI, in a Berlin restaurant. The court stated that the government of Iran had followed a policy of liquidating the regime's opponents who lived outside Iran, noting that the murders had been approved at the most senior levels of the Iranian government by an extralegal committee whose members included the minister of intelligence and security, the foreign minister, the president, and the supreme leader. While Khatami's government staffed these positions with individuals not involved in the murders, in September 1997 Iran's new leadership still affirmed the fatwa on Salmon Rushdie, which had been in effect since 1989.

In the fall of 1997, Tehran hosted numerous representatives of terrorist groups, including Hamas, Lebanese Hizballah, the PIJ, and the Egyptian AL-GAMA'AT AL-ISLAMIYYA at a conference on liberation movements. Participants reportedly discussed jihad, establishing greater coordination between certain groups, and an increase in support for some groups. The PKK, a Turkish separatist group that has carried out numerous terrorist attacks in Turkey and on Turkish targets in Europe, continued to enjoy safe haven in Iran even after Turkey invaded northern Iran in late 1997 in pursuit of PKK cadres.

Iran remained the most active state sponsor of terrorism through 2004. Its Islamic Revolutionary Guard Corps and Ministry of Intelligence and Security were involved in the planning and support of terrorist acts and continued to encourage a variety of groups to use terrorism in pursuit of their goals. Although it detained senior AL-QAEDA members in 2003, it continued to refuse to identify them publicly or to transfer custody of any of its al-Qaeda detainees to either their countries of origin or to third countries for interrogation and/or trial.

Supreme Leader Ali Khamenei praised Palestinian terrorist operations in 2004, and the government provided a variety of groups—including Hizballah, Hamas, Palestinian Islamic Jihad, the AL-AQSA MARTYRS' BRIGADE, and the POPULAR FRONT FOR THE LIBERATION OF PALESTINE–GENERAL COMMAND—with funding, safe haven, training, and weapons. Iran provided Hizballah with an unmanned aerial vehicle, which it sent into Israeli airspace on November 7, 2004.

Iraq

In spite of the controls imposed on Iraq after its unsuccessful invasion of Kuwait during the 1990s, Iraq continued to provide safe haven to a variety of Palestinian groups that engaged in terrorism, including the ABU NIDAL ORGANIZATION (ANO) and the Arab Liberation Front. It also provided bases, weapons and safe haven for the MUJAHIDEEN-E-KHALQ, a group that opposes the Iranian regime. Its alleged attempts to generate weapons of mass destruction, including chemical and biological weapons, became the basis for the U.S.-led war in Iraq.

In the wake of the U.S.-led war in Iraq in 2003, this country has become the central battleground in the global war on terror. Former elements of the regime as well as foreign fighters and Islamic extremists conduct terrorist attacks on civilians but also fight as insurgents in attacking coalition and Iraqi security forces. Terrorist attacks against a variety of targets mingled with insurgent attacks against the emerging Iraqi government make it difficult to determine the exact level of terrorism occurring in this country at this time.

Jordanian-born ABU MUSAB AL-ZARQAWI and his organization, Jama'at al-Tawhid wa'al-Jihad, emerged in 2004 to play a leading role in terrorist activities in Iraq. In October of that year, Zarqawi announced the merger of his group with BIN LADEN's AL-QAEDA organization, and in December, bin Laden endorsed Zarqawi as his official emissary in Iraq. Zarqawi claimed credit for the March 2004 simultaneous bomb attacks in Baghdad and Karbala that killed more than 180 pilgrims as they celebrated the Shia festival of Ashura and also for the suicide attack on the offices of the leader of the Supreme Council for the Islamic Revolution in Iraq, which killed 15 and wounded over 50. These attacks were, according to Zarqawi, part of a sectarian war in Iraq, focusing on creating a rift between Shias and Sunnis through attacks on the Iraqi Shia.

In August 2004, the Kurdish group Ansar al-Sunna claimed responsibility for the kidnapping and murder of 12 Nepalese construction workers. This group is believed to be an offshoot of the ANSAR AL-ISLAM group founded in Iraq in September 2001. Al-Sunna claimed responsibility for bomb attacks on the offices of two Kurdish political parties in Irbil that killed 109 Iraqi citizens. PKK/KADEK/KONGRA-GEL also maintains an estimated 3,000 armed militants in northern Iraq, according to Turkish government sources, although no terrorist incidents by this group in Iraq have been reported.

Iraq was removed from the list in the United States of states sponsoring terrorism in the wake of the 2003 invasion and the subsequent formation of a democratically elected government in 2005.

Libya

Libya was accused in the courts of several nations of sponsoring bombing attacks during the 1980s and early 1990s. Germany held the trial of five defendants in the 1986 La Belle Discotheque bombing in Berlin, which killed three people and wounded more than 200, many seriously. In opening remarks at that trial, the German prosecutor stated that the bombing was "definitely the act of an assassination commissioned by the Libyan state." German authorities issued warrants for four other Libyan officials for their role in the case. Tripoli's involvement in the bombing of Pan Am flight 103 in 1988 was the source for serious international concern, including UN Security Council resolutions ordering Libya to turn over the two bombing suspects for trial. In 1992, UNSCR 748 was adopted as a result of Libya's refusal to comply with an earlier resolution (UNSCR 731) ordering the country to turn over the two Libyan bombing suspects for trial in the United States or the United Kingdom, pay compensation, cooperate in the ongoing investigations into the Pan Am 103 and UTA 772 bombings, and cease all support for terrorism. UNSCR 748 imposed sanctions that embargoed Libya's civil aviation and military procurement efforts and required all states to reduce Libya's diplomatic presence. UNSCR 883, adopted in November 1993, imposed further sanctions, including a limited assets freeze and an oil technology ban on Libya.

French officials on January 29, 1998, officially completed their investigation into the 1989 bombing of UTA 772. The officials concluded that the Libyan intelligence service was responsible and named Qadhafi's brother-in-law, Muhammad al-Sanusi, as the mastermind of the attack.

Libya decreased its sponsorship role significantly by the turn of the century, including the yielding of two of its citizens accused of complicity in the bombing of Pan Am 103 over Lockerbie, Scotland, to trial at an international tribunal in The Hague. It nevertheless continued to provide safe haven for several Palestinian groups engaged in terrorism, including the Abu Nidal Organization, the Palestinian Islamic Jihad, and the Popular Front for the Liberation of Palestine–General Command.

Libya remained designated as a state sponsor of terrorism during the first five years of the 21st century, in spite of curtailment of support for international terrorism. In 2003, Libya concluded a deal with the families of the 270 victims of the 1988 Pan Am 103 bombing over Lockerbie, Scotland. The deal included payments by Libya of $10 million per family, contingent upon the lifting of UN and U.S. sanctions against Libya and removal of Libya from the state sponsors of terrorism list. By the end of 2004, UN and U.S. sanctions were lifted, and the families had received a total of $8 million each, but Libya remained designated as a state sponsor of terrorism. A remaining $2 million per family remained in a third-country escrow account, pending Libya's removal from the terrorism list.

North Korea

According to U.S. reports on state sponsorship of terrorism in 2004, North Korea has not been conclusively linked to any international terrorist attack in almost two decades. The 1987 midair bombing of Korean Airlines flight 858, which killed all 115 persons aboard, is the last known case of North Korean involvement in terrorism, but the state is alleged to still offer sanctuary to terrorists from neighboring countries. Lacking financial resources, it no longer openly supplies weapons or training to terrorists. Four JAPANESE RED ARMY members remain in the Democratic People's Republic of Korea following their involvement in a jet hijacking in 1970.

Sudan

Sudan's connection with terrorist financier Osama bin Laden and its willingness to harbor members of several of the most violent international groups engaged in terrorism continue to hold this state on the list of states sponsoring terrorism. It served through the end of the 20th century as a haven, meeting place, and training facility for a variety of international terrorist organizations, usually those of Middle Eastern origin.

Although Sudan ordered the departure of bin Laden in 1996, in compliance with UN Security Council resolutions, it has struggled over the issue of safe haven for others accused of terrorism. The three Egyptian al-Gama'at members linked to the 1995 assassination attempt on Egyptian president Hosni Mubarak in Ethiopia provoked demands that Sudan turn these individuals over to Egypt for trial, since the three fugitives were enjoying sanctuary in Sudan. Sudan also continued to harbor members from Lebanese Hizballah, the Palestinian Islamic Jihad, the Abu Nidal Organization, and HAMAS, as well as regional Islamic and non-Islamic opposition and insurgent groups from Ethiopia, Eritrea, Uganda, and Tunisia. Sudan's sponsorship includes paramilitary training, indoctrination, money, travel documentation, safe passage, as well as refuge. The country serves as a transit point and meeting place for several terrorist groups, a base to organize some of their operations and to support compatriots elsewhere.

The ongoing violence in Darfur and the unwillingness of the government to accept responsibility for, or to effectively restrain and punish, the Janjaweed whose attacks on non-Arab citizens provoked international condemnation for genocide, continues to mar Sudan's efforts to counter terrorism. The government has increased cooperation with Ugandan authorities to diminish the capabilities of the LORD'S RESISTANCE ARMY (LRA), a Ugandan group that has terrorized civilians in northern Uganda and claims to seek to overthrow the current Ugandan government.

In March 2004, a new Hamas representative arrived in Khartoum. According to press reports, he was received by the Sudanese government in an official capacity, although the government later closed a Hamas office in the capital.

Syria

Syria continues to provide safe haven and support for several groups engaged in planning or executing international terrorist attacks. Several such groups maintain training camps or other facilities in Syrian territory, including Ahmad Jabril's POPULAR FRONT FOR THE LIBERATION OF PALESTINE–GENERAL COMMAND, the PALESTINE ISLAMIC JIHAD, HAMAS, and the KURDISTAN WORKERS' PARTY. Syria granted a variety of these groups basing privileges or refuge in areas of Lebanon's Bekáa valley under Syrian control. It has not made efforts to stop anti-Israeli attacks by Hizballah and other Palestinian groups operating in Lebanon through Damascus, but Syria has made attempts to restrain the activities of some of these groups as the peace process in this region progresses.

In May 2003, Syria announced that the groups had voluntarily closed their offices in Damascus, although the groups continue to operate from Syria. The Syrian government insists that the Damascus-based offices undertake only political and informational activities. Syria also continues to permit Iran to use Damascus as a transshipment point for resupplying Lebanese Hizballah in Lebanon. Syrian officials have publicly condemned international terrorism, but they make a distinction between terrorism and what they consider to be the legitimate armed resistance of Palestinians in the occupied territories and of Hizballah.

The Syrian government has not been, as of the close of 2004, implicated directly in an act of terrorism since 1986, in spite of Israel's claim that Syria was indirectly involved at least in the August 31, 2004, Beersheva bus bombings that left 16 dead. Accusations have also been leveled from Lebanese officials of Syrian government involvement in two assassinations of leaders in Lebanon in 2005.

References: Council on Foreign Relations. State Sponsors of Terrorism. Available online. URL: http://www.cfr.org/issue/458/state_sponsors_of_terrorism.html. Accessed February 16, 2006; U.S. Department of State. Counterterrorism Office. "Country Reports on Terrorism." 2004. Available online. URL: http://www.state.gov/s/ct/rls/crt/c14818.htm. Accessed on March 27, 2006.

state terrorism

Individuals and groups are not the only perpetrators of terrorism. Political leaders have used terrorism as an instrument of both domestic and foreign policy for centuries. From the time when centralized governments were first organized, rulers have resorted to the use of terror tactics to subdue their subjects and to spread confusion and chaos among their enemies.

Terrorism remains a formidable weapon in the hands of a ruthless state. It is still used primarily for those two purposes: to subdue a nation's own people or to spread confusion and chaos among its enemies.

INTERNAL TERRORISM, practiced by a state against its own people, has produced some of the most flagrant violations of human rights that the world has ever known. External terrorism, practiced by one state against citizens of another, is less often cited as a form of state terrorism. Its perpetrators tend, as a rule, to try to conceal their roles as the instigators or supporters of the terrorists.

Throughout history, states have used terrorist acts of violence to subdue groups or individuals. States have, from time to time, used such violence to create a climate of fear in which citizens will do whatever the government wants.

The history of state terrorism stretches back at least into the legacy of ancient Rome. The Roman emperor Nero ruled by fear. He ordered the deaths of anyone who either opposed him or constituted a threat to his rule, including members of his own family. He was responsible for the slaughter of many of the nobility and for the burning of Rome in A.D. 64. To him, everyone was an "enemy," and with his power, he made them all victims of his terrorism.

What a state does to its own people was, until very recently, strictly its own business. Neither the rulers nor concerned citizens in other countries usually interfered with what a sovereign government chose to do with its citizens. Even today, such interference is largely limited to diplomatic or economic pressures and to the problematic effects of an informed world opinion.

In the wake of discovering just how ruthless some rulers could be in dealing with their subjects, leaders of victorious nations after World War II tried to create international laws that would restrict the ability of governments to use terrorism against their citizens. Attempts to create such laws by consensus were only marginally successful.

On December 10, 1948, the General Assembly of the United Nations adopted the Universal Declaration of Human Rights without dissent, calling on all member countries to publicize the text of the declaration and to "cause it to be disseminated, displayed, read and expounded principally in schools and other educational institutions, without distinction based on the political status of countries or territories."

This document states that "everyone has the right to life, liberty, and security of person" and that these rights may not be taken away by any institution, state, or individual. According to this declaration, it is not acceptable for states to administer collective punishment or to punish any person for a crime that he or she did not personally commit. The declaration, too, emphasizes the necessity of fair trials and equal justice before the law. Since terrorism by a state often involves the summary punishment of individuals, not for any specific crime, but because their deaths or incarceration will result in a climate of fear among other citizens, this declaration would appear to be significant in the effort to curb state terrorism. However, it has no binding effect in international law. It is, in some respects, only a statement of concern among some states about the presence of state terrorism.

If this declaration is only a statement of principles lacking mechanisms for enforcement involving state terrorism, the subsequent International Covenant on Civil and Political Rights tried to remedy that flaw. But while this covenant has more explicit provisions for enforcing compliance, it has a much worse record for ratification. The United States refused for decades to ratify this covenant, just as it also refused for over 40 years to become a party to the convention outlawing genocide. The United States eventually ratified the covenant in 1992, but with reservations.

The problem, both in terms of ratification and enforcement, is largely a political one. States do not openly interfere in the domestic affairs of other states since such interference would leave them open to similar intrusions. Conventions such as those protecting human rights are often viewed as dangerous, even by states with relatively clean records in terms of state terrorism, in that these conventions open avenues for hostile governments to interfere with the internal affairs of the nation.

George M. Kren and Leon Rappoport argue that:

> Within certain limits set by political and military power considerations, the modern state may do anything it wishes to those under its control. There is no moral-ethical limit which the state cannot transcend if it wished to do so, because there is no moral-ethical power higher than the state. Moreover, it seems apparent that no modern state will ever seriously interfere with the internal activities of another solely for moral-ethical reasons.

Most interference in the internal affairs of a sovereign state is done for reasons of national security rather than on ethical or moral grounds. Although the Nuremberg Trials offered some evidence that the principle of nonintervention was being challenged by nations motivated by moral-ethical concern, since that time, few nations have indicated that "crimes against humanity" undertaken within a nation's own borders are a basis for international intervention. Even evidence of "ethnic cleansing" in Bosnia during the early 1990s, although generating the formation of an international criminal tribunal, did not produce on the part of nations a willingness to send indicted criminals to succumb to the justice process of The Hague. Justice remains largely within the purview defined by the rulers of the individual nation-states. State terrorism remains an unpunished crime.

If it is true, as Leon Trotsky declared at Brest-Litovsk, that "every state is based on violence," this does not imply that a state retains the right to continue to perpetrate violence indefinitely. This would extend the rights of the state to implausible lengths.

The linkage between revolution and violence has been discussed at length by many authors for decades. A similar relationship exists with respect to the right of a state to protect itself from revolutionary violence. Most modern states have experienced a period of revolutionary violence. During and after such periods, the right of a state to protect itself remains restricted by even more rules than those that apply to its revolutionary enemies. In addition to abiding by the laws of warfare, states are entrusted with the responsibility for preserving and protecting human rights and freedoms.

Thus, a state has an abiding obligation to restrain its use of violence against its citizens. Whether at war or at peace, a state is supposed to recognize a legal commitment toward the preservation of the rights of the individual. If it is true that insurgent terrorists frequently try to provoke government repression in the hope of generating greater sympathy and support for the terrorists' cause, then it is obviously extremely important that governments not respond in kind.

This does not mean that governments are or should be held to be impotent in the face of flagrant attacks on law and order. Certainly a state is responsible for protecting its citizens from violence. But the means used to ensure law and order must be carefully balanced against the responsibility of the government to insure the maximum protection of civil rights and liberties. Too great a willingness to sacrifice the latter in order to preserve stability within a state would not only be giving the terrorist the impetus for his/her cause but would also be placing the state in the invidious position of breaking international law in order to stop someone else from breaking it.

A state that violates international law by committing acts of genocide, violently suppressing fundamental freedoms, or breaking the laws of war or the Geneva Convention on the treatment of prisoners of war and civilians can be considered guilty of state terrorism. If TERRORISM is defined to include acts of political violence perpetrated without regard to the safety of innocent persons in an effort to evoke a mood of fear and confusion in a target audience, then surely states have been as guilty of such acts as have individuals and groups.

It is useful to remember that the word "terror" derives from the actions of a government—the Jacobin government of revolutionary France. In fact, "terrorist" regimes have been far more deadly than group or individual actors in this century, even after the end of World War II. The word *totalitarian* became part of the political lexicon of the 20th century as a result of state terrorism in Nazi Germany and Stalinist Russia. Both systems relied upon organized, systematized indiscriminate terror to create a bondage of the mind as well as of the body.

If, as Hannah Arendt suggests, "lawlessness is the essence of tyranny, then terror is the essence of totalitarian domination." In her essay "On Violence," this same expert notes that "terror is not the same as violence; it is, rather, the form of government that comes into being when violence, having destroyed all power, does not abdicate but, on the contrary, remains in full control." State terrorism, thus described, is the quintessential form of terrorism.

State terrorism frequently comprises a nasty combination of personality and ideology. Nazism and Stalinism were personifications of the evil genius of their leaders. Totalitarianism and state terrorism aim not only at the transmutation of society but also at a fundamental change in human nature itself. The basic goal of terrorist states is mass disorientation and inescapable anxiety. Modern governments whose actions have earned for themselves the soubriquet "terrorist," such as Indonesia in the 1960s or Chile in the 1970s, have employed terror-violence as an integral part of the governing process.

Governments have been, and will no doubt continue to be, as likely to commit terrorist acts as individuals and groups. Moreover, it appears logical that "as violence breeds violence, so terrorism begets counter-terrorism, which in turn leads to more terrorism in an ever-increasing spiral," as a UN study on this subject noted. State domestic terrorism not only transgresses international law, but it often creates the political, economic, and social milieu that precipitates acts of individual and group terrorism. It is thus a causal factor in the perpetration of further terrorism.

Even the United States, in its war on terror, has not escaped this vicious cycle of violence. In 1987, the United Nations Convention against Torture and Other Cruel, Inhuman or Degrading Treatment or Punishment entered into force, with most of the world's nations as signatories, including the United States. In 2004, the United States was accused of the use of torture in the Abu Ghraib prison in Iraq. In the era of Saddam Hussein, Abu Ghraib, 20 miles west of Baghdad, was one of the world's most notorious prisons, with torture, weekly executions, and vile living conditions. As many as 50,000 men and women—no accurate count is possible—were jammed into Abu Ghraib at one time, in 12-by-12-foot cells that were little more than human holding pens.

In the looting that followed the regime's collapse in 2003, the huge prison complex, by then deserted, was stripped of everything that could be removed, including doors, windows, and bricks. The coalition authorities had the floors tiled; cells cleaned and repaired; and toilets, showers, and a new medical center added. Abu Ghraib was now a U.S. military prison. Most of the prisoners—by the fall there were several thousand, including women and teenagers—were civilians, many of whom had been picked up in random military sweeps and at highway checkpoints. They fell into three loosely defined categories: common criminals, security detainees suspected of "crimes against the coalition," and a small number of suspected "high-value" leaders of the insurgency against the coalition forces.

In June 2003, Janis Karpinski, an army reserve brigadier general, was named commander of the 800th Military Police Brigade and put in charge of military prisons in Iraq. General Karpinski, the only female commander in the war zone, was an experienced operations and intelligence officer who had served with the special forces and in the 1991 Gulf War, but she had never run a prison system. Now she was in charge of three large jails, eight battalions, and 3,400 army reservists, most of whom, like her, had no training in handling prisoners.

In January 2004, General Karpinski was formally admonished and quietly suspended, and a major investigation into the army's prison system, authorized by Lieutenant General Ricardo S. Sanchez, the senior commander in Iraq, was under way. A 53-page report, obtained by the *New Yorker,* written by Major General Antonio M. Taguba and not meant for public release, was completed in late February. Its conclusions about the institutional failures of the army prison system were devastating. Specifically, Taguba found that between October and December of 2003 there were numerous instances of "sadistic, blatant, and wanton criminal abuses" at Abu Ghraib. This systematic and illegal abuse of detainees, Taguba reported, was perpetrated by soldiers of the 372nd Military Police Company and also by members of the American intelligence community. (The 372nd was attached to the 320th M.P. Battalion, which reported to Karpinski's brigade headquarters.) Taguba's report listed some of the wrongdoing:

> Breaking chemical lights and pouring the phosphoric liquid on detainees; pouring cold water on naked detainees; beating detainees with a broom handle and a chair; threatening male detainees with rape; allowing a military police guard to stitch the wound of a detainee who was injured after being slammed against the wall in his cell; sodomizing a detainee with a chemical light and perhaps a broom stick; and using military working dogs to frighten and intimidate detainees with threats of attack, and in one instance actually biting a detainee.

There was stunning evidence to support the allegations, Taguba added—"detailed witness statements and the discovery of extremely graphic photographic evidence." Photographs and videos taken by the soldiers as the abuses were happening were not included in his report, Taguba said, because of their "extremely sensitive nature."

The photographs—several of which were broadcast on CBS's *60 Minutes 2*—showed leering G.I.s taunting naked Iraqi prisoners who were forced to assume humiliating poses. The photographs tell it all. In one, Private Lynndie England, a cigarette dangling from her mouth, is giving a jaunty thumbs-up sign and pointing at the genitals of a young Iraqi, who is naked except for a sandbag over his head, as he masturbates. Three other hooded and naked Iraqi prisoners are shown, hands reflexively crossed over their genitals. A fifth prisoner has his hands at his sides. In another, England stands arm in arm with Specialist Charles Graner; both are grinning and giving the thumbs-up behind a cluster of perhaps seven naked Iraqis, knees bent, piled clumsily on top of each other in a pyramid.

Yet another photograph shows a kneeling, naked, unhooded male prisoner, head momentarily turned away from the camera, posed to make it appear that he is performing oral sex on another male prisoner, who is naked and hooded. Such dehumanization is unacceptable in any culture, but it is especially so in the Arab world. Homosexual acts are against Islamic law, and it is humiliating for men to be naked in front of other men, according to Bernard Haykel, a professor of Middle Eastern studies at New York University. "Being put on top of each other and forced to masturbate, being naked in front of each other—it's all a form of torture," Haykel said.

Prosecutions of the soldiers and commanders involved in this abuse occurred but was not enough to diminish the glaring evidence of prisoner torture and abuse by U.S. soldiers and civilians. Clearly, torture is still a weapon used by governments today to intimidate, coerce, and even kill those suspected of opposing a government.

The Bush adminstration has argued that it needs to be able to use "tough interrogation techniques" against a determined enemy. In September 2006, reports charged that the Bush administration had authorized the use of "waterboarding"—a form of physical torture—against detainees from the War on Terror. This type of torture is prohibited under the Geneva Conventions with regard to prisoners of war and under the United Nations Convention on Torture, on both of which the United States is a signatory. President Bush argued that the captured terrorists being held are not in fact "prisoners of war" but "unlawful enemy combatants" and as such are not afforded the protections given to POWs in the Geneva Conventions, such as protection against torture and the right to fair and speedy trial in a court of law. In June 2006, the U.S. Supreme Court ruled in *Hamdan v. Rumsfeld* that military commisions set up in to try detainees in Gauntanamo Bay "violate both the Uniform Code of Military Justice and the four Geneva conventions." In October 2006, President Bush signed into law the Military Commisions Act to help make the military tribunals stay within the U.S. Constitution and meet treaty obligations. Critics charge that the law still allows for holding people without charge, permits torture, and denies the right of appeal, which in effect makes the United States a terrorist state in its own right and only breeds more terrorists.

State terrorism, then, whether it is internal or external, offers a real threat to international peace and security. Internal terrorism breeds resistance movements, which often resort to terrorist tactics. This cycle of terror-violence can result in a whirlwind that will destroy all within its reach, innocent and guilty.

References: Bowden, Mark. "The Dark Art of Interrogation." *The Atlantic* (October 2003). Available online. URL: http://www.theatlantic.com/doc/200310/bowden. Accessed March 28, 2006; Strasser, Steven. *The Abu Ghraib Investigations: The Official Independent Panel and Pentagon Reports on the Shocking Prisoner Abuse in Iraq* (New York: Perseus Books, 2004); United Nations. Office of the High Commissioner for Human Rights. "Convention against Torture and Other Cruel, Inhuman or Degrading Treatment or Punishment." Available online. URL: http://www.unhchr.ch/html/menu3/b/h_cat39.htm. Accessed March 28, 2006.

Stern Gang

A group organized by Avraham Stern during the last years of the British presence in Palestine (1918–48) in an attempt to expedite the British departure. The Stern Gang was so vehemently anti-British that some of its members even attempted during World War II to make contact with the virulently anti-Semitic government in Germany to cooperate in defeating the British. The Germans refused to have anything to do with the Sternists. Most of the Jewish community in Palestine disowned the Stern Gang and its violent methods that were directed against Arabs, Britons, and Jews considered to be too accommodating to the latter groups.

Avraham Stern was eventually killed by the British. His followers continued their opposition to the British presence until the end of the British Mandate. Some of them were involved in the attack in 1947 on Deir Yassin, an Arab village, in which nearly 300 men, women, and children were killed. The Sternists had worked with the IRGUN ZVAI LEUMI, another extremist but somewhat less violent Jewish organization, to coordinate the attack in the belief that the village harbored Palestinian terrorists. Another explanation is that the Sternists and Likud wanted to use Deir Yassin as an example to encourage Arabs to leave Palestine. The Jewish authorities condemned the attack.

After Israel achieved statehood in 1948, the Stern Gang dissolved and joined the Irgun in parliamentary opposition. The Israeli government also indicated it would not tolerate any armed groups that were not sanctioned by the state, thus outlawing the Irgun and the Stern Gang. A few of the Stern Gang's members became members of the Israeli parliament. One of its activists, Yitzak Shamir, eventually became prime minister (1983–84 and 1986–92). The Stern Gang at its height probably claimed no more than a few hundred followers. It never achieved popularity or legitimacy within the Jewish community, which consistently disavowed the organization, its activities, and its goals.

Reference: Gelvin, James L. *Israel-Palestine Conflict: One Hundred Years of War* (New York: Cambridge University Press, 2005).

Stockholm syndrome

This is the term used to describe the "identification" of victims with their captors, which is the psychological condition that occurs when a victim held under duress seems to understand and empathize with his/

her captors. It draws its name from an incident that occurred at the Kreditbanken in Stockholm, Sweden, in the summer of 1973, when four hostages were taken in a bank robbery that resulted in a six-day standoff. At the end of the six days of captivity, the hostages actively resisted rescue, refused to testify against their captors, and actually raised money for their captors' legal defense. According to some reports, one of the hostages eventually became engaged to one of her jailed captors. From this unusual behavior, the term *Stockholm syndrome* came to be used to describe similar captive/captor relationships.

In the United States, the term was used to describe the behavior of Patty Hearst in 1974, when she was kidnapped and tortured by the SYMBIONESE LIBERATION ARMY, a radical political group of the 1970s. Ms. Hearst, while still a "captive" of the SLA, took up arms and joined their cause, adopting the name of "Tania" and assisting the group in bank robberies. Ms. Hearst, after her capture, denounced the group and her involvement in it, and used the Stockholm syndrome in her defense.

Generally, this psychological pattern comes into play when a captive cannot escape and is isolated and threatened with death but is shown token acts of kindness by the captor. It typically takes about three or four days for the psychological shift to take hold. Captives begin to identify with their captors initially as a defensive mechanism, out of fear of violence. Small acts of kindness by the captor are magnified, since finding perspective in a hostage situation is by definition impossible. Rescue attempts are also seen as a threat, since it is likely the captive would be injured during such attempts. These symptoms occur when the victim is under enormous emotional and often physical duress. The behavior, according to psychologists, is considered a common survival strategy for victims of interpersonal abuse and is observed in battered spouses, abused children, prisoners of war, and concentration camp survivors. Thus, victims of terrorist capture and abuse may be expected to exhibit similar symptoms.

Sudan, pharmaceutical plant, bombing of

See OPERATION INFINITE REACH.

suicide terrorists

On October 23, 1983, two explosions at barracks of the American and French peacekeeping forces in Beirut inaugurated the modern phenomenon of suicide terrorism. Seventeen years later, a suicide attack on the USS *Cole* anchored off the port city of Aden in Yemen provided a grim reminder of the effectiveness of terrorists willing to die for their cause. For nearly two decades suicide terrorism has been a tactic pursued by a variety of terrorist organizations from Algeria to Sri Lanka. The weapon of choice is a bomb that is in easy proximity to the suicide terrorist or, more usually, strapped to the terrorist's body.

During the last two decades of the 20th century, the low cost and high lethality of the tactic have made it a favorite with not only terrorists but also guerrilla and insurgent groups, particularly in the Middle East, but also in Sri Lanka. The LTTE were, according to an expert from the Institute for Counter-Terrorism in Israel in 2000, "unequivocally the most effective and brutal terrorist organization ever to utilize suicide terrorism." After the LTTE signed a cease-fire with the Sri Lankan government in 2001, suicide bombings by Islamic militants, belonging to groups such as HAMAS and the Al-Aqsa Martyrs' Brigade, have taken the lead in the use of this tactic, although it is important to note that the ATTACK ON AMERICA on September 11, 2001, involved the largest and most destructive individual suicide terrorist attacks on a single day.

Suicide terrorists tend to belong to an organization that regularly sponsors and commits terrorist acts. Organizations that have resorted to suicide terrorism include HIZBALLAH, Egyptian ISLAMIC JIHAD, HAMAS, the Algerian ARMED ISLAMIC GROUP (GIA), and the Sri Lankan LIBERATION TIGERS OF TAMIL EELAM (LTTE), or Black Tigers. While most of these groups inspire potential suicide terrorists with religious doctrines, a few, such as the Black Tigers, do so with extreme secular messages.

It is important to note that most terrorist organizations that use suicide terrorism as a tactic are not consistent practitioners of this form of terror. Military retaliation is the normal result of an act of suicide terrorism. The retaliation may be so massive that terrorist leaders will frequently suspend suicide terrorism for lengthy periods of time, as was the case when the United States attacked al-Qaeda bases in Afghanistan after the attacks on 9/11. But the cost of the attack for the group initiating the attack is initially low and the gain in destruction of its target high. For an expenditure of around $100,000, al-Qaeda effected a trillion-dollar drop in global markets within one week and triggered massive increases in military and security

Masked Hamas militants dressed as suicide bombers march in a rally in the southern Gaza Strip, 2002. (GETTY IMAGES)

expenditure in response. The destruction wreaked by the United States in Afghanistan in response may have offset those gains but not sufficiently to make such tactics unattractive, as became evident in the LONDON and MADRID bombings.

Generally, suicide terrorist bombings are initiated by a group for what it perceives as a vital, but temporary, tactic. Hamas, for example, authorized a series of suicide terrorist incidents on Israeli civilian buses during 1994–96 to discourage the success of a peace process between ISRAEL and PALESTINE that was then gaining momentum. Hamas accepted and encouraged martyrdom to attack the enemies of Islam. "Martyrs," recruited to destroy themselves along with as many other people as possible, were often sincere individuals very committed to their cause who genuinely believed they were pursuing justice. They were often motivated by the belief that their martyrdom would result in immediate transport to Paradise. According to Israeli counterterrorism authorities, Hamas, Islamic Jihad, and Fatah operated "Paradise Camps," training children as young as 11 to become suicide bombers.

During what was called the Second INTIFADA, suicide bombings in Israel increased, with frequent attacks on cafés or crowded buses at rush hour. Using suicide belts, explosive devices (often including shrapnel), the would-be martyrs chose buses packed with civilians or crowded marketplaces and restaurants to maximize the effects of the blast and the loss of life in the enclosed locations. Typically, a young person would board a civilian bus, wait several stops until the bus was full of students, shoppers, and children, and then detonate him- or herself. The cost in lives was usually very heavy. The intended impact was to cause a maximum loss of life and physical injury and to intimidate rank-and-file Israelis to stay home. Military targets were seldom chosen, unless it was possible to hit soldiers awaiting roadside transport.

"The method of martyrdom operation is the most successful way of inflicting damage against the opponent and the least costly to the mujahidin in terms of casualties," according to al-Qaeda leader Ayman al-Zawahiri. Certainly, suicide terrorism has become increasingly popular in the wake of the U.S.-led invasion of Iraq in 2003. The low-cost/high-yield nature of this form of attack, as noted by the al-Qaeda leader, has led to waves of suicide bombings and to considerable confusion as to whether the attacks are insurgent- or terrorist-initiated. If the targets are military, regardless of the strategic intent, the attacks are considered acts of war. If such acts violate the laws of war in any way, then the attack may be considered a crime (of war) but not a terrorist act. However, if the attacks deliberately involve civilian, noncombatant targets, then the terrorist nature of the act is clear. Since many of the attacks in Iraq have involved civilian targets (Shiite mosques, international offices of the United Nations and the Red Cross, Iraqi men waiting in line to apply for jobs with the police force, etc.), such attacks are properly considered terrorist acts. Attacks on U.S. military personnel, equipment, and bases, however, remain acts of war, whose legality must be assessed in that context.

Suicide terrorist attacks have occurred in more than 30 countries in recent years and appear to be gaining popularity as the cost/benefit analysis for this tactic is clearly attractive to groups with limited resources facing large and powerful enemies.

See also AL-QAEDA; AL-AQSA MARTYRS' BRIGADE.

References: Bloom, Mia. *Dying to Kill: The Allure of Suicide Terror* (New York: Columbia University Press, 2005); Oliver, Anne Marie. *Road to Martyrs' Square: A Journey into the World of the Suicide Bomber* (New York: Oxford University Press, 2005); Pape, Robert A. *Dying to Win: The Strategic Logic of Suicide Terrorism* (New York: Random House, 2005).

surrogate terrorism

Like state-sponsored terrorism, this type of action is taken by a state that does not wish to be openly linked to terrorist acts by a group or individual but is willing to discreetly help such actions occur if they enhance the state's foreign policy goals. Since war between states is legally not acceptable following the signing of the United Nations Charter, states may engage in a form of surrogate war by giving assistance to another state or organization engaged in violent actions against an enemy state.

IRAN, under the AYATOLLAH KHOMEINI, engaged in this practice throughout the Middle East. LIBYA has used this form of terrorism as an instrument to help the state track down and eradicate exiled dissidents or to intimidate them into silence. Essentially, surrogate terrorism involves one state using another state or a terrorist group to carry out acts of violence against an enemy that the aforesaid state would like to strike but cannot do so openly.

Symbionese Liberation Army (SLA)

The SLA was a group in the United States that considered itself to be a "revolutionary vanguard army," propounding a radical ideology and occasionally committing assassinations, bank robberies, and other acts of violence between 1973 and 1975. Although this group never had more than 13 members, it became well known during its lifetime, primarily because of its headline-generating kidnapping of newpaper millionaire heiress Patty Hearst, who during her captivity joined the group and participated in its robberies. Hearst's trial also popularized the term STOCKHOLM SYNDROME, used to explain the psychological identification of a hostage with his or her captors.

The Symbionese Liberation Army was formed by Donald DeFreeze, who adopted the name of "Cinque" (from the reported leader of the slave rebellion that took over the Spanish slave ship *Amistad* in 1839). DeFreeze escaped from Soledad State Prison in March 1973 and ended up at a commune in the San Francisco Bay Area, sharing living quarters first with Willie Wolfe and Russ Little, and then with Patricia Soltysik, all of whom became members of the SLA. Although the SLA considered themselves leaders of the black revolution, DeFreeze was the only African-American member of the organization.

After spending a few months acquiring, storing, and training in the use of firearms at various public shooting ranges, the SLA took its first violent action in November 1973, with the murder of Oakland, California's superintendent of schools, Marcus Foster, who was, ironically, black. In assassinating Foster, and seriously wounding his deputy, Robert Blackburn, as the men left an Oakland school board meeting, the SLA claimed to be striking out against Foster's plan to introduce identification cards into Oakland's schools, a move DeFreeze called "fascist." Since Foster had actually opposed the use of identification cards in his schools and instead offered a watered-down version of such a plan and was himself very popular in the black community and with the political left (for whom the SLA claimed to be fighting), the assassination was considered pointless and counterproductive by most of the community. The media attention gained by the group for its action garnered no support and was predominantly negative.

Two months later, Joe Remiro and Russ Little were arrested and charged with Foster's murder. Both were convicted and sentenced to life in prison, although Little was later acquitted on a retrial. Subsequently, the SLA began to try to negotiate a prisoner swap, kidnapping publishing heiress Patricia Hearst, a Berkeley college student, in February 1974, one month after Remiro and Little's arrest. The initial demand of the SLA for a prisoner swap did not generate success, so the group changed the demand to that of a food-distribution program in return for her release, with the demand for the value of the food escalating dramatically from $4 million to $43 million. Although some free food was actually distributed, this ceased when one of the four distribution points experienced a riot.

Hearst was apparently "indoctrinated" into the SLA ideology, and tapes were released within 13 days of her capture in which she expressed this ideology in her own words. The tapes indicated Hearst's apparent espousal of the aims of the SLA and eventually included her denunciation of her former life as a media heiress, her parents, and her fiancé. She stated on the tapes that the SLA had given her the option of being released or of joining the SLA and that she had decided to join the group, taking on the name of "Tania."

Hearst participated actively in the next action taken by the SLA, a robbery of the Hibernia Bank, in which two civilians were shot. Following this robbery, the SLA moved its operations to the Los Angeles area, with catastrophic results for the group, which commandeered a house and supplies from the very community that it was allegedly "supporting" in its radical struggles. A subsequent violent confrontation at a neighborhood sporting goods store led police to a house in a black community that the group had commandeered after abandoning their safe house. In a siege of the house the following day by Los Angeles police, FBI, the California Highway Patrol, and the LA Fire Department, members of the group in the house were killed or captured. Ms. Hearst was not in the house at that time. She was later captured, tried, and pardoned for her actions, based on her Stockholm syndrome defense.

In 1975, Kathleen Soliah, an SLA member, failed in her attempt to kill officers of the LAPD when the bombs she put under a police car did not detonate. Soliah remained a fugitive, first abroad, and then in Minnesota where, under the alias of Sarah Jane Olson, she married a doctor and had several children. Soliah was arrested in 1991, and in 2001, she pleaded guilty to possession of explosives with the intent to murder. She was sentenced to 13 years, plus six for her role in a killing during a bank robbery. The remaining members of the SLA have also been arrested, charged, and convicted and are currently serving sentences.

References: Boulton, David. *The Making of Tania Hearst* (Bergenfield, N.J.: New American Library, 1975); Hearst, Patty, with Alvin Moscow. *Patty Hearst: Her Own Story* (New York: Avon, 1982).

T

tactical terror

This type of terror is used by revolutionary movements or groups engaged in GUERRILLA WARFARE against politically attractive targets, usually part of the government. Such attacks are directed solely against the ruling government, not just its citizens or supporters, and it constitutes a part of a "broad revolutionary strategic plan." A tactical terrorist attack is thus only a tactic to gain a specific end against a clearly defined enemy, one step in a plan for action against a target (the government), not a random selection of a location in which innocent bystanders could be killed.

taggants

See EXPLOSIVES, TAGGANTS FOR.

targeted killings

After the 1972 Munich Olympics massacre of 11 Israeli athletes by the radical Palestinian organization BLACK SEPTEMBER, the Israeli government sanctioned the tracking down and killing of those who had planned (but not necessarily participated in) the operation. The Israelis believed that the practice of holding responsible those who inspired, financed, and organized attacks against Israeli citizens did not exempt any Palestinian organization's political leadership from reprisals. ISRAEL referred to this policy as "focused preventive acts," a euphemism for assassinations. Not even YASIR ARAFAT was or considered himself to be immune, though he was left alone by the Israelis, if only because of pressure from the United States. It was clear, especially during the Netanyahu and Sharon governments (1996–99 and 2001–06, respectively), that most of the Israeli political leadership believed that Arafat should be killed.

In recent years, Israel has focused its targeted killing policy on top HAMAS leaders. Top people, such as Abdul Aziz Rantisi and Sheikh Ahmed Yassin, were killed within 25 days of one another. Hamas then adopted a policy of not revealing its top leader's name. In June 2006, within days after Hamas operatives kidnapped an Israeli soldier, the Israeli military responded in kind by essentially abducting 21 Hamas members of the Palestinian Authority's Legislative Council and seven cabinet ministers as well. A total of 84 people were arrested and confined by Israeli authorities, at least 60 of whom were affiliated with Hamas. Moreover, Israel warned the PA's prime minister, Ismail Haniyeh, that he should not consider himself immune from arrest or harm. "Targeted kidnappings" or "targeted detentions" of Palestinian leaders seems to have become a spin-off of targeted killings.

Israel has continued the policy of targeted killings despite an outcry of international condemnation. The United States, during the second Bush administration (2005–09), officially maintained its opposition to targeted killings but was either mild in its criticism of them or silent altogether. In fact, in November 2002, an automatically piloted American *Predator* drone attacked and killed the then top AL-QAEDA leader in Yemen along with five of his associates. The United States, however, was careful to distance itself from the notion that this was another example of targeted killings and argued that it was engaged in a war with al-Qaeda killers and that this was the only way to conduct it. In April 1986, the United States had launched an air strike on LIBYA in an unsuccessful attempt to kill Libya's MU'AMMAR QADHAFI as a response to the Libyan's regime sponsorship of terrorism directed against American soldiers stationed in Europe. The British have never admitted doing so, but there were apparent assassinations of IRISH REPUBLICAN ARMY leaders during the 1970s and 1980s. Israel is far from being the only country that follows a practice of targeted killings, though it may be the only one that publicly acknowledges the practice as official policy.

It is difficult to speculate how successful the policy of targeted killings has been. The point of targeted assassinations is to keep the groups of terrorists, particularly and especially at the leadership level, off balance. This reasoning suggests that if the leading planners of terrorists attacks are kept occupied trying to survive, they will have less opportunity and even less incentive to pursue attacks if their own lives, and sometimes the lives of family members, might be forfeited in the process. At least, that is the theory. Of course, many fanatical terrorists, particularly religiously inspired ones, expect to die anyway and even look forward to the event because of their belief of a reward in the hereafter.

The Israelis have occasionally interrupted the policy of targeted killings in informal and casual ways and resumed the policy in much the same manner, basically whenever it suited them to do so. Israelis across most of the political spectrum believe that the policy has enhanced their security and discouraged more terrorism than they have already suffered. The Hamas leadership, the most frequent target of the policy, has attempted to retaliate, but without success. The security apparatus that surrounds Israeli leaders is far tighter than their Palestinian counterparts'. But Israelis are still vulnerable: Operatives from the POPULAR FRONT FOR THE LIBERATION OF PALESTINE, for example, were able to assassinate an Israeli cabinet member, minister of tourism Rechavam Ze'evy, on October 17, 2001, in a Jerusalem hotel.

In July and August 2006, during the 34-day-long Israeli incursion into Lebanon in an effort to stop HIZBALLAH from launching rockets on Israeli territory, retrieving two soldiers Hizballah had kidnapped, and perhaps even disarming Hizballah terrorists, the Israelis unsuccessfully targeted Hassan Nasrallah, Hizballah's secretary-general. Nasrallah was apparently not where the Israeli military thought he would be located and proceeded to taunt Israelis with frequent television appearances to announce that he was still alive and well.

targets, hardening of

This involves efforts to make targets less accessible. These strategies include installing metal detectors and X-ray machines at points of entry, using sensor or closed-circuit television to monitor accessways, and employing other similar technical devices. Such measures can also include the erection of fences, vision barriers, and heavy barriers around the perimeters of the installation. Related security measures can involve increased use of such items as armored cars, security guard forces, and bulletproof vests. Executives of international companies are increasingly enrolling employees in training programs designed to teach skills in such things as high-speed car chases, surviving a kidnapping, and how not to look like a businessperson traveling abroad.

It is neither possible nor popular to harden all targets. The erection of heavy barriers and armed guards around public buildings, while perhaps effectively hardening the targets to some degree, are usually extremely unpopular measures in a democratic society, where public access is fundamental to the system. As the United States learned in the OKLAHOMA CITY BOMBING, moreover, it is neither popular nor practical to seek security by hardening security around federal buildings that are there to serve the public. A determined assault can usually get past the security, and the efforts to harden such targets often offend the public whom the offices are designed to serve. In the wake of the events of 9/11, efforts at hardening the target have focused on actions such as reinforcing cockpit doors, equipping pilots with weapons, and including air marshals on random flights. All of these options, while potentially useful, are not fail-safe and may, in the view of some experts, engender a false sense of security.

Reference: Thomas, Andrew R. *Aviation Insecurity: The New Challenges of Air Travel* (Amherst, N.Y.: Prometheus Books, 2003).

target search teams

Target search teams constitute a vital part of Germany's counterterrorism (CT) efforts. These teams, comprised from a special unit of investigators drawn from the BKA (the Federal Criminal Investigation Department), use the PIOS information system to study known and suspected terrorists. Although every police officer in the Federal Republic carries at all times a set of cards bearing the photographs and identification data on all of these "targeted" persons (about 15 of the most violent offenders), it is the target search teams who focus absolutely on these individuals.

Each target search team takes one terrorist and immerses itself in his or her life, using THE KOMMISSAR, as the computer system at Wiesbaden is affectionately known. All of the information about a subject, however trivial it may seem, can be useful to the search team. If they know, for instance, that a suspect always telephones his or her mother on her birthday, the mother's phone can be wiretapped. Support for a certain soccer team indicated by the subject can lead the search team to attend that team's matches.

These intensive "target searches" have had documented success. Using these methods, 15 terrorists were located in a six-week period in 1978. But the ability to locate terrorists in other countries has made the arrest and trial record of these teams less impressive since apprehension of the suspects depends on the cooperation of the other countries.

Four of the aforementioned terrorists sought in 1978 were traced to Bulgaria. According to the lawyer for Till Meyer, Gabrielle Rollnick, Gudrun Sturmer, and Angelika Loder (the four suspects), four hired cars containing heavily armed German police drew up at a café in Sonnenstrand, a Bulgarian resort. The four suspects were taken to a bungalow not far away and tied up. At 2 A.M., they were taken to Bourgas Airport in a minibus with German customs license plates and put onto a plane with 25 other armed German police. The cooperation of the Bulgarian government in this "kidnapping" of terrorists offers an interesting example of a joint effort, during the cold war, between a communist country (Bulgaria) and a noncommunist state (Germany) in the apprehension of terrorists.

Similar cooperative success was achieved by Germany with France in May 1980 when five women wanted on terrorism charges in Germany were arrested in an apartment in the Rue Flatters on the Left Bank in Paris. French police simply arrested the women and sent them to Germany for trial.

However, the French were far less cooperative in the case involving Germany's efforts to apprehend Abu Daoud, one of BLACK SEPTEMBER's commanders. Dauod arrived in Paris (under an assumed name) for the funeral of the PALESTINE LIBERATION ORGANIZATION's representative. The French, who had photographed the funeral, circulated the pictures to friendly governments, including Germany, asking for information to assist French police in solving the murder of the representative. When British intelligence identified Daoud, French police promptly arrested him, much to the chagrin of the French government. Although Germany immediately requested his extradition, the French authorities quietly set him free, outside of their borders.

The former Yugoslavia, too, failed significantly to cooperate when it refused to arrest CARLOS "THE JACKAL" after being informed (in detail in an intelligence report) of his presence and his crimes by a German target search team. Yugoslav officials did arrest four of [West] Germany's most wanted terrorists (Rolf-Clemens Wagner, Brigitte Mohnhaupt, Sieglinde Hofmann, and Peter Boock) on information given by another German target search team, but they later released these suspects without either a trial or an extradition proceeding, failing to follow through on Germany's efforts.

Target search teams, then, have been a useful tool of Germany's counterterrorism efforts in many respects. While their success record in tracking and finding suspects has been very good indeed, their ability to complete the process with an arrest and trial has been less stellar, in part due to a lack of complete cooperation of the authorities in other states. German efforts to apprehend members of the Hamburg cell of AL-QAEDA believed to be responsible for planning the ATTACK ON AMERICA in 2001 were partly successful. According to U.S. and German investigators, there were 11 core members of this group. Of those, three died in the attack, two are in U.S. military custody, one is imprisoned in Syria, and two are facing trial in Germany. The other three remain at large. However, prosecution

Members of the 86th Transportation Group put up concrete barriers around the 86th Airlift Wing Headquarters Building on Ramstein Air Base, Germany in response to the 9/11 attacks on America, 2001. (DEPARTMENT OF DEFENSE)

of these individuals in trials has a mixed record. After three years of failing to hold anyone accountable for the attacks of September 11, 2001, Germany prepared to expel accused members of the Hamburg-based cell and send them to countries with more aggressive records of prosecuting terrorism.

terrorism

Working Definition of Terrorism

While it has not been possible, yet, to create a universally acceptable definition of "terrorism," it is both possible and necessary to specify certain features common to the phenomenon. This, in turn, makes it feasible to create an operational definition of this term. Acts possessing *all* of these attributes could then be identified as "terrorist" acts with some consistency. Without falling into the political quagmire of attempting to label individuals or groups as terrorist, certain types of *actions* could be identified as terrorism, regardless of who commits them for however noble a cause.

Consider a loose definition of contemporary terrorism. It must of necessity be "loose" since its elements tend to form a wide variety of compounds that today fall within the rubric of terrorism. For the purposes of this investigation, terrorism will be defined as a synthesis of war and theater, a dramatization of the most proscribed kind of violence—that which is perpetrated on innocent victims—played before an audience in the hope of creating a mood of fear for political purposes.

Crucial Components of Terrorism

There are, in this description of terrorism, a number of crucial components. Terrorism, by this definition, involves an act of violence, an audience, the creation of a mood of fear, innocent victims, and political motives or goals. Each of these elements deserves some clarification in order to formulate a clear set of parameters for this frequently misunderstood and misused term.

Violence: First, it is important to note that terrorism is fundamentally a violent act. Sit-ins, picket lines, walkouts, and other similar forms of protest, no matter how disruptive, are *not* terrorist acts. Violence—the threat of violence where the capacity and the willingness to commit violence are displayed—is endemic to terrorism. The violence need not be fully perpetrated, that is, the bomb need not be detonated or all of the passengers aboard an airliner killed, in order for it to be considered a terrorist act. But the capacity and the willingness to commit a violent act *must* be present.

Audience: This means, then, that it is the *perception* of the audience of that violent potential that is crucial to classifying an act as terrorism. Terrorism is, essentially, theater, an act played before an audience, designed to call the attention of millions, even hundreds of millions, to an often unrelated situation through shock—producing situations of outrage and horror, doing the unthinkable without apology or remorse. Unlike similar acts of murder or warfare, acts of terrorism are neither ends in themselves nor are they often more than tangentially related to the ends sought. They are simply crafted to create a mood of fear or terror in that audience.

Mood of Fear: This mood is not the result, moreover, of the *numbers* of casualties caused by the act of violence. Automobile accidents cause greater numbers of injuries and deaths each year in the United States without necessarily invoking a mood of terror among other drivers (or pedestrians). Nor is it the deliberate nature of the death inflicted that causes the audience's response. Individuals are murdered in nonpolitical, nonterrorist acts throughout the world each year, without provoking widespread fear.

Victims: Instead, the creation of this mood of intense anxiety seems to be specifically linked to the nature of the victim of terrorist acts. As Irving Howe noted:

> To qualify as an appropriate victim of a terrorist today, we need not be tyrants or their sympathizers; we need not be connected in any way with the evils the terrorist perceives; we need not belong to a particular group. We need only be in the wrong place at the wrong time.

Terrorism is thus distinguished from guerilla warfare by deliberate attacks upon *innocent* persons and the separation of its victims from the ultimate goal—the "playing to an audience" aspect of a terrorist act. Terrorism *can* be distinguished from legal acts of warfare and ordinary crimes of murder. David Fromkin pointed out:

> Unlike the soldier, the guerilla fighter, or the revolutionist, the terrorist . . . is always in the paradoxical position of undertaking actions the immediate physical consequences of which are not particularly desired by him. An ordinary murderer will kill someone because he wants the person to be dead, but a terrorist will shoot somebody even though it is a matter of complete indifference to him whether that person lives or dies.

Put more simply, the difference between a "terrorist" act and a similar crime or war activity is that terrorist acts are perpetrated *deliberately* upon innocent third parties in an effort to coerce the opposing party or persons into some desired political course of action. Victims are thus chosen not primarily because of their personal guilt (in terms of membership in an opposing military or governmental group) but because their deaths or injuries will so shock the opposition that concession can be forced to prevent a recurrence of the incident or in order to focus attention on a particular political cause. Terrorist acts, in other words, are deliberately constructed to "make war" on innocent persons.

This distinction will need some explanation. The laws of war permit waging war between national armies, within certain humanitarian limits. Even for the enemy in a violent protracted conflict, some types of behavior (such as genocide and torture) are expressly forbidden, and certain basic amenities are required to be preserved (regarding such issues as the treatment of prisoners of war). "War" as waged by terrorist acts violates these rules in that those deliberately destroyed are not principally armed military opponents but the hapless civilians. Rules of international behavior, particularly those that pertain to political responsibility and military obligations, offer maximum protection to the innocent person. Terrorism makes a practice of persistent, deliberate harm to precisely that type of person.

The distinction between a terrorist act and a legitimate act of guerrilla warfare is not always clear. General George Grivas, founder and head of the Cypriot EOKA asserted in his memoirs, "We did not strike, like a bomber, at random. We shot only British servicemen who would have killed us if they could have fired first, and civilians who were traitors or intelligence agents." The French Resistance, the Polish Underground, and the Greek Guerrillas were called "terrorists" by Nazi occupation forces; yet they, like the EOKA, attacked primarily military personnel, government officials, and local collaborators.

During World War II, the Polish-Jewish Underground planted explosives at the Café Cyganeria in Cracow, a meeting place for Nazi officers, which no doubt resulted in injury to Polish waiters as well as to the desired military targets. The point here is that the terrorist deliberately chooses to invoke injury on the innocent in an effort to shock the "guilty" political or military audience. Injury to the innocent thus is not an undesirable accident or by-product but the carefully sought consequences of a terrorist act.

A terrorist act is committed, not against a military target necessarily—as the individual or group perpetrating the act does not seek to defeat an enemy by military force—nor against the person in direct opposition to the perpetrators, as the ultimate goal is not usually the death of one leader. Unlike the terrorism practiced by 19th-century anarchists, 20th-century terrorist acts are deliberately aimed against noncombatants, unarmed third parties whose loss of well-being can be expected to evoke a desired response from the opposition or from the "audience" watching the event throughout the world.

Until recently it appeared that, although most of the victims of terrorism were "innocent" of any crime, they were also relatively few in number. In those terrorist incidents recorded in the 1950s and 1960s, the actual number of casualties was relatively small. It has been speculated that perhaps the terrorists felt a need to avoid alienating certain groups of people or portions of society. Perhaps it was also true that terrorists want a lot of people watching, not a lot of people dead.

However, the bombing of crowded passenger airplanes and the slaughter of family groups at airports would appear to herald a loosening of the threads that have constrained terrorists in their search for victims. As the craving for a worldwide audience increases among groups utilizing terrorism, the increasing tolerance of that audience for violence may actually be pushing terrorists to widen their target range, to create a more "spectacular" event for their audience.

Thus, as the violence becomes more randomized, it is being directed against a wider range of "innocent" persons. Children are becoming targets, as the massacres at the Rome and Vienna airports demonstrated. Ironically, this increase in innocent targets may well be a direct result of a viewing audience that is no longer as interested in attacks on military attachés or political figures.

Political Motivation or Goal: Terrorism, then, is an act of violence perpetrated on an innocent person in order to evoke fear in an audience. There is, though, one further component necessary to this definition. As it stands, such a definition could reasonably be applied to actions taken by professional sportsmen on the playing field!

However, the addition of a "political purpose" to the concept of terrorism continues to create enormous legal problems. While it is obviously crucial to establish parameters for this concept of political purpose, particularly in light of the fact that political crimes and criminals have enjoyed special status under international law for centuries, the concept remains largely undefined.

Much of the confusion today results from a misconception that the presence of political *motivation* is sufficient to establish the political character of an action. A recent extradition case clearly stated that an offense does not have a political character simply because it was politically motivated. The prevailing Anglo-American rule of law has been derived from *in re Castroni,* in which two basic criteria were given for determining the political quality of an action. These requirements, simply stated, were that (a) the act at issue must have occurred during a political revolt or disturbance, and (b) the act at issue must have been incidental to and have formed part of that same revolution or disturbance.

A political motive thus may be termed *necessary,* but it is not *sufficient* to earn for an action a political offense status under international law. Nicholas Kittrie suggested that a "pure political offense" would consist of acts that challenge the state but do not affect the private rights of innocent parties. By this definition, a political revolution or disturbance is an essential ingredient, in which the political offense plays only a part. Moreover, the offense must bring harm *only* to the state while protecting innocent parties from harm through reasonable precautions. This has the effect of narrowing the classes of acceptable victims and eliminating random acts of lone assassins.

Political assassination by committed revolutionaries careful to cause as little harm as possible to innocent persons remains thus protected to some extent within the political offense provisions of international law. Hence, the assassination of the Grand Duke Sergius might qualify for political offense status, while the mob violence of the Paris Commune would certainly not.

Obviously, the political element of an act of terrorism adds considerable confusion, both in the legal and the political realm. While it is a necessary component to a definition of terrorism, it is so ambiguous a concept that it is often a two-edged sword, offering insights into the causes of an act while providing gaping loopholes in the law through which perpetrators of heinous acts continue to slither.

Nicholas Kittrie described the problem in this manner:

> In order to maintain a proper balance between human rights and world order, it is imperative that the world community in rejecting the proposition that all forms of violence are justified if supported by political goals, avoid the trap of supporting the other extreme, that violent opposition to an established regime is never permissible by international standards. Consequently, the principles of self-defense and the requirement of proportionality need to be re-examined, refined and injected more vigorously into this area.

What distinguishes terrorism, then, from purely political actions may be the illegality of the violence employed, primarily in terms of the victims of the offenses. Many activities, including some sports and many movies, have as a goal the instilling of fear in an audience or opponent. What distinguishes the "terrorist" of today from the football player, the political assassin, and the revolutionary engaged in regular or irregular warfare may be the *lack* of legitimacy that his/her actions enjoy under international norms. By its very nature, terrorism involves the deliberate disruption of norms, the violation of generally accepted standards of decency, including the laws of war as they apply to the innocent and helpless.

Since this is a very confusing and contradictory area of the definition of terrorism, it is useful to review the issue once more. What is it, then, that distinguishes the terrorist act from other acts of war as well as from other political or common crimes? Few would argue that wars, whether between or within states, could or should occur without violence, without the inflicting of injury and death. As individuals we may deplore the violence, but as nations we have recognized its inevitability and accorded it a limited legitimacy.

However, international rules have been created and accepted that govern the acceptable types of violence, even in war. The international community does not forbid the use of *all* violence; it does, however, suggest basic rules for the use of violence. Many of these rules are directed toward the protection of innocent persons. Even in the life-and-death struggles between nations, these laws focus on the minimizing of danger of injury or death to noncombatants, civilians with neither military nor political rank or involvement in the conflict.

Political motivation, then, is *not* a lever by which acts of terrorism can be justified under international law. On the contrary, international law makes it clear that, regardless of the motive, there are some acts of political violence that are never acceptable.

In spite of the dramatic interest inspired in "defining" terrorism by the events of 9/11, and the completion to date of at least 12 conventions by the international community dealing with this subject, there remains some conflict over developing a universally accepted definition for the term. This conflict is made clear by the differing definitions offered by various states and agencies, some of which exclude states from being "terrorists," and others which preclude attaching the term to actions of national liberation movements. A working definition is the only option available at this point.

References: Combs, Cindy C. *Terrorism in the Twenty-First Century* (Upper Saddle River, N.J.: Prentice Hall, 2005); Howard, Russell B., and Reid L. Sawyer. *Defeating Terrorism: Shaping the New Security Environment* (Guilford, Conn.: McGraw Hill/Dushkin, 2002).

terrorism, financing of

Terrorism is, in many respects, a business venture, with a great deal of widely dispersed capital from a wide range of sources. A quick examination of a few organizations that engage in terrorism makes this clear.

A Multinational Corporation

If the PALESTINE LIBERATION ORGANIZATION were an American corporation, it would have been on the list of Fortune 500 companies during the 1980s. British journalist James Adams calculated the organization's financial empire at $5 billion in the mid-1980s. Return on investments was the group's largest source of income at that time, bringing in about $1 billion per year; its financial headquarters in downtown Damascus resembled a modest government office building but was the base for one of the wealthiest multinational corporations in the world.

On the top floor of this building were banks of Honeywell computers, tended by white-coated young Palestinians, most of whom were computer experts trained in the United States, some at MIT and some at Harvard. From this high-tech and superefficient world, the

Palestinian National Fund managed investments that generated a total annual income that was greater than the total budget of some Third World countries, an income that made the PLO the richest and most powerful terrorist group in the world during the 1980s.

Almost all of the PLO's assets were held indirectly through private individuals and in numbered bank accounts in Switzerland, [West] Germany, Mexico, and the Cayman Islands. Its primary banking institution was the Palestinian-owned Arab Bank, Ltd., headquartered in Amman, Jordan. PLO financiers invested money in the European market, as well as some blue-chip stocks on Wall Street, and the PLO held large amounts of lucrative money certificates in the United States. These and other investments reportedly provided as much as 20% of all of the group's revenues.

The PLO, like many multinational corporations, was also involved in a wide variety of business ventures, not all of which generated a monetary profit. Some were primarily political, made to win friends for the PLO. PLO money flowed covertly, through dummy corporations established in such places as Liechtenstein and Luxembourg, into investments in Third World countries. Much of this investment money passed through the Arab Bank for Economic Development in Africa and the Arab African Bank.

The PLO owned dairy and poultry farms and cattle ranches in the Sudan, Somalia, Uganda, and Guinea. It reportedly purchased a duty-free shop in Tanzania's Dar es Salaam International Airport and acquired similar shops in Mozambique and Zimbabwe. This organization not only had cash assets of staggering proportions, but it also succeeded in investing them for capital, political, and strategic gains. Its stock and bond investments were exemplary and brought in considerable revenue; its investment in Third World ventures brought it considerable support and goodwill from many nations; and its ventures into such operations as duty-free airport concessions provided it with security-proof access through which to transfer materials from country to country. The PLO not only had money—but learned how to use much of it wisely.

Revolutionary Taxes

Not all groups carrying out terrorist acts are so well endowed. Most have to depend on the largesse of patrons or on their own success in staging robberies and ransom situations. ETA, which had close ties with the IRISH REPUBLICAN ARMY and the Palestine Liberation Organization, adopted one of the PLO's less publicized methods of raising money. Funds for this group, which received training and support from Libya and the PLO, were generate through "revolutionary taxes." These taxes were levied on Basque businessmen. The PLO levied such a tax against the wages of Palestinians working abroad throughout the Arab world.

Bin Laden's al-Qaeda Network

OSAMA BIN LADEN, son of a billionaire Saudi construction magnate with an estimated worth of hundreds of millions of dollars, ran a portfolio of businesses across North Africa and the Middle East. Companies in sectors ranging from shipping to agriculture to investment banking threw off profits while also financing AL-QAEDA's movement of soldiers and procurement of weapons and chemicals. Saudis, Pakistanis, Yemenis, Egyptians, Algerians, Lebanese, Mauritanians, Palestinians, and more have carried out al-Qaeda–linked terror operations. Many of these men were originally affiliated with a specific national organization such as EGYPTIAN ISLAMIC JIHAD or Algeria's ARMED ISLAMIC GROUP, but their allegiance shifted to bin Laden, and they fought for his causes.

Some of bin Laden's money is in mainstream institutions, as investigations after the September 11th attack indicated when the United States requested that banks worldwide cooperate in freezing al-Qaeda's assets. But al-Qaeda also clearly makes use of Hawala, an informal Islamic banking network that links brokers around the world who advance funds to depositors on a handshake and, sometimes, a password. Hawala, Hindi for "in trust," has operated for generations in Asia and the Middle East. In remote areas, a broker may have little more than a rug and a phone, and the transfers leave little or no trail for investigators to follow, since they involve no wire transfers, balance sheets, or financial statements.

Hawala is used to transfer small amounts of money—usually less than $1,000—around the world. The transaction is almost immediate, based entirely on trust and requires no certification that might leave a paper trail. This system is an excellent example of the Islamic world's unique approach to finance. Services and training are provided interest-free for rich and poor, personal relationships and trust replace collateral, and accounting is a luxury often not included. Donating money for the advancement of Islam—building a mosque or funding an Islamic exhibit—is a religious obligation.

Financial services like Hawala are a quick and inexpensive way for Muslims in the West to send funds to poorer relatives back home. For example, Al-Barakaat, a Somali-based organization, has outlets in cities across Europe and North America through which Somalis abroad send vital cash to families at home.

Extremists have begun exploiting the religious rather than the financial motives of Hawala, and its lack of detailed bookkeeping makes it difficult to track the source of money used by groups engaged in terrorist acts. Islamic charities also take in billions each year, most of which is used for good causes, but not all. Some of these funds make it into the hands of Islamic fighters and terrorists

In Sudan, where bin Laden established himself in 1991, he launched several companies. One of these, the Al Shamal Islamic Bank, had a complete website with a list of correspondent banking relationships, including institutions in New York, Geneva, Paris, and London. Bin Laden also set up agricultural and construction companies.

One former al-Qaeda member, Jamal Ahmed al-Fadl, a Sudanese man, suggested in testimony at the trials of those accused of the bombing of the U.S. embassies in Kenya and Tanzania that bin Laden's organization has been beset by the usual office politics, ruthless cost-cutting and even corruption by some of its members. Al-Fadl complained bitterly about his $500 monthly salary, which was lower than other members', particularly certain Egyptians who seemed to enjoy preferential treatment. Bin Laden's response, according to al-Fadl, was that the Egyptians were paid more because they had more skills than the Sudanese, like the ability to obtain forged documents.

In this sense, terrorism in the al-Qaeda network resembles a warped mirror image of an international corporation, in its financial structure with corporate chieftains who manage lean, trimmed-down firms and bring in consultants and freelancers to perform specific jobs. As Don van Natta, Jr., noted in his article "Running Terrorism as a Business," which was published in the *New York Times* on November 11, 2001, "The specialists work as a team to complete an assignment, then move on to other jobs, often for other companies. In this image, too, bin Laden is much like a terror 'mogul,' a man with the power to approve projects suggested to him, who has final veto over the content or timing but often little to do with the project's actual creation. His most important contribution is the money."

The formalized merging of al-Qaeda with the Egyptian Islamic Jihad in 1998 greatly enhanced bin Laden's global reach and organizational ability. In early 1998, when the two groups announced that they had formed the World Islamic Front for Jihad against Jews and Crusaders, the focus of Islamic Jihad shifted from overthrowing the current Egyptian government to attacking U.S. interests, bin Laden's focus. The scope of the network is illustrated by the countries where 107 defendants in the 1999 trial were arrested—Albania, Bulgaria, Azerbaijan, the United Arab Emirates, and Egypt.

The leaders of this expanded network used the Muslim pilgrimages to Islamic holy sites in Saudi Arabia as a cover for recruiting new members or passing cash from one member to another. They shifted money around the world to bail members out of jail in Algeria or Canada and to finance applications for political asylum to enable the planting of terrorist cells in western Europe.

One example of such a cell is emerging from a trial in Spain of an individual accused of assistance in the September 11 attacks. The cell began to take shape in 1994, when a group of radicals sought to take over a mosque in central Madrid in order to impose more fundamentalist teachings. The attempt failed when the insurgents argued among themselves, splitting into rival factions, one of which coalesced under the leadership of Anwar Adnan Mohamed Saleh, a Palestinian. This group, known as the Soldiers of Allah, distributed literature at the mosque about the activities of Muslim militants in Algeria, the Palestinian territories, Egypt, and Afghanistan, as well as communiqués issued by Osama bin Laden. According to a report submitted in the trial, Saleh and his associate, Imad Eddin Barakat Yarkas, a Syrian, began to indoctrinate young Muslims who expressed an interest in the literature, recruiting several to fight in Bosnia, where Muslims were at war with the Serbs.

Saleh left Spain abruptly in 1995, moving to Peshwar, Pakistan, where he began to work with the fledgling organization that would become al-Qaeda, moving Muslim militants across the border into Afghanistan for training in terrorist camps established there by bin Laden. In Spain, Yarkas took over the cell created under Saleh's leadership. Eventually, Spanish authorities charged eight men with complicity in the September 11 attack. The officials marveled that these men had posed patiently for years as middle-class householders, occasionally moving into the shadows to recruit young Muslim fighters for bin Laden's camps or to commit crimes to raise money for guns and explosives. The bombing attacks on the Madrid train system in March 2004 offered evidence of the expertise clearly developed by such cells, as well as suggested the linkage of such al-Qaeda units with local groups like ETA, whom local authorities initially blamed for the attacks.

Evidence of al-Qaeda cells emerged in more than 40 countries after the September 11 attack, as the United States urged other states to work to "follow the money" to determine the extent of the network of terrorism and its financial support structure. Bin Laden's degree in economics and his experience as part of a multibillion-dollar, multinational construction company, has made this task quite challenging.

Al-Qaeda resources have been invested in industries as diverse as honey and diamonds. American officials noted that there is evidence that bin Laden used a network of shops that sell honey—a staple of Middle Eastern life since biblical times—to generate income, as well as to secretly move weapons, drugs, and agents throughout his terrorist network. Honey is deeply rooted in Middle Eastern culture, religion, and trade. In Saudi Arabia, which produces relatively little honey, families consume on average more than two pounds a month, according to a 1998 report by the U.S. Department of Agriculture.

The honey business is less significant for the income it generates, however, than for the operational assistance it provides. The shops allow al-Qaeda to ship contraband such as money, weapons, and drugs. "The smell and consistency of honey makes it easy to hide weapons and drugs in shipments. Inspectors don't want to inspect that product. It's too messy," according to Judith Miller and Jeff Gerth in their article "Trade in Honey Is Said to Provide Money and Cover for bin Laden," *New York Times,* October 11, 2001.

Al-Qaeda, like other groups, has exploited the corruption and chaos endemic to the Democratic Republic of the Congo (DRC) to tap into the diamond trade and funnel millions of dollars into their organizations. U.S. officials investigating the financing of al-Qaeda indicated that they had greatly underestimated the amount of money this group and others organizations controlled, not only in the diamond trade, but also in the trade of gold, uranium, and tanzanite in this troubled region. The diamonds and other precious and semiprecious materials are bought at a small fraction of their market value, then smuggled out of the country and sold, frequently in Europe, for sizable profits.

Viewed in this context, al-Qaeda is clearly a financial structure willing to break laws to further its cause. Preying on the failed or collapsed states like the DRC, Liberia, and Sierra Leone, this organization profits from the chaos, violence, and intimidation of this region to secure funds for its operatives to carry out terror in other states.

Financing Terror

Under MU'AMMAR AL-QADHAFI, Libyan agents dispersed huge amounts of aid during the 1970s and 1980s to various terrorist groups. That this dispersal appeared to depend greatly on whim, and consequently caused a great deal of frustration among terrorists dependent upon his support, does not detract from the substantial contributions he made to the financing of terrorism worldwide.

Qadhafi supported Palestinian groups, including the POPULAR FRONT FOR THE LIBERATION OF PALESTINE, the DEMOCRATIC FRONT FOR THE LIBERATION OF PALESTINE, and the POPULAR FRONT FOR THE LIBERATION OF PALESTINE–GENERAL COMMAND, with donations of as much as $100 million a year. He also assisted the IRA, ETA, the Baader-Meinhof gang, the JAPANESE RED ARMY, the RED BRIGADE, the TUPAMAROS, and the Moros (in the Philippines).

His assistance was not confined to the financing of only terrorist operations. Israeli intelligence suggested that Qadhafi paid a $5 billion bonus to the BLACK SEPTEMBER terrorists who were responsible for the MUNICH MASSACRE in 1972. Western intelligence also believed that Qadhafi paid CARLOS "THE JACKAL" a large bonus, around $2 billion, for his role in the seizure of the OPEC oil ministers in Vienna in December 1975.

Bonuses were payments given for success, such as that paid to Carlos, and for "injury or death on the job." By the 1990s, these significantly decreased in amount. Qadhafi reportedly paid only between $10,000 and $30,000 to the families of terrorists killed in action, in the late 1980s, down considerably from the $100,000 reportedly paid to a terrorist injured in the OPEC incident in 1972.

So Qadhafi gave money to support terrorist groups and he furnished monetary incentives for participating in terrorist events. Other leaders throughout history have supported dissident groups and provided for the survivors of their military or quasi-military activities.

But Qadhafi took his support of terrorists to greater lengths. When the United States carried out air raids on LIBYA on April 15, 1986, Qadhafi was, of course, furious. He offered to buy an American hostage in Lebanon, so that he could have him killed. On April

17, Peter Kilburn, a 62-year-old librarian at American University who had been kidnapped on December 3, 1984, was executed after Qadhafi paid $1 million to the group holding him. He paid $1 million to be able to kill an elderly librarian, in order to punish the United States.

Declining oil revenues, particularly due to UN sanctions, diminished Libya's role in financing terrorism. In six years, this income fell from $22 billion to about $5.5 billion, seriously reducing Qadhafi's ability to bankroll terrorism. Although after this loss he remained involved in the training of terrorists, his role as "godfather" of terrorism decreased dramatically during the last decade of the 20th century, making it difficult to predict his role for the 21st century.

This assistance extended into the Western Hemisphere in the 1970s. Long before they came to power in 1979, Sandinista leaders had been training in PLO camps in Libya and Lebanon. When the Sandinistas finally seized power, Qadhafi promised political and financial aid, promises that he kept over the years.

In the early years, the Sandinistas received a $100 million "loan" from Libya. In 1983, Brazilian authorities inspecting four Libyan planes bound for Nicaragua discovered that crates marked "medical supplies" actually contained some 84 tons of military equipment. This "military assistance" included missiles, bombs, cannons, and two unassembled fighter planes.

"Fighting funds" for Terrorists

Iran is the home of the Shiite branch of Islam, which has been in conflict with the majority Sunni branch for centuries. When AYATOLLAH KHOMEINI came to power after the fall of the shah, he began to rally Shiites globally to this ancient conflict. In March of 1982, clergy and leaders of Shiite revolutionary movements from all over the world came to Tehran. At this meeting, in addition to agreeing to establish a number of training camps for terrorists in Iran (which was after all the home of the Assassins), it was agreed that $100 million would be immediately allocated as a "fighting fund," established by Iran to support worldwide terrorism. Moreover, an additional $50 million was designated to be spent each year for an indefinite period of time to bankroll specific acts of terrorism.

From this capital outlay have come a variety of terrorist activities. Several powerful groups operating in Lebanon were financed by IRAN during the last two decades of the 20th century. Bomb attacks on moderate Arab states, including Kuwait, Saudi Arabia, and Egypt, caused serious personal and monetary damage. Islamic fundamentalism rose rapidly in southern Asia, supported by substantial cash infusions. Hit squads were dispatched throughout Europe to eliminate "enemies" of Shiite Islam. And a global network of clergy-dominated religious groups was formed, whose purpose was to mastermind further terrorism and recruit new "Assassins" to serve in Iran's "holy war."

Aid—to a Charity?

Michael Flannery, a former member of the IRISH REPUBLICAN ARMY living in New York, established in 1969 Irish Northern Aid—generally known as NORAID. Its purpose was to facilitate the giving of assistance to the IRA. Headquarters were established at 273 East 194th Street, in the Bronx, New York City.

Conflicting reports are offered about the importance of NORAID for the IRA during the last three decades of the 20th century, but certainly in the early 1970s, NORAID could be considered crucial to the Provisional IRA's survival, since it supplied over 50% of the cash needed by the PIRA. By the end of the 20th century, however, the PIRA could expect to receive less that $200,000 of their estimated $7 million budget from NORAID.

During the late 1980s, NORAID no longer supplied only cash to the PIRA. Instead, cash raised at traditional annual "dinners" was frequently used to purchase arms, which were then smuggled to Ireland. Since each dinner was expected to generate between $20,000 and $30,000, and such dinners were held in cities throughout the United States during the 1980s, the supply of arms that could be purchased and smuggled was substantial.

The financing of terrorism continues to take many forms, even in the wake of legislation designed to combat the problem. The U.N. Convention for the Suppression of Terrorist Financing has made possible greater government effort to track direct cash flows and investments but has had little impact on the practice of Hawala. But such counterterrorism legislation has made open state support for terrorism, through "fighting funds" or "revolutionary taxes" more costly and thus less attractive to most states today. A series of articles from the *New York Times* in June 2006 revealed the details behind a U.S. Treasury Department program called the Terrorist Finance Tracking Program (TFTP). This program was designed to take advantage of international computer databases that recorded billions of financial transactions and use these records to track transactions between terrorist groups. The Treasury Department and the CIA had been using the program since the 9/11 ATTACK ON AMERICA, and some claim that the program helped capture the al-Qaeda operative in 2003 who was responsible for the 2002 Bali bombing. Concerns were raised by some that this tracking was a violation of U.S and European privacy laws, while others condemned the media for exposing details of the program to the public.

References: Combs, Cindy C. *Terrorism in the Twenty-First Century.* 4th ed. (Upper Saddle River, N.J.: Prentice Hall/Pearson, 2005); Napoleoni, Loretta. *Terror Incorporated: Tracing the Dollars behind the Terror Networks* (New York: Seven Stories Press, 2005).

terrorists, characteristics of "successful"

Some scholars have attempted to create a profile of a "typical terrorist." Their success is mixed, at best, but offer some ideas that help not only to understand what a typical terrorist may be like (if such a person can be said to exist) but also to evaluate how terrorists as well as terrorism have changed in recent years.

Edgar O'Ballance offered one such critique of what he calls a "successful" terrorist (by which he appears to mean one who is neither captured nor dead). In his book, *The Language of Violence,* O'Ballance suggested several essential characteristics of the "successful" terrorist. These include:

1. *Dedication:* To be successful, a terrorist cannot be a casual or part-time mercenary, willing to operate only when it suits his convenience or his pocket. He must become a FEDAYEEN, a "man of sacrifice." Dedication also implies absolute obedience to the leader of the political movement.
2. *Personal bravery:* As the terrorist must face the possibility of death, injury, imprisonment, or even torture if captured, O'Ballance regarded this trait as important, to varying degrees, depending upon one's position within the terrorist group's hierarchy.
3. *Without the human emotions of pity or remorse:* Since most of his victims will include innocent men, women, and children, whom he must be prepared to kill in cold blood, the terrorist must have the "killer instinct," able to kill without hesitation on receipt of a code or signal. As this expert noted, many can kill in the heat of anger or in battle, but few, fortunately, can do so in cold blood.
4. *Fairly high standard of intelligence:* As the would-be terrorist has to collect, collate, and assess information, devise and put into effect complex plans, and evade police, security forces, and other hostile forces, intelligence would appear to be a requisite.
5. *Fairly high degree of sophistication:* This is essential, according to O'Ballance, in order for the terrorist to blend into the first-class section on airliners, stay at first-class hotels, and mix inconspicuously with the international executive set.
6. *Be reasonably well educated and possess a fair share of general knowledge:* By this, O'Ballance meant that the terrorist should be able to speak English as well as one other major language. He asserted that a university degree is almost mandatory.

O'Ballance noted that not every terrorist measures up to these high standards, but he contends that the leaders, planners, couriers, liaison officers, and activists must. This is an assertion that is difficult to challenge effectively since if the terrorist is "successful," the implication is that he/she has succeeded in evading law enforcement, security, and intelligence officers, and hence the information about the individual is necessarily either scant or unconfirmed.

One could conclude, with some justice, that most of O'Ballance's assertions, like most generalizations, are at least half-true, half-false, and largely untestable. But these generalizations, with their grains of truth, are still useful in analyzing terrorism and terrorist behavior. Examination of each of his suggested "attributes" of a terrorist may reveal they can be substantiated by insights into contemporary behavior.

Dedication appears, on the surface, to be characteristic of modern terrorists. Palestinians involved in various groups have indicated a willingness to wait for as long as it takes them to realize their dream of a return to a nation of PALESTINE. They have been willing to wait as long as the Zionists waited, or longer, and many are reluctant to accept the current peace settlements since that represents at this point less than full national independence for Palestine. Like the Zionists, they have unbounded faith in the justice of their cause and seem willing to die to achieve it.

The progress toward a comprehensive peace settlement in the Middle East in the last years of the 20th century indicated that this tenacity may have been a liability to the emerging government established by YASIR ARAFAT in the Gaza Strip and parts of the West Bank since this represented only a portion of the land that was Palestine and did not constitute full sovereignty from Israel for the Palestinians. Anger by the Palestinian group of HAMAS, a radical Islamic movement supported throughout the Middle East by IRAN, indicated that a significant portion of the Palestinians remained committed to full restoration of "Palestine" to the Palestinian people. The suicide bombings in 1994 and 1995, which claimed the lives of many innocent men, women, and children, gave credence to this resolve.

Nor is such dedication limited to Palestinians. Observers in Northern Ireland suggested that religious fanaticism is handed down from generation to generation in this region as well, carrying with it a willingness to fight and die for a cause. Schoolchildren in NORTHERN IRELAND have exhibited an intolerance and a bitterness that often gets translated into violence. Where children, preachers, and priests join in willingness to commit murder in a "holy" cause, dedication has produced countless bloody massacres and apparently endless terrorism.

However, as in the Middle East, progress has been made toward a political settlement of the problem of Northern Ireland. Like the situation of Palestine, though, the solution will probably not satisfy all of the truly "dedicated" terrorists. The IRISH REPUBLICAN ARMY's willingness to negotiate a "peace" has angered radical elements in the Catholic community, and the movement of the British to negotiate with the IRA openly has raised equal anger in militant Protestant groups. If a resolution of the dispute of the British with the IRA is reached and a unity government representing both Catholic and Protestant citizens becomes functional, there is reason to fear that a similarly "dedicated" group of terrorists will emerge, determined to force either the United Kingdom into retaining sovereignty (thus retaining Protestant control) or Irish nationalists into a quick union with the Republic of Ireland (desired by Catholics).

Such "dedication" is not always directed at specific nationalist cause. Members of the JAPANESE RED ARMY, founded in 1969, described themselves as "soldiers of the revolution" and pledged themselves to participate in all revolutions anywhere in the world through exemplary acts. This group was responsible for the massacre of 26 tourists at LOD AIRPORT in Tel Aviv, Israel. These dedicated revolutionaries undertook numerous terrorist attacks, many of which, like the Lod Airport massacre, were essentially suicide missions since escape was scarcely possible.

Personal bravery is also a characteristic that has often been attributed to modern terrorists. There are, however, two views of the "bravery" with which terrorists may be said to be endowed. One might argue that it can scarcely be termed brave to use weapons mercilessly against unarmed and defenseless civilians. The men, women, and children at Lod Airport were unable to defend themselves against the attack of the Japanese Red Army. Was it "brave" of the JRA to slaughter these innocent and unarmed people?

The opposing view, which does in fact attribute bravery to those perpetrating acts of terrorism, suggests that to be willing to carry out missions in which one's own death or at least imprisonment are inevitable outcomes argues no small degree of personal courage. A willingness to give one's life for a cause has, throughout history, commanded at the very least a reluctant admiration, even from enemies.

Bravery is, in fact, a very subjective term. One may feel oneself to be very cowardly but be perceived by others to be quite fearless. The audience for one's deeds are often able to judge one's "bravery" only by the commission of the deed and are unaware of the inner doubts or demons that may have driven one to the act. Nor is the individual necessarily the best judge of his or her own personal bravery since a person's capacity for self-deception makes it so that one does not consciously admit (or refuses to be aware of) true motives and fears.

The question as to whether or not terrorists who murder innocent persons, with the knowledge that their own survival is problematic, are brave may never be answered to anyone's satisfaction. Much depends on the way in which one evaluates the situation.

According to O'Ballance, a "successful" terrorist should be *without the human emotions of pity or remorse*. Given the necessity of being able to kill, in cold blood, unarmed and innocent persons, this would appear to be a reasonable assumption regarding terrorist personality. Unlike the criminal who may kill to prevent someone from capturing him, or to secure some coveted prize, a terrorist must, by the very nature of the act that he is often called upon to commit, kill persons against whom he has no specific grudge, whose life or death is not really material to his well-being or security.

Frederick Hacker in his book, *Criminals, Crusaders, Crazies: Terror and Terrorism in Our Time,* states that:

> Often, the terrorists do not know whom they will hurt, and they could not care less. Nothing seems important to them except they themselves and their cause. In planning and executing their deeds, the terrorists are totally oblivious to the fate of their victims. Only utter dehumanization permits the ruthless use of human beings as bargaining chips, bargaining instruments, or objects for indiscriminate aggression.

This description creates a vivid portrait of a ruthless and, one would think, thoroughly unlikable killer. Yet those guilty of such acts have not always presented to the world such a vision of themselves.

Just as there is no safe generalization with regard to the personal bravery of terrorists, so there seem to be pitfalls in making too broad a characterization of a terrorist as "incapable of pity or remorse." Perhaps concerning this particular aspect of a terrorist's characteristics, it is accurate to say only that terrorists appear to have a "killer instinct" simply in that they are willing to use lethal force.

Some may indeed kill without pity or remorse and may in fact be incapable of such emotions. But to say that terrorists as a whole are so constructed is a generalization for which there is insufficient data and conflicting indicators in known cases.

The characteristics that O'Ballance suggests of sophistication and education are less true of post-1970s terrorists than they were of terrorists prior to that time. Many 19th-century revolutionary ANARCHISTS were indeed intelligent, sophisticated, university educated, and even multilingual. Those responsible for the murder of Czar Alexander II of Russia in March 1881 were men and women who possessed a much higher level of education and sophistication than most other young people of their nation. They were led by Sophia Perovskaya, daughter of the wealthy governor-general of St. Petersburg, the empire's capital.

Similarly, the TUPAMAROS (URUGUAY FACTION) were primarily composed of the young, well-educated liberal intellectuals, who sought, but never fully gained, the support of the less educated masses. The Baader-Meinhoff gang in West Germany, which terrorized that nation throughout the 1970s, was composed of middle- and upper-class intellectuals. This gang's master strategist was Horst Mahler, a radical young lawyer, and it drew its membership and support system heavily from the student body of German universities.

The founder of one of Italy's first left-wing terrorist bands, the Proletarian Action Group (GAP), was Giangiacomo Feitrinelli, the heir to an immense Milanese fortune and head of one of Europe's most distinguished publishing houses. Like the RED BRIGADES (BR), which would succeed this group as Italy's leading left-wing terrorist group, Feitrinelli drew much of his initial membership from young, often wealthy, intellectuals.

Terrorists until the 1980s tended to be recruited from college campuses. Many came from well-to-do families, so that sophistication and an ability to mix with the international set were well within their grasp. Intelligence, sophistication, education, and university training: not only the leaders but also many of the practitioners of both 19th-century anarchism and contemporary terrorism possessed these attributes.

However, standards and modes of behavior among terrorists in the 21st century are changing. The French anarchists would not have abducted children and threatened to kill them unless ransom was paid. The NARODNAYA VOLYA would not have sent parts of their victims' bodies with little notes to their relatives as the right-wing Guatemalan MANP and NOA did. Neither French nor Russian anarchists would have tormented, mutilated, raped, and castrated their victims, as many terrorist groups have done in the latter part of the 20th century.

As Walter Laqueur pointed out: "Not all terrorist movements have made a fetish of brutality; some have behaved more humanely than others. But what was once a rare exception has become a frequent occurrence in our time." According to Laqueur, the character of terrorism has undergone a profound change. Intellectuals, he contended, have made "the cult of violence respectable." In spite of the violence that characterized their movement, he asserted that no such cult existed among the Russian terrorists, a difficult claim either to prove or to disprove.

Nevertheless, Laqueur is correct in his assertion that the terror of the latter decades of the 20th and the early 21st century is different. Modern terrorists are significantly different, and the difference in the type of person becoming a terrorist today has a great deal to do with the difference in terrorism.

References: Hacker, Frederick J. *Crusaders, Criminals, Crizies: Terror and Terrorism in Our Time* (New York:

Norton, 1976); Laqueur, Walter. *The Age of Terrorism* (Boston: Little, Brown, 1987); O'Ballance, Edgar O. *The Language of Violence: The Blood Politics of Terrorism* (San Rafael, Calif.: Presidio, 1979).

threat assessment

Three types of indicators are used by governments and businesses today to assess the possibility of successful terrorist attacks within their territory. These include general threat indicators, local threat indicators, and specific threat indicators. General threat indicators are used to determine whether, within a nation or state, conditions exist that might stimulate or provoke terrorism. Such indicators are extremely general and consequently of little use in predicting the likelihood of a specific terrorist attack. They are used instead to assess the climate—political, ideological, economic, religious, etc.—that might influence the willingness of a portion of the population to resort to terrorism. Politically, the presence of a corrupt or extremely unpopular leadership is considered to be a positive indicator for the probability of terrorism. Economically, the presence of extreme poverty and/or high unemployment is regarded as conducive to terrorism.

Local threat indicators, in contrast, are used to assess more localized possibilities for terrorism, focusing on the forms that dissent tends to take on the local level and the degree of violence involved in the expression of that dissent. Such things as the formation of radical groups; reports of stolen firearms, ammunition, and explosives; violence against local property, including looting and arson; violence against individuals, including murders, beatings, and threats; and the discovery of weapon, ammunition, and explosive caches are all local threat indicators.

Specific threat indicators are instruments intended to evaluate the vulnerability of a particular target to terrorism. These indicators do not predict the likelihood of terrorism within a neighborhood or nation. The tactical attractiveness of a target (its accessibility, public visibility, etc.), the history of attacks on similar targets, its counterterror and communications capability, and the availability of security personnel are types of specific threat indicators.

None of these types of indicators can accurately predict the probability of a successful terrorist attack against the facility or nation. But they may be useful in security preparedness issues.

threat/hoax, as terrorist tactic

This is a low-cost tactic for terrorists, with varying potential for disruption, without making innocent victims out of anyone. This tactic forces governments to assess the vulnerability of the targets and the history of the group claiming responsibility. The cost of reacting to such a hoax may well be crippling to the authority involved, while the consequences of not responding could be equally unacceptable.

A threat/hoax of nuclear terrorism has become an increasingly feasible tactic of terrorists in modern times. In such cases, leaders are frightened or blackmailed into acceding to terrorist demands based on the threat of detonating a hidden nuclear device in a crowded area, such as a city. Although such a threat sounds more like science fiction than serious threat, such threats have in fact already been made. Leaders in several nations, including the United States, have already had to deal with such threats.

torture *See* STATE TERRORISM.

totalitarianism *See* STATE TERRORISM.

training camps for terrorists

Until the 1990s, more than a dozen nations offered training camps for terrorists. Some of the camps were set up specifically for terrorists, while others were camps used by the host country for its own military and/or intelligence training. A number of countries during the 1960s through the 1980s operated training facilities within the structure of their own military services. Nations such as IRAN, IRAQ, AFGHANISTAN, and SUDAN offer both training and arming for a variety of terrorist groups in the new century. The dramatic changes in the world in the early 1990s, with the demise of the Soviet Union, seriously impacted the ability of many other states to support terrorist training camps. CUBA, for example, could no longer financially or politically afford to train and equip terrorists openly, lacking the Soviet political and economic shield against Western disapproval. Syria and North Korea were similarly unable and unwilling, in the late 1990s, to continue offering training and weapons to terrorist groups.

Nevertheless, the existence of such camps continues to be an issue of international concern. The U.S.

bombing of such a camp in Afghanistan in 1998 highlighted the depth of the concern still experienced by the presence of active terrorist training camps.

trends in terrorist demography

It is unlikely that the search for a "terrorist personality" could be successful in creating a set of common denominators that could span several continents, time periods, cultures, and political configurations. All that most experts seem to agree on regarding terrorists today is that they are primarily young people. There are very few old terrorists.

There are, however, some demographic trends in modern terrorist affiliations that offer some clues as to who is currently becoming a terrorist. While this falls short of providing a profile of a modern terrorist, it does yield insights into not only who modern terrorists are but also the impact of such a demographic configuration on contemporary terrorism.

Age

Terrorism is a pursuit not only of the young; it became in the late 1970s and 1980s a pursuit of the *very* young. While terrorists during the time of the Russian anarchists tended to be at least in their mid-20s, in the late 20th century, the average age steadily decreased. During the turbulent 1960s, many terrorists were recruited from college campuses throughout the Western world. This brought the average age down to around 20, give or take a year, since the leaders were several years older, often in their early 30s.

Research in 1977 indicated that the usual urban terrorist was between 22 and 25 years of age. Among the TUPAC AMARU REVOLUTIONARY MOVEMENT (MRTA), the average age of arrested terrorists was around 24.1, while in Brazil and Argentina, the average was 23 and 24, respectively. These figures remained true for the BASQUE FATHERLAND AND LIBERTY (ETA), the IRISH REPUBLICAN ARMY (IRA), and groups in IRAN and Turkey during that time.

As early as the spring of 1976, however, evidence of a change in the age level of terrorists began to emerge. Arrests of Spanish ETA members revealed a number of youths in their teens. In NORTHERN IRELAND, some of the terrorists apprehended were as young as 12 to 14.

Today, while the majority of active terrorists are in their 20s, there has been a tendency, particularly among the Arab and Iranian groups, to recruit children of 14 or 15 years of age. These children are used for dangerous, frequently suicidal, missions partly because their youth makes them less likely to question their orders and partly because their extreme youth makes them less likely to attract the attention of the authorities.

One explanation of this phenomenon is that the anarchistic-revolutionary philosophy that had begun to infiltrate the province of the university students has begun to infiltrate the secondary school level. While this may explain part of this demographic trend, another explanation may lie in the number of children growing up in cultures in which violence is indeed a way of life.

In the Middle East and Northern Ireland, children growing up in violent community struggles could easily become a part of terrorist activities that span successive generations within the same family. Children were thus recruited, not by philosophy learned at university or secondary school, but by the dogma and lifestyles of their parents, facilitating a potentially more comprehensive assimilation into the terrorist group.

By the 1990s, this trend began to reverse as peace within those two regions came closer to reality. Religious fanaticism is less likely to be the motivating factor compelling a 12 year old into terrorism; instead, as HAMAS membership indicates, most members are closer in age to the early 1970s terrorist profile. The individuals responsible for the bombing of the Pan Am flight over LOCKERBIE, and those involved in the WORLD TRADE CENTER BOMBING in New York City, were certainly not 12 or 13 years of age, nor were the perpetrators of the ATTACK ON AMERICA in 2001.

Sex

During the earlier part of the 20th century, while the leaders of terrorist cadres included some women among their numbers, the rank and file were usually predominately male. In many such groups, women were assigned the less life-threatening roles of intelligence collection, courier, nurse or medical personnel, and maintenance of "safe houses" for terrorists on the run.

Terrorism of the late 20th century, however, has been an equal-opportunity employer. The commander of the JAPANESE RED ARMY for years, FUSAKO SHIGENOBU, was a woman, and of the 14 most wanted West German terrorists in 1981, 10 were women. Moreover, studies have shown that female members of terrorist groups have proved to be tougher, more fanatical, more loyal, and possessors of a greater capacity for suffering. Women have also, in some terrorist groups, tended to remain a member longer than men, on the average.

Two examples serve to demonstrate the difference in the roles played by women in terrorism today. It was a pregnant woman who was given the task of carrying a suitcase loaded with explosives aboard an airplane in the 1980s. Only a few decades ago, she might have been allowed to provide a safe haven for the man entrusted with that task. This is not to suggest that this is in any way "progress" but to indicate a marked difference in the role women now play in terrorism. Similarly, women in the Middle East have taken on the role of suicide bombers, a role that a few generations ago would never have been assumed by a woman. While a female suicide bomber is still the exception rather than the rule, the role of women in carrying out terrorist acts is clearly changing from the supportive role of previous centuries to an active leadership role today.

Education

Until the mid-1970s, most of the individuals involved in terrorism were quite well educated. Almost two-thirds of the people identified as terrorists were persons with some university training, university graduates, or postgraduate students. Among the Tupac Amaru, for example, about 75% of their membership were very well educated, and of the Baader-Meinhof gang in West Germany, the figure reached almost 80%.

In the Palestinian groups, most members were university students or graduates, frequently those who had, by virtue of their middle-class wealth, been able to study at foreign universities. By 1969, several thousand Palestinians were studying abroad at universities, particularly in Europe, where they were exposed to anarchistic-Marxist ideas. This group became an important recruiting pool for the POPULAR FRONT FOR THE LIBERATION OF PALESTINE (PFLP). Indeed, the chief of the PFLP for decades, George Habbash, was a medical doctor who obtained his degree abroad.

However, the level of education of the average terrorist is declining today. This is due in part to the trend in recruitment age of the last two decades of the 20th century already noted. If young people are being recruited out of secondary school rather than out of college, then the number of individuals in terrorist groups with a college education will necessarily decline as well.

This trend brings with it another important decline: a diminishing of the understanding by the rank and file among terrorists of the political philosophies that have supposedly motivated the groups to adopt terrorist activities. Elementary schoolchildren are clearly unable, as a rule, to grasp the impetus of Marxist philosophy toward social revolution. Unlike the college students of the 1960s, who studied and at least half-understood the radical political philosophies, today's new terrorist recruits are fed "watered down" versions of Marx and Lenin by leaders whose own understanding of these philosophers is certainly suspect.

This downward trend in education and understanding of political philosophy is exhibited by terrorist leadership figures as well as by the cadres' rank-and-file memberships. The notorious terrorist, Abu Nidal, leader of the group bearing his name, attended college in Cairo for only two years. Contrary to his claim in subsequent years, he never obtained an engineering degree or indeed any other degree. He dropped out and went home to teach in the local school in Nablus.

In contrast, the men recruited to participate in the 9/11 suicide/hijacking attacks were grown men, with at least secondary educations and in some cases specialized training. Thus, the "trend" in declining age and education levels is not consistent, particularly among suicide terrorists, where the age range varies greatly.

Economic Status

During the 1960s, many young people joined terrorist organizations as a way of rejecting the comfortable, middle-class values of their parents. They were often children of parents who could afford to send them to private colleges, and they were rejecting the comparative wealth of their surroundings to fight for "justice" for those less fortunate.

Today's terrorists tend to be drawn more from the less fortunate than from comfortable middle-class homes. While some come from families who have had wealth but lost it through revolution or confiscation, most have roots in absolute destitution, for whom terrorism represents the only way to lash out at society's injustices. In the terrorist group, these individuals find a collective wealth and ability to improve one's financial situation that is enormously appealing to the impoverished.

Again, Abu Nidal provides insight into the change in the economic circumstances of the type of person who becomes a terrorist today in many parts of the world. Nidal, born SABRI AL-BANNA, was the son of wealthy Palestinian parents who lost everything. From the lap of luxury, his family moved into the extreme poverty of the refugee camps. The bitterness and frustration of this life of endless poverty and statelessness may well have been the catalyst for the terrorist he was to become.

Osama bin Laden, however, clearly does not fit the pattern of economic destitution. The son of a multimillionaire, inheriting substantial wealth, bin Laden was, in this respect, more like the terrorists of the 1970s, rejecting the life of wealth and perceiving himself as fighting on behalf of those "victimized" by the very economic system from which his family benefited. This is remarkably similar to the attitude of the founders of the Tupamaros in Uruguay and stands in stark contrast to the example of Nidal.

Socialization toward Violence

Intellectuals have, during the past few decades, helped to make the cult of violence "respectable." But today's terrorists have been socialized toward violence in ways never experienced before in civilized society. Intellectual terrorists of the 1960s were, for the most part, first-generation terrorists. There are an increasing number of third- and even fourth-generation terrorists. Young people recruited in such circumstances have been socialized to accept violence as a normal pattern of life. Peace, as much of the rest of the world knows it, has no meaning for them, and the related values of a civilized society have equally little relevance in their lives.

In Northern Ireland, and in parts of the Middle East, until the peace efforts of the 1990s, this pattern of successive generations of terrorism has produced terrorists who have no understanding of the kind of limits on the use of violence that much of the world regards as customary. Violence is not only a normal pattern of life, it is a means of survival, and its successful use offers a means of security and enhancement of one's own and one's family's lives.

This role of violence is made vividly clear by remarks made by the Reverend Benjamin Weir, a former U.S. hostage held by terrorists in LEBANON. He suggested that, for many Lebanese youths, the only employment open to them, which offered both an income and some form of security for their families, was with one of the warring militia factions. College was for decades either unavailable or unaffordable, and alternative employment in a nation whose economy was in a shambles was unlikely. Life as a terrorist was, in some respects, the *only* alternative for many young people in that war-torn country.

These trends present an alarming portrait of modern terrorists. Many are younger, much younger. As any parent (or older sibling) knows, younger children are harder to reach by logical argument. Their values are less clearly formed or understood. They are, as a whole, less rational, more emotional than their elders. They are also less likely to question the orders of their leaders, more likely to follow blindly where their trust is given.

Individuals committing terrorist acts today are less likely to have a comfortable home to fall back upon or to cushion their failure. Instead, their families are increasingly likely to be extremely poor. For these new recruits, membership—and success—in a terrorist group offers a necessary basis for behavior, a "legitimate" vent for anger and frustration, as an increasingly globalized world makes clear the glaring economic and political disparities that exist, over which they have little control. Growing up in these conditions, these young men and women are used to violence; it is for them a daily occurrence.

They neither understand nor recognize the need for limits on that violence. They have seen homes destroyed, families killed, in endless wars of attrition. The idea that civilization wishes to impose limits on the types or victims of violence is beyond their understanding, because they have seen almost every type of violence used against almost every conceivable victim.

In examining trends in terrorist demography, it is useful to note the anomaly posed by suicide terrorists, who fit few of the "trends" described here. Suicide bombers are more likely to be male, but female suicide bombers are common among the LIBERATION TIGERS OF TAMIL EELAM (LTTE), the CHECHEN rebels, and the KURDISTAN WORKERS' PARTY (PKK). They are most often from middle-class backgrounds and live in countries with little political freedom, where their relative economic freedom chafes at the lack of comparable political choice. They are usually well educated and hold strong political or more often religious beliefs, since it is such religious beliefs that offer hope of a reward in another life for their suicide. Suicide bombers are generally neither economically destitute nor mentally ill, although many have come from dysfunctional homes and have had difficult childhoods. They are therefore only marginally within the "trends" identified here and may in fact offer better insights into the future demographic trends of tomorrow's terrorists.

References: Bloom, Mia. *Dying to Kill: The Allure of Suicide Terror* (New York: Columbia University Press, 2005). Reich, Walter. *Origins of Terrorism: Psychologies, Ideologies, Theologies, States of Mind* (Princeton, N.J.: Woodrow Wilson Center Press, 1998).

TREVI

Existing in Europe, this is a permanent though comparatively secret structure whose code name derives from the words "terrorism, radicalism, and violence, international." This is a formalization of the "old boy" police network that exists in many countries. TREVI regularly brings together police chiefs from European Union countries. It also engages in day-to-day consultations through national bureaus. At a meeting in April 1978, the EU countries, plus Austria (not an EU member at that time) and Switzerland, agreed to pool resources to combat terrorism on the continent. Members of TREVI are all from European Economic Community nations except Ireland, plus Israel and Switzerland.

The operating definition of terrorism used in most treaties today defines terrorism as the use of illegitimate means, typically involving the exercise of violence against innocent people, to gain political power. It has therefore been argued that Interpol cannot be authorized within the parameter of its own constitution, especially Article 3, to exchange information regarding political terrorists. Responding to such concerns, police cooperation with respect to terrorism has in the European context been legally and formally secured in Articles K-K.9 (Title VI) of the Treaty on the European Union concerning cooperation in the fields of justice and home affairs. One of the articles provides for "police cooperation for the purposes of preventing and combating terrorism, unlawful drug trafficking and other serious forms of international crime, including customs cooperation in connection with a Union-wide system for exchanging information within a European Police Office." TREVI, as a part of this system of exchange, has a vital role in combating international terror.

Túpac Amaru Revolutionary Movement (MRTA)

This traditional Marxist-Leninist revolutionary movement was founded in 1983 and formed from the remains of the Movement of the Revolutionary Left, a Peruvian insurgent group active in the 1960s. The group was initially composed primarily of young, well-educated liberal intellectuals who sought, but never fully gained, the support of the less-educated masses. It has often been overshadowed by the larger Maoist-influenced SENDERO LUMINOSO (Shining Path) rebel group. Túpac Amaru, whose ideology was inspired by Fidel Castro's CUBA, probably never had more than 1,800 members and is now believed to have no more than a few hundred.

Túpac Amaru was named for Túpac Amaru II, an indigenous rebel who was executed for an uprising against the Spanish in the late 1700s. The rebel had taken his name from the last ruler of the Inca Empire before Spain conquered Peru.

Most of Túpac Amaru's attacks focused on urban warfare, including bomb attacks on fast-food restaurants, bank robberies, and kidnapping of businesspeople. This differed sharply from Shining Path attacks, which occurred primarily in mountain villages, towns, and poor urban areas.

In 1992, the leader of the Túpac Amaru, Victor Polay, was captured by Peruvian police and sentenced to life in prison. Whereas in the latter decade of the 20th century the top commanders in this group had stated that the Túpac Amaru were "giving up the fight" and many surrendered their weapons to President Alberto Fujimori, an attack occurred in December of 1996 that brought this group once more to international attention as an active insurgency. The assault on the Japanese ambassador's residence, during a large party hosting guests from many countries, began a siege that lasted for more than 100 days. One of the key purposes of this attack, according to the guerrillas involved, was the release of Polay and other Túpac members held in Peruvian jails. Fourteen MRTA members occupied the Japanese ambassador's residence, holding 72 hostages for more than four months, until Peruvian forces stormed the residence in April, carrying out OPERATION CHAVÍN DE HUÁNTAR.

In rescuing the hostages, the Peruvian forces also killed most of the group's leaders on site at the residence. The group has not conducted a significant terrorist operation since that event, and it now appears more focused on obtaining the release of imprisoned MRTA members by other means. It is believed to have no more than 100 members at this time, consisting mostly of young fighters who lack leadership skills and experience. It controls no specific territory, unlike the Shining Path, and operates only in Peru, although it has supporters throughout Latin America and Western Europe.

Although Peru has aggressively prosecuted terrorist suspects, in January 2003 the Constitutional Tribunal overturned numerous provisions in Fujimori-era decree laws on terrorism, in conformance with decisions of the Inter-American Court of Human Rights.

Military court convictions in approximately 2,000 cases were vacated and reviewed for retrial. President Toledo issued decree legislation revising Peru's antiterrorism legislation in line with the Constitutional Tribunal decision and established the procedures for reviewing and retrying terrorism cases. Some were dropped because sentences were nearing completion, and some 750 cases were sufficiently strong to be retried beginning in 2004.

In September 2003, four Chilean defendants were retried and convicted of membership in the Túpac Amaru Revolutionary Movement and participation in an attack on the Peru–North American Cultural Institute and a kidnapping-murder in 1993. The retrial of 13 MRTA leaders, including its founder Victor Polay, began in December 2004.

Peru is a party to all 12 of the conventions and protocols relating to terrorism. The Peruvian government and civil society are working to implement the 2002 recommendations of the Truth and Reconciliation Commission to heal wounds from the terrorist conflict of the 1990s. The Peace and Development Commissions, formed in 2002 by President Toledo, continue to promote cooperation between police, military, and residents in the areas where SENDERO LUMINOSO and MRTA conflicts had been the greatest.

Reference: National Memorial Institute for the Prevention of Terrorism (MIPT). "Tupac Amaru Revolutionary Movement." Available online. URL: http://www.tkb.org/Group.jsp?groupID=121. Accessed February 15, 2006.

Tupamaros (Uruguay faction) (Túpac Amaru)

The Tupamaros, named for Túpac Amaru, a Peruvian rebel Indian leader of that name who was burned at the stake in the 18th century, began as a nationalist movement in 1962. It was led in the beginning by Raúl Sendic, born in 1925 in the Flores province of Uruguay in an upper-middle-class family. Sendic became unhappy with his law studies and dropped out of school, heading to the northern part of Uruguay to work among poor sugar beet laborers. In 1962, Sendic went to CUBA for a few months, returning to organize the sugar plantation laborers in their first march to the captial, Montevideo. As support grew for Sendic and the sugar beet laborers engaged in protesting for better wages and working conditions, the Tupamaros movement was launched.

The Tupamaros protested against what they considered to be an undemocratic, quasi-welfare state, viewing it as an attempt to destroy the political soul of the masses with economic incentives. The first terrorist act of this group occurred in 1963, in a raid on a Swiss rifle club. Following this incident, Sendic fled to Argentina.

The Tupamaros viewed themselves as fighting capitalism and democracy. They were, as a whole, a highly educated group, consisting mostly of university students and other rebellious middle-class youth. Most were between 18 and 30 years of age, and a large number of the members were women. Among its membership were prominent engineers, architects, and teachers, who often led a double life of public rectitude and private revolution. By 1972, their membership was estimated to be around 6,000.

The structure of the Tupamaros was difficult for law enforcement to infiltrate. The group operated in an interlocking cell structure, in which groups of four or five member, called firing groups, were directed by a group leader. This leader had contact only with the member directly above him/her in the hierarchy of the group. Thus, infiltration was limited to one cell at a time, minimizing the group's potential loss.

Training as the Tupamaros did in Uruguay, Argentina, and Cuba, their leaders were also members of the JRC (Revolutionary Coordinating Committee) an inter-American guerrilla organization founded by the four most prominent insurgency groups in Latin America at that time: Chilean MIR, Uruguayan Tupamaros, Bolivian ELN, and the Argentine ERP. The JRC was a joint effort to mobilize the leftist movement in Latin America. Thus, the Tupamaros developed close ties with each of the other JRC members, sharing training, offering hideouts, and providing intelligence for each other. They also developed strong links with ETA of Spain.

The Tupamaros were clearly influenced by the Cuban revolution, believing that this revolution was the pattern for all Latin American leftist groups to follow. Their ideology was based on their understanding of Marxist-Leninist philosophy, with several differences. Tupamaros advocated agrarian reform, seeking to establish a socialist society.

Tupamaros engaged in two types of warfare: a guerrilla war against the government and a propaganda war designed to topple the "bourgeois capitalist order" by persuasion. Their guerrilla war was patterned on that of Abraham Guillen of Spain, involving hit-and-run tactics designed to force the government to surrender territory a little at a time. Seeing themselves as the "Robin Hood" of their country, they robbed banks and corporations, then distributed the money to the poor. Kidnapping was another profitable method of financing their activities, often yielding enormous sums for only one victim. Victims included a Brazilian consul, a U.S. adviser to the Uruguayan police (whom they later killed in 1970), and the British ambassador to Uruguay (in 1971). They also assassinated leading figures, including Colonel Artigas Alvarez, chief of civil defense forces in Uruguay.

The propaganda war involved forcing their way into a radio or television station, interrupting the broadcast, and playing their own message, providing them with two important GOALS OF TERRORISTS, CONCERNING MEDIA: access to a platform to explain their cause and demonstration of the weakness of the government (in its inability to prevent such actions). When the Tupamaros carried out a violent act, the government would denounce it to the public, satisfying an important GOAL OF GOVERNMENT, CONCERNING MEDIA IN A TERRORIST EVENT: focus on the illegality of the act committed by the group. Then, the Tupamaros would counter by broadcasting their version of the event, often using a mobile transmitter.

The leadership of the Tupamaros sought, according to their statements, to create a revolutionary consciousness in the general population through their actions. In 1969, they raided Financera Monty, a lending institution, seizing cash and account books providing evidence of the misuse of public funds by public officials. The resulting scandal led to the resignation of the minister of agriculture.

Convinced that the Tupamaros constituted a threat to democracy in Uruguay, President Gestido banned the Socialist Party in 1967, and the government declared an internal war against the Tupamaros. Two years later, when workers tried to strike, they were called up to serve in the Uruguayan army; they were then told to go back to work or risk being tried for military desertion. By 1972, more than 4,000 Tupamaros sympathizers had been arrested, and the government passed the "Law of State Security," suspending the normal time period allowed for the holding of suspects. It also permitted military trials of suspected Tupamaros supporters. Free press and free speech were also suspended by the government in order to curb the media coverage of the Tupamaros.

The climate of change the Tupamaros sought came, but not in the form that they sought. When Tupamaros leaders were arrested by the military, they often revealed secrets discovered by the group about corrupt politicians. The military in turn began to accuse government leaders of corruption, and the government retaliated by accusing the military of being allied with the Tupamaros. In 1973, the military overthrew the government of Uruguay, ending democracy in that state and crushing the Tupamaros movement. By the end of that year, members who were not in jail fled the country and joined other groups engaged in similar antigovernment movements.

Finally, in 1985 the Uruguay Supreme Court reviewed the cases of the jailed Tupamaros and released all of them. In that year, the military surrendered control of the government to civilian politicians. On September 4, 1985, existing members of the Tupamaros released a statement indicating that they had given up armed struggle and were joining the Frente Amplio coalition and the Movimiento 26 de Marzo.

References: Gilespie, Charles. *Negotiating Democracy: Politicians and Generals in Uruguay* (New York: Cambridge University Press, 1991); Radu, Michael, and Vladimir Tismaneanu. *Latin American Revolutionaries: Groups, Goals, and Methods* (New York: International Defense Publishers, 1990).

Turner Diaries, The

Written by American NEO-NAZI William Pierce, this book offers a blueprint for revolution in the United States based on a race war. It became the operational profile for the ARYAN NATIONS. It is available on the open market, and the book is used by many groups that have splintered from the Aryan Nations for tactical reasons.

William Pierce was a longtime racist and anti-Semite who began his career of right-wing extremism in the 1960s as an aide to George Lincoln Rockwell, founder and leader of the American Nazi Party. Pierce is a former academic who holds a doctorate in physics. The novel is a violent scenario that imagines the global murder of Jews and includes a nuclear attack on Israel and the salvation of the United States for the minority of the population that is genuinely Aryan. Pierce's book is said to have inspired Timothy McVeigh to carry out the OKLAHOMA CITY BOMBING in 1995. McVeigh apparently read and reread *The Turner Diaries* and was fond of quoting entire passages of it to anyone who would listen. Pierce's scenario was scripted to occur during the 1990s. The fact that it didn't has not diminished his enthusiasm for cleansing America of impure elements such as blacks, Hispanics, Jews, and Asians. In addition, the federal government is a primary target since it is viewed by Pierce and his supporters as representative of and controlled by non-Aryans.

The novel has received a wide distribution among and has inspired portions of the militia movement. Among some militia groups, such as The Order, *The Turner Diaries* has become a motivation and a hope for defending the integrity of the white race. The novel is seen by its adherents as a blueprint for extremist activities. Pierce's ultimate hero was Adolf Hitler whom *The Turner Diaries* refers to as "the Great One." While it is unlikely that the novel will ever appear on the *New York Times* best-seller list, its influence should not be underestimated. For substantial numbers of people, perhaps in the many thousands, *The Turner Diaries* is a persuasive and convincing political fantasy.

TWA flight 847

On the morning of June 6, 1985, less than a half-hour into the flight, two Shiite Muslim members of ISLAMIC JIHAD brandished guns and grenades to hijack TWA flight 847, a Boeing 727 traveling from Athens to Rome. The plane, carrying more than 150 passengers and crew members, contacted the Beirut tower, reporting that the hijackers had pulled a hand-grenade pin and were prepared to blow up the aircraft if they "had to." The pilot insisted that the plane must be allowed to land in Beirut.

Beirut, not desiring any involvement with the terrorists, attempted to prevent flight 847 from landing, ordering airport crews to block the runways with trucks and buses. The pilot, John Trestake, however, radioed that the hijackers were beating up passengers, making landing essential, and reiterating the hijackers' threats to blow up the plane. The hijackers reportedly threatened to fly the plane into the airport tower or into the presidential palace if landing rights were refused. Faced with these threats, the tower in Beirut gave reluctant permission to "land quietly."

The next demand was for fuel, with threats again to kill the passengers and to blow up the plane. Flight 847 was allowed to refuel, and the hijackers then released about six women and children and departed for Algiers. The authorities in Algiers responded by shutting down the airport in an effort to keep flight 847 from landing there. U.S. president Ronald Reagan contacted Algerian president Chadli Bendjedid at that point and persuaded the Algerian authorities to allow the plane to land. Most of the male passengers and crew, except for the pilot, were released at that point, and flight 847 departed Algiers and returned to Beirut.

Upon landing in Beirut for the second time, the hijackers killed a passenger, U.S. Navy diver Robert Stetham. Radio broadcasts while the plane was on the tarmac in Beirut alerted the hijackers aboard the jet that the pilot was transmitting information to authorities on the ground. The hijackers then killed the captain, threatening to kill another in five minutes. Within minutes, an Amal official and his bodyguard boarded the plane in an effort to prevent further killings. The hijackers then demanded the release of 50 Lebanese Shiites held in Israeli jails and the release of Shiites imprisoned in Cyprus and Kuwait, the withdrawal of Israeli forces from southern Lebanon, international condemnation of the United States and Israel, and that the airport lights be turned off. Unfortunately, the airport lights were soon turned off, giving the two hijackers the opportunity to board additional gunmen for reinforcements without the airport officials' knowledge. During this time, the hijackers also obtained the passports from the hostages on board, which they used to identify those passengers with Jewish-sounding names. These passengers were smuggled in the darkness out of the aircraft and taken to a site where they were held by members of Islamic Jihad.

After making their demands to Israel and the international community, gathering reinforcements and dispersing part of the passengers to Islamic Jihad control on the ground, flight 847 departed Beirut and returned to Algiers. In Algiers, the hijackers released 50 more hostages after Algerian negotiators met with the hijackers, then the flight returned for the third time to Beirut. However, this time the Beirut tower refused to give permission to flight 847 to land. The pilot, in desperation, informed Beirut tower that the aircraft only had five minutes of fuel on board. He continued on his flight plan and landed the aircraft in Beirut.

The United States, in the meantime, had dispatched the antiterrorist Delta Force units, who rescued the Jewish passengers that had been taken off the aircraft and held by Islamic Jihad. After several more threats, the hijackers freed the remaining hostages, blew up the aircraft, and fled into the Shiite neighborhoods.

See also AERIAL HIJACKING; GOALS OF MEDIA, IN TERRORIST EVENT; CENSORSHIP, OF MEDIA CONCERNING TERRORIST EVENTS.

tyrannicide

Assassination has become both an ideological statement and a powerful political weapon, using the doctrine of tyrannicide, the assassination of a (tyrant) political leader. Throughout Italy during the Renaissance, tyrannicide was fairly widely practiced, while in Spain and France during the Age of Absolutism, it was at least widely advocated. The leading advocate of the doctrine of tyrannicide as an acceptable solution to political repression was a 16th-century Spanish Jesuit scholar, Juan de Mariana, one of whose principal works, *De Regis Institutions,* was banned in France.

In the words of Mariana is found much of the same political justification as that used by leaders of national liberation movements. Mariana asserted that people necessarily possessed not only the right of rebellion but also the remedy of assassination, stating that "if in no other way it is possible to save the fatherland, the prince should be killed by the sword as a public enemy."

Only 10 years after Mariana's words were uttered, King Henry III of France was assassinated by the monk François Ravaillac. Many leaders since that time have been struck down by persons who claimed to have acted as instruments of justice against a tyrant. Even President Lincoln's assassin, John Wilkes Booth, saw his act in such a light, as evidenced by his triumphant shout, *"Sic semper tyrannis!"* (Thus always to tyrants!)

Political assassins, like those committing murder in the name of religion, have frequently claimed to be acting as "divine instruments" of justice. At the very least, such assassins have viewed themselves as the chosen instruments of popular legitimacy, rightly and even righteously employed in the destruction of illegitimate regimes and tyrannical rulers. The robes of martyrdom have been donned as readily by political as by religious zealots. Like the religious fanatics, political assassins have had no hesitation in acting as judge, jury, and executioner, assuring themselves and others that their appointment to these offices was made, not by themselves, but by a "higher" will or authority.

During the latter part of the 18th century and early 19th century, the "divine right of kings" theory, that kings rule by divine appointment, began to lose its political grip on Europe. As the theory of the existence of a social contract between a people and their government began to gain acceptance, those who carried out political offenses such as tyrannicide gradually found a more benign atmosphere in which to act.

As one acting to "right the wrongs" committed by government, the political assassin was no longer regarded with universal disfavor. Vidal, a leading French legal scholar, noted that:

> Whereas formerly the political offender was treated as a public enemy, he is today considered as a friend of the public good, as a man of progress, desirous of bettering the political institutions of his country, having the laudable intentions, hastening the onward march of humanity, his only fault being that he wishes to go too fast, and that he employs in attempting to realize the progress which he desires, means irregular, illegal, and violent.

Not until the middle of the 20th century was the murder of a head of state, or any member of his/her family, formally designated as "terrorism." Even today, those who commit the "political" crime of murder of a head of state can often enjoy a type of special protection, in the form of political asylum, which constitutes a type of sanctuary or refuge for a person who has committed such a crime granted by one government against requests by another government for extradition of that person to be prosecuted for this political crime.

References: Hurwood, B. *Society and the Assassin: A Background Book on Political Murder* (London: International Institute for Strategic Studies, 1970); Vidal. *Cours de Droit Criminel et de Science Penitentiare.* 5th ed. (Paris: Institut de Presse de Paris, 1916); Zasra, O., and J. Lewis. *Against the Tyrant: The Tradition and Theory of Tyrannicide* (Boston: Little, Brown, 1957).

U

Uganda *See* IDI AMIN.

Ulster Defense Association

Since the early 1970s, the Ulster Defense Association (UDA) has been struggling for the independence of Ulster from both the United Kingdom and the Republic of Ireland. Members have randomly massacred hundreds of Catholics while proclaiming their message of Ulster's freedom. It has used, from time to time, other names, including the Ulster Freedom Fighters, in order to carry out terrorist attacks without incurring the danger of being identified by the authorities.

This group was extremely active in the 1970s and early 1980s, acting often to kill anyone, especially Catholics, who did not agree with their goals. By the end of the 1990s, it had begun to target members of the IRISH REPUBLICAN ARMY (IRA) and the Catholic community. One UDA spokesman commented to the British and Irish: "Hands off Ulster! We are growing more disillusioned toward the British . . . because they have shown neither the willingness nor the will to root out the Provisional IRA (PIRA)."

The UDA used "death squads" whose main mission was to kill and the cause chaos for all who stood in the way of achieving their goal of independence for Ulster. Between 1972 and 1977, the UDA murdered approximately 440 people; it wounded and seriously injured thousands more.

The UDA/Ulster Freedom Fighters (UFF) declared a series of cease-fires between 1994 and 1998, but in September 2001, its Inner Council withdrew its support for Northern Ireland's Good Friday Agreement. The following month, after a series of murders, bombings, and street violence, the British government ruled the UDA/UFF's cease-fire defunct. The dissolution of the organization's political wing, the Ulster Democratic Party, soon followed, but in early 2002, the UDA created the Ulster Political Research Group to serve in a similar capacity. The UDA/UFF has evolved into a criminal organization, deeply involved in drug trafficking and other profitable criminal activities, primarily operated through six essentially independent "brigades."

In November of 2004, the UDA announced that it would disengage from paramilitary activities and reenter the political peace process. The group also announced its intention to work with the Independent International Commission on Decommissioning as part of its cease-fire activities. The UDA removed several prominent members from positions of leadership in 2005 in what appeared to be an attempt to clean up an image tarnished with racketeering and drug trafficking. While these are positive developments, the Ulster Defense Association remains the largest sectarian paramilitary organization in Northern Ireland.

Reference: National Memorial Institute for the Prevention of Terrorism (MIPT). "Ulster Defence Association/Ulster Freedom Fighters." Available online. URL: http://www.tkb.org/Group.jsp?groupID=122. Accessed February 15, 2006.

Unabomber

An unusual serial killer in the United States in the 1990s was the individual known as the Unabomber. Before his identity was known, the FBI referred to him as the UNABOM (from "university" and "airline bomber"). Variants of the code name appeared when the media started using it, including Unabomer, Unibomber, and Unabomber. He was born Theodore John Kaczynski in Chicago, on May 22, 1942, son of Wanda and Richard Kaczynski, and has a younger brother, David. His mother Wanda was widowed in 1990 when her husband learned he had terminal cancer and took his own life.

Ted was intellectually gifted as a child and known to be extremely shy and aloof. A severe allergic reaction to medication that resulted in several weeks of hospitalization and isolation when he was an infant may have altered his personality. His parents were only allowed infrequent visits during this illness and were barred from holding Ted; and his mother reported that the once-happy baby was "never the same," incessantly crying and pleading for her comfort. Friends and neighbors noticed young Ted's intellectual gifts but thought his social skills were severely lacking, considering him "very unsociable" and "an old man before his time." At the age of 10, his IQ was found to be 170, and he skipped two grades, graduating from high school in 1958 and entering Harvard at the age of 16, majoring in mathematics. While there, Kaczynski participated in psychological experiments. He is mentioned in an article about a long-ignored personality profile of Adolf Hitler, written by Dr. Henry A. Murray, who worked for the Office of Strategic Services during World War II. The article notes that "Lawyers for Mr. Kaczynski, who pleaded guilty in 1998 to letter bomb attacks that killed 3 people and wounded 28 others, traced some of his emotional instability and fear of mind control to those tests."

In 1962, Kaczynski graduated from Harvard and earned a master's degree and a Ph.D. in mathematics from the University of Michigan in Ann Arbor, where he began a research career. He earned his Ph.D. by solving, in less than a year, a math problem that one of his professors himself had been unable to solve. He received, in 1967, a $100 prize recognizing his dissertation, entitled "Boundary Functions," as the school's best in math that year. At Michigan, he held a National Science Foundation fellowship, taught undergraduates for three years, and published in mathematical journals two articles related to his dissertation, publishing four more papers after he left Michigan. He was hired in the fall of 1967 as an assistant professor of mathematics at the University of California, Berkeley, where his aloofness and reserve made students rate him poorly, probably contributing to his decision to resign, without explanation, in 1969, in spite of efforts by department staff to persuade him to stay.

After leaving his position at Berkeley, Kaczynski held no permanent employment, living a simple life in a remote shack on very little money, occasionally working odd jobs, with some financial support from his family. Nine years later, in 1978, he worked briefly with his father and brother at a foam rubber factory.

That same year, he sent his first mail bomb, in late May, to Professor Buckley Crist at Northwestern University. The package was found in a parking lot at the University of Illinois at Chicago, with Professor Crist's return address and a "send to" address of Prof. E. J. Smith at Rensselaer Polytechnic Institute. The package was sent "back" to Crist, who, suspicious of a package he never sent, notified campus police. Campus police officer Terry Marker, responding to the call, opened the package, and it exploded, causing Marker minor injuries.

This initial bombing was followed by bombs to airline officials, and in 1979, a bomb was placed in the cargo hold of a commercial airplane. Fortunately, a faulty timing mechanism prevented the bomb from exploding, instead causing it to begin to smoke and forcing the pilot to make an emergency landing, where many of the passengers were treated for smoke inhalation. Authorities said that the bomb had had enough firepower to obliterate the plane, had it exploded.

The FBI became involved after this incident and came up with the code name UNABOM. Initially, they believed that the culprit was a disgruntled airline mechanic, although Agent John Douglas, the father of "profiling" criminals, disagreed with this assessment, since he claimed that the bombs were much too sophisticated and that the bomber was most likely an academic. Profiling was a new investigative tool at the time, and so Douglas's theory was largely ignored.

The first serious injury caused by the Unabomber occurred in 1985, when a Berkeley graduate student, Captain John Hauser, lost four fingers and the vision in one eye, destroying his chances for the astronaut training for which he had been accepted. The bombs were all handcrafted and were made with some wooden parts, some of which carried the inscription "FC" (later found to mean "Freedom Club"). A California computer store owner was killed by a nail-and-splinter-loaded bomb lying in his parking lot in 1985. A similar attack occurred on February 20, 1987, against a computer store in Salt Lake City, Utah. After a six-year break, Kaczynski struck again in 1993, mailing a bomb to David Gelernter, a computer science professor at Yale University. Another bomb in the same year maimed geneticist Charles Epstein. In 1994, an advertising executive was killed by another mail bomb, which was followed by the 1995 murder of California Forestry Association president Gilbert B. Murray in Sacramento, California.

In 1995, Kaczynski mailed several letters, some to his former victims, outlining his goals, demanding that his 35,000-word paper *Industrial Society and Its Future* (commonly called the "Unabomber Manifesto") be printed verbatim by a major newspaper and stating that he would then end his bombing campaign. After much controversy, and more threats to kill people, the Justice Department recommended publication out of concern for public safety, and the *New York Times* and the *Washington Post* published it on September 19, 1995, with the hope that someone would recognize his writing style, as indeed happened.

David, Ted's younger brother, recognized his writing style and notified authorities. After a team of forensic linguists compared text samples provided by David and his mother with the Unabomber's writings and determined that they had been written by the same person, officers went to arrest Ted Kaczynski on April 3, 1995, at his remote cabin outside Lincoln, Montana.

While not clearly a terrorist, in that the political agenda that motivated his actions was unclear, even after the publication of his "manifesto," Ted Kaczynski certainly generated a mood of fear in his audience and caused serious security concerns throughout the nation. His threats generated long delays at airports, as authorities sought to reduce the possibility of a bomb attack, and several of his mail bombs caused serious injury or death to the individuals targeted, or to their family members. Theodore Kazcynski was arrested in 1996. The federal court in Montana found him guilty of the charges and sentenced him to life in prison.

Police officers bring Theodore Kaczynski, the Unabomber, to court for arraignment, 1996. (CORBIS)

Reference: Chase, Alston. *A Mind for Murder: The Education of the Unabomber and the Origins of Modern Terrorism* (New York: W. W. Norton & Company, 2004).

unholy triangle *See* NARCO-TERRORISM.

United Kingdom anti-terror legislation

Periodic outbreaks of violence in Northern Ireland prompted the British Parliament to enact the Northern Ireland (Emergency Provisions) Act in 1973.

Parliament renewed this act each year for the next two decades, retaining in its title the term *emergency*, even though it had been in effect for more than a decade. This measure:

1. Allows suspects to be detained by the executive authority;
2. Gives police powers of arrest without warrant for up to 72 hours;
3. Gives security forces broad authority for search and seizure; and
4. Makes it possible for those charged with terrorism to be tried by a judge, without benefit of a jury.

This legislation was followed in 1974 by an act called the Prevention of Terrorism (Temporary Provisions) Act. Under this act, the home secretary was given special powers:

1. To exclude from the United Kingdom, without court proceedings, persons "concerned with the commission, preparation, or instigation of acts of terrorism" and
2. To detain a suspect for up to seven days without bringing him or her to court (after arrest by police officers without a warrant, as allowed under the Emergency Provisions Act).

The Temporary Provisions Act also allowed the prohibition in the United Kingdom of organizations considered to be connected with terrorism. Both of these acts were renewed annually by Parliament, though often with heated debates. Although they carried the titles of "Temporary" and "Emergency," such terms are not appropriate. "Emergency" by definition refers to "a sudden condition or state of affairs calling for immediate action."

In 2000, the parliament of the United Kingdom passed the Terrorism Act, which constituted an attempt to "define" a terrorist act, primarily by citing actions that would constitute "terrorism." The legal definition in this act included three parts: the act, or threat of destructive action; the intent to influence the government; and the purpose of advancing a political or ideological cause. It gave the police, when undertaking a terrorist investigation, the power to cordon off an area (and order people to leave) for up to 14 days (with the ability to extend that authority for up to a maximum of 28 days). They were also given the power to arrest anyone reasonably suspected of being a terrorist and to hold that person for up to 48 hours, with access of the prisoner to a lawyer denied during that time. This act also extends police stop-and-search powers, allowing them to stop and search if a person has anything on them to prove that they are a terrorist. It also gives police the authority to use "reasonable force."

After the events of the fall of 2001, the United Kingdom passed another major piece of legislation relating to terrorism, the Anti-Terrorism Crime and Security Act (ATCSA). This act expanded the government's ability to confiscate and/or block the transfer of funds from individuals suspected of being involved with terrorism—a broad mandate that allowed the enforced "forfeiture" of "terrorist cash" suspected of being used for the purposes of terrorism, belonging to a proscribed organization, and/or property obtained through terrorism. A "terrorist" is defined, in this act, as being one whom the Home Secretary reasonably suspects of being involved in the preparation, commission, or instigation of acts of international terrorism; belonging to a terrorist organization (which is not defined in the act); or being linked with such an organization. Thus, under this act, a person or organization can be certified to forfeit resources/cash if he/she/it is suspected of involvement in, or linkage to (by support or participation), acts of terrorism (undefined). The certificate of forfeiture may be challenged in court.

The portion of this act (Part 4) justifying the detention of a suspected international terrorist caused considerable legal controversy in the context of requirements of the European Convention on Human Rights. Ordinarily, non-British citizens suspected of involvement in terrorism would be prosecuted with criminal offenses associated with those activities; if insufficient admissable evidence is available to prosecute them, such persons would normally be deported as a "threat to national security." But, according to Article 3 of the European Convention on Human Rights, it is illegal to deport a person to another country if there are substantial grounds for believing that the person would be subjected to torture or degrading treatment.

Part 4 of the ATCSA was justified, from the British point of view, by the fact that, if a foreigner was suspected of being involved in international terrorism, but could not be prosecuted because there was a lack of admissable evidence to sustain a prosecution, and could not be deported to their country of origin because of Article 3 of the European Convention, then that person remained a security risk for the country and must therefore be detained until the person no longer presented a risk to national security, or until a third country was willing to take him or her.

Following a series of legal challenges to the powers and processes established by the ATCSA, the House of Lords ruled in the fall of 2004 that the powers of detention of suspected international terrorists as described in Part 4 were incompatible with the European Convention on Human Rights and therefore not acceptable in British law. This led, in 2005, to the Prevention of Terrorism Act, which replaced Part 4 of the ATCSA, which authorized restrictions commensurate with "house arrest" on British citizens as well as foreigners suspected of being involved in international terrorism. The compatiblity of this act with U.K. obligations under the European Convention on Human Rights and other international agreements remains under debate.

In response to the LONDON BOMBINGS of 2005, the British Parliament passed the Terrorism Act 2006, part of which is aimed at curtailing violent speech and publishing. The goal of this law was to criminalize speech that encourages terrorism, such as the public remarks and websites produced by certain radical Islamist leaders in the United Kingdom that praise suicide bombers and celebrate the deaths of British and American soldiers in Iraq and Afghanistan. In February 2006, the radical Islamic cleric Abu Hamza al-Masri was convicted and sentenced to seven years in prison for soliciting murder and racial hatred under the Terrorism Act 2000.

See also LONDON BOMBINGS.

References: MI5. Resources and Links. Key Legislation. Available online. URL: http://www.mi5.gov.uk/output/Page134.html. Accessed April 11, 2006; Walker, Clive. *Blackstone's Guide to Anti-Terrorism Legislation* (New York: Oxford University Press, 2002).

United Nations, response to terrorism

The issue of terrorism was brought before the UN General Assembly in 1972 after the massacre of Israeli athletes at Munich by a Palestinian group. Sporadically since that time, the UN has worked on measures to combat the global problem. In the 1970s, the ad hoc committee tasked with generating consensus for action on the issue deadlocked in a struggle to define the term "terrorism."

After a decade of effort, the committee reported that the issue was "too politically difficult" to define, making consensus on appropriate actions in response not possible. The problem for the General Assembly lay in differentiating between the legitimate struggles of peoples under colonial rule, or alien domination and foreign occupation, and terrorism. Self-determination and national liberation were processes that many member states had experienced, and most were reluctant to create law that could impinge on these fundamental rights.

The General Assembly's Sixth (Legal) Committee struggled with a greater degree of success to generate legal responses to this issue. By the end of the 20th century, 11 legal documents were drafted. Each draft treaty dealt with a specific aspect of terrorism since a focused approach to a particular issue was easier to promulgate than general antiterrorism legislation. The earlier treaties involved attacks on civil aviation, making aerial hijacking an international crime. Two of the most recent treaties focus on the threat of nuclear terrorism and on efforts to restrict financial support for terrorist acts.

Terrorism appeared on the agenda of several other UN organizations, with less clarity or successful action. Consensus that terrorism constitutes a violation of human rights made the topic an agenda item in the General Assembly's Third Committee as well as the Economic and Social Council (ECOSOC) and several of its subunits, particularly the Commission on Human Rights.

On November 26, 1997, the Third Committee condemned terrorisms. The committee drafted a resolution that condemned violations of the rights of life, liberty, and security and reiterated its condemnation of terrorism. Provisions of this resolution, approved by a recorded vote of 97 in favor to none against, with 57 abstentions, called on states to take all necessary and effective measures to prevent, combat, and eliminate terrorism. It also urged the international community to enhance regional and international cooperation for fighting against terrorism and to condemn incitement of ethnic hatred, violence, and terrorism. The resolution carried no method of enforcement and thus was similar to most action taken by the UN on this issue, simply issuing a call for cooperation, condemning terrorist acts, but entailing no further action or obligation.

Using the General Assembly Plenary Declaration in 1994, which stated that acts of terrorism could also threaten international peace and security, the Security Council became more involved in the struggle to deal with this issue. Unanimously adopting Resolution 1269 (1999), the council stressed the vital role of the United Nations in strengthening international cooperation in combating terrorism and emphasized the importance of enhanced coordination among states and international and regional organizations. It called upon all states to take steps to cooperate with each other through bilateral and multilateral agreements and arrangements, prevent and suppress terrorist acts, protect their nationals and other persons against terrorist attacks, and bring to justice the perpetrators of such acts. The Security Council continues to advocate exchange of information in accordance with international and domestic law, cooperation on administrative and judicial matters to prevent the commission of terrorist acts, and use of all lawful means to prevent and suppress the preparation and financing of any such acts in member states' territories.

In other resolutions passed in the 1990s, the Security Council called on all states to deny safe havens for those who planned, financed, or committed terrorist acts by ensuring their apprehension and prosecution or extradition. These resolutions also stressed that, before granting refugee status, states should take appropriate measures in conformity with national and international law, including international standards of human rights, to ensure that the asylum seeker had not participated in terrorist acts.

The Security Council has been careful not to initiate action on this issue that would replace the efforts of the General Assembly but rather has sought to interact with the latter on the basis of the competence granted to it within the charter. Noting that the degree of sophistication of terrorist acts, and the increasingly globalized nature of those acts, were new trends and that the extensive international networks of organized criminals were creating an infrastructure of "catastrophic terrorism," the Security Council resolved that terrorism posed a serious threat to international peace and security, making it an issue that needed action by the Security Council as well as the General Assembly and ECOSOC.

On September 28, 2001, acting under Chapter VII of the United Nations Charter (concerning threats to international peace and security), the Security Council adopted Resolution 1373 (2001), reaffirming its unequivocal condemnation of the terrorist attacks that took place in New York, Washington, D.C., and Pennsylvania on September 11, 2001, and expressing its determination to prevent all such acts. Resolution 1373 also established the Counter-Terrorism Committee (known by its acronym, the CTC), made up of all 15 members of the Security Council. The CTC monitors the implementation of resolution 1373 by all States and tries to increase the capability of States to fight terrorism. The CTC is an instrument to monitor the implementation of resolution 1373, but it is not a sanctions committee and does not have a list of terrorist organizations or individuals.

The United Nations Policy Working Group on Terrorism was established by the secretary-general in October 2001 to identify the implications and broad policy dimensions of terrorism for the United Nations and formulate recommendations. The Policy Working Group identified how the UN's activities should be part of a tripartite strategy supporting global efforts to dissuade disaffected groups from embracing terrorism, deny groups or individuals the means to carry out acts of terrorism, and sustain broad-based international cooperation in the struggle against terrorism.

In resolution 56/261, the General Assembly adopted plans of action for the implementation of the Vienna Declaration on Crime and Justice: Meeting the Challenges of the Twenty-first Century. The Centre for International Crime Prevention within the United Nations Office on Drugs and Crime was asked to, in cooperation with other relevant international and regional organizations, in coordination with the Office of Legal Affairs of the Secretariat, as appropriate, and in accordance with the present resolution:

a. Take steps to raise awareness of the relevant international instruments, encourage States to sign and ratify such instruments, and, where feasible, provide assistance in implementing such instruments to States, upon request;
b. In cooperation with Member States, take measures to raise public awareness of the nature and scope of international terrorism and its relationship to crime, including organized crime, where appropriate;
c. Continue to maintain existing databases on terrorism;
d. Offer analytical support to Member States by collecting and disseminating information on the relationship between terrorism and related criminal activities;
e. If further developments so require, draw up concrete proposals for consideration by Member States to strengthen the capacity of the centre to develop, within its mandate, and administer the terrorism prevention component of its activities.

From the Sixth Committee, after September 2001, came a new convention on terrorism: the International Convention for the Suppression of Acts of Nuclear Terrorism, deposited with the secretary-general on April 13, 2005. With the International Convention for the Suppression of the Financing of Terrorism, adopted by the General Assembly of the United Nations on December 9, 1999, the legal groundwork for international cooperation through the UN to combat terrorism became significantly stronger.

References: *A Global Agenda: Issues before the 60th General Assembly of the United Nations* (New York: UNA-USA, Rowman & Littlefield, 2005); United Nations. UN Action against Terrorism. Available online. URL: http://www.un.org/terrorism. Accessed April 7, 2006.

United Self-Defense Forces of Colombia (a.k.a. Autodefensas Unidas de Colombia [AUC])

Since the middle of the 1960s, the government of Colombia has combated a number of Marxist guerrillas, the largest two being the REVOLUTIONARY ARMED FORCES OF COLOMBIA (FARC) and the NATIONAL LIBERATION ARMY (ELN). As these groups grew in strength and influence, the Colombian government conceded control of many areas to these guerrillas or to local self-defense forces comprised of armed citizens. These local self-defense forces grew out of the government's willingness to allow citizens to defend themselves in the rural areas, where the guerrilla's influence is stronger than that of the official Colombian military; however, they have taken on the shape of paramilitary forces that operate outside the law. Many have been accused of terrorism and of doing much to derail any peace negotiations between guerrilla forces and the Colombian government. Today most of these paramilitaries are united under a single umbrella organization known as the Autodefensas Unidas de Colombia (AUC), or United Self-Defense Forces of Colombia.

In 1981, the first Colombian paramilitary group, Muerte a Secuestrados (MAS) ("Death to Kidnappers") was formed using a 1968 law that allowed legal local self-defense groups to create as a pretense an illegal vigilante militia that could operate outside the law to combat the guerillas. This local defense force quickly changed its posture from a defensive to an offensive one, attacking not armed guerrillas but unarmed civilians suspected of guerrilla activity. Hundreds of other paramilitary groups and death squads rapidly spawned from MAS's example, due to the perception of the Colombian public that these groups provided them with a means of striking back at the guerrillas. By 1988, the number of paramilitary groups had expanded to 300, and at least 140 death squads were active.

In 1997, most of the local and regional paramilitary groups united as the umbrella organization AUC, under the command of former leader of MAS, Carlos Castaño. The fundamental charge of each group to combat insurgents locally remained, but this is now orchestrated through a flexible network on the national level.

AUC members are part of a right-wing vigilante terrorist organization, seeking to defend the status quo or return to that of an earlier period by using terrorist tactics on a population without legitimate authority to do so. Members believe that the use of violence is justified, given the Colombian government's inability defend its citizens from the Leftist rebels. Landowners have created their own form of justice, in which leading citizens exact revenge on the offenders for disrupting civil society, in an attempt to restore order to the system. These vigilantes seek personal gain, and many of the leaders of the AUC have amassed considerable fortunes through the protection of criminal enterprise.

However, the nature of the violence between the guerrillas and the paramilitaries has created a type of extremism among AUC members that is similar to a "crusader" mentality. The hatred felt by some paramilitaries for the Marxist guerrillas has become so all-consuming that it has caused them to seek not personal gain but prestige and power for a collective cause. This was particularly true of the motivations of early paramilitaries, who were uncorrupted by the riches provided by narco-terrorism. The involvement of the paramilitaries in providing protection for traffickers and producers of drugs is aptly described as narco-terrorism, because of the codependent nature of the relation between Colombian drug lords and paramilitaries that has provided funding to the AUC necessary to carry out attacks on guerrillas. In a sense the AUC is also a tool of state terrorism, as it has been used by the Colombian government to indirectly terrorize the Leftist guerrillas. The legal and conventional methods employed by the Colombian government to combat the guerrillas have been stymied by corruption, internal politics, and international restraints. Many within the Colombian government and the military have supported mass terrorism through support of the AUC.

According to 1992 estimates, 70% of political killings carried out were attributable to security forces and paramilitary groups.

Paramilitaries of Colombia abandoned the premise of providing defense for local citizens, adopting instead an offensive approach predicated on the displacement of guerrilla sympathizers by means of massacres and terror. Immediately following the formation of the AUC, its members began campaigns against entire villages, operating more and more like an army—attacking with hundreds of fighters and then occupying captured territories. The typical tactics of these AUC units are to arrive in a village with a death squad and a list of suspected collaborators. The individuals named on the list are rounded up and publicly questioned with the use of torture and then executed in bizarre manners, often in front of family members. A favorite form of execution among AUC death squads is decapitation by chainsaw.

In 1983, Amnesty International credited the AUC's predecessor MAS with more than 800 extrajudicial killings, over a multiyear period. In contrast, the Colombian National Police reported the AUC carried out 804 assassinations, 203 kidnappings, and 75 massacres in the year 2000 alone. In 2001, human rights groups estimated that the AUC murdered more than 1,000 unarmed civilians. In May of 2004, a mass grave was discovered in the Arauca province, containing 11 bodies of individuals who had been reported missing two days earlier when they were picked up by AUC members. The men were believed to have been killed for having collaborated with guerrilla forces. Army officials reported that the bodies of the men showed signs of torture.

On several occasions, the AUC prevented or derailed peace negotiations between the Colombian government and guerrillas. In 2000, President Andreas Pastrana attempted to award the ELN control of a demilitarized zone as a precondition to peace negotiations. The AUC advanced on the area, easily defeating ELN forces, which were unprepared to combat this threat during the truce. The violation of the demilitarized zone by the AUC not only hampered the success of negotiations with the ELN but also destroyed a fragile truce that had been established against FARC. While the AUC usually avoids conflict with government security forces, clashes have increased as the AUC has interfered with the government's attempts to handle the guerrillas.

The violence created by leftist insurgent terrorists produced an environment ripe for recruitment for the AUC. After 40 years of struggle between the government and guerrillas, there are many disaffected soldiers and civilians willing to step in and provide security where the Colombian government is unable. Due to the legal tradition of using civilians to provide for local defense, as provided by legislation in 1968, civilians have access to training and equipment. For MAS founder Fidel Castaño and his brother, and successor, Carlos Castaño, the violence used against guerrilla forces is born out of a search for revenge for the kidnapping and murder of their father by FARC. Like the Castaño family, most Colombians have been affected directly by the violence, a fact that has begun to create a cycle common with terrorist activities. This cycle of violence is exacerbated by the willingness of government security forces to provide clandestine support for the AUC as a counterinsurgency tool; such support has created a situation in which vigilantes are able to escalate the violence in response to terrorism of the guerrillas.

The paramilitary groups were originally supported by right-wing businessmen who feared both the personal danger that the leftist guerrillas posed to their own security, as well as the damage that the instability caused by these groups' conflicts with security forces brought to their business interests. The paramilitaries received training and arms from members of the military who considered them an effective counterinsurgency tool. They also received support from ranchers who had become targets when the guerrillas turned to kidnapping and extortion to fund their own expanding operations, including drug lords who themselves owned over 3.5 million hectares of agricultural land. Almost immediately, MAS allied itself with drug lords, specifically the notorious Medellín drug cartel.

The right-wing elements that initially funded the paramilitaries lost control, however, as they became progressively like a private army answering only to Castaño. Their connection with drug cartels grew as they came to control large parts of coca-producing areas. The AUC replaced the guerrillas as providers of protection to traffickers and producers and in return levied heavy taxes on drug lords. This new revenue source afforded the AUC the opportunity to purchase modernized equipment and weapons and the ability to pay fighters a wage higher than that of the average Colombian. These funds were essential to intelligence gathering, as they could be used to create informants among guerrilla forces. Today the AUC openly admits that about 70% of its budget comes directly from

NARCO-TERRORISM, with the other 30% being made up of private donations.

A major supporter of the paramilitaries has always been the official military security forces; however, the extent to which this support is approved of by the Colombian government is difficult to gauge. One example of apparent collusion took place in 2001, when the AUC attacked a village, provoking no response on the part of the Colombia military. The military later claimed that they were unaware of the attack until it was too late to do anything; however, critics point out that a similar attack in the area by FARC received an immediate response.

The U.S. State Department added the AUC to its list of terrorist organizations on September 10, 2001. In the wake of the September 11th tragedy, U.S. policy toward Colombia changed. In 2002, the administration of President George W. Bush requested that Congress increase military aid to Colombia. Unlike the previous $1.3 billion aid package, this package focused mainly on combating the guerrilla threat. The perception that military aid would inevitably favor the AUC, which has clandestine support from the military, is credible. Recent U.S. policy toward the AUC seemed to favor negotiations and peaceful demobilization amnesty.

Efforts to demobilize the AUC have been met with mixed success. While AUC leaders seem anxious to secure a seat at negotiations in the hope of gaining amnesty, many seem reluctant to relinquish their control, as that would mean losing access to the wealth brought through their connections with drug lords. By spring of 2005, 3,600 AUC members had voluntarily demobilized, according to reports from the U.S. State Department. However, AUC forces continue to carry out operations. In 2005, the UN announced that it intended to use International Court of Justice authority to intervene in legal matters pertaining to human rights violations by the AUC.

References: National Memorial Institute for the Prevention of Terrorism (MIPT). "United Self-Defense Forces of Colombia (AUC)." Available online. URL: http://www.tkb.org/Group.jsp?groupID=126. Accessed February 15, 2006; U.S. Navy. Naval Post Graduate School Country Reports on Terrorism (2004). Country Reports on Terrorism United Self-Defense Forces/ Group of Colombia (AUC). Available online. URL: http://library.nps.navy.mil/home/tgp/auc.htm. Accessed February 21, 2006.

C. M.

United States, recent patterns of terrorism in

While the United States has experienced relatively little domestic terrorism, even in the turbulent 1960s, compared with other democratic systems, the 1990s witnessed dramatic changes. The lethality of international attacks as well as attacks on U.S. citizens and facilities escalated; right-wing groups grew in number and levels of activity; and the potential for the use of weapons of mass destruction also appeared to increase.

Lethality of International Attacks

While the United States had experienced some lethal attacks on its citizens in previous decades, the number and intensity of these attacks increased substantially. The large number of casualties in the attack on the U.S. Marine barracks outside of Beirut in the early 1980s were described, in later years, as casualties of war rather than victims of terrorism since the casualties were soldiers in a war zone in which their country was involved in launching missile attacks. No such designation could be given, though, to those killed or injured in the bombing of the U.S. embassies in Nairobi, Kenya, and Dar es Salaam, Tanzania, in August 1998. The blast in Tanzania killed at least 116 people and injured over 4,300, while the bomb in Kenya killed at least 221 and injured almost 5,000 more, including the U.S. ambassador to Kenya. Timed to coincide within minutes of each other, the events were clearly linked, and U.S. intelligence eventually linked them to OSAMA BIN LADEN's agents. This precipitated the U.S. bombing of AFGHANISTAN and SUDAN in response.

The OKLAHOMA CITY BOMBING of a federal building by a man linked to the MONTANA FREEMEN, which again caused numerous deaths and injuries including many children, made the nation aware of its vulnerability to attack by its own citizens. Intense scrutiny by federal agencies of ARMED RIGHT-WING GROUPS and particularly ARMED MILITIA groups followed. The standoff in WACO, TEXAS, which ended in a large number of casualties, also alerted the nation of a need for a more coherent response to internal groups threatening violence. While a nation whose history included the activities of hate groups like the KU KLUX KLAN and the linking of RACISM AND TERRORISM that had permeated the South after the Civil War could not be unaware of its potential for problems from WHITE SUPREMACIST GROUPS such as the ARYAN NATIONS and the CHRISTIAN IDENTITY MOVEMENT, the nation and much of its law enforcement forces were unprepared for the terrorism of the 1990s. The need arose

People stand among the charred ruins following the bomb blast at the United States Embassy in Nairobi, 1998. (CORBIS)

to adjust to potential dangers in AIRPORT SECURITY as well as attacks that made even school sites not secure from terrorist attacks.

The WORLD TRADE CENTER BOMBING in New York City also offered a learning experience in terrorism, as the United States experienced a SPILLOVER EVENT of Middle Eastern terrorism as well as an attempt to create a weapon of mass destruction. Court records after this event indicated that the individuals responsible had intended to create a lethal gas in the explosion, packing sodium cyanide into the vehicle used. Cyanide gas, if released as intended by the terrorists, would have potentially killed thousands, not the few killed in the bomb blast. The United States had, in a sense, been lucky that time in that the terrorists did not make the device work properly. It was left to wonder how long that luck would last.

That question was answered on September 11, 2001, when two hijacked airliners crashed into the Twin Towers of the World Trade Center in New York City and a third hijacked airliner crashed into the Pentagon in Washington, D.C. A fourth, possibly bound for another target in the capital, crashed in Somerset County, Pennsylvania, after passengers attempted to overpower the hijackers. The magnitude of destruction in this attack, with an estimated 3,000 civilian deaths, went far beyond anything that had previously occurred in the United States, or in the world, for that matter. The Federal Bureau of Investigation (FBI), the Central Intelligence Agency (CIA), and other law-enforcement agencies were forced to admit that they had no previous knowledge that this type of attack would occur. Many officials pointed out that this type of attack went far beyond the usual terror scenarios and that the open society of the United States makes it even more difficult to prevent this type of attack. As a result, the United States is seeing changes in its homeland security, such as heightened airport security, immigration restrictions, and expanded powers for law enforcement to pursue suspected terrorists.

Some argue that these developments raise the issue as to whether the rights of U.S. citizens might be infringed by the U.S. government's new powers, while others argue that the potential loss of certain freedoms is far outweighed by the benefits if it means the prevention of future terrorist attacks. While the devastation of the September 11 attacks was high, many experts agree that if the terrorists had somehow been able to use biological, chemical, or nuclear weapons instead, the outcome would have been far more horrific.

Reference: Talbott, Strobe, and Nayan Chanda, eds. *The Age of Terror: America and the World After September 11* (New York: Basic Books, 2001).

USA PATRIOT Act

Officially named "Uniting and Strengthening America by Providing Appropriate Tools Required to Intercept and Obstruct Terrorism" (U.S. Public Law 107-56), the PATRIOT Act was introduced, passed, and signed into law in October of 2001 in response to the September 11th attacks. This act, which gives the U.S. government much broader authority to conduct surveillance within the United States, was passed with very little debate in either house of Congress in response to a cry from the public to do something to catch those responsible for the 9/11 attacks and to keep anything like that from happening again. However, as the horror of the 9/11 attacks fades, concerns have increased that the PATRIOT Act gives the U.S. government too much

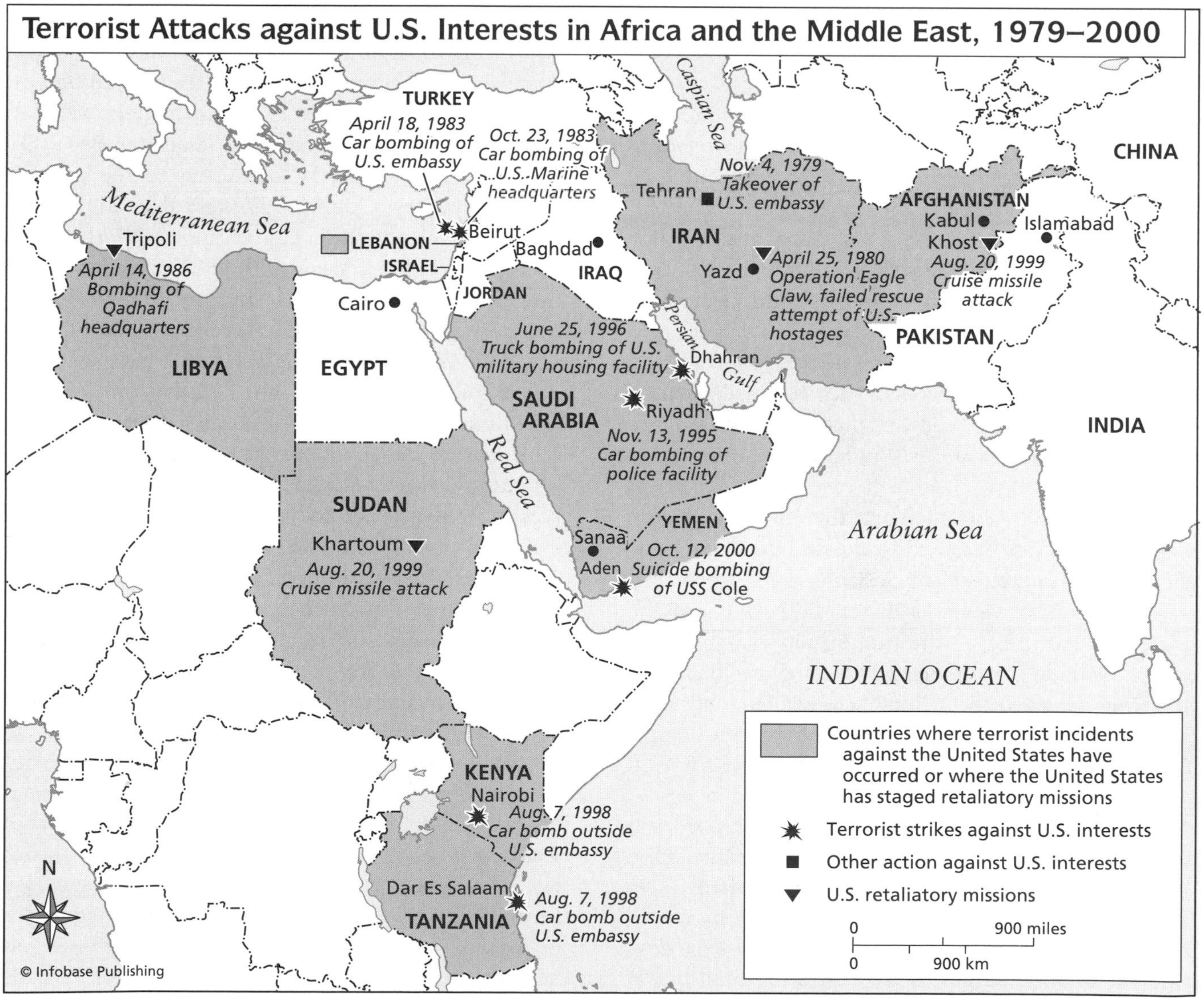

authority and that it breaks Fourth and Fifth Amendment protections.

The stated purpose of the PATRIOT Act is to ease restrictions on domestic law-enforcement personnel and agencies. Law-enforcement agencies complained they were not able to pick up on the hijackers before they attacked because of various operational constraints. Agencies were often not allowed to talk to each other about people they suspected of being involved in illegal acts. Even if they did talk to each other, agencies were hampered in coordinating because different agencies had different goals and regulations. Even if the CIA informed the FBI that a person was in the country that they had evidence wanted to carry out a terrorist act, the FBI often could not seek a warrant to conduct surveillance. This is because the CIA (and most other federal/state law-enforcement agencies) often did not have evidence that could be used in a U.S. court, since that evidence might have been obtained illegally or because using that evidence in open court would put ongoing operations and personnel at risk.

The PATRIOT Act sought to alleviate this problem by relaxing the requirements for warrants to conduct search and/or surveillance (physical or electronic), as provided in section 214 of the act. In order to protect ongoing operations, the PATRIOT Act allows for law enforcement to conduct searches without the suspect's knowledge, requiring that he or she only be notified at a later date (section 213). The PATRIOT Act also gives all federal agencies permission to share foreign intelligence as deemed necessary for national security. It should be noted that these changes are meant to pertain only to foreign nationals and are not supposed to affect U.S. citizens.

The PATRIOT Act also allows for the attorney general or his or her designee to detain and deport any alien that he or she has concluded is going to commit a terrorist act or otherwise harm the security of the United States. If he or she cannot deport the person quickly, and the person's release is thought to endanger American security, the federal government may hold the individual for up to six months without charge. The only appeal the individual can make is to a federal court for a writ of habeas corpus.

The PATRIOT Act also defined domestic terrorism as ". . . acts dangerous to human life that are a violation of the criminal laws of the United States or of any state; that appear to be intended—to intimidate or coerce a civilian population to influence the policy of a government by intimidation or coercion; or to affect the conduct of a government by mass destruction, assassination, or kidnapping; and occur primarily within the territorial jurisdiction of the United States."

The FBI itself gives much of the credit for the successes it has had in finding and convicting or expelling terror suspects to the PATRIOT Act. In its annual report on the success of its criminal division, the FBI spoke at length of its many successes. It claimed that since 9/11 up to the end of 2004 it had charged 375 individuals and convicted 195 on terror-related charges. It also claimed to have removed 515 people related to the 9/11 investigation from the United States. The FBI makes clear in its report that the PATRIOT Act enabled it to achieve much of its success quickly.

Concerns remain about the impact of the PATRIOT Act on civil rights and liberties. Civil libertarians criticize the PATRIOT Act as giving too free a hand to law enforcement. They argue that the FBI is correct in stating that the PATRIOT Act allows it to remove many people from the United States whom it suspects of terrorism that it otherwise would not be able to deport. Civil libertarians argue that this is not an improvement. Opponents of the act claim that, under the PATRIOT Act, the U.S. government has damaged the people's right to appropriate due process and that this betrays core values of the U.S. Constitution and the Fifth Amendment, since it seems to hold the government to a low threshold of evidence when deciding to expel a student or religious leader. Libertarians argue that in the United States people are presumed innocent until proven guilty in an open court and that this assumption of innocence should not be traded for short-term security, since this is vital to U.S. civil society.

Critics of the PATRIOT Act also claim that the act gives the government too much ability to take away an individual's right to privacy. Civil libertarians argue that changes in requirements for issuance of warrants and allowing law enforcement to not notify targets that their effects have been searched go too far. They argue that the new rules invite abuse of authority from government personnel and break the Fourth Amendment to the Constitution.

Most provisions in the PATRIOT Act are permanent, but several surveillance portions were set to expire at the end of 2005. Both the Senate and the House of Representatives voted in March 2006 to make all but two provisions permanent. Those two provisions are the authority to conduct "roving" surveillance under the Foreign Intelligence Surveillance Act (FISA) and the authority to request production of business records under FISA. These provisions will expire in four years. In March 2006, President George W. Bush signed the reauthorization of the act.

References: Baker, Stewart A. *Patriot Debates: Experts Debate in the USA PATRIOT Act* (New York: American Bar Association, 2005); Library of Congress. Thomas Home. Bills and Resolutions. "H.R. 3162." Available online. URL: http://thomas.loc.gov/cgi-bin/bdquery/z?d107:h.r.03162: Accessed April 7, 2006.

R. B.

USS *Cole,* bombing of

Nearly a year before the 9/11 attacks, an American warship, the USS *Cole,* was attacked and nearly sunk by two suicide bombers. On October 12, 2000, terrorists blew a 40-by-40-foot hole in the *Cole*'s hull. Seventeen sailors were killed, and 39 were injured in the blast. The *Cole* had docked in the harbor of Aden in Yemen for a fuel stop. In the late morning, a small boat approached the *Cole* carrying two men. The men, visible from the *Cole*'s deck, appeared friendly and even smiled and waved at the sailors before detonating their cargo. The suicide bombers were identified as Ibrahim al-Thawr and Abdullah al-Misawa. They had rented a house in a neighborhood in which Yemeni government and military officials lived. For several weeks prior to the attack, the two had carefully prepared their strategy and were frequently observed on the nearby beach speaking with fishermen and determining the distance they could travel in the fiberglass boat they had secured.

The attack and its perpetrators were quickly linked to AL-QAEDA. A great deal of meticulous planning had preceded the attack. Two and possibly three previous attacks were planned but did not succeed. One attempt to blow up the USS *The Sullivans* failed because the bombers' boat nearly sank when the explosives on board overloaded it. The attack on the *Cole* was successful in great part because of the ability of the bombers to learn from past mistakes. Many blamed OSAMA BIN LADEN directly, though he denied knowing the bombers. Bin Laden, however, warned that another attack on his training camps, such as the one that followed the 1998 bombings of the U.S. embassies in Kenya and Tanzania, would not stop his battle against those he considered to be "enemies of Islam."

Investigations that followed the attack drew interesting and helpful conclusions. The two bombers were not alone. On November 3, 2002, the Central Intelligence Agency used an AGM-114 Hellfire missile to kill two Yemenis linked to the bombing, Abu Ali al-Harithi and Ahmed Hijazi. Two others, Abd al-Rahim al-Nashiri and Jamal al-Badawi, were sentenced to death by a Yemeni court after their capture, though al-Nashiri was turned over to the United States and remains in American custody.

Several dozen FBI agents were sent to Yemen to investigate the attack. Before the investigations were completed, the number of FBI agents rose to around 150. Yemeni government officials denied that Yemen sponsored or in any way supported terrorist enterprises on its soil. This denial may have been accurate since some evidence provided by the investigations conducted by Yemeni security forces and the FBI determined that Saudi Arabia might have been the base for the operation. There were some disagreements between the Americans and Yemenis over what the latter regarded as their sovereign territorial integrity. In any case, no reliable claims for responsibility for the attack were forthcoming.

Reference: CRS Report for Congress. "Terrorist Attack on USS Cole: Backgound and Issues for Congress." Available online. URL: http://www.mipt.org/pdf/CRS_RS2072.pdf. Accessed April 7, 2006.

V

Venice Statement on Taking of Hostages

Issued by the heads of state and government of the Seven Summit Countries (often referred to as the G7) during their meeting in Venice in 1980, this statement not only expressed grave concern about the Iranian hostage situation but also called upon nations to ratify the recently completed Convention Against the Taking of Hostages. This convention had just been adopted by the UN General Assembly on December 17, 1979. Completed shortly after the seizure of the American embassy in Teheran, this convention effectively made it a crime to take any person a hostage. The document extended the protection of international law to every individual, regardless of his or her position (or lack of one), with the exception of those in armed forces engaged in armed conflict.

The G8 (the G7 plus Russia), in a statement made at a meeting in 2002 in Ottawa, Canada, noted that it attaches the highest importance to preventing and combating terrorism. To assist in the effort, the G8 defined a series of principles that provide guidance to strengthen capacities to combat terrorism, including full adherence to the following instruments relating to the prevention and suppression of terrorism:

a. The 12 United Nations conventions and protocols addressing counter-terrorism issues listed in the annex;
b. All relevant United Nations Security Council Resolutions, in particular, United Nations Security Council Resolution 1373 (2001).

In this new declaration, the G8 also committed itself and urged all other States to

a. Work within the United Nations system to complete the draft UN Comprehensive Convention on International Terrorism and coordinate their efforts in this regard.
b. Promote appropriate action in multilateral organizations of which they were members, including at the regional level, in order to usefully supplement counterterrorism measures already taken or under development at the global level.

On the opening day of the 2005 G8 summit in Scotland, July 7, 2005, a synchronized series of bombings were detonated in the LONDON Underground and on a London double-decker bus, claiming more than 50 lives and wounding hundreds. Credit for the attacks was immediately taken by the "Secret Group of Al-Qaeda's Jihad in Europe." The attacks are assumed to be in retaliation for the United Kingdom's participation in military action in Afghanistan and Iraq, although terrorism has been perpetrated against Western states by Islamic fundamentalists prior to those actions. The global attention focused on the G8 summit was presumably leveraged by the terrorists for maximum symbolic effect.

Vienna Convention on Diplomatic Relations

This convention, signed in April 1961, demonstrated a broadening concern for diplomats as well as heads of state in terms of vulnerability to attack. Under this convention, signatory states were to assume responsibility to prevent attacks on a diplomatic agent's person, freedom, or dignity. It did not, however, describe the need for a constant vigilance on the part of states, acting either individually or collectively, to prevent the occurrence of incidents of violence against these "protected people."

W

Waco, Texas, incident

On February 28, 1993, the Bureau of Alcohol, Tobacco and Firearms (ATF) attempted to serve an arrest and search warrant at the Mount Carmel compound of the Branch Davidians for Vernon Howell. Vernon Howell, also known as David Koresh, was the leader of the Branch Davidians, an apocalyptic religious group. Their compound, which was located just northeast of Waco, Texas, off Route 7, occupied 70 acres of land.

Seventy-six ATF officers attempted to enter the compound. The ensuing melee of gunfire, in which an estimated 6,000 to 10,000 rounds were fired, left both sides reeling. Four ATF agents died and another 20 were injured along with an unknown number of Branch Davidians in the 45-minute confrontation. Local media had been alerted and had positioned themselves to watch the raid.

Following the failure of the initial raid, the ATF withdrew to a safe position and alerted the Federal Bureau of Investigation (FBI). The FBI allocated its Hostage Rescue Team, Critical Incident Negotiations Team, and other experts to the operation while securing a perimeter around the Mount Carmel compound. A 51-day standoff began.

David Koresh considered himself to be the herald of the second coming of Christ and a messenger of God. After the raid, Koresh and his followers were waiting for a sign from God to leave their Mount Carmel compound. Koresh was also writing his interpretation of the Seven Seals in the book of Revelations in the Christian Bible. Until both the sign from God was received and Koresh's interpretation of Revelations was completed, the Branch Davidians were committed to maintaining the impasse with the FBI.

Throughout the standoff, constant negotiations between senior members of the FBI and the Davidians occurred by way of telephone. Overall, a total of 21 children and 14 adults left Mount Carmel during the standoff. In FBI attempts to coerce the Branch Davidian members to leave the compound, varied tactics were used, including the cutting off of electricity and water, the use of high-power halogen lamps to illuminate the compound at night, and loud music. Negotiations were fruitful early in the standoff for both sides. Fourteen children were released after a recorded tape was aired on a local radio station. However, by the end of March, progress slowed and negotiations began to stall.

After FBI officials decided that negotiations could not resolve the standoff, a plan to use CS gas, a form of tear gas, became a viable option. The plan to introduce CS gas was finalized on April 17. Senior FBI officials consulted the army's antiterrorist group, Delta Force,

Black smoke erupts from the compound in Waco, Texas, where Branch Davidian cultists had been surrounded by federal agents. (CORBIS)

on the plan's formulation and feasibility. Furthermore, professional medical advice about the possible harm to the children from CS gas exposure was considered. Early on the morning of April 19, 1993, combat engineer vehicles (CEVs) began pumping CS gas into certain areas of the compound, coupled with another 300 rounds of CS canisters. Fires set by Branch Davidians erupted from multiple points within the compound at 12:00 P.M. Not long after, explosions from ammunition and other combustibles totally engulfed the Branch Davidian structure. Nine people survived the blaze, and 75 bodies were recovered.

In August 1999, documents were uncovered that indicated that during the raid on the Branch Davidian compound the FBI used a limited number of flammable tear-gas canisters. This revelation contradicted assertions of the FBI and the Department of Justice that the government had done nothing that could have contributed to the start or spread of the fire. In response, Attorney General Janet Reno appointed a special counsel, former Republican senator John C. Danforth, to reexamine the assault to determine how the fire started and whether there was a cover-up of information implicating law-enforcement officials or the Justice Department.

On July 21, 2000, after a 10-month investigation, Danforth issued a preliminary report exonerating the government and its agents. His report concluded that federal agents did not start the fire, direct gunfire at the complex, or improperly employ U.S. armed forces. Danforth assigned responsibility for the tragedy to the Branch Davidians and David Koresh. According to the report, they contributed to the tragedy by refusing to exit the compound during the 51-day standoff, directing gunfire at FBI agents, shooting members of the compound, and ultimately setting the fire that burned the compound down.

Danforth did find, however, that an FBI agent fired three pyrotechnic tear-gas rounds at a concrete pit 75 feet from the living quarters of the compound. Although these rounds did not start the fire, government officials did not admit their use until August 1999, more than six years later. Danforth found that this negligence was at best a mishandling of evidence and at worst a criminal attempt to conceal the truth from investigators.

As a result of the standoff, changes were made in the way federal law-enforcement agencies dealt with future crises. The FBI was denoted as the lead agency in hostage/barricade situations and incidents of domestic terrorism. Greater resources were allocated to the FBI to deal with high-risk operations and raids as well as an increase in research operations.

A call to arms for many ultraright groups emerged in response to this standoff. Government involvement in the private lives of individuals and groups was decried by extremist groups as becoming unbearable. Federal law-enforcement abuses became "prevalent" in the eyes of many of these groups. This confrontation, combined with the Ruby Ridge incident, has been cited as a stimulus in the later OKLAHOMA CITY BOMBING of the Alfred P. Murrah Federal Building.

Reference: Reavis, Dick J. *The Ashes of Waco: An Investigation* (Syracuse, N.Y.: Syracuse University Press, 1998).

War Measures Act *See* CANADA AND THE FLQ.

weapons, conventional terrorist

Modern terrorists use a wide variety of conventional weapons, from guns to car bombs, grenades to missiles. A brief look at the potential arsenal of contemporary terrorists gives perspective to the diversity of the threat with which security systems must cope. Since most terrorists today use conventional weapons rather than weapons of mass destruction, these are the weapons that constitute the most common threat from terrorists today.

Bombs and guns, the terrorist's most common weapons of choice, are found in almost infinite variety, are both "homemade" and manufactured professionally, and may be used for selective assassination or mass destruction. Clearly, understanding the conventional arsenal of terrorists is essential to grasping, and coping with, contemporary terrorism in all of its many forms.

Guns (and Other Firearms)

The majority of contemporary terrorists have access to, and use, manufactured firearms made professionally by arms factories all over the world. These types of guns come in three general categories: small arms (including pistols, revolvers, rifles, both sub- and light machine guns, and assault rifles), medium-sized infantry weapons (generally belt-fed machine guns, smaller mortars, rocket-propelled grenades, and some of the smaller caliber wire-guided missiles), and heavy infantry weapons (such as heavy-caliber machine guns and mortars, shoulder-held antitank missile launchers, and certain types of rockets).

These types of guns are produced by a wide range of manufacturers, including A. Kalashnikov, Beretta, Walther, Browning, Glock, Uzi, Sterling-Enfield, Ruger, Mauser, Springfield, Armalite, SIG, Luger, and dozens of others. The guns produced by these well-known manufacturers include the AK-47, a rifle from the former Soviet Union supplied to anti-Western insurgents globally for more than half a century. It is perhaps the most widely used rifle in the world.

Certain types of medium- to heavy-infantry weapons are also becoming more available to terrorist groups today. The RPG-7 (rocket-propelled grenade) used by the former Soviet forces, those of the Chinese and the North Korean military, and many of the eastern European countries receiving Soviet weapons, has been extensively used by terrorist groups in the Middle East and is increasingly used in Latin America and among other insurgent groups today. It is available, illegally, on the international arms market and is believed to be in the inventory of many groups, since it is a simple and functional weapon, requiring little training to use, and is useful against vehicles as well as fixed emplacements. U.S. troops in Iraq in 2005 have been attacked by groups using this type of weapon.

The U.S.-manufactured Stinger (FIM92A) is another lethal conventional weapon often found in the hands of insurgents in the Middle East as well. This is a man-portable infrared-guided shoulder-launched surface-to-air missile (SAM) that Americans trained Afghan guerrillas to use during their insurgency against the Soviets. Those guerrillas who took their commitment home (as in Libya) or turned it against America (at the call for jihad issued by OSAMA BIN LADEN), have now both the training and often a substantial cache of these SAMs, courtesy of the American support for the mujahideen in their fight against communism in Afghanistan. This weapon has been used to target high-speed jets, helicopters, and even commercial airliners, making terrorist threats to aircraft quite credible, even from the ground.

Bombs (and Other Types of Explosives)

While some types of guns have been improvised by groups, or local industries seeking to copy the weapons of larger states, many types of bombs today are improvised rather than manufactured. The "bomb" that destroyed the federal building in Oklahoma City was improvised, but clearly effective. These types of bombs are known as improvised explosive devices (IEDs) and are the contemporary terrorist's most diverse weapon today, as the variety and success of suicide bombings have made clear. IEDs have a basic structure: There is a main charge, which is attached to a fuse, which is in turn attached to a trigger, which activates the fuse, which ignites the charge, causing the explosion. There are, of course, infinite variations to these linked actions, and materials that can be added to intensify or radically alter the impact, such as scraps of metal for shrapnel or radioactive material to create a "dirty bomb."

The type of explosive incorporated in the IED also varies, from modern forms of plastic explosives, such as C4 or Semtex, to TNT and dynamite. The availability of these types of explosives varies, but a material as simple and easy to acquire as fertilizer, used as a base, can certainly generate a devastating blast, as demonstrated in Oklahoma City by Timothy McVeigh. IEDs thus range from pipe bombs—the most common type of terrorist bomb—to Molotov cocktails (simple devices originally used by Russian resistance fighters consisting of glass containers filled with combustible liquid, such as gasoline, with a cotton fuse) to barometric bombs (which are detonated when an altitude meter reaches a designated point).

Iraqis gather at the scene of a car bomb that targeted a passing U.S. military patrol in Baghdad, 2006. (GETTY IMAGES)

On August 11, 2006, British authorities uncovered a terror plot that involved the detonation of explosive liquids (which could be disguised as ordinary items) on flights originating from the United Kingdom and the United States, adding yet another challenge for airport security. As a result, airports have placed tighter restrictions on the amount of liquid material that passengers can bring on a plane.

Reference: United Nations Office on Drugs and Crime. Terrorism, Corruption, and Human Trafficking. "Terrorism: Conventional Terrorist Weapons." http://www.unodc.org/unodc/terrorism_weapons_conventional.html. Accessed April 29, 2006.

weapons of mass destruction *See* BIOLOGICAL AND CHEMICAL ATTACKS; NUCLEAR TERRORISM.

white supremacist groups

These are mostly found in but are not restricted to the United States and, to a lesser extent, Europe. In the United States, white supremacist groups have appeared throughout the country, most notably in the Pacific Northwest. Their common characteristics include anti-Semitism, racism, and a distrust of as well as contempt for the federal government. Many, perhaps most, white supremacists also consider themselves to be the last line of defense of Christianity. Several groups subscribe to the notion that the American government is completely controlled by ZOG, the Zionist Occupation Government.

White supremacists became more sophisticated during the 1990s. There are a large number of websites that regularly deliver messages that suggest conspiracies determined to destroy white Christians are being hatched by Jews, communists, and blacks. A favorite book is *THE TURNER DIARIES*, a white supremacist fantasy of a successful rebellion by whites that violently eliminates the threat to white purity posed by Jews and blacks. Some white supremacists see themselves as the descendants of the Ten Lost Tribes of Israel, the real Israelites that established the white countries of northern Europe.

Most white supremacists may in fact not be violent, whereas a hard-core minority fully expects and is preparing for a final confrontation with a Jewish-controlled government. Federal and state authorities have more than once expressed a concern that white supremacists could attempt to establish by force a white homeland in the sparsely inhabited western states. There is also some apprehension that white supremacists are stockpiling weapons and are training to use them.

See also AMERICAN FRONT; ARIZONA PATRIOTS; ARYAN NATIONS; CHRISTIAN IDENTITY MOVEMENT; CHRISTIAN PATRIOTS; CHRISTIAN MILITIA MOVEMENTS, IN THE UNITED STATES; COVENANT, SWORD, AND ARM OF THE LORD; MILITIAS IN THE UNITED STATES.

Reference: Ridgeway, James. *Blood in the Face: The Ku Klux Klan, Aryan Nations, Nazi Skinheads and the Rise of a New White Culture* (New York: Thunder's Mouth Press, 1995).

Wilmington Coup and Massacre of 1898

This was one of the more prominent examples of the political terror waged against African Americans by white supremacists in the late 19th and early 20th centuries. It is also considered by many scholars to be the only example of a political coup within the United States, in which a duly elected government was forced by threat of violence to relinquish power. The coup was the cornerstone of a movement by Democrats in North Carolina to wrest political control from a Republican/Populist coalition and to eliminate the black political participation that bolstered this coalition. It was a key component in a white supremacy campaign that culminated in the disenfranchisement of African Americans in North Carolina by 1900 and part of a larger movement of black disfranchisement and legal segregation that swept the South at the turn of the last century. The incident is mentioned in, or has been the subject of, numerous historical studies on race relations in the post-Reconstruction South, from articles and full-length monographs to novels.

Even before the end of Reconstruction in 1877, southern white "redeemers" sought to deprive African Americans of the political power they had gained after the Civil War. This movement for disfranchisement accelerated after 1890 when Mississippi became the first southern state to revise its constitution to eliminate the black vote. In order to accomplish this, southern "redeemers" had to get around the 15th Amendment to the Constitution, which said that a person could not be deprived of the right to vote because of race. Thus, they came up with ostensibly race-neutral measures, such as "literacy tests," "grandfather" clauses, and poll taxes to eliminate black voting. With a literacy test, a person had to read and interpret some document, often the state constitution, to the satisfaction of the registrar before he could register to vote. The tests were not really a means of determining literacy but a means of preventing African-American men from voting, as evidenced by the fact that whites did not have to take the literacy tests. They were exempted by "grandfather" clauses or "good character," clauses, which basically stated that if one's grandfather could vote before 1867 or if the registrar could attest that the potential voter was a person of "good character," they did not have to take the literacy tests. Since few African Americans could vote before 1867 and since registrars could arbitrarily exclude blacks on the character clause, African Americans had to take the literacy tests. Sometimes race-specific measures were utilized such as the "white" primary, in which blacks were excluded from participating in the Democratic Party primary. Since the South was a one-party region with the Democratic Party being the dominant political party, blacks were effectively shut out of the process. These measures were upheld by a conservative Supreme Court, which acquiesced to state power and by a U.S. Congress and successive presidents who likewise eschewed intervention.

However, these extralegal measures were undergirded by use of political violence and terror. Even before the official end of Reconstruction, southern whites resorted to violence and intimidation to eliminate the black vote. Organizations like the KU KLUX KLAN terrorized potential black voters through the use of lynchings and assassinations. Democratic Party "clubs" would sometimes train a cannon on the polling place or have target practice next to the polls to scare away African-American voters. This violence and intimidation increased in the late 19th and early 20th centuries as efforts at disfranchisement intensified throughout the South. There was an increase in the number of lynchings and a change in the characteristics of lynch victims. In the early 1880s, when statistics on lynchings began to be kept, most of the victims were white. However, by 1889, more blacks than whites were being lynched. Between 1893 and 1904, an average of 100 blacks a year were lynched, compared with 29 whites. From 1906 through 1915, 10 times as many blacks (620) as whites (61) were lynched. Ostensibly acts of "justice," lynchings were really acts of terror designed to keep African Americans in "their place," which in part, meant out of the voting booth.

Lynchings and antiblack riots swept the South at the turn of the 20th century. In Lake City, South Carolina, in 1898, the home of a black postmaster was burned to the ground by a mob, and he and most of his family were shot as they tried to escape the flames. In Atlanta in 1906, an antiblack riot took the lives of 10 African Americans. In 1908 a similar riot took place in Springfield, Illinois. It so horrified many in the nation that it led to the creation of the National Association for the Advancement of Colored People in 1909. Other such racial conflagrations occurred in East St. Louis, Illinois, in 1917 and Chicago in 1919.

Often these acts of violence were instigated by the inflammatory rhetoric of race-baiting politicians, such as "Pitchfork" Ben Tillman of South Carolina or James K. Vardaman of Mississippi as well as by lurid headlines and stories in the press about alleged black rapists. White supremacist politicians, including Tillman, Vardaman, Georgia's Tom Watson, and others, raised the specter of so-called Negro domination, employing the stereotypes of the criminal, brutish Negro, to gain political support from whites already predisposed to such views by generations of prejudice. J. K. Vardaman, campaigning for governor in 1900, declared, "We would be justified in slaughtering every Ethiopian on the earth to preserve unsullied the honor of one Caucasian home," and he said that the Negro was a "lazy, lying, lustful animal which no conceivable amount of training can transform into a tolerable citizen." Alluding to blacks he went on to say, "We do not stop when we see a wolf to find if it will kill sheep before disposing of it, but assume that it will." Tom Watson said that blacks simply had "no comprehension of virtue, honesty, truth, gratitude and principle" and that the South had "to lynch him occasionally, and flog him now and then, to keep him from blaspheming the Almighty by his conduct, on account of his smell and his color." Ben Tillman summed up the views of these politicians toward depriving blacks of political rights when he said, "We have done our level best. We have scratched our heads to find out how we could eliminate the last one of them [blacks]. We stuffed ballot boxes. We shot them. We are not ashamed." With the urgings of such politicians, Jim Crow and disfranchisement became established fixtures in the South, and political violence was a vital tool in accomplishing their ends.

It was in this atmosphere that the Wilmington Coup and Massacre of 1898 took place. In 1898 the seaport of Wilmington, situated along the Cape Fear River in southeastern North Carolina, was the largest city in the state as well as a key commercial center. It was also a mecca for African Americans, who outnumbered the white population 11,324 to 8,731. Blacks held significant political and economic power in Wilmington. Three seats on the 10-member board of aldermen were held by African Americans. One out of five members of the powerful board of audit and finance was black. There was a black justice of the peace, deputy clerk of court, superintendent of streets, and coroner. There were several black policemen and a black mail clerk and mail carriers. An African American, John Campbell Dancy, had been appointed by President William McKinley as collector of customs at the Port of Wilmington, a plum position whose salary was $1,000 more than the state's governor. Dancy had replaced a prominent white Democrat in this position, which was a source of consternation to many local whites.

In addition to their political prowess, African Americans in Wilmington had considerable economic clout. All but one of the city's restaurants were owned by blacks, and they had a virtual monopoly on the barber trade. Blacks owned numerous other small businesses and were active in the trades. Some blacks, such as architect Frederick C. Sadgwar and real estate agent Thomas C. Miller, were major businessmen in the city. Wilmington boasted one of the few black newspapers in the South, the *Daily Record* owned and coedited by Alex Manly, the "octoroon" acknowledged grandson of a former governor of North Carolina. His paper was said to be the only black daily newspaper in the country at the time.

The main reason that blacks were able to exercise such political and economic authority was the presence in Raleigh of a fusionist government of Republicans and Populists. In the 1894 election, this interracial fusionist ticket gained control of both houses of the state legislature. According to the North Carolina constitution, the legislature exercised extensive control over local government charters and ordinances. It had complete power to change any city ordinance. The Democrats had used this authority to create election laws and gerrymandered districts that limited the representation and participation of African Americans. The new fusion government reversed this trend, liberalizing election laws and making them more democratic. Loosed from the straitjacket of discriminatory election ordinances, Wilmington's black majority was able to gain some political power. It was the purpose of the Democratic Party in North Carolina to regain control of state government, and Wilmington became the focal point of that effort.

In order to accomplish this, Furnifold Simmons, chairman of the state Democratic Executive Committee and his lieutenants, Josephus Daniels, editor of the Democratic *Raleigh News and Observer,* and Charles B. Aycock, the future governor, orchestrated a white supremacy campaign playing on fears of "Negro domination." The *News and Observer* and other Democratic newspapers hammered at this theme by constantly running stories and editorials that portrayed blacks as "insolent" and disrespectful of whites. They particularly focused on the supposed sexual interest of black men in white women. Democratic orators like future governors Aycock and Robert Glenn and former governors Thomas J. Jarvis and Cameron Morrison crisscrossed the state warning voters of the perils of "Negro domination." They hoped to create a tide that would sweep the fusionists out of office and terminate black political participation, and in this they were quite successful.

Spurred on by this statewide effort, plans were laid for a Democratic takeover in Wilmington. At least six months before the November 8, 1898, election, plans were being made by a group of prominent white citizens known as the "Secret Nine" to seize control of the government of Wilmington. In the weeks leading up to the coup, the Democratic *Wilmington Messenger* published a profusion of articles on the alleged insolence and criminality of blacks in Wilmigton, designed to help whip the white population into a frenzy. It was inadvertently aided in this purpose by the black editor of the *Daily Record,* Alex Manly. Manly wrote an editorial replying to a widely publicized speech by Georgia feminist and white supremacist Rebecca Felton in which she called on white men to "lynch a thousand times a week if necessary" to protect white womanhood. Manly replied that many white women who claimed to be raped by blacks were not in fact raped and that some of those liaisons were consensual. He also pointed out that white men had historically seduced and raped black women and did not receive the same condemnation for their actions. Parts of Manly's editorial, especially those that spoke of consensual sexual relations between black men and white women, were circulated throughout the South, enraging many whites. The conspirators had the match to ignite their fire.

About three weeks before the election, a huge Democratic rally was held in nearby Fayetteville. The keynote speaker was none other than fiery Senator Ben Tillman of South Carolina. He was accompanied by a contingent of Red Shirts, a white supremacist terrorist group. In his book on the Wilmington massacre, H. Leon Prather described the scene:

> A delegation from Wilmington led the parade, followed by 300 Red Shirts riding in military formation. A float carrying twenty-two beautiful young ladies in white trailed the Red Shirts, as if to justify the latter's claims of protecting the sanctity of white womanhood. Next came the carriage bearing Fayetteville's mayor and Democratic committee chairman, the editor of the *Fayetteville Observer,* and Senator Tillman himself. Arriving amid the boom of cannons, the great throng assembled at the speaker's stand and listened to the music of the Wilmington brass band. It would not be the last time that Wilmington set the rhythm of Democratic politics across the state.

In his speech, Tillman railed against blacks, Republicans, and fusionist politics. But his deepest invectives were saved for Alex Manly and his notorious editorial. "Such articles as written by the negro editor in Wilmington were an insult to the women of North Carolina," he said. "Why don't you kill that damn nigger editor who wrote that? Send him to South Carolina and let him publish any such offensive stuff, and he will be killed."

Stoked by this rally, white supremacist activity in eastern North Carolina increased in the weeks before the election. Speakers fanned out across eastern North Carolina to spread the fear of "Negro domination" and the salvation of "white supremacy." Chief among these speakers was Alfred Waddell of Wilmington, an ex-Confederate officer and ex-U.S. congressman. He electrified large crowds as he inveighed against the supposed "insolence," "arrogance," and "criminality" of black men. Red Shirt terror against African Americans increased. According to Republican governor Daniel Russell, the Red Shirts had broken up several political meetings in Halifax and Richmond counties. He said, "Several citizens have been taken from their homes at night and whipped . . . several citizens have been intimidated and terrorized by threats of violence to their persons and their property, until they were afraid to register themselves preparatory to the casting of a free vote at the ballot box." In Wilmington, the Red Shirts held a series of marches and rallies organized by an unemployed fireman, Michael Dowling. Prather wrote, "Dowling led the mounted white men through the streets of Wilmington as if they were ranks of cavalry. White women waved flags and handkerchiefs as the long columns of armed riders passed. The parade stopped in front of Democratic Party headquarters . . . where Democratic politicians spoke to swelling crowds, after which the Red Shirts and others whooped it up far into the night." As the election day approached, Wilmington became more and more an armed camp. However, blacks were prevented from buying arms. Local merchants would not sell them to African Americans, and even efforts to order them from national outlets proved fruitless.

Election Day, November 8, passed quietly. Most blacks stayed away from the polls due to the threat of violence, and whites voted overwhelmingly Democratic. Thus, the hated Republican government in Wilmington was voted out of office. However, the Democratic conspirators were not yet pleased. They realized that the newly elected Democratic government could not actually take office until the spring. This was unacceptable; they wanted immediate power. The next day, November 9, a public meeting was held at the courthouse. There, the city's white citizens adopted a series of resolutions known as the "White Man's Declaration of Independence." The resolutions held, among other things, that black office holding was unnatural and that never again would the white men of New Hanover County allow black political participation. Furthermore, the *Daily Record* should cease publication, and its editor, Alex Manly, should be banned from the city. The document, composed by the Secret Nine, was read to the throng by Alfred Waddell to uproarious applause. A committee of 25 leading white citizens, with Waddell as the head, was chosen to carry out the terms of the resolutions. The committee summoned a group of 32 prominent African Americans, distributed the resolution, and demanded a reply be brought to Waddell's house by 7:30 the next morning.

The group of black leaders composed a conciliatory reply, saying that they did not agree with Manly's editorial but had no control over forcing him to leave. However, they would use what influence they had to try to effect his departure. Manly, sensing the danger he was in, had already slipped out of town. The letter was given to prominent black attorney Armond Scott, who chose to mail it rather than deliver it in person to Waddell. Consequently, when the letter did not arrive by 7:30 the next morning, a mob of 2,000 whites, led by Waddell, marched to the offices of the *Daily Record* to expel (or probably lynch) Manly. Finding him absent, they burned the building down. Skirmishes broke out between whites and blacks. Finally, the Red Shirts, Rough Riders, and members of the Wilmington Light Infantry entered the fray. They invaded the black section of town known as Brooklyn like a military operation, firing at blacks. Many African Americans were shot dead in the streets. One black man who fought back was captured and made to run a gauntlet in which his body was filled with "a pint of bullet," according to one observer.

Appeals to the state's Republican governor and to President McKinley went unanswered. When it was all over, scores lay dead, and many prominent blacks and white Republicans were banished from the city. Conservative estimates put the death toll at from nine to 20, but some claim that hundreds died, their bodies tossed in the Cape Fear River or buried secretly in nearby marshy areas. The current mayor and aldermen were forced to resign their offices immediately, and Alfred Waddell became the mayor.

The effects of the Wilmington Massacre reverberated throughout North Carolina for years beyond the event. In 1900, Charles B. Aycock was elected governor, and the Democrats regained both houses of the General Assembly by running a statewide white supremacy campaign. The centerpiece of their campaign was a constitutional amendment intended to disfranchise African Americans. Aycock argued that such an amendment must be passed to prevent violence, such as that which had occurred in Wilmington. The lesson of Wilmington, Aycock said, was that blacks must be disfranchised for the sake of peace. Disfranchisement, he argued, would prevent future bloodshed. As for Wilmington, African Americans never regained the political or economic power they possessed before 1898. The black middle class of the city was eviscerated and never recovered. No African American was again elected to the city council until the 1970s. And though the massacre was rarely discussed publicly, it left a lasting taste of bitterness between whites and blacks.

With the Wilmington Massacre, North Carolina joined the pantheon of other southern states to disfranchise African Americans at the turn of the last century. And as was the case in many of those other states, political violence and terror played prominent roles.

References: Bennett, Lerone, Jr. *Before the Mayflower: A History of Black America* (New York: Penguin, 1993); Cecelski, David S., and Timothy Tyson, eds. *Democracy Betrayed: The Wilmington Race Riot of 1898 and Its Legacy* (Chapel Hill: University of North Carolina Press, 1998); Gossett, Thomas F. *Race, The History of an Idea in America.* 2nd ed. (New York: Oxford University Press, 1997); Litwack, Leon F. *Trouble in Mind: Black Southerners in the Age of Jim Crow* (New York: Vintage, 1999); Logan, Rayford W. *The Betrayal of the Negro: From Rutherford B. Hayes to Woodrow Wilson.* 2nd ed. (New York: Da Capo, 1997); Luebke, Paul. *Tar Heel Politics 2000* (Chapel Hill: University of North Carolina Press, 2000); Mulrooney, Margaret. "The 1898 Coup and Violence," in "The Centennial Record," *A Journal of the 1898 Centennial Foundation* (Wilmington: 1998); Prather, H. Leon, Sr. *We Have Taken a City: Wilmington Racial Massacre and Coup of 1898* (Wilmington: NU World, 1998); Woodward, C. Vann. *The Strange Career of Jim Crow* (New York: Oxford University Press, 1989).

E. S.

World Trade Center bombings, 1993

On February 26, 1993, at approximately 12.18 P.M., an improvised explosive device exploded on the second level of the World Trade Center parking basement. The resulting blast produced a crater, approximately 150 feet in diameter and five floors deep, in the parking basement. The structure consisted mainly of steel-reinforced concrete, 12 to 14 inches thick. The epicenter of the blast was approximately eight feet from the south wall of Trade Tower Number One, near the support column K31/8. The device had been placed into the rear cargo portion of a one-ton Ford F350 Econoline van, owned by the Ryder Rental Agency, Jersey City, New Jersey. Approximately 6,800 tons of material were displaced by the blast.

The main explosive charge consisted primarily of approximately 1,200 to 1,500 pounds of a homemade fertilizer-based explosive, urea nitrate. The fusing system consisted of two 20-minute lengths of a nonelectric burning type fuse such as green hobby fuse. The hobby fuse terminated in the lead azide, as the initiator.

Also incorporated in the device and placed under the main explosive charge were three large metal cylinders (tare weight 126 pounds) of compressed hydrogen gas. The resulting explosion killed six people and injured more than 1,000. More than 50,000 people were evacuated from the Trade Center complex during the hours immediately following the blast.

The initial inspection on February 27 was described as "a scene of massive devastation, almost surreal." It was like walking into a cave, with no lights other than flashlights flickering across the crater. There were small pockets of fire, electrical arcing from damaged wiring, and automobile alarms whistling, howling, and honking. The explosion ruptured two of the main sewage lines from both Trade towers and the Vista Hotel and several water mains from the air-conditioning system. In all, more than 2 million gallons of water and sewage were pumped out of the crime scene.

After an initial inspection of the underground parking area, FBI explosive unit personnel were able to determine that a crater had been formed, measuring approximately 150 feet in diameter at its widest point and over five stories deep. The damage done to automobiles and concrete and structural steel, for example, suggested that the explosive had a velocity of detonation of around 14,000 to 15,500 feet per second. It is known that there are several commercial explosives that fall within that range of detonation, including some dynamites, water gels, slurries, and fertilizer-based explosives. The explosive damage constituted more of a pushing and heaving type rather than the damage one would expect from a more intense shattering and splitting explosive, such as TNT or C-4. Also, by an initial assessment of the type of damage and the size of the crater, it was determined that the explosive main charge must have been between 1,200 and 1,500 pounds.

On February 27 three teams were assembled and the entrance and exit ramps to the parking basement were secured and cleaned while contract engineers were rapidly securing the structural support of the crime scene. By February 28 approximately 200 law enforcement officers from at least eight different agencies were on hand to begin the monumental task of collecting evidence.

On February 28, four FBI forensic chemists and four ATF (Bureau of Alcohol, Tobacco, and Firearms) chemists arrived to begin explosive residue collection. A transient chemistry explosive residue laboratory was

A massive crater lies underneath the World Trade Center after a blast killed five people and injured 300, 1993. (REUTERS/CORBIS)

put together in the already existing New York City Police Department laboratory. Later that evening, six forensic chemists, two from each agency (FBI, ATF, NYPD) were dispatched to the crater area to collect explosive residues. A bomb technician from the NYPD and an ATF agent were also assigned to provide safety support for the chemists.

During the early-morning hours of this residue collection, the bomb technician discovered a fragment from a vehicle frame that displayed massive explosive damage. The ATF agent and bomb technician placed the 300-pound fragment onto a litter and carried it to a police vehicle. The fragment was transported to the laboratory for analysis. Due to sewage contamination, the piece was of no value for explosive residue analyses. A closer inspection of the fragment displayed a dot matrix number. The number was identified as the confidential vehicle identification number of a van reported stolen the day before the bombing. The vehicle was a 1990 Ford, F-350 Econoline van owned by the Ryder Rental Agency, rented in New Jersey, and reported stolen in New Jersey. The frame fragment displayed explosive damage consistent with damage from a device exploding inside the vehicle.

Also by Tuesday, February 28, four assistant U.S. attorneys were assigned to the prosecution. It was fortunate that the attorneys were assigned at that time because late on Monday night, the vehicle fragment had been identified by the FBI laboratory as constituting a portion of the vehicle that contained the device and as having been reported stolen on February 25, 1993. FBI agents traveled to the Ryder Rental Agency in Jersey City, New Jersey, which had rented out the vehicle, and interviewed the station manager. While the interview was under way, an individual by the name of Mohammad Salameh telephoned Ryder and wanted his security deposit returned. A meeting was arranged so that Salameh would return to the Ryder Agency on March 4. When he returned for the $400 deposit, FBI agents were on hand to place him under surveillance. As Salameh was leaving, numerous media personnel were observed outside, setting up their photography equipment. It was then decided that Salameh would be arrested on the spot.

His arrest and the subsequent search of his personal property led to Nidel Ayyad, a chemist working for the Allied Signal Corporation in New Jersey. Ayyad was connected to Salameh through telephone toll records and joint bank accounts. At the time of Ayyad's arrest, his personal computer was seized from his office. Also through toll records and receipts, a safe house or bomb factory was located on Pamrappo Avenue, in Jersey City. A search of his bomb factory revealed that acids and other chemicals had been used at that apartment to manufacture explosives. Traces of nitroglycerine and urea nitrate were found on the carpet and embedded in the ceiling. It appeared that a chemical reaction involving acid had occurred in the apartment. At the same time, telephone toll records from Salameh and Ayyad showed that calls had been made to a self-storage center not too far from the bomb factory.

An interview with the manager of the self-storage center indicated that Salameh had rented a space and that four "Arab-looking" individuals had been observed using a Ryder van several days before the bombing. The manager also said that the day before the bombing, AGL Welding Supply from Clifton, New Jersey, had delivered three large tanks of compressed hydrogen gas. The storage manager had told Salameh to remove them that day. During the search of the storage room rented by Salameh, many chemicals and items of laboratory equipment were located. The items seized included 300 pounds of urea, 250 pounds of sulfuric acid, numerous one-gallon containers, both empty and containing nitric acid and sodium cyanide, two 50-foot lengths of hobby fuse, a blue plastic trash can, and a bilge pump. While examining the trash can and bilge pump, a white crystalline substance was found. A chemical analysis identified urea nitrate.

On March 3, a typewritten communication was received at the *New York Times*. The communiqué claimed responsibility for the bombing of the World Trade Center in the name of Allah. The letter was composed on a personal computer and printed on a laser printer. Very little could be identified as to the origin of the printer, but a search of the hidden files in Ayyad's computer revealed wording identical to that of the text of the communiqué. Saliva samples from Salameh, Ayyad, and a third man, Mahmud Abouhalima, were obtained and compared with the saliva on the envelope flap. A DNA Q Alpha examination concluded that Ayyad had licked the envelope on the communiqué received by the *Times*. Abouhalima, who was an integral part of the conspiracy, had fled the United States the day after the bombing.

In September 1992, a man named Ahmad M. Ajaj had entered the United States from Pakistan at New York's JFK airport. He was arrested on a passport violation. In his checked luggage, Ajaj had numerous manuals and videocassette tapes. These tapes and manuals described method of manufacturing explosives, including urea nitrate, nitroglycerine, lead azide, TNT, and other high explosives.

Interviews and latent fingerprint examinations identified two other individuals who were an integral part of the bombing conspiracy. The first, Ramzi Yousef, had entered the United States on the same flight as Ajaj. Yousef was identified through fingerprints and photospreads as having been associating with Salameh immediately prior to the bombing. His fingerprints were also found in the explosives manuals located in Ajaj's checked luggage. The second individual, Abdul Rahman Yasin, was identified in much the same manner and was probably involved in the packaging and delivery of the bomb on the morning of February 26.

The FBI laboratory was under orders to complete all scientific examinations by July 7, 1993, in compliance with the Speedy Trial Act. A trial date was set for September 6, 1993. During the examination of evidence in the laboratory, the remains on three high-pressure gas cylinders belonging to the AGL Welding Company were identified. A small fragment of red paint with a gray primer was located on one of the metal fragments of the gas cylinder. This paint fragment was compared with the red paint used by AGL on their hydrogen tanks and was found to be the same. On one portion of a fragment of the Ryder truck bed, several fragments of blue plastic, the size of a pinhead, were located. These fragments were compared with the plastic from the trash container at the self-storage center premises Salameh had rented and were found to be alike. Fragments of all four tires were found at the crime scene and compared with the data on the maintenance scheduled at Ryder. All four tires were accounted for in the research.

Prior to the trial, the FBI laboratory's Special Project Section constructed a scale model of the portion of the Trade Center that was damaged by the blast. The model incorporated push-button fiber-optic lighting to depict the location at the crime scene where pertinent items of evidence were found. Once illuminated and described to the jury during the trial, the lights and the model told a very clear and precise story.

During the six-month trial, more than 200 witnesses introduced over 1,000 exhibits. On March 4, 1994, exactly one year after Salameh's arrest, the jury found Salameh, Ajaj, Abouhalima, and Ayyad guilty on all 38 counts.

Abouhalima was identified during neighborhood investigations at the bomb factory and storage center through a photospread. It was later determined that he was an integral part of the conspiracy. He had fled the United States the day after the bombing and was arrested in Egypt. He was thereafter extradited to the United States.

Ramzi Ahmed Yousef and Eyad Ismoil were also indicted on federal charges. Both managed to flee the United States and elude authorities until Ismoil was apprehended in Jordan in 1995, and Yousef, in Pakistan in 1997. Prosecutors claimed that Yousef built the bomb and orchestrated the attack. The indictment stated that Yousef, using a phony Iraqi passport, flew to New York from Pakistan in September 1992 to hook up with Mohammed Salameh and later purchased chemicals. In January and February 1993, the indictment said, Yousef and other coconspirators mixed chemicals in a Jersey City, New Jersey, apartment to produce explosive materials. Ismoil was charged with driving the van carrying the bomb into the building's parking garage and setting it off. In November 1997, after three days of deliberation, a federal jury convicted Yousef and Ismoil on murder and conspiracy charges.

Abdul Rahman Yasin, although detained by the FBI for questioning right after the bombing, was released and left the country for Baghdad. He was then indicted in August 1993, charged with helping mix chemicals for the bomb.

Yousef is believed to have returned to Pakistan, where he began plotting to fulfill part of his unsuccessful Bojinka plot, which entailed the destruction of planes on United and Northwest flights out of Bangkok. He recruited a South African Muslim, Istaique Parker, but Parker got "cold feet" at the last minute and could not check-in the luggage containing the bombs. After returning to Pakistan, Parker heard about the $2 million bounty being offered by the United States for the capture of Yousef and contacted the United States embassy in Islamabad with information. Yousef was arrested by Pakistani intelligence and turned over to U.S. Diplomatic Security Service agents on February 7, 1995. Pakistani intelligence raided the Su-Casa Guest House in Islamabad where Yousef was staying and recovered plans for the failed Bojinka project.

Yousef was flown back to the United States, sent to a prison in New York City, and held there until his trial. On September 5, 1996, Yousef, Murad, and Shah were convicted for planning Bojinka and sentenced to life in prison without parole.

On November 12, 1997, after three days of deliberation, a federal jury found Yousef guilty of masterminding the 1993 bombing, and in 1998, he was convicted of "seditious conspiracy" to bomb the towers. He is currently being held in the high-security prison in Florence, Colorado, the same prison in which the UNABOMBER and TIMOTHY MCVEIGH were imprisoned.

Reference: Reeve, Simon. *New Jackals: Ramzi Yousef, Osama Bin Laden, and the Future of Terrorism* (Boston: Northeastern University Press, 1999).

A. S.

Y

Yassin, Sheikh Ahmed (1936–2004)

Sheikh Yassin was the main founder of HAMAS that officially emerged on December 14, 1988. He left the Palestinian village of al-Jura in 1948 with his family after ISRAEL occupied the area. They moved to the Gaza Strip, where Yassin studied and later taught Arabic and Islamic studies. As a youth, he was influenced by the Muslim Brotherhood and partially modeled Hamas after it. For his advocacy and planning of violent attacks against Israeli citizens, he was imprisoned by Israel intermittently over several years, beginning in 1983 and ending with his final release in 1998. Yassin used his freedom to immediately renew his plans for attacks on Israel and continue to inspire suicide missions.

Yassin was known as a hard-line opponent of the Israeli-Palestinian peace process and continued to call for a relentless jihad against Israel and its destruction as a state. After 1998, Yassin traveled to several Arab states to insist that the struggle against Israel continue until the "Zionist entity" was completely eliminated and a Palestinian state, governed by Islamic law, was established over the entire region of PALESTINE. The tour was a financial success: Yassin raised tens of millions of dollars, mostly from wealthy Persian Gulf states, to finance Hamas operations. Yassin also applauded the Pakistani ability to create and sustain a nuclear weapons system.

Sheikh Yassin relied on support from wealthy Arab regimes and was adept at exploiting their internal weaknesses. While most of these regimes are not in total agreement with the goals of Hamas, and a few developed some sort of relationship with Israel, many felt the need to demonstrate in some tangible way their support for the goals of Islamic radicalism. This may have been done to satisfy public opinion in their own countries, much of which remains hostile to Israel, and to discourage terrorism within their own borders. The destruction of Israel was only a part of Yassin's long-term strategy, which included a full-fledged theocratic state that would apply the full measure of Islamic law. He was as much concerned with a revival of orthodox Islam as he was with the creation of a Palestinian state.

Both Israel and some Arab regimes perceived Yassin to be a counterweight to YASIR ARAFAT. Israeli regimes apparently believed that Arafat could become more reasonable if he believed that Hamas was a primary rival. Arafat and Yassin both died in 2004, the former from natural causes, the latter from an Israeli assassination. The Israeli government acknowledged that it planned and executed Yassin's death and argued that he had been responsible for "sending children and women to explode themselves" in Israel. Yassin remained, until his death, insistent that negotiation with Israeli authorities could not happen since, in his mind, negotiation itself was a form of recognition of a state which he believed should not exist.

References: Hirst, David. "Sheikh Ahmed Yassin." *Guardian* March 23, 2004; Keinon, Herb. "Hamas's Sheikh Ahmed Yassin: Is He a Genuine Threat?" *Jerusalem Post*. June 20, 1998, p. 7.

Yousef, Ramzi (1964?–)

The precise background of Ramzi Ahmed Yousef is disputed. His birth name might have been Abdul Basit Karim. Yousef used numerous aliases during his career as a terrorist in an attempt to both confuse authorities and conceal his true identity. Yousef apparently grew up in Kuwait, though his actual nationality is also uncertain. He traveled with a false Iraqi passport and spent considerable time in Pakistan, where he has relatives and where he also received an education in bomb-making.

Yousef arrived in the United States in 1992. His traveling companion was arrested by customs authorities after bomb-making instructions were found in his luggage. Yousef was not detained, though he was asked to return in a few weeks. He did not and instead proceeded to get in touch with Sheikh Omar Abdel Rahman, a Muslim leader in Brooklyn, originally from Egypt, who eventually went to prison for conspiring to bomb New York City landmarks that included the Holland Tunnel.

By the end of 1992, Yousef and at least three associates were meticulously planning to bomb the World Trade Center. The bombing occurred on February 26, 1993. Even though six people were killed and over a thousand were injured, Yousef, who fled the United States only hours after the bombing, was disappointed. He had hoped to kill tens of thousands by causing one of the World Trade Center towers to collapse onto the other. Yousef maintained after his arrest that he had hoped to kill the equivalent of the number of Japanese who were destroyed in the atomic bombings of Hiroshima and Nagasaki, perhaps a total of a quarter of a million people. He considered this toll a fitting gesture of justice for what he considered to be a long record of American cruelty to Muslims and other peoples. Interestingly, during his flight back to the United States after his arrest in 1995 in Pakistan, Yousef got an opportunity to view the towers as his plane prepared to land in New York City. An FBI agent remarked that the towers were still standing, and Yousef responded that the next time would be more successful.

For the next two years, Yousef pursued terrorist objectives that included unsuccessful attempts to bomb the Israeli embassy in Bangkok, Thailand, and to plant bombs on United and Northwest airline flights leaving Bangkok. He was finally arrested on February 7, 1995, in Islamabad, Pakistan, after a Muslim he was trying to recruit informed on him. Yousef was turned over to American officials who transferred him to the United States for indictment and trial. He was convicted of "seditious conspiracy" to bomb the towers and sentenced to a maximum term of 240 years along with six other Islamic militants who were involved in the conspiracy.

Yousef's career as a terrorist is over, but he remains unrepentant. His only regret seems to be his lack of complete success. Yousef freely admitted his desire to destroy American and Israeli targets that would have involved great loss of life. In fact, loss of life was his primary objective. In this sense, he almost anticipated OSAMA BIN LADEN, whose strategy and tactics include causing great loss of life in order to impress the United States with his resolve. There is no evidence or admission that the two ever met or even communicated, though they did have common acquaintances.

Z

al-Zarqawi, Abu Musab (1966–2006)

Born October 30, 1966, in Zarqua, Jordan, Zarqawi was a part of a 28-member cult uncovered by Jordanian authorities in 1999 that had ties to AL-QAEDA and to its leader, OSAMA BIN LADEN. The cult planned an attack for the millennium celeberation in Jordan that included the bombing of the Radisson Hotel in Amman, Jordan's largest and capital city, as well as other American, Israeli, and Christian targets, but the plot was discovered before it could be carried out. Zarqawi was sentenced in abstentia to 15 years in prison, along with 11 others who also escaped capture, while six members were apprehended and sentenced to death.

Al-Zarqawi was also linked to ANSAR AL-ISLAM, the militant group with ties to al-Qaeda that operates in northern Iraq, as well as to al-Qaeda cells in the United Kingdom that apparently attempted to manufacture RICIN. Although Zarqawi ran a poison-training camp in 2000 in Afghanistan, specializing in chemical and biological weapons, the precise nature of his network's relationship to al-Qaeda remains unclear. Money appears to have changed hands between the two. Apparently, Zarqawi and bin Laden met several years ago and each took an immediate dislike to the other. For the most part, Zarqawi and his followers, who numbered only in the few hundreds, tended to operate independently within the world of Islamist terror. He maintained close ties with Iran (though he frequently murdered Shiite Muslims in Iraq) and with Qatari royalty as well as with the Chechen rebel movement.

In October 2001, Zarqawi fled to Iran with a wounded leg (reportedly shattered in the post-9/11 U.S./Northern Alliance campaigns). He then dispatched three members of his group (two Palestinians and a Jordanian) to Israel to conduct bombing attacks. By May 2002, he had traveled to Iraq, where he had his injured leg amputated and a prosthetic limb put in its place, spending time recovering in Baghdad and reestablishing his base of operations with nearly two dozen other extremists. Then U.S. Secretary of State Colin Powell, in detailing for the United Nations Security Council in February 2003, the concerns the United States had with Iraq's development of weapons of mass destruction, noted that Zarqawi had already developed a poison and explosive training center in northeastern Iraq. In fact, Zarqawi's movement into Iraq to seek medical treatment was cited as the basis of the U.S. administration linking SADDAM HUSSEIN's regime to terrorism in general and to al-Qaeda in particular.

Lawrence Foley, a U.S. official with the Agency for International Development was assassinated in Jordan on October 28, 2002. Zarqawi provided the murder weapon, a 7-mm pistol with a silencer, along with $18,000 to the man who carried out the assassination.

In January 2003, Zarqawi returned to the Ansar al-Islam camp in northern Iraq, where he was known for his work with various toxins prepared for use in Britain, France, Georgia, and CHECHNYA. Indeed, several individuals linked to Zarqawi were arrested in Britain for plotting to introduce ricin into the military food supply.

Zarqawi prepared an audio recording for Osama bin Laden in January 2004. The message was divided into three parts. The first, which was about 30 minutes long, was devoted to Koranic verses and hadiths extolling jihad and martyrdom. In the second part, he talked about his friend, Abd al-Hadi Daghlas, whom he regarded as a martyr since he was killed by American forces in Iraq at the beginning of the war. This part also began with accusations of Muslim clerics who "abandoned" mujahideen as they confronted "the strongest power in the world." This continued to be his primary theme in the third part of the message, as he strongly chastised Muslim clerics who were silent as "hundreds of thousands of Muslims were slaughtered by the infidels." In March 2004, Zarqawi was indirectly linked to the bombings of the MADRID commuter trains. Jordanian authorities arrested a number of suspected person plotting attacks for April using chemical weapons and explosives. This plot involved an elaborate scheme in which funding, weapons, and detailed instructions for the group came from Zarqawi, who remained a Jordanian citizen (and a fugitive) while living in Iraq. In June of the same year, Zarqawi murdered Nicholas Berg, an American civilian hostage. Berg was beheaded, and the murder was taped for a later video webcast, setting a new threshold for the MEDIA SHOWCASING of terrorism.

Abu Musab al-Zarqawi (PETRA/EPA/CORBIS)

After the Iraqi insurgency got underway during the spring of 2003, Zarqawi quickly surfaced as a top leader. His group kidnapped and murdered several, mostly civilian, workers and contractors, Westerners, as well as East Asians. While a variety of groups launched or later participated in the insurgency, Zarqawi and his group became the most notorious and were held responsible for large numbers of suicide bombings and beheadings. Zarqawi became the most-wanted terrorist in Iraq. Apparently, American and allied forces came close on several occasions to finding him. He was, however, able to slip away before being captured or killed. Zarqawi often traveled with groups of women and children to minimize suspicion and apparently moved through military checkpoints that way without difficulty. He met with some success in his efforts to lure foreign jihadists into Iraq to fight as his allies.

Zarqawi hated Americans, but most of his victims were Iraqis. His network of terror targeted Shiite Muslims whom he believed to be apostates and unIslamic. His murderous activities did not spare women or children who were Shiites or even Sunnis who cooperated with the United States and its allies. Zarqawi's goal was the exact opposite of what the United States desired: He focused on initiating and sustaining a civil war between Sunnis and Shiites.

On June 14, 2006, after months of near misses, Zarqawi was located and killed. Ironically, his safe house had been revealed to U.S. military intelligence by al-Qaeda informants who probably had their own reasons for betraying him. His methods had become too radical even for al-Qaeda. The location was a farmhouse near Baqubah, a small town about 30 miles north of Baghdad. A small surveillance team hid in a nearby grove and watched the house for any sign of movement while two U.S. Air Force F-16s were ordered away from a previous assignment to launch two precision-guided 500-pound bombs on the target. The result was the complete destruction of the farmhouse and the death of its seven occupants, who were apparently just sitting down to dinner several minutes after six in the evening. Zarqawi's dining companions included Sheik Abdul-Rahman, his spiritual adviser; two other men, probably bodyguards; and three women, including his 16-year-old wife.

When American and Iraqi operatives made their way to the rubble that had been the farmhouse, they were surprised to find Zarqawi terribly injured but still alive. He was placed on a stretcher, from which he made a weak attempt to escape. He died of his injuries several minutes later. It should be noted that, while there was brief celebration that Zarqawi's career of murder had been stopped, the killing that he had encouraged and practiced continued. If anything, the situation in Iraq became worse. By the middle of summer 2006, as many as 100 Iraqis each day were losing their lives in what had become for the most part a sectarian conflict between Sunni and Shiite Muslims.

Reference: BBC News. Middle East. "Obituary: Abu Musab al-Zarqawi." June 8, 2006. Available online. URL: http://news.bbc.co.uk/2/hi/middle_east/5058262.stm. Accessed August 25, 2006.

Zionism

A political movement with religious undertones that was established in its modern manifestation during the last years of the 19th century and early years of the 20th. The goal was to establish a homeland or state for Jews to remove them from the discrimination and persecution that was in ample evidence in Europe. Theodore Herzl (1860–1904) was the motivating force of the early Zionist movement. He and his colleagues created the World Zionist Organization, visited PALESTINE, then an impoverished province of the Ottoman Empire, and organized the first Jewish settlements.

Zionism's goal was achieved in 1948 with Israeli statehood. However, several trends in Zionism are still in ample evidence. Herzl's plan was to create a Jewish commonwealth. As a secular Jew, he gave little consideration to the religious component that would naturally be associated with his mission. The most orthodox members of the Jewish community believed that only with the coming of the Messiah could the Israeli polity be restored. A small residue of this school of thought still refuses to recognize modern Israel's legitimacy.

Others do not believe that the work of Zionism will be completed until most, if not all, Jews have returned to Israel. Most religious Jews accept Israel's legitimacy, but they and many secular allies argue that the goal of returning to the ancient homesite of Israel, much of which is in the West Bank, must be pursued. To help guarantee that it will be attained, tens of thousands of religious Jews have moved there. This goal has made negotiations by the Israeli government with the Palestinians very difficult.

Reference: Laqueur, Walter. *A History of Zionism* (New York: Holt, Rinehart, and Winston, 1972) is probably the best introduction to this complicated and enduring subject.

APPENDIX

Incidents of Terrorism Worldwide, 2005

Incidents of terrorism worldwide	11,111
Incidents resulting in death, injury, or kidnapping of at least one individual	8,016
Incidents resulting in the death of at least one individual	5,131
Incidents resulting in the death of zero individuals	5,980
Incidents resulting in the death of only one individual	2,884
Incidents resulting in the death of at least 10 individuals	226
Incidents resulting in the injury of at least one individual	3,827
Incidents resulting in the kidnapping of at least one individual	1,145

**All cases limited to incidents targeting noncombatants.*

Individuals worldwide killed, injured or kidnapped as a result of incidents of terrorism	74,087
Individuals worldwide killed as a result of incidents of terrorism	14,602
Individuals worldwide injured as a result of incidents of terrorism	24,705
Individuals worldwide kidnapped as a result of incidents of terrorism	34,780

**All cases limited to incidents targeting noncombatants.*

Incidents of Terrorism in Iraq and Afghanistan, 2005*

Incidents of terrorism in Iraq	3,474
Incidents in Iraq resulting in death, injury, or kidnapping of at least one individual	2,839
Individuals in Iraq killed, injured, or kidnapped as a result of incidents of terrorism	20,711

**All cases limited to incidents targeting noncombatants.*

Incidents of terrorism in Afghanistan	489
Incidents in Afghanistan resulting in death, injury, or kidnapping of at least one individual	365
Individuals in Afghanistan killed, injured, or kidnapped as a result of incidents of terrorism	1,533

**All cases limited to incidents targeting noncombatants.*

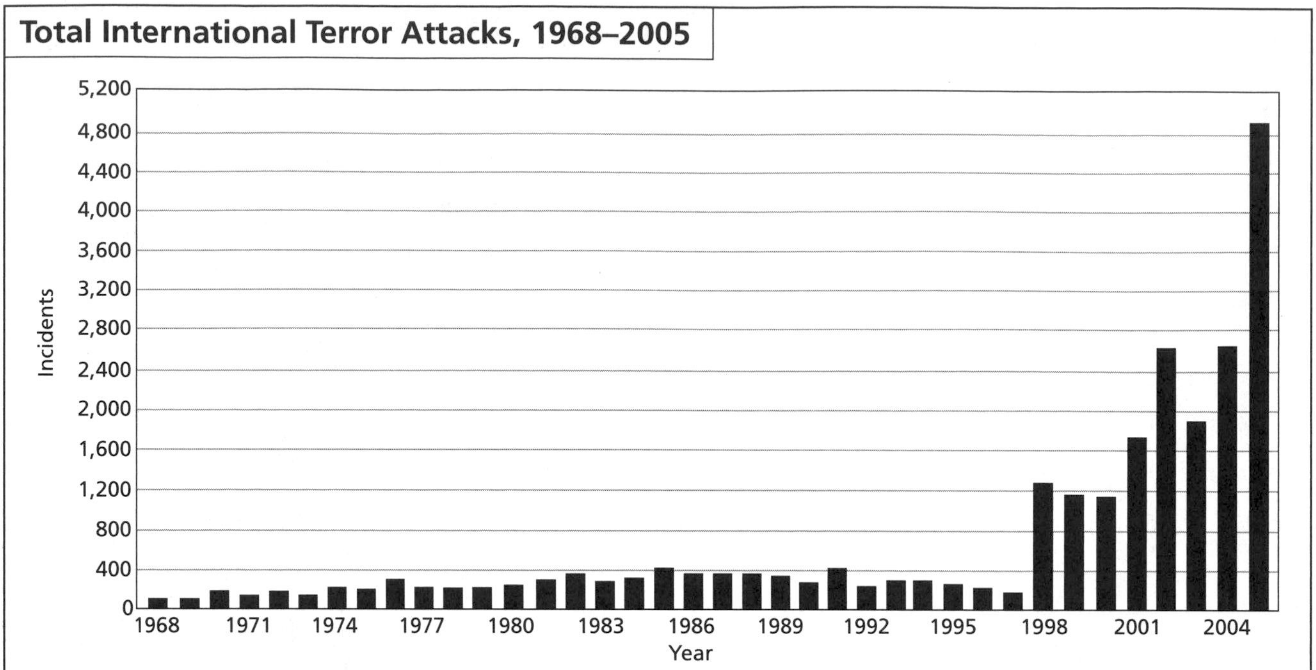

Note: Data for 1968–1997 cover only international incidents.
Data for 1998–Present cover both domestic and international incidents.

Total International Attacks by Region, 1968–2005

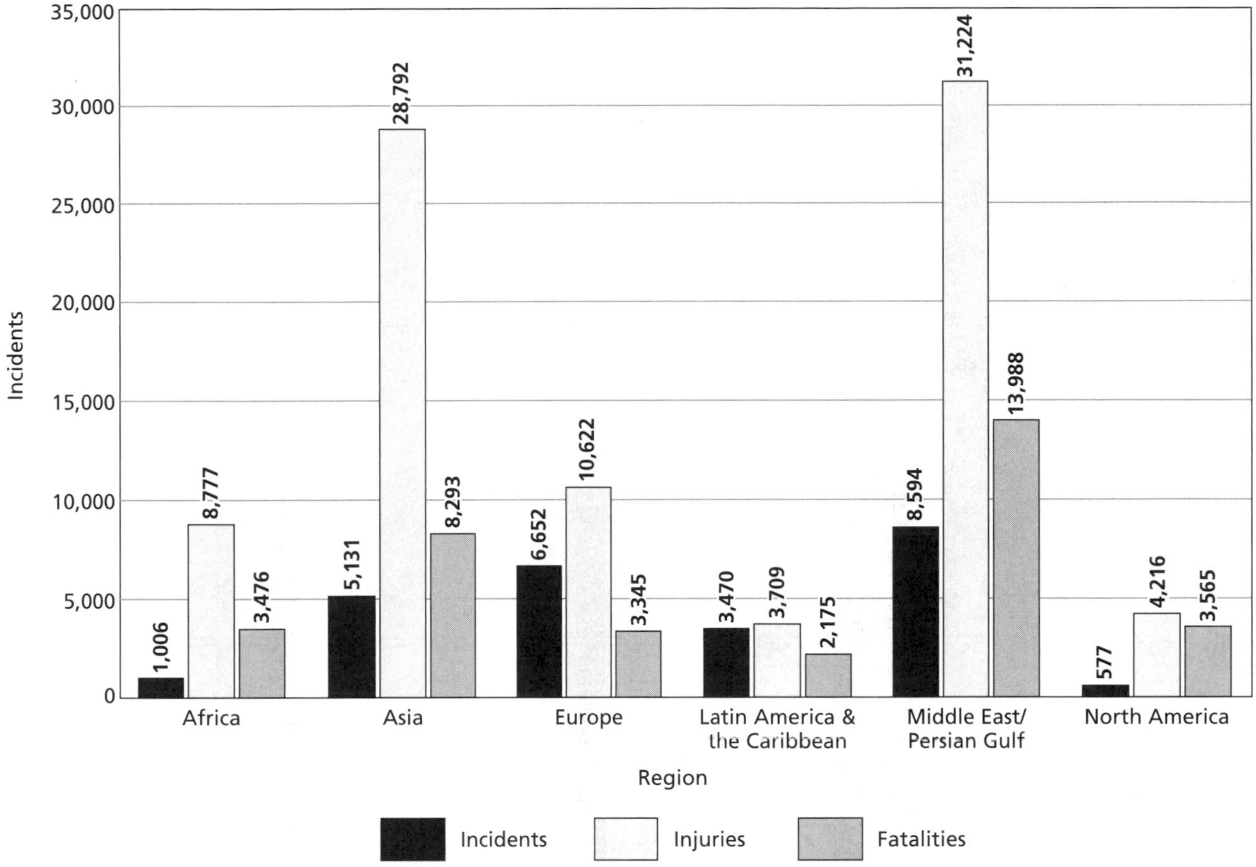

Note: Data for 1968–1997 cover only international incidents.
Data for 1998–Present cover both domestic and international incidents.

Total International Attacks by Group, 1968–2005

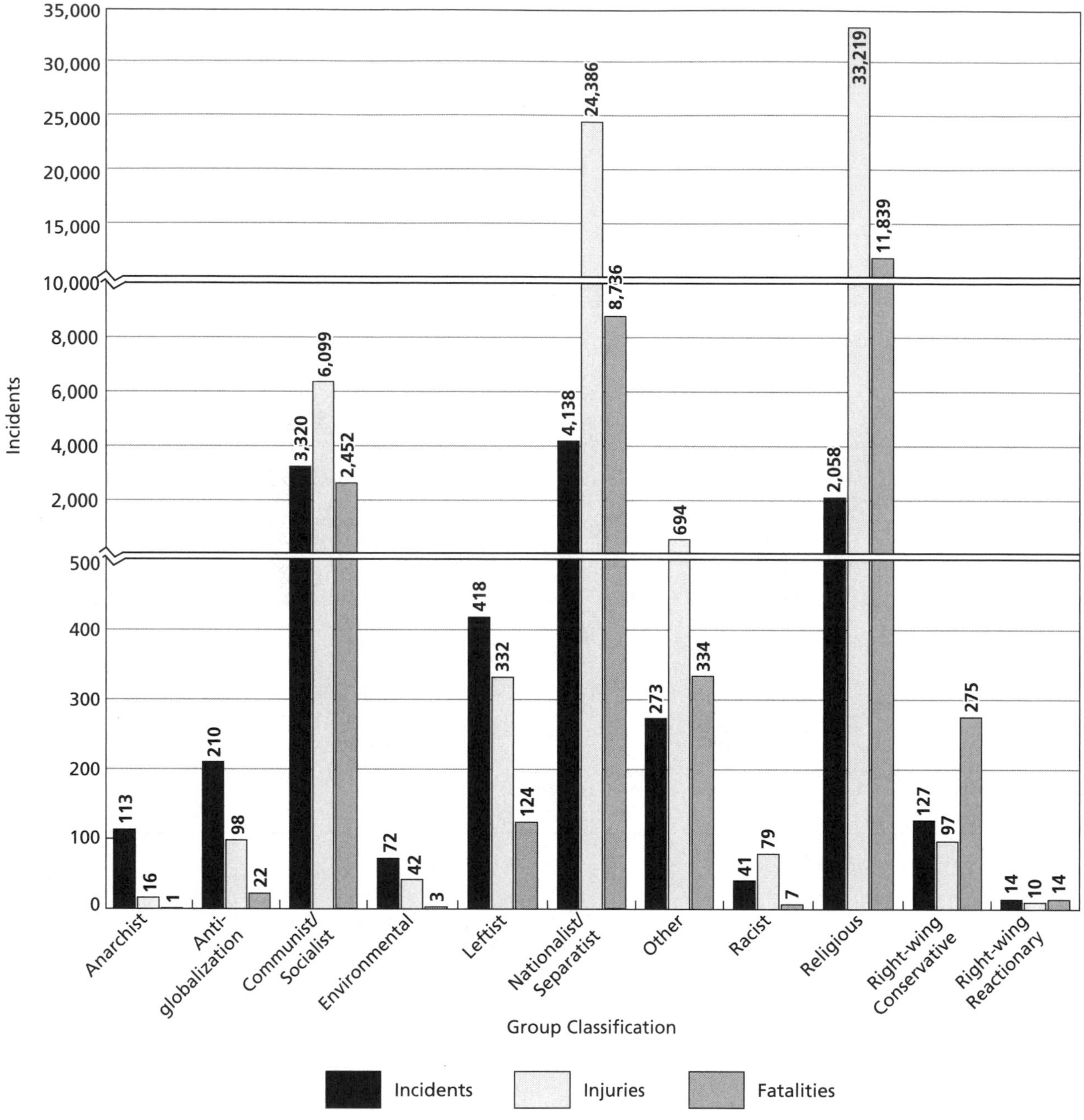

Note: Data for 1968–1997 cover only international incidents.
Data for 1998–Present cover both domestic and international incidents.

Total Facilities Struck by International Attacks, 1968–2005

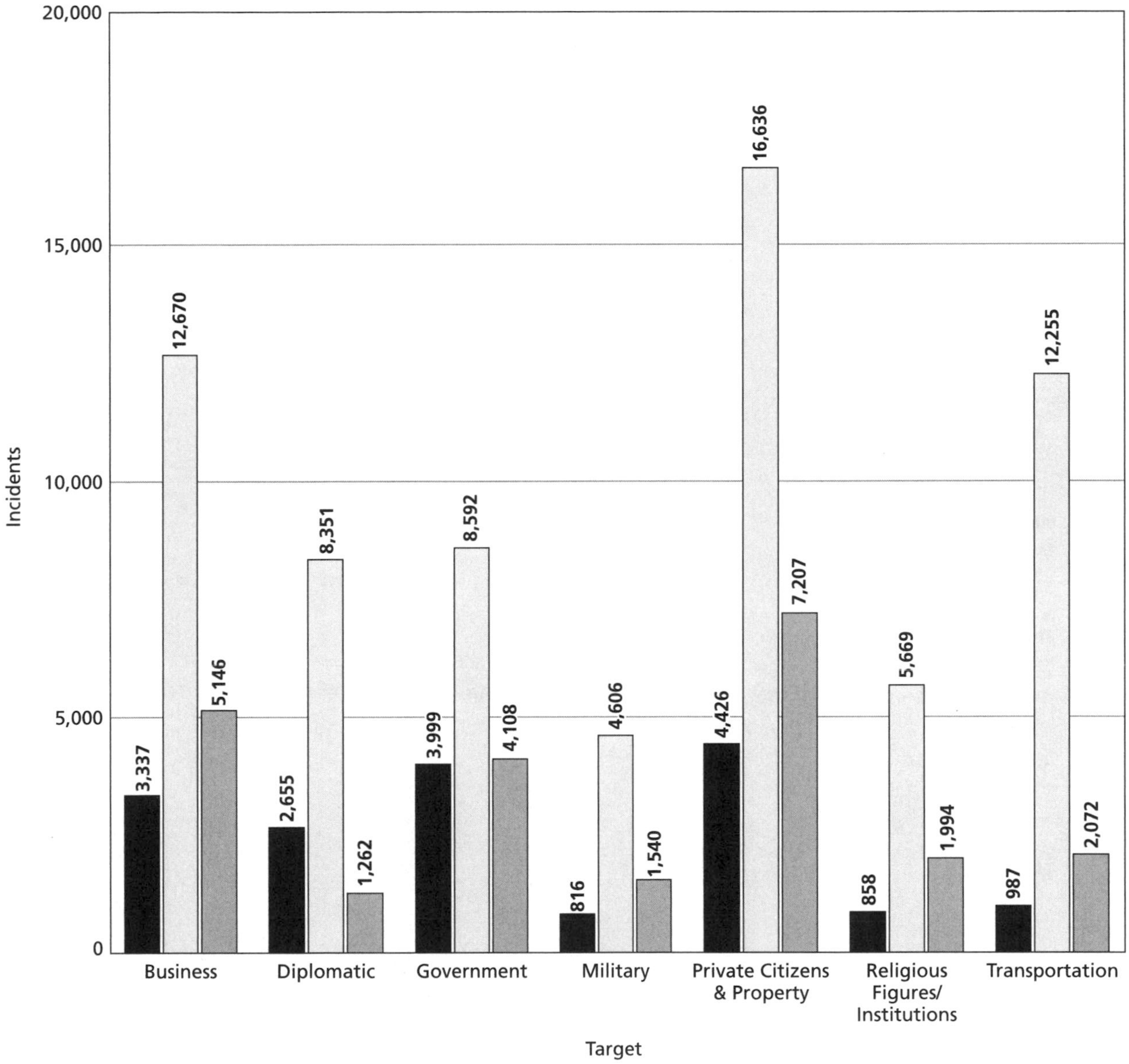

Note: Data for 1968–1997 cover only international incidents.
Data for 1998–Present cover both domestic and international incidents.

MAJOR ACTS OF TERRORISM 1946–2006

Author's Note: No time line on terrorism can be truly comprehensive. Instead, it represents information currently available, and we anticipate that the chronology will be updated as more data on terrorism emerges. Because terrorism is a continually occurring phenomenon and the description of what constitutes this phenomenon is still in flux in the international community, the revisions of the future will necessarily reflect both new events and revised assessments of past actions by individuals, groups, and states.

1946

January 7
Germany: Nazi sympathizers murder two U.S. occupation officials in Passau, in the U.S. Zone.

July 22
Palestine: A bomb explodes in the King David Hotel in Jerusalem, killing 91 people. Responsibility is claimed by the Irgun Zvai Leumi (Irgun), the Jewish terrorist organization led by Menachem Begin.

1947

February 10
Italy: British General R. W. M. De Winten is shot to death by an Italian nationalist over the loss of Italian territory to Yugoslavia in the postwar settlement.

July 30
Palestine: Jewish terrorists kill two British soldiers, one of many similair incidents in an attempt to pressure the British government to turn Palestine over to the Jewish settlers.

December 25
Sweden: Alberto Bellardi Ricci, an Italian diplomat, is attacked and killed by an Italian Fascist.

1948

January 30
India: Mohandas K. Gandhi, the Indian nationalist, is assassinated by a Hindu militant.

April 9
Palestine: At the Arab village of Deir Yasin, the Jewish terrorist organizations Lehi and Irgun kill more than 200 Arab men, women, and children.

September 17
Israel: Count Folke Bernadotte of Sweden, acting as United Nations mediator between Israel and the Arabs, and French colonel Andre Serot are killed by the Stern Gang.

December 28
Egypt: Prime Minister of Egypt Mahmoud Fahmy el-Nokrashy Pasha is assassinated by a member of the Muslim Brotherhood.

1949

February 13
Egypt: Sheikh Hassan Albanna, leader of the Muslim Brotherhood, is assassinated in Cairo.

December 3
Malaysia: Ducan Stewart, British colonial governor of Malaysia, is attacked and mortally wounded by Malay nationalists.

1950

November 1
United States: Puerto Rican nationalists fail in an attempt to assassinate President Harry S. Truman.

1951

March 30
Philippines: John Hardie, a U.S. citizen, and his wife are murdered at their farm outside Manila by the Huks.

July 20
Trans-Jordan: King Abdullah I of Jordan is shot and killed by a Palestinian gunman.

October 25
Philippines: The Huks kill two Americans near Olongapo.

1952

December 5
Tunisia: Red Hand, a pro-French terrorist group in North Africa, assassinates Farhat Hached, a leader of the Tunisian Labor Federation.

1954

March 1
United States: Four Puerto Rican nationalists open fire on members of the U.S. House of Representatives. Five representatives are wounded in the attack, and all the terrorists are later apprehended.

1955

August 20
Algeria: Known as the "Philippeville Massacre," the FLN (Algerian National Liberation Front) murder 37 men, women, and children.

1956

March 15
Algeria: The Secret Army Organization (OAS) executes six men.

October 21–22
Algeria: FLN assassins murder 49 people over a two-day period.

1958

November 28
Cyprus: Two British soldiers are killed by Cypriot nationalists outside a nightclub in Nicosia.

1960

March 20
South Africa: Police open fire on civil rights demonstrators in what becomes known as the "Sharpeville Massacre." Sixty-nine demonstrators are killed.

October 8
Algeria: One person is killed and 16 are injured (including five French soldiers) when an FLN terrorist throws a hand grenade into a café.

1962

January 25
France: The homes of 14 well-known French citizens are bombed by the OAS. There are no casualties.

1963

November 27
Venezuela: A U.S. military attachi is kidnapped by FALN (Armed Forces for National Liberation) terrorists, demanding that 70 political prisoners be released as ransom. The government releases the prisoners, and the attaché is returned.

1964

September 10
Uruguay: The Tupamaros bomb the home of the Brazilian ambassador.

1965

May 6
Uruguay: The offices of two American businesses are bombed by the Tupamaros.

1967

February 27
Ethiopia: The Eritrean Liberation Front attacks and severely damages the Mobile petroleum plant in Aseb.

1968

July 23
Air Piracy: An Israeli El Al Boeing 707, en route from Rome to Tel Aviv, is hijacked over Italy by three members of the Popular Front for the Liberation of Palestine (PFLP) and forced to fly to Algiers. The Algerian government releases the hostages in groups, the last on August 31, and lets the plane go on September 1.

August 28
Guatemala: John G. Mein, U.S. ambassador to Guatemala, is killed by gunmen in Guatemala City.

October 12
Brazil: Captain Charles R. Chandler of the U.S. Army is killed by two gunmen as he leaves his home in Sao Paulo.

November 22
Israel: A car bomb explosion in the Jewish sector of Jerusalem kills 12.

December 26
Greece: Two Palestinians attack an Israeli El Al Boeing 707 at Athens airport with grenades and small arms, killing one passenger.

December 28
Lebanon: Israeli commandos take over Beirut airport and destroy 13 civilian aircraft belonging to three Arab airlines.

1969

February 18
Switzerland: Four Arab gunmen attack an Israeli El Al Boeing 720 at Zurich airport, injuring six passengers and crew.

July 18
Great Britain: Bombs planted by Palestinians explode in the Marks and Spencer store in London.

August 29
Air Piracy: A U.S. Trans World Airlines Boeing 707, en route from Rome to Athens and Tel Aviv, is hijacked by two PFLP terrorists and forced to fly to Damascus. The plane is destroyed by a bomb after landing. Two Israeli passengers held as hostages are exchanged on December 5 for 13 Syrian prisoners in Israel.

September 4
Brazil: U.S. ambassador to Brazil, Charles Elbrick, is kidnapped in Rio de Janeiro. He is released after 15 prisoners are released and flown out to Mexico.

December 12
Italy: A bomb explosion in the National Bank of Agriculture in Milan kills 16 and injures 90.

1970

February 10
West Germany: A grenade attack by three Arabs on a bus at Munich airport kills one Israeli and wounds 11 others.

March 31
Guatemala: Count Karl von Spreti, West German ambassador to Guatemala, is kidnapped in Guatemala City and later found dead on April 5.

May 29
Argentina: Lieutenant General Pedro Aramburu, a former provisional president of Argentina, is kidnapped from his home by four men and found shot on July 16.

July 31
Uruguay: Two diplomats are kidnapped by Tupamaros guerrillas in Montevideo. Dan Mitrione of the U.S. Agency for International Development is found shot on August 10. Aloysio Gomide, Brazilian vice consul, is released on February 21, 1971, after a ransom is paid by his family.

September 6
Air Piracy: PFLP terrorists seize three planes en route to New York—a Swissair DC-8 from Zurich, a TWA Boeing 707 from Frankfurt, and a Pan American World Airways 747 from Amsterdam. An attempt to seize a fourth plane, an El Al Boeing 707, fails when a hijacker is shot dead by security guards. The Swissair and TWA planes are flown to Dawson's Field in the Jordanian desert. The Pan Am plane is flown to Beirut and then on to Cairo, where it is evacuated and blown up. A further plane, a BOAC VC10, en route from Bombay to London, is hijacked on September 9 and flown to Dawson's Field. The three planes are destroyed on September 12. The hostages are freed during the remainder of September as part of a deal for the release of Arab terrorists held in Europe.

October 5
Canada: James Cross, a British diplomat, is kidnapped by French-Canadian separatists in Montreal. He is released on December 3, 1970, in return for safe passage to Cuba for hijackers.

October 10
Canada: Pierre Laporte, Quebec labor minister, is seized by separatists in Montreal and found dead on October 18.

December 1
Spain: Eugen Beihl, West German honorary consul, is kidnapped from his home in San Sebastian by Basque nationalists. He is released on December 25 on condition that death sentences on six Basques on trial at Burgos be commuted to imprisonment.

1971

January 8

Uruguay: Geoffrey Jackson, the British ambassador, is kidnapped by Tupamaros guerrillas in Montevideo. He is released on September 9, three days after the escape of 106 Tupamaros from prison.

March 14

Netherlands: Fuel tanks in Rotterdam are blown up by Palestinians and their French sympathizers.

April 7

Sweden: Viadunir Rolovic, Yugoslav ambassador to Sweden, is shot in Stockholm by two Croatians and dies on April 15.

May 17

Turkey: Ephraim Elrom, Israeli consul-general in Istanbul, is kidnapped by the Turkish People's Liberation Army and found dead on May 23.

July 27

France: A Palestinian bomb attack occurs at the Jordanian embassy in Paris.

August 21

Philippines: Ten are killed and 74 are wounded by terrorist grenades at a preelection rally of the opposition Liberal Party in Manila.

November 28

Egypt: Wasif Tell, Jordanian prime minister, is assassinated in Cairo by Black September guerrillas.

December 15

Great Britain: Zaid Rifai, Jordanian ambassador in London, is wounded when shots are fired at his car by Black September guerrillas.

December 16

Switzerland: A parcel bomb attempt on the life of Ibrahim Zreikat, Jordanian ambassador to Switzerland, injures two policemen in Geneva.

1972

February 6

Netherlands: Two gas-processing plants in Rotterdam are blown up by Black September guerrillas.

February 8

West Germany: A factory making electric generators for Israeli aircraft is damaged in Hamburg.

February 21

Air Piracy: A West German Lufthansa jumbo jet en route from New Delhi to Athens is hijacked by five PFLP terrorists and diverted to Aden. The passengers are released, and the 16 crew are freed on February 23 when the West Germans pay a $5 million ransom.

February 22

Great Britain: A Provisional IRA bomb attack on the Officers' Mess of the Parachute Regiment in Aldershot kills seven.

March 18

Canada: A bomb explosion in a supermarket in Toronto kills two.

March 21

Argentina: Oberdan Sallustro, Fiat executive president in Argentina, is kidnapped in Buenos Aires by Ejército Revolucionario Popular (ERP) and shot dead on April 10 as police surround the kidnappers' hideout.

March 27

Turkey: One Canadian and two British NATO radar technicians are kidnapped in Ankara by the Turkish People's Liberation Army and murdered when police discover the kidnappers' hideout. Ten terrorists are killed by police.

May 8

Air Piracy: A Belgian Sabena Airlines plane en route from Vienna to Tel Aviv is hijacked by four Black September terrorists and diverted to Lod airport, Tel Aviv. Israeli paratroopers disguised as mechanics enter the plane, shoot dead two hijackers, and wound a third on May 9.

May 11
West Germany: Bombs explode at headquarters of the Fifth U.S. Army Corps in Frankfurt, killing Colonel Paul Bloomquist and wounding 13 others.

May 31
Israel: Three Japanese Red Army terrorists attack passengers at Lod airport near Tel Aviv, killing 26 and wounding 76 others.

July 8
Lebanon: Ghassan Kanafani, a leader of the PFLP, is killed, together with his niece, by a car bomb in Beirut.

July 21
Northern Ireland: Nine are killed in Belfast in a coordinated series of at least 20 bombings by the Provisional IRA.

September 5
West Germany: Black September terrorists seize the Israeli quarters in the Olympic Games village in Munich. Two Israeli athletes are killed initially, and a further nine hostages, five terrorists, and a policeman die in a shoot-out at the airport.

September 19
Great Britain: Dr. Arni Shachori, counselor for agricultural affairs at the Israeli embassy in London, is killed by a letter bomb sent from Amsterdam by Black September.

October 29
Air Piracy: A Lufthansa Boeing 727 en route from Beirut to Ankara is hijacked by two Black September terrorists and forced to fly to Munich. Without landing, it returns to Zagreb in Yugoslavia and circles the airport until a smaller plane carrying three Arabs held for the Munich massacre arrives. The three terrorists then board the hijacked aircraft and fly to Tripoli in Libya.

December 8
France: Mahmoud Hamshari, PLO representative in Paris, is killed by an electronically triggered bomb attached to his phone by Israeli agents.

1973

March 1
Egypt: The Saudi Arabian embassy in Khartoum, Sudan, is seized by Black September during a party for an American, George C. Moore. The Belgian chargé d'affaires, Guy Eid; the U.S. ambassador, Cleo Noel; and Moore are killed.

March 8
Great Britain: Car bombs in London outside the Old Bailey and the Army Recruiting Office off Trafalgar Square kill one person and injure some 200 others.

April 15
Lebanon: Israeli commandos attack the homes of Palestinian guerrillas in Beirut, killing 17.

May 17
Italy: Four are killed and more than 40 are injured in a grenade explosion at the entrance to police headquarters in Milan.

June 28
France: Mohammed Boudia, an infamous Arab terrorist, is killed by a car bomb planted in his car in Paris.

July 1
United States: Colonel Yosef Alon, Israeli military attaché in Washington, is shot dead outside his home.

July 20
Air Piracy: A Japan Air Lines 747, en route from Amsterdam to Tokyo, is hijacked by three PFLP and one Japanese Red Army terrorists. A female hijacker accidentally kills herself with a grenade. The plane lands at Dubai and is then flown to Benghazi, Libya, on July 24. The plane is evacuated and then blown up.

August 5
Greece: At Athens, Palestinians kill five and wound more than 50 in a machine-gun and grenade attack on passengers disembarked from a TWA flight from Tel Aviv.

September 28

Austria: Palestinian guerrillas seize three Soviet Jewish emigrants on a Moscow-Vienna train, releasing them when Austrian chancellor Bruno Kreisky agrees to close facilities for emigrants awaiting transfer to Israel at Schonau Castle.

November 22

Argentina: John A. Swint, general manager of a subsidiary of Ford Motor, Argentina, is killed with two bodyguards in Córdoba by terrorists of the Peronist Armed Forces.

December 6

Argentina: Victor Samuelson, an American manager with Esso, Argentina, is kidnapped in Buenos Aires by the ERP. He is released on April 29, 1974, after payment of a $14.2 million ransom.

December 17

Italy: Five Palestinians, members of Arab Nationalist Youth Organization for the Liberation of Palestine, murder 33 Pan Am passengers as their plane sits on the ground at Rome's Leonardo da Vinci Airport. The terrorists then hijack a Lufthansa jet to Kuwait, where they surrender and are turned over to the PLO.

December 18

Great Britain: Two IRA car bombs and a parcel bomb injure some 60 people in London.

December 20

Spain: Spanish premier Luis Carrero Blanco is killed when Basque terrorists explode a bomb beneath his car in Madrid.

December 31

Great Britain: Edward Sieff, president of Marks and Spencer, survives an assassination attempt at his home in London by Carlos, the Venezuelan terrorist.

1974

February 3

Great Britain: An IRA suitcase bomb hidden in the luggage department of a bus traveling through Yorkshire with soldiers and their families kills 11 and wounds 14.

February 5

United States: Patty Hearst, 19-year-old granddaughter of newspaper magnate William Randolph Hearst, is kidnapped in Berkeley, California, by members of the Symbionese Liberation Army (SLA), who demand that her father provide millions of dollars to feed the poor. On April 3, the kidnappers release a tape in which Patty announces she has joined the SLA. She is finally arrested in San Francisco on September 18, 1975, after allegedly taking part in a bank robbery and other operations. Although claiming she had acted under duress, she is sentenced to two years' imprisonment.

April 11

Israel: Three Arab guerrillas enter the town of Kiryat Shmona and kill 18 people in an apartment block. The terrorists are killed when explosives they are carrying are set off.

May 15

Israel: Three Palestinian commandos attack the village of Maalot, killing 25 people, mainly students. Israeli jets attack targets in southern Lebanon in retaliation the following day.

May 17

Ireland: Car bombs explode in Dublin and Monaghan, killing 30 and injuring some 200 others.

May 28

Italy: A bomb explosion at an antifascist rally in Brescia kills seven and injures 93.

June 13

Israel: Three women are killed in a Palestinian raid on Shamir, a northern Israeli kibbutz.

June 17

Great Britain: The Provisional Irish Republican Army bombs the Houses of Parliament, causing extensive damage and injuring 11 people.

June 24

Israel: Three people are killed in a Palestinian guerrilla attack on the town of Nahariya, near the Lebanese border.

July 15

Argentina: Arturo Roig, former interior minister of Argentina, is shot dead in Buenos Aires.

July 17

Great Britain: An IRA bomb explosion in the armory of the Tower of London kills one tourist and injures 36.

August 4

Italy: A bomb planted by an Italian neofascist group, the Black Order, on a Rome-Munich train explodes between Florence and Bologna, killing 12 people.

August 30

Japan: A bomb explosion in front of the Mitsubishi Heavy Industries building in Tokyo kills eight and wounds more than 300.

September 13

Netherlands: Three Japanese Red Army terrorists seize 11 hostages at the French embassy in The Hague. They secure the release of a comrade, Yukata Furuya, from a French prison, and the four are flown to Damascus, Syria.

November 19

Israel: Four are killed in a guerrilla raid on an apartment building in the northern town of Bein Shean, near the Jordanian border.

1975

January 24

United States: Puerto Rican nationalists bomb a Wall Street bar, killing four and injuring 60 people.

February 26

Argentina: John P. Egan, U.S. honorary consul in Córdoba, is kidnapped by Montoneros guerrillas and murdered when the government refuses to negotiate for his release.

February 27

West Germany: Peter Lorenz, chairman of the West Berlin Christian Democratic Union, is kidnapped. He is set free on March 4 when the government releases five Baader-Meinhof terrorists.

March 5

Israel: Eight Palestinian guerrillas attack a shorefront hotel in Tel Aviv, killing 11.

April 24

Sweden: Six Red Army Faction members occupy the West German embassy in Stockholm and demand the release of 26 Baader-Meinhof terrorists. They blow up the embassy as police prepare to attack, then surrender.

July 4

Israel: A Palestinian bomb explodes in Zion Square, Jerusalem, killing 14 and wounding some 80 others.

August 4

Malaysia: Five Japanese Red Army guerrillas attack the American and Swedish embassies in Kuala Lumpur. The terrorists and four hostages are flown to Libya.

September 5

Great Britain: Two are killed and 63 injured by an IRA bomb at the London Hilton Hotel.

October 3

Ireland: Tiede Herrema, a Dutch industrialist, is kidnapped in Limerick in an attempt to secure the release of three IRA prisoners. He is freed on November 7 when police surround the kidnappers' hideout at Monastervin.

October 22

Austria: Danis Tunaligil, Turkish ambassador, is shot dead at his embassy in Vienna by three terrorists.

October 24

France: Ismail Frez, Turkish ambassador in Paris, and his chauffeur are killed by two gunmen.

November 13

Israel: Six are killed and 42 wounded by a bomb blast near Zion Square, Jerusalem.

November 27

Great Britain: Ross McWhirter, editor of the *Guinness Book of Records,* is shot dead by the IRA at his north London home after he establishes a reward fund for information leading to the arrest of terrorists.

December 2

Netherlands: South Moluccan terrorists (Free South Moluccan Youth Movement) demanding independence from Indonesia for their homeland seize a train near Beilin in the Netherlands, killing two people and holding 23 hostages. The six terrorists surrender on December 14.

December 4

Netherlands: South Moluccans seize the Indonesian consulate in Amsterdam. One hostage is killed, but terrorists surrender on December 19.

December 12

Great Britain: Four IRA gunmen surrender after a six-day siege in an apartment on Balcombe Street in central London.

December 21

Austria: The headquarters of OPEC in Vienna is seized by Palestinian and Baader-Meinhof terrorists led by Carlos, the Venezuelan terrorist chief.

December 23

Greece: Richard S. Welch, CIA station chief, is murdered in Athens.

December 29

United States: Eleven people are killed and 70 injured when a bomb explodes in a baggage-claim area at LaGuardia Airport, New York.

1976

January 4

Northern Ireland: Five Catholics are murdered in Belfast.

January 5

Northern Ireland: Ten Protestant workmen are shot dead by the IRA in Belfast.

June 16

Lebanon: Francis E. Meloy, U.S. ambassador to Lebanon, and Robert O. Waring, his economic adviser, are kidnapped and killed, along with their Lebanese driver, in Beirut.

June 27

Air Piracy: Palestinian and Baader-Meinhof terrorists hijack an Air France A3OOB airbus en route from Tel Aviv to Paris shortly after it leaves Athens. The terrorists force the plane to fly to Entebbe in Uganda, where they demand the release of 53 prisoners from jails in Israel, Kenya, West Germany, Switzerland, and France. On July 3, some 200 Israeli commandos, transported in three Cl 30 Hercules aircraft, make a surprise assault on Entebbe and rescue the hostages.

July 21

Ireland: Christopher Ewart-Biggs, British ambassador in Ireland, and his secretary, Judith Cooke, are killed by an IRA land mine as he is driving near his home in Dublin.

August 11

Turkey: Two Palestinian terrorists kill four and wound more than 30 passengers waiting to board an El Al plane at Yesilkoy airport, Istanbul.

August 20

Argentina: Forty-seven people are killed by right-wing death squads in two suburbs of Buenos Aires.

October 28

Northern Ireland: Maire Drumm, former vice president of the Provisional Sinn Féin, is shot dead in a Belfast hospital, while recuperating from cataract treatment, by members of the Ulster Volunteer Force, a Protestant paramilitary group.

November 17

Jordan: Four Palestinians attack the Intercontinental Hotel in Amman but are overrun by Jordanian troops. Three terrorists and five others are killed.

1977

April 7

West Germany: Siegfried Buback, chief federal prosecutor, and his driver and bodyguard are shot dead in a car in Karlsruhe by Baader-Meinhof terrorists.

April 10

Great Britain: Palestinian terrorists assassinate the former Yemeni prime minister Abdullah al-Hejiri, his wife, and the minister at the Yemeni embassy in London.

May 23

Netherlands: South Moluccans seize a train at Assen and a school at Bovinsmilde. The siege at the school ends on May 27. Two hostages and six terrorists are killed in an army attempt to rescue train hostages on June 11.

July 30

West Germany: Jurgen Ponto, chairman of the Dresdner Bank, is shot and killed at his home near Frankfurt.

September 5

West Germany: Hans-Martin Schleyer, president of the Federation of Industry, is kidnapped in Cologne by terrorists who kill his driver and three of his police guards. The kidnappers demand the release of 11 left-wing terrorists. Schleyer's body is found in the trunk of a car in Mulhouse, France, on October 19.

September 28

Air Piracy: A Japan Air Lines DC-8 en route from Paris to Tokyo is hijacked by five Japanese Red Army terrorists off Bombay and forced to land at Dacca in Bangladesh. The aircraft is eventually flown to Algiers after stops at Kuwait and Damascus. The passengers are then set free in return for the release of six prisoners in Japan and a ransom of $6 million.

October 11

Yemen: Colonel Ibrahim al-Hamdi, president of Yemen, and his brother, Abdullah Mohammed al-Hamdi, are assassinated in San'a.

October 13

Air Piracy: A Lufthansa Boeing 737 en route from Majorca to Frankfurt is hijacked by four Arab terrorists, who take the aircraft to Rome, Cyprus, Babrain, Dubai, and Aden, where they shoot dead the pilot, Jurgen Schumann. Finally, the plane lands at Mogadishu in Somalia, where it is stormed by German commandos on October 17. Three terrorists are killed, and 86 passengers are released.

December 7

Egypt: David Holden, Middle East expert of the *Sunday Times* (London), is murdered in Cairo.

1978

January 4

Great Britain: Said Hammami, representative of the PLO in London, is shot dead in his office by Palestinians opposed to Yasir Arafat's policy of negotiating with Israel.

February 14

Israel: Two are killed and 35 wounded when a bomb explodes on a crowded bus in Jerusalem.

February 17

Northern Ireland: Twelve are killed and 30 injured in an IRA firebomb explosion at the Le Mon House restaurant in Belfast.

February 18

Cyprus: Two Palestinian gunmen murder Yusuf el-Sebai, editor of Cairo's daily newspaper, *Al Ahram,* and seize 30 hostages at the Hilton Hotel in Nicosia. Terrorists fly out in a Cyprus Airways plane but are refused landing rights elsewhere and return to Larnaca airport. Egyptian troops attempt to seize terrorists on February 19, but 15 of the 74 commandos die in a gun battle with the Cyprus National Guard and PLO.

March 10
Italy: Judge Rosano Berardi is murdered by Red Brigades in Rome.

March 11
Israel: Palestinian terrorists kill 35 people on a bus traveling between Haifa and Tel Aviv.

March 13
Netherlands: South Moluccans seize a government building in Assen, killing one man and taking 71 hostages. Marines storm the building on March 14 and capture the terrorists; five hostages are wounded.

March 16
Italy: Aldo Moro, former Italian premier, is kidnapped in Rome by Red Brigades, who kill five bodyguards. His body is found in a stolen car in the center of Rome on May 10.

May 20
France: Three Arabs open fire on passengers waiting to board an El Al flight at Orly airport. One policeman and the three terrorists are killed.

June 15
Kuwait: Ah Yasin, representative of the PLO, is murdered by Black June terrorists.

July 9
Great Britain: General al-Naif, former premier of Iraq, is assassinated outside the Intercontinental Hotel in London.

July 31
France: Gunmen invade the Iraqi embassy in Paris, taking hostages. They surrender, but an attempted ambush by the Iraqi secret service as they leave the building results in the deaths of a French police inspector and an Iraqi diplomat.

August 3
France: Ezzedine Kalak, PLO representative, and his deputy, Hamad Adnan, are killed by Black June terrorists at the Arab League office in Paris.

August 6
Pakistan: Gunmen attack the PLO office in Islamabad, killing three PLO members and a police guard.

August 6
Zimbabwe: An explosion in a crowded store in Harare kills 11 and injures 76.

August 13
Lebanon: Bombing of headquarters of PLO in Beirut kills 150.

August 19
Iran: Some 430 people are killed by Muslim arsonists in a crowded theater in Abadan.

August 20
Great Britain: An attack on an El Al aircrew bus outside the Europa Hotel in London leaves one stewardess dead and nine injured.

August 22
Nicaragua: Twenty-five Sandinista guerrillas seize the National Palace in Managua, killing six people and holding 1,000 hostages. The guerrillas fly to Panama on August 24 with 59 released prisoners and a $500,000 ransom.

September 11
Great Britain: Georgi Markov, a Bulgarian exile working for the BBC, is murdered by an injection of a powerful poison in a London street.

1979

January 29
Italy: Emiho Alessandri, public prosecutor, is assassinated by Red Brigades in Milan.

February 14
Afghanistan: Adolph Dubs, U.S. ambassador, is kidnapped by Muslim extremists and dies, together with the four kidnappers, when Afghan police storm the room in the Kabul Hotel where he is held.

March 22

Netherlands: Sir Richard Sykes, British ambassador, is shot at the door of his residence in The Hague by the Provisional IRA.

March 30

Great Britain: Airey Neave, Conservative MP for Abingdon and opposition spokesman on Northem Ireland, is killed by an IRA bomb in his car as he leaves the House of Commons garage in London.

June 16

Syria: Sixty-three cadets are killed and 23 are wounded by the Muslim Brotherhood at a military academy in Aleppo.

June 25

Belgium: An attempt on the life of General Alexander Haig, supreme commander of Allied Forces in Europe, fails when a bomb in a culvert near Mons explodes just after his car has passed.

July 13

Turkey: Palestinians seize the Egyptian embassy in Ankara. Two Turkish policemen and an Egyptian hostage die.

August 27

Northern Ireland: Eighteen British soldiers are killed by a remote-controlled bomb at Warren-Point, County Down.

August 27

Ireland: Lord Mountbatten, together with his grandson, Nicholas Knatchbull; Lady Brabourne; and a local boy, Paul Maxwell, are killed when an IRA bomb blows up their fishing boat off the coast of County Sligo.

September 21

Italy: Carlo Ghiglieno, a Fiat executive, is murdered by Red Brigades in Turin.

November 4

Iran: The United States embassy in Teheran is seized by Iranian militants and 90 hostages are taken, including 60 Americans.

November 20

Saudi Arabia: Some 300 Muslim extremists invade the Grand Mosque in Mecca. Fighting to evict them continues until December 4 and leaves 161 dead.

December 14

Turkey: Three American civilians employed by the Boeing Aircraft Company and a U.S. Army sergeant are shot while waiting for a bus in Florya, near Istanbul, by the Marxist-Leninist Armed Propaganda Squad.

December 15

Cyprus: Ibrahim Ah Aziz, PLO head of guerrilla operations in the occupied West Bank, and Ah Salem Alimed, second secretary of the PLO diplomatic mission, are shot dead in Nicosia.

1980

January 31

Guatemala: Thirty-five people are killed when police storm the Spanish embassy in Guatemala City, where guerrillas held the ambassador and other diplomats hostage.

February 29

Colombia: Terrorists seize the embassy of the Dominican Republic in Bogotá and take 60 hostages; the terrorists fly to Cuba with 12 hostages on April 27.

March 24

El Salvador: Oscar Romero, Roman Catholic archbishop of San Salvador, is shot dead by four gunmen in a hospital chapel. During a gun battle at his funeral on March 30, 39 people are killed.

April 7

Israel: Five Palestinians are killed by Israeli commandos after taking hostages in a kibbutz near the Lebanese border; two Israeli civilians die.

April 30

Great Britain: Gunmen demanding the release of political prisoners in Iran seize the Iranian embassy in London and kill two hostages. The SAS storm the embassy on May 5; five terrorists are killed, and one is arrested.

July 19

Turkey: Nihat Erin, former prime minister, is assassinated in Istanbul.

July 21

France: Salah al-Din Bitar, former prime minister of Syria, is assassinated in Paris.

August 2

Italy: Eighty-four are killed and 200 injured in a bomb explosion at Bologna's central railway station.

September 26

West Germany: Twelve are killed and 300 wounded in a bomb explosion at the Munich beer festival.

October 3

France: A bomb explodes outside a synagogue in Paris, killing four.

October 3

Spain: Basque terrorists shoot dead three policemen and then three civil guards the following day.

December 31

Kenya: Sixteen die in a bomb explosion at the Norfolk Hotel, Nairobi, owned by a family of Jewish origin.

1981

January 21

Northern Ireland: Sir Norman Strange, former Stormont Speaker, and his son are shot dead by the IRA at their home in South Armagh.

March 2

Air Piracy: A Pakistan International Airlines Boeing 720 on an internal flight from Karachi to Peshawar is hijacked by three Al-Zullikar terrorists and forced to land at Kabul in Afghanistan. A Pakistani diplomat, Tariq Rahim, is shot dead. The aircraft is flown to Damascus, where the hostages are set free on March 14 in return for the release of 55 prisoners in Pakistan.

March 28

Air Piracy: An internal Indonesian flight is hijacked by five armed men and forced to fly to Bangkok, Thailand. On March 30, the aircraft is stormed by Indonesian and Thai commandos, who kill four of the hijackers and release the hostages.

May 13

Italy: Pope John Paul II is shot and badly wounded by a Turkish terrorist, Mehmet Ali Ağca.

May 19

Northern Ireland: Five soldiers die in a land-mine explosion in South Armagh.

October 6

Egypt: Soldiers who are secretly members of the Takfir Wal-Hajira sect attack and kill Egyptian President Anwar Sadat during a troop review.

October 10

Great Britain: An IRA nail bomb attack on a bus carrying Irish Guards in London kills two passers-by and wounds 35 people.

November 28

Syria: A car bomb planted by the Muslim Brotherhood kills 64 people in Damascus.

December 4

El Salvador: Three American nuns and one lay missionary are found murdered outside San Salvador. They are killed by members of the National Guard.

December 17

Italy: Brigadier General James Dozier, NATO deputy chief of staff, is kidnapped by Red Brigades terrorists but freed by an Italian antiterrorist squad on January 28, 1982.

1982

March 30

France: Six are killed and 15 wounded by a bomb explosion on a Paris-Toulouse train.

June 3
Great Britain: Shlomo Argov, Israeli ambassador, is shot and critically wounded in London.

July 20
Great Britain: Eleven soldiers are killed and more than 50 people injured by IRA bombs in Hyde Park and beneath the bandstand in Regent's Park.

August 7
Turkey: Eleven are killed in an attack by Armenian terrorists at Ankara airport.

August 9
Paris: Six die and 22 are injured in a gun attack on a Jewish restaurant.

September 14
Lebanon: President Bashir Gemayel is assassinated (along with 25 others) by a car bomb outside of his party's Beirut headquarters.

December 6
Northern Ireland: Seventeen people, including 11 soldiers, are killed in an explosion at a public house in Ballykelly.

1983

April 18
Lebanon: A bomb attack on the American embassy in Beirut leaves some 60 dead and 120 injured.

May 20
South Africa: A car bomb explosion in central Pretoria kills 18.

July 15
France: A bomb planted by Armenian terrorists at Orly Airport, Paris, kills seven and injures 50.

July 27
Portugal: Armenian terrorists seize the Turkish embassy in Lisbon. When commandos storm the embassy, five Armenians and the wife of the Turkish chargé d'affaires are killed.

October 9
Burma: A bomb explosion in Rangoon kills 21 people, including four South Korean ministers on an official visit.

October 23
Lebanon: Suicide truck bomb attacks on the U.S. Marine headquarters and French paratroop barracks in Beirut kill 241 Americans and 58 French nationals.

November 4
Lebanon: Sixty are killed in a suicide bombing of Israeli military headquarters in Tyre.

December 17
Great Britain: Six are killed and 90 injured by an IRA car bomb outside Harrods department store in London.

1984

February 15
Italy: Leamon Hunt, director-general of the Sinai multinational peacekeeping force, is assassinated by Red Brigades terrorists in Rome.

March 16
Lebanon: Political Officer William Buckley, a U.S. citizen, is kidnapped and later murdered by Islamic Jihad in Beirut.

April 12
Spain: Eighteen U.S. servicemen are killed and 83 people injured in a bomb attack on a restaurant near a U.S. Air Force Base in Torrejon.

April 17
Great Britain: Policewoman Yvonne Fletcher is killed by shots fired from the Libyan People's Bureau in London at anti-Qadhafi demonstrators; Libyan diplomats are expelled after a 10-day siege.

June 5
India: Sikh terrorists seize the Golden Temple in Amritsar. One hundred people die when Indian security forces retake the Sikh holy shrine.

July 31

Air Piracy: An Air France Boeing 737 en route from Frankfurt to Paris is hijacked by three armed men and forced to fly to Tehran. The hijackers demand the release of five terrorists jailed in France for the attempted murder of Dr. Chapour Bakhtiar in 1980. The French government refuses to comply with the demands of the hijackers, who surrender to the Iranians on August 2.

August 2

India: A bomb explosion at Madras airport kills 29 people.

August 23

Iran: A bomb planted near Tehran's central railway station kills at least 17 and injures 300.

September 20

Lebanon: A truck bomb attack on the American embassy in Beirut kills nine people.

October 12

Great Britain: An IRA bomb planted in the Grand Hotel, Brighton, where Prime Minister Margaret Thatcher and members of her cabinet are staying for the Tory Party Conference, kills five people and injures 32.

October 31

India: Indian Prime Minister Indira Gandhi is shot to death by members of her security force, as a reprisal for India's bloody assault on the Golden Temple in Amritsar.

December 3

Air Piracy: A Kuwaiti airliner bound for Karachi is hijacked by Shiite terrorists demanding the release of 13 Shiite Muslims imprisoned in Kuwait. The aircraft is taken to Tehran, where two officials of the American Agency for Development are shot dead. Iranian security forces disguised as cleaners enter the aircraft on December 9, releasing the remaining passengers and capturing the hijackers.

December 23

Italy: A bomb explosion on a train near Florence kills 15 passengers.

1985

February 7

Mexico: Under orders from narcotrafficker Rafael Caro Quintero, Drug Enforcement Administration agent Enrique Camarena Salazar and his pilot are kidnapped, tortured, and executed.

February 28

Northern Ireland: Eight policemen and one civilian are killed in an IRA mortar attack on Newry police station.

April 12

Spain: Eighteen die and 82 are injured in a bomb explosion in Madrid; responsibility is claimed by Shia Muslim extremists.

June 14

Air Piracy: An American Trans World Airlines jet en route from Athens to Rome is hijacked by Lebanese Shiite terrorists attempting to secure the release of Shiite prisoners in Israel. The aircraft is diverted to Beirut and twice flown to Algiers. In Beirut, an American passenger, U.S. Navy diver Robert D. Stethem, is killed, and a further 39 Americans are transferred to the control of the Shiite militia, Amal. On June 24, Israel releases a number of Shiite prisoners, and on June 30, the American passengers are set free. The remaining Shiite prisoners are freed by Israel in July, August, and September.

June 19

West Germany: Three are killed and 42 injured in a bomb attack at Frankfurt airport.

June 23

Air Piracy: A bomb destroys an Air India 747 flight from Canada over the Atlantic, killing all 329 people aboard. Sikh separtists are blamed. Several suspects are brought to trial, but only one person is convicted.

July 24

Burma: Some 70 people are killed when a mine explodes under a passenger train traveling from Rangoon to Mandalay.

September 25
Cyprus: One British and two Arab gunmen kill three Israelis onboard a yacht in Larnaca harbor after demanding the release of Palestinians held in Israel.

September 30
Lebanon: Four Russian diplomats are kidnapped in West Beirut; one of them is later found murdered, while the others are released.

October 7
Italy: Palestinians hijack an Italian cruise liner, *Achille Lauro,* in the Mediterranean and murder an invalid American passenger. The hijackers surrender in Egypt on October 9. American jets intercept the aircraft taking the hijackers to Tunis on October 10 and force it to land in Sicily, where the Italian authorities arrest them.

November 6
Colombia: M-19 Movement guerrillas seize the Palace of Justice in Bogota and hold senior judges hostage. When troops storm the building the next day, all the guerrillas, 12 judges, and 50 others die.

November 23
Air Piracy: An Egypt Air plane, en route from Athens to Cairo, is hijacked by five members of a PLO splinter group, Egypt's Revolution, and forced to land at Luqa airport, Malta. An American woman passenger is murdered by the terrorists, and some 60 people die when Egyptian commandos storm the aircraft on November 24.

December 27
Italy: An Arab terrorist attack at Rome airport kills 14 people.

December 27
Austria: An Arab terrorist attack at Vienna airport kills three.

1986

February 28
Sweden: Prime Minister Olof Palme is shot dead by an unknown assassin in a Stockholm street.

April 5
West Germany: An explosion in a West Berlin discotheque kills a U.S. serviceman and a Turkish woman, and injures 200 people.

April 25
Spain: A bomb explosion in Madrid kills five members of the Civil Guard.

May 31
Sri Lanka: At the end of a month of violence, a bomb planted by Tamil extremists on a Colombo-bound train kills eight passengers.

July 14
Spain: Eleven Civil Guards are killed and more than 50 injured by a car bomb detonated by Basque separatists in Madrid.

September 5
Air Piracy: Four Arab terrorists seize an American Pan Am Boeing 747 at Karachi airport in Pakistan and demand to be flown to Cyprus, intending to secure the release of three men imprisoned for the murder of Israelis at Larnaca harbor in September 1985. The crew escapes, but some 20 people are killed when the hijackers open fire, believing that a commando assault on the plane is in progress.

September 6
Turkey: Twenty-one worshipers at a synagogue in Istanbul are killed by machine gun and hand grenade by two terrorists, who themselves die in the explosions.

September 7
Chile: An unsuccessful attempt on the life of President Pinochet leaves five bodyguards dead.

September 14
South Korea: A bomb blast at Seoul's Kimpo airport kills five and wounds 26 people.

October 15
Israel: One person is killed and 70 are injured in a grenade attack on army recruits and their relatives taking part in a ceremony at the Wailing Wall in Jerusalem.

October 25
Spain: Provincial military governor General Rafael Garrido Gil, his wife, and son are killed by a bomb placed in their car by a motorcyclist in San Sebastian.

November 17
France: Georges Besse, chairman of the state-owned Renault automobile company, is shot dead by Action Directe terrorists in Paris.

1987

March 20
Italy: Terrorists shoot dead a senior air force general, Licio Giorgieri, in Rome.

March 23
West Germany: An IRA bomb at the U.K. military base at Rheindalen injures 31.

April 17
Sri Lanka: Tamil separatists ambush three buses and two trucks near Trincomalee, killing 120.

April 21
Sri Lanka: A bomb explosion in Colombo kills more than 100.

April 25
Northern Ireland: Lord Justice Maurice Gibson and his wife are killed by a car bomb as they cross from Eire into Northern Ireland at Killen.

June 1
Lebanon: Premier Rashid Karami is killed by a bomb planted in his helicopter.

June 19
Spain: A bomb planted by Basque separatists in the underground parking garage of a department store in Barcelona kills 19.

July 6
India: Sikh militants kill 40 Hindu bus passengers in the Punjab. A further 32 are killed in the neighboring state of Haryana on July 7.

July 14
Pakistan: Two bomb explosions in Karachi, blamed on Afghan agents, kill 70.

July 24
Air Piracy: An Air Afrique jet flying from Brazzaville to Bangui is hijacked to Geneva by a Lebanese Shiite, Hussain al-Hariri, who demands the release of a Lebanese being held in West Germany. Swiss security forces storm the aircraft and capture the hijacker. One French passenger killed.

July 30
South Africa: A bomb explosion near military barracks in Johannesburg injures 68 people.

August 18
Sri Lanka: A grenade attack in the parliament fails to assassinate the president but kills one MP and injures 15.

November 8
Northern Ireland: A bomb explosion at a Remembrance Day service at Enniskillen kills 11 and injures 31.

November 9
Sri Lanka: A Tamil separatist bombing in Colombo kills 32, injures more than 100.

November 29
Air Piracy: A bomb on a Korean plane kills all 116 passengers.

December 11
Spain: A Basque separatist bomb in Zaragoza kills 12.

1988

February 14
Cyprus: Three PLO officials are killed in a car bomb explosion in Limassol.

February 19
Namibia: A bomb attack kills 14.

March 7
Israel: Three Palestinians, who hijacked a bus in the Negev, are killed by Israeli troops; three bus passengers die.

March 8
Air Piracy: Five of the 11 hijackers of an Aeroflot plane are killed when Soviet security forces storm the craft at Leningrad.

March 16
Northern Ireland: Three are killed and 50 injured in a grenade and pistol attack by a loyalist gunman at the funeral of three IRA men killed by the SAS in Gibraltar on March 6.

April 5
Air Piracy: A Kuwaiti airliner en route from Bangkok to Kuwait is hijacked to Iran by gunmen demanding the release of 17 terrorists imprisoned in Kuwait. The plane is ordered to Cyprus, where two passengers are killed, then on to Algiers, where the remaining hostages are released on April 20 in return for safe passage for the hijackers.

April 14
Italy: Five people are killed by a bomb at the U.S. Navy Club in Naples.

April 16
Italy: Senator Robert Ruffilli is murdered by Red Brigades terrorists.

April 16
Tunisia: Khalil al-Wazir (Abu Jihad), second-in-command of the PLO, is assassinated in Tunis.

April 23
Lebanon: A car bomb in Tripoli kills 69 and injures more than 100.

May 1
Netherlands: Three off-duty British soldiers die in two IRA attacks.

May 1
Sri Lanka: More than 26 bus passengers are killed by a land mine.

June 15
Northern Ireland: Six soldiers are killed when their van is blown up by the IRA at Lisburn.

June 28
Greece: U.S. naval attaché Captain William E. Nordeen is killed by anti-NATO terrorists in Athens.

July 11
Greece: A terrorist attack on the cruise ship *City of Poros* kills 11.

August 1
Great Britain: One soldier is killed and nine injured by an IRA bomb at army barracks in North London.

August 17
Pakistan: President Zia is killed by a bomb planted on his aircraft, together with more than 30 others, including the U.S. ambassador, Arnold L. Raphel.

August 20
Northern Ireland: Eight British soldiers are killed when their bus is blown up by the IRA near Omagh.

October 30
Israel: A gasoline bomb attack by Palestinians in Jericho kills 4.

December 21
Air Piracy: Pan Am Boeing 747, flying from London to New York, is blown up over Scotland, killing 259 passengers and crew and 11 residents of Lockerbie.

1989

March 17
Lebanon: A car bomb in Beirut kills 12.

April 13
Sri Lanka: Forty-five are killed in a Tamil bombing in Trincomalee.

September 7
West Germany: Heidi Hazell, German wife of a British soldier, is shot by the IRA in Dortmund.

September 19
Air Piracy: A DC-10 airliner of the French Union de Transport Aérien crashes in Niger following a bomb explosion on board, killing 171.

September 22
Great Britain: An IRA bomb attack on Royal Marines' barracks at Deal in Kent kills 11 bandsmen.

November 22
Lebanon: New president of Lebanon René Mouawad is killed by a car bomb.

November 30
West Germany: A Red Army Faction car bomb kills Alfred Herrhausen, chief executive of the Deutsche Bank, at Bad Homburg near Frankfurt.

December 6
Colombia: A bomb planted at the security and intelligence agency by drug traffickers kills 50.

1990

January 2
Northern Ireland: A loyalist is killed by car bomb in East Belfast.

January 20
Northern Ireland: An IRA bomb kills a boy during a "Bloody Sunday" anniversary march.

February 4
Israel: Nine are dead in an attack on a tourist bus near Ismalia. Many are wounded.

February 20
Great Britain: A bomb explodes in an army vehicle in Leicester, injuring three.

March 28
Peru: Maoist guerrillas use car bombs and assassination to disrupt a presidential and congressional election.

April 3
India: A bomb planted by Sikh separatists kills 32 and injures 50 in Punjab.

April 4
Northern Ireland: A huge IRA bomb near Downpatrick kills four UDA soldiers.

April 11
Great Britain: Teeside Customs seize parts of a suspected "supergun" destined for Iraq. Trucks carrying suspected parts are later seized in Greece and Turkey.

July 30
Great Britain: Conservative MP Ian Gow assassinated by IRA car bombs at his Sussex home.

1991

February 7
Great Britain: An IRA mortar bomb attack on the British cabinet occurs at 10 Downing Street.

February 17
Colombia: A bomb at Medellín kills 22 and injures 140.

February 18
Great Britain: The IRA bombs Paddington and Victoria railroad stations, London. All London rail terminals are temporarily closed.

March 2
Sri Lanka: Ranjan Wijeratne, deputy minister of defense, is killed by a car bomb.

May 21
India: Leader of the Congress (I) Party Rajiv Gandhi is assassinated near Madras in a bomb attack during an election rally.

June 15
India: Sikh terrorists in Punjab kill 74 in an attack on two passenger trains.

August 8
France: Former Iranian prime minister Shahpour Baldatiar and his secretary are assassinated in Paris by Iranian agents.

November 2
Northern Ireland: The IRA bombs Musgrave Park Hospital, Belfast; two British soldiers are killed.

December 25
Turkey: Eleven are killed in an Istanbul clothing store firebombed by Kurdish terrorists.

1992

February 5
Northern Ireland: Five Catholics are killed in a Belfast betting shop. The British government begins a review of Protestant Ulster Defence Association (UDA) activities. The UDA is proscribed in August.

February 16
Lebanon: Sheikh Abbas Mussawi (leader of pro-Iranian Hizballah), his wife, son, and bodyguards are assassinated in an Israeli raid.

March 17
Argentina: The Israeli embassy in Buenos Aires is bombed; 29 people are killed and 252 wounded. The Iranian-backed Islamic Jihad claims responsibility.

April 10
Great Britain: The IRA bombs the Baltic Exchange building in London; three are dead, 80 are injured.

May 23
Italy: The assassination of a senior Italian judge occurs in a continuing Mafia campaign.

June 29
Algeria: President Mohamed Boudiaf of Algeria is assassinated; this is presumed to be the work of Muslim fundamentalists.

July 17
Peru: A Shining Path car bomb kills 18 in Lima.

August 28
Algeria: A bomb kills nine and injures 128 at Algiers airport.

November 14
Northern Ireland: The IRA "Bookmaker's Shop Massacre" occurs in North Belfast. Three are killed, 12 are injured. IRA bombing also devastates the center of Coleraine.

1993

January 22
Peru: Terrorists detonate a van bomb at a Coca-Cola plant in central Lima. The bomb causes serious damage to the plant. At least two persons are killed and two injured. Later that day, a car bomb is detonated at another Coca-Cola facility in Lima, causing only slight material damage.

January 24
Turkey: Well-known Turkish journalist Ugar Muncu, noted for his criticism of Islamic extremism and separatism, is killed when a bomb explodes under his car outside his apartment in Ankara.

January 28
Turkey: Police bodyguards foil an attempt to ambush the motorcade of a prominent Jewish businessman and community leader in Istanbul. Police recover an RPG-18 rocket at the scene, and on January 30, arrest two of the terrorists as they flee toward the Iranian border.

January 28
Peru: Terrorists explode a car bomb in front of the IBM headquarters building in Lima. Major damage is caused, and 11 passersby and employees are injured.

January 30
Colombia: A massive car bomb kills 11; scores more are injured. This is believed to be the work of drug baron Pablo Escobar.

February 4
Egypt: A molotov cocktail bomb is lobbed at a tour bus as South Korean passengers wait to embark at a

hotel outside Cairo. The extremist Islamic terrorist group Al-Gama'at al-Islamiyya claims responsibility for the attack.

February 23
Colombia: Eight ELN (National Liberation Army) terrorists kidnap U.S. citizen Lewis Manning, an employee of the Colombian gold-mining company Oresom, in the Choco area.

February 26
Egypt: A Swedish, a Turkish, and an Egyptian citizen are killed when a bomb explodes inside a cafe in downtown Cairo. Eighteen others, including U.S. citizens Jill Papineau and Raymond Chico, a Canadian, and a Frenchman, are wounded.

February 26
United States: Seven are killed and 1,000 are injured (some seriously) in car bomb explosion at the World Trade Center, New York.

February 26
Great Britain: The IRA bombs gas works in Warrington.

March 8
Costa Rica: Four terrorists take 25 persons hostage in the Nicaraguan embassy in San José, including the Nicaraguan ambassador. The hostage situation continues for several days while negotiations are conducted. On March 21, the occupation of the embassy is concluded peacefully. After the hostages are released, the terrorists are permitted to leave the country.

March 12
India: Three hundred die and more than 1,300 are injured by a coordinated series of bombings in the heart of Bombay.

March 16
India: Eighty die in bombings in the congested Bow Bazaar area of Calcutta.

March 16
Italy: Two terrorists on a motor scooter are shot and killed by a leading Iranian dissident while traveling in his car in Rome.

March 20
Great Britain: The IRA strikes again at Warrington.

March 22
Iraq: A Belgian official from a nongovernmental organization involved in relief efforts in northern Iraq is shot and killed on the road between Irbil and Sulaimaniyah.

April 10
South Africa: Leading ANC figure Chris Hani is assassinated by a right-wing extremist.

April 20
Egypt: Terrorists attempt to assassinate Egyptian Information Minister Safwat Sharif in Cairo by firing at his motorcade. The minister is slightly injured and his bodyguard seriously wounded. Al-Gama'at al-Islamiyya claims responsibility for the attack.

April 24
Great Britain: London is bombed by the IRA for the second time (in Bishopsgate), leaving one dead and 36 injured.

May 1
Sri Lanka: President Premadasa is assassinated by a Tamil Tiger suicide bomber.

May 13
Chile: Three terrorists enter a Mormon church in Santiago, overpower the bishop, douse the church with fuel, and set it afire. The church is completely destroyed. The terrorists leave pamphlets at the scene in which the Mapu Lautaro group—United Popular Action Movement—claims responsibility.

May 27
Italy: The Uffizi Gallery in Florence is devastated by bomb.

May 29
Germany: Five Turks are killed at Solingen after arson attacks by neo-Nazis.

June 8
Egypt: Terrorists explode a bomb underneath an overpass as a tour bus conveys visitors to the Giza pyramids. Two Egyptians are killed, and six British

tourists, nine Egyptians, three Syrians, and at least three others are injured.

June 24
Western Europe: Terrorists from the Kurdistan Workers Party (PKK) stage a wave of coordinated attacks in more than 30 cities in six Western European countries. The attacks consist primarily of vandalism against Turkish diplomatic and commercial targets and included the takeover of one Turkish consulate.

June 27
Turkey: Terrorists throw hand grenades at a number of hotels and restaurants frequented by tourists in the Mediterranean resort area of Antalya. Twelve foreigners are among the 28 persons injured.

July 1
Japan: A few days before President Clinton's arrival at the base prior to the Group of Seven summit in Tokyo, terrorists fire two homemade rockets at the U.S. Air Force base at Yokota, causing minimal damage but no casualties.

July 7
Peru: Police discover the bodies of two European tourists in a remote area of Ayacucho. The two were traveling together in a region contested by Sendero Luminoso (Shining Path) terrorists.

July 7
Japan: Terrorists fire four homemade projectiles at the headquarters of the U.S. Air Force in Japan at Camp Zama. None of the projectiles explode, and little damage is caused.

July 5–October 14
Turkey: In eight separate incidents within this period, the PKK kidnap a total of 19 Western tourists traveling in southeastern Turkey. The hostages, including U.S. citizen Colin Patrick Starger, are released unharmed after spending several weeks in captivity.

July 25
Turkey: A terrorist bomb planted in a trash can next to an automatic teller machine in the Hagia Sophia district of Istanbul explodes and wounds two Italian tourists.

July 27
Peru: After first spraying the building with bullets from automatic weapons, terrorists explode a van bomb outside the U.S. embassy in Lima. One embassy guard is injured.

July 28
Italy: Terrorist bombs leave five dead in Milan; 20 are injured in Rome.

August 18
Turkey: Terrorists throw a hand grenade underneath a Hungarian tourist bus in front of a hotel. Three foreign tourists and five Turkish bystanders are injured.

August 18
Egypt: A motorcycle bomb kills five persons and wounds 15 others on a street in Cairo. The bomb is directed at Egyptian interior minister Alfi, who is slightly injured. The Islamic extremist group New Jihad claims responsibility.

August 25
Turkey: Four terrorists masquerading as Turkish security officials kidnap Iranian dissident Mohammad Khaderi from his residence. On September 4, his body is discovered by the side of the Kiursehir-Boztepe highway.

August 28
Turkey: Iranian dissident Behram Azadfer is assassinated by terrorists in Ankara.

September 2
Italy: Three terrorists throw a hand grenade over the fence and also fire shots at the U.S. Air Force base at Aviano. The Red Brigades terrorist group later claims responsibility.

September 8
South Africa: Nineteen are killed and 22 injured in a shooting at Wadeville industrial zone, east of Johannesburg.

September 20
Algeria: One Moroccan and two French surveyors are kidnapped by terrorists as they drive between Oran and Sidi Bel Abbes. The Morrocan citizen is released unharmed, but the two Frenchmen are later found murdered.

September 21
Israel: PLO peace advocate Mohammed Hashem Abu Shaaban is assassinated.

September 22
South Africa: The "Day of Terror" occurs as 31 die on the day Parliament debates formation of a Transitional Council.

September 26
Iraq: A United Nations truck carrying 12 tons of medical supplies is destroyed by a bomb while traveling near Irbil. The bomb was attached to the truck's fuel tank. The driver and 12 civilians are injured.

October 11
Norway: The Norwegian publisher of Salman Rushdie's book *Satanic Verses* is shot and seriously wounded at his home near Oslo.

October 16
Algeria: Terrorists shoot and kill two Russian military officers and wound a third outside an apartment building near the Algerian military academy. The Russians were instructors at the academy.

October 19
Algeria: Terrorists kidnap a Peruvian, a Filipino, and a Colombian from the cafeteria of an Italian construction firm in Tiaret. The three are technicians employed by the firm. On October 21, the three are found dead some 50 kilometers from the abduction site. On October 26, the extremist Armed Islamic Group claims responsibility for this and other attacks against foreigners.

October 23
Northern Ireland: An IRA bomb kills 10, injures 56, in an attack on UDA headquarters in Shankhill Road, West Belfast.

October 24
Algeria: Three French diplomats are kidnapped as they leave their apartment in Algiers. A police officer who attempts to prevent the kidnapping is shot and killed. On October 26, the Armed Islamic Group claims responsibility for the incident. The three diplomats are released unharmed on the night of October 30.

October 24
Israel: Two small explosive charges are detonated near the French embassy in Tel Aviv. It causes no damage or casualties. A member of the Jewish extremist Kahana Hay movement claims responsibility for the explosions, saying the attack is carried out to protest PLO leader Yasir Arafat's visit to France and agreements he signed there.

October 25
Nigeria: Four members of a Nigerian dissident group hijack a Nigerian Airways Airbus-310 airliner with 150 passengers and crew on board shortly after it takes off from Lagos. After trying unsuccessfully to land the aircraft at Ndjamena, Chad, the terrorists order the plane to land at Niamey, Niger. The hijackers then release two groups of passengers. After lengthy but fruitless negotiations, Nigerien police storm the aircraft on October 28. All four of the hijackers surrender, but one of the crew is killed, as is one of the hijackers during the rescue operation.

October 25
Peru: Terrorists explode a large bomb under a minibus in the parking lot near the departure terminal at Lima's international airport. The driver of a hotel shuttle bus is killed, and about 20 other persons are injured. The American Airlines cargo office, which is located nearby, sustains some damage.

October 29
France: Three terrorists throw a firebomb into the Turkish-owned Bosphorus Bank in central Paris. No serious damage is caused, but four people are injured, one seriously.

October 30
Northern Ireland: Seven people are killed as loyalist gunmen attack Rising Sun pub, Greysteel.

November 8
Iran: Two hand grenades are thrown into the courtyard of the French embassy in Tehran, causing no casualties and little damage. On the same day, a French citizen is injured when a hand grenade is thrown into the Tehran offices of Air France. A group called the Hizballah Committee claim responsibility for both attacks, saying they are carried out to protest the French government's support for the Mujahideen-e-Khalq.

November 14

Philippines: Terrorists from the Islamic extremist group Abu Sayyaf kidnap a U.S. missionary, Charles M. Watson, in Pangutaran Island, Sulu Batu. The missionary works for the Summer Institute of Linguistics. He is released unharmed in Manila on December 7.

November 25

Egypt: A car bomb explodes near the motorcade of Prime Minister Atif Sedki; the prime minister is unhurt but one bystander, a teenage girl, is killed and at least 18 other persons wounded. The Jihad Group later claims responsibility.

December 9

Egypt: A police officer is killed and six others are injured when a group of terrorists open fire on two movie houses that are showing foreign films. On December 12, Al-Gama'at al-Islamiyya claims responsibility for the murders, stating that the attack is in retaliation for the screening of "immoral" films.

December 11

Egypt: Libyan dissident, human rights activist, and former foreign minister Mansour Kikhia is kidnapped from his hotel in Cairo. Ambassador Kikhia is visiting Cairo to attend a human rights conference. He has not been heard from since.

December 13

Iraq: One person is killed and six others are injured in Sulaimaniyah when a terrorist bomb destroys a relief center operated by the Belgian humanitarian group Handicap International.

December 14

Algeria: A large group of armed terrorists attacks a work camp of a hydroelectric project in Tamezguida. Fourteen Croatian citizens are removed from the camp. Twelve are murdered, but two others escape with injuries. On December 16, the Armed Islamic Group claims responsibility, stating that the attack is part of an ongoing campaign to rid Algeria of all foreigners and to avenge Muslims killed in Bosnia.

December 27

Egypt: Seven Austrian tourists and eight Egyptians are wounded when terrorists fire on a tour bus traveling in the old district of Cairo. A small bomb that is thrown at the bus rolls near a cafe and explodes.

December 29

Algeria: Terrorists murder a Belgian husband and wife in their sleep at their home in Bouira.

1994

January 4

Ireland: The Ulster Volunteer Force (UVF) claims responsibility for two mail bombs sent to Sinn Féin's Dublin offices.

January 10

Italy: A bomb is detonated in front of the NATO Defense College building in Rome. That evening, copies of an eight-page Red Brigades bulletin claiming responsibility on behalf of the "Combatant Communist Nuclei" (NCC) is found in several Italian provinces.

January 14

Colombia: Suspected members of the National Liberation Army (ELN) kidnap U.S. citizen Russell Vacek, his wife Elizabeth, and other family members as they are traveling in El Playon.

January 29

Lebanon: A Jordanian diplomat is shot and killed outside his home in Beirut. The government of Lebanon arrests and prosecutes Abu Nidal Organization (ANO) terrorists for the attack.

February 3

Greece: A bomb is detonated at the German Goethe (culture) Institute in Athens. A local newspaper receives a warning from the Revolutionary People's Struggle (ELA) terrorist group a half-hour before the detonation.

February 19

Egypt: Unknown assailants fire upon a passenger train and wound a Polish woman, a Thai woman, and two Egyptian citizens in Asyut. The al-Gama'at al-Islamiyya (Islamic Group) claims responsibility for the attack.

February 23

Egypt: A bomb explosion aboard a passenger train in Asyut injures six foreign tourists—two New Zealanders, two Germans, and two Australians—and five Egyptian citizens. The Islamic Group claims responsibility for the attack.

February 25

West Bank: Jewish right-wing extremist and U.S. citizen Baruch Goldstein machine-guns Muslim worshippers at a mosque in the town of Hebron, killing 29 and wounding about 150.

March 4

Egypt: Unknown gunmen open fire on a Nile cruise ship and wound a German tourist near the Sohag Governorate. The Islamic Group claims responsibility for the attack.

March 9–13

United Kingdom: The Provisional Irish Republican Army fires mortars at London's Heathrow airport in three separate attacks. There are no injuries because the fully primed mortars fail to detonate.

March 27

Turkey: A bomb is detonated in the gardens of the Saint Sophia Mosque and Museum in Istanbul, injuring three tourists: one German, one Spanish, and one Dutch. The Metropole Revenge Team of the political wing of the PKK claims responsibility.

April 1

Colombia: Six members of the Revolutionary Armed Forces of Colombia (FARC) kidnap U.S. citizen Raymond Rising, security chief of the Summer Linguistic Institution, as he rides his motorcycle from the municipal capital of Puerto Lleras.

April 2

Turkey: The PKK claims responsibility for bombing the IC Bedesten, the old bazaar at the center of the newer complex, in Istanbul. Two foreign tourists, one Spanish and one Belgian, are killed, and 17 others are injured.

April 6

Rwanda: The presidents of Rwanda and Burundi are assassinated in a missile attack on their airplane.

April 6

Israel: A suicide attack on a school bus by the Hamas organization occurs in Afula (in revenge for the Hebron massacre). Seven die; 50 are injured.

April 13

Lebanon: Five individuals, including two Iraqi diplomats, are arrested for assassinating Iraqi opposition figure Shaykh Talib Ali al-Suhayl in his house near West Beirut.

April 13

Israel: The second revenge attack by Hamas occurs on the commuter bus at Hadera, central Israel. Six die; 25 are wounded.

April 27

South Africa: A car bomb explodes at Jan Smuts Airport in Johannesburg, injuring 16 persons, including two Russian diplomats and a Swiss Air pilot. Although no group has claimed responsibility, white separatists opposed to South Africa's first multiracial election are believed responsible.

May 8

Algeria: Two French priests are shot and killed by two male assailants in the lower Casbah district of Algiers. In its weekly publication, the Armed Islamic Group (GIA) claims responsibility.

May 17

Greece: A time-detonated rocket is fired at an IBM office in downtown Athens. The 17 November terrorist group claims responsibility in a warning call to a radio station.

May 29

Iraq: At least two unknown assailants are shot and killed by an Iranian dissident, Seyeed Ahmad Sadr Lahijani, as he drives his car through Ghalebieh.

June 17

Uganda: A driver for the Catholic Relief Services is badly beaten by Lord's Resistance Army (LRA) rebels who ambush the truck he is driving.

June 21–22

Turkey: In the coastal towns of Fethiye and Marmaris, bombs kill one foreign national and injure 10 others at tourist sites. The PKK claims responsibility for the attacks, on German television.

July 18
Argentina: A car bomb explodes at the Israeli-Argentine Mutual Association, killing nearly 100 persons and wounding more than 200 others. The explosion causes the seven-story building to collapse and damages adjacent buildings.

July 26
Cambodia: The Khmer Rouge attacks a train traveling in Kompong Trach and kidnaps a number of passengers, among them an Australian, a Briton, and a Frenchman.

August 3
Algeria: Five French embassy employees are killed and one is injured when guerrillas from the AIG attack a French residential compound in Algiers.

August 8
Turkey: The PKK kidnaps two Finnish nationals, stating that they did not have "entry visas for Kurdistan." The Finns are held for 22 days before being released unharmed.

August 18
Chile: A bomb explodes at a Santiago office building that houses the American company Fluor Daniel. The Manuel Rodriguez Patriotic Front (FPMR) claims responsibility and states that the incident is carried out in solidarity with Cuba and against the U.S. economic blockade of the island.

August 26
Angola: A Portuguese priest and four nuns are kidnapped by suspected National Union for the Total Independence of Angola (UNITA) rebels near Choba.

August 27
Philippines: Seven South Korean engineers and 30 Filipino workers are taken captive by the Moro Islamic Liberation Front (MILF).

September 23
Colombia: Twelve terrorists from the FARC kidnap U.S. citizen Thomas Hargrove when he is stopped at a guerrilla roadblock.

September 27
Egypt: Three persons are killed and two are wounded when an assailant fires on a downtown tourist area in Hurghada. Two Egyptians and one German are killed in the attack. The IG claims responsibility for the attack.

October 9
Israel: Two Arabs armed with assault rifles and grenades attack pedestrians in Jerusalem. The gunmen kill two people and injure 14 others. Two U.S. citizens are among the injured. Hamas claims responsibility for the incident.

October 18
Algeria: Approximately 30 members of the AIG attack an oil base, killing a French and an Italian worker.

October 23
Egypt: Assailants shoot and kill a British tourist and wound three others in an attack on a bus near Luxor. The Islamic Group is believed to be responsible for the attack.

December 11
Philippines: The Abu Sayyaf Group (ASG) claims responsibility for an explosion aboard a Philippine airliner. One Japanese citizen is killed, and at least 10 others are injured.

December 24
Algeria: Members of the AIG hijack an Air France flight in Algeria. The plane arrives in Marseille, France, on December 26. A French antiterrorist unit storms the plane, ending the 54-hour siege in which three hostages have been killed by the terrorists. All four terrorists are killed during the rescue.

December 25
Israel: An American is among 12 persons injured when a Hamas supporter carrying a bag of explosives blows himself up at a West Jerusalem bus stop.

December 27
Algeria: The AIG claims responsibility for the murders of four Catholic priests. The murders are apparently in retaliation for the deaths of four AIG hijackers the previous day in Marseilles.

1995

January 15
Cambodia: A U.S. tourist is killed and her husband is seriously wounded when Khmer Rouge rebels attacked their sightseeing convoy. A tour guide is also killed when the assailants fire a rocket at the van.

January 18
Colombia: Members of the People's Liberation Army kidnap a U.S. citizen working as an administrative support officer for Cerrejon Coal Mine of Riohacha in La Guajira.

January 26
Colombia: Seven guerrillas of the ELN kidnap three Venezuelan Corpoven engineers and kill a fourth near La Victoria.

February 27
Greece: Khidir Abd al-Abbas Hamza, a defecting Iraqi former nuclear scientist, is abducted in Athens while he is attempting to call a newspaper office from a phone booth. The Iraqi ambassador in Athens denies any Iraqi involvement, but the incident is similar to other Iraqi government-sponsored abductions.

March 8
Pakistan: Two unidentified gunmen armed with AK-47 assault rifles open fire on a U.S. consulate van in Karachi, killing two U.S. diplomats and wounding a third. The Pakistani driver is not hurt.

March 20
Japan: Twelve persons are killed and 5,700 injured in a Sarin nerve gas attack on a crowded subway station in the center of Tokyo. A similar attack occurs nearly simultaneously in the Yokohama subway system. The Aum Shinrikyo cult is responsible for the attacks.

April 9
Gaza Strip: A suicide bomber crashes an explosive-rigged van into an Israeli bus, killing a U.S. citizen and seven Israelis. More than 50 other persons, including two U.S. citizens, are injured. A faction of the Palestine Islamic Jihad claims responsibility for the attack.

April 19
Colombia: Members of the ELN kidnap two Italian oil workers from their car and kill their Colombian driver near Barrancabermeja.

April 19
United States: A car bomb blows up the Alfred P. Murrah Federal Building in Oklahoma City, Oklahoma, killing 168 people.

April 22
Netherlands: Two Turkish citizens are shot by Kurdish extremists at a coffeehouse in The Hague. Four men are arrested in connection with the attack.

May 5
Algeria: Suspected members of the AIG attack employees of a pipeline company, killing two Frenchmen, a Briton, a Canadian, and a Tunisian.

May 15
Peru: Five alleged Shining Path members hold up a bus near Chimbote and rob some 50 passengers, including three U.S. citizens.

May 23
Sierra Leone: Revolutionary United Front (RUF) rebels abduct three Lebanese businessmen during attacks on towns in the Lebanese community of the diamond district of Kono.

May 31
Colombia: Seven ELN guerrillas kidnap a U.S. citizen and three Colombians at the Verde Limon Gold Mine in Zaragoza. Shortly afterward, the Colombian army frees the captives in a confrontation that leaves one Colombian hostage and two guerrillas dead.

June 24
Colombia: Unknown guerrillas abduct the son of a British Exxon employee in Formeque and demand a ransom of $500,000. On August 12, during the course of negotiations, the victim's body is found.

June 25
Pakistan: Five gunmen kidnap three German engineers and a Pakistani driver in the North-West Frontier Province. The kidnappers demand a ransom of 10 million rupees. One of the Germans and the Pakistani are released on July 3, at which time

the kidnappers add the release of four prisoners in Peshawar to their demands. The other two hostages are freed unharmed on July 13. It does not appear that the demands have been met.

June 26
Ethiopia: The IG claims responsibility for a failed assassination attempt against Egyptian president Hosni Mubarak in Addis Ababa.

July 4–8
India: Six tourists—two U.S. citizens, two Britons, a Norwegian, and a German—are taken hostage in Kashmir by the previously unknown militant group al-Faran, which demands the release of Muslim militants held in Indian prisons.

July 25
France: A bomb detonates aboard a Paris subway train as it arrives at St. Michel station, killing seven commuters and wounding 86.

August 17
France: A nail-filled bomb detonates in a trash bin near a subway entrance in Paris, injuring 17 people. Among those injured are four Hungarians, four Italians, three Portuguese, one German, and one Briton.

August 21
Israel: A bomb explodes on a bus in Jerusalem, killing six persons, including one U.S. citizen, and wounding two other U.S. citizens and more than 100 others. The Izz al-Din al-Qassem Brigades, the military wing of Hamas, claims responsibility.

September 7
India: A woman claiming to be from the militant group Dukhtaran-e-Millat delivers a mail bomb to the office of the BBC in Srinagar, Kashmir. The bomb explodes later in the hands of an Agence Francé-Presse freelance photographer, who dies from his injuries on September 10. Dukhtaran-e-Millat denies responsibility for the bombing.

October 20
Croatia: A car bomb is detonated outside the local police headquarters building in Rijeka, killing the driver and injuring 29 bystanders. The Egyptian IG claims responsibility, warning that further attacks will continue unless authorities release an imprisoned Gama'at militant, Tala'at Fuad Kassem, arrested in September 1995.

October 27
Angola: UNITA soldiers kill two people and kidnap 32 others in Lunda Norte. Four of the hostages are South African citizens employed by the SA Export Company, Ltd.

November 4
Israel: Prime Minister Yitzhak Rabin is assassinated by a Jewish extremist at a peace rally.

November 8
Egypt: Islamic extremists open fire on a train en route to Cairo from Aswan, injuring a Dutchman, a Frenchwoman, and an Egyptian. The IG claims responsibility for the attack.

November 13
Saudi Arabia: A car bomb explosion in the parking lot of the Office of the Program Manager/Saudi Arabian National Guard (OPM/SANG) in Riyadh kills seven people and wounds 42 others. The deceased include four civilian U.S. federal civilian employees, one U.S. military person, and two Indian government employees. Three groups, including the Islamic Movement for Change, claim responsibility for the attack.

November 13
Switzerland: An Egyptian diplomat is shot and killed in the parking garage of his apartment building in Geneva. On November 15, the International Justice Group claims responsibility for the attack.

November 19
Pakistan: A suicide bomber drives a vehicle into the Egyptian embassy compound in Islamabad, killing at least 16 persons and injuring 60 others. The bomb destroys the entire compound and causes damage and injuries within a half-mile radius. The IG, Jihad Group, and the International Justice Group all claim responsibility for the bombing.

November 21
India: A powerful bomb explodes outside a restaurant in the Connaught Place shopping area in New Delhi. The blast injures 22 persons, includ-

ing two Dutch citizens, one South African, and one Norwegian, and causes major damage to shops and parked cars. Both the Jammu and Kashmir Islamic Front, a Kashmiri Muslim separatist group, and the Khalistan Liberation Tiger Force, a Sikh separatist group, claim responsibility for the bombing.

December 10

Ecuador: Three FARC militants kidnap the treasurer for the Nazarine missions, who is a U.S. citizen. A captured member of FARC leads a rescue team to a mountainous area near Quito, where they free the victim. Three kidnappers are killed, and two others escape.

December 16

Spain: Several bombs detonate in different areas of a department store in Valencia, killing one person and wounding eight others, including a U.S. citizen. Basque Fatherland and Liberty (ETA) claims responsibility for the attack.

December 23

Germany: A bomb is detonated outside an office building in Duesseldorf that houses the Peruvian honorary consulate, causing major damage. On December 27, the Anti-Imperialist Cell (AIZ) claims responsibility for the attack in a letter stating that the Peruvian government's domestic policies are "unbearable for the majority of Peruvians."

December 27

Philippines: Twenty Abu Sayyaf militants kidnap at least 16 vacationers, including six U.S. citizens, at Lake Sebu, Mindanao. Two of the hostages escape; four are released, carrying a ransom demand of $57,700. On December 31, the kidnappers release the remaining hostages in exchange for government promises of improvements in the south.

1996

January 8

Indonesia: Two hundred Free Papua Movement (OPM) guerrillas abduct 26 individuals in the Lorenta nature preserve, Irian Jaya Province. The hostages are on a research expedition for the World-wide Fund for Nature. Among the hostages are seven persons from the United Kingdom, the Netherlands, and Germany. The OPM demands the withdrawal of Indonesian troops from Irian Jaya, compensation for environmental damage and for the death of civilians at the hands of the military, and a halt to Freeport Indonesia mining operations. On May 15, Indonesian Special Forces members rescue the last nine hostages after locating them with a pilotless drone.

January 16

Turkey: Seven Turkish nationals of Chechen origin hijack a Russia-bound Panamanian ferry in Trabzon. The hijackers initially threatened to kill all Russians on board unless Chechen separatists being held in Dagestan, Russia, are released. On January 19, the hijackers surrender to Turkish authorities outside the entrance to the Bosporus. The passengers are unharmed.

January 18

Ethiopia: A bomb explodes at the Ghion Hotel in Addis Ababa, killing at least four persons and injuring 20 others. The injured include citizens from the United Kingdom, Mali, India, and France. In March, al-Ittihaad al-Islami (The Islamic Union), an ethnic Somali group, claims responsibility for the bombing.

January 19

Colombia: Six suspected FARC guerrillas kidnap a U.S. citizen and demand a $1 million ransom. The hostage is released on May 22.

January 31

Sri Lanka: Suspected members of the Liberation Tigers of Tamil Eelam (LTTE) ram an explosives-laden truck into the Central Bank in the heart of downtown Colombo, killing 90 civilians and injuring more than 1,400 others. Among the wounded are two U.S. citizens, six Japanese, and one Dutch national. The explosion causes major damage to the Central Bank building, an American Express office, the Intercontinental Hotel, and several other buildings.

February 6

Colombia: ELN rebels kidnap three cement industry engineers, including a Briton, a Dane, and a German, and their Colombian companion in San Luis. They are abducted from their vehicle at a makeshift roadblock. The hostages are later freed.

February 9

United Kingdom: A bomb is detonated in a parking garage in the Docklands area of London, killing two persons and wounding more than 100 others, including two U.S. citizens. The IRA claims responsibility.

February 25

Jerusalem: A suicide bomber blows up a bus, killing 26 persons, including three U.S. citizens, and injuring some 80 others, among them three other U.S. citizens. Hamas's Izz al-Din al-Qassem Battalion claims responsibility for the bombing in retaliation for the Hebron massacre two years previously, but later denies involvement.

March 4

Israel: A suicide bomber detonates an explosive device outside the Dizengoff Center, Tel Aviv's largest shopping mall, killing 20 persons and injuring 75 others, including two U.S. citizens. Hamas and the Palestine Islamic Jihad (PIJ) both claim responsibility for the bombing.

March 26

Cambodia: Suspected Khmer Rouge guerrillas abduct 26 Cambodian mine-disposal experts, their British supervisor, and his translator near the Angkor Wat temple complex. Six of the hostages escape, leaving the British national and his interpreter captive. At least five police officers and soldiers are killed by land mines while searching for the hostages.

April 18

Egypt: Four IG militants open fire on a group of Greek tourists in front of the Europa Hotel in Cairo, killing 18 Greeks and injuring 12 Greeks and two Egyptians. The IG claims that it intended to attack a group of Israeli tourists it believed were staying at the hotel in revenge for Israeli actions in Lebanon.

May 13

West Bank: Arab gunmen open fire on a bus and a group of Yeshiva students near the Bet El settlement, killing a dual U.S./Israeli citizen and wounding three Israelis. No one claims responsibility for the attack, but Hamas is suspected.

May 31

Nicaragua: A gang of former contra guerrillas kidnap a U.S. employee of USAID who was assisting with election preparations in rural northern Nicaragua. She is released unharmed the next day after members of the international commission overseeing the preparations intervene.

June 9

Israel: Unidentified gunmen open fire on a car near Zekharya, killing a dual U.S./Israeli citizen and an Israeli. The PFLP is suspected.

June 25

Saudi Arabia: A fuel truck carrying a bomb explodes outside the U.S. military's Khubar Towers housing facility in Dhahran, killing 19 U.S. military personnel and wounding 515 persons, including 240 U.S. personnel. Several groups claim responsibility for the attack, which remains under investigation.

July 12

Austria: Four Kurdish militants occupy a Reuters news agency office in Vienna and hold two employees hostage for several hours before surrendering. The attackers are suspected PKK sympathizers.

July 25

United States: A bomb explodes at the Summer Olympic games in Atlanta, Georgia.

August 1

Algeria: A bomb explodes at the home of the French archbishop of Oran, killing him and his chauffeur. The attack occurrs after the Archbishop's meeting with the French foreign minister. The AIG is suspected.

August 17

Sudan: Sudan People's Liberation Army (SPLA) rebels kidnap six missionaries in Mapourdit, including a U.S. citizen, an Italian, three Australians, and a Sudanese. The SPLA releases the hostages on August 28.

November 1

Sudan: A breakaway group from the SPLA kidnaps three International Committee of the Red Cross (ICRC) workers, including a U.S. citizen, an Australian, and a Kenyan. On December 9, the rebels release the hostages in exchange for ICRC supplies and a health survey for their camp.

December 11
Colombia: Five armed men claiming to be FARC members kidnap a U.S. geologist at a methane gas exploration site in La Guajira Department. The geologist is killed, and his body is retrieved by Colombian authorities in February 1997.

December 17
Peru: Twenty-three members of the Tupac Amaru Revolutionary Movement (MRTA) take several hundred people hostage at a party given at the Japanese Ambassador's residence in Lima. Among the hostages are several U.S. officials, foreign ambassadors and other diplomats, Peruvian government officials, and Japanese businessmen. The group demands the release of all MRTA members in prison and safe passage for the ex-prisoners as well as themselves. The terrorists release most of the hostages in December but still hold 81 Peruvians and Japanese citizens at the end of the year.

1997

January 2–13
United States: A series of letter bombs with Alexandria, Egypt, postmarks are discovered at *Al-Hayat* newspaper bureaus in Washington, D.C.; New York City; London; and Riyadh, Saudi Arabia. Three similar devices, also postmarked in Egypt, are found at a prison facility in Leavenworth, Kansas. Bomb disposal experts defuse all the devices, but one detonates at the *Al-Hayat* office in London, injuring two security guards and causing minor damage.

January 18
Rwanda: Hutu militants shoot and kill three Spanish aid workers from Doctors Without Borders and wound one U.S. citizen.

February 23
United States: A Palestinian gunman opens fire on tourists at an observation deck atop the Empire State Building in New York City, killing a Danish national and wounding visitors from the United States, Argentina, Switzerland, and France before turning the gun onto himself. A handwritten note carried by the gunman claims that the act is meant as punishment against the "enemies of Palestine."

March 7
Colombia: FARC guerrillas kidnap a U.S. mining employee and his Colombian colleague who are searching for gold in Colombia. On November 16, the rebels release the two hostages after receiving a $50,000 ransom.

April 11–12
Bosnia: Several hours before his arrival, police discover and defuse 23 land mines under a bridge that is part of Pope John Paul II's motorcade in Sarajevo.

July 7
Sri Lanka: LTTE guerrillas hijack a North Korean food ship, killing one North Korean crew member, and hold 37 others hostage. On July 12, the LTTE releases the hostages to the International Committee of the Red Cross.

July 30
Israel: Two bombs detonate in the Mahane Yehuda market in Jerusalem, killing 15 persons—including two suspected suicide bombers—and wound 168 others.

September 4
Israel: Hamas suicide bombers claim the lives of more than 20 Israeli civilians.

October 15
Sri Lanka: LTTE guerrillas detonate a massive truck bomb in the parking lot of a major hotel next to the new World Trade Center in Colombo, killing 18 persons and injuring at least 110 others. Among the injured are seven U.S. citizens and 33 other foreign nationals. The explosion causes extensive damage to several international hotels and the World Trade Center.

November 17
Egypt: Islamic militants kill 62 at Luxor.

December 23

Pakistan: Unidentified assailants fire shots at the teachers' residential compound of the Karachi American School, wounding one Frontier Constabulary guard. The compound, home to nine U.S. citizen and six Canadian teachers, is one block from the school in a neighborhood with seven other consulate residences. The guard post has been in place since the November 12 murders of four Union Texas Petroleum employees.

1998

February 3

Greece: Bombs are detonated at two McDonald's restaurants in the Halandri and Vrilissia suburbs of Athens, causing extensive damage. Authorities suspect anarchists of carrying out the attacks in retaliation for the arrest of the alleged leader of the Fighting Guerrilla Formation (MAS).

March 22

Chad: Gunmen kidnap six French and two Italian nationals in the Tibesti region. Chadian forces free all but one hostage within hours. A group called the National Front for the Renewal of Chad (FNTR; the French acronym) claims responsibility.

April 15

Somalia: Multiple media sources report the abduction by militiamen of nine Red Cross and Red Crescent workers at an airstrip north of Mogadishu. The hostages include a U.S. citizen, a German, a Belgian, a French citizen, a Norwegian, two Swiss, and one Somali. The gunmen are members of a subclan loyal to Ali Mahdi Mohammed, who controls the northern section of the capital. On April 24, the hostages are released unharmed, and no ransom is paid.

May 27

Colombia: In Santa Marta, 20 ELN rebels bomb the offices of a subsidiary of the U.S.-owned Dole company. The guerrillas overpower the guards, gag the employees, and destroy files before detonating four bombs, partially destroying the headquarters.

July 18

Ecuador: The Indigenous Defense Front for Pastaza Province (FDIP) kidnaps three employees of an Ecuadorian pipeline maker subcontracted by a U.S. oil company in Pastaza Province. The group accuses the company of causing environmental damage in its oil field developments. On July 28, the FDIP releases one hostage, and it releases the remaining two hostages the next day.

August 1

Northern Ireland: A 500-pound car bomb explodes outside a shoe store in Banbridge, injuring 35 people and damaging at least 200 homes. Authorities received a warning telephone call and are evacuating the area when the bomb goes off. The Real IRA, the Republic of Ireland-based military wing of the 32 County Sovereignty Council, claims responsibility.

August 7

Kenya: U.S. embassies in Kenya and Tanania are bombed (see the following entry); Islamic extremist Osama bin Laden is believed to have been responsible.

August 7

Tanzania: A bomb detonates outside the U.S. embassy in Dar es Salaam, killing seven FSN members and three Tanzanian citizens; one U.S. citizen and 76 Tanzanians are injured. The explosion causes major structural damage to the U.S. embassy facility. The U.S. government holds Osama bin Laden responsible.

August 15

Northern Ireland: A 500-pound car bomb explodes outside a local courthouse in Omag's central shopping district, killing 29 persons and injuring more than 330. Authorities are in the process of clearing the shopping area around the courthouse when the bomb explodes. On August 17, authorities arrest five local men suspected of involvement in the bombing. The Real IRA claims responsibility.

August 20

Afghanistan: U.S. cruise missiles hit suspected terrorist bases in Sudan and Afghanistan.

August 25
South Africa: A bomb explodes in the Planet Hollywood restaurant in Capetown, killing one person and injuring at least 24 others—including nine British citizens—and causing major damage. The Muslims Against Global Oppression (MAGO) claims responsibility in a phone call to a local radio station, stating that the bomb is in retaliation for the U.S. missile attacks on terrorist facilities in Sudan and Afghanistan.

August 29
Belgium: Arsonists firebomb a McDonald's restaurant in Puurs, destroying the restaurant and causing up to $1.4 million in damage. The Animal Liberation Front (ALF) claims responsibility for the attack.

October 5
Ecuador: Three employees of the Santa Fe Oil Company, two U.S. citizens and one Ecuadorian, are kidnapped, according to local press accounts. One U.S. citizen escapes the next day.

November 15
Colombia: Armed assailants follow a U.S. businessman to his family home in Cundinamarca Department and kidnap his 11-year-old son after stealing money, jewelry, one automobile, and two cell phones. The kidnappers demand $1 million in ransom. On January 21, 1999, the U.S. embassy reports that the kidnappers have released the boy to his mother and uncle in Tolima Department. It is not known if any ransom is paid. The kidnappers claim to be members of the Leftist Revolutionary Armed Commandos for Peace in Colombia.

December 28
Yemen: Armed militants kidnap a group of tourists traveling on the main road from Habban to Aden. The victims include two U.S. citizens, 12 Britons, and two Australians. On December 29, Yemeni security forces undertake a rescue attempt, during which three Britons and one Australian are killed, and one U.S. citizen is injured seriously. Yemeni officials report that the kidnappers belong to the Islamic Jihad.

1999

January 2
Angola: A United Nations plane carrying one U.S. citizen, four Angolans, two Philippine nationals, and one Namibian is shot down, according to a U.N. official. No deaths or injuries are reported. Angolan authorities blame the attack on UNITA rebels. UNITA officials deny shooting down the plane.

February 16
Austria: Kurdish protesters storm and occupy the Greek embassy in Vienna, taking the Greek ambassador and six other persons hostage. Several hours later, the protesters release the hostages and leave the embassy. The attack follows the Turkish Government's announcement of the successful capture of PKK leader Abdullah Ocalan.

March 1
Uganda: According to French diplomatic reports, 150 armed Hutu rebels attack three tourist camps, killing four Ugandans and abducting three U.S. citizens, six Britons, three New Zealanders, two Danish citizens, one Australian, and one Canadian national. On March 2, U.S. embassy officials report that the Hutu rebels have killed two U.S. citizens, four Britons, and two New Zealanders. The rebels release the remaining hostages.

April 5
Netherlands: Two Libyan suspects are tried on charges of having planted the bomb that blew up Pan Am flight 103 over Scotland in 1988 that killed 270 people.

May 30
Colombia: The Cali local press reports that heavily armed ELN militants attacked a church in the neighborhood of Ciudad Jardín, kidnapping 160 persons, including six U.S. citizens and one French national. The rebels release approximately 80 persons, including three U.S. citizens, later that day. On June 3, the ELN releases an additional five hostages. On June 15, the rebels release 33 hostages, including two U.S. citizens, according to U.S. embassy reports. On December 10, the local press reports that the rebels have released the remaining hostages unharmed.

June 22

India: The United Liberation Front of Assam, with the backing of Pakistan's Inter-Service Intelligence, claims responsibility for the bombing at the Julpaiguri railroad station that kills 10 persons and injures 80 others, according to senior government officials.

September 29

India: According to press reports, unidentified militants throw grenades at a government building in Srinagar, killing one police officer and causing undetermined damage. The Harakat al-Mujahideen (HUM) claims responsibility.

October 27

Armenia: Gunmen attack the parliament while it is in session, killing the prime minister and six others.

November 12

Pakistan: U.S. and UN buildings are targeted in a rocket attack allegedly coordinated as retaliation for sanctions against Afghanistan for its failure to turn over Osama bin Laden.

December 24

India: Muslim terrorists hijack an Indian Airlines jet with 189 onboard. On December 31, the Indian government agrees to release three imprisoned militants in exchange for the hostages' safe return. The plane and remaining hostages are released unharmed later that day.

2000

January 8

Sudan: Humanitarian Aid Commission officials report that SPLA rebels attacked a CARE vehicle in Al Wahdah State, killing the CARE office director and his driver and abducting two others. An SPLA spokesperson denies the group's involvement.

March 21

India: Armed militants kill 35 Sikhs in Chadisinghpoora Village, according to press reports. Police officers arrest Muslim militants, who confess to helping two groups suspected in the massacre—the Lashkar-e-Tayyiba and the Hizb ul-Mujahidin—two of the principal militant Muslim groups in Kashmir.

May 5

Sierra Leone: RUF militants kidnapp 300 UNAMSIL peacekeepers throughout the country, according to press reports. On May 15, in Foya, Liberia, the kidnappers release 139 hostages. On May 28, on the Liberia and Sierra Leone border, armed militants release unharmed the last of the UN peacekeepers.

June 8

Greece: In Athens, the press reports two unidentified gunmen killed British Defense Attaché Stephen Saunders in an ambush. The Revolutionary Organization 17 November claims responsibility.

July 27

Colombia: In Bogotá, suspected Guevarist Revolutionary Army (ARG) militants kidnap a French aid worker affiliated with Doctors Without Borders, according to press reports. The ARG is a suspected faction of the ELN.

August 12

Kyrgyzstan: In the Kara-Su Valley, according to press accounts, Islamic Movement of Uzbekistan rebels take four U.S. citizens and one Kyrgyzstani soldier hostage. The rebels kill the soldier, but the four U.S. citizens escape on August 18.

September 7

Guinea: Suspected RUF rebels kidnap three Catholic missionaries—one U.S. citizen and two Italian priests—in Pamlap, according to press accounts. In early December, the two Italian priests escape.

October 12

Yemen: In Aden, a small dinghy carrying explosives ram the U.S. destroyer, USS *Cole,* killing 17 sailors and injuring 39 others. Supporters of Osama bin Laden are suspected of the attack.

Ecuador: In Sucumbios Province, a group of armed kidnappers led by former members of defunct Colombian terrorist organization the Popular Liberation Army (EPL) take hostage 10 employees of Spanish energy consortium REPSOL. Those kidnapped include five U.S. citizens, one Argentine, one Chilean, one New Zealander, and two French pilots who escape four days later. On January 30, 2001, the kidnappers murder American hostage Ronald Sander. The remaining hostages are released on February 23 following the payment of $13 million in ransom by the oil companies.

November 19

Jordan: In Amman, armed militants attempt to assassinate the Israeli vice consul, according to press reports. The Movement for the Struggle of the Jordanian Islamic Resistance Movement and Ahmad al-Daqamisah Group both claim responsibility.

December 30

Philippines: A bomb explodes in a plaza across the street from the U.S. embassy in Manila, injuring nine persons, according to press reports. The Moro Islamic Liberation Front is possibly responsible.

2001

May 27

Muslim Abu Sayyaf guerrillas seize 13 tourists and 3 staff members at a resort on Palawan Island and take their captives to Basilan Island. The captives include three U.S. citizens: Guellermo Sobero and missionaries Martin and Gracia Burnham. Philippine troops fight a series of battles with the guerrillas between June 1 and June 3 during which nine hostages escape and two are found dead. The guerrillas take additional hostages when they seize the hospital in the town of Lamitan. On June 12, Abu Sayyaf spokesman Abu Sabaya claims that Sobero has been killed and beheaded; his body is found in October. The Burnhams remain in captivity until June 2002.

September

A global "war on terrorism" is declared in the wake of the September 11 attacks on the United States. Letters containing anthrax are sent through the U.S. postal system in Washington, D.C., and New York areas. Several people are infected, a few fatally.

October–November

On October 7, the U.S. Centers for Disease Control and Prevention (CDC) report that investigators have detected evidence that the deadly anthrax bacterium is present in the building where a Florida man who died of anthrax on October 5 had worked. Discovery of a second anthrax case triggers a major investigation by the Federal Bureau of Investigation (FBI).

December 11

The chairman of the Jewish Defense League and another JDL member are arrested on charges of conspiring to bomb an Islamic mosque and the offices of a U.S. congressman in Los Angeles.

December 13

A bus carrying 45 Jewish civilians traveling in the West Bank is hit by two bombs, raked by gunfire, and hit with grenades. Hamas claims responsibility for the attack, which kills 10 and wounds more than 30.

2002

January

Prisoners captured by U.S. forces in its "war on terrorism" begin to arrive in military custody at the U.S. base in Guantánamo Bay, Cuba. The prisoners are from many different countries, and hundreds are eventually held for "interrogation."

January 23

Armed militants kidnap *Wall Street Journal* reporter Daniel Pearl in Karachi, Pakistan. Pakistani authorities receive a videotape on February 20 depicting Pearl's murder. His grave is found near Karachi on May 16. Pakistani authorities arrest four suspects. Ringleader Ahmad Omar Saeed Sheikh claims to have organized Pearl's kidnapping to protest Pakistan's subservience to the United States; Saeed Sheikh belonged to Jaish-e-Muhammad, an Islamic separatist group in Kashmir. All four suspects are convicted on July 15. Saeed Sheikh is sentenced to death, the others to life imprisonment.

February

Muslim extremists kill scores of Hindu activists aboard a train in India. Hindu mobs retaliate by killing hundreds of Muslims.

March 27

A suicide bomber kills 29 people and wounds more than 100 in an attack on a hotel in the Israeli city of Netanya.

April 11

A synagogue in Tunisia is firebombed, killing 19 and wounding more than 20. Al-Qaeda is blamed for the attack.

May 8

A suicide bomber detonates a car bomb next to a shuttle bus at a hotel in downtown Karachi, Pakistan, killing 14, including 11 French civilians. The bomber allegedly had ties to al-Qaeda.

June

Israel begins construction on a fence system to seal off the West Bank from Israel. Called the "Separation Wall" by some and the "Security Barrier" by others, the wall is purportedly to block terrorist infiltration routes.

June 7

Philippine Army troops attack Abu Sayyaf terrorists on Mindanao Island in an attempt to rescue U.S. citizen Martin Burnham and his wife Gracia, who were kidnapped more than a year before. Burnham is killed but his wife, though wounded, is freed. A Filipino hostage is killed, as are four of the guerrillas. Seven soldiers are wounded.

June 18

A 22-year-old member of Hamas detonates a suicide bomb in a bus in Jerusalem, killing 19 people and wounding at least 55, many of whom are high school students.

July 31

A bomb hidden in a bag in the Frank Sinatra International Student Center of Jerusalem's Hebrew University kills nine persons and wounds 87. The dead include five U.S. citizens and four Israelis. The wounded include four U.S. citizens, two Japanese, and three South Koreans. The Islamic Resistance Movement (HAMAS) claims responsibility.

August 7

Members of FARC attack Colombia's presidential palace during the inauguration of president Álvaro Uribe, killing 19 people.

October 12

A bomb explodes in a pub in Kuta, a town on the Indonesian island of Bali. As patrons and others rush into the street, a more powerful second bomb hidden inside a van is detonated. 202 people are killed and 209 injured in these attacks, most of them tourists. Jemaah Islamiya Organization claims responsibility.

October 28

Gunmen in Amman assassinate Laurence Foley, Executive Officer of the U.S. Agency for International Development Mission, in Jordan. Jordan arrests two men who claim to be acting on the orders of Abu Musab al-Zarqawi. In April 2004, the two gunmen are sentenced to death.

November 28

A hotel in Mombassa, Kenya, is bombed, killing 15 people and wounding 40. Al-Qaeda is implicated in the attack.

2003

February 8

A car bomb in Bogotá, Colombia, kills 20 and injures 114. FARC members are blamed for the attack.

May 12

Three housing compounds for expatriate workers in Riyadh, Saudi Arabia, are bombed, killing dozens and wounding about 140. Al-Qaeda cells are implicated.

May 16

Synchronized bombs, including suicide devices, explode in Casablanca, Morocco, killing more than 40 and wounding about 100. Al-Qaeda is linked to the attacks.

August 5

Bombs as the J. W. Marriott Hotel in Jakarta, Indonesia, kill at least 17 and wound nearly 140. Jemaah Islamiya Organization is responsible.

August 19

A suicide bomber kills 22 on a Jerusalem bus. The United Nations headquarters in Baghdad is bombed, killing 22. The Abu Hafs al-Masri Brigades, an al-Qaeda–affiliated group, claims responsibility.

October 15

A remote-controlled bomb explodes under a car in a U.S. diplomatic convoy passing through the northern Gaza Strip. Three security guards, all employees of DynCorp, are killed. A fourth is wounded.

October 23–26

Chechen rebels take more than 700 people hostage at a Moscow theater, demanding that Russian troops leave Chechnya. After nearly three days, special forces troops pump an aerosol anesthetic gas into the theater and attack. All of the rebels and 129 of the hostages are killed, with most of the hostages dying from the gas.

October 26

Iraqis using an improvised rocket launcher bombard the al-Rashid Hotel in Baghdad, killing one U.S. Army officer and wounding 17 persons. The wounded include four U.S. military personnel and seven American civilians.

November 9

A bomb explodes in Riyadh, Saudi Arabia, at a compound housing primarily non-Saudi Arab families, killing at least 17 and injuring more than 120. Militant Islamists are blamed.

November 11

Two synagogues in Istanbul, Turkey, are bombed, killing 23 and wounding about 200. An al-Qaeda–affiliated group, the Abu Hafs al-Masri Brigades, claims responsibility.

November 15

Grenade attacks on two bars frequented by Americans in Bogotá kill one person and wound 72, including four Americans. Colombian authorities suspect FARC (the Revolutionary Armed Forces of Colombia).

November 20

The British consulate and HSBC Bank's local headquarters are bombed in Istanbul, Turkey, killing 27 and wounding more than 450.

2004

February 6

A bomb in a Moscow subway car kills 39 and wounds more than 100. Chechen rebels are implicated in the attack.

March 2

Sectarian suicide bombings in Iraq at Shia holy sites kill 181 and wound about 500.

March 11

Ten bombs are detonated on several commuter trains in Madrid, Spain, killing 191 and wounding more than 1,500. Al-Qaeda cells are responsible for the attacks.

March 14

Suicide bombers kill 10 people in the Israeli port of Ashdod. The bombers had been hidden in a container exported from the Gaza Strip.

March 22

An Israeli missile attack in the occupied territory of the West Bank kills Sheik Ahmed Yassin, founder of Hamas.

April 17

An Israeli missile attack in the occupied territory of the West Bank kills Hamas leader Abdel Aziz Rantisi.

April 21

A car bomb in Riyadh, Saudi Arabia, kills five and wounds 147. An al-Qaeda–affiliated group, calling itself the Brigade of the Two Holy Shrines, claims responsibility.

June 12

In Riyadh, Saudi Arabia, attackers abduct American contractor Paul Johnson. On June 19, 2004, an Islamist website posts pictures of the victim's decapitated body, which is later found on a street in eastern Riyadh. The al-Qaeda organization in Saudi Arabia claims responsibility.

May 29

Four Islamic radicals attack a foreign residential compound and oil installation in Al-Khobar, Saudi Arabia, taking hostages. Twenty-two are killed and 25 injured in the attack.

August 24

Two Russian airliners crash, almost simultaneously. Investigators find the same explosive residue at both crash sites. Chechen suicide bombers are suspected, but a group calling itself the Islambouli Brigades of al-Qaeda claims responsibility.

August 31

Hamas suicide bombers detonate on two buses almost simultaneously in the Israeli city of Beersheba, killing at least 15 and wounding dozens.

A Chechen woman detonates a bomb near a Moscow subway station, killing nine and wounding about 100. The Islambouli Brigades of Al-Qaeda claim responsibility.

September 1–3

Heavily armed Chechen rebels seize a school in Beslan, North Ossetia, taking 1,200 hostages. As explosives are detonated and Russian special forces retake the school, more than 330 people are killed, most of them schoolchildren.

September 29

In the Israeli town of Sderot two young children are killed by Hamas rocket fire, the first fatalities recorded as a result of the Qassam rocket.

October 7

In Taba, Egypt, Islamic assailants drive a car bomb into the lobby of the Hilton Hotel, detonating the explosives, killing 34 people, and wounding 159 others.

November 2

A Dutch citizen of Moroccan descent murders filmmaker Theo van Gogh, shooting van Gogh multiple times, and then slitting his throat. Van Gogh had been a critic of Islam.

2005

January 19

In Che, Democratic Republic of the Congo, armed assailants attack civilians with guns and machetes, killing 16 people, kidnapping 34 girls, and burning 220 homes. No group claims responsibility, although it is widely believed that the Lendu-Ndouchi Ethnic Group is responsible.

February 14

Rafik Hariri, former prime minister of Lebanon, is assassinated by a car bomb, which also kills 20 others. Syrian agents are suspected.

March 19

At about 10:30 P.M., in Fatehpur, Balochistan, Pakistan, an improvised explosive device explodes at a Sufi memorial, killing 50 Pakistani civilians and wounding 40 others. Shortly after the explosion, a second device is found at the shrine and disarmed. Approximately 10,000 people had gathered for the annual Urs celebration. No group claimed responsibility.

April 15

In Sobhani, Nepal, gunmen shoot and kill 10 Nepalese civilians, including one child, and wound two others. The attackers set fire to nine houses and detonate improvised explosive devices in four other homes. No one claims responsibility, although it is widely believed that the Communist Party of Nepal (Maoist)/People's Front is responsible.

April 18

Near Buenaventura, Valle del Cauca, Colombia, assailants kidnap four children and eight civilians. On April 21, authorities discover their bodies. No group claims responsibility, although the Revolutionary Armed Forces of Colombia (FARC) are believed to be responsible.

May 3

In Mogadishu, Somalia, a timed improvised explosive device explodes in a soccer stadium where the interim prime minister is giving a speech, killing 15 civilians and injuring 40 others. No group claims responsibility.

May 5

In the early morning, in Gulu, Uganda, assailants attack villagers with machetes and hoes, killing 10 villagers and wounding 14 others. No group claims responsibility, but a Ugandan army spokesman states that the Lord's Resistance Army is responsible.

May 7

Unknown attackers detonate three powerful bombs in a coordinated attack against a trade fair held at a convention center and two upscale shopping centers in Yangon, Myanmar, killing at least 25 civilians and injuring an estimated 200 civilians. No group claims responsibility for the attacks, although the military government of Myanmar blames several nationalist groups, including the Shan State Army.

May 23

In Nidja, Democratic Republic of the Congo, armed assailants attack a village, killing 18 people, injuring 11, and kidnapping 50 others. The interim governor of Sud-Kivu Province says the members of the Democratic Forces for the Liberation of Rwanda are responsible.

May 27

At about 11:20 A.M., in Islamabad, Pakistan, assailants detonate an improvised explosive device on the Bari Imam Shia Shrine compound, killing 19 civilians and wounding 86 others. No group claims responsibility.

May 28

In Tentena, Indonesia, attackers detonate an improvised explosive device (IED) in a crowded market in a predominantly Christian town and detonate another IED nearby 15 minutes later, killing 19 civilians and injuring at least 57. No group claims responsibility.

June 1

In Deukoue, Côte d'Ivoire, assailants armed with 12-caliber shotguns and machetes attack sleeping villagers, killing 41 civilians, wounding 64 others, and burning 30 huts. No group claims responsibility.

At about 9:00 A.M., in Kandahar, Afghanistan, an improvised explosive device is detonated inside a mosque during a funeral ceremony, killing the police chief of Kabul and 20 civilians and wounding 69 other civilians. No group claims responsibility, although al-Qaeda is believed to be responsible.

June 13

In Pulwama, Jammu and Kashmir, India, assailants detonate a vehicle-born improvised explosive device near a high school, a state bank of India, a post office, a shopping center, office complexes, and a Central Reserve Police Force camp. The explosion kills two schoolchildren and at least 10 civilians, injuring at least 12 schoolchildren and 88 other civilians. No group claims responsibility, but Hizb ul-Mujahidin (HM) and Harakat ul-Mujahidin (HUM) are believed to be responsible.

June 21

George Hawi, former head of Lebanon's Communist Party, is assassinated by a remotely controlled car bomb. Syrian agents are suspected.

June 28

Dhari Ali al-Fayadh, a member of Iraq's newly constituted parliament, is assassinated by a suicide car bomb in Baghdad.

July 3

Gunmen kidnap Ihab Sherif, Egypt's senior diplomat in Baghdad. He was to become the first Arab ambassador to the newly formed Iraqi government.

In Kokambo, Democratic Republic of the Congo, armed assailants fire upon and kill 15 civilians, many of whom are fishermen. No group claims responsibility.

July 7

Four bombs explode in London, three simultaneously aboard London Underground trains and one aboard a bus. The attacks, carried out by suicide bombers, kill more than 50 people and injure more than 700.

July 9

In Kalonge Chiefdom, Bukavu, Democratic Republic of the Congo, armed assailants force residents into their homes, lock them in, and set fire to the houses, killing 15 children and 24 other civilians, mostly women. No group claims responsibility, although the Democratic Forces for the Liberation of Rwanda (FDLR) are believed to be responsible for the attack.

July 10

In Kitgum District, Uganda, assailants ambush a vehicle traveling to market, killing 14 occupants, stealing their food, and setting fire to the vehicle. Although no group claims responsibility, the Lord's

Resistance Army is believed to have carried out the attack.

July 21
An identical bombing attack to that of July 7 is attempted in London, but it fails when the explosives misfire. Four bombs—three aboard Underground trains and one aboard a bus—fail to detonate because the explosives had degraded over time. British-based cells sympathetic to al-Qaeda were responsible for both attacks.

July 23
Three suicide bombers detonate bombs at the Egyptian resort town of Sharm el-Sheikh in Sinai. More than 60 people are killed, including more than 40 Egyptians and at least 15 foreign tourists, mainly Europeans. The assault is the latest in a series of attacks against the Egyptian tourist industry.

July 28
Near Harpalganj, Uttar Pradesh, India, assailants detonate explosives on the Patna-Delhi Shramjeevi express train, killing 12 civilians and wounding 57 others. No group claims responsibility.

August 23
In Paloma, Colombia, attackers shoot and kill 15 civilians and wound six others. No group claims responsibility, but the Revolutionary Armed Forces of Colombia (FARC) are believed to be responsible.

September 5
In Bhelwa Village, Giridih, Jharkhand, India, assailants fire on a group of villagers who are meeting to form a self-defense group to fight the Communist Party of India–Maoist (CPI-Maoist). The attack kills 11 civilians. No group claims responsibility.

September 11
In Bheluaghati, Giridih, Jharkhand, India, approximately 100 people attack Village Defense Committee members, killing at least one child and 14 civilians and injuring at least six others. The assailants cut the throats of their victims. No group claims responsibility, but the Communist Party of India–Maoist is believed to be responsible.

September 26
Armed assailants attacked a village in Ouaddai, Chad, killing 56 civilians. No group claims responsibility, but the Janjaweed militia are believed to be responsible.

September 30
In Darfur, Sudan, a group of 300 armed assailants attack a camp for displaced people, killing 29 civilians, wounding 10 others, and destroying 80 temporary shelters. No group claims responsibility.

October 1
Suicide bombers in Kuta, Bali, Indonesia, and Jambaran Bay, Bali, Indonesia, simultaneously detonate three improvised explosive devices at three restaurants (one in Kuta, two in Jambaran Bay), killing at least 26 civilians and wounding 129 others. Although it does not claim responsibility, the Jemaah Islamiya Organization is believed to have carried out the attacks.

October 2
In Vista Hermosa, Meta, Colombia, assailants launch grenades at a farm, killing 13 civilians and wounding at least 11 others. No group claims responsibility, but the Revolutionary Armed Forces of Colombia are believed to be responsible.

October 10
At night, in the eastern part of the Democratic Republic of the Congo, armed assailants attack a village, killing 25 civilians and wounding several others. No group claims responsibility, although the Democratic Forces for the Liberation of Rwanda are believed to be responsible for the attack.

October 15
In Jengka, Karbi Anglong, Assam, India, two passenger buses are attacked by armed assailants who kill 23 civilians by slitting their throats and injure two children. No group claims responsibility.

October 29
In New Delhi, India, assailants launch coordinated attacks using improvised explosive devices, killing at least 62 civilians and injuring between 155 and 210 others. Authorities believe Lashkar-e-Tayyiba is responsible.

November 1

At about 11:10 A.M., in Nowgam, Srinagar, Jammu and Kashmir, India, a suicide bomber detonates a car full of explosives, killing six civilians, one child, and wounding 15 civilians. Jaish-e-Mohammed claims responsibility.

November 9

Three hotels are bombed in Amman, Jordan, killing 59, including more than 20 people who are at a wedding reception. Al-Qaeda in Iraq claims credit for the attacks, via an Internet posting. The posting states that all of the attacks were carried out by suicide bombers, including a husband-and-wife team. Tanzim Qa'idat al-Jihad fi Bilad al-Rafidayn (QJBR) (al-Qaeda in Iraq) claims responsibility.

November 21

In Pader District, Uganda, armed assailants attack a bus, killing 12 civilians and wounding five others. No group claims responsibility, but the Lord's Resistance Army is believed by authorities to be responsible.

December 3

In César, Colombia, approximately 24 civilians are kidnapped by armed assailants, and at least 13 are tortured and killed. No group claims responsibility, but Colombian authorities attribute the attack to the AUC.

December 8

Assailants in Jandola, Pakistan, detonate an explosive device in a market, killing 12 civilians and wounding 40 others. No group claims responsibility.

December 19

In the Darfur province of Sudan, armed assailants attack a village, killing two children and 18 civilian adults and burning 50 huts. No claim of responsibility is made.

December 20

On the waters of Rivers State, Nigeria, assailants in speedboats throw explosive devices at a Royal Dutch Shell oil pipeline. The ensuing explosion kills about 20 civilian adults and eight children and destroys 20 homes. No group claims responsibility, but the Nigerian Government suggests that the Niger Delta People's Volunteer Force is responsible.

December 26

In the Darfur province of Sudan, armed assailants attack a village, killing 20 civilians and wounding 13 others. No group claims responsibility.

2006

January 19

Bin Laden warns Americans in an audiotape that al-Qaeda is planning more attacks on the United States. There have been more than 15 audio and video messages from him since the September 11 attacks.

March 3

An Iranian-born graduate of the University of North Carolina–Chapel Hill drives his car into a crowded part of campus, injuring nine people, to "avenge the deaths of Muslims worldwide."

June 15

The Liberation Tigers of Tamil Eelam detonate two claymore mines targeting a bus in Sri Lanka. A total of 68 civilians are killed and 60 are wounded.

July 11

A series of explosions rocks commuter trains in Mumbai, India, killing 209 and injuring 714 civilians.

July 31

Two suitcase bombs are discovered in trains near the German towns of Dortmund and Koblenz, undetonated because of an assembly error. Video footage from the Cologne train station, where the bombs were put on the trains, leads to the arrest of two Lebanese students in Germany, Youssef al-Hajdib and Jihad Hamad, and subsequently of three suspected co-conspirators in Lebanon.

August 10

British intelligence officials say they have disrupted a plot by British-born young men of Pakistani descent to explode bombs on as many as 10 London–United States jetliners during midflight.

Immediately, liquids are banned from carry-on luggage on flights to and from the United States and the United Kingdom.

September 12

Four attackers armed with grenades and machine guns attempt to storm the U.S. embassy in Damascus, Syria. Three of the gunmen and one Syrian guard are killed during a battle between the attackers and Syrian security forces. One Syrian employee of the embassy and at least 10 bystanders are wounded, among them, seven Syrian telephone company workers and a senior Chinese diplomat.

November 1

The Real IRA detonates a series of firebombs in two stores. Both buildings are completely destroyed, but no injuries are reported.

December 29

A car bombing at Madrid Barajas Airport, which wounds about 20 people, is attributed to Basque Fatherland and Liberty (ETA).

U.S. AND INTERNATIONAL REACTION TO SEPTEMBER 11, 2001, DAY BY DAY

September 11

Two hijacked airliners crash into the Twin Towers of the World Trade Center in New York City. Thousands are feared dead when the towers collapse more than an hour after the impacts. A third hijacked airliner crashes into the Pentagon, outside Washington, D.C. A fourth, possibly bound for another target in Washington, D.C., crashes in Somerset County, Pennsylvania, apparently after passengers attempt to overpower the hijackers.

The Federal Aviation Administration (FAA) suspends all air traffic in the United States and diverts international flights to Canada. Federal offices and public buildings in Washington, D.C., New York City, and other major cities are closed.

President George W. Bush, in Florida at the time of the attacks, flies first to Barksdale Air Force Base in Louisiana and then to Offutt Air Force Base in Nebraska before returning to the White House. During his first stop, he says, "The resolve of our great nation is being tested, but make no mistake: We will show the world that we will pass this test." That evening, he says that "the full resources of our intelligence and law-enforcement communities" are to be used to find the terrorists and bring them to justice. "We will make no distinction between the terrorists who committed these acts and those who harbor them."

Secretary of State Colin L. Powell cancels visit to Colombia and returns from a meeting of the OAS General Assembly in Lima, Peru. Before returning, he says that terrorists "will never be allowed to kill the spirit of democracy. They cannot destroy our society. They cannot destroy our belief in the democratic way."

The North Atlantic Council holds a special meeting in which it declares its solidarity with the United States and pledges its support and assistance. The Euro-Atlantic Partnership Council makes a similar pledge.

September 12

President Bush meets with his national security advisers and with leading members of Congress. He also telephones the leaders of Great Britain, Canada, France, Germany, China, and Russia as the first steps toward building an international coalition against terrorism. He calls the attacks "acts of war" and announces that he will ask Congress for additional funds to protect the nation's security.

Secretary of State Powell announces that he has authorized U.S. ambassadors to close their missions or suspend operations if they believe the threat level justifies it. Twenty-five percent do so. He also telephones the secretaries general of the United Nations and NATO and the president of the European Union. He expects to have active support from "friendly Muslim states" in the fight against terrorism and speaks to officials in Saudi Arabia and to the chairman of the Arab League.

The North Atlantic Council invokes Article 5 of the North Atlantic Treaty, thereby considering the terrorist attacks on the United States to be an attack on all member states, and pledges any necessary assistance.

Department of State spokesman Richard Boucher says during a briefing that the United States will make careful preparations before responding to terrorist attacks. He says that Secretary of State Powell has called the foreign ministers of Israel and the United Kingdom.

U.S. Congress meets to approve a joint resolution pledging support to President Bush in his efforts to find and punish the terrorists.

Both the UN General Assembly and Security Council approve by acclamation resolutions condemning the terrorist attacks on New York and Washington and calling on member states to cooperate to bring the "perpetrators, organizers, and sponsors of the outrages" to justice.

Finance ministers of the G-7 countries pledge their financial resources to ensure that the terrorist attacks on the United States do not destabilize the world economic community.

President Pervez Musharraf of Pakistan pledges his country's "unstinted cooperation in the fight against terrorism."

September 13

President Bush proclaims September 14 a National Day of Prayer and Remembrance and announces plans to visit New York City that day. He calls on Congress to approve a $20-billion supplemental appropriations bill to provide assistance to victims and their families, relief and recovery efforts, investigations, and precautions against further attacks.

During a White House daily briefing, Press Secretary Ari Fleischer says that President Bush will seek a resolution from Congress authorizing the use of military force in retaliation for the attacks on New York and Washington. Fleischer says that Bush has called various foreign leaders, including the prime ministers of Japan and Italy, the secretary general of NATO, and Crown Prince Abdullah of Saudi Arabia. President Bush later says that he has also talked with the presidents of Russia and China, and Secretary of State Powell adds that the president has spoken to Egyptian president Mubarak and King Abdallah II of Jordan.

President Bush and Attorney General John Ashcroft urge Americans not to hold Arab Americans and Muslims responsible for the terrorist attacks and pledge a swift response to violence against them.

Secretary of State Powell tells the Public Broadcasting System that the United States is creating an antiterrorism coalition that seeks to include the UN, NATO, the European Union, the OAS, and the Organization of Islamic States. He says that Osama bin Laden is a prime suspect in the terrorist attacks and notes that according to Saudi Arabian ambassador Prince Bandar, his government has revoked bin Laden's citizenship. His contacts with Islamic states include the president of Pakistan and officials in Saudi Arabia and Qatar. Powell says that the U.S. consul general in Jerusalem has been swamped with calls from Palestinians expressing their sympathy and condolences and disavowing any association with those who rejoice at the terrorist attacks.

During a special briefing at the State Department, Powell expresses his sympathy to other nations who lost citizens in the destruction of the World Trade Center and declares, "Terrorism is a crime against all civilization." He says that the United States has provided Pakistan with a list of areas for cooperation, and he intends to discuss that list with President Musharraf. Deputy Secretary of State Richard L. Armitage has already spoken with Pakistani representatives. Powell has also spoken with the prime minister and foreign minister of Israel and with Chairman Yasir Arafat in an effort to promote a cease-fire between Israel and the Palestinians.

Deputy Secretary of Defense Paul Wolfowitz says that a response to the terrorist attacks will be a sustained military campaign, "with the full resources of the U.S. government."

The State Department announces that Deputy Secretary of State Armitage, Assistant Secretary for European and Eurasian Affairs Elizabeth Jones, Assistant Secretary of State for South Asian Affairs Christina Rocca, and Coordinator for Counterterrorism Francis Taylor will visit Moscow and Brussels on September 19–20 to discuss cooperation against terrorism. The meeting in Moscow will include a meeting of a bilateral Afghan Working Group.

Secretary of the Treasury Paul O'Neill says that disruptions to the U.S. economy resulting from terrorist attacks will be short term, and prospects for a recovery remain good. The New York Stock Exchange is to reopen on September 17.

Secretary of Transportation Norman Mineta announces that U.S. airspace will be reopened to commercial air traffic. Airports will reopen on a case-by-case basis under more intense security. The only major airport that remains closed is Reagan National, in view of its proximity to downtown Washington.

The NATO-Russia Permanent Joint Council announces intensified cooperation to defeat terrorism.

September 14

After attending a memorial service at the Washington National Cathedral, President Bush visits the ruins of the World Trade Center in New York City.

President Bush orders the mobilization of up to 50,000 National Guard and Reserve personnel for port operations, medical and engineer support, and home defense. The Defense Department plans to mobilize 35,000 from all services.

Congress authorizes President Bush to use all necessary military force against the perpetrators of the September 11 attacks, their sponsors, and those who protect them. The Senate approves the resolution by a vote of 98-0; the House of Representatives' vote is 420 to 1. The House and Senate unanimously approve a supplemental spending bill authorizing up to $40 billion for disaster relief, counterterrorism, and military operations.

Secretary of State Powell enumerates his conversations with his counterparts in North Africa, the Middle East, and South Asia during a press briefing. These include the foreign ministers of India, Portugal, Saudi Arabia, Morocco, Tunisia, and Japan. He expects to hear from Israel's defense minister and Syria's foreign minister shortly. He also instructs U.S. ambassadors to talk to their foreign colleagues to convey the seriousness with which the government views the crisis. The assistant secretaries of state for Near Eastern Affairs, European and Eurasian Affairs, and Western Hemisphere Affairs invite foreign ambassadors to the State Department for further discussions. President Assad of Syria sends President Bush a letter of support. He warns Afghanistan's Taliban government that continued support for bin Laden will have consequences and also warns that lack of support for the struggle against terrorism may effect U.S. relations with certain countries.

During a visit to Washington to commemorate the 50th anniversary of the ANZUS Treaty, Australian prime minister John Howard says that the collective security provision of Article IV applies to the terrorist attacks on the United States.

Parliamentary leaders of the 19 NATO countries endorse a statement supporting the North Atlantic Council's pledge of solidarity with the United States.

U.S. trade representative Robert Zoellick announces that the World Trade Organization meeting in Qatar will be held in November as scheduled.

September 15

President Bush meets with his national security advisers at Camp David, in Maryland. He tells reporters: "This act will not stand; we will find those who did it; we will smoke them out of their holes; we will get them running and we'll bring them to justice." He also confirms that Osama bin Laden is a "prime suspect."

Secretary of State Powell praises Pakistan's willingness to cooperate and expresses gratification at worldwide expressions of support. "Dozens of countries lost lives [at the World Trade Center], and they realize that this was an attack against them, as well."

The House of Representatives approves a Concurrent Resolution urging that in the struggle against terrorism, the rights of Arab Americans, American Muslims, and Americans from South Asia be protected and that acts of violence or discrimination against them will be condemned.

September 16

After returning to the White House from Camp David, President Bush expresses satisfaction at positive responses from the leaders of Pakistan, India, and Saudi Arabia. He warns the American public that "this war on terrorism is going to take a while," and that they must be patient.

Vice President Richard B. Cheney states on NBC-TV's *Meet the Press* that nations harboring terrorist groups will "face the full wrath of the United States." He says that no evidence has been found linking Iraq to bin Laden and his al-Qaeda organization, and it is not known whether bin Laden is still in Afghanistan. Terrorist attacks will not change U.S. relations with Israel or force a withdrawal from the Middle East.

On the CBS-TV show *Face the Nation,* Secretary of State Powell says that Pakistan's president Musharraf has agreed to support the U.S. antiterrorist campaign. Syria and even Iran have made fairly positive statements. Nothing has been heard from Iraq, but no links had been found between Iraq and bin Laden. Existing sanctions against Iraq will remain in place. Powell later tells CNN's *Late Edition* that the United States will insist that Afghanistan's Taliban government cooperate with the United States against bin Laden or face the consequences. Saudi Arabia and the Gulf states have been "supportive" and "ready to cooperate."

Secretary of Defense Donald H. Rumsfeld tells reporters that the campaign against terrorism will be a years-long international effort. He hints that countries harboring terrorists could face a U.S. military response.

September 17

President Bush addresses Pentagon employees and discusses the employment of mobilized reserves and National Guards. When he pledges to find "those evil-doers," he reminds his audience of the posters in the Old West that read, "Wanted, dead or alive." In the afternoon, he addresses Muslim community leaders at the Washington Islamic Center and tells them: "The face of terror is not the true faith of Islam. . . . Islam is peace. These terrorists don't represent peace. They represent evil and war." He urges Americans to treat their Muslim neighbors with respect.

Secretary of State Powell expresses satisfaction with U.S. progress toward assembling an antiterrorist coalition. His most recent conversations have been with President Salih of Yemen and Foreign Minister George Papandreou of Greece. Powell urges the people of Afghanistan not to "put their society at risk" by harboring bin Laden and the al-Qaeda organization.

The State Department issues a travel warning for Pakistan and authorizes the departure of nonessential diplomatic and consular personnel and their families.

The World Bank and the International Monetary Fund announce the cancellation of their annual meetings scheduled for September 29–30 in Washington, D.C.

The White House announces that French president Jacques Chirac will make a working visit on September 18, and that British prime minister Tony Blair will do so on September 20. The emir of Qatar will make a working visit on October 4. The visits are part of the U.S. effort to build an international coalition against terrorism. President Bush's most recent conversation has been with the president of the United Arab Emirates.

The Treasury Department announces that it will form an interagency Foreign Terrorist Asset Tracking Center to identify foreign terrorist groups and their sources of finance.

September 18

The White House announces that President Bush has conversed with the secretary general of the United Nations, the president of Brazil, and the prime minister of Canada. Later in the day, Bush meets with French president Jacques Chirac, who expresses "total solidarity" with the United States while expressing concern about the appropriateness of using the term "war." Bush also signs into law the congressional resolution authorizing the use of force to respond to terrorist attacks and the $40-billion emergency appropriation bill.

Secretary of State Powell meets with South Korean foreign minister Han Seung-Soo and expresses thanks for his country's support. Powell says that the death toll at the World Trade Center includes citizens of 62 nations. He later attends the swearing-in of John D. Negroponte as U.S. permanent representative to the United Nations. Negroponte presents his credentials to Secretary General Kofi Annan the next day.

Deputy Secretary of State Armitage, Assistant Secretary of State Jones, and Coordinator for Counterterrorism Taylor meet with Russian officials in Moscow to discuss measures to be taken against terrorists based in Afghanistan.

Secretary of Defense Rumsfeld says that the United States is "moving in a measured manner" in "a very new type of conflict." The al-Qaeda network may have connections in 50 to 60 countries, which makes a "very broadly based campaign" necessary.

At the United Nations, Ambassador A. G. Ravan Farhadi says that the Islamic State of Afghanistan, which opposes the Taliban's government, is willing to cooperate against the United States in the hunt for Osama bin Laden. The Security Council, meanwhile, issues a statement demanding that the Taliban comply with an existing Security Council Resolution (UNSCR 1333 of December 19, 2000) and surrender bin Laden to appropriate authorities and close terrorist training camps. The UN also announces that it is indefinitely postponing the ceremonial opening of the General Assembly.

In Afghanistan, Taliban leader Mohammad Omar refuses a Pakistani demand to surrender Osama bin Laden and calls a meeting of Muslim clerics to decide his fate. As Taliban leaders urge their countrymen to prepare for a holy war with the United States, thousands flee Afghan cities. Pakistan attempts to close its border to stem the flood of refugees.

September 19

President Bush and Secretary of State Powell meet with Indonesian president Megawati Sukarnoputri, Russian foreign minister Igor Ivanov, and German foreign minister Joschka Fischer. Ivanov says that Russia will not object to U.S. efforts to enlist former Soviet republics in Central Asia for the campaign against bin Laden. President Bush plans to address a joint meeting of Congress on September 20 to outline his plans for diplomatic and military action.

U.S. military preparations for Operation Infinite Justice begins as the air force starts deploying fighters and bombers to Saudi Arabia, Oman, Kuwait, and Diego Garcia Island. Some will operate from the former Soviet republics of Tajikistan and Uzbekistan. A 14-ship navy task force led by the aircraft carrier USS Theodore Roosevelt leaves Norfolk, Virginia, for the Persian Gulf. A Marine amphibious ready group is to leave Camp Lejeune, North Carolina, for the Mediterranean on September 20.

In Pakistan, President Musharraf warns his people that his country faces "very grave consequences" if it does not cooperate with the United States in the campaign against terrorism.

Prime Minister Junichiro Koizumi says that Japan's Self-Defense Forces will assist U.S. armed forces by collecting intelligence and providing logistical support.

The Organization of American States agrees to activate the 1947 Inter-American Treaty of Reciprocal Assistance (Rio Treaty). It also schedules a meeting of foreign ministers of member states for September 21 to discuss possible measurers against terrorism.

September 20

President Bush addresses a joint session of Congress, proclaims that "freedom and fear are at war," and warns the Taliban to hand over bin Laden and all other al-Qaeda leaders, free its prisoners, and close its terrorist training camps or face the consequences. He talks of a long campaign against terrorism and warns all countries that they will be regarded as hostile regimes if they continue to support terrorism. Bush announces the establishment of a cabinet-level Office of Homeland Security and nominates Governor Tom Ridge of Pennsylvania as director.

British prime minister Tony Blair meets with President Bush and pledges to stand "shoulder to shoulder" in the conflict against terrorism. Saudi foreign minister Prince Saud promises support, while hoping that the Taliban will hand over bin Laden and that military actions will not create "an unbridgeable gap" between Islam and the West. Chinese foreign minister Tang Jiaxuan meets with Vice President Cheney. Secretary of State Powell meets with EU president Louis Michel.

Secretary of State Powell tells Fox News that citizens of 80 nations are among the victims at the World Trade Center and that "the world is coming together." He does not rule out the possibility of cooperation with Syria or Iran, pointing out that there are many ways to participate in the coalition.

The United Nations announces that the General Assembly will hold a special session about terrorism on October 1. Secretary General Annan hopes that the session will lead to a convention against terrorism.

The United States and the European Union issue a joint ministerial statement on combating terrorism.

After a two-day meeting, a council of Islamic religious leaders in Kabul urge bin Laden to leave Afghanistan. They set no deadline for his departure and promise a jihad in reply to any U.S. military action. Secretary of State Powell says that the United States wants action, not statements, concerning bin Laden.

September 21

In Pakistan, at least two persons die amid large-scale demonstrations against the government's support for the U.S. antiterrorism campaign. Abdul Salaam Zaeef, the Taliban's ambassador to Pakistan, says that bin Laden will not be given up without evidence linking him to the attacks. White House spokesman Ari Fleischer is unimpressed, stating, "There will be no negotiations and no discussions. The war preparations continue."

President Bush telephones the presidents of Turkey and Nigeria and the sultan of Oman before traveling to Camp David for the weekend.

Secretary of State Powell meets with Chinese foreign minister Tang Jiaxuan, who promises nonmilitary cooperation and the sharing of intelligence with the United States. Powell also meets with Canadian foreign minister John Manley, who promises support but warns of the adverse economic effects of tightening border controls. Manley says that his government has found no evidence that any of the hijackers had entered the United States by way of Canada.

September 22

While spending the weekend at Camp David, President Bush assures the public that the U.S. economy is "fundamentally strong." He also mentions discussions that he has had with Russian president Vladimir Putin and announces that he is waiving sanctions that Congress imposed on India and Pakistan after their 1998 nuclear tests.

The Defense Department announces the mobilization of more than 5,000 additional Air National Guard and Air Force Reserve personnel, for a total of 10,303. It declines to comment on Taliban reports that a remotely piloted vehicle was shot down over Afghanistan.

In Afghanistan, fighting begins between the Northern Alliance and the Taliban.

September 23

After the Taliban claim that bin Laden has disappeared, Secretary of State Powell urges it to "come to its senses" and give him up. Powell says that the Bush administration plans to publish evidence linking bin Laden to the terrorist attacks on Washington, D.C., and New York City, as well as to earlier attacks on the U.S. embassies in Kenya and Tanzania and on the USS *Cole*. There will also be a secret report.

In Jidda, Saudi Arabia, the foreign ministers of the Gulf Cooperation Council states condemn the terrorist attacks on the United States and promise "total support and cooperation."

Russian president Putin contacts the leaders of five former Soviet Central Asian republics. Meanwhile there are unconfirmed reports of U.S. military transport planes landing at Tashkent, Uzbekistan.

National Security Adviser Condoleezza Rice says that the United States, not the UN, will be in charge of military actions against terrorists. The United States does not rule out the possibility of cooperating with Iran and Syria, both of which have been designated as states sponsoring terrorism.

Secretary of Defense Rumsfeld hints that the United States is seeking the cooperation of opposition groups within Afghanistan, and even that of dissident factions among the Taliban. The FAA grounds all crop-dusting flights in the United States for a day in view of a report that one suspected hijacker had asked questions about the performance of crop-dusting planes.

September 24

President Bush signs an executive order freezing the assets of 27 organizations and persons known to be linked to al-Qaeda and suspected of funding terrorism. He calls on foreign banks to follow his example or have their U.S. assets frozen.

Bush also meets with Canadian prime minister Jean Chrétien and thanks him for sheltering diverted international flights.

Secretary of State Powell says that the United States has "an abundance of evidence" linking bin Laden to the terrorist attacks but sets no date for releasing unclassified information.

The House of Representatives approves U.S. payment of $852 million in back UN dues by a voice vote. An amendment intended to protect U.S. military personnel from the International Criminal Court is deleted.

The Senate approves a trade agreement with Jordan by a voice vote.

President Putin announces the opening of Russian air space to humanitarian flights and more aid to Afghan groups opposing the Taliban. He does not rule out U.S. use of air bases in the former Soviet Central Asian republics but calls for a broader role for the UN and other international organizations in the fight against terrorism.

Vatican spokesman Joaquín Navarro-Valls says that although nonviolent solutions are preferred and that military actions should be directed against terrorists rather than against Islam, Pope John Paul II recognizes the right of the United States to use force in self-defense.

September 25

President Bush meets with Japanese prime minister Junichiro Koizumi, who offers nonmilitary support. Bush says that one way to "rout terrorists" might be "to ask for the cooperation of citizens within Afghanistan who may be tired of having the Taliban in place." However, he denies any interest in "nation-building," and Press Secretary Fleischer denies that military actions are "designed to replace one regime with another."

The White House announces that President Bush will limit his first trip to Asia as president to attending the APEC summit meeting in Shanghai on October 20–21. Visits to Beijing, Tokyo, and Seoul will be postponed.

Secretary of Defense Rumsfeld describes the U.S. war on terrorism as an "unusual conflict that cannot be dealt with by some sort of massive attack or invasion." The campaign will be renamed Operation Enduring Freedom, suggesting that it will take a long time to achieve its goals. It may involve "revolving coalitions" since international support for specific U.S. military actions against terrorists could be selective. He and Secretary of State Powell later give a two-hour, top-secret briefing to members of Congress, including 90 senators.

Secretary of State Powell meets with Italian foreign minister Renato Ruggiero.

The Saudi Arabian government breaks diplomatic relations with the Taliban.

Russian defense minister Sergei Ivanov says that the United States can use bases in Tajikistan to attack targets in Afghanistan "if the need arises."

Pakistani foreign minister Abdul Sattar warns against supporting opponents of the Taliban in order to impose a government on Afghanistan.

During an interview on the French television network France 3, Egyptian president Hosni Mubarak says that bin Laden threatened to assassinate President Bush during the G-8 Summit Meeting in Genoa.

September 26

During a meeting of NATO defense ministers in Brussels, Deputy Secretary of Defense Paul D. Wolfowitz says that no military actions against terrorists are likely until more information has been collected. At present, NATO allies can be most helpful by sharing intelligence information and helping to trace the financial assets of terrorist groups. Secretary General George Robertson of NATO says that evidence has been collected linking bin Laden and al-Qaeda to the attacks on Washington, D.C., and New York City. Russian defense minister Ivanov also attends the meeting.

Egyptian foreign minister Ahmed Maher meets with President Bush and Secretary of State Powell and says that Egypt will require more proof of bin Laden's role in terrorist attacks before endorsing U.S. military actions. Powell also meets with Irish foreign minister Brian Cowen.

Iran's spiritual leader Ayatollah Ali Khameini says that his country will not join the U.S. coalition against terrorism, stating that the United States was "not sincere enough" to lead such a campaign in view of its continued support for Israel.

In Kabul, a mob sacks the former U.S. embassy compound, which was abandoned in 1989. In Pakistan, the U.S. consulate in Lahore is closed for security reasons.

September 27

Turkish foreign minister Ismail Cem meets with Secretary of State Powell and pledges his country's support for the war on terrorism.

U.S. and Pakistani military officers conclude a meeting about the situation in Afghanistan. A Pakistani spokesman says there is a "complete unanimity of views" but does not give details.

Also in Pakistan, the Taliban's ambassador says that a message was delivered to bin Laden asking him to leave Afghanistan.

At the UN, Secretary General Annan seeks $584 million in emergency aid for Afghanistan. The United States seeks support for a Security Council draft resolution calling for freezing the assets of terrorist groups and for closer international cooperation against terrorism.

After anti-American demonstrations in Jakarta, Indonesia, the State Department authorizes the voluntary departure of family members and nonessential personnel from the embassy there.

September 28

King Abdullah II of Jordan meets with President Bush, who signs a U.S.-Jordan free trade agreement. Bush assures the king "that our war is against evil, not against Islam," praises Jordanian and Saudi cooperation, and pledges $25 million in aid to Afghan refugees.

President Bush also speaks with the leaders of Australia and the Philippines. Spanish foreign minister Josep Pique meets with Secretary of State Powell.

The UN Security Council unanimously adopts a U.S.-sponsored resolution calling on member states to end financial, political, and military connections with terrorist groups and to freeze their assets. Member states will report every 90 days to a 15-member compliance council. The United States abstains as the rest of the Security Council votes to lift economic sanctions imposed on Sudan in 1996 following an assassination attempt against Egyptian president Mubarak. Deputy Representative James Cunningham cites Sudan's recent cooperation against terrorism.

In Afghanistan, the Taliban turns away a delegation of nine Pakistani religious leaders who seek bin Laden's extradition.

September 29

President Bush spends the weekend at Camp David, where he video-conferences with the NSC. In his weekly radio address, he speaks of "a different kind of war," adding that the United States condemns the Taliban and welcomes the support of others in isolating it. He announces that retired army general Wayne Downing will be called on to join the NSC as a special assistant on terrorism. General Downing criticized U.S. security lapses following the June 1996 bombing of the Khobar Towers barracks in Saudi Arabia.

The NSC and the State Department prepare an Afghanistan Declaratory Policy that calls for an international effort to stabilize the country and to assist those who seek to make it peaceful, developed, and terrorist free should the Taliban be removed from power.

Approximately 4,500 protesters march through downtown Washington to protest possible U.S. military action. They had originally planned to protest the World Bank and IMF meetings. Eleven are arrested.

Undersecretary of State for Arms Control and International Security Affairs John R. Bolton discusses antiterrorism with Russian deputy foreign minister Georgii Mamedov in Moscow. Bolton had previously visited Uzbekistan.

September 30

Administration officials announce that $100 million has been authorized for the relief of Afghan refugees and that a covert program of support for opposition groups in Afghanistan has been approved.

On various Sunday television news programs, Secretary of Defense Rumsfeld, Attorney General Ashcroft, and White House Chief of Staff Andrew H. Card Jr. warn that terrorist groups may eventually attack the United States with chemical or biological weapons.

Mohammad Zahir Shah, former king of Afghanistan, meets with leaders of the Northern Alliance and with an 11-member U.S. congressional delegation in Rome. The king has no interest in restoring the monarchy but proposes that he might convene a loya jirgah, or national assembly, to form a new government.

In London, Prime Minister Tony Blair says that he has seen "incontrovertible evidence" linking bin Laden to terrorist attacks on the United States. Chancellor of the Exchequer Gordon Brown announces that Great Britain has frozen $88 million worth of Taliban assets in a London-based bank.

October 1

In an address to employees of the Federal Emergency Management Agency (FEMA), President Bush says that 27 countries have granted overflight and landing rights to U.S. forces; 29,000 military personnel have been deployed overseas; 19 countries have agreed to freeze terrorist assets; $6 million in assets have been frozen in 50 bank accounts (including 20 foreign accounts); 241 threats have been analyzed by the Justice Department; and 150 persons in more than 25 countries have been arrested or detained. He also announces the arrest of a Pakistani who had taken part in a 1986 hijacking in which two Americans were killed.

New York mayor Rudolph W. Giuliani addresses a special UN General Assembly meeting on terrorism and calls on member states to decide whether they are "with civilization or with terrorism."

The Defense Department announces that the aircraft carrier USS Kitty Hawk will leave Yokosuka, Japan, for the Persian Gulf, where it may serve as a mobile base for ground troops. It also announces that 3,427 more National Guard and Reserve personnel have been activated, for a total of more than 20,000.

In Pakistan, President Musharraf tells the BBC that he expects that the United States will soon attack the Taliban and predicts a quick end to the Taliban's rule.

In Rome, former king Mohammad Zahir Shah and Northern Alliance representatives agree to convene a Supreme Council to which 120 Afghan political leaders will be invited. This will serve as a first step in convening a Grand Assembly to form a new government for Afghanistan.

October 2

President Bush meets with congressional leaders and warns that "there will be a consequence" if the Taliban does not surrender bin Laden and destroy his terrorism network. He also announces that Reagan National Airport will reopen the next day under stricter security procedures. Aircraft needed for resumption of service begin arriving on October 3; flights resume on October 4.

Secretary of Defense Rumsfeld orders the deployment of U.S. forces to Uzbekistan and Tajikistan. He then departs for the Middle East, where he plans to visit Egypt, Saudi Arabia, Oman, and Uzbekistan. Earlier in the day, he meets with Indian foreign and defense minister Jaswant Singh. The Defense Department later denies a report that 1,000 soldiers from the 10th Mountain Division have deployed to Tajikistan and Uzbekistan; the unit has only been placed on alert.

Greek foreign minister Papandreou meets with National Security Adviser Rice. British prime minister Blair warns the Taliban to "surrender the terrorists or surrender power" when he addresses a Labour Party conference in Brighton. He warns that British forces are within striking distance of Afghanistan as part of routine military exercises with Oman.

After a briefing by Coordinator for Counterterrorism Francis Taylor, NATO secretary general Robertson says that the United States has provided "clear and compelling" evidence of bin Laden's role in the terrorist attacks. As a result of the briefing, NATO concludes that the attacks are directed from abroad and will "therefore be regarded as an action covered by Article 5 of the Washington Treaty, which states that an armed attack on one or more of the allies in Europe or North America shall be considered an attack against them all." NATO is therefore prepared to provide unconditional support for U.S. military actions.

October 3

Secretary of Defense Rumsfeld visits Saudi Arabia, where he meets with King Fahd, Crown Prince Abdullah, and Defense Minister Prince Sultan. He declines to comment on whether permission has been given for U.S. forces to use Saudi bases for antiterrorist missions.

Secretary of State Powell lunches with members of the Senate Foreign Relations Committee and discusses humanitarian aid to Afghanistan (Senator Joseph R. Biden Jr. calls for a pledge of $1 billion) and removal of remaining sanctions against Pakistan (Senator Sam Brownback has introduced a bill to that effect). Powell also meets with the emir of Qatar and the foreign minister of Portugal.

Assistant Secretary of State William J. Burns meets with British and Libyan officials in London in the hope of inducing Libya to sever its terrorist connections. U.S. officials brief Pakistani officials on bin Laden's role in the terrorist attacks.

Russian president Putin visits Brussels and says that his country will hold monthly meetings with EU officials about counterterrorism. He claims that bin Laden was aiding Chechen rebels. He also says that Russia will reconsider its opposition to the expansion of NATO if it is consulted.

Northern Alliance foreign minister Abdullah Abdullah says that Afghan opposition groups met regularly with U.S. officials outside Afghanistan. He expresses willingness to meet with Rumsfeld in Uzbekistan.

October 4

In a speech at the State Department, President Bush announces an additional $320 million in humanitarian aid to Afghanistan. He says the coalition against terrorism is strong because it is not a religious war but "a war between good and evil." Bush later visits the Labor Department, where he announces an extended program of unemployment benefits for those who lost jobs as a result of the terrorist attacks.

President Bush meets with Emir Sheik Hamad bin Khalifa al-Thani of Qatar, who says that Arab governments need more proof of bin Laden's role before supporting military actions against him. He also warns against attacks on targets that have no definite links to terrorism or against groups engaged in resistance to Israel.

Bush also meets with President Vicente Fox of Mexico and discusses security concerns along the countries' border.

National Security Adviser Rice talks of an extensive U.S. contribution to "the reconstruction of Afghanistan" once the Taliban has been replaced by a more representative government.

Richard Haass, director of policy planning, meets with former king Mohammad Zahir Khan in Rome.

British prime minister Blair tells Parliament about the U.S. case against bin Laden and his followers, stating that the evidence against them is "overwhelming." The British government releases an 18-page summary of the evidence.

In Pakistan, foreign ministry spokesman Riaz Muhammad Khan says that the evidence shown to his government "provided sufficient basis for indictment" of bin Laden.

After Secretary of Defense Rumsfeld visits Oman, the Defense Department announces that the United States will sell 12 F-16s with precision-guided weapons to Oman. Rumsfeld goes to Cairo to discuss Egypt's role in the antiterrorist coalition. He says that relief supplies may be dropped into Afghanistan.

NATO announces that it will grant to U.S. forces unlimited access to member states' airspace, ports, air bases, and refueling facilities. Naval maneuvers are scheduled in the eastern Mediterranean. Financial aid will be offered to states facing additional terrorist threats. NATO will also replace U.S. peacekeeping forces in the Balkans if necessary.

Japan announces that it will provide $160 million in aid to Afghan refugees and will use Self-Defense Force aircraft to transport relief supplies. Prime Minister Koizumi plans to visit South Korea to reassure the government about his country's peaceful intentions.

October 5

After a visit by Secretary of Defense Rumsfeld, Uzbekistan offers to allow U.S. forces to conduct humanitarian and combat search-and-rescue missions from its bases. President Islam Karimov is not yet ready, however, to allow attacks on Taliban forces to be launched from Uzbekistan. A reinforced battalion from the 10th Mountain Division arrives in Uzbekistan the next day.

While returning from Central Asia, Rumsfeld visits Ankara, where he meets with Turkish prime minister Bulent Ecevit and senior officials and thanks Turkey for its assistance to the antiterrorist campaign.

The State Department issues its biennial list of groups designated by the Secretary of State as foreign terrorist organizations. Hamas, Hizballah, al-Qaeda, the Egyptian Islamic Jihad, and the Islamic Movement of Uzbekistan are among the 28 groups currently designated.

The Japanese government introduces bills to allow its Self-Defense Forces to ferry ammunition and operate field hospitals overseas. Personnel could carry weapons for self-defense during operations outside the immediate area of Japan. These emergency measures would last for two years. Relief flights to Pakistan begin the next day.

British prime minister Blair visits Pakistan. He and President Musharraf agree that any post-Taliban government in Afghanistan must be "broad-based."

October 6

In his weekly radio address, President Bush warns the Taliban that "time is running out" unless it gives up terrorist suspects. White House spokesperson Claire Buchan dismisses a Taliban offer to free eight jailed aid workers (two are Americans) in return for an agreement not to use force. Bush also urges Congress to make funds available for the postwar reconstruction of Afghanistan.

In Washington, G-7 finance ministers and central bank presidents meet to promote economic recovery and to devise means for tracking terrorist assets. They schedule a meeting of the Financial Action Task Force for October 29–30.

In Geneva, the UN-sponsored Afghan Forum pledges $608 million in humanitarian aid.

A bomb explosion in Khobar, Saudi Arabia, kills two persons and wounds four. One of the dead is an American. There is no clear connection to bin Laden.

October 7

U.S. and British forces attack Taliban military targets throughout Afghanistan with bombers and cruise missiles. The 30 targets include airfields, air defense systems, terrorist training camps, and troop concentrations facing Northern Alliance forces. President Bush announces the strikes from the White House Treaty Room at 1 p.m. Eastern Standard Time and says that he consulted with congressional leaders the day before. He says that more than 40 countries provided air transit or landing rights and even more shared information. Canada, Britain, Australia, France, and Germany pledged military support.

Secretary of Defense Rumsfeld and General Richard B. Myers, chairman of the Joint Chiefs of Staff, add that relief supplies will be dropped into Afghanistan and that there will be radio broadcasts and leaflet drops to encourage defections from the Taliban. Rumsfeld speaks of cooperation with the Northern Alliance, and Myers hints that covert operations are in progress in Afghanistan.

Bin Laden, meanwhile, issues a taped broadcast in which he urges Muslims to join in a jihad against the United States and vows that "neither America nor the people who live in it will dream of security before we live it in Palestine, and not before all the infidel armies leave the land of Muhammad."

The State Department announces a "worldwide caution," warning Americans overseas of possible retaliatory attacks. The U.S. embassy in Saudi Arabia is closed.

October 8

U.S. forces continue their attacks on Taliban targets in Afghanistan, with some being conducted by day. Secretary of Defense Rumsfeld says progress has been made but warns against the "mistaken understanding that some sort of cruise missile" can defeat terrorism. Military operations will continue until "the terrorist networks are destroyed" and the Taliban has been overthrown. An additional 1,000 soldiers from the 10th Mountain Division are scheduled to deploy to Uzbekistan.

The government of Tajikistan opens its air space to U.S. forces and offers to make its airfields available for operations against terrorism.

President Bush warns of a "long war" in which "America is not immune to attack." He then signs an executive order establishing the Office of Homeland Security. Governor Tom Ridge is sworn in as its director. The president also phones the prime minister of New Zealand and the presidents of China and South Korea.

At the UN, Ambassador Negroponte presents a letter to the Security Council stating that the attacks in Afghanistan are acts of self-defense under Article 51 of the UN Charter. The letter adds: "We may find that our self-defense requires further action with respect to other organizations and other states." British foreign secretary Jack Straw, however, suggests that the United States and Great Britain have agreed to limit military operations to Afghanistan.

The United States does not contest the UN General Assembly's election of Syria to a two-year term on the Security Council.

The UN's World Food Program announces that it will suspend food distributions in Afghanistan until the bombing campaign ends.

NATO announces that five of its AWACS aircraft will patrol the East Coast of the United States. Canada announces that it will commit 2,000 military personnel, six warships, and six aircraft to the campaign. Australia offers 1,000 troops. France offers the use of its naval forces in the Indian Ocean and says that French intelligence agents are in contact with the Northern Alliance.

In Pakistan, rioters burn UN and foreign relief offices, police stations, and movie theaters in Quetta to protest the attacks in Afghanistan. President Musharraf tells reporters that he "is very positive the vast majority of Pakistanis are with me" but hopes that the campaign will be short; he warns that his country has only limited ability to accept Afghan refugees.

The Palestinian Authority condemns the terrorist attacks on the United States; however, there is widespread rioting in the Gaza Strip, where at least two persons are killed as Palestinian security forces fire on demonstrators sympathetic to bin Laden. The Palestinian Authority then declares a state of emergency.

Japanese prime minister Koizumi meets with Chinese president Jiang Zemin in Beijing. He finds Zemin to be "understanding" of Japan's support for the U.S. antiterrorism campaign and privately supportive of the campaign itself. Koizumi also visits a museum dedicated to Chinese resistance to Japan before and during World War II, where he delivers a "heartfelt apology" for his country's past aggression.

October 9

As the air campaign continues in Afghanistan, Secretary of Defense Rumsfeld hints that direct air support may be provided to the Northern Alliance and other opponents of the Taliban. General Myers reports that U.S. forces have achieved "air supremacy over Afghanistan."

President Bush meets with German chancellor Gerhard Schroeder and urges the public to "feel comfortable going about their lives." He announces the appointments of Richard A. Clarke as a special adviser for cybersecurity and of retired general Wayne A. Downing as deputy national security adviser for combating terrorism.

At the UN, Ambassador Negroponte presents a letter to his Iraqi counterpart, Mohammed Douri, warning him that if Iraq aids the Taliban, uses weapons of mass destruction, or cracks down on its opposition groups, "There will be a military strike against you, and you will be defeated."

The UN coordinator for humanitarian affairs in Afghanistan reports that four civilian guards working for a land-mine removal group called Afghan Technical Consultants were killed by a bomb or missile near Kabul.

Egyptian president Mubarak expresses his support for the U.S. campaign against terrorism but urges the United States to avoid causing civilian casualties and to promote a Palestinian state.

Foreign ministers of 22 Arab countries meet at Doha, Qatar, on the eve of a meeting of the Organization of the Islamic Conference. They reportedly seek to minimize the chance that Arab states become targets in the war against terrorism and to exclude groups fighting for "national liberation" from any definition of terrorism.

Qatar's Al-Jazeera network broadcasts a videotape in which bin Laden aide Suleiman Abou-Gheith threatens further hijackings and attacks by "thousands of young people who look forward to death like the Americans look forward to living."

October 10

President Bush holds a press conference at the FBI's headquarters and releases a list of the 22 Most Wanted Terrorists, who are linked to events as far back as the 1985 hijacking of TWA flight 847. The list includes Osama bin Laden and 12 members of al-Qaeda. The State Department offers rewards of up to $5 million for information leading to their capture.

President Bush also meets with NATO secretary general George Robertson and thanks him for NATO's cooperation in the campaign against terrorism. The deployment of five NATO AWACS aircraft marks the first time that NATO has come to the defense of the United States.

The air campaign in Afghanistan concentrates on targets around Kabul and Kandahar. The Defense Department announces that Pakistan is allowing U.S. forces to operate from air bases at Pasni and Jacobabad. The first U.S. fatality occurrs when Master Sergeant Evander Earl Andrews of the U.S. Air Force is killed in a forklift accident in Qatar.

State Department spokesman Richard A. Boucher says that terrorist suspects have been arrested or detained in 23 countries: 10 in Europe, 7 in the Middle East, 4 in Africa, and 1 each in Latin America and East Asia. Steps have been taken against terrorist financial assets in 112 countries. U.S. embassies have been ordered to stockpile at least a three-day supply of ciprofloxacin in the event of an anthrax attack.

National Security Adviser Rice contacts the executives of five television networks and urges them not to broadcast taped messages by bin Laden and his colleagues. They agree to review and edit such messages in advance. White House spokesman Fleischer says that the messages may contain coded messages to terrorists in the United States. Taliban leader Muhammad Omar, meanwhile, urges "every Muslim [to] resolutely act against the egotistic power."

The Northern Alliance agrees not to attack Taliban forces outside Kabul until an interim government has been established for Afghanistan.

In Doha, the Organization for the Islamic Conference expresses concern about "deaths of innocent civilians" in Afghanistan. The OIC calls the September 11 attacks "opposed to the tolerant and divine message of Islam" and opposes attacks on "Islamic or Arab state[s] under the pretext of fighting terrorism." It urges the United Nations to lead future antiterrorist campaigns and that terrorism be defined in such a way that it excludes Palestinian and Lebanese groups fighting Israel.

October 11

President Bush holds his first prime-time news conference. He tells the Taliban that they still have second chance; if they give up bin Laden and his followers, "We'll reconsider what we're doing to your country." He also says that the United States is prepared to help the UN establish a stable and representative Afghan government that will be involved in neither terrorism nor the drug trade. The United States will support a Palestinian state if it recognizes Israel's right to exist and is prepared to live in peace with Israel. Bush is prepared to meet with Yasir Arafat if he believes that it will promote peace. Bush urges Saddam Hussein to allow UN inspectors to return to Iraq and is conciliatory toward Syria. He also urges each American child to contribute $1 to the relief fund for Afghan children.

The FBI says that terrorist attacks on the United States and/or U.S. interests are likely "over the next several days."

Secretary of Defense Rumsfeld says that the U.S. air campaign is now targeting cave complexes with laser-guided "bunker buster" bombs. In response to Taliban claims of up to 300 civilian deaths, he regrets any "unintended loss of life." Major General Henry P. Osman says that U.S. forces have refrained from directly coordinating air strikes with the Northern Alliance.

Deputy Secretary of State Armitage says that the United States is campaigning against all groups that threaten its interests or those of its allies. Consequences to states that support terrorists might range from isolation to military action.

October 12

Vice President Cheney tells PBS, "The U.S. homeland now is open to attack in ways that we've only speculated about before."

The Treasury Department orders a freeze on the assets of 39 more people and organizations, most of them linked to bin Laden.

The air campaign over Afghanistan slackens in deference to the Friday Muslim sabbath. In Pakistan there is rioting in Karachi, but demonstrations elsewhere are smaller and more peaceful.

The United States and Uzbekistan issue a joint statement about consultation on security matters.

Canadian transportation secretary David Collenette announces that armed members of the Royal Canadian Mounted Police will travel aboard Air Canada flights to Reagan National Airport.

NATO AWACS aircraft begin patrols off the East Coast of the United States.

Philippines defense secretary Angelo Reyes says that U.S. military advisers will assist his country's campaign against the Abu Sayyaf Muslim rebels in the southern islands. Abu Sayyaf has been linked to al-Qaeda and has executed one American and is holding two more hostage.

October 13

As the air campaign resumes, President Bush holds a video conference with the NSC at Camp David. In his weekly radio address, he says that the Taliban was "paying a price" for harboring bin Laden.

Al-Qaeda spokesman Suleiman Abou-Gheith broadcasts another vow of vengenace over the Al-Jazeera news network, in which he warns Muslims in countries attacking Afghanistan to stay away from airplanes and tall buildings.

The Defense Department admits that a bomb aimed at the Kabul airport hit a residential area by mistake. It cannot confirm Taliban reports of civilian casualties.

States of the Gulf Cooperation Council agree to freeze the assets of persons and groups connected to bin Laden.

October 14

Afghan deputy prime minister Haji Abdul Kabir offers to negotiate the transfer of bin Laden to a neutral third country if the United States stops bombing Afghanistan. President Bush rejects the offer and insists that bin Laden and his followers must be given up.

Demonstrations continue in Pakistan. One protester is killed by police in Jacobabad, where U.S. forces are using an airfield.

The Taliban brings foreign journalists to Karam, a village in eastern Afghanistan, where they claim that a U.S. air strike killed 200 civilians.

October 15

Secretary of State Powell visits Pakistan, where he praises the "bold and courageous" measures that President Musharraf has taken. He announces that Richard N. Haass, director of policy planning, will serve as a special assistant for Afghanistan. Haass will meet soon with UN officials in New York. Powell also plans to urge both Pakistan and India to resolve the Kashmir dispute.

The Defense Department announces that an air force AC-130 gunship took part in the air campaign directed at a Taliban stronghold near Kandahar. Secretary of Defense Rumsfeld announces that U.S. forces are dropping leaflets into Afghanistan along with food. Some urge the finders to tune into "Information Radio." Rumsfeld calls Taliban charges of 300 civilian deaths "ridiculous," although he admits that the United States has not made an effective presentation of its case in the Middle East and South Asia. Rumsfeld and General Myers say that the attack on Karam targeted a cave complex that apparently contains large amounts of ammunition.

Former king Mohammed Zahir Shah addresses a letter to members of the UN Security Council in which he urges them to establish a UN peacekeeping force for Afghanistan should the Taliban government collapse.

National Security Adviser Rice is interviewed on Al-Jazeera. She seeks to assure her audience that the United States is not at war with Islam, expresses concern at Saddam Hussein's quest for weapons of mass destruction, and says that different means will be used with different countries in the fight against terrorism.

Italian prime minister Silvio Berlusconi meets with President Bush at the White House.

October 16

At the Pentagon, Lieutenant General Gregory Newbold says that U.S. air attacks have "eviscerated" the Taliban's armed forces. Northern Alliance forces claim to be about to capture the city of Mazar-e Sharif.

Secretary of State Powell concludes his visit to Pakistan and continues to India. President Musharraf admits that a majority of his people oppose the U.S. air campaign in Afghanistan but says that Pakistan will stay in the coalition for as long as necessary. Powell and Musharraf agree that there is a role for moderate elements of the Taliban in a postwar Afghan government and urge Afghan opposition groups to hasten their efforts to form one. In northern Afghanistan, Northern Alliance foreign minister Abdullah Abdullah rejects any Taliban role in a postwar government.

Raymond C. Offenheiser, president of Oxfam America, says that U.S. air attacks and increasing lawlessness inside Afghanistan are preventing the delivery of humanitarian aid. The Defense Department, meanwhile, admits that a navy plane accidentally bombed a warehouse used by the International Committee of the Red Cross in Kabul. Taliban military forces are believed to be storing equipment in nearby buildings.

The House of Representatives approves by a voice vote a two-year waiver of U.S. restrictions on economic aid to Pakistan. Secretary of State Powell sends a letter to the Senate Foreign Relations Committee in which he recommends that restrictions on financial aid to Azerbaijan be lifted in view of that country's assistance to the U.S. antiterrorist campaign.

At the UN, special envoy Lakhdar Brahimi advises the Security Council against sending a peacekeeping force to Afghanistan without first assuring political and financial support. He envisions the UN's postwar role as supplying humanitarian aid, helping the Afghans to form a broadly based government, and aiding with reconstruction.

CNN announces that it plans to submit six questions to bin Laden through Al-Jazeera. These questions will be about bin Laden's and al-Queda's role in the September 11 attacks and in later outbreaks of anthrax; whether al-Qaeda had trained or financed the hijackers; whether other foreign governments had been involved; whether bin Laden had weapons of mass destruction and planned to use them; how bin Laden would respond to Islamic leaders who called his attacks on the United States unjustified; and "how can you and your followers advocate the killing of innocent people."

October 17

During a stop at Travis Air Force Base on his way to the APEC Summit in Shanghai, China, President Bush says, "We're paving the way for friendly troops on the ground to slowly, but surely, tighten the net" around the Taliban. He admits that the war on terrorism could take more than two years and that there could be political consequences if the public gets tired of it.

In New Delhi, India, Secretary of State Powell assures officials that the United States stands "shoulder to shoulder" with India in the campaign against terrorism, including that directed against the South Asian country. He reportedly carries a promise from President Musharraf that Pakistan will curb extremists in Kashmir.

While flying from New Delhi to Shanghai, Powell endorses a strong UN role in the postwar political reconstruction of Afghanistan and does not rule out a peacekeeping force. UN special envoy for Afghanistan Brahimi, however, believes that a UN military force probably will be resisted and says that the secretary general is not interested in involving the UN in either forming an interim government or with reconstruction.

The Defense Department admits to two new developments in the air campaign in Afghanistan: F-15E fighters based in Persian Gulf states are taking part, and armed unmanned drones (Predator planes equipped with Hellfire missiles) have been used for the first time. Rear Admiral John D. Stufflebeem denies that U.S. forces are making any special effort to coordinate their attacks with the Northern Alliance but says that U.S. planes began patrolling designated "engagement zones" in search of mobile targets. They also are "flex-targeting" adjacent areas if nothing appears in a designated zone.

In Afghanistan, reinforced Taliban forces counterattack Northern Alliance forces at Mazar-e Sharif. Taliban forces also seize World Food Program warehouses in Kabul and Kandahar to the alarm of international relief organizations.

Iran announces that it will conduct search-and-rescue missions if U.S. pilots operating over Afghanistan should crash in its territory.

October 18

President Bush meets with Chinese president Jiang Zemin at the APEC Summit in Shanghai and says that China has agreed to share intelligence and to help with the financial campaign against terrorism.

The Defense Department admits that U.S. Special Forces are operating in southern Afghanistan. Secretary of Defense Rumsfeld and General Myers hint that the war in Afghanistan will become more intense. Rumsfeld says that the United States is prepared to aid the Northern Alliance. Commando Solo EC-130 aircraft are broadcasting messages urging civilians to stay away from potential targets and not to interfere with U.S. forces.

Special U.S. representative for Afghanistan Haass meets with UN officials in New York to discuss a possible UN role in postwar Afghanistan.

The government of Uzbekistan announces that it will allow relief supplies to be delivered to northern Afghanistan.

Japan's House of Representatives approves a bill allowing the Self-Defense Forces to provide logistical support for the antiterrorist campaign. Related bills allow the Self-Defense Forces to protect U.S.

bases in Japan and the Coast Guard to use force against suspicious ships in Japanese waters.

October 19

In the first acknowledged action by U.S. ground forces in Afghanistan, army Rangers and Special Forces seize an airfield in the south and attack Mullah Mohammed Omar's headquarters near Kandahar. One helicopter on a supporting mission crashes in southern Pakistan, killing two soldiers. The Defense Department denies Taliban claims that the helicopter was damaged over Afghanistan and that the U.S. raiders were quickly driven off. General Myers later says that there are no U.S. casualties, resistance has been light, Taliban losses are unknown, no Taliban leaders are on the premises, but potentially useful information has been captured.

Secretary of Defense Rumsfeld admits that the United States is supplying money and ammunition to Northern Alliance forces and that there is good "coordination" with them.

After meeting with President Zemin at the Shanghai APEC Summit, President Bush announces a new "constructive and cooperative relationship" with China. President Zemin urges the United States to minimize civilian casualties in Afghanistan and to seek a wider UN role in the conflict. Russian president Putin declares his "outright support" for the United States.

UN special envoy Brahimi arrives in Washington to discuss the UN's role in postwar Afghanistan with Vice President Cheney and Deputy Secretary Armitage.

EU heads of government meet at Ghent and declare their support for the U.S. campaign in Afghanistan and pledge to help reconstruct the country once the Taliban has been replaced by a stable and representative government.

October 20

At the APEC Summit meeting, President Bush calls the September 11 attacks "an attack on all civilized countries." He meets with Malaysian prime minister Mahathir Mohammed, who says that the two have agreed to disagree about the U.S. air campaign. The presidents and foreign ministers of Russia and China express their hopes for a peaceful solution in which the UN Security Council can play a major role. President Bush also praises Japanese prime minister Koizumi's cooperation.

In Islamabad, a foreign ministry spokesman confirms that Pakistani officials met with Mullah Jalaluddin Haqqani, a Taliban leader from Khost Province, to discuss a possible role in a postwar Afghan government.

October 21

As U.S. planes attack Taliban forces north of Kabul, Secretary of State Powell said that he expects Northern Alliance forces to "start moving on Kabul more aggressively" and eventually "invest" it. He declines to speculate about reports that President Bush directed the CIA to destroy bin Laden and al-Qaeda or about the origins of anthrax outbreaks in the United States. He hopes that the campaign in Afghanistan can be concluded before winter and says that while "there is no place for the current Taliban leadership" in a postwar government, Taliban followers have to be included.

APEC leaders issue a statement condemning the September 11 attacks on the United States and agreeing on the need to deny terrorist access to money and arms and to expand cooperation between customs systems. Participants decline to comment about the U.S. air campaign in Afghanistan.

President Putin stops in Tajikistan while returning from the APEC Summit. He meets with Burhanuddin Rabbani of the Northern Alliance and pledges that Russia will supply arms. He later says that Russia recognizes the Northern Alliance as the only legitimate government of Afghanistan.

October 22

As U.S. planes attack Taliban positions near the Bagram air base and Mazar-e Sharif, Secretary of Defense Rumsfeld denies Taliban claims that U.S. helicopters have been shot down, prisoners taken, and a hospital in Herat bombed. He also says that U.S. air attacks are now in direct support of Northern Alliance forces.

During an interview for CNN's *Larry King Live*, President Musharraf warns of wider opposition in the Muslim world if the U.S. air campaign continues into Ramadan. In his news conference, however, Secretary Rumsfeld notes that there are many instances in which Muslim countries have fought one another or other countries during religious holidays.

Afghan opposition groups announce that they will meet in Istanbul as a first step toward forming a postwar government.

The United States signs an agreement with Uzbekistan to help it clean up a site where Soviet biological weapons were tested on an island in the Aral Sea.

Senator Joseph R. Biden Jr., chairman of the Senate Foreign Relations Committee, addresses the Council on Foreign Relations. He fears that the air campaign in Afghanistan makes the United States look like "a high-tech bully" and that the longer it lasts, the more vulnerable the United States will be to criticism in the Muslim world.

October 23

Defense Department spokesman Victoria Clarke admits that U.S. planes accidentally bombed a senior citizens' home near Herat and a residential district near Kabul but declines to comment on Taliban claims that the first attack killed 100 civilians.

After meeting with Security Council representatives, UN special envoy Brahimi announces that he plans to visit South Asia to meet with representatives of various Afghan political groups.

October 24

At the Pentagon, Admiral Stufflebeem says that the Taliban appears ready for a long struggle. Stufflebeem also says that the Taliban could poison food supplied by international agencies and blame it on the United States and is using civilians as human shields in efforts to shelter personnel and equipment from U.S. air attacks.

British foreign secretary Jack Straw visits Washington and meets with Secretary of State Powell, who says that military operations in Afghanistan may continue through Ramadan. Powell appears before the House International Relations Committee in his first congressional appearance since September 11 and discusses prospects for assembling a postwar government for Afghanistan. He says that the makeup of such a government is unclear, except that the Taliban would have no place in it. He expects the UN to play an important role. He also says that an airlift of food aid into Afghanistan may be necessary.

The presidents of Uzbekistan and Turkmenistan agree to open their borders to UN relief supplies bound for Afghanistan.

More than 1,000 representatives of Afghan opposition groups meet in Peshawar to discuss a possible postwar government. Representatives of former king Mohammed Zahir Shah, however, boycott the meeting. Northern Alliance representatives are also conspicuously absent.

The Turkish government offers to host a meeting of Afghan opposition groups at a time and place to be determined.

Pakistani officials say that a U.S. air raid on October 23 killed 22 Pakistani guerrillas who were fighting alongside the Taliban near Kabul. The dead were members of the Harakat ul-Mujahedeen, which also fought Indian forces in Kashmir; their group had been placed on the State Department's official list of terrorist organizations in 1995.

October 25

President Bush meets with Crown Prince Sheikh Salman bin Hamad Khalifa of Bahrain and designates Bahrain a "major non-NATO ally." He also calls Crown Prince Abdullah to thank him for Saudi Arabia's cooperation in the antiterrorist campaign.

Secretary of Defense Rumsfeld takes exception to a headline in USA Today that implies that the United States expects bin Laden's escape. He says that the hunt will continue and will be eventually successful. During the daily Defense Department briefing, Rumsfeld says that U.S. air strikes are mainly against Taliban forces facing the Northern Alliance and that a B-52 had carpet bombed Taliban positions.

In London, Prime Minister Blair briefs Conservative Party leaders on plans to commit British ground troops to Afghanistan.

The U.S. government forms a 100-member team in New York to track the financial assets of terrorists. Most of the team will be from the customs service and has had prior experience in tracking funds from drug trafficking and related activities.

October 26

The Taliban claims to have captured and executed Abdul Haq, a prominent opposition leader among Afghanistan's Pashtun community. Haq and two companions were apparently trying to persuade tribal leaders to defect. The Defense Department declines to comment on reports that Americans were with Haq before his capture or that he had sought air support. State Department spokesman Boucher calls Haq's death "regrettable" but not a fatal setback to efforts to topple the Taliban regime.

In London, Armed Forces minister Adam Ingram announces that 200 Royal Marine commandos will be made available for service in Afghanistan and that 400 more will be placed on alert. An 11-ship Royal Navy task force will join U.S. forces in the Indian Ocean after completing maneuvers near Oman.

In Pakistan, President Musharraf expresses concerns that "anarchy and atrocity" will follow the collapse of the Taliban unless the coalition devises a "political strategy."

The State Department issues its annual report on religious freedom in the world. The report criticizes practices in Saudi Arabia, Tajikistan, and Uzbekistan, although it does not place them among states of "particular concern" (for example, Iran, China, Burma, Sudan, Iraq, and, most recently, North Korea). It mentions Afghanistan's Taliban, even though the United States never recognized the Taliban as a legitimate government.

October 27

The Taliban claims to have captured and executed five leaders and 10 soldiers of the Northern Alliance. Northern Alliance leader Rabbani confirms the death of Abdul Haq.

The London *Sunday Telegraph* interviews Iraq's deputy prime minister Tariq Aziz, who says that he expects the United States and Great Britain to use the "war on terrorism" as an excuse to attack his country and overthrow Saddam Hussein. He predicts that such an attack will break up the coalition.

President Bush signs into law a bill allowing him to waive sanctions imposed on Pakistan after General Musharraf's seizure of power in 1999.

The government of Pakistan announces that it has turned a suspected al-Qaeda member over to U.S. authorities. Jamil Qasin Saeed Mohammad of Yemen is suspected of involvement in the October 2000 attack on the USS *Cole* in Aden.

October 28

Secretary of Defense Rumsfeld tells CNN's Late Edition that the United States has been assisting the Northern Alliance with air strikes, will support occupation of Kabul by the Northern Alliance, and plans to continue the air campaign through Ramadan. When asked about civilian casualties, Rumsfeld notes that the Taliban is using mosques, schools, and hospitals to shelter military equipment and supplies.

The Army of Omar claims responsibility for the massacre of 16 Pakistani Christians worshiping in a Catholic church in Bahawalpur, Pakistan. President Musharraf condemns the attack.

UN high commissioner for refugees Ruud Lubbers announces that Pakistan will open its borders to the neediest Afghan refugees.

October 29

Attorney General John Ashcroft and FBI director Robert S. Mueller III warn that more terrorist attacks can be expected against U.S. interests at home or overseas within the next week.

After a meeting with U.S. Army general Tommy R. Franks in Islamabad, President Musharraf calls for a bombing pause during Ramadan. In Washington, Secretary of Defense Rumsfeld says that the terrorists "are unlikely to take [a] holiday" and observes that there are many historical examples of Muslim countries continuing to wage war during Ramadan. In London, however, British secretary of defense Geoff Hoon tells reporters that a bombing pause will not be ruled out.

The White House announces that President Bush plans to meet with President Musharraf at the UN General Assembly on November 10. The State Department announces that more than $1 billion in economic aid will be offered to "strengthen" Pakistan.

During a Defense Department briefing, Rumsfeld says that U.S. planes are dropping ammunition to Northern Alliance forces. He does not rule out the possibility of establishing a forward base in Afghanistan. General Myers says, "We are in the driver's seat," and U.S. forces are setting the pace for the campaign.

Rumsfeld also says that about 30 U.S. military personnel are serving as advisers to the Philippine army against Abu Sayyaf Muslim rebels on the island of Basilan.

Japan's Diet approves legislation that will allow its Self-Defense Forces to provide logistical support for the U.S. campaign against terrorism.

October 30

Secretary of Defense Rumsfeld acknowledges that "a very modest number of" U.S. troops are in Afghanistan to coordinate air strikes and to provide logistical support for the Northern Alliance. He says that 80% of the day's attacks are on Taliban frontline units in northern Afghanistan. Senior officials say that deployment of air and ground units to Central Asia is being considered. Rumsfeld declines to comment about reports of possible defections or supply problems among Taliban forces. He also announces plans visit Russia and Central Asia.

General Franks, chief of the U.S. Central Command, visits Uzbekistan and meets with President Karimov and senior officials.

British defense secretary Hoon visits Washington and meets with senior officials and members of Congress. He suggests that the United States take Ramadan into account when conducting the air campaign.

In Britain, Prime Minister Blair addresses the Welsh National Assembly in Cardiff, calls the antiterrorism campaign "a principled conflict," and pledges to use all possible means. Admiral Sir Michael Boyce, chief of the British defense staff, says that the conflict could last three or four years. Brigadier Roger Lane of the Royal Marines recommends that his forces not be sent to Afghanistan until they receive additional training and intelligence.

In Pakistan, High Commissioner for Refugees Lubbers of the UN meets with President Musharraf and Taliban ambassador Zaeef in hopes of assuring the security of UN relief workers and supplies in Afghanistan. Lubbers urges the United States and Britain to show "self-restraint" to minimize civilian casualties.

At the UN, Secretary General Kofi Annan also calls for a bombing halt to facilitate the delivery of urgently needed humanitarian aid.

October 31

General Franks meets with Northern Alliance general Mohammed Fahim in Dushanbe, Tajikistan, to discuss further military cooperation. Meanwhile U.S. air attacks include a B-52 strike against Taliban positions near Bagram. Admiral Stufflebeem says the preferred term for such an attack was *long stick* rather than *carpet bombing*.

The Defense Department announces that Reserve call-ups will exceed 50,000. Secretary of Defense Rumsfeld will leave on November 2 to visit Moscow and various countries near Afghanistan.

AID announces that it will supply the UN and other humanitarian agencies with $11.2 million to buy up to 30,000 tons of wheat from Central Asian countries for relief in Afghanistan. Administrator Andrew Natsios briefs President Bush on the impending food crisis in Afghanistan.

The European Union agrees to reinterpret its understanding of UN sanctions against Afghanistan so that arms can be supplied to opponents of the Taliban.

Saudi Arabia announces that it will freeze the assets of 66 persons and organizations on the U.S. list of sponsors of terrorism.

The U.S. Mission at the UN rejects a French proposal to seek Security Council condemnation of the anthrax attacks in the United States on the grounds that there is no clear proof that the attacks are of foreign origin.

In Kabul, Taliban spokesman Emir Khan Muttaqi says that negotiations with the United States are possible if it provides proof of bin Laden's involvement in the September 11 attacks.

November 1

Secretary of Defense Rumsfeld says that he plans to increase the number of Special Forces troops operating with the Northern Alliance as soon as possible. U.S. forces are currently directing 80% of their sorties against targets in northern Afghanistan. The Defense Department also announces plans to deploy a JSTARS surveillance aircraft and an experimental Global Hawk drone to Afghanistan.

National Security Adviser Rice says that the air campaign will continue through Ramadan.

Azerbaijan and Armenia offer to extend over-flight rights to U.S. aircraft during the campaign against terrorism. The administration in turn urges a House-Senate conference committee to approve a Senate provision in the Foreign Aid Appropriations Bill that would allow President Bush to waive a ban on military aid to Azerbaijan.

Turkey announces that it will send 90 of its Special Forces troops to train the Northern Alliance.

President Bush proposes a plan to enforce the 1972 Biological Weapons Convention by calling on signatories to enact laws against developing biological weapons, as well as a UN procedure to investigate reports of their use.

Bin Laden sends a handwritten letter to Al-Jazeera in which he urges Pakistan's Muslims to resist the "Christian crusade."

November 2

After a meeting with Nigerian president Obasanjo, President Bush says that the United States is "slowly but surely tightening the net" around bin Laden.

Secretary of Defense Rumsfeld leaves for Russia and Central Asia. He admits that a navy air strike was called in to successfully protect Hamid Karzai, a Pashtun opposition leader who was being pursued by Taliban forces.

The Defense Department admits that an army helicopter crashed in northern Afghanistan during bad weather. Four injured crew members were rescued, and an air strike destroyed the wreck. Admiral Stufflebeem admits that freezing rain is hampering efforts to fly more Special Forces teams into Afghanistan.

The State Department announces the freezing of the financial assets of 22 foreign terrorist organizations, including Hamas, Hizballah, Islamic Jihad, the Popular Front for the Liberation of Palestine, the Basque ETA, the Real IRA, and three Colombian groups.

In Kabul, Muslim clerics denounce Muslim states, particularly Turkey, that have failed to support the Taliban.

November 3

Secretary of Defense Rumsfeld visits Moscow to discuss missile defense, nuclear arms reductions, and cooperation against terrorism with Russian officials. He then proceeds to Tajikistan, which authorizes U.S. military engineers to survey three former Soviet air bases for possible use in the air campaign in Afghanistan.

Al-Jazeera broadcasts another taped message by bin Laden, in which he calls on Muslims to defend Afghanistan against the U.S. "crusade" and terms Muslim leaders who relied on the UN as "hypocrites." Al-Jazeera also broadcasts a 15-minute rebuttal by former U.S. ambassador Christopher W. S. Ross.

November 4

Secretary of Defense Rumsfeld visits Uzbekistan and then continues to Pakistan. In Islamabad, President Musharraf cautions him that bombings during Ramadan may offend the Muslim world. He privately offers to let the United States use three air bases in western Pakistan. Rumsfeld says that the Taliban has ceased to function as a government although "concentrations of power" still exist.

General Franks appears on ABC-TV's *This Week* and denies an article by Seymour Hersch in the *New Yorker* that claims that 12 Delta Force soldiers were wounded by enemy fire in an attack on a Taliban stronghold. Franks says that all injuries were minor and not the result of hostile action. On NBC-TV's *Meet the Press*, General Myers says that more Special Forces teams arrived in Afghanistan to direct air strikes, and that logistical support will make the Northern Alliance forces better prepared for winter warfare than the Taliban. Both say that although the war will be a long one, it is proceeding on schedule.

The State Department has no comment on a Taliban report that an American citizen, identified as John Bolton, was arrested on October 26 and died while in captivity in Kandahar. ICRC officials later turn over documents to the U.S. embassy in Islamabad.

As Arab League foreign ministers meet in Damascus, Secretary General Amr Moussa and Egyptian foreign minister Ahmad Maher deny that bin Laden speaks for all Arabs or Muslims.

November 5

President Abdelaziz Bouteflika of Algeria visits President Bush and endorses the U.S. antiterrorism campaign but also calls for action to improve the conditions that terrorists exploit.

Secretary of Defense Rumsfeld concludes his Central Asian tour with a visit to India. He praises Indian cooperation, calls for closer political and military ties, and pledges support for India's campaign against terrorists in Kashmir.

The State Department announces the appointment of the former assistant secretary of state James Dobbins as a special envoy to Afghan opposition groups.

November 6

Northern Alliance forces claim to have captured villages south of Mazar-e Sharif. Secretary of Defense Rumsfeld says that more Special Forces units will be sent to locate targets and that the air campaign will intensify. The Defense Department says that it used two BLU-82 15,000-pound bombs on Taliban targets on November 4.

French president Chirac visits President Bush and reaffirms his support for the U.S. antiterrorist campaign. They discuss humanitarian aid to Afghanistan and the need to continue the Middle East peace process.

President Bush addresses an antiterrorism conference in Warsaw by satellite video. He compares militant Islamic terrorists to the totalitarian regimes of the 20th century, says that their access to weapons of mass destruction will pose a "dark threat" to civilization, and that no nation can be neutral in the struggle.

Secretary of State Powell is interviewed by Egyptian television. When asked whether Iraq is a possible target in the campaign against terrorism, he says, "There are no plans at the moment to undertake any other military action." Links between the September 11 terrorists and Iraqi intelligence have not been proven.

Chancellor Gerhard Schroeder announces that Germany will provide up to 3,900 troops for support duties in the U.S. campaign in Afghanistan. These will include up to 100 from a "special unit." The deployment will require approval by the lower house of Parliament.

In Islamabad, embassy spokesman Mark Wentworth says that there is no evidence that a supposed relief worker who died in Kandahar was an American citizen.

November 7

The United States freezes the assets of 62 organizations and persons with suspected terrorist connections. Most are offices or affiliates of al-Barakaat and al-Taqua, which are informal financial exchange institutions linking the United States with the Middle East and Somalia. FBI and customs agents raid the offices of al-Barakaat in Alexandria and Falls Church, Virginia; Minneapolis, Minnesota; Boston, Massachussets; Seattle, Washington; and Columbus, Ohio. Similar raids take place in Liechtenstein, Austria, the Netherlands, Italy, and Switzerland. President Bush holds a press conference at the Treasury Department's financial crimes center and tells the world's financial institutions that failure to act against terrorism will prevent them from doing business with the United States.

President Bush also holds a joint press conference with British prime minister Blair, in which they reaffirm their commitment to the campaign against terrorism.

Secretary of State Powell replies to criticisms of Saudi Arabia's role in the antiterrorism campaign. He tells reporters at the State Department that Saudi Arabia has "excommunicated" bin Laden, severed relations with the Taliban, and responded positively to U.S. initiatives. Powell also meets with Kuwait's acting prime minister, who says that his country is and will remain "allied to the United States."

The Defense Department announces that the USS *John C. Stennis* and its escorts are being readied for duty in the Indian Ocean, which will bring the number of U.S. aircraft carriers in the region to four.

The House of Representatives votes 405-2 to establish a Radio Free Afghanistan to broadcast news and entertainment to the country in local languages.

Pakistan asks Taliban diplomats to stop holding news conferences and restricts domestic broadcasts by al-Jazeera in an effort to hamper the Taliban's propaganda campaign. President Musharraf calls once more for the suspension of the U.S. air campaign during Ramadan while on a stop in Istanbul on his way to a meeting of the UN General Assembly.

The UN and Pakistan reach an agreement to establish camps for Afghan refugees in Pakistan's North-West Frontier Province.

The Italian parliament votes to commit a naval task force and up to 2,700 troops to the U.S. antiterrorism campaign.

November 8

President Bush gives a speech in the George World Congress Center in Atlanta in which he stresses the public's responsibility for preventing terrorism. He proposes mobilizing members of the Senior Corps and AmeriCorps to assist police departments, health agencies, and areas hit by terrorists and concludes, "My fellow Americans, let's roll."

National Security Adviser Rice says that President Bush will not meet with Palestinian Authority chairman Yasir Arafat during the UN General Assembly in view of Arafat's failure to prevent terrorism in Israel.

The government of Lebanon rejects U.S. requests to freeze the assets of Hizballah on the grounds that "resistance groups" are not terrorist organizations.

The government of Pakistan forbids the Taliban's ambassador to hold press conferences and orders the Afghan consulate in Karachi to close.

Indian prime minister Atal Valpayee begins his visit to the United States. He expresses concern about the slow progress of the war in Afghanistan and predicts that the United States will need to commit substantial numbers of ground troops.

Three Japanese naval Self-Defense Forces ships leave Sasebo for the Indian Ocean.

November 9

Northern Alliance forces capture Mazar-e Sharif and claim that Taliban forces in northern Afghanistan are in retreat. Secretary of State Powell says that he prefers to see Kabul declared an "open city" than occupied by the Northern Alliance.

President Bush meets with Indian prime minister Valpayee and expresses satisfaction with Indian and Saudi cooperation in the campaign against terrorism. Saudi foreign minister Prince Saud, however, expresses frustration with Bush's failure to seek a new Middle East peace initiative.

At the UN General Assembly, Organization of the Islamic Conference members postpone action on an antiterrorism treaty until November 19. They seek an exemption for "national liberation movements." U.S. ambassador Negroponte attends an Iranian-sponsored Dialogue Among Civilization, during which he urges Muslim states not to accept bin Laden's claim that the United States is at war with Islam.

Czech foreign minister Milos Zeman meets with Secretary of State Powell on his way to the UN General Assembly. Zeman says that Mohamed Atta, mastermind of and participant in the September 11 attacks, talked about attacking the headquarters of Radio Free Europe and Radio Liberty during a meeting with a suspected Iraqi intelligence agent in Prague. Zeman also says that there is no record that Atta discussed attacks on targets in the United States.

November 10

President Bush addresses the UN General Assembly and says that each nation will be expected to play its part in the war against terrorism and that the "allies of terror" will be held accountable. He also says that his administration is working for the day that "two states—Israel and Palestine—could live peacefully together within secure and recognized borders."

Bush also meets with President Musharraf and says that he will seek an additional $1 billion in aid for Pakistan. Bush says that he will encourage the Northern Alliance to move south, but not into Kabul. When Musharraf addresses the UN General Assembly, he says that Pakistan has taken measures to ensure the security of its nuclear weapons. Musharraf also meets with Iranian president Mohammad Khatami to discuss their countries' policies in Afghanistan.

Two Pakistani newspapers publish an interview by journalist Hamid Mir with bin Laden, in which bin Laden claims to have chemical and nuclear weapons that he will use if the coalition uses weapons of mass destruction on his forces. Bin Laden claims ignorance of anthrax outbreaks in the United States.

November 11

With Northern Alliance forces claiming to have liberated six northern provinces, the Taliban concedes the loss of three of them and claims to be making a "strategic withdrawal." The Northern Alliance claims a major victory over the Taliban at Taloqan. Foreign Minister Abdullah says that the Northern Alliance intends to fight "up to the gates of Kabul" but will only enter the capital to prevent a breakdown of law and order or the entry of Pakistani troops.

In New York, President Musharraf warns of anarchy and atrocities if the Northern Alliance captures Kabul and insists that the Pashtuns be involved in a postwar political settlement. He says that debt relief from the United States depends on a new agreement between Pakistan and the IMF. Secretary of State Powell says on NBC's *Meet the Press* that the United States has no plans to release F-16s that were purchased by Pakistan and impounded after Pakistan tested nuclear weapons.

Secretaries Powell and Rumsfeld and National Security Adviser Rice all express skepticism that bin Laden has nuclear weapons. Rumsfeld tells ABC's *Face the Nation* that bin Laden probably has chemical and biological weapons and that U.S. forces bombed sites where they may have been kept. Rice says that the prospect of bin Laden getting nuclear weapons makes his defeat all the more imperative.

President Bush and Secretary General Annan attend a memorial service at Ground Zero. Before returning to Washington, Bush meets with the presidents of South Africa, Colombia, and Argentina. Powell meets with Arafat and stays in New York to meet with the foreign ministers of Syria and the Gulf Cooperation Council states.

The UN announces that its first shipment of humanitarian aid from Uzbekistan to Afghanistan is ready to be delivered.

England's defense secretary Geoff Hoon confirms that British troops are operating in Afghanistan.

Johanne Sutton of Radio France Internationale, Pierre Billaud of RTL Radio, and Volker Handloik of the German magazine *Stern* become the first foreign journalists to die in the Afghan conflict when Taliban forces ambush the Northern Alliance troops they were accompanying.

November 12

The Northern Alliance announces the liberation of Herat. Its forces are said to be closing in on Kunduz, the last Taliban stronghold in the north, and to be approaching Kabul. Pakistani officials urge the United States and the UN to establish an interim government and to impose security on the Afghan capital.

At the UN, Secretary of State Powell attends a conference of foreign ministers of the Six-Plus-Two Group, states bordering Afghanistan. At the start of the meeting, he publicly shakes hands with Iranian foreign minister Kamal Kharrazi. Powell urges his colleagues to quickly organize a peacekeeping force and a provisional administration for Kabul. He tells the *New York Times* that Muslim countries like Turkey, Indonesia, and Bangladesh could have a role to play.

AID administrator Natsios visits Tashkent and says that the liberation of Mazar-e Sharif will simplify the delivery of humanitarian aid to Afghanistan.

Defense Department officials say that the United States is considering the use of at least one air base in Tajikistan to support the air campaign in Afghanistan.

November 13

Taliban forces abandon Kabul and Northern Alliance forces take control of the Afghan capital. Eight foreign aid workers, two of them American women accused of promoting Christianity, remain in captivity and are reportedly taken to Kandahar. Before the entry of Northern Alliance forces, mobs loot government offices and the Pakistani embassy and kill any foreign Taliban supporters they can find. Foreign Minister Abdullah says that the Northern Alliance has sent its security forces into Kabul to prevent disorder and that General Mohammed Fahim will lead a "military and security council." In Kandahar, Mohammad Omar urges the Taliban to "resist, put up resistance, and fight."

Secretary of Defense Rumsfeld says that U.S. Special Operations forces are operating in southern Afghanistan in pursuit of al-Qaeda and Taliban leaders. Special Forces teams are currently in Kabul to observe the Northern Alliance. U.S. aircraft continue to harry fleeing Taliban forces. Rumsfeld urges other countries not to give sanctuary to fugitive terrorists and says that the struggle against terrorism is far from over.

Al-Jazeera reports that its Kabul office was bombed before the Northern Alliance entered the city. A U.S. Central Command spokesman says that the building is thought to be used by al-Qaeda.

President Bush issues a directive to authorize the establishment of military tribunals to try foreign terrorist suspects and their accomplices. The secretary of defense will appoint the tribunals and determine their rules and procedures.

Bush also holds a joint press conference with Russian president Vladimir Putin at the White House. Putin hopes that the war on terrorism will make possible closer cooperation between the United States and Russia. Bush says, "We will continue to work with the Northern Alliance commanders to make sure they respect the human rights of the people that they are liberating."

As President Musharraf returns from the United States, he calls for the immediate deployment to Kabul of a UN peacekeeping force from Muslim nations so that a hostile government will not establish itself on Pakistan's border. Pakistani spokesmen say that their government may contribute troops to a peacekeeping force.

At the UN, Brahimi proposes to the Security Council that a conference of Afghan representatives be held under UN protection. This conference would establish a provisional council to select an interim government, which would in turn outline a program to draft a new constitution to be endorsed by a national council (*loya jirga*). Brahimi envisions a two-year transition period between an interim and a permanent government. Secretary General Annan instructs Brahimi to send UN political advisers to Kabul as soon as "security conditions permit."

U.S. special envoy James F. Dobbins meets with former king Zahir Shah in Rome. Although Zahir Shah has been mentioned as possible chairman of a provisional council, Northern Alliance leader Rabbani says that the king can only return to Afghanistan as a private citizen. In Kabul, Northern Alliance foreign minister Abdullah says that all factions except the Taliban will be welcome to help form a coalition government.

The State Department announces that it will institute a stricter screening program for men from 25 Arab and Muslim countries who are seeking visas to enter the United States.

In Germany, Chancellor Schroeder calls for a vote of confidence when the lower house of Parliament votes on his decision to contribute up to 3,000 troops to the antiterrorism campaign.

November 14

Taliban forces continue to flee southward toward Kandahar. Some Pashtun tribes in southern Afghanistan reportedly have taken up arms against the Taliban. U.S. Special Forces teams are said to be setting up roadblocks in the search for followers of bin Laden, and air force planes are dropping leaflets offering a $25 million reward for bin Laden's capture. A Taliban spokesman says that bin Laden and Mohammad Omar are still alive and well in Afghanistan.

The Taliban abandons eight foreign relief workers who had been under arrest in Afghanistan since August. The workers are freed by residents of the town of Ghazni, who then contact the International Committee of the Red Cross, which arranges for their evacuation to Pakistan by U.S. Special Forces helicopters.

The UN Security Council approves a resolution calling on all parties in Afghanistan to attend a conference to settle the country's future, urging member states to provide humanitarian aid and calling for a central role for the UN in the reconstruction process. The UN also authorizes member states to provide peacekeeping forces.

Great Britain offers to commit 5,000 troops to peacekeeping in Afghanistan. Prime Minister Blair tells Parliament that bin Laden admitted his guilt in a video recorded on October 20. Bin Laden boasted that al-Qaeda had attacked the United States "in self-defense" and as "revenge for our people killed in Palestine and Iraq."

U.S. special envoy Dobbins arrives in Islamabad to discuss the political future of Afghanistan.

November 15

Presidents Bush and Putin agree that the United States and Russia will cooperate against terrorism and in the political reconstruction of Afghanistan. After their summit meeting at Bush's ranch in Crawford, Texas, Putin visits Ground Zero of the World Trade Center in New York before returning to Moscow.

The United States announces plans for an international conference for the reconstruction of Afghanistan, to be held at the White House later in November. A larger conference, sponsored by the World Bank, the UN Development Program, and the Asian Development Bank, is scheduled for Islamabad on November 27–29. AID administrator Natsios flies to northern Afghanistan to assess relief needs.

The first peacekeeping forces arrive in Afghanistan as 100 British marines land at the Bagram airfield. President Chirac notifies Secretary General Annan that France will send troops to secure the airport at Mazar-e Sharif. Canada and the Netherlands also express their willingness to send troops. Turkey is expected to supply peacekeeping forces for Kabul but is awaiting Security Council authorization.

As fighting continues around Kandahar and Kunduz, General Franks says, "We are tightening the noose. It's a matter of time." A Taliban envoy in Pakistan asks UN representatives for help in arranging the surrender of his forces in Kunduz; they are noncommittal. Bin Laden's whereabouts are unknown, but a defiant Mohammad Omar vows to fight on until "the destruction of America."

In the Philippines, Muslim Abu Sayyaf rebels release seven of their 10 hostages. A Filipina nurse and an American missionary couple remain in captivity.

November 16

The Taliban admits that Osama bin Laden's deputy, Muhammad Atef, was killed in an air raid near Kabul earlier in the week. Atef, a native of Egypt, was wanted in the United States for his involvement in the 1998 embassy bombings in Kenya and Tanzania.

The Defense Department announces that 300 Special Forces personnel are in Afghanistan: 200 in the north and the rest, along with allied personnel, in the south. Although Admiral Stufflebeem says that the Special Forces' chief task was "strategic reconnaissance," Secretary Rumsfeld admits that they are taking part in ground combat as they hunt for information and fugitive members of the Taliban and al-Qaeda. Forty U.S. soldiers arrive at Bagram to join British forces in repairing the airfield.

In Berlin, Chancellor Schroeder's Social Democratic–Green Party coalition survives a vote of confidence by two votes when it approves commitment of German troops to support the antiterrorism campaign in Afghanistan.

In Afghanistan, a Taliban spokesman denies a report that Taliban leaders are trying to work out a deal for the evacuation of Kandahar. In Kabul, the Northern Alliance occupies Radio Kabul and government offices.

Secretary of State Powell discusses a possible humanitarian aid package for Uzbekistan with Foreign Minister Kamilov.

November 17

Former Afghan president Burhanuddin Rabbani makes a triumphal return to Kabul. He invites all Afghan groups except the Taliban to meet in Kabul to form a new government. He tells reporters that he welcomes the formation of a broad-based government and says that the Northern Alliance will respect the decision of a *loya jirga*. Two planeloads of UN officials, led by Deputy Special Representative Francesc Vendrell, arrive at Bagram to reestablish a UN presence in Afghanistan and to help arrange a conference among Afghan political groups.

Taliban ambassador Zaeef says that bin Laden and his family left Afghanistan for parts unknown. He later says that the bin Ladens had only left the Taliban-controlled part of the country.

First Lady Laura Bush delivers the weekly presidential address, in which she denounces the Taliban's oppression of Afghan women and children.

The French defense ministry announces that up to 10 French aircraft will be available for missions in Afghanistan in two weeks.

The G-20 finance ministers meet in Ottawa to discuss means of shutting down terrorist financial networks. They also discuss plans for the reconstruction of Afghanistan. Further discussions will be held during the IMF and World Bank meetings.

November 18

Northern Alliance foreign minister Abdullah meets with U.S. special envoy Dobbins in Tashkent and announces that the Northern Alliance is willing to meet with other Afghan political groups in Europe to discuss a postwar government. No date or location is set.

As fighting continues around Kunduz and Kandahar, Secretary of State Powell, National Security Adviser Rice, and Deputy Secretary of Defense Wolfowitz tell TV news programs that they believe bin Laden's options are shrinking along with the Taliban-controlled portions of Afghanistan. They doubt that bin Laden has fled the country or that neighboring countries would agree to take him in. Powell suggests that if bin Laden does escape, the United

States will try to "coordinate" his capture with local authorities.

USAID administrator Natsios concludes a visit to five Central Asian republics. He is confident that USAID will be able to avert famine in Afghanistan by arranging for the delivery of 55,000 tons of food per month from Iran, Turkmenistan, Uzbekistan, and Tajikistan. The United States is also considering a program to rebuild roads, wells, and irrigation systems.

Russia sends a 12-member delegation to Kabul to meet with the Northern Alliance.

November 19

Secretary of Defense Rumsfeld says that the United States is counting on Afghan opposition groups to help find bin Laden and that a $25-million reward for his capture could provide an incentive. There are as yet no plans to commit large numbers of U.S. troops to the search for bin Laden. Rumsfeld is also cool to the notion of a negotiated surrender of Taliban forces in Kunduz.

The air campaign around Kunduz and Kandahar continues, with Taliban leaders in Kunduz seeking a way to arrange an orderly surrender to the Northern Alliance and safe passage to an undisclosed third country for the Taliban's foreign contingents.

Special envoy Dobbins meets with Northern Alliance officials at Bagram and says that they are willing to attend an international conference on the future of Afghanistan. Germany offers to host the conference. Northern Alliance spokesmen remain noncommittal, and UN officials have not said which other parties will be invited to attend. Pakistani foreign minister Abdul Sattar claims the Northern Alliance's occupation of Kabul unacceptable and calls for the deployment of an international force. The Northern Alliance complains that it was not consulted about the dispatch of British troops to the Bagram airfield and says that France will have to negotiate sending troops to the airport at Mazar-e Sharif. Britain and France postpone plans to send additional troops to Afghanistan.

Six armed men ambush a caravan of vehicles that is traveling between Jalalabad and Kabul. Four foreign journalists are kidnapped, stoned, and then killed. It is not known whether their assailants were Taliban members or ordinary bandits.

In Geneva, Undersecretary of State for Arms Control and International Security John R. Bolton says that Iraq is pursuing a biological weapons program, while North Korea, Libya, Syria, Iran, and Sudan are suspected of doing so. The United States still favors enactment of domestic bans on biological weapons activities, international investigations of suspicious outbreaks of diseases, and more cooperation with the World Health Organization instead of the draft protocol for enforcement of the Biological Weapons Convention.

President Bush signs into law a bill federalizing U.S. airport security personnel. In the evening he hosts a dinner at the White House for Muslim diplomats in honor of Ramadan.

Secretary of State Powell addresses representatives of women's advocacy groups and says that the United States is committed to ensuring that Afghan women have their rightful place in any postwar government.

November 20

The United States hosts a conference at the State Department to discuss the postwar reconstruction of Afghanistan. Secretary of State Powell tells the delegates that the United States expects to play a major role. U.S. and Japanese officials say that they have developed a long-term "action program."

President Gloria Macapagal-Arroyo of the Philippines meets with President Bush and the secretaries of state and defense, who promise to supply her country with $92.3 million in military equipment. She also seeks economic aid and the opening of U.S. markets to Filipino products. President Bush will consider adding the Communist New People's Army and various Muslim insurgent groups to the list of terrorist organizations whose assets will be frozen.

Northern Alliance foreign minister Abdullah meets with UN special envoy Vendrell in Kabul. They announce that the Northern Alliance will attend a UN-sponsored conference in Berlin about the political future of Afghanistan. Former president Rabbani says that the Berlin conference will be "mostly symbolic." Special envoy Brahimi says that all major Afghan political groups except the Taliban will attend. Abdullah still insists that the Northern Alliance must approve further deployments of foreign peacekeeping troops.

The UN announces that it will provide air transportation between Islamabad and Bagram to journalists, diplomats, and aid workers. A one-way ticket will cost $2,500.

The Defense Department announces that 4,400 U.S. Marines from the 15th and 26th Marine Expeditionary Units are available for deployment in Afghanistan. Admiral Stufflebeem says that the United States has no plans for a Thanksgiving bombing pause but does not rule out a cease-fire during possible negotiations for the surrender of Taliban forces in Kunduz. The Northern Alliance, meanwhile, gives the Taliban forces three days to surrender or face the consequences. The most likely sticking point is the fate of foreign members of the Taliban.

Pakistan's foreign ministry announces that the Taliban's consulates in Quetta and Peshawar will be closed. The U.S. embassy in Islamabad opens a Coalition Information Center. Kenton Keith serves as the center's director.

November 22

President Bush visits the 101st Airborne Division at Fort Campbell, Kentucky, and speaks of a long and desperate struggle against terrorism in which "the most difficult steps in this mission still lie ahead."

At Spin Boldak, Taliban spokesman Tayab Agha tells the United States to "forget the September 11 attacks," while vowing to fight on and refusing to take part in any postwar government. He denies any knowledge of bin Laden's whereabouts.

Taliban commander Mullah Faizal says that his forces in Kunduz are ready to surrender to the Northern Alliance, though details remain to be worked out.

General Myers attends a meeting of senior NATO military leaders in Brussels and says that even if bin Laden is killed or captured, the hunt for other al-Qaeda leaders will continue. Secretary of Defense Rumsfeld says during a visit to Fort Bragg that his personal preference is that bin Laden be killed rather than captured. The U.S. deputy chairman of the joint chiefs of staff, General Peter Pace, says that navy ships will be searching foreign ships off the coast of Pakistan for fugitive terrorists.

In London, International Development Secretary Clare Short claims that differences with the United States have delayed the deployment of more British troops to Afghanistan. Prime Minister Blair denies it. Further deployments, even for humanitarian purposes, still await approval by the Northern Alliance. Interior Minister Yunus Qanuni announces that he will lead the Northern Alliance delegation to the Berlin conference on the future of Afghanistan.

In Kuala Lumpur, Malaysia, Admiral Dennis Blair, chief of the U.S. Pacific Command, doubts that U.S. forces will be involved in combat against terrorist groups in Southeast Asia. The United States will assist area governments in identifying terrorists, shutting off their funds, and preventing their movement.

The Northern Alliance resumes bombardment of Kunduz after surrender negotiations with the Taliban break down. President Musharraf contacts Prime Minister Blair, Secretary of State Powell, and UN secretary general Annan in an effort to ensure the safety of Pakistanis fighting with the Taliban. Pakistan also closes the Taliban's embassy.

November 23

Northern Alliance foreign minister Abdullah says that Kunduz will be attacked if no agreement is reached by November 24 for its surrender. The sticking point is still the fate of the 3–4,000 foreign Taliban members. British foreign secretary Straw visits Islamabad and says, after meeting with senior Pakistani officials, that a Taliban surrender should be accepted. UN spokesman Eric Falt also calls for a cease-fire.

UN spokesman Ahmad Fawzi says that the peace conference, now to be held in Bonn, will open November 27 to allow delegates some more travel time. The four major Afghan groups are the Northern Alliance, the Rome Group (followers of former king Zahir Shah), the Peshawar Group (Pashtuns with ties to Pakistan), and the Cyprus Group (non-Pashtuns with ties to Iran).

November 24

In his weekly radio address, President Bush warns of "difficult times ahead" and hints at preemptive strikes against terrorists.

Although no general surrender agreement is reached at Kunduz, more than 1,000 Taliban members surrender to Northern Alliance forces. Another large surrender takes place at Maidan Shahr.

President Musharraf says that it is unlikely that bin Laden has escaped to Pakistan.

The Defense Department says that captured al-Qaeda members may be held on Guam. Former UN war crimes prosecutor Richard Goldstone calls U.S. plans to try foreign terrorist suspects before military tribunals "second- or third-class justice."

Former president Rabbani says that he will step down if the Bonn conference agrees upon a leader for an Afghan provisional government. He also calls for "a new friendship, based on mutual respect, noninterference, and territorial independence" with Pakistan. UN high commissioner for refugees Mary Robinson calls for excluding Afghan leaders from the provisional government if their followers have committed atrocities.

November 25

About 1,200 U.S. Marines establish a base near Kandahar after opponents of the Taliban seize an airfield. The marines are expected to take part in the search for bin Laden and other leading terrorists.

Captured Taliban soldiers revolt at the Qala Jangi prison near Mazar-e Sharif. Hundreds are believed to have been killed in several hours of fighting that included U.S. air strikes directed by U.S. Special Forces and British Special Air Service troops. Most of the captives are believed to have been foreign members of the Taliban. The Defense Department first denies that any U.S. military personnel are casualties but says that a CIA officer has been wounded. The CIA declines to comment. The Defense Department later admits that five U.S. soldiers are have been wounded by a stray bomb.

Meanwhile, Northern Alliance forces begin occupying Kunduz.

November 26

Northern Alliance forces complete the occupation of Kunduz. President Musharraf expresses concern about the fate of Pakistani nationals who were serving with the Taliban in view of reports that foreign members of the Taliban were shot during the fall of Kunduz.

U.S. Marines continue to build a forward base near Kandahar. Navy fighters and marine helicopter gunships attack a Taliban armored column. Secretary of Defense Rumsfeld says that the new base will allow U.S. forces and their allies to interdict roads leading out of Kandahar and that no more than 2,000 marines will be deployed. The base had been attacked by army Rangers on October 19.

Former Afghan president Rabbani says that the Bonn conference will not be a summit council and that major councils and meetings will take place within Afghanistan. He makes these remarks in the United Arab Emirates. UN spokesman Eric Falt says that 32 delegates from four major groups are expected to attend. The Northern Alliance and the Rome Group plan to send eight negotiators and three advisers each. The Peshawar and Cyptus Groups will each send three delegates and two advisers.

British defense secretary Hoon announces that most of the 6,000 troops alerted for deployment to Afghanistan will not be deployed. He admits that four British soldiers were injured while operating with U.S. forces but gives no details.

Pakistani officials say that they have initiated a search for bin Laden and other al-Qaeda leaders in Afghanistan.

Russia begins flying officials, technicians, and relief supplies to Afghanistan. President Bush says that other countries that try to develop weapons of mass destruction will "be held accountable." Countries that harbor, fund, or shelter terrorists will be counted as terrorists. He urges Saddam Hussein to readmit UN inspectors to Iraq or face the consequences and links the establishment of relations with North Korea to the admission of weapons inspectors.

SELECTED BIBLIOGRAPHY

BOOKS AND ARTICLES

Aberlin, Mary Beth. "Trace Elements: Taggants Can Help Finger Terrorists and Counterfeiters." *The Sciences* 36, no. 6 (November–December 1996): 8–10.

Adams, James. *The Financing of Terror.* New York: Simon & Schuster, 1986.

Alali, A. Odasuo, and Kenoye K. Eke. "Terrorism, News Media and Democratic Political Order." *Current World Leaders* 39, no. 4 (August 1996): 64–72.

Alexander, Yonah, and Allan S. Nanes, eds. *Legislative Responses to Terrorism.* Boston: Martinus Nijhoff Publishers, 1986.

Alexander, Yonah, and Robert Patter. *Terrorism and the Media: Dilemma for Government, Journalism, and the Public.* Washington, D.C.: Brassey's, 1990.

Ali, Tariq. *The Clash of Fundamentalisms: Crusades, Jihads and Modernity.* London: Verso, 2002.

Bassiouni, M. C. "Media Coverage of Terrorism." *Journal of Communication* 32: 128–143.

———. "Terrorism and the Media." *Journal of Criminal Law and Criminology* 72: 1–55.

———. *Terrorism, Law Enforcement, and the Mass Media.* Rockford, Md.: NCJRS.

Beaton, Leonard. "Crisis in Quebec." *Roundtable* 241 (1971).

Begin, Menachem. *The Revolt.* Rev. ed. New York: Dell, 1977.

———. *White Nights: The Story of a Prisoner in Russia.* New York: Harper & Row, 1977.

Bell, J. Bowyer. *Terror out of Zion: Irgun Zvai Leumi, LEHI, and the Palestine Underground, 1928–1949.* New York, 1977.

———. *A Time of Terror: How Democratic Societies Respond to Revolutionary Violence.* New York: Basic Books, 1978.

———. *Transnational Terror.* Washington, D.C.: American Institute for Public Policy Research; and Stanford, Calif.: Hoover Institute on War, Revolution, and Peace, 1975, 10–25.

Benesh, Peter. "The Growing Menace from Traders in Terror." In *Violence and Terrorism 98/99.* 4th ed., edited by Bernard Schechterman and Martin Slann. Guilford, Conn.: Dushkin/McGraw-Hill, 1998.

———. "Many Terrorists Are Seduced by Thoughts of Becoming a Martyr." In *Violence and Terrorism 98/99.* 4th ed., edited by Bernard Schechterman and Martin Slann. Guilford, Conn.: Dushkin/McGraw-Hill, 1998.

Bering-Jensen, H. "The Silent Treatment for Terrorists." *Insight.* November 21, 1988, 27–41.

Bremer, L. Paul, III. "Terrorism and the Rule of Law." U.S. State Department, Bureau of Public Affairs, Current Policy No. 847, April 23, 1987.

Burleigh, Michael. *The Third Reich: A New History.* New York: Hill & Wang, 2000.

Carr, Caleb. "Terrorism as Warfare: The Lessons of Military History." *World Policy Journal.* Winter 1996/97, 1–12.

Clarke, Richard A. *Against All Enemies: Inside America's War on Terror.* New York: Simon & Schuster, 2004.

Clarke, Thurston. *By Blood and Fire: The Attack on the King David Hotel.* New York: Putnam, 1981.

Cole, David, and James X. Dempsey. *Terrorism and the Constitution: Sacrificing Civil Liberties in the Name of National Security.* New York: New Press, 2002.

Combs, Cindy C. *Terrorism in the Twenty-First Century.* Upper Saddle River, N.J.: Prentice Hall, 2000.

Convention for the Suppression of Unlawful Acts Against the Safety of Civil Aviation, signed in Montreal, Canada, September 23, 1971.

Convention on Extradition, December 13, 1957, 24 Europe T.S.

Convention on Offenses and Certain Other Acts Committed on Board Aircraft, signed in Tokyo, Japan, September 14, 1963.

Convention Relative to the Protection of Civilian Persons in Time of War, U.S.T. 3516, T.I.A.S. No. 3365, 75, U.N.T.S. 28 (1949).

Crelinsten, Ronald D., Danielle Laberge-Altmjed, and Dennis Szabo, eds. *Terrorism and Criminal Justice.* Lexington, Mass.: D.C. Heath, 1978.

Crenshaw, Martha, ed. *Terrorism, Legitimacy and Power: The Consequences of Political Violence.* Middletown, Conn.: Wesleyan University Press, 1983.

Denby, David. "No Rules: New Interpretation of the Massacre at the Munich Olympics." *New Yorker,* August 21 and 28, 2000, 160–164.

Deutch, John. "Fighting Foreign Terrorism: The Integrated Efforts of the Law Enforcement Community." *Vital Speeches of the Day,* October 1, 1996, 738–740.

———. "Terrorism." *Foreign Policy* (Fall 1997): 10–22.

Dobson, Christopher, and Ronald Payne. *The Carlos Complex: A Study in Terror.* New York: Putnam, 1977.

———. *Counterattack: The West's Battle against the Terrorists.* New York: Facts On File, 1982.

Encyclopaedia Britannica, 11th ed. S. V. "Bakunin, Mikhail Alexandrovich."

Fenelo, Michael J. "Technical Prevention of Air Piracy." *International Conciliation* 585 (1971) 117–124.

Finn, John E. "Media Coverage of Political Terrorism and the First Amendment: Reconciling the Public's Right to Know with Public Order." In *Violence and Terrorism 98/99,* 4th ed., edited by Bernard Schechterman and Martin Slann. Guilford, Conn.: Dushkin/McGraw-Hill, 1998.

Fitzpatrick, T. E. "The Semantics of Terror." *Security Register* 1, no. 14 (November 4, 1974): 17–35.

Friedlander, Robert. *Terrorism: Documents of International and National Control.* Dobbs Ferry, N.Y.: Oceana Publications, 1979.

———. "Terrorism and National Liberation Movements: Can Rights Derive from Wrongs?" *Case Western Reserve Journal of International Law* 13, no. 2 (Spring 1981) 47–69.

Fromkin, David. "The Strategy of Terror." *Foreign Affairs* 53 (July 1975): 689.

"Gaping Holes in Airport Security." *U.S. News and World Report,* April 25, 1988.

Goldman, Emma. *Anarchism and Other Essays.* New York: Dover Press, 1969.

Goldstein, A., and M. H. Segall, eds. *Aggression in Global Perspective.* New York: Pergamon Press, 1983.

Gow, James. *Triumph of the Lack of Will: International Diplomacy and the Yugoslav War.* New York: Columbia University Press, 1997.

Grant, Marvin. "What Is the PLO Worth?" *Parade Magazine,* September 21, 1986.

Gross, Felix. *Political Violence and Terror in Nineteenth and Twentieth Century Russian and Eastern Europe.* New York: Cambridge University Press, 1990.

Grossman, Lawrence K. "The Face of Terrorism." *Quill* (June 1986): 24–41.

Gunaratna, Rohan. *Inside al-Qaeda: Global Network of Terror.* New York: Columbia University Press, 2002.

Gurr, Ted. *Why Men Rebel.* Princeton, N.J.: Princeton University Press, 1970.

Hacker, Frederick J. *Crusaders, Criminals, and Crazies: Terror and Terrorism in Our Time.* New York: Bantam, 1978.

Harris, Jonathan. *The New Terrorism: Politics of Violence.* New York: Messner, 1983.

Hecht, David. "African Women: Standing up to Ancient Custom." *The Christian Science Monitor,* June 3, 1998, 1–7.

Hewitt, Christopher. *The Effectiveness of Antiterrorist Policies.* New York: University Press of America, 1984.

Hickey, Neil. "Gaining the Media's Attention." In *The Struggle against Terrorism,* edited by William P. Lineberry. New York: Wilson, 1977, 45–62.

Hodgson, M. *The Order of the Assassins.* San Rafael, Calif.: Presidio Press, 1960.

Hoffman, Bruce. *'Holy Terror': The Implications of Religion Motivated by Religious Imperative.* Santa Monica, Calif.: The RAND Corp., P-6450, 1993.

———. "Recent Trends and Future Prospects of Iranian Sponsored International Terrorism." In *Middle Eastern Terrorism: Current Threats and Future Prospects,* edited by Yonah Alexander. New York and Toronto: G. K. Hall, 1994.

———. "Responding to Terrorism Across the Technological Spectrum." *Terrorism and Political Violence.* Autumn 1994, 366–390.

Hopple, Gerald W., and Miriam Steiner. *The Causal Beliefs of Terrorists: Empirical Results.* McLean, Va.: Defense Systems, 1984.

Horowitz, Irving Louis. "Can Democracy Cope with Terrorism?" *Civil Liberties Review* 4 (1977).

Howard, Michael. "Combatting Crime & Terrorism: International Solutions." *Vital Speeches of the Day,* October 1, 1996, 741–743.

Howard, Russell D., and Reid L. Sawyer. *Defeating Terrorism: Shaping the New Security Environment.* Guilford, Conn.: McGraw-Hill/Dushkin, 2004.

Howe, Irving. "The Ultimate Price of Random Terror," *Skeptic: The Forum for Contemporary History* 11 (January–February 1976): 10–19.

Huffman, Stanley, "International Law and the Control of Force." *International and Comparative Law Quarterly* 32 (June 1995).

Hurwood, B. *Society and the Assassin: A Background Book on Political Murder.* London: International Institute for Strategic Studies, 1970.

Jain, Vinod K. "Thwarting Terrorism with Technology." *The World and I* no. 11 (November 1996): 149–155.

Jenkins, Brian. "High Technology Terrorism and Surrogate War: The Impact of New Technology on Low-Level Violence." In *Contemporary Terrorism: Selected Readings,* edited by J. D. Elliott and L. K. Gibson. Gaithersburg, Md.: International Association of Chiefs of Police, 1978.

———. *International Terrorism: A New Kind of Warfare.* Santa Monica, Calif.: RAND, 1974, P-5261, 4.

———. "International Terrorism: The Other World War." A Project AIR FORCE Report Prepared for the United States Air Force, November 1985.

———. *The Likelihood of Nuclear Terrorism.* Santa Monica, Calif.: RAND, P-7119, July 1985.

———. *Terrorism: Trends and Potentialities.* Santa Monica, Calif.: RAND, 1977.

———. *The Terrorist Mindset and Terrorist Decisionmaking: Two Areas of Ignorance.* Santa Monica, Calif.: RAND, 1979.

———. "Will Terrorists Go Nuclear?" P-5541. Santa Monica, Calif.: RAND, November 1975.

Jenkins, Brian, and Janera Johnson. *International Terrorism: A Chronology, 1968–74.* A Report Prepared for the Department of State and the Defense Advances Research Projects Agency, R-1587-DOSIAPRA (March 1975). Santa Monica, Calif.: RAND, 1975.

Jenkins, Roy. *England: Prevention of Terrorism (Temporary Provisions)—A Bill.* London: Her Majesty's Stationery Office, 1974.

Joyner, Christopher C. "Offshore Maritime Terrorism: International Implications and the Legal Response." *Naval War College Review* 36, no. 4 (July/August 1983): 17–32.

Joyner, Nancy D. *Aerial Hijacking as an International Crime.* Dobbs Ferry, N.Y.: Oceana, 1974.

Judgment of the International Military Tribunal, Nuremberg, September 30, 1946, vol. 22. Trial of the Major War Criminals Before the International Military Tribunal Proceedings (1948).

Kahler, Miles. "Rumors of War: The 1914 Analogy." *Foreign Affairs* 58, no. 2 (1979–80), 374–396.

Karsh, Efraim, and Isari Rauti. *Saddam Hussein: A Political Biography.* New York: Free Press, 1988.

Kegley, Charles W., Jr. *The New Global Terrorism: Characteristics, Causes, Controls.* Upper Saddle River, N.J.: Prentice Hall, 2003.

Kehler, C., G. Harvey, and R. Hall. "Perspectives of Media Control in Terrorist-Related Incidents." *Canadian Police Journal* 6: 225–243.

Kidder, Rushworth M. "Manipulation of the Media." In *Violence and Terrorism: Annual Editions, 98/99,* 4th ed., edited by Bernard Schechterman and Martin Slann. Guilford, Conn. Dushkin/McGraw-Hill, 1998.

———. "Unmasking State-Sponsored Terrorism." *Christian Science Monitor,* May 14, 1986, 18–20.

Kittrie, Nicholas N. "Patriots and Terrorists: Reconciling Human Rights with World Order. *Case West-*

ern Reserve Journal of International Law 13, no. 2 (Spring 1981) 300–04.

———. "Response: Looking at the World Realistically." *Case Western Journal of International Law* 13, no. 2 (Spring 1981).

Knickerbocker, Brad. "Latest Tactic against Hate Groups: Bankruptcy." *The Christian Science Monitor,* August 25, 2000, 3.

Kupperman, Robert H., and Darrell M. Trent. *Terrorism: Threat, Reality, and Response.* Stanford, Calif.: Hoover Institute Press, 1979.

Kushner, Harvey. *Holy War on the Home Front: The Secret Islamic Terror Network in the United States.* New York: Penguin Group, 2004.

Kyemba, Henry. *A State of Blood: The Inside Story.* New York: Grosset and Dunlap, 1977.

Laqueur, Walter. *The Age of Terrorism.* Boston: Little, Brown, 1987.

———. *The New Terrorism: Fanaticism and the Arms of Mass Destruction.* New York: Oxford University Press, 1999.

———. "Post-Modern Terrorism." *Foreign Affairs,* September/October 1996, n.p.

Laqueur, Walter, ed. *Voices of Terror: Manifestos, Writings and Manuals of Al-Qaeda, Hamas, and other Terrorists from around the World and Throughout the Ages.* New York: Reed Press, 2004.

Leeman, Richard W. "Terrorism." In *Morality and Conviction in American Politics: A Reader,* edited by Martin Slann and Susan Duffy. Upper Saddle River, N.J.: Prentice Hall, 1990.

Levi, Werner. *Contemporary International Law: A Concise Introduction.* Boulder, Colo.: Westview, 1989.

Lewis, B. *The Assassins: A Radical Sect in Islam.* San Rafael, Calif.: Presidio Press, 1968.

Lipstadt, Deborah. *Denying the Holocaust: The Growing Assault on Truth and Memory.* New York: Plume, 1993.

Liston, Robert A. *Terrorism.* New York: Elsevier/Nelson. 1977.

Livingstone, N. C. "Taming Terrorism. In Search of a New U.S. Policy." *International Security Review: Terrorism Report 7,* no. 1 (Spring 1982): 12–17.

Livingstone, W. D. "Terrorism and the Media Revolution." In *Fighting Back: Winning the War against Terrorism,* edited by N. C. Livingstone and T. E. Arnold. Lexington, Mass.: Heath, 1986, 213–227.

Maoz, Moshe. *Syria and Israel: From War to Peace Making.* New York: Oxford University Press, 1995.

McCormick, Gordon H. *The Shining Path and Peruvian Terrorism.* Santa Monica, Calif.: RAND, 1987.

———. *The Shining Path and the Future of Peru.* Santa Monica, Calif.: RAND, 1990.

McGurn, William. "Indonesia's Kristallnacht." *The Wall Street Journal,* July 10, 1998, A14.

Memorandum of Understanding of Hijacking of Aircraft and Vessels and Other Offenses. 24 U.S.T. 737, T.I.A.S. no. 7579 (1973).

Metzer, Milton. *The Terrorists.* New York: Harper & Row, 1983.

The Middle East. 9th ed. Washington, D.C.: Congressional Quarterly Press, 2000.

Midlarsky, Manus I., Martha Crenshaw, and Fumihiko Yoshida, "Why Violence Spreads: The Contagion of International Terrorism." *International Studies Quarterly* 24 (1980).

Miller, A. H. "Terrorism and the Media: Lessons from the British Experience." In *The Heritage Foundation Lectures.* Washington, D.C.: Heritage, 1990.

———. "Terrorism, the Media, and the Law: A Discussion of the Issues." In *Terrorism, the Media, and the Law,* edited by A. H. Miller. Dobbs Ferry, N.Y.: Transnational Publishers, 1982, 13–50.

Miller, Judith. "Even a Jihad Has Its Rules." *The New York Times,* August 29, 1998.

Miller, Judith, Stephen Engelberg, and William Broad. *Germs: Biological Weapons and America's Secret War.* New York: Simon & Schuster, 2001.

Moore, Brian. *The Revolution Script.* New York: Holt, Rinehart & Winston, 1971.

Moranto, Robert. "The Rationality of Terrorism." In *Multidimensional Terrorism,* edited by Martin Slann and Bernard Schechterman. New York: Reinner, 1987.

Mydans, Seth. "Pol Pot, Brutal Dictator Who Forced Cambodians to Killing Fields, Dies at 73." *New York Times,* April 17, 1998, 12A.

Nanes, Allan S. *The Changing Nature of International Terrorism.* Washington, D.C.: Congressional Research Service, March 1, 1985.

The 9/11 Commission Report: Final Report of the National Commission on Terrorist Attacks upon the United States. Authorized Edition. New York: W. W. Norton & Co., 2004.

Norton, A. R., and M. H. Greenberg, eds. *Preventing Nuclear Terrorism: The Report and Papers of the International Task Force on Prevention of Nuclear Terrorism.* Lexington, Mass.: 1987.

O'Ballance, Edgar O. *The Language of Violence: The Blood Politics of Terrorism.* San Rafael, Calif.: Presidio Press, 1979.

O'Brien, Connor Cruise. "Reflecting on Terrorism." *New York Review of Books,* September 16, 1978.

Oots, Kent Layne. *A Political Organization Approach to Transnational Terrorism.* Westport, Conn.: Greenwood Press, 1986.

Osterholm, Michael T., and John Schwartz. *Living Terrors: What America Needs to Know to Survive the Coming Bioterrorist Catastrophe.* New York: Random House, 2000.

"Ottawa Ministerial Declaration on Countering Terrorism." Released at the Ottawa Ministerial on December 12, 1995.

Parry, A. *Terrorism from Robespierre to Arafat.* New York: Vanguard Press, 1976.

Perl, Ralph T. *Terrorism, the Media, and the 21st Century.* Washington, D.C.: Congressional Research Service, 1998.

Pipes, Daniel. "Syria's 'Lion' Was Really a Monster," *The Wall Street Journal,* June 12, 2000.

"Profile: Mujahid Usamah Bin Laden." *The Call of Islam Magazine.* Australia, 1996.

Rapoport, David. "Fear and Trembling: Terrorism in Three Religious Traditions." *American Political Science Review* 78, no. 3 (September 1984): 658–676.

Raynor, Thomas P. *Terrorism.* New York: Franklin Watts, 1982.

"Religious Fanaticism as a Factor in Political Violence." *International Freedom Foundation.* December 1986.

Reuven, Paz. "Abu Nidal: Coming in from the Cold?" *ICT,* May 22, 2000.

Rivers, Gayle. *The Specialists: Revelations of a Counterterrorist.* New York: Stein & Day. 1985.

Rose, Paul. "Terror in the Skies." *Contemporary Review* 248 (June 1986).

Rozakis, Christos L. "Terrorism and the Internationally Protected Person in Light of the ILC's Draft Articles." *International and Comparative Law Quarterly* 23 (January 1974): 33–41.

Russell, Charles, and Bowman Miller. "Profile of a Terrorist." *Terrorism: An International Journal* 1, no. 1 (1977): 42–59.

Safer, Sasson. *Begin: An Anatomy of Leadership.* Oxford, Eng.: Oxford University Press, 1988.

Schecherman, Bernard. "Specific Trends and Projections for Political Terrorism." *Violence and Terrorism 98/99.* 4th ed., edited by Schechterman and Martin Slann. Guilford, Conn.: Dushkin/McGraw-Hill, 1998.

Schmid, A. P., and J. de Graff. *Violence as Communication: Insurgent Terrorism and the Western News Media.* Beverly Hills, Calif.: Sage, 1982.

Schmid, Alex. *Political Terrorism.* New Brunswick, N.J.: Transaction, 1983.

Schultz, G. P. "Terrorism and the Modern World." *Terrorism* 12 (January 1985): 431–447.

Schultz, George. "Low-Intensity Warfare: The Challenge of Ambiguity." Address to Low-Intensity Warfare Conference. Washington, D.C., January 15, 1986.

Sederberg, Peter C. "Explaining Terrorism." In *Terrorism: Contending Themes in Contemporary Research,* edited by Peter Sederberg, 1991.

———. *Terrorist Myths: Illusion, Rhetoric and Reality.* Upper Saddle River, N.J.: Prentice Hall, 1989.

Segaller, Stephen. *Invisible Armies: Terrorism in the 1990s.* New York: Harcourt, Brace Janovich, 1987.

Seib, Gerold F. "Why *Terror Inc.* Puts Americans in the Cross Hairs." *Wall Street Journal,* August 26, 1998.

Shaw, Paul, and Yuwa Wong. *Genetic Seeds of Warfare: Evolution, Nationalism, and Patriotism.* Boston: Unwin Hyman, 1989.

Simon, Jeffrey D. *Terrorists and the Potential Use of Biological Weapons: A Discussion of Possibilities.* Santa Monica, Calif.: RAND, 1989, R-3771-AF-MIC.

Slann, Martin. "The State as Terrorist." In *Multidimensional Terrorism,* edited by Martin Slann and Bernard Schechterman. New York: Reinner, 1987.

———. "Tolstoyan Pacifism and the Kibbutz Concept of *Hagannah Azmit* [Self-Defense]." *Reconstructionist,* vol. XLIV, no. 7 (November 1978) 13–21.

Sofaer, Abraham D. *The Political Offense Exception and Terrorism.* U.S. Department of State, Bureau of Public Affairs, Current Policy No. 762, August 1, 1985.

Sprinzak, Ehud, and Larry Diamond, eds. *Israeli Democracy under Stress.* Boulder and London: Lynn Reinner Publisher, 2000.

Stancel, Sandra. "Terrorism: An Idea Whose Time Has Come." *Skeptic: The Forum for Contemporary History* 11 (January–February 1976): 4–5.

Stephens, Maynard M. "The Oil and Gas Industries: A Potential Target for Terrorists." In *Terrorism: Threat, Reality and Response,* edited by Robert Kupperman and Darrell Trent. Stanford, Calif.: Hoover Institute Press, 1979.

Sterling, Claire. *The Terror Network.* New York: Holt, Rinehart, & Winston, 1981.

Stern, Kenneth A. "Militia and the Religious Right." *Freedom Writer* (October 1996).

Talbott, Strobe, and Nayan Chanda, eds. *The Age of Terror: America and the World after September 11.* New York: Basic Books, 2001.

Tarazona-Sevillano, Gabriela. *Sendero Luminoso and the Threat of Narcoterrorism.* New York: Praeger, 1990.

Technology Against Terrorism. U.S. Government Office of Technology Assessment Study (January 1992 and September 1991).

Terrorist Group Profiles. Dudley Knox Library. Monterey, Calif.: Naval Postgraduate School, April 2000.

Thomas, Andrew R. *Aviation Insecurity: The New Challenges of Air Travel.* Amherst, N.Y.: Prometheus Books, 2003.

Thorton, Thomas. "Terror as a Weapon of Political Agitation." In *Internal War,* edited by H. Eckstein. London: International Institute for Strategic Studies, 1964, 77–78.

"Usamah Bin Laden Bides His Time; To Strike the USA Again?" ERRI Risk Assessment Services. Daily Intelligence Report vol. 3 (July 25, 1997): 206.

"Usamah Bin Laden Special Report." *NBC News.* January 1997.

U.S. Congress. Senate. Hearing Before the Subcommittee on Near Eastern and South Asian Affairs of the Committee on Foreign Relations. *Iraq: Can Saddam Be Overthrown?* One Hundred Fifth Cong. 2d sess., March 2, 1998.

U.S. Department of State, *Global Terrorism Report.* Washington, D.C.: Government Printing Office (published annually).

Van Dam, Nikolaos. *The Struggle for Power in Syria: Politics and Society under Asad and the Ba'ath Party.* London: I. B. Taurus, 1996.

Van Evera, Stephen. "The Cult of the Offensive and the Origins of the First World War." *International Security* 9 (1984): 58–107.

Venturi, F. *Roots of Revolution: A History of the Populist and Socialist Movements in Nineteenth Century Russia,* translated by F. Haskell. New York: Norton, 1966.

Wardlaw, Grant. *Political Terrorism: Theory, Tactic, and Counter-measures.* Cambridge: Cambridge University Press, 1982.

———. "State Response to International Terrorism: Some Cautionary Comments." Paper Presented to the Symposium on International Terrorism, Defense Intelligence Agency, Washington, D.C., 1988.

Webster, William. "Can We Stop the Super-Terrorists?" *Violence and Terrorism 98/99.* 4th ed., edited by Bernard Schechterman and Martin Slann. Guilford, Conn.: Dushkin/McGraw-Hill, 1998.

Weinberg, Leonard B., and Paul B. Davis. *Introduction to Political Terrorism.* New York: McGraw-Hill, 1989.

Weinberg, Leonard, and William Lee Eubank. "Recruitment of Italian Political Terrorists." In *Multidimensional Terrorism,* edited by Martin Slann and Bernard Schechterman. Boulder, Colo.: Lynne Rienner Publishers, 1987, 78–94.

Whiteman, Marjarie M. *Digest of International Law.* Washington, D.C.: Department of State, 1988.

Wilcox, Ambassador Philip, Jr. "Terrorism Remains a Global Issue." *USIA Electronic Journal,* February 1997.

Wilkinson, Paul. *Political Terrorism.* Cambridge, Mass.: Harvard University Press, 1974.

———. *Terrorism and the Liberal State.* New York: New York University Press, 1986.

Zasra, O., and J. Lewis. *Against the Tyrant: The Tradition and Theory of Tyrannicide.* Boston: Little, Brown, 1957.

SELECTED WORLD WIDE WEB SITES

http://abcnews.go.com Articles on groups including, but not limited to, Earth Liberation Front, PETA, and others active in the United States.

www.animalliberation.net Animal Liberation Front homepage.

www.cfr.org/issue/135/terrorism.html.articles form the Council On Foreign Relations concerning differents aspects of terrorism.

www.cnn.com/world This site offers news stories about terrorist and counterterrorist events.

www.fbi.gov U.S. Federal Bureau of Investigation homepage, with information on domestic terrorist incidents and groups.

www.hamas.org Regularly updated material about Hamas.

www.hizbollah.org Information on the group, including purpose, profile, and structure, updated frequently.

www.i-cias.com This site has a wide variety of links, including the *Encyclopedia of the Orient.*

www.militia-watchdog.org Information on militia groups in the United States from the Anti-Defamation Le

www.state.gov/s/ct/rls/ U.S. Department of State Report on the Patterns of Global Terrorism, produced annually by the Office of the Coordinator for Counterterrorism. It contains a comprehensive look at the year, with overviews of each region, of state-sponsored terrorism; usually includes chronologies of terrorist events and background information on terrorist groups.

www.terrorism.com The Terrorism Research Center offers original research, documents on counterterrorism, a fairly comprehensive list of other web links related to terrorism, and profiles of terrorist and counterterrorist groups that are updated monthly.

www.tkb.org/Home.jsp A comprehensive database of global terrorist incidents and organizations.

INDEX

Note: Page numbers in **boldface** indicate major treatment of a subject. Page numbers in *italic* refer to illustrations and photographs. Page numbers followed by *c* indicate entries in the chronology.

Q